Instead of modernity

Manchester University Press

Series editors: Anna Barton, Andrew Smith

Editorial board: David Amigoni, Isobel Armstrong, Philip Holden, Jerome McGann, Joanne Wilkes, Julia M. Wright

Interventions: Rethinking the Nineteenth Century seeks to make a significant intervention into the critical narratives that dominate conventional and established understandings of nineteenth-century literature. Informed by the latest developments in criticism and theory the series provides a focus for how texts from the long nineteenth century, and more recent adaptations of them, revitalise our knowledge of and engagement with the period. It explores the radical possibilities offered by new methods, unexplored contexts and neglected authors and texts to re-map the literary-cultural landscape of the period and rigorously re-imagine its geographical and historical parameters. The series includes monographs, edited collections, and scholarly sourcebooks.

Already published

Engine of modernity: The omnibus and urban culture in nineteenth-century Paris
Masha Belenky

Spain in the nineteenth century: New essays on experiences of culture and society
Andrew Ginger and Geraldine Lawless

Creating character: Theories of nature and nurture in Victorian sensation fiction   Helena Ifill

Margaret Harkness: Writing social engagement 1880–1921   Flore Janssen and Lisa C. Robertson (eds)

Richard Marsh, popular fiction and literary culture, 1890–1915: Re-reading the fin de siècle   Victoria Margree, Daniel Orrells and Minna Vuohelainen (eds)

Charlotte Brontë: Legacies and afterlives   Amber K. Regis and Deborah Wynne (eds)

The Great Exhibition, 1851: A sourcebook   Jonathon Shears (ed.)

Interventions: Rethinking the nineteenth century   Andrew Smith and Anna Barton (eds)

Counterfactual Romanticism   Damian Walford Davies (ed.)

Instead of modernity

The Western canon and the incorporation of the Hispanic (*c.* 1850–75)

Andrew Ginger

Manchester University Press

Copyright © Andrew Ginger 2020

The right of Andrew Ginger to be identified as the author of this work has been asserted by them in accordance with the Copyright, Designs and Patents Act 1988.

Published by Manchester University Press
Oxford Road, Manchester M13 9PL

www.manchesteruniversitypress.co.uk

British Library Cataloguing-in-Publication Data
A catalogue record for this book is available from the British Library

ISBN 978 1 5261 4784 4 hardback
ISBN 978 1 5261 7903 6 paperback

First published 2020

The publisher has no responsibility for the persistence or accuracy of URLs for any external or third-party internet websites referred to in this book, and does not guarantee that any content on such websites is, or will remain, accurate or appropriate.

Typeset by
Servis Filmsetting Ltd, Stockport, Cheshire

For Conchita, it was ours both

Both in and out of the game and watching and wondering at it
                                                    Walt Whitman

Contents

List of illustrations	viii
Acknowledgements	x
Abbreviations and conventions	xi
Introduction: from modernity to the aesthetic appreciation of history	1
1 Meeting: coming together and taking shape	34
2 Departure: to leap beyond yet nearer bring	98
3 Sacrifice: everyone must die	142
4 Repose: forms of shared distraction	205
References	271
Index	296

Illustrations

Plates

1. Mariano Fortuny, *Fantasia on Faust* (1866), © Archivo Fotográfico Museo Nacional del Prado, Madrid
2. *Pompeii: Street of Tombs* (image for megalethoscope), Museo del Romanticismo, Madrid, Inventory Number CE6203, photograph by Miguel Ángel Otero
3. Édouard Manet, *The Execution of Maximilian* (1869), oil on canvas, 252 × 302 cm, Kunsthalle Mannheim, Germany, photograph Kunsthalle Mannheim/Cem Yücetas
4. Eugenio Lucas Velázquez, *Felipe IV, His Court, and the Meninas* (1858), Museo Nacional de Bellas Artes de La Habana, Cuba, courtesy of Alamy
5. Prilidiano Pueyrredón, *Siesta* (1865), private collection
6. Gustave Courbet, *The Wrestlers* (1852–53), Museum of Fine Arts, Budapest, © Museum of Fine Arts, Budapest, 2019
7. Rosa Bonheur, *Spanish Muleteers Crossing the Pyrenees* (1857), photograph courtesy of Sotheby's, Inc. © 2007
8. William Holman Hunt, *The Scapegoat* (1854–55) – Lady Lever Art Gallery, Liverpool
9. Jean-François Millet, *The Angelus* (1859), Musée D'Orsay, Paris, photograph © Musée D'Orsay, Dist. RMN-Grand Palais/Patrice Schmidt
10. Antonio Gisbert, *The Comuneros Padilla, Bravo and Maldonado on the Scaffold* (1860), Archive of the Congreso de los Diputados, Madrid
11. James McNeill Whistler, *Nocturne in Blue and Gold: Valparaíso Bay* (?1874), Freer Gallery of Art, Smithsonian Institution, Washington, DC: Gift of Charles Lang Freer, F1909.127a-b
12. Insects from the Pacific Expedition, Museum of National Sciences Madrid, photograph by the author
13. José Agustín Arrieta, *Disorderly Table – Green Glass Decanter, Bell-Glass Vase and Candelabra*, private collection
14. Hermenegildo Bustos, *Still Life with Frog, Watermelon, and Scorpion* (1874), Museo Nacional de Arte, Mexico City
15. Mariano Fortuny, *Old Man Naked in the Sun* (1874), © Archivo Fotográfico Museo Nacional del Prado, Madrid
16. Mariano Fortuny, *Choosing the Model* (1874), Courtesy National Gallery of Art, Washington, DC
17. Gustave Courbet, *The Painter's Studio: Real Allegory* (1855), Musée D'Orsay, Paris, photograph © Musée D'Orsay, Dist. RMN-Grand Palais/Gérard Blot/Hervé Lewandowski

Illustrations

18 Eduardo Rosales, *Presentation of Don Juan de Austria to the Emperor Carlos V in Yuste* (1869), © Archivo Fotográfico Museo Nacional del Prado, Madrid
19 Francisco Laso, *The Three Races (Equality before the Law)* (c.1859), Museo de Arte de Lima
20 Eduardo Rosales, *Isabel the Catholic Dictating Her Will* (1864), © Archivo Fotográfico Museo Nacional del Prado, Madrid

Figures

1 Juan Laurent, *Dolores Custodio in Entre mi mujer y el negro* (1863), Museo de Historia de Madrid	68
2 Juan Laurent, *Matilde Díez*, Museo de Historia de Madrid	71
3 Juan Laurent, *Actors in Venganza Catalana*, Museo de Historia de Madrid	74
4 José Martínez Sánchez, *Self-Portrait* (c.1360–62), collection of Mario Fernández Albarés	81
5 José Martínez Sánchez, *Guadalfeo Bridge* (?1867), Biblioteca Nacional de España, Madrid, photograph © Biblioteca Nacional de España	84
6 José Martínez Sánchez, *Tómalos Bridge* (?1867), Biblioteca Nacional de España, photograph © Biblioteca Nacional de España, Madrid	86
7 Jane Clifford, *Armour of Christopher Columbus* (c.1865), Victoria and Albert Museum, London, © Victoria and Albert Museum	89
8 Charles Clifford, *San Miguel de Lillo* (1854), Victoria and Albert Museum, London, © Victoria and Albert Museum	92
9 Juan Laurent, *Las Meninas* (1875), Fototeca IPCE/Archivo Ruiz Vernacci	96
10 Julia Margaret Cameron, '*Call, I follow, I follow, let me die!*' (1867), Victoria and Albert Museum, London, © Victoria and Albert Museum	148
11 José Martínez Sánchez, *Mummies of the Lovers of Teruel* (1867), Biblioteca Nacional de España, Madrid, photograph © Biblioteca Nacional de España	164
12 Early photograph of Rossend Nobas, *The Nineteenth Century* (a.k.a. *The Wounded Bullfighter*) (1871) from *Ilustración Non Plus Ultra*, 9 September 1886 (p. 4), © Hemeroteca Muncipal, Madrid	166
13 Juan Laurent, *Saturn Devouring His Son* (c.1863–66), Ruiz Vernacci Photographic Archive IPCE, Ministerio de Cultura y Deporte, Madrid [CC BY-SA 2.5 es (https://creativecommons.org/licenses/by-sa/2.5/es/deed.en)]	174
14 Jules Luys, *Photographic Iconography of the Nervous Centres* (1873), Plate XVIII – BIUS Santé, Original data downloaded from www.biusante.paris descartes.fr/histoire/medica/resultats/index.php?do=livre&cote=06429, updated on 25 October 2019	197
15 Francisco Ortego y Vereda, 'Each one with their one each' / 'There are no more Pyrenees', author's collection	238

Acknowledgements

The origins of this book lie over twenty years before its publication, when my research first turned to the mid-nineteenth century. Through those many years, my thinking and the project have undergone many metamorphoses. Over so much time, through so many conversations and so many papers given and discussed, it is impossible to list every person to whom I owe a debt of gratitude. I will not attempt to do so here. There are, even so, a series of individuals in nineteenth-century studies whose support and encouragement have meant a great deal, and I hope the mention of them will not be felt to be to the detriment of others. The late Susan Manning was generous with her insights at moments when the direction of my research was changing. Claudia Hopkins and Henriette Partzsch have been thoughtful, open-minded interlocutors. Carol Tully has been an ever-supportive voice, always able to see the funny side. Geraldine Lawless has been so important and incisive a presence over more than a decade that I would not know where to begin summing up all that she has done. Lee Fontanella has been a wonderful conversationalist and companion through these years, as well as the source of my interest in photography.

I would like to thank the editors of the book series *Interventions: Rethinking the Nineteenth Century* and Manchester University Press for their faith in and support for this project. I have especially valued the opportunity to test out and develop ideas among two groups of people. The first is the international nineteenth-century Hispanists network and its annual meetings. I would particularly like to mention Gregorio Alonso, Raquel Sánchez and Adrian Shubert, constant figures in that dance to the music of time. The second is the succession of I+D+i projects on utopias under the inspiring leadership of Juan Pro, and the workshops, conferences, publications and discussions these have involved. This present project has come to fruition under the auspices of *Emotional Spaces: The Places of Utopia in Modern History* (Proyecto PGC2018–093778-B-I00 del Plan Estatal de Investigación Científica y Técnica e Innovación del Gobierno de España: *Espacios emocionales: los lugares de la utopía en la Historia Contemporánea* (HISTOPIA-II), 2019–2021). The many seminars I have had with my students over the years have been a constant source of stimulation. As the project came together in its definitive form, I was particularly grateful for the opportunity to give papers at a series of events: in the concluding conference of the HERA Travelling Texts project at Glasgow; at the Edinburgh College of Art; at a session on death at the MLA Austin, and at a workshop on the same theme at Columbia University; and in a public event on changing sociability at the Museum of Romanticism in Madrid.

But Conchita alone knows what these years have really meant. This book is for her, with all my love.

AG

Abbreviations and conventions

In references to Wittgenstein's philosophy, I have followed the convention of using the initials of the work concerned followed by the number of the aphorism (*PI* § = *Philosophical Investigations*; *OC* § = *On Certainty*; *TLP* § = *Tractatus Logico-Philosophicus*).

Where I have used a text in an original language that I read, I have provided the original language version, along with my own translation. I have not done so with texts in German, but have relied there on existing translations. While, for the most part, I have sought to confine this monograph to languages that I know, I concluded that the subject matter of the study – the integration of the Hispanic with some key canonical writers for 'modernity' – demanded the inclusion of Nietzsche and Marx.

With the proliferation of e-publishing, many books are now habitually read and accessed in digital form. I have used the Kindle referencing system of locations in the form: loc.x.

Introduction: from modernity to the aesthetic appreciation of history

COOPER *Laura and I had the same dream.*
ANDY *That's impossible.*
COOPER *Yes, it is.*
Twin Peaks, Series 2 (dir. David Lynch)

A perspicuous representation ...
Ludwig Wittgenstein, *Philosophical Investigations §122*

Preliminary remarks

To make a thaumatrope, you need a disc-shaped piece of card, some string, a pen, and something to make a hole with. On either side of the card, you draw a different image – say, a bird and a cage. You make a hole in the top of the disc, and thread the string through it, so that you can dangle the card. Then you spin the disc. If you do this right – if only now and then – you will see the two pictures as if they were one – say, a bird in a cage. The two images are actually in different places and times: each are on either side of the card, and when one of them is facing you, the other is not. For that reason, the thaumotropic picture can be thought of as an optical illusion, its effect dispelled by an understanding of how human vision works. Equally – and this is so obvious it can easily be overlooked – when you see the picture as one – a bird in a cage, say – you do, in fact, see that picture. You have, in fact, experienced two different places and times as of the same place and time.

It is worth keeping this in mind.

Instead of modernity; or, how this book came about

This is a book concerning connections that intimately join places and times. It explores notions of sameness, of finding something in common between what seems disparate, of being possessed by something else. It dwells on such experiences of commonality across history and geography, valuing them in their own right. It approaches these things in an open and flexible spirit, not foreclosing on narrow distinctions between sameness, similarity and commonality, but rather exploring possibilities for realising intimate connections through all these variously. It deals in the aesthetic appreciation of these interconnecting patterns. Its contents stretch out from Spain and Spanish America through France, the United States, Britain and (to a lesser degree) the German states, conjoining the 'Hispanic' world with supposed cultural powerhouses of the 'West'. But the book began life as something somewhat different. It was to be a study of the rise of a key notion of cultural modernity (Post-Romantic modernity) in the middle of the nineteenth century – *c.*1850 to *c.*1875. According to many theorists, this was when there was a decisive shift from an interest in how things are represented or expressed (mimesis), to the means and media by which these things were represented (signs), from a Romantic and pre-Romantic paradigm to Post-Romantic Modernity. My idea was to put the 'Spanish-speaking' world into this story, so that accounts of Spanish and Latin American artists and writers intermingled with those of better-known Europeans and North Americans. This was not simply because a vast swathe of the world and its population had been neglected in this narrative. It was in response to the special place habitually assigned to the 'Hispanic' within histories and understandings of all that is deemed 'modern'. On the one hand, the 'Hispanic', its cultures and ideologies, have long been considered foundational to, constitutive of the 'modern' from the time of Columbus's crossing of the Atlantic, the establishment of a transcontinental state and commerce and the Habsburgs' participation in the formation of continental statehood in Europe. On the other hand, from the Enlightenment, scientific revolution, and the Age of Revolutions, the Hispanic has often been deemed marginal to, an obstacle to, or simply an exemplary failure to embody the 'modern'. It is for this reason that it is often given so little attention in relation to supposed turning points in the nineteenth century. The emphasis, then, was twofold: on integration, by identifying what was held in common; and on disruption, by showing how theoretical conclusions about Post-Romantic cultural modernity, drawn without full consideration of Spain and Latin America, would have to be revised.

The transformation – from a book about modernity to one concerning commonality – was an undoing and recasting of the book's fundamental subject from within. It was not simply a change in focus, a reflection of mutating interests on my part. It was a statement that the very quest for the origin of cultural modernity would lead us instead to the experience of commonality. A moment of supposed rupture with the culture of the past would be explored – and would appear – instead as an outpouring of connections throughout place and time. Where we might seek an obsession with 'representation', with the sign in its own right, autonomous of the world, we would find instead sensations of profound intimacy. The change in the book came about through its twin concern with integration and disruption. On the one hand, these preoccupations themselves took shape as explorations of connectedness. If the Spanish-speaking world was to be integrated with the rise of cultural modernity in the 'West', we would need to identify what it had in common with developments elsewhere. If its integration disrupted our notion of modernity, a connection would form between us and the Spanish-speaking past, altering our worldview, offering an alternative sense of what we might share with the mid-nineteenth century. On the other hand, if integration with the Spanish-speaking world disrupted the notion of cultural modernity, the latter concept might itself come undone, become unsustainable. Its visions of rupture and exceptionalism might be overshadowed by a dynamic sense of what places and times have in common. This would not mean the total disappearance of such notions. Rather, in their very place, in their stead, we would find their own involvement in their expression of sameness and commonality.

The new book would be 'instead' (in the stead) of modernity, not born of the idea's utter erasure. It would have two distinct, but inseparable facets. It would set forth expressions of intimate connectedness across place and time stemming from the mid-century. And it would explore ways of tracing and writing about commonality across the writers and artists who figure on its pages. Both aspects of the book would flow from and through each other. The way I write about commonalities – imagery, turns of phrase – would employ figures of speech and images from mid-century writing and art. And the way I write about mid-century writers and artists would be shaped through the ways I find to express commonality across them. The very prose of the book would be an expression of something shared dynamically beyond periodisation or geographical divides. The act of writing would be a form of practice, crafted through contact with material from the mid-century and its legacy.

Theory and the mid-nineteenth century

From Clement Greenberg (1993a; 1993b: 86, 89) through Walter Benjamin (1997: 105, 172) and Michel Foucault (1977a: 91–3), to Pierre Bourdieu (1992: 149, 162, 196), the mid-century has been held to herald a crucial shift from an interest in how things and meanings are represented or expressed, to the autonomous means and media by which things are represented and constructed (signs). Such a transformation became fundamental, not just to many accounts of modernism, but to canonical theorisations of cultural study that were well entrenched by the late twentieth century. So much is this so that Toril Moi was once moved to remark: 'if you want to be a really radical student today, one that annoys the professors terribly, you can just start claiming that words have meanings' (2003: 166). As much as philosophical arguments about the autonomy of signs, the foundations of much canonical Theory were interpretations of that particular historical moment and its consequences. They asserted a supposed recognition – *anagnorisis* – of what truly mattered in the mid-century. In practice, they often evoked a well-established proto-modernist canon of writers and artists, not least the Parisian patriarchy of Baudelaire, Flaubert and Manet. For Foucault (1984), in 'What Is Enlightenment?', Baudelaire's notion of modernity involves acceptance that there is no substantive, pre-existing human subject, but rather that any sense of selfhood must be produced aesthetically. In 'Fantasia of the Library', he invokes Manet and Flaubert in recounting the rise of modern culture, where the arts are based purely on signs, bringing about an 'indefinite murmur', for better or for worse (1977a: 92–3). Such developments point to the possible erasure of the face of man – the presence of a universal human subject – that he famously contemplates at the end of *The Order of Things* (1970). If Roland Barthes in his 'The Death of the Author' and Foucault in 'What Is an Author?' dwell on the role of the poet Stéphane Mallarmé, both take time once more to allude to Flaubert (1988: 168, 170; 1977b: 117, 120). In 'Fantasia of the Library', Foucault specifically describes Flaubert as opening the way for Mallarmé, such that 'modern literature is activated' (1977a: 92). In turn, Mallarmé – whose relevant work falls chronologically beyond this present book – looms large in Jacques Derrida's *Dissemination* and that philosopher's account of signs without the presence of the subject (1981: 54–5, 206).

'All that is solid melts into air', Marshall Berman (1983) famously affirmed, echoing Karl Marx. Berman seeks to renew a vision of modernism that emerges from the mid-nineteenth century, with particular reference to Baudelaire and Marx, as well as Nietzsche (1983: 19, 88–164). A notion of being firmly rooted within the world is replaced – for good and ill – by fluid, changing experiences, in which 'there will no longer by any illusion of a real self underneath the masks' (1983: 110). For Berman, Baudelaire confronts a world where everything can be ironised (1983: 162–3). With this narrative of an historical transformation comes a supposed decentring of Man: an offsetting, if not erasure, of the notion that the world revolved around a fundamental unchanging human nature. By the early 1870s, the young Friedrich Nietzsche – so influential on Foucault as on others – appeared to repudiate the legacy of classical Greek philosophy and of Christian thought. He rejected their supposed efforts to provide an immutable foundation for human being and for knowledge, ontology and epistemology. Charles Darwin's *Origins of the Species* left humanity as but an accidental outcome of vast, blind processes of evolution across the ages. Karl Marx's *Capital* put human agency at the mercy of forces of production; it recognised the power of abstract concepts made real in mid-century economic life: commodities, capital, exchange. On the one hand, the autonomy of the sign was one more instance of such decentring: put at its crudest, language spoke humans rather than the other way around. On other other hand, the emphasis on representations may be thought consistent with and a consequence of the various decentrings that were afoot. If there were no foundation rooting humanity, no universal shared human nature – it might appear – all experiences of being human would be constructs of representations, accumulations of signs without any secure, fixed meaning.

While high theorists of Post-Romantic modernity entertain debate about the specific significance of the mid-nineteenth century, they offer few doubts about the period's world-historical resonance. Disputes are instead about the nature of that shift, and its corresponding implications for good and ill. For example, Walter Benjamin's work on Baudelaire as a 'lyric poet in the age of high capitalism' links the concern with autonomous signs to the dazzling effect of commodities as the capitalist process of production became ever more remote from consumers. At the same time, that autonomy putatively resists the use-value of commodities (1977: 105, 172). T.J. Clark (1984) offers a not dissimilar, social-historical line in his discussion of Manet's concern with the medium of painting, rejecting Clement Greenberg's account. Greenberg had famously seen modernism primarily in formal terms, as a recognition that painting should be concerned with the realities and potential of its own medium, not primarily with representing the world. For Greenberg, Manet is the initiator of this development (1988a: 234; 1988b; 1993a: 242; 1993b: 86). It is not unusual to link cultural modernity to a wide-ranging pattern of nineteenth-century social and economic changes, variously conceived, and often to do with a crucial juncture in capitalism. Such is the overarching argument of Berman's volume, where mid-century modernism is a response to the perplexing contradictions thrown up by capitalist modernisation (1983: 102, 123). For the sociologist Bourdieu, the autonomy of the medium as established decisively by Baudelaire, Flaubert and Manet marks a challenge to and a transformation of the institutional structures of culture, overthrowing the power of the official Academies and, more broadly, the role of authority in governing the arts (1993: 190–1, 149). For Jonathan Crary, autonomy from any grounded foundations of being or fixed external reality was a product of new technologies, linked in turn to a notion of individuality that served a bourgeois economic order. The new development at once served and resisted the disciplinary forces of modernising societies. Courbet emerges within this wider cultural transformation, as does Manet's rejection of reference to an inner subject (1990: 126–32, 150; 2000: 83). For Foucault, the erasure of the face of Man was primarily a discursive phenomenon, with the capacity to become a near-pervasive change in the structure and discipline of our experience of the world, overpowering the dominant nineteenth-century order of things. Ranging against Clark's view of Manet, Michael Fried (1996) plays down socioeconomic factors, looking to a conjunction of debates around 'theatricality' and 'absorption', which he links in turn to discussions of the interplay of national and 'universal' cultures in France. There are many such variants through the bibliography about canonical writers and artists of the time, as critic and theorist after critic and theorist seek to establish what 'modernity' was and what its implications are. Put another way, the recognition of modernity's true significance would entail the identification and elucidation of the most fundamental motor of cultural change in the mid-nineteenth century and its enduring transformation of the world.

In returning to this matter, my starting point was – and is – to underline how key totems of these theorisations – so widely insinuated that they have taken on a character almost of neutrality – are forged in a narrow and exclusionary vision of the mid-nineteenth century. In part, this is because notions of the autonomy of the sign and related decentring are historically contingent worldviews. So much is perhaps implied by Foucault's deadpan, ambiguous tone at the end of 'What Is an Author?': he may be describing rather than advocating the coming 'anonymous murmur'. Some critics, like William Keach, have sought to lend some historical distance to Paul de Man's viewpoint in *Rhetoric of Romanticism*. Keach shows how the supposed problem of autonomous signs and their referents came to be imagined through very specific nineteenth-century debates, rather than being sempiternal philosophical preoccupations (2004: ix, xii, 20). The problem is larger still: the vision of the mid-century that underpins such theorisations rests both on a highly selective canon with a particularly dominant Parisian male cohort, and on a specific series of interpretations of that canon and its context. Even when theorists – like Jonathan Crary in *Techniques of the Observer* – seek to generalise to a wider field of activity, it is striking how little their sources tend to stray from languages and cultures whose prestige has tended to dominate (English, French, German). The exclusive nature of these foundations is all the more ironic given that the theory following from them is so often deployed against exclusivity.

From the perspective of a Hispanist, the absence of the vast geographical stretch and major population areas of the Spain and Spanish America is very apparent. Such an exclusion clearly supposes that, by the mid-nineteenth century, these places were intellectually and culturally backward compared to places where people spoke, say, French or English or, for that matter, German. They were of no real account at this supposed foundational moment. Underpinning putatively radical Theories lies a familiar pattern from stadial histories, such as the German philosopher G.W.H. Hegel's *Phenomenology of Spirit* (1807). Leadership of the human spirit passes from one location and people to another, in an eschatological shift from one era to another, until it reaches its culmination in European states bordering the North-West Atlantic coastline (Sharman 2013: 15, 34). Since the influential histories of Ferguson and Robertson during the Scottish Enlightenment, it has been widely assumed that the destiny of the Hispanic world was to have laid foundations for the 'modern' after 1492: the bringing together of oceanic commerce, the establishment of large-scale state apparatus on continental Europe and globally. Its fate was then to be superseded by the dynamism of societies to the north.

It was as if the Spanish domains had opened the door to the modern world only to be shut outside. In the cultures of those places and among Hispanists studying them, a parallel notion became ideologically effective and potent for a full range of political and intellectual positions. It was claimed that efforts in Spain and Spanish America at all manner of modernisations (cultural, political, socioeconomic) were fundamentally flawed, and had only periodic successes. Napoleonic invasion of Spain in 1808 had drastically disrupted the Ancien Régime, leading to a succession of revolutions and uprisings. With these came cultural and societal changes, including the ultimate independence of much of Spain's American lands (1826), though not the Caribbean islands of Cuba and Puerto Rico. There was an attempt at constitutional parliamentary government across Spain and its overseas territories (the Cádiz Constitution of 1812), and there were continuous struggles over the establishment of liberal constitutional order, the nature of states, and even which states should exist and with what boundaries. These efforts at change have been characterised in a vocabulary that populates commentary on the century: *fracaso* (a failure through falling short), *retraso* and *atraso* (backwardness in relation to progress elsewhere), *cursilería* (kitch as a result of attempting to emulate something thought modern, but either poorly imitated, or already passé or both). In another all-too-familar pattern in historiography, we are thus left with an origin story. In short, the nineteenth century was envisaged both as the source of a new modern order in the Hispanic world, and of its fatal flaws.

Unravelling towards sameness

While the narrative about the supposed protagonists of Post-Romantic modernity has been pervasive, there have been few research monographs dealing with any significant number of these writers and artists together, across national boundaries. Berman's *All That Is Solid Melts into Air*, published nearly 40 years ago now, is one exception; Jonathan Crary's two monographs have something of a wider-ranging approach. Most major studies confine themselves to a particular country, a single-language culture or, often as not, one or two protagonists. This is true from Michael Fried on Manet to Frederic Jameson (2014) on Marx. I wanted instead to take a comparative approach, placing many supposed leading-lights once more together in a single volume. Nietzsche, Marx, Darwin, Flaubert, Baudelaire and Courbet all make appearances here, alongside such other canonical giants as Whitman and Whistler. I wanted to do so too in a way that stepped beyond the confines of a collection of patriarchs, by including female artists and authors such as Rosa Bonheur, Julia Margaret Cameron, Juana Manuela Gorriti and Rosalía de Castro.

Through this comparative framework, I wanted to address and – as it were – assist in undoing the constitutive but ambiguous relationship between the 'Hispanic' and notions of the 'modern'. Both terms have often been constituted, on the one hand, by the supposedly crucial role of the 'Hispanic' in founding the 'modern', and, on the other, by the supposedly marginal or even oppositional role of the 'Hispanic' in the subsequent development of the 'modern'. Put another way, the 'Hispanic' is often deemed both 'modern' and 'not-modern', and the 'modern' is at once founded on and excludes the 'Hispanic'. A comparative approach that puts Hispanic culture back into the picture of the supposed key moment of 'modernity' in the mid-century brings to the fore this fundamental double-edged relationship. There are a series of interrelated reasons for my adopting this approach, each from a critical stance of the picture as it was. First, the inclusion of Hispanic writers and artists challenges the dominant narrative about Spain, Latin America and the modern world set out above. Rather than fading into the background, they would form a dynamic, active presence at this putatively world-historical moment. In turn, the notion of the torch of the modern – or of Spirit – passing from one set of peoples to another would be disrupted. A major stream of historiography since at least the 1990s has emphasised how the Hispanic world after 1808 was highly integrated into and resembled the pattern of revolution, reform and reaction across European and the American culture and society, for better and for worse. In relation to Spain, for example, understandings of political, social and economic history have been revised by intellectuals such as Isabel Burdiel (1998), Adrian Shubert (1990) or David Ringrose (1996). As regards mid-nineteenth-century Latin America, James E. Sanders has underlined the prominence of radical notions of republican modernity that have subsequently been occluded (2014: 12–13). The direction of travel is neatly signalled in the Spanish subtitle of Ringrose's study of economic change, 'the myth of failure': *El mito del fracaso*.

The consequent emphasis on – even longing for – a kind of normalisation may sit uneasily with the celebration of difference in Anglophone cultural studies, so suspicious of the oppressive and exclusionary effect of European and US notions of normality (and with good reason). Such preoccupations find a widespread echo in Hispanic studies too, given both the conflictive encounter in the Americas of European peoples with the indigenous and those of African descent, and the multiplicity of languages and cultures in metropolitan Spain, from the Basques to the Catalans to the legacy of Islam. The complexities, fusion and violence are teased out in studies from Mary Pratt's *Imperial Eyes* (1992) to the essay collection *Spain Beyond Spain* (2005) by Bradley Epps and Luis Fernández Cifuentes (to offer just two examples). For many, like Ángel Rama (2004), modern Latin America is characterised by the mutually transforming tension of incoming 'Western' influences and local conditions. In Spain, the struggle over integration with Western Europe could be experienced as a clash between national identities, as Jesús Torrecilla has it ('enfrentamiento de identidades nacionales') (1996: 13). Yet, as even this implies, the appeal of some kind of normalisation with the 'West' remains compelling – and for its own good reasons, culturally, socially, politically, economically and as a matter of historical fact. The notorious slogan 'Spain Is Different' epitomises all that provoked the converse assertion, that Spain and Latin America were not, in fact, a world apart. It evokes the resented insinuation that these peoples were not fully part of the modern world, were incapable of so being, and that prosperity, intellectual and cultural energy and political and social freedom belonged in, say, France, Germany, the UK and the United States. The wish for normalisation kicks against the same insult by which southern Europeans have more recently been designated PIGS (Portugal, Italy, Greece, Spain). Frustration with the exclusionary narrative does not simply fuel love of local particularity: it may stimulate a wish to show that others too can participate and have done so.

A notion of sameness implicitly pervades the revised historiography of nineteenth-century Spain and Latin America, though rarely surfaces explicitly as a subject in its own right. The practice of teasing out commonalities with France, Germany, Britain and the United States implies the subtleties involved in tracing sameness. It is in no way a matter of conflating all these situations and treating them as homogeneous, but rather of finding things in common through varying and uneven circumstances. We can see this, for example, in work by Guy Thomson (2009) on the political cultures of Spain. Thomson underlines how the armed internal conflict to which an unstable state was particularly susceptible – like Spain's Carlist civil war of absolutists and liberals (1834–39) – could lead to political engagement and radicalisation of a mobilised, militarised population, sharing ideas with democrats elsewhere (Thomson 2009). In his work on mid-century Latin America, James Sanders emphasises how the extreme weakness of the state there – even by nineteenth-century standards – was accompanied by a dynamic culture of appeals to new collective identities among the wider populace as new countries formed and developed. Not least in the aftermath of the US-Mexican war and with the persistence of older social hegemonies in Europe, there emerged a form of universalism that, while echoing European revolutionary ideals, looked beyond them to a notion of the Spanish Americas as the source of global democratic renewal (2014: 12–13, 16–17, 64, 81). In practice, 'many parts of Latin America would far surpass the United States and Europe in extending citizenship to all men, regardless of race or class' (2014: 54). My aim is likewise to weave strands of sameness through unevenness and variation, in redescribing mid-century Post-Romantic 'modernity'.

In this respect at least, my undertaking echoes developments in the writing of nineteenth-century world history, such as C.A. Bayly's *The Birth of the Modern World* (2004) or, subsequently, Jürgen Osterhammel's vast *The Transformation of the World* (2009). Both seek to integrate into the narrative of the 'modern' a wide array of societies and actors from around the globe, recognising the marked power and projection of a small number of 'Western' states like Britain and France, but showing how patterns of historical development arose and were inflected across the planet. Bayly speaks of 'a complex parallelogram of forces' (2004: 7), and observes how 'different agencies and ideologies across the world empowered it [modernity] in different ways' (2004: 12). For that very reason, he 'rejects the view that any type of contradiction exists between the study of the social fragment ... and the study of the broad processes which constructed modernity' (Bayly 2004: 9). Like Osterhammel, Bayly envisages what is shared in the 'modern' as a multi-layered, multi-faceted narrative, but not for that any less a story held in common.

To integrate Hispanic writers and artists into the story of mid-century modernity entails explicitly setting them in a relationship of commonality with their better know peers elsewhere, the supposed founders of a new era in culture. Not to do so would leave them not visibly integrated at all – and, by the same token, would not integrate better-known figures from elsewhere with them either. Belatedly perhaps, I have come to realise both the tactical and intellectual advantages of including nineteenth-century Hispanic culture within a wider comparative study, rather than primarily elucidating the importance of nineteenth-century Hispanic writers and artists by using comparative reference points. A great deal of scholarly work now forcefully asserts the originality and significance of Hispanic writing and visual art that is much less known beyond Spain and Latin America. The claim is that these works deserve to be better known and to be taken fully into account. Such scholarly writing seeks to reach out to an audience beyond those specifically interested in the Hispanic world, but often ends up largely reaching those who are, because those are the kinds of people who read those sorts of publication. It is a sad truth that there are remarkably few crossover articles or books on lesser-known dimensions of Hispanic culture. At the level of readership and audience, this situation mirrors the main historiographical problem. Contributions of such Hispanic writers and artists have not, in practice, been presented to wider audiences as part of the larger story of culture, as sharing in it. It is through the act of writing Hispanic actors into a wider story of subtle sameness that inclusion can be effected. María del Pilar Blanco's *Ghost-Watching American Modernity* (2012), James Dunkerley's *Americana: The Americas in the World, around 1850* (2000), Elizabeth Amann's *Importing Madame Bovary* (2006) and Pratt's earlier *Imperial Eyes* (1992) are signal examples of such a practice of writing the narrative of the nineteenth century.

Disruption goes hand in hand with commonality and inclusion. Once what was excluded from 'modernity' becomes part of the 'same' story, the historical narrative is fundamentally changed. The contingency and exclusivity of the previous version is exposed and transformed. Given how much has been at stake in a recognition of the mid-century's significance, the foundations of Post-Romantic theories would be altered, and their starting point for reflection on culture would change. Even their account of the exclusive canon on which they rested might be transformed, taking on new emphases and priorities. This is what has happened in other fields of study of the nineteenth century. For instance, in Bayly's account of economic change, the core notion of an 'industrial revolution' is offset by a much amplified concept of an 'industrious revolution' which did not need to include industrialisation as such (2004: 52). The emphasis on disruptive commonality is pointedly distinct from a much-touted notion of 'plural modernities'. The latter is the more modest claim that deep-set assumptions about what counts as modernity, based on a limited canon, prevent us from appreciating what is important elsewhere, and in other modern countries and cultures. So, for example, Albert Boime (1993) and Norma Broude (1987) argue that the mid-century Italian *machiaiolli* had been dismissed for not fulfilling criteria for modern art set by French Impressionism. Instead, they offer a distinct aesthetic, rooted in social activism and even feminism. Italian art had its own modernity, unlike that of the 'Francocentric' vision.

Such a notion of 'plural modernities' is problematic. The canonical view of mid-century modernity never denied that there were other strands to culture at the time. It claimed only that these did not offer a fundamental, compelling change in what culture was understood to be. Relatedly, the use of the noun *modernities* in the phrase *plural modernities* serves no obvious purpose, and potentially creates a self-contradiction. We could only be sure that each of the plural strands was a *modernity* if there were a shared understanding of how that term is to be employed, expressing some compelling claim about fundamental change. So, even in *plural modernities* there would need to be one *modernity*. The search for disruptive commonalities in mid-century 'modernity' offers, instead, a critical comparative approach. It is *critical*, on the one hand, because attention centres on challenging what is really at stake in the claims made by the more exclusionary narrative. On the other hand, it is *critical* because this process takes the heart of that narrative to a point of crisis through which it is transformed. In cultural study, something of the desired effect may be seen in Lynda Nead's *Victorian Babylon* (2005). Nead points out how theorisations of modern urban experience so often derive from Baron Haussmann's mid-century rebuilding of Paris; she asks how that vision might be if it incorporated the vast metropolis that is Victorian London. Likewise, Martina Lauster (2007) explores how theoretical assumptions about modernity are disrupted if Benjamin's focus on Baudelaire's myth of the flâneur is replaced by a more inclusive treatment of visions of nineteenth-century urban experience.

Treated in this way, the mid-century would become a 'dynamic moment', to borrow Siegfried Zielinski's phrase (2006: 11). Rather than being confined to an interpretation of the past that has mastered it, it would continually unsettle present-day assumptions about cultural theory. For there to be 'modernity', there needs to be a step-change to a new era founded on a new basis, a radical principle or set of principles, but this notion runs into serious problems when we seek disruptive commonalities. Let us take the key notion of a turn to the medium of representation in itself. Through this, I once found it possible to link together a common interpretation of Manet and Flaubert in Paris with their contemporary Eugenio Lucas Velázquez in Madrid. As we have seen, Manet and Flaubert have been said to launch a new, Post-Romantic era in culture, the anonymous murmur of signs. This is ultimately an eschatological vision: a rupture from one epoch to another. For all its boldness, it mirrors an extremely conventional nineteenth-century notion that, while artists should imitate others, they should do so with a new voice and style for their time. Conversely, I argued that Lucas's concern with autonomous signs was a rejection of any notion that an artist could step into a new era. Rather, they would be utterly immersed in the past, forever constituted by the legacy of signs from across place and time, and could do no more than navigate pragmatically among these. Lucas's work amounted to a fundamental rejection of the conventional notion that art should seek to establish a new style and voice for their time (Ginger 2007a).

A commonality certainly exists between Manet and Lucas, because of their shared attention to autonomous signs. But if both are consequently classed as 'modernity', the notion of *modernity* pulls in quite different directions – and, paradoxically, one of these would constitute a denial of the very possibility of a fundamentally new era, of something radically 'modern'. Moreover, what supposedly made, say, Manet and Flaubert special was that they putatively presented a challenge to the most fundamental, radical core of how culture was imagined to be, by a focus on the mode of representation itself, as if at last recognising what culture was made of. It is not clear why this goes more fundamentally to the heart of culture, to a radical principle, than might other substantial innovations in the mid-century. The Argentine painter Prilidiano Pueyrredón's *Siesta* (Plate 5) presents two separate moments in time simultaneously and as if fused in a single moment on the canvas: an identical woman awake and asleep. It has something in common with Baudelaire's 'Seven Old Men' ('Les Sept vieillards') where the same aged individual appears in the same place seven times consecutively, as if following himself. If such effects were classed as a less fundamental alteration of art and writing, that was because of a key assumption underpinning the supposed recognition, the *anagnorisis*, of what really mattered in mid-century culture, indeed in culture as a whole.

The circular supposition is that culture is made up of autonomous signs, of means of representing things – or at least in the new era is taken so to be. So, only those works of art that support such a view truly went to the heart of the problem of what culture was. This attitude is to a degree in line with Clifford Geertz's influential *The Interpretation of Culture*: only a semiotic account – one constituted around signs and their interpretations – rigorously and coherently constitutes an explication of culture, as opposed to what is proper to other fields, or to a loose eclectic approach to the matter. Geertz himself quite properly tempered the claim, resisting the notion that there was a closed system of signs, and looking to the latters' roles in lives (1973: 4–5, 17–20, 24, 27, 30). In her *Revolution of the Ordinary*, Toril Moi points out that the semiotic approach rests on an 'almost mystical belief in "the materiality of the signifier"', and with it a 'craving for generality'. The latter is exemplified in the wish for a generalisable theory of signs through which culture can be analysed, 'the idea of language as a closed system' (2017: 116, 4). Moi finds a genealogy for these attitudes in a very particular interpretation of the early twentieth-century linguistician Ferdinand de Saussure, and for his own assumptions amid the influence of the French Symbolists (2017: 118). Shining through the latter is an established vision of the supposed Post-Romantic turning point, the mid-century. But the canonical view of mid-century modernity is just one picture of how culture might be, with its own presuppositions about what matters most. There are many other such pictures. Moi points out that if one has been institutionalised to believe only the semiotic one, it becomes very difficult to see beyond it and engage with alternatives (2017: 10). If one does not accept the privileging of the 'materiality of the signifier', there are indeed other large, compelling claims about the nature of culture, made in the nineteenth century. For instance, scholars such as Susan Manning (2002) or Cairns Craig (2007) have emphasised continuous innovations in English-speaking culture linked to Associationism. Here, language, thought and feeling are assembled psychologically through the apparent, contingent similarity of one experience to another.

The notion of a new cultural era founded on a radical set of principles flounders as we incorporate diverse, compelling visions of culture from the mid-century into the core narrative. With it, so does the notion of a step change to a new epoch in culture. To treat the mid-century as a 'dynamic moment', throwing out numerous critically challenging viewpoints to present-day assumptions, is to say that these 'abound and revel in heterogeneity', to borrow Zielinski's words once more (2006: 11). This is at odds with stating that what matters in the mid-century onwards is a bounded set of principles constituting and establishing a discrete historical period, set apart from others. At all events, whether something appears to be a step change involves a relative judgement that one kind of bold innovation is more fundamental than another. This, in turn, is dependent on a given vantage point. We have seen how slippery such a judgement is, when wondering if Manet, or Lucas, or Pueyrredón or the inheritors of Associationism make the more marked difference to the conception of cultural activity. Even if we confine ourselves to the 'materiality of the signifier', it is difficult to discern so clear a divide between a Post-Romantic sensibility and what preceded it. To do so would require that we know what degree and kind of attention to the 'materiality of the signifier' counts as a really fundamental way of attending to it. Narratives of the nineteenth century such as those developed by Foucault create the effect of such a break by describing earlier attitudes as failing denials of the constructed nature of language and culture, founded on a belief in some essential, universal human subject.

Scholars revisiting the first part of the nineteenth century have spoken instead of complex and subtle attitudes to how culture is assembled and historicised. For example, alongside the renewed attention to Associationism, James Chandler (1998) explores how later critical outlooks on the nineteenth century such as Foucault's depend intimately and subtly upon early nineteenth-century practice. Many academics – like Terence Cave in *The Cornucopian Text* (1979) – have found parallels between Theory's preoccupation with the autonomy of signs and previous medieval and early modern ideas about literary imitation. Such similarities, and their doubling back across history, might serve to undo any claim of a step change, replacing it instead with a myriad of comparisons back and forth over time. 'The modernist historical frame is lifting only now', Alexander Nagel remarks in *Medieval Modern* (2012: 12). Periodising separations in art between a medieval epoch, a later era and the vanguard deserve to be 'criss-crossed to oblivion' (2012: 21).

Surveying this intellectual morass, I wonder if anything would be lost in taking the term *modernity* out of the study of the mid-century, except in referencing how the term was used at the time. I wonder if there is any sentence about mid-century culture, and perhaps in general, in which the word might not be substituted by something else, or simply omitted. For all his vast efforts and after hundreds of pages, Osterhammel acknowledges that 'the concept of modernity has to this day remained enigmatic' (2014: 836). 'We have never been modern', Bruno Latour (1993) has famously said (though even he seems attracted by the notion that something called *modernity* did fundamentally reshape human experience, for all that it occluded). I mean instead that the term *modernity* may not be very helpful at all, at least so far as culture goes. Like Susan Stanford Friedman in *Planetary Modernisms* (2015), we could launch a rescue attempt for the term, stripping it of any substantial definition. We could simply use it relationally, to express any relative novelty with respect to any previous state of affairs, at any point in time or place. But, I have not, for myself, felt the imperative to do so.

After all, what is compelling about the term, as used by cultural historians, is precisely its supposed specificity, its unique world-historical significance. It is presumably some residue of this resonance, some lingering belief that the word confers truly totemic recognition, that accounts for its still persistent use. It is as if, in wielding it, we truly show that something is important (but why not just say it is important?). This surely is its use in that otherwise uninformative phrase 'plural modernities', translating as something like: 'but these things matter too'. Bayly – and others – would grasp for one or another version of *modernity* as a solid guarantor of periodisation (2004: 10–11). But its real significance – in the mid-century and now – lies in the very urge to use or claim the term, to assert some fundamental change. It is in this respect only that a notion of *modernity* or, more widely, of an eschatologically distinct new epoch appears in this book: as something advocated or described by people in the mid-century. Where it is discussed, the notion is subsumed in the larger topic of this book, figuring instead as a contributory element to the pursuit of commonality.

Commonality instead of modernity: the cultural supernova

This unravelling of the notion of mid-century modernity unfurls four preoccupations, each related to the other. In summary, the first is the tracing of subtle sameness, of disruptive commonality, essential to integrating mid-century canonical art and writing with 'Hispanic' culture. The point may be generalised. Given that any account of cultural history – conventional or otherwise in its narrative form – requires some kind of weaving together of disparate parts, any inclusive account of cultural history would involve the drawing of disruptive commonalities. After all, any comparative study of culture requires linking comparisons to be made. Second, the mid-century past would not form or initiate a delineated period, but rather would be a 'dynamic moment', a heterogeneous source of culture. It would not stand clearly apart from other periods. It would present a continual, stimulating challenge to our present-day theorisation of culture. This approach would involve an emphasis on 'the conditions under which the absent past can be said to have "presence" in the present', as Vivian Sobchack says of media archaeology (2011: 323). This connectedness across stretches of time would mirror the tracing of disruptive commonality through the mid-century. In turn, other junctures in history would be 'present' to the mid-nineteenth century as dynamic moments, criss-crossing any effort at periodisation, as we will see, for instance, in Chapter 1, with invocations of the Germanic myth of Faust.

Third, the stimulating resonance of works of the mid-century – from Marx's *Capital I* to Nietzsche's *Birth of Tragedy* – would not primarily depend on any strong commitment to periodisation. None of the excitement is lost simply because these works do not together form the shared foundations of a new modernity. Just as importantly, there would be no need to emphasise, in its own right, any effort in such works to establish a new era apart from others, for such a notion would no longer be of primary significance. With that preoccupation set to one side, the focus moves to their capacity to open up dynamic relationships interconnecting places, tracing what Wai Chee Dimock calls 'Deep Time'. Dimock finds through US literature of the nineteenth century and beyond a multiplicity of multi-directional 'pathways' interweaving cultures and times (2006: 3). The very assertion of a new epoch or of a modernity could form part of that phenomenon, as we will see in Chapter 2 of this book (*Departure*) through an exploration of Marx, Manet and Baudelaire.

Fourth, there would be no reason to fixate on the notion of autonomous signs, the 'materiality of the signifier', the supposed Post-Romantic sensibility, in its own right. Lifting the mid-century out of this frame enables exploration of a range of compelling visions of culture. In particular, it gives oxygen to notions of some more intimate connection between sign and world, and might enable us to perceive these where they had been previously occluded. This is something I explore as much with Herman Melville's *Moby-Dick* as with the Argentine Estanislao del Campo's *Fausto*. In turn, the capacity for communication, intimated in such works, enables dynamic communion across place and time through writing and visual art. By the same token, concerns other than the autonomy of signs – or for that matter, the de-centring of the subject – take prominent shape in the subtle sameness, the disruptive commonalities that I trace through works of the mid-century. Accordingly, the emphasis shifts in the treatment of canonical works of the time. For instance, where Paul de Man reads Nietzsche's *The Birth of Tragedy* as an allegory of representation, I dwell on an experience of intimate encounter, a passage through equivalence in the realm of the gods.

Our encounter with the mid-century becomes – as it were – a cultural supernova. The vision of modernity implodes, but is transformed into one of energetic commonality, stretching out across place and time. We attend now to compelling forms of connectedness. To the fore is the very question of what is happening when such connections are made, an issue that goes to the heart of comparative study. In her magisterial study of notions of 'likeness' – *Poetics of Character* – Susan Manning aptly notes that 'we still lack a sufficiently complex comparative poetics'. In cultural study, our vocabulary for similitude, commonality, or simply persistence through place and time, is somewhat depleted. 'If all judgment is comparative', Manning wonders, '... what is the "texture of likeness" in a particular case?' (2013: xi–xiii). In turn, the 'dynamic moments' of the past enrich us – link to us – by offering ways of imagining connectedness that we may have discarded. The history of culture is a Pandora's box of commonality, there to be opened, once the Post-Romantic frame is removed. A range of historians of culture have begun to explore this possibility. Deborah Jenson (2001) points to the 'social life of mimesis in post-revolutionary France', Tim Ingold (2016) looks to the complex legacy of efforts to draw 'lines', James E. Sanders (2014) evokes democratic universalism in mid-century Latin America.

In this book, I study images and texts from the mid-nineteenth century through the connections that resonate among them and out across place and time. In so doing, I look also to the experiences of connectedness that they themselves suggest. In the place of 'modernity' come echoes of resemblance and persistence, and disclosures of possibility. There is a deliberate heterogeneity to this undertaking. The book ranges across modes, from Rosa Bonheur's painterly vision of dominance and submission on the Franco-Spanish frontier at the end of Chapter 2, or, the pained gazing across history and empire in Julia Margaret Cameron's photographs at the start of Chapter 3, or, at that chapter's end, the reflections and transparencies of the world in glasswork in the Crystal Palace and in Mexico. The recovery of past sensibilities involves a reckoning with longer legacies, often forged in cruelty, that resonate through the mid-century imagination. The bringing together of worlds under Spain, that fateful crossing of the Atlantic from 1492, recurs, from Marx's vision of

Capital in Chapter 2, through Columbus's ghostly armour floating in Jane Clifford's photograph during Chapter 1, or, in Chapter 3, the reversal of his voyage in *La Peregrinación de Bayoán* (*The Pilgrimage of Bayoán*), a novel by the Puerto Rican Eugenio de Hostos. I echo here recent efforts to rediscover the place of Spain's imperial venture – the notion of a Universal Monarchy, and debates about it – in the development of Western and American notions of universalism and internationalism, for worse as well as for better, whether in Pagden (1995), Headley (2008: 75–96, 102–7) or Mignolo (2000). In turn, I seek to bring into confluence attempts across diverse scholarly fields to ponder likeness, persistence and an intimate connectedness. I draw from the comparative cultural study in which I have my roots (Manning, Dimock), as I do from sexuality studies (Tim Dean or Lisa Downing, for example), or the study of trauma and the arts (Griselda Pollock and Dominic LaCapra, among others), or the debate on sacrifice in continental philosophy (Derrida, Kristeva and Agamben, for instance), or discussion of visual studies and of optical technology (Michael Fried, Mary Ann Doane and Jonathan Crary). In a corresponding spirit, we encounter across these pages the scientific slicing of brains in France (Chapter 3), a stage performance in Mexico (Chapter 1), taxidermic practices in natural history (Chapter 3) and an obsessive dwelling on donkeys (Chapter 4).

The tracing of such varied 'textures of likeness' echoes Dimock's scepticism that modern people experience time and place as homogeneous empty things (2006: 2). To open up past visions of commonalities is to relax such assumptions about the nature of sameness in the modern world. This is the case even where one might expect geography and history to be most homogeneous and empty, as in the geometry that I explore through the final part of Chapter 1. Even as Marx himself evokes Capital's imagined flattening of the world, he conjures up a rich hotchpotch of time and place, from medieval chivalry, through classical Greek verse, and fetishes, as we see in Chapters 2 and 3. In their *Timespace*, Jon May and Nigel Thrift find a 'radical unevenness' in the putative 'modern' world (2001: 5). People lived, as they had for centuries, 'according to a multiplicity of times and rhythms, learning to adapt to changes in those rhythms' (2001: 16). Even as mutations in experience and perception occurred, these were such that 'space is seen to both expand and to contract, time horizons to both foreshorten but also to extend, time itself to both speed up but also slow down and even to move in different directions' (2001: 10). In Chapter 4, we meet Darwin pottering in his garden so as to find scientific vistas on great ages of evolution, connecting the small to the vast. Conversely, in the Spanish writer Ros de Olano (Chapter 3), we encounter a crushing compression of distance and time by technology to a single point that discloses an ancient, global pain.

An aesthetic approach to history

I attend here to experiences of likeness, connectedness and persistence themselves and for their own sake, in their own right as a subject. I explore their sensual and emotional textures. 'Even the most fundamental conceptions of reason are imagined in sensual form', said the Spanish logician José María Rey y Heredia in 1849, '… we cannot conceive of a similarity without imagining sort of parallel lines' (Hasta las concepciones más fundamentales de la razón son imaginadas bajo una forma sensible: … no concebimos una semejanza, sin imaginar cierto paralelismo) (1849: 90). The approach I take to connections across place and time is aesthetic, in the sense that I attend to what it is like to have the experience of these.

'Esthetic experience is experience in its integrity', John Dewey once remarked. To comprehend it, 'the philosopher must go to understand what experience is' (1934: 274). This focus on the aesthetic experience of connections has a number of implications, entwined with its rationale.

The similarities we may experience across the histories of culture, or even in the persistence of parallel ways of making art and literature, do not arise solely from direct influence or transmission, or through immediate and apparent chains of cause and effect. Susan Manning and Andrew Taylor have commented on the impoverishment that results when studies 'are formulated in terms of one-way influence, or reception' or of 'the structure of implied priorities and progressions' (2007: 7, 10). The value and rigour of tracing cultural connections are not vouchsafed and justified by the search for such 'priorities'. In practice, comparativists of many kinds consider likenesses that do not emerge in those ways, or at least cannot be shown so to do. When we turn to immediate causes, it is not at all clear that similar developments in culture have the same systemic origin. We have seen that Manet's use of pastiche has similarities to Lucas, but it is far from apparent that there was any flow of influence from the one to the other. Manet is hardly discussed in Spain in the 1860s. The reasons for Lucas's interest in pastiche can be reconstructed with reference to more local debates in Spain about history and nationhood, and very different French painters (Delacroix, Delaroche and the *genre historique* painters, for example). Francisco Laso in Peru combines echoes of the Renaissance nude with a socially and painterly realism, as do Courbet and Manet; but Laso despised the rise of Realism in France, with which Courbet was associated (Ginger 2007a, 2013).

A surface effect of patterns observed in the history of culture does not always map onto a cohesive social, economic, political or even discursive system that produced it or to which it responded. Many accounts of cultural modernity have supposed that there must be some connection to a deeper system in some way, however complex: we find this in Berman's *All That Is Solid Melts into Air*, just as in Crary's monographs on perception and attention. It often underpins the view that Latin America was a site for the transmutation of modernity, as described by Rama: an expanding modern social, economic and political system encounters new conditions in the Americas. It is reasonable to doubt the very existence of such a causal system in the first place. Historical modernity has been described variously in relation to a range of factors: industrialisation, revolutionary liberal politics (supposed) European-style nation states, European imperialism and its legacy, capitalism, urbanisation, the rise of a 'bourgeoisie'. It is less than clear that these categories are internally cogent, that they actually map to historical realities, or that, even if they did, they would form a cogent system. Writing in the volume of essays, *When Was Latin American Modern?*, the historian Alan Knight states bluntly: 'The notion of "modernity" embodied in late twentieth-century modernisation theory … is not historically much use.' The concept 'lumps' things together, Knight observes, when they are actually disparate (2007: 106). Osterhammel's vast opus – one of only a few global histories of the modern world seriously to cover Spanish-speaking peoples – tries to provide a panoramic and thematic view of the 'transformation' (2014: xxi–xxii). It seeks to take into account the many different perspectives and nuances of the nineteenth-century world. This huge undertaking ends up in perhaps inadvertent testimony to the impossibility of such a task. Despite centuries now of thinking about global economic change, 'investigation and reflection by the very best minds in history and the social sciences has not produced any kind of general theory of industrialisation' (2014: 637). While talk of nationhood seems to have been important, 'the nineteenth-century was not an "age of nation-states"' (2014: 407).

By the same token, this present book is not an attempt to reconstruct the causal processes and structures of a system of cultural production and distribution over a large geographical area. Approaches of this kind have proved appealing in articulating a variety of visions of world or global literature, from David Damrosch (2014: 9), to Pascale Casanova's *World Republic of Letters* (2007) or Franco Moretti's distant readings of historical patterns over a large corpus of literature (2007). Within the sphere of Latin American studies, for example, Christopher Conway (2015) has likewise sought patterns of nineteenth-century cultural life in relation to social class, identity and context. Nor have I quite sought to delineate historically and geographically a defined historical culture – however complex – with cosmopolitan or universalist aspirations, in the fashion of Sheldon Pollock's *The Language of the Gods in the World of Men* (2009). This difference arises more from emphasis than direct disagreement with these extraordinary analyses. There are fragments of such things scattered across this book, as there are of the relationships between world art history and other socio-historical factors, such as we find elaborated (say) in Julian Bell's subtly interwoven *The Mirror of the Mirror* (2007: 7). I note here, not the impossibility of such historiographical undertakings, but rather the need to look to historical patterns that might exceed their kinds of historicisation.

More specifically, to reintegrate the cultures of the Spanish-speaking mid-nineteenth century into a larger story is not just to make the important point that, historically, they did come to notice or had direct contact beyond their local circumstances, as was the case (for example) with the internationally influential painter Mariano Fortuny in relation to artists of the United States and beyond (Boone 2007: 63–4, 79, 108–9). Nor is simply it to repeat the impressive findings of researchers, such as David Howarth, who have shown how much of a reference point Spain's early Golden Age was for 'modern' European cultures (for example, Howard 2010; Howarth et al. 2009; Tinterow et al. 2003). This important observation – on which I will touch once and again in this book – does not, after all, overcome the paradigm in which the Hispanic world mattered in its own right in the early modern era, but, in later decline, was subsequently relevant primarily with reference to that past. Nor is my purpose solely to trace the exclusionary structures of production and distribution that – both then and now – ensured that most mid-nineteenth-century Spanish-language writers and artists remained largely marginal beyond their homelands. Rather, the tracing of similarities between the mid-century 'Hispanic' world and more canonical art and literature affords nineteenth-century 'Hispanic' cultures a visibility that they were habitually denied historically. The point is to write the history of culture differently, so as retrospectively to reactivate their resonances and possibilities.

An alternative way to account for patterns of similarity across cultures has been to link these to certain fundamental cultural 'forms' available to human beings, repeated in continual variation across the expanses of place and time. Such 'forms' have what Caroline Levine calls 'affordances': they exist as latent possibilities, rather than as pre-defined outcomes (2017: iv). In *Structural Intuitions*, Martin Kemp has gone so far as to attribute 'historically recurrent patterns of thought' to five fundamental shapes of solids in the universe, identified as early as in Plato and Euclid (2016: 1, 14, 23). Likewise, the emergence of similitudes may be explained in terms of a large philosophical theory, as seems implied in Kaja Silverman's *The Miracle of Analogy* (2015). Silverman draws here on Heidegger's vision of how Being is disclosed in the world (Dasein). The observation of 'forms' with 'affordances' does not, however, require any such fundamental explanation, nor any commitment to some encompassing philosophical or scientific account of the world, nor to a finite number of such possible patterns.

While causality is not insignificant, it is important to explore what the resemblances and persistences are actually like in their fullness, above and beyond what brought them about. It was, after all, the fact of these resemblances that drew us to any comparative investigation in the first place. I compare, for example, the Argentine Pueyrredón's *Siesta* (Plate 5) with Courbet's *Wrestlers* (Plate 6) and *Sleep* because both feature two closely paired undressed figures in a narrow confine (Chapter 2). I place Estanislao del Campo's *Fausto* close to Nietzsche's *Birth of Tragedy* because both intimate the return, through music, of atavistic creatures in the contemporary world (Chapter 1). I see parallels between Thoreau's *Walden* and the Spaniard Juan Valera's *The Illusions of Dr Faustino* (Chapter 4) because both suggest a global vision born of rural retreat. Cause has too often been privileged over effect, when effect is the point of interest. Perhaps *cause* stands here as a putative guarantor of academic 'standards' while, in practice, deflecting from the subject at hand. If the notion of 'forms' and 'affordances' matters, it is not least because these may draw attention back to effect. More broadly, we might be alert to the risk that, in establishing guidelines for which resemblances and persistences we should properly pursue (which of them 'count', which are 'irrelevant'), we may stop attending to the effects of similarity and recurrence in their own right. Presumably, what lies behind any aversion to so doing is a kind of fear or anxiety. Causality provides 'depth' to what is otherwise literally 'superficial', a matter of surface similitude; guidelines prevent us wantonly associating disparate things, and ward off the ancient question, 'is analogy argument?' (Manning 2013: xi). I do not wish simply to dismiss such worries, but I do want to note their emotive content. Rita Felski, among others, has underlined how easily the affect of established styles of academic prose may be conflated with assertions of rigour (2015: 1–3).

There is a difference in disposition between those attracted to explanatory systems and firm guidelines, and those who, in their philosophies, suppose that releasing one's hold on these presents fewer dangers than might be anticipated. To borrow words from Thoreau's *Walden*, 'we may safely trust a good deal more than we do. We may waive just so much care of ourselves as we honestly bestow elsewhere' (2012: 205–6). When Richard Rorty (1979) spoke controversially of philosophy as simply the 'conversation' of humankind, he was making just such a gambit: that we would not more likely imperil (say) knowledge or morality by lacking an epistemology or ethical system, than we would if we had these things. So far as the present book is concerned, our experiences of resemblances and persistences in culture's history offer us their textures and their own realities: we can work our way through them, finding possible vocabularies. We can gamble – either way it is a gamble – that this may prove worthwhile. It would be better to describe this as the appreciation of the history of culture, than its analysis.

Writing in *More Investigations* (*Otras inquisiciones*) (1952) and pondering his own essays, the Argentine writer Jorge Luis Borges remarks that he had tended to be more interested in the aesthetic interest of historical ideas than in their apparently intellectual content (1985: 192). However, this need not be a sceptical stance: quite the contrary, we may assume that the resemblances and persistences are indeed there in our experience of them, and that we may indeed attend to them as realities. This involves a practice, not a theory:

that is, we explore and discover these things in the act of experiencing them through the words and images, and, not least, by writing them. We might compare this path to that of a craftsperson, finding their way through a material: Richard Sennett has spoken in this vein of 'the value of experience understood as craft' (2008: 288–9). All this involves a supposition not unlike that of Stanley Cavell when he speaks of the virtue of not clutching and grasping at the world (2013: 85–8, 108), or of Jean-Luc Marion – after Courbet – when he talks of how 'the unseen surged to the eye' such that 'the glory of the phenomenon in itself is manifest to the *ego*' (l'invu a surgi à l'oeil; la gloire du phénomène en soi se manifeste à l'*ego*) (2014: loc.2625, 2646). On that account, we could be open to the textures of resemblance and persistence in the history of culture, and our experience could be shaped through them, without our prior outlook forcibly shaping them. Vivian Sobchack has spoken in this vein of the notion that 'historiography is … transformed … in *narrated* acts of discovery and description that open up our senses as well as our intellect to the world … its always marvellous "otherness" from the way we would think it' (2011: 327).

Considerations of whether there are notable resemblances and persistences, and what we make of them, undertaken in this manner, are not underpinned by some schematic criterion against which we can test them. They cannot, in that very specific sense, be proven. Rather, things are established by showing, sharing, inviting – in conversation, as Rorty had it. That does not necessarily make them less robust or less real: whether we judge that to be the case depends, once more, on the extent of our faith in this approach, on whether we make this gambit. The aesthetic approach to history, in this present book, is an exploration of that possibility.

Aesthetic pedagogy

The approach I take in this book is pedagogical, not didactic. The book offers a series of experiences of resemblance and persistence. As in a humanities classroom, these are presented for exploration, to see, as if in conversation, where they might take us, what their possibilities involve. They are not urged on anyone as the correct point of view. In the words that Isaiah Berlin was fond of quoting, 'je n'impose rien, je ne propose même rien; j'expose' (2013: 91): 'I am not imposing anything, I am not even proposing anything, I am setting things out.' This is a corollary of the relaxing of causal and systematic explanation, the turning to the appreciation of effects: we open ourselves to their potential and see where it bears us. The patterns traced are, in that sense, 'weak', as Dimock would have it: they are deliberately incapable of 'yielding any theory with enough predictive (or even descriptive) authority to be called sovereign' (2013: 738). In the end, anyone may take or leave them.

Running through this aesthetic pedagogy is a double-edged relationship with some readings of Wittgenstein's late philosophy. The appeal of this Wittgenstein lies in his efforts to release us from the pursuit of a single grand theory, as from a dogmatic or assumed view of signs and language, and his corresponding appreciation of the diversity of practices that take shape in forms of life in human culture. We may entertain a whole range of ways of experiencing the world, understanding what they enable us to do. The interest is less in epistemology as such – in ascertaining the right way of knowing things – than in whether we are at 'home' in the world, as the American philosopher Stanley Cavell puts it (Cavell 2013: 33). On this account, Wittgenstein's primary concern is to relieve us of 'deep disquietudes' (Cavell 2013: 32) brought about by how we construe the world and our lives ('pictures' of the world), by how we live our 'forms of life'. The hope is that we may come to feel 'at home' amid the diversity of practices that constitute our forms of life.

It matters to anyone who seeks to find commonalities across place and time whether they feel 'at home' amid vast diversity, or whether they experience many forms of life with 'deep disquietudes'. At least, this is so if they do not seek to find commonality by stripping away all that is uncomfortable to themselves. It matters likewise to any historian of culture for whom the primary task is not to pass defining judgement on what they survey or to distil their own intellectual or aesthetic position, but for whom the imperative is to open the Pandora's box of human possibility. Conversely, my doubt about this Wittgenstein is whether his vision of release actually ends up making it difficult to be at 'home' amid such vast possibilities, the heterogeneous 'forms of life' proffered across place and time in the cultures of our world. This is because his version of being 'at home' involves trying to release us therapeutically from the entrancements of many ways of thinking, feeling and being. Many – perhaps nearly all – the forms of experience that we find in cultures across place and time are at odds with this therapeutic Wittgenstein. They appear as harbingers of sickness, tempters into madness; they bewitch us; they take us 'on holiday' (*PI* §38), away from 'home' and into exile (Cavell 2013: 34).

This book is close to Cavell's account of Wittgenstein in its exploration of release from inhibiting visions of culture. In particular, it shares a desire to escape the obsession with the autonomy of signs and representations and referents, forming an endless system of differences. That is just one picture of the world, characteristic of a particular cultural disposition – a variety of scepticism – which is contingent and could be renounced (Cavell 2013: 50). I likewise share Wittgenstein's suspicions of any quest for ultimate, rational justifications of things that we are manifestly able to do, and of our asking questions that seem unprovoked – all fruits of an inclination to doubt. For instance, some philosophers discuss whether and how they know that there is a tree before them, when there is no obstacle in the way, no indication of an optical illusion, and they have no defects of sight. We have taken phrasing used under certain circumstances, generalised it, then subjected it to doubt, which we seek to overcome (*OC* §347, 553). Once we realise that such questions – do I 'know' there is a tree? – are used only where there is a situation that provokes doubt – I could not initially quite make out the shape, for example – then we are back 'at home' in that specific 'form of life'. A futile, all-or-nothing quest for grand, single theories that master all aspects of our forms of life is the twin of a corresponding all-embracing doubt that impels and undermines it (and vice versa). Our ability to be at 'home' in the world is continuously deferred by such impulses, but that endless deferral becomes in turn a kind of mirror longing for the infinite. In contrast, Wittgenstein famously affirms that 'explanation comes to an end somewhere' (*PI* §1).

If we recognise that explanation comes to an end, our attention turns to exploring what is involved in our doing or saying particular things, in carrying out particular 'forms of life'. This is apparent in my interest less in whether a given cultural outlook or activity has some ultimate justification, or might be doubted, than in what it might enable us to do. This is so from a cowboy's claim to have seen the Devil in Chapter 1, through people seeing two images as one vision in optical devices during Chapter 2, or the refusal to renounce traumatic pain in Chapter 3. In a similar spirit, Wittgenstein suggests that forms, concepts and words are not useless or invalid simply because we cannot precisely pin down their boundaries or with precision state their meaning, so that they can withstand any doubter's questions (*PI* §71). Rather, 'vagueness' plays an important role in some forms of life because it enables us to do things that 'precision' prevents: what matters is the 'use' to which 'vague' things can be put. This viewpoint is apparent in the notion of 'taking shape' that recurs from the second part of Chapter 1 of this book onwards, beginning with the forms of actors' poses, the patterns found in photographs and those projected in occult practices. Imperfect outlines are presented here as ways of transmitting and communing with cultures and persons in spite of boundaries of place and time, and without losing particularity.

Forms of life can 'go on' across a myriad of situations because they are not schemata and they are not based on a fixed set of rules with precise boundaries to which things we subsequently encounter must be subjected. In the words of Wittgensteinian educationalist Nicholas Burbules, we learn forms of life 'through participation and activity', and we 'go on' with them in that manner, through their 'openness and indeterminacy' (2017: 131–2). Once I learn to say 'chair' (for example), I may encounter things I had never previously experienced as ways a chair could be, but this does not mean they are not chairs. The larger implication for cultural study is that to adopt a particular form of life, a pattern, shape or discourse is not inherently exclusionary, nor does it suppose absolute limits to a capacity to adapt and change. Such an outlook has its parallel in my practice in writing this book. Tracing a series of deliberately vague forms of life, the text 'goes on' from one place, time, or thing to another. In Chapter 4, for example, we go on through 'repose', traversing Flaubert's *Sentimental Education* from post-1848 France, through Darwin mulling on science in his English garden, and the Spaniard Rosales's paintings of national and classical history. Phrases and imagery taken from the mid-century enable us also to 'go on': Whitman's 'to leap beyond yet nearer bring' and 'Me myself' offer a path through Eugenio Lucas's paintings (Chapter 2) or the murderous destiny of Martín Fierro (Chapter 3). If only implicitly, the forms of this book as a whole do not seek to limit their subject matter to what I am able to discuss, but are an invitation to go on beyond its bounds. As Cavell notes, the fact that there is more that I can say is not the same as my withholding or deferring something (2013: 23).

On this account, Wittgenstein's approach is 'therapeutic': he aims to 'show the fly the way out of the fly bottle' (*PI* §309). Yet it is this very Wittgenstein, so appealing as a guide to release, that poses a challenge for an historian of culture and thought such as myself. On the therapeutic reading, Wittgenstein's interest in culture centres on philosophy's capacity repeatedly to cure us of the entanglements into which our forms of life lead us. Applied to the histories of thought, feeling and expression, this would imply that we should study such things primarily so as to disabuse ourselves of their confusions, and to return to what Wittgenstein calls the 'bedrock' (*PI* §217). It is this emphasis in Wittgenstein's thought that Cavell describes as a cult of 'poverty': an almost monastic self-purgation in the face of culture's sickness (Cavell 2013: 69–70). Taken with all seriousness, the therapeutic approach would at best leave vast swathes of the histories of culture as sterilised curios, observed now in such a manner that they may no longer infect us. Borges's sceptical take on the aesthetic appreciation of thought sometimes seems not far removed from such a conclusion. At worst, the therapeutic outlook would imply mastery over the past: the history of culture could only be tolerated where purified. Such an approach presupposes a commitment to deprivation, whereby, at the very outset, we renounce feeling 'at home' amid the multitudinous outpourings of culture and thought. To accept this is to strip much of culture's history (and present) of its inherent value. It ends, or severely curtails, any notion of time as a series of 'dynamic moments'. Put at its strongest, it forecloses the positive study of the history of cultures; perhaps despite itself, it shuts down human possibility. I find it hard to imagine that a therapeutic Wittgenstein would countenance much of what is explored in this book. In the face of our cowboy's claim to have seen the Devil at the theatre in Chapter 1, his preoccupation would surely have been to unpack the uses of the verb *to see* so as to clear up the misapprehension.

The notion of 'acknowledgement' – as advanced by Cavell and recently by Toril Moi – seems to address my dilemma, while in practice underlining the problem. Moi casts *acknowledgement* within a broad Wittgensteinian account of language and culture. 'To acknowledge your expressions and behavior is to show that I understand how it is with you', Moi explains (2017: 208). It is primarily a way of doing something: of responding to a claim made upon us by someone or something else (such as: 'I am in pain' (Cavell 2012: 246–66)). *Acknowledgement* is an alternative to assuming either that we know from a master theory how it is with other persons or cultures, or its sceptical twin assumption that we cannot possibly know how it is. Cavell characteristically observes that 'the anti-skeptic's motivation is at least as questionable as the skeptic's' (Cavell 2012: 248). The notion that human beings are separate from each other and from the rest of the world has been confused with the idea that there is an unbreachable epistemological gap between them (Moi 2017: 206). Unencumbered by a theoretical template, without a predictable guide to how we should read or view things, and unconstrained by doubt about our capacity to 'acknowledge', we may embark on 'a discovery of the unexpected and the new … an adventure' (Moi 2017: 217).

On the face of it, this might seem to enable us to feel 'at home' amid a whole diversity of cultures, texts and images, because we are able to 'acknowledge' them. Our apparent separation from them is no obstacle to our keeping them company, showing our understanding, or being transformed through our close encounter with them. Even so, that very notion of *acknowledgement*, for all its apparent openness to diversity, is through and through informed by 'poverty'. We can acknowledge what we wish, but our manner of doing so can never be fundamentally compromised by what we acknowledge, or we would end up back 'on holiday': we would be exposed to all the philosophical errors that this Wittgenstein seeks to avoid. For that matter, we would end up being unable to 'acknowledge' at all in Moi or Cavell's sense, because the notion of 'acknowledgement' derives from their specific philosophical stance. The prescription of this Wittgenstein really is 'stern', as Cavell puts it: he describes it as 'starvation' (2013: 69). We are only able to acknowledge all that diversity by being purged of it in the first place, as if sterilising ourselves against its most pernicious effects. A scholar of religion, Tyler Roberts, has aptly remarked that Cavell's 'acknowledgement' is essentially a 'spiritual exercise' (2013: 120).

I explore my dilemma explicitly in Chapter 2 through the opposition between 'lavishness' and 'poverty'. Cavell draws this distinction in *This New Yet Unapproachable America* (2013: 69–70, 72, 74–7), where he discusses Wittgenstein and nineteenth-century American thought. On Cavell's account, the discipline of 'poverty' involves the purifying return 'home': it entails not departing 'on holiday', not heading into exile and madness. It involves avoiding an 'endlessness of deferral' (Cavell 2013: 74), such as Theory had so often invoked in its account of modernity: the impossibility of ever establishing definitively how a sign should be used, a relentless infinite differing. 'Lavishness' – such as that of the 'endlessness of deferral' – is the result as much of efforts to create all-encompassing systems of knowledge meant to exclude doubt, as it is of their twin, absolute scepticism, which they provoke. Chapter 2 (Departure) crystallises the issue around Whitman's 'Me myself', Baudelaire's 'Mal', and the notion of a promiscuous gallery in the Prado, among other instances. There, I am interested in exploring whether humanity might forever 'lavishly' depart from one experience of culture to the next, and one linguistic or visual sign to the next, across place and time, without this amounting to an 'endlessness of deferral' in which we never find ourselves at home amid our own forms of life (Cavell 2013: 74).

The alternative gambit is that we might seek a way to feel 'at home' amid all the outpouring of human possibility, without committing to 'poverty' (or, at least, to that version of 'poverty'). Cavell toys with a distinct kind of 'lavishness', which he attributes to the philosopher Richard Rorty, 'a lavishness different from the ones of the great philosophers … a general post-philosophical cultural conversation' (2013: 72). Letting go of any prior philosophical commitment at all, and unperturbed by scepticism, we might truly inhabit the conversation of humankind, and be unafraid in so doing. In this book, I experiment with just such lavishness, as a manner in which connections might be forged across place and time. The supposition is that there are ways of doing so that enable us to explore and appreciate rich possibilities in connectedness through the history of culture, and that doing this need not ultimately prove harmful. Pedagogically, this endeavour often involves what, in Chapter 2, I call *ventriloquism*, drawing in part on the work of Steven Connor (2011). That means adopting forms used by past writers and artists, so as to make utterances, even to the extent of carrying on with the potential of what they did ('going on', in that sense), rather than what they actualised in their life's work. Some recur through the book, expansively extending beyond their originator: 'Look at your sister', words of a hypnotist in Chapter 1, or Marx's shove and kick from Chapter 2. This is akin to what the ventriloquist does with their doll (and its character). The ventriloquist need not be distanced, in the sense of being bodily and sensually or even emotionally remote, from what their *alter ego* says and does, its manner of talking and being. On the contrary, they will feel the words and movement physically in their own body: in their larynx, their mouth or their arm, for example. The voice that is heard is both and at once that of the doll and that of the ventriloquist. At the same time, this does not mean that the latter is then forever unable not to be the doll, to cease speaking and moving as it does. Like the 'Me myself' of Chapter 2, we find ourselves both 'in the game' and 'out of the game'. Ventriloquists, on the whole, slip easily between those two, as if they enter and exit states of possession. It is thereby possible to inhabit many forms of life across the history of culture, and for them to inhabit us, without that involving either an ironic distancing of oneself from these, or an unending embrace of them.

On the face of it, being 'at home' in such 'lavishness' would involve feeling no 'deep disquietudes' in any form of life, on holiday or otherwise. Even amid chains of endless difference, we would not feel 'deferral', at least as Cavell describes it. But the call to 'poverty' is not some mere inconvenient impediment to such expansive sentiments. Cavell aptly notes of Rorty's appeal to 'conversation' that it claims to be able to 'afford not to care whether the path of philosophy may be lost' (2013: 72). There really would be no safety net, nothing to fend off cultures that made us ill or drove us insane or simply, utterly misled us. The appeal of Wittgensteinian 'poverty' is that it allows us to keep to a 'path of philosophy' without having to commit to a theory, or to scepticism, or to deferral. It allows us to acknowledge diversity, to explore possibilities, without lacking judgement, or proving unable to state some kind of criteria. Rorty is all too sanguine about the 'conversation of humankind', and the risks to which its endless chatter and imagery expose us. He is all too confident that it is robust enough without such safeguards. Contemplating Rorty's conclusions, the Pragmatist philosopher Susan Haack speaks evocatively of 'a nasty muddle' and 'the very debauchery of thought'. Where 'truth "drops out"', she warns, 'the disaster is quite general' (1998: 20, 65) The assumption of this present book is that the risks are very real, and are inherent to being 'at home' in 'lavishness'. In such an outpouring, we would need to assume them and to travel through them, but not for that to experience them less as risks, as terrifying even. In that spirit, Chapter 3 (Sacrifice) dallies overtly with sickness and danger, ending in the maddening mirrors and glass reflections of mid-century Mexican art, images of dizzying analogy. It skirts what I call 'history's edge-play', a courting of destruction and self-destruction, a deliberate embrace of pain, in a quest for release from a given time and place. The threat of insanity looms from the very outset of the book in Chapter 1: a cowboy who saw the Devil, or a magnetised woman encountering her dead sister.

Mood and experience

In that spirit, the present book looks beyond what Felski calls 'the limits of critique' and its stance of '*professional suspicion*', its 'detached, dispassionate, and skeptical demeanor' which 'singularly fails to surprise' (2015: 46, 115; original emphasis). The very sophistication of probing ironies may deflect from the rich resonances of things that might seem more direct or apparent or even simple, giving us instead an *Infinite Jest*, as David Foster Wallace (1996) put it in the novel of that title. The constant Brechtian feeling of distantiation risks an attitude of implicit and ultimately invincible superiority towards all that is said and done. With that comes further risk of deprivation in our experience of the history of culture. 'The alternatives', Felski observes, '… are not limited to gullibility, blind faith, and slavish compliance' (Felski 2015: 50).

The four chapters of this book are more akin to the evocation of four moods and practices than they are to four arguments in the manner of academic critique. 'At bottom, in the phenomenon of transnational cultural experiences, is the possibility of shared emotions', the Japanese historian Akira Iriye has remarked (2013: 48). The observation holds of all the connections explored in this book (whether or not one baulks at the specific term *transnational*). I work my way across meeting, departure, sacrifice and repose, words that emerged out of the craftwork of my writing through the texts and images that I consider here. Each of the sections, taken as a whole, is a kind of ventriloquism of the forms of life explored through its pages. In turn each section is multi-faceted, and explores multiple voices and images. Each of these forms of life goes on through its myriad of possibilities, because it is not fixed to some pre-established definition or schemata. The emphasis is upon the experiences that the texts and artwork offer, upon what they suggest and evoke, more than on the interpretation of their meaning as such. Even when considering a work of thought, such as Marx's *Capital I*, my interest is in the sensations of connectedness that are opened up, over the reconstruction of the thinker's discursive reflection. There the depths of time give shape to the economic system of the present, atavisms haunt modern universalism.

In general, I have sought more to explore the dispositions that texts and art might enable – the emotional and even bodily stances in which we might inhabit the world – than to seek to extract ideological treatises from what I study here. I look beyond efforts (for example) to reconstruct out of Manet's paintings 'an unmistakable statement' on contemporary behaviour, or 'a way to probe the rottenness of society's belly from underground', or any such thing (Boime 2007: 668, 700). This book is not the child of interpretation, at least not if interpretation is understood in that sense. In the case of Manet, for example, I linger rather on the sensation of a tug and pull between violent rejection and attraction in his art. The classicist Shane Butler has memorably described interpretation as 'constitutionally deaf' to things 'that do not themselves constitute meaning', and 'a remarkably unfeeling lover of the Muses' (2015: 54–5). He recalls Susan Sontag's essay 'Against Interpretation' and her wish for 'an erotics of art' (2015: 87). Decades earlier John Dewey wryly remarked that 'there is always something stupid about turning poetry into a prose that is supposed to explain the meaning of the poetry' (1934: 165). Dewey saw that this need not be a matter of either/or: meaning is not excluded from what we appreciate aesthetically, rather the question, as with many distinctions, is one of emphasis, and not for that less important.

I have spoken repeatedly here of *experience*, as I do throughout this book. 'To account for one's experience of a work of art', Moi comments, 'requires willingness to pay close attention to that experience. It requires us to trust it, and to find it worth expressing' (2017: 217). *Experience* is a 'fuzzier word' than some alternatives, Richard Sennett observes, and deliberately so, richly spanning from 'emotional inner impress' and 'sensitivity' to matters of 'skill' and 'thinking', subsuming what is instrumental and what is an end in itself (2008: 288). It does not seek to disaggregate the many things it may include. Nor must it involve a subjection of everything one encounters to how one has previously experienced the world. Moi emphasises that the experience is not a set of fixed patterns; rather existing patterns can be broken (2017: 219). In speaking of experience as craft, Sennett remarks that it involves a 'not knowing quite what you are about when you begin' (2008: 262). *Culture* in the present book likewise indicates something more multi-faceted, and more inherently emotive, than the systems of signs and representations themselves, semiotics. I set aside any such rigourist definition of the proper object of cultural study. Moi finds herself perplexed by what use is served by defining *literature*; the same may be said of *culture* (2017: 213). We are able to 'go on' in employing the term *culture*, roughly distinguishing it from emphases on other things such as (say) chemical elements. In so doing we may appreciate its many dimensions above and beyond the pursuits of interpretation or the assembling and disassembling of systems of signs. If we were to think of this as 'thick description', we would look perhaps even more to the philosopher Gilbert Ryle's original coinage of the phrase than to Geertz's now famous redeployment of the words. Ryle's point in 'The Thinking of Thoughts' (1968) is that cogitating, like teaching, is not understood as a single thing, but rather is constituted by and observed in a bundle of attitudes, behaviours, gestures, techniques and boxes of tricks, in relation to one another.

Running through experience and culture are their moods, which Felski summarises as 'an overall atmosphere or climate that causes the world to come into view in a certain way' (2015: 21). As moods change, so do the experiences of connectedness that we have. What matters is more what those feelings and practices make possible – their affordances – than a test of philosophical or empirical truth. That is not because I hold truth in general to be relative – I really do not – but rather because the manner in which one feels connected to something, or has a mood, is not of itself falsifiable. Pedagogically, and through ventriloquism, these variations offer diverse experiences, to explore and consider, take them or leave them. This is what we encounter in tracing connections through the history of culture. Early in Chapter 1 (*Meeting*), it is the firm embrace of two friends that discloses companionship across German, French and Argentine culture, and between the medieval and the modern. In *Sacrifice*, we meet the sight of a political martyr at the point of death (the Spaniard Juan de Padilla) calling out across the centuries, compelling them to turn to him, and propelling him out of his place and time. In contrast, in *Repose*, Gorriti turns her gaze away from the risk of endlessly repeated pain, suffering and vengeance. Her stories deflect us into multiple, mobile, partial viewpoints that form networks of connections across time and place.

The gambit is that tracing links through moods is worthwhile in some way that is not reducible to the purification of those experiences, nor to an unending embrace of them, nor to ironic distance from them, even at their most apparently deluded. The psychiatrist R.D Laing once suggested that the way to engage with subjective experience is to find oneself 'going or being conducted – one cannot clearly distinguish active from passive here – on a journey' through it (1990: 104–5). While there may be entry and exit points to such immersive travelling, there is not necessarily a pre-existing map. Describing Wittgenstein's accounts of forms of life, Cavell talks of 'a dream-like quality', of there being 'no prior paths … no footprints' (2013: 18). The language we use to speak of this journeying would arise in the practice of undertaking it or of writing it. Laing warns of trying to shape those words forcibly into the kinds of frameworks familiar from scientific theorising (1990: 102–3). In a not dissimilar vein, in *Shamanism, Colonialism, and the Wild Man*, Michael Taussig cautions against reliance on 'the magic of academic rituals of explanation … with their alchemical promise of yielding system from chaos' (1987: xiv). (Taussig notes in more than passing his debt to the psychiatric nurse Frank Atkin (1987: xv), who was crucial to the Villa 21 experiment in alternative practice, and became known to Laing (Clarke 2004: 138).) For better or for worse, Laing himself had grandiose aspirations for his own supposedly shamanic journeys: that, taking us back beyond even some primal humanity, they could save people from being utterly lost. He talked portentously of the discovery of an 'inner realm' (1990: 104–7). I doubt my book will save anyone, and in talking of *experience*, I am not particularly concerned with notional inner realms.

But this book shares with Laing a gambit: that the very act of working through experiences may change us (however slightly) with the awareness that comes from engaging in such practices, and with the repository of dispositions and forms of life that it gives us. Laing talks of a 'natural healing process' (1990: 105). Stripped of its grander claim, this supposes that the alteration does not depend on and cannot be explicated by anything other than itself. Of the nature of the case, it is not possible to state systematically, less still in advance of the fact, how a person would be before or after following given trails of connectedness. One does not have to commit to a particular system of psychiatry to echo the words of queer theorist and philosopher Tim Dean: 'The psychoanalytical rule of free association … requires a suspension of judgment that permits different forms of thinking to emerge' (2009: 28). If such a suspension of judgement is declared impossible – Dean avers – 'psychoanalysis cannot exist' (2009: 29). The forms of life of connectedness are multifarious and variegated; to trace them is a practice and a craft, not a theory; we work with the specificities of the material; there is no safe, distanced vantage point for critique. This is pedagogy, not didacticism: it is not about stating with which experiences we should identify, which are right or wrong. The supposition is that to offer them, to ventriloquise them, to bring them into conversation, is enough; more still, that this is what is needed. 'Communication is not announcing things', John Dewey once said, 'even if they are said with great sonority.

Instead of modernity

Communication is the process of creating participation, of making common what had been isolated and singular' (1934: 242).

Intimacy and drama

The four chapters of this book share a quality of experience that I will call *intimacy*. I use the word, in a manner not unlike Cavell, so as to evoke the notion that signs, images and words may enable us to experience 'the world' (2013: 80), and thus other people, places, times and outlooks. Here signs offer us 'forms of *life*', 'not *forms* of life', as Cavell puts it (2013: 42–3). Such a possibility arises if we are not faced with 'an endlessness of deferral'. Such intimacy subsumes – but is not exhausted by – the feeling of closeness associated in recent cultural theories with the haptic, the sensation of touch. Speaking of aspects of contemporary culture, visual theorist Giuliana Bruno observes, 'an ever-stronger haptic desire to come into contact and be contacted' (2002: 117). In influential writings, Laura Marks has explored 'sensuous similarity' through 'contact', 'mediated by the body', in intercultural encounters (2000: 140, 168, 139). 'Mimesis ... is a ... relation of similarity', she says, evoking 'mimetic knowledge that does not posit a gulf between subject and object' (2000: 138, 151). Such sensual resemblances and correspondences are found throughout the erotics of this book, from sailors gathered to squeeze sperm in *Moby-Dick* (Chapter 3), to the collision and joining of same-sex bodies in Courbet and Pueyrredón's art or in Nietzsche's marriage of Apollo and Dionysus (Chapters 1 and 2). Through her *Atlas of Emotion*, Bruno traces multiple haptic passages across space, an 'experience ... involving a knowledge of surface, geometry, material, location, energy, and dynamics' (2002: 254). We find something of this in the sensual geometrical patterns transferred to photography from the bold body of the actress Matilde Díez or from landscapes (Chapter 1), as in the forms of matter across the universe (Chapter 4).

At the same time, the book's 'intimacy' goes beyond the haptic. It extends to sensations other than touch, from the outset when the two cowboys' bodies all but merge in the force of their embrace. It is unconstrained by the limits sometimes found in 'contact'. Whereas Marks focuses on the skin (one of her titles is *The Skin of the Film*), in Chapter 3 we encounter the rending of the bounds of the body, in a book opened with chisel blows to palpitating entrails (Antonio Ros de Olano's *Dr Lañuela*). Marks often seems wary of straying beyond a continual to-ing and fro-ing, familiar from the play of presence and absence, and the corresponding cult of difference and even of signs, found in many versions of modernity. She warns against a preoccupation with 'prediscursive' accounts of touching (2000: 144–5). 'What the works of art, the writing, and the world in which they exist have in common is not as valuable as the *differences* among them are', she declares (2002: loc.43). She prefers it when she has 'brushed, almost touched' something (2002: loc.34–9). It is not that such emphases are wholly lacking in this book. The final chapter explores delicate myriads of sensual juxtapositions, through the paintings of Fortuny, for example. The second (Meeting) finds us amid an erotic to-and-fro in Manet's relationship to past art. But these arise as passages, however apparently paradoxical, to an undeferred intimacy.

Culture that connects intimately does so by extending and persisting beyond any supposed confines of a place and time, beyond any narrow delineation of its 'context'. It might do so as much into earlier history as across what comes after: in this respect, there would be 'no past or future in art', to borrow Picasso's words (cited in Cowling 2002: 336). Culture of this kind would not simply be a series of signs that are received in other contexts, to be construed according to the outlooks and circumstances of each place and time, their sense forever deferred. Mulling reception theories of that latter kind, the art historian Christopher S. Wood points to 'a certain lack of drama'. Wood suggests that such approaches to interpretation deny us the 'conundrum of how to explain historically the transhistorically valuable' (2012: 171), that is, of how something could be experienced as classic. 'Classical texts', he says, 'are those that remember that the significant messages are borne in, instantaneously or even violently, though not always intelligibly. They measure the clumsy realities of human communication, time-bound and dependent on relays and inscriptions, against the angel-borne messages' (2012: 170). 'A strong concept of the classics', Wood avers, '… is nothing other than a strong concept of poetry' (2012: 170). The poet Alice Oswald has spoken likewise in *Memorial* (2011) of her desire to 'retrieve the … *enargeia*' of *The Iliad*, the '"bright, unbearable reality" … when the gods come to earth not in disguise but as themselves' (2011: loc.11). The experience of something beyond the bounds of any mortal life – at a minimum of something transfigured and projected beyond any such finite context – recurs throughout this book. In Chapter 2, I take seriously the presence of Satan in Baudelaire, as, in Chapter 1, I urge the importance of Nietzsche's invocation of two gods. In Chapter 3, the death of the artist – the actress Sarah Bernhardt posing in her coffin, the laurelled corpse of Mariano Fortuny – places them among the immortals.

Along with that sense of 'drama' – of the very highest stakes in the connectedness of place and time – comes an emotive force, expressed in 'the language of experience', of mood, and, at times, in rhetoric that evokes an epic scale. A god kicks out in Marx's *Capital*; vast violent gaps open in time across Manet's art; figures return from ancient mythos like the Devil in *Fausto*; the dead rise up, like Goya's restless spirit on his writhing walls; with Darwin, we serenely contemplate the greatest depths of history. In experiences of this kind, times and places may flow through one another, without apparent bounds, as they do through the thick paint of Lucas's art; creatures may persist in spite of history's passage, slaughtered for immortality as they are in Madrid's Cabinet of Natural History. This can doubtless prove unsettling, not just because of the overt atavism, but because the latter is symptomatic of the dissolving confines of any given person's world. 'We defend ourselves violently even from the full range of our egoically limited experience', Laing remarks, 'How much more are we likely to react with terror, confusion and "defences" against ego-loss experience' (1990: 104). In the writing of the history of culture, the effect may at times come close to a kind of academic dreaming, in which apparently sharp distinctions give way; I suggest, for example, that *The Birth of Tragedy* may be read as a scholarly hallucination. My interest lies in wondering what connections and persistences of that kind would be like, how it might be to have experiences of that sort, what might make them appear plausible. This seems worthwhile exploring, given that, amid the 'lack of drama' and with our depleted vocabulary for similitude, such things may be treated, almost unquestioningly, as unavailable and undesirable.

I do not say this by way of didactic recommendation of what follows, rather in a spirit of experimentation, of 'what if'. Rational argument cannot decide for us whether artworks and texts are indeed, in this sense, intimately connected, or whether they are only ever what they are to any given place and time. Attempts to exit the dilemma by using the term *transnational* are, in practice – and if the word amounts to anything substantive – a qualified bet on narrow contextualisation. Transnationalism pictures the world as a series of criss-crossed boundaries (Stanford Friedman 2015: 7). In pointing to the decision over whether any such intimacy exists, I am suggesting that what is at stake is a difference between two distinct dispositions, rather than asserting some form of relativism about the ultimate truth of the matter. In telling phrases, glossing Cavell, Michael Fischer remarks of 'intimacy' that it is 'remarkable because nothing seems to account for it'. By 'starting from the fact of our intimacy', Cavell 'emphasises the astonishing reality of our attunement' (1989: 61). Pedagogically, aesthetically, as journeys in appreciation, as practice and craft, as ventures through risk, the chapters of this book elaborate possible ways in which a disposition to believe in those things might play out. In that spirit, the first words of each chapter are 'Let us imagine …'.

Historical context is subsumed within intimacy, in its projection outwards and its persistence across place and time. If we are to suppose that things born of history may project, extend and persist, we must imagine that they do so out of and through their own historical conditions and make-up, in their own historicity. In this book, art and writing are intertwined with their immediate circumstances without being limited to them. I attend to the claims that the works themselves urge upon other places, other periods, which is a key aspect of what historically they were. We encounter the infrastructure of global communications, whether in *Walden* or *Dr Lañuela*; we meet the tensions between colonial Puerto Rico and the Iberian metropolis in *The Pilgrimage of Bayoán*; we view British imperialism and nationalism in Cameron's photographs, and the global positioning of the Ante-Bellum United States in *Moby-Dick*; in the writings of Colonel Mansilla, we approach the limits of 'Greater Europe' at the Argentine frontier. We likewise hear the plea for a future global order in *The Pilgrimage*, or for a transfigured belonging in the world through Thoreau.

From this perspective, context does not 'stink', as Rem Koolhaas so vividly asserted (Latour 2005: 147). In the broadest sense, to *contextualise* something involves apprehending it through its connections with times and places, and to judge some of these to be especially pertinent. That includes what, in *History in Transit*, Dominick LaCapra calls 'responsive understanding', which must supplement efforts to understand them through their immediate circumstances (2004: 17). Relationships may stretch back and forth across geography and history, forming the webs of 'deep time', the 'global civil society' of which Dimock has spoken (2006: 5). The point is to appreciate these trails as they take shape in the works of art reaching out over place and time, not to focus upon causes of the text and images through them. The latter emphasis involves the fallacy in cultural study – neatly stated by Jurgen Pieters – that 'if we want to gain an accurate understanding … we will need to understand the historical context out of which it [the work] grew and of which it is a manifestation. The more information we can get about this context, the deeper our understanding' (2001: 143). Perhaps we might speak rather of *context spread thin*: the painstaking reconstruction of a moment in time is not the sole priority, and we attend instead to patterns that spread in connections and resonances over swathes of geography and history, beyond cause and influence and even transmission.

Narrative form and language

There is no necessary contradiction between reconstructing notions from past 'contexts' (the 1850s, say), and using them to write in ways that deny such contextualisation. In his foreword to Manning's *Poetics of Character*, James Chandler ponders for a moment whether, by looking to 'the cultural influence of her Scottish Enlightenment paradigm ... her method ultimately shares something of the historiographical impulse that she polemically dismisses' (2013: viii). Yet, if a person accepts the gambit that things may persist and extend and project across place and time, it follows that past notions are not inherently bound to their narrow 'contexts', even as we may rediscover and recover them through history. To assume that an historic work of art or literature or belief may 'go on' is to suppose that it is not constitutively and for all time defined systemically by the characteristics of its origins. It is to assume that any such limitations are not of themselves exclusionary. Historic works of art and literature are likewise not simply defined by those aspects that later audiences have overcome, found to be ethically unacceptable, and therefore deem anachronistic in their own era. This is in part because such limitations are often contested in terms of the claim for justice that those very works urge upon the future. The sociologist Jeffrey C. Alexander emphasises this viewpoint on past thought in his study, *The Civil Sphere* (2006: 65, 153–4). So, while Whitman might express discriminatory views, these may be challenged through an appeal to his own notion of 'Me myself'. Habitually, when exploring experiences of likeness and persistence, I look to what Carol Armstrong calls the 'subideological' (1998: 220), and even to what Biman Basu, in a study of sadomasochism and African American literature, terms 'an encrypted utopian trajectory' (2012: 12). That is to say that, even given some degree of complicity with oppression, forms of expression may subsume an alternative to that very repression: they may offer alternate possibilities through their own affordances. As José Esteban Muñoz suggests in his *Cruising Utopia*, we can mine the historical evidence critically, with a view to undisclosed, unrealised potential (2009: 9, 16–18). Domination itself may resonate with liberation from confines, as we find with the images of actors and actresses and audiences that appear in Chapter 1, subjecting themselves to forces that break them out of gender and out of narrow context.

The sense in which such works 'go on', though, is larger still than all this. Were it limited to judgements of that kind, our purpose in encountering the past would, once more, be to denude it of all that we found alien, to reduce it to terms acceptable to our own, and in that sense to limit its 'going on'. Surveying 'departures' in Chapter 2, I emphasise rather the very experience of 'going on' that such works disclose, the longing and desire for sameness and connectedness that they transmit, and which, if accepted, compel us to relinquish any notion of a narrow contextualisation. In that chapter, I take Pueyrredón's doubled, masturbating woman of his *Siesta* (Plate 5) as one emblematic (and problematic) instance of this sensation. Notions, images and phrases flow back and forth across geography and time. In this book, I freely intermingle and fuse such things from the mid-nineteenth century with other descriptions of cultural forms. These too are presented as as 'affordances': patterns that can appear in any number of places and times, without direct influence, and that make specific kinds of connection possible. Precisely because they are potential configurations of our experience of place and time, they can recur in very different circumstances. I talk, for example, of *pulsations* – where one perceived shape continually mutates into others – such as we find in the patterned photographs by Juan Laurent and Martínez Sánchez in Chapter 1. I evoke *flickers* – where two separate images seem alternately to fuse and separate – as in Marx's and Manet's superpositions of past and present, and in optical toys, during Chapter 2. I speak of *bubbles* – where a place and time, as if in a Foucauldian heterotopia, seems to encompass non-chronological phenomena – such as I find in the Gallery of Isabel II in Madrid's Prado Museum. I talk of *looping* – where something is caught in endless painful repetition, like José Vilches's ever-screaming statue of Andromache in Chapter 3. I treat notions, images and phrases from the mid-nineteenth century in a similar fashion, invoking them as affordances in a range of circumstances beyond their origin: to leap beyond yet nearer bring (Whitman), for instance, or to shove and kick away (Marx), or two horses riding out together (Estanislao del Campo), or everything as a centre with respect to everything (*The Total Organisation of Matter*, in Chapter 4). In so doing, I at once evoke specific kinds of connectedness while also myself effecting a non-causal link: by repeating a phrase, image or notion, I connect disparate works that offer analogous effects. Among taxidermied animals we encounter a cone of copies from *Dr Lañuela*. Later phrases appear and reappear in a similar vein, evoking their own affordances: Cavell's *lavishness* and *poverty*, Wittgenstein's *family resemblances* and *to go on*, *telluric force* from Umberto Eco, *limbo* from the contemporary Spanish novelist Agustín Fernández Mallo.

Through the aesthetic appreciation of the history of culture, I work these layers together, as if textures of interconnection were being threaded ('one cannot clearly distinguish active from passive here', said Laing). If we follow this gambit, phrases, notions and images are not pinned down to a precise sense in an originary place and time. That is as true of secondary as well as of primary sources. The very titles of the chapters are not offered as tight definitions: I have no interest in presenting a disquisition on the proper usage of the word *sacrifice*, for example. By the same token – if we follow this experiment – the present book does not treat such phrases, notions and images as arbitrary signs to be used and reused freely. Rather, it redeploys them according to the potential inherent in them to effect specific affordances, the kinds of connection that they suggest as possibilities. To have confidence in the aesthetic appreciation of history – not to be afraid of its lack of systematic guidelines or foundations – is to suppose that, in finding a way through the textures of interconnections and affordances, 'we may safely trust a great deal more than we do. We may waive just so much care of ourselves as we honestly bestow elsewhere.'

There are elements of pastiche in this book, as there was to that last sentence, if by *pastiche* is understood, not just the copying out of hollowed signs, but that same capacity of extant phrases, words and images to suggest affordances, that dilation of possibility. (Such a practice may be infused with our own mortality, Chapter 3 implies: it may become a journey through death.) I am interested in what such phrases and imagery may effect, how they might, for example, 'allow[s] for a complex conception of sameness and for versions of solidarity that do not need to repress the differences', to borrow words from Paul Gilroy's *Against Race* (2000: 252). Many serve as a form of 'strategic universalism', in Gilroy's famous phrase (2000: 326). They appear, not as compellingly reasoned theories of human commonality, but as ways of imagining that might bring about connections across time and place. The tendency to pastiche is apparent in the specific way the book draws upon a range of fields of study and theories: gender studies and queering, trauma studies, interest in the haptic, discussion of nineteenth-century visuality. Such allusions matter here frankly for what they enable in the narrative of this present book, not so as to make claims to authority in those areas of enquiry or to establish a theoretical stance on them. My primary interest is in possible intimate experiences of connectedness, sameness, commonality, persistence per se; my main points of reference are discussions in Atlantic, global and hemispheric study concerning the notions of likeness and transhistorical endurance. Notions, phrases, images are significant here for the possibilities that they unfold for those specific kinds of intimate connectedness. When I evoke (for instance) same-sex desire in Courbet's *Sleep* and *Wrestlers* (Plate 6) (Chapter 2), it is in an effort to elucidate notions of sameness, not vice versa; that is, I am not seeking to research same-sex desire and whether and to what extent a notion of likeness is or is not helpful there.

Through the affordances, I work together brain images from France, preserved insects from the Americas, glass in London, poetry from Argentina; Flaubert and Nietzsche find themselves in the company of Rosalía de Castro from Spain and Juana Manuela Gorriti from Latin America. The flotsam and jetsam of history – optical toys found in Madrid, say – sit with now famous names like Melville or Marx. All of these things become classic: persistent, resistant to the confines of a place and time. The tracing of interconnections brings about the two key substitutions with which this introduction began. The story of modernity fades before a spectacle of linkages, stretching from and into the depths of history, the breadths of place. And, rather than lurking on the peripheries, the former Spanish Empire's vast territories thread through the narrative. We set out from Estanislao del Campo's poem *Fausto* in Argentina and end, in an echo, with Juan Valera's novel *Don Faustino* in southern Spain. The technique is not unlike that of Joaquín Torres García's famous inverted map of the world, with Latin America at the top and the United States and Europe below, pointedly reversing the dominance of the cultures of the North-West Atlantic. The perspective here is that of a Hispanist, looking outwards from their main specialism, with other texts and images looming up on the horizon, sometimes coming into view: bits and pieces of Britain, France, the United States, Germany. (This is perhaps as frustrating to non-Hispanists as the reverse so often is to us; the frustration is part of the experience.) But, in the flowing back and forth of connections, there can be no simple inversion. Nor does integrating the Hispanic world effect a clear, overarching transformation of our visions of the history of culture: the effect is necessarily more piecemeal (Ginger 2007b). So, there are many points of entry: Chapter 2 begins with Marx, Chapter 3 with Julia Margaret Cameron. The Spanish Empire and its successor states alternately come to the fore and fade, but return persistently through the book like a motif, without their role being reduced to a single, simple explanation.

The tracing of such intimate interconnections beyond cause and influence and transmission, of forms and things that persist across place and time, of journeys through mood and experience, of multiple points of exit and entry, gives this book its narrative structure. The supposedly standard humanities essay format, with its chains of cause and effect, of reasons and their consequences, in its very veneer of 'rigour', risks deflecting from such other ways in which the history of culture may be apprehended. In the final words of her final book, Manning looked to a way of structuring transatlantic history around analogy as a form of argument (2013: 269). 'To structure an argument aimed towards a conclusion in a regular academic style', Khadija von Zinnenburg Carroll has likewise remarked, 'would not revise the pace and linearity of … time and its classifications' (2014: 6). Speaking of her own monograph, Stanford Friedman observes that '*Planetary Modernisms* is, for the most part not written in conventional academic prose. It experiments with alternate forms of argumentation …. The logical progression of a Ciceronian argument seldom structures an oftentimes dialogic or associational processions of ideas and examples' (2015: 13). The four chapters of this present book could be ordered into other sequences, as, in places, could their component parts. Even read continuously, the prose does not advance in a simply linear form, but echoes backwards and forwards through repeated phrases ('the other night I saw the Devil', 'to leap beyond', for example); at the end of Chapter 4 we come to words from the ending of the first part of Chapter 1, which in turn are a quotation from Umberto Eco. These repetitions do not form a robust and overt structure, overarching the book, like some tightly woven set of leitmotifs, but come and go, disappearing in places entirely from view.

To find one's way from one text or image to another is simply to do that. 'It is in the groping that the valuable work lies', says Mieke Bal in her *Travelling Concepts in the Humanities* (2002: 11). It is to reach out to the next thing, but also to be receptive to a suggestion, to an emerging notion, of what might join in. It involves the releasing of our clutching at the world, to borrow Cavell's image (2013: 108): it is an opening of our hand. There is no defined corpus here, and no compulsory reading list. It is easy to deceive ourselves otherwise, and to suppose that we may or should bring such things, one way or another, under control. Yet insights in the humanities depend very much upon unpredicted conjunctions. They involve what the philosopher Nicholas Davey has called 'the creative uncertainty ... upon which the movement of all understanding rests' (2006: 210). Talking of her own version of 'deep time', Dimock advocates 'an archive that errs on the side of randomness rather than on the side of undue coherence ... if only to allow new permutations to come into being' (2006: 79). The groupings of images and texts that we discover may become apparent only after the event of our tracing connections: just as Minerva's owl flies at dusk, the sense of our doing things may be often manifest only in their own wake.

In the practice and the craft of appreciating linkages, the specificity of our experience of each image and text is retained: it is through the textures of these that we are able to find connections to others. Often in this book, the juxtapositions are starkly apparent: in Chapter 1 we shift abruptly from one starting point to another: August 1866 outside Buenos Aires; a studio in Madrid in the summer of the same year; late 1871 in Basle, Switzerland; Mexico City in the mid-1850s. Intimacy does not eliminate specificity and flatten out difference, but rather exists through these things in what Estanislao del Campo calls *mixtura* (blending). In the absence of a system, or grand theory, it is only possible to work from and through the textures of experience, in openness to it. The very energy of 'dynamic moments', the disruptive effect of integrating the Hispanic world into a large narrative, depends upon the force of specificity as these things enter into juxtapositions. The case study thus looms large in this book's narrative form. The very notion of such a thing – a 'case study' – supposes that something evinces at once specificity and a relevance to larger matters, individuality and exemplarity, both held together, without loss of either. In dwelling at length on the value of the genre, Chandler has evoked 'its peculiar mediation of particularity and generality' (1998: 197). It was to this form that James Dunkerley looked in his great history, *Americana*, so as to weave together the mid-nineteenth-century south and north continent. The result, he remarks laconically, is 'unusual in its format and approach' (2000: xxi). In some lengthy sections, the cases come together in something like an essay form, but not so much through 'Ciceronian argument' or a predefined corpus. Rather, the process is, as Dimock puts it, 'cumulative' (2006: 79), with resonances joining suggestively, the textures of words, phrases and images combining to form a mood or disposition.

This book as a whole has – I hope – its own aesthetic. I mean not that it sets out didactically a view of what literary and artistic form should be, but that, through its phrasing, images and recurrences, in its textures, it offers an experience of its own: the beating of the hooves, the return of the ancients, the kick and the shove, the penetrative woman, the promiscuity, the bubbles, the flickers, the looping, the slippage, the soothing dispersing points of vision, the tangential apprehension of vastness, the chiselled heart, the meeting, the departure, the sacrifice, the repose, the spinning thaumatrope.

1

Meeting: coming together and taking shape

... your feet I'm following
In soft steps on a path the way you lead ...
Au Revoir Simone, 'A Violent Yet Flammable World'

Let us imagine a coming together, a meeting of here and there, or then and now, of one and another, of things that might be thought bounded within their own worlds. Some such notion of a meeting is frequently apparent in ways of talking about how diverse people, societies and cultures have come to inhabit the world. It is present in the oft-used concept of an *encounter*, whether it evokes something good or ill. Mary Louise Pratt has famously spoken of 'the *contact* zone' not least to describe what happens between colonial European, or European-descended and other peoples (1992: 6; emphasis added). In reviving neglected Asian thinking about such things, Kris Manjapra talks of 'zones of *conversation* ... between different cultural, linguistic and political communities' (2010: 3; emphasis added). Exploring the expanses of time, Alexander Nagel evokes 'mutual relations' instead of stark divisions of time periods that are seemingly distant from one another (2012: 25). In her *Planetary Modernisms*, Susan Stanford Friedman speaks of how 'polycentric, recurrent modernities ... develop not in isolation but always *relationally* through *encounters* with other societies and civilizations' (2015: 62; emphasis added). If only in its denial, some notion of meeting is suggested too by the talk of 'presence' and 'absence' that has so frequently characterised discussion of language, signs, representations, and thence of 'modernity'. This issue is directly implicated in the potential meeting of people, societies and cultures. In his influential *Voice and Phenomenon* [*La voix et le phénomène*], the French philosopher Jacques Derrida suggests that, wherever signs are used to communicate between people, and across time – ultimately beyond the death of anyone who made any utterance – the originator of what is represented cannot ever be fully present to their interlocutor. They cannot even be fully present to themselves (1967: 60, 72–6, 104–8).

On this account, if there is an encounter, it must be characterised by an absence, and with it a deferral. *Must* here means either *necessarily does* or *obligatorily should*, or both these things. The notion is that, otherwise, the encounter would be either impossible or oppressive (or both these things): a denial that the parties involved are actually 'other' than one another. The 'absence' offers guarantees against any such refusal of otherness – or so it is supposed – because neither side is overwhelmingly present in the encounter. For this reason, many accounts of meetings, whether between people, societies and cultures, or between language, signs, representations and the world, emphasise a to-ing and fro-ing (a *vaivén* in Spanish), an endless, transformative motion between incommensurable things. At a minimum, it is often supposed that the contact means that something on each side is discarded or lost or missed out, even as something is gained when some new arrival is adapted by a culture and the culture altered by it. Hence in Dipesh Chakrabarty's *Provincializing Europe*, we read of the importance of a 'politics of translation' arising from the key notion of 'difference'. This would give rise to what Chakrabarty calls 'translucence – and not transparency – in the relation between non-Western histories and European thought and its categories' (2001: 17–18). In the absence of any single meaning that would be the precise equivalent of terms from the two (or more) cultures – a 'universal middle term' – there is instead a bartering, not an exact exchange, between the diverse outlooks brought to the table (2001: 83–5). Likewise, Pratt emphasises the ethnological notion of transculturation where marginalised groups select inventively from more dominant cultures (1992: 6).

Let us imagine, though, that it might be otherwise: that there might be no 'deferral' as such in the meeting. Let us imagine that in some meetings, the here-ness and now-ness, the then-ness and there-ness might not separate peoples, cultures and societies. Rather, they might bring about an intimate companionship. The two (or more) parties might be fully present to one another and fully open to one another's presence. Or, at least, one party would willingly prove itself able fully to accept the presence of the other: that is to say, there would be no alienation in its so doing. Or, out of a meeting there would arise something new, beyond either of the parties, but which involved no loss at all: the two (or more) would still be entirely present even as they were exceeded in the new blend. To borrow words from Tim Dean on barebacking and its implications, this would be 'an experience of unfettered intimacy, of overcoming the boundaries between persons' (2009: 2). Were a meeting of this kind to take place, it would not always, necessarily involve the absence of features familiar from the notion of a *vaivén*. Irony may signal difference, whether that be between one culture and another, or one culture and another's version of it, or between a representation and what is represented or intended. Such irony could be subsumed by something larger than it – by the meeting, the companionship itself – in which the presence of all parties would be felt. In turn, we would not be entitled to assume, simply because there was an ironic touch to something, that it involved 'deferral'.

We might find realised, in a particularly acute form, what has been intimated by a variety of theorists of global history: the 'possibility of shared emotion' of which Iriye speaks (2013: 48), the potential – as Gilroy sees it – for the local or national not to be compromised within an internationalist outlook (2000: 350). The neo-Hegelian Bruce Mazlish has argued that 'it seems requisite for a global society to accept the cultural particular, as well as its accompanying ethnic and national differences, as part of the very universality of globalization' (2006: 91). Kris Manjapra has remarked similarly on the need to return to 'the different kinds of cosmopolitanism that exist outside the assimilationist versus particularist dichotomy' (2010: 3). Looked at over time rather than place, such meetings would involve the thoroughgoing replacement of the 'modernist historical frame' (Nagel 2012: 12). In the meeting itself, there could be no delineated periodisation between a 'modern' and an earlier, or later, epoch. The chronologically earlier party would be as if alive once more in the encounter, because no longer confined to their originary time. Following Warburg, Philippe-Alain Michaud has spoken of how someone seeking to engage with the past might 'displace his [*sic*] body and his point of view, proceed to a sort of transfer by which the "timbre of those unheard voices" … would be suddenly revealed' (2007: 18). We would thus revitalise our relationship with classical antiquity and early modern culture

Instead of modernity

(Michaud) or with the medieval (Nagel), among other periods. In the first part of this chapter, we will re-encounter medieval myth, early modern culture and characters, and Greek divinities in nineteenth-century Argentina, Spain and Germany: Faust, Apollo, Dionysus. Aesthetically, we would encounter something akin to the 'pure embodiment of value' that Manning finds in Robert Burns' 'A Red, Red Rose'. What is entirely specific, personal even – and thus without justification or explanation in terms of general principles – would be experienced as something shared and unlimited by its originating circumstances (2013: 265–7).

A meeting of this kind would be experienced as an *intimate culture*, to use the phrase I will take up later in this chapter. Or, perhaps better put, experiencing the meeting in that way would constitute an *intimate culture*. We would avoid emphasising any framework of causal explanation for, or moral judgement on the experience of the other, even as these things would not be utterly irrelevant. To prioritise either would be *per se* to distance ourselves from that experience by localising it in a context, whether ethical or historical. It would mean, as it were, looking behind or beyond it, as if that in some way offered some justification for our having had the experience. Above all, it would mean understanding it primarily within our own frame of reference. Renouncing such things would be the condition for the degree of attunement necessary for this kind of intimacy. The supposition would be that such a renunciation were possible. In Tim Dean's words, 'no account of experience necessarily constitutes a recommendation, a justification, or, conversely, an expression of regret concerning that experience'. 'Judgment' (in those specific senses) can indeed be 'suspended or deferred' (2009: 29). All that we would have would be 'affordances' from each meeting whose ramifications we might explore.

In a chapter that dwells on actors, storytellers, dancers and spectacles of entertainment, it is tempting to reach for the word *performance* to describe what it would be like to adopt any such possibility. In Part 2, we will meet leading Spanish artists of the mid-century, especially the celebrated actress Matilde Díez, who travelled to Mexico in the 1850s, alongside others such as the soprano Dolores Custodio in drag. If I have shied somewhat here from the term *performative*, it is because it has so often been conflated with a notion of the 'constructedness' of cultural experience. The latter derives from a notion of a divide between representation and the world that is at odds with the sense of intimacy that is entertained here. Conversely, I take it that such intimate experiences might be said to be performative in the broader spirit of the term stemming from Judith Butler's *Gender Trouble*: that they do not require justification in terms of some supposedly prior and hierarchically more important frame of reference. No given sensual or erotic experience (same-sex desire, say) needs a psychoanalytical explanation, or serves some pre-ordained purpose (a teleology) within an overall scheme of things (Butler 2007). From the perspective of an intimate culture, it would no more be a question of pathologising any experience of the meeting with the other, than of de-pathologising it. It would not be about disabusing ourselves of some ethical error. None of these things would ultimately be at stake (though they may, like any thing, rear their heads): that is simply not the focus.

In such a spirit of engendering meetings beyond prior frameworks, this chapter (like its successors) sets together disparate encounters, bringing them each into a kind of companionship with one another. The first part of the chapter forms as if a triptych with a slimmer middle panel, Argentine cowboys and operagoers are on one side, and on the other, Nietzsche, Wagner and the Greek gods Dionysus and Apollo; between these two is situated a group of Spanish friends meeting Mephistopheles, Faust and their victim through music. We begin with Estanislao del Campo's poem *Fausto* on the outskirts of Buenos Aires after a performance of Gounod's *Faust*; we turn to the same opera reworked as a fantasia among the painter Mariano Fortuny's friends and depicted in his art; before moving to Germany and Switzerland for Nietzsche's *The Birth of Tragedy*. We shift from here to the arrival of Díez in Mexico, her photographic image as produced by the transnational company Laurent & Co., and thence to encounters opened by the photographic medium, translating Spain across place and time, through Laurent and his Spanish collaborator José Martínez Sánchez, traversing occult practices as we touch on Browning's poetry and a version of Poe's account of the death of Mr Valdemar. We will dwell on the fraught encounters and relationships of German, French, Anglophone and Hispanic cultures, of north and south, of the ancient and modern in the mid-century. We will pass through the internal divisions of post-independence Argentina, the war between Argentina and Paraguay, the Franco-Prussian War and German unification, the efforts of Spaniards to project a renewed image of its place in the modern world, the attempts by Spaniards and others to come to terms with the country's imperial legacy, and the presence of contemporary Spanish culture in independent Mexico.

We will dwell particularly on nineteenth-century obsessions with (geometrical) 'shape' and its role in transmission and communication, in a putative universal language, a kind of craft, that aims to overcome dichotomies between what is particular and what is shared, between what is taken and what received, between the animate and inanimate, dead and alive, past and present. The then relatively new medium of photography has a significant role here, but it is not treated as a medium apart, and I move freely in and out of specific reference to it. I take it that the indexical character of photograph, its actual preservation of light from the physical world, rather than setting it apart, makes it an instance of the ways that forms are articulated in the world. The chapter provocatively interweaves its account of mainstream nineteenth-century performance practice and the interest in the occult with extreme sexual experiences and the transfiguration of the human body. Encounters may be contingent and casual, and not for that less valuable. To state this sensually and erotically, the chapter offers a variety of historical and geographical 'cruising' with a continual 'openness to alterity' (Dean 2009: 176). The sensual encounters evoked in this chapter range from the blending of bodies in embrace, through experiences of domination and submission, to penetration by and of men and women, the configuration of bodies and objects into patterns, and the power of mesmeric forces.

An intimate erotics of culture of this kind may not simply be assimilated to (say) the liberal-minded views of an early twenty-first-century Anglophone academic. It is one thing to queer the past, or – perhaps better put – to disclose the past's queerness; we will see such things in the two *gauchos*' embrace in *Fausto*, in the marriage of Apollo and Dionysus in Nietzsche, and in the suggestions of a phallic woman with the actress Matilde Díez. It is quite another thing to write out, or quarantine behind a screen of ethical judgement, what proves less comfortable in the past: for example, a nineteenth-century emphasis in some quarters on the special qualities of male friendship, or (for that matter) the much maligned interest in the straight lines of classical geometries. If we are to imagine an intimate culture, it would and must extend to what we find alien, however much this may involve some 'self-abolition'. We would be confronted by what it would be to embrace things utterly other than ourselves, to be blended with them. Conversely, that prospect – of itself – would tell us nothing about how we might afterwards feel disposed towards the world, in what may prove a troubling experience.

Coming together parts 1 and 2, with interlude

Part 1

It is August 1866. Outside Buenos Aires, one Argentine cowboy, or *gaucho* – El Pollo – by chance meets his old friend, Laguna, and recounts the experience he has had at the Colón Theatre in the city. There he has heard the opera *Faust* by the French composer Charles Gounod. The two *gauchos* appear in a poem, written by the Argentine author Estanislao del Campo, apparently the day after seeing the spectacle himself, on the 24th of that month. The story has it that he did so at the behest of his own friend Ricardo Gutiérrez, as they joked during the performance (Lamborghini 2008: 113). The poem was titled: *Fausto: Impressions of the Gaucho Anastasio el Pollo on the Performance of This Opera (Fausto: Impresiones del gaucho Anastasio el Pollo en la representación de la Ópera)*.

Fausto is a poem of coming together, but a poem also of apparent irony. The coming together flows from an initial meeting through multiple further levels. I say *flows* because the first level enables all the others, and, once this begins, each level comes to involve every other one. The first to be joined are the two *gauchos*. When they embrace, they do so with such intense physical force that 'their two souls in one / may even have blended' (sus dos almas en una / acaso se misturaron) (2000: 26). Out of this warm welcome comes a close relationship between the city life of an educated Europeanising Argentine elite, and the rural world of the cowboys. The long conversation and storytelling between the men comes to centre and linger on the opera performance in Buenos Aires that El Pollo has attended, and which he now conveys beyond the city limits. Conversely, it is through the voice of an educated, European opera-going member of the urban elite – Estanislao del Campo – that we hear the *gaucho*'s dialogue. In turn, this encounter gives us a mixing of European opera and elite culture, with the countryside of the Americas. The reader now beholds Gounod's opera only through El Pollo's conversation with Laguna, in his *gaucho* voice, through his eyes and ears. Likewise, El Pollo's tale is shaped utterly, through and through, by the *Faust* libretto: of the six parts of the poem, five correspond to the acts of the opera (the first offers us Laguna's encounter with El Pollo).

In turn, in the outlines of Gounod's work, we find a meeting across the heart of Europe, between French and Germanic culture: we discern in its plot and preoccupations the shape of Goethe's great poem *Faust I*. The comings together occur across the depths of time as well as the expanse of place: by extension, through Goethe – as through Gounod – we are visited by a medieval Germanic myth, that of Faust. Finally, in the course of the poem, artistic representation is confounded with external reality, just as the souls of El Pollo and Laguna were squeezed together through the force of their hug. Such is the power of the staging in El Pollo's eyes and ears that he talks of what he witnessed as if it were a simple fact: 'the other night I saw / the Devil' (la otra noche lo he visto / al demonio) (2000: 33). (Or, so he claims.) In this way – putatively at least – the blending of sign and referent is associated with the merging of cultures, times, places and individuals. All in all, these transformations are worthy of Mephistopheles himself, turning the old into the young, or dressing the farm girl as a princess – 'Ce n'est plus toi!', it is no longer you, the libretto says.

In the critical essays that accompany the poem in its 1870 edition, an early commentator, Carlos Guido y Spano, remarks that only the numen – the presiding spirit – of the Devil himself could have inspired del Campo to this most bizarre of undertakings, and, above all, enabled him to get away with it (del Campo 1870: 222). The breaking of bounds throughout the poem – between people, times, places, world and representation – echoes Satan's releasing of Faust from the finite limits of his own mortality, so as to roam across geography and history.

Fausto thus goes to the heart of this present book, and especially the notion of a 'meeting'. It offers at least the prospect of undeferred intimacy. And it does so by integrating the Spanish-speaking world into the wider 'West': it treats the 'Hispanic' as an equal participant, a co-creator, and dispenses with the distinction between a culturally hegemonic 'centre' (Gounod's Paris, North-West Europe) and a 'periphery'. By the same token, it seems to look beyond the opposition – often perceived as internalised within Argentina and Spanish America – between a Europeanising urban elite looking out across the Atlantic, and a hinterland population that is not simply assimilable to such forces. In his study of the warlord Juan Facundo Quiroga, the influential Argentine politician and intellectual Domingo Faustino Sarmiento famously crystallised this divide as that between civilisation and barbarism, with the *gauchos* on the latter side (1845–51). Del Campo's poem projects a vision of a new unity, emerging out of Argentina, in the face of the recurrence of war around the new borders of the post-independence Spanish Americas: the work was sold to finance military hospitals during a bloody war against Paraguay. At the same time, the poem also suggests the prospect of deferral and distancing through irony. Taking these two aspects of the work together as we read *Fausto*, we encounter a potential opposition and a choice between an intimate encounter, as described above, and its opposite. Put slightly differently, the poem explores relationships between potentially undeferred intimacy, and the acknowledgement of irony. The fusion of sign and referent may seem undermined even as it is affirmed. El Pollo perhaps protests too much that he truly observed the extraordinary events of the opera, and, like his companion, is increasingly inebriated as he does so. Laguna's cries of astonishment serve in turn to underline the reasonable question: 'What are you saying? … Bleedin' amazing! / By Christ the father! … Can it be true?' (¿Qué dice? … ¡barbaridá! … / ¡Cristo padre! … ¿Será cierto?) (2000: 58).

In turn, the blending of cultures and of places and times may either be a comic misapprehension – a failure to make appropriate distinctions – or a deliberate deceit or joke on El Pollo's part. Either way, apparent fusion once more might point to ultimate difference. Margarita's brother, for instance, is described as an Argentine solider on his way to battle with Paraguay, as if a medieval German could be a nineteenth-century child of the Americas (2000: 67). Within Argentina, not all may be well either in the encounter between the Europeanising urban elite, and the rural *gaucho*, on a social or a literary level. When El Pollo reaches the theatre, the city crowds dirty his boots and his knife is stolen from him (2000: 43). In the midst of the vast conflict waged by the Argentine government against Paraguay (1864–70), we hear of the economic struggles of the *gauchos*, due to the war (2000: 30). Within the poem, the voice of Estanislao del Campo, for all its apparent imitations of gauchesque voices, is manifestly not that of a *gaucho*. Even if his errors go unnoticed – the poet Lugones famously slammed him for supposing a cowboy would ride about on an 'overo rosao' – he is obviously a member of an urban elite, an educated military officer, a theatregoer, imitating Gounod and Goethe, as well as a multitude of other literary sources. Rafael Bonilla Cerezo (2010), for example, has mined the poem for allusions from *Orlando Furioso* through Cervantes to the great seventeenth-century Spanish poet Luis de Góngora.

For these reasons, *Fausto* has come to seem emblematic of a widespread vision of Argentine and, indeed, Latin American culture: it is a quintessential text for a widespread vision of Latin American modernity. First, Argentina and Latin America offer their own, alternate path to modernity, where the latter is understood as an awareness that signs are signs, and thus autonomous of the world. Second, there is at once a close relationship with and immersion in hegemonic European culture, and a self-conscious distance from the latter which causes it to be transformed on American shores. This occurs as much within the Americas – it is said – as in their direct encounter with Europe, because of the tendency of Europeanising cities to come into contact with much less Europeanised hinterlands. The influential Argentine novelist and intellectual Ricardo Piglia places *Fausto* at the heart of a cultural trend that culminates in the most celebrated of the country's writers, Jorge Luis Borges. The interplay and contrast of Europeanising culture and of the gauchesque creates a 'system of quotations, cultural references, allusions, plagiarisms, translations, pastiches' (sistema de citas, referencias, culturales, alusiones, plagios, traducciones, pastiches) (Piglia 1986: 41–2, 53–4; the quotation is on page 41). As European culture is obsessively pursued in a land where it is not entirely at home, so it breaks into a multitude of fragmentary representations unrooted from their referent.

Parody and pastiche thus give us both a version of cultural modernity and the unstable interplay of multiple cultures: these latter two amount to the same thing, and depend on one another. In her seminal book on the gauchesque genre, another Argentine literary theorist, Josefina Ludmer, emphasises the poem's 'coming-and-going', its *vaivén*. On such accounts, *Fausto* seems neither to commit to the many connections it evokes, nor entirely to deny them: it is shot through with ambivalence (1988: 274). Ludmer points to the dubious contracts evoked in the poem, so as to underline the uncertain faith we might likewise place both in the relationships forged and the signs that stand for them. El Pollo is not paid by the city dweller who ordered wool from him; the Devil's pact with Faust is, of course, at the cost of the latter's soul and of Margarita's death. We can take *Fausto* at face value only as a work of literature, in which all the pairs that are connected form parodies of and jokes about one another, and all are fictitious and theatrical. The only thing that truly joins the various parts is literary language itself, the act of storytelling, the playfulness and play of ambivalence between its component stories, which is the real subject of the poem (1988: 244–5, 255–69).

Irony, here, at once opens a breach in time – creating a modern era – and undoes any pure similarity or commonality across cultures. Lamborghini comments of *Fausto* that 'in parody, the similarity between the derivation and its model has nothing reverential about it; on the contrary, it is taken in jest so as to neutralise its paralysing power' (En la parodia, la semejanza del derivado con su modelo no tiene nada de reverencial; por el contrario, se lo toma en solfa para neutralizar su poder paralizante) (2008: 112). Truly to share likeness, then, would be to be oppressed: ironic transculturation enables the possibility of a free Latin American culture, even as it emerges from close ties to Europe. *Fausto*'s parody, Antonio Carreño-Rodríguez remarks, is a 'sign of emancipation', characteristic of modernity (signo de emancipación) (2009: 17). Geographical as well as temporal separation is thus realised. Ludmer's use of the word *vaivén* – *coming-and-going* – indicates what is habitually privileged: a kind of ping-pong, in which for every connection we make, there is a corresponding disconnection, and vice versa. Irony and tension reign supreme, if only as the facilitators of change, enabling cultural metamorphosis. Parody and pastiche are frequently understood as ironic in that sense. Even where irony is not quite emphasised, there is – in Mariano Siskind's words – a 'constitutive lack' which accompanies the 'longing for universal belonging'. That is to say, where Latin Americans might affirm their belonging to a wider global, or even just Western, culture, they can only make that claim in a way that acknowledges the inability to realise this absolutely in concrete, specific ways, because of 'differential identity' (2014: 9). In this way, just as Piglia's account of Latin American pastiche provides a route to modernity's destabilised signs, so the historical 'constitutive lack' provides a road to recent radical leftist universalisms. Thus, there are echoes here of the attempt by the Argentine political theorist Ernesto Laclau to envisage a claim to universality as at once absolutely necessary, and inherently empty of pre-defined specific meaning, like a floating signifier, *'an empty place'* (2000: 58; original emphasis). This is, at least, a get-out-of-jail for those seeking to assert universal justice while at the same time fearing that universalisms might, of their nature, crush particularity and cause oppression.

Such accounts of del Campo's poem resonate with the broader viewpoint of some of Spanish America's most influential cultural theorists. The Argentine thinker Beatriz Sarlo describes Borges's work in similar terms as 'a game on the edge of two shores' which 'destabilises the major Western traditions' (un juego en el filo de dos orillas; desestabiliza las grandes tradiciones occidentales) (1993: 12–13). A not dissimilar vision is enshrined in Ángel Rama's seminal account of narrative transculturation in Latin America (*La transculturación narrativa en Latinoamérica*). Here, the originality of Latin American literature is said to lie in the often tense interplay between its lettered cities (*ciudad letrada*) such as Buenos Aires, and its hinterland, such that a modernising, internationalising culture is received and transformed continually through contact with contrasting non-urban societies, and vice versa (Rama 2004). In short, as Carlos Alonso puts it in *The Burden of Modernity*, 'To paraphrase José Martí: our modernity may be a conflicted modernity, but it is out modernity nonetheless; and if we are to study it in all its specificity we must eschew all critical approaches that interpret that complexity as a symptom of deficiency, as a sign of a modernity manqué' (1998: 40). The effect is as Julio Ortega describes in his *Transatlantic Translations*: 'Latin American texts follow a different route. This is one of heteroclite appropriations which displace codes ... and in the end begin to construct representations of fusion, combination and the site of the subject of a new culture' (2006: 30).

While such musings have become quite orthodox, the question, aptly posed by *Fausto*, is whether we could (for better or for worse) imagine things otherwise, such that similarity and commonality were less equivocally affirmed between people, places, times and between representations and the world. The great twentieth-century Argentine writer, Jorge Luis Borges – whose shadow falls over much of the above – found something more bluntly decisive in *Fausto*. He saw in it a joyful expression of friendship (1985: 21). He has a point: fundamentally, the entire poem evokes an encounter between two men who are very fond of one another, El Pollo and Laguna. The scene for the work is set by the intense, physical embrace between the two *gauchos* at the opening, and their pleasure in meeting. Looked at this way, it is companionship that ultimately frames *Fausto*, and sets its tone, not irony, not *vaivén*, at least not *per se*, because whatever else is ironised, friendship ultimately is not. Pointedly, the poem ends – not as do Goethe's verses or Gounod's opera with the ascent of Margarita to heaven – but with the two men riding off together in unison, and the one buying the other a meal. In the final *décima*, a single line stands out, separated from all the others by its lack of a verb, and containing only the words 'as good ol' companions' (como güenos compañeros) (2000: 140).

The question is not simply what this might mean for our appreciation of *Fausto*, but what *Fausto* might thereby offer by way of affordances in the interconnection of peoples, places and times, and of representation and the world. At stake likewise is whether it opens a portal – as it were – to somewhere other than a now quite orthodox account of Latin American modernity and its place in the 'West' and the world. It is in a spirit of friendship that the story of the opera is told and discussed, and thus that all the connections of cultures, places and times unfold. Without the embrace of the two *gauchos*, which unleashes El Pollo's tale, we could not experience that succession of other meetings: Europe–Argentina, city–country, France–Germany, present–medieval, sign–referent. The suggestion is that all of these are to be experienced fundamentally as kinds of companionship. They would be felt to be in company with one another just as are those 'güenos compañeros', El Pollo and Laguna. What is more, the meeting that frames the entire poem is one that occurs quite by chance, just as El Pollo happens to be in Buenos Aires on other business when the Gounod opera is performed. This suggests that the companionship evoked throughout the poem may arise as much as anything through contingent connections, the happenstance of things crossing one another's paths, bumping into one another. We are invited, then, to value cultural encounters for something other than their arising from some underlying pattern of causes, whether through influence or through some global socioeconomic and political system.

To that extent at least, *Fausto*'s vision of cultural companionship resembles the approach taken by Susan Manning in her work on relations between the literature of the Americas and that of the British Isles. In her own masterpiece, *Poetics of Character*, Manning is inspired not least by aspects of north Atlantic thought and literature of the eighteenth and nineteenth centuries in evoking 'a poetics-led comparison' that 'supplements the historical lacunae of connection' (2013: 232). Manning underscores the importance of a notion of friendship in the forging of such associations, dedicating an entire chapter to 'literary friendship and transatlantic correspondences' (2013: 152–82). Following the Scottish philosopher David Hume, she begins by noting the notion that 'character is produced in relation and stabilised by mirroring from others' (2013: 152). The philosopher Anthony Appiah has likewise mused that larger cultural allegiances – a 'rooted cosmopolitanism', even – may need to stem from personal and kinship relationships. These, like El Pollo and Laguna's opening embrace and their riding off together, may of their nature overshadow more abstract frameworks and commitments. They involve what Appiah calls 'special obligations': 'an individual friend', notes Appiah, is 'not an instantiation of the general good' (2005: 224, 230). That is to say, in turn, that such relationships do not find their justification in some framework beyond them, in some 'structure of implied priorities and progressions', in this case one of morality or an abstract philosophical system. The experience of companionship on every level matters in its own right.

Fausto points to an experience of intimate meeting in friendship that is much less qualified even than that described by Manning. Manning emphasises the importance of 'likeness' in cultural encounters (2013: xi). At the same time, she evokes a play between presence and absence, a continuing *vaivén* inherent to 'likeness', that expresses a nervousness about conflating distinct things. In the circumstances of the post-independence

Americas, Manning notes, such conflation could raise the spectre of *translatio imperii et studi*, and with it a legacy of controlling imperialism, of incorporation into European hegemony by other means (2013: 152). Both the distance and the reserved style involved in Anglophone literary correspondence across the Atlantic thus become exemplary. Such writing is 'limited by prudence and punctuated by interruption' (2013: 159). It balances 'a contagion of language and ideas between two minds' with 'a kind of inoculation against the other mind' (2013: 172). Manning is not alone in lacing a vision of companionship with reservations that are putatively inherent to it. In her *Cultivating Humanity*, which looks to the ancient Stoics, the philosopher Martha Nussbaum affirms that, while 'world citizenship' entails not even 'thinking of enemies as other', it also involves 'patient critical scrutiny of the imagery and speech we employ'. It 'does not, and should not, require that we suspend criticism towards other individuals and cultures' (1998: 65). For better or for worse, this take us back, beyond Manning, to a potential 'structure of implied priorities'.

'Their two souls in one may even have blended', we read instead in *Fausto*: 'sus dos almas en una / acaso se misturaron'. For those with a proclivity towards *vaivén*, the *acaso – maybe, perhaps* or even *by accident* – emphasises a qualification and doubt, as if suspending belief in the fusion even as it seems to be affirmed (Bonilla Cerezo 2010: 54): once more we would be in a world of emotional ping-pong. Yet the emphasis of del Campo's words is less on reservation than it is on astonishment: that an embrace could be so forceful it might even have eliminated the boundaries that divide two souls. If it did not quite do so utterly – and there is no certainty that it did not – the embrace leads us forcefully to the possibility of such an occurrence. Afterwards, the two men had to 'disentangle' themselves (se desenredaron) (2000: 27). The matching together is echoed by their horses, the one saluting the other on arrival, and, after the men embrace, the mane of the first rubbing the ear of the second (2000: 26–8). The animals' intimacy matters all the more because there is no neat boundary to separate the men from the world of their horses: El Pollo's first remark is to say that he *is* an old nag (yo soy jaca vieja) (2000: 26), and when we first observe Laguna, he seems to be stuck to his mount (parecía / pegao en el animal) (2000: 24).

This is a state of affairs in which commonality has the upper hand, and is valued in its own right. The emphasis is decisively on oneness or near-oneness, not difference. This is no balancing act where what cuts across a boundary is weighed evenly against what still divides, a kind of equilibrium in diversity. More still, it is clear that nothing would be lost in such a blending: there is no selectiveness in what is kept or discarded from either side as they mix. The 'two souls' are both still there. By the same token, the notion of their oneness is not '*an empty place*', in Laclau's words, any more than their friendship could be expressed in terms of a generic abstraction as 'an instantiation of the general good'. Here, the blend offers a gain, something more than existed previously – as typically is the case in the notion of 'transculturation' – but without a corresponding subtraction. In this forceful impact of two men's bodies on another, there is something of what Tim Dean finds in 'erotic intimacy': 'a means for encountering something wonderfully strange to the self – something that neither the self nor the other properly possess but that emerges in the contact between them' (2009: 181). The verb that del Campo uses is *misturar* (now spelt *mixturar*, as it was sometimes then): *to blend* (2000: 26). The Spanish Royal Academy dictionary of 1852 tells us that *mixturar* is 'to mix, incorporate and confound one thing with another' (mezclar, incorporar y confundir una cosa con otra). *Confundir* is literally *to melt together with* (*con – fundir*). Once they press themselves together, and their boundaries give way, they emerge as a mix, as a newly found commonality.

It is in this specific spirit of intimate friendship that we are invited to take the relationship between country and lettered city, Europe and Latin America, past and present, sign and referent throughout the poem, fused across time and place and into the world. Poetry and the poetic – as rhythm and pattern – are at the heart of this: we have in *Fausto* a 'poetics-led comparison', in Manning's words. If *Fausto* begins with a meeting, it ends with the parallel beat of hooves, of the mounts to which the 'good companions' are so attached: 'juntos al trote', trotting together (2000: 140). Such a pairing of sounds is manifestly crucial to the music of poetry. In his *Ancient Phonograph*, in which he explores the sounds present in ancient verse, the classicist Shane Butler suggests we look to Echo rather than to Narcissus as the source of poetry in ancient myth. The one – Narcissus – gazing in a mirror, evokes a basic theory of imitation (mimesis): that art should be a copy of the world, that it is primarily a way of knowing it. Echo, instead, invites us to value the repetition of sounds for their own sake, as music (2015: 81–2, 84, 86–7).

The noise of the hooves pairs companionship with poetry's sonorous echoing, treating the two as one and the same. In rhythmic sound such as that of the horses' trot, we are offered a patterning of lived experience in which two things are fused into one, without loss on either side. Because it is not a Narcissus-like copy, this fusion is not a reduction of one thing to the other (say, of the mirror image to the 'original'). For Shane Butler, the mixing of echoing sounds surpasses, takes us beyond what we are being told, even beyond the words that are being said. Looking to Carolyn Abbate's account of opera, he notes how that art form, while ostensibly a kind of narrative, resists narration in its music (2015: 81). The patterned sounds, Butler says, 'come to make some scholars slightly uncomfortable: they seem like child's play, or indeed, baby talk'. Via Echo, he thus evokes Susan Sontag in her railing *Against Interpretation*, and her advocacy of an 'erotics of art': an appreciation of its sensual textures rather than a search for its meaning (2015: 87; citing Sontag).

In turn, in her *Gauchos and Foreigners*, Ariana Huberman recalls the German thinker Walter Benjamin's recourse to sound so as to evoke cultural transmission, as she ponders transculturation between Argentine cowboys and outsiders. 'Walter Benjamin's formulation of translation', she observes, 'reminds us of the definition of *glossa* in relation to music as a variation that a musician skilfully executes over the same notes, but without rigorously adhering to them. To gloss is to translate and clarify in a way in which the original inevitably changes' (2011: 8). In Benjamin's 'The Task of the Translator', to which she alludes, we read that 'translation must in large measure refrain from wanting to communicate something, from rendering the sense' (1970: 78). This is because 'in all language and linguistic creations there remains in addition to what can be conveyed something that cannot be communicated' (1970: 79). Thus, translation at its best is not an attempt to tell us what its source means, but rather to evoke 'in embryonic or intensive form' a pure, ideal language in which the unconveyable may be encountered, precisely because it has avoided direct communication (1970: 72). Transculturation, on this account, might best offer us an experience of incommensurability itself. In that respect, it is akin to Shane Butler's account of sound, and music in poetry. Insofar as each version of a work – del Campo's of El Pollo's of Gounod's of Goethe's of the myth of Faust – is an echo of another, what is conveyed in the 'gloss' is irreducible to and beyond meaning. It runs 'against interpretation'.

Meeting: coming together and taking shape

Certainly, in *Fausto*, all the pairings that make up the poem are subsumed into its patterned sound, as the final trotting of hooves suggests. But, equally, the framing of the poem – the opening embrace, the sound of the parting horses – invites us to experience all the parallels, not as things from which the music abstracts, but rather as taken up in the subsuming, like souls blended into one mixture, or voices that come together in an opera. Reality and its representation, Argentina and Europe, the French and the Germanic, past and present, lettered city and countryside are transfigured within it, not left behind. In one of the early critical commentaries, Juan Carlos Gómez alludes to Estanislao del Campo in terms that recall a vagabond singer calling at the home, not even of Gounod, but of the illustrious Goethe, who had been dead for over thirty years. The image captures their distinct poetic worlds while at the same time evoking a kind of encounter: the complex verse forms and intricate allusions of the German with the simpler, song-like gauchesque octosyllables of del Campo. 'The door of the powerful was not closed this time ... to the call of the beggar', we are told (la puerta del poderoso no se ha cerrado esta vez ... al llamado del mendigo) (del Campo 1870: 209). Just as *Fausto* evokes the shared trotting of the *gaucho*'s horses together in time, and just as it binds characters and narrators together in its verse forms, so Gómez speaks of something fundamental and specific in common that persists in utterly different kinds of poetry, like music across quite distinct instrumentation: 'as Mozart's chords and Bellini's melodies keep their harmony or cadence when played on the vihuela' (como los acordes de Mozart y las melodías de Bellini guardan su armonía o su cadencia al resonar en una vihuela) (1870: 210). Likewise, and in a converse direction through time in the poem *Fausto* itself, medieval Germany and its myths echo with the sounds of the Argentine: 'The Devil', we hear at one point, 'is as much a guitar player / as our most American of countrymen' (el Diablo es tan guitarrero / como el paisano más criollo) (del Campo 2000: 118).

The entire structure of the poem, after all, echoes with the form of the libretto of Gounod's *Faust*, even as it does not replicate it. To put it another way, *Fausto* sounds like the opera (and the opera, in consequence, like *Fausto*) – and not just like the incommensurable sounds of the opera but its narrative and characters and words and settings. In turn, the voices of El Pollo, Laguna and del Campo himself all sound like each other, without ceasing to be identified with their originators. The soundscape of the poem as a whole forms through this blending: it is the 'one' into which their diverse souls might 'blend'. While their personalities differ – el Pollo is more given than Laguna to comparisons and to overt emotions – and at times they disagree, though never for long, the two *gauchos*' turns of phrase are very alike. Often as not, when they speak, their dialogue shares a stanza, and sometimes even a single line that flows across the two of them: 'We can make ourselves a cigarette / if you like... – How could I not!' (Armemos un cigarillo / si le parece... – ¡Pues no!) (2000: 77). Likewise, del Campo's voice echoes El Pollo's, the two main storytellers sounding exactly alike, as the gauchesque urban poet emulates a rustic character who served as his own alter ego. The eight-syllable line and full, close rhymes of del Campo's narration through song-like *décimas* blend into and out of El Pollo's speech in *redondillas*, octosyllabic full-rhyming verses in stanzas of four lines. Representation and reality, theatre and the external world, equally sound alike in El Pollo's *redondillas*: fiction is in beat with external reality, and vice versa. Take these two stanzas: 'In the little green trees / glass droplets shone, / and to the ground swang down / birds in song' (En los verdes arbolitos / gotas de cristal brillaban, / y al suelo se descolgaban / cantando los pajaritos) (2000: 101). 'It's pretty to see at the times / when the sea's gone out, / droppin' in flight ta the open beach / gulls, herons, and ducks' (Es lindo ver en los ratos / en que la mar ha bajao / cáir volando al desplayao / gaviotas, garzas y patos) (2000: 65). The first speaks of the stage set, the second of the coastline of Buenos Aires.

What we experience here runs against the now widespread tendency – we see it in Piglia as we do in Benjamin – to suppose that apparent difference mars obvious commonality. At best, resemblance could then be found only in the very incommensurability that this implies. The latter is a supposition, one way of envisaging an encounter, and there are others. A test case is the obsession, since at least Lugones, with del Campo's literary departure from authentic *gauchismos*. One of the early commentators, the poet Ricardo Gutiérrez, avers that the error would have lain rather in following too closely the *gaucho*'s turns of phrase. This would have given us only 'the construct of the language' (la construcción del idioma) (1870: 217). By leaving that behind, del Campo can through his own poetry bring forth another kind of person's way of beholding and experiencing the world. Evoking the name of the first *gauchesque* poet, Gutiérrez affirms, 'Hidalgo did not copy the *gaucho*; he looked through the eyes of the *gaucho*; he did not become mannered by his sentiment, he felt through his heart' (Hidalgo, no ha copiado al gaucho; ha mirado por los ojos del gaucho; no se ha amanerado a su sentimiento, ha sentido por su corazón) (1870: 218). Gutiérrez does not seem to be drawing a simple distinction here between the letter of the writing and some disembodied spirit of meaning: Hidalgo actually looks through the *gaucho*'s eyes. Rather, what is at stake is *mannerism* and *copying* as opposed to a shared *seeing* and *feeling*, a sensual experience of something in common. Gutiérrez is invoking basic elements of many nineteenth-century artists' training. To *copy* something – in this sense – is a technical exercise, a direct mimicking of the surface appearance of another's work, useful for learning about artistic styles but not of itself enough for the student to paint well in their own right or, for that matter, fully to appreciate the model. *Mannerism*, likewise, is the fault of attending more to stylistic devices for their own elaborate sake than to the larger effect of a work of art. To imitate minutely the language of another, rather than finding a different voice, would risk missing what is important about them. It would be a sort of distraction from true likeness.

Difference here becomes a way of enabling commonality in a thoroughgoing sense, not its impediment. Such an outlook entails a disposition in which we are not lured by the notion of incommensurability. Guido y Spano tackles this issue head on. In so doing, he highlights character and outlook – in this case, that of the poem's *gauchos* – as of critical importance in the translation of culture. He acknowledges – from the vantage point of the educated elite – the sort of response to irony that might later be found in Ludmer: the apparent incommensurability of rich literary texts when they are interpreted, and the notion that products of one context (say, the German lands) may resist understanding in the terms of another (say, mid-nineteenth-century Argentina). He dwells on the poem's humour and calls the work a *parody* (1870: 222). He toys with the notion that Goethe's *Faust* is enclosed within an alien, inaccessible cultural world, acknowledging the claim that this chaos of a complex poem can be understood only in the German lands for which it was intended. He goes so far as to say that 'no one can speak [of it] appropriately except in Teuton, for in Romance [languages] there is no explaining its delirious beauties' (nadie puede hablar con propiedad salvo en tudesco, porque en romance no hay quien esplique sus delirantes bellezas) (1870: 221).

Meeting: coming together and taking shape

But after saying all this, he stresses, with some amusement, how imperturbable El Pollo is in the face of the challenge: 'Apparently Anastasio did not suffer the nausea which that vertiginous composition inflicts upon the mind' (por lo visto, Anastasio no ha sufrido el mareo que causa en el ánimo esta vertiginosa composición) (1870: 221). Beyond any wryness here, Guido y Spano conjures up a vision of parallel nebulous landscapes traversed by the *paisanos*, the countrymen: the Germanic and the Argentine. While these retain distinct aspects – the one a world of philosophical abstraction, the other of physical immediacy – their shadows blend, the *gauchos* find their way through both, and the journeys follow a like path across their doubled-up surroundings.

> The two *paisanos* whom you make known to us, wend their way amid the nebulous metaphysics of the *highest poet* just as our *gauchos* are wont gallantly to cross through the fog of our *pampa*, interrupting the songs with which they lighten their passage, to gaze here and there upon the fantastical perspectives cast by the mirage.[1]

Unencumbered by modes of thinking and patterns of language that lead us to perceive something as incommensurable, the *gauchos* here offer a blithe confidence in riding through obscurity, a shared delight in gazing upon fantasias – a singing together once more – that makes them adept at navigating at once Goethe's poem and their native Argentina, two apparently disparate contexts. They present a setting aside of the disposition towards the world out of which the supposed problem was formulated in the first place.

A key aspect of this alternative disposition is a tendency to find through the apparent difference of context a fundamental resemblance. The point is not simply to be able thereby to engage in comparison, observing what is alike as well as what is not. Rather, in this disposition, the experience of convergence becomes the basis of the transfiguration set out above, such that by attending to it, we no longer experience contexts as bounded locations at all, not even in a qualified sense with criss-crossings over their borders. Instead, we experience both as an actual sharing of location, and a seamless running together of places and times, a fusion enabled by the resemblances that they do have. Thus, in *Fausto*, a medieval German character is indeed an Argentine soldier on his way to war with Paraguay. In a fundamental way, this outlook is at odds with the tendency – however qualified – to seek the 'location of culture', in Homi Bhabha's famous words (Bhabha 1994): the understanding of cultures through their situatedness in specific, discreet places and times, disparate contexts. In Guido y Spano's account, the manner in which *gauchos* might travel through 'the fog of our *pampa*' is what enables them likewise to traverse 'the nebulous metaphysics of the *highest poet*'. In Juan Carlos Gómez's evocation of *Fausto*, del Campo is welcomed by Goethe like a travelling singer such as a *gaucho*. Reciprocally, it is this relationship that once more enables those from one landscape – the world of *Faust* – so smoothly to traverse another: 'The genius of the north has permitted the Argentine folksinger to walk the blonde Margarita through the boundless Pampa' (El jenio del norte ha permitido al payador argentino pasear a la rubia Margarita por la pampa incomensurable) (1870: 209). In Ricardo Gutiérrez's account of the relationship of the educated poet to the *gaucho*, we find even the shared occupation of

---

[1] Los dos *paisanos* que Vd nos hace conocer, atraviesan por entre la nebulosa metafísica del *altísimo poeta*, como suelen hacerlo gallardamente a través de las brumas de nuestra pampa, nuestros gauchos, interrumpiendo los cantos con que entretienen el camino, para fijarse aquí y allí en las perspectivas fantásticas que produce el miraje (1870: 222).

the same body: looking through the same eyes, feeling with the same heart. These ways of envisaging commonality conjure up sensual, physical, embodied experiences of transfigured locations once more, not '*an empty place*'.

But what, then, of all the ironies? The poem does not seem to invite us simply to ignore them: they are all too obvious. Rather, they are presented as bonding the intimate friendship of the two *gauchos*, which frames and flows into all the other companionships. Rafael Bonilla Cerezo has observed how the intense embrace and its fusion has as its corrollary the sharing of *patrañas*, shaggy-dog tales between the two old men (2010: 54–5). In their opening dialogue, the two *gauchos* exclaim, and tease each other, on the joys of exaggeration and lying. Laguna claims his own horse is so calm that when his brother-in-law fell unconscious upon it for three days long, the animal did not move, and was still where it had been when he came to. 'Played like the lying *gaucho* you are!', El Pollo celebrates (¡Bien haiga gaucho embustero!) (2000: 28). In reply, he suggests that if the man had died, the horse would have been found waiting patiently at the end of the world. 'Look how he flipped / it over … well played, El Pollo!', Laguna responds (Vean como le buscó / la guelta … ¡bien haiga el Pollo!) (2000: 29). There are hints that there is no great difference between this behaviour and the writing of Gounod's opera or, for that matter, Goethe's poem, and by extension the arts and culture in general. More than once Laguna wonders how on earth a learned doctor like Faust could fall for Mephistopheles' trickery (2000: 50, 55), and, of course, he repeatedly questions whether the tale El Pollo recounts – that is, the plot of *Faust* – could possibly be true. Such is the very substance of their friendship as we encounter it, exchanged between them like the gin they swig together. Once and again we are reminded of the joy of narrating and listening: 'Mr Pollo, I won't have you / cutting short even the teensiest bit / the story that you've started', Laguna says (don Pollo, no le permito / que me merme ni un chiquito / del cuento que ha comenzao) (2000: 83).

We are invited to experience irony here not so much as a way of distancing things, not as a coming-and-going, a *vaivén*, but as effecting an embrace so forceful that it might blend two souls into one. This is not a matter of saying anything as qualified as that irony enables us to mediate between two others, to explore their interplay of sameness and difference. That would not give us the prospect of 'unlimited intimacy' (if only the prospect) that we have been proferred. If the emphasis is tipped decisively to fusion through friendship, then the role of the humour, far from disrupting delicate relationships, lends them their necessary nuance – just as when we drink a blend, a *mixtura*, we must taste the coming together of its distinct elements, just as when we listen to horses ride together we must hear the different sets of hooves. Irony becomes a means to discern what Susan Manning memorably called 'the 'texture' of likeness' (2013: xiii). El Pollo's at times laconic renderings into *gauchesque* verse are distinguishable from Goethe's and Gounod's elaborations, bringing a smile to the reader. At the same time, with their colloquialism and concision, the words are forcefully immediate, presenting starkly the resonance of del Campo's antecedents, so that he and they are both conflated and separately discernible in the words. Faust 'said he could do nothin'' / with the learnin' he studied; / he said he loved a blonde, / but the blonde did not love him' (Dijo que nada podía / con la cencia que estudió; / que él a una rubia quería, / pero que a él la rubia no) (2000: 47).

There remains, even so, the question of the credence that we are to give to any of what we read here. 'The other day I saw the Devil', El Pollo claims; 'Can it be true?' asks his interlocutor. It may seem – it has come to seem – axiomatic that if we doubt the claim, then we will experience the words as constructs, and in turn, we will be distanced from them, perceiving them as the collection of linguistic signs that they actually are. It may seem – it has come to seem – that this would involve a continual questioning of our attachment, even of the world's attachment, to the signs that are being used. The influential art historian and theorist Michael Fried has drawn a distinction between 'theatricality' and 'absorption' deriving from European art of the eighteenth and nineteenth centuries (Fried 1980, 1990, 1996). In the first, we are so aware of the falsity, the staging of a scene that we cannot connect affectively to it. In the other, we become so involved that we become oblivious to the fact of a work of art being a work of art. The question is how to navigate between these, and whether they can be reconciled. El Pollo's telling of the tale seems to embody both: his narration suggests he is so absorbed as to treat what he is seeing as part of his own reality, while yet he is still able to register – as he always notes – that the curtain rises and falls. Seen this way, El Pollo, and his telling of the tale, points to an emotional state beyond theatricality and absorption, acknowledging and subsuming both. In turn, his attainment of these feelings is, in a more antique sense, a parody of the performance of Gounod's opera: that is to say, the poem's comedy is offered not to criticise but in affectionate hommage to the success of the production. Charlotte Lange has observed how easily one may overlook the legacy of this historic notion of parody in the discussion of Latin American fiction (Lange 2008).

If intimate companionship both subsumes and transcends theatricality and absorption, the question of whether something is or is not false, of whether it is or is not credible or plausible, simply does not arise. We are in a realm of experience where that issue just does not exist. It is worth distinguishing this notion from the rather more limited claim that what El Pollo says about the Devil is true insofar as it tells us about his subjective experience, or insofar as it refers solely to perception. Certainly, it is undeniable that El Pollo did see the Devil, because he went to the theatre and saw the Devil on stage: 'Don't go thinkin' I'm lying to you: 'Alf the city saw it' (No crea que yo le miento: / Lo ha visto media ciudá) (2000: 53). But the question of whether that was a subjective or perceptual experience autonomous of other realities could only arise where that question is asked. Conversely, culture – as we are invited to experience it through *Fausto* – could not, in that sense, be a construct. It could not be a semiotic system – a collection of signs – because this would mean it primarily exhibited 'theatricality'. *Fausto* sets itself against such a 'separation of art from the objects and scenes of ordinary experience', in the words of the American philosopher John Dewey (1934: 6). Art – and, with it, culture – is not a construct, nor is it a representation of or about something. Rather 'it is *an* experience' in its own right (1934: 34).

'The other night I saw the Devil.' We are invited to encounter what it would be to have that alien, atavistic experience in its own right. We do so, not so as to believe in it or disbelieve in it, but rather so as to keep it company, to be intimate with it, to feel the 'texture of likeness' that binds us to it, however strange, however other to us. We ride alongside it, echoing it, keeping it company, as El Pollo did Laguna. Writing of the film director David Lynch, the essayist and novelist David Foster Wallace reflects on what it is to encounter scenes that we find disturbingly alien. 'I like to judge', Foster Wallace mused, '... we (I) like to feel powerful' (1997: loc.3387). The alternative, he said, 'requires that these features of ourselves and the world not be dreamed away or judged away or massaged away but *acknowledged*' (1997: loc.3437). The verb in italics is – probably uncoincidentally – one that was used in discussions between Michael Fried and the philosopher Stanley Cavell; Foster Wallace had attended classes with Cavell. For Cavell, to be in attunement with another's feelings is not a matter of epistemology – of a framework for knowing what is true or false – but rather a way we treat others and ourselves: 'To know you are in pain is to acknowledge it, or to withhold the acknowledgement. —I know your pain the way you do' (2012: 266; see Fried 1990: 285 for their conversations).

If, in this way, there is to be intimate companionship between ourselves and others, between things that are disparate, if we are to move through and beyond irony into the bonds of companionship, we will leave behind what Manning and Taylor call the 'structure of implied priorities and progressions'. We will not be concerned with reducing culture to some explanatory framework or frame of morality: for example, that El Pollo is a liar, or that the 'Devil' is a singer and actor on a stage, a 'theatrical construct', a 'representation'. Such are the terms of an intimate culture. For, as Appiah says, friendship is not 'an instantiation of the general good', and it may not be assessed as such, that is with regards to a prescriptive or explanatory framework. Instead, we will live among the sounding echoes. Take the two *gauchos* as we might experience them now. It is tempting – and not of itself an error – to latch on to their queerness as something now familiar. We may dwell upon the force of an embrace between two men that breaks the bounds between them, such that two become one. We may smile in recognition as Laguna contrasts himself to Faust: 'I don't lose my way over females' (Por hembras yo no me pierdo) (2000: 85). But if we were intimately to encounter the *gauchos*, we would experience a world of values that is likely not our own, but rather alien and uncomfortable. If a *gaucho* receives an offence from another man – we hear – he can knife him, flee to a new life, and return to a welcome. But if a cowboy seduces and deceives a woman, and she is left pregnant and alone, all she can do is dampen the hair of her child with tears (2000: 110–13). The *gauchos* could already feel foreign to the educated urban elite of the 1860s, even beyond the pale for some. 'Pariahs of our society', Guido y Spano calls them (parias de nuestra sociedad) (del Campo 1870: 222), and, sure enough, they are depicted violating the Rural Code of 1865 with their outdoor drunkenness and perhaps with their gambling. They are two uncouth old men (del Campo 2000: 32–3, 36–7; 1870: 293–4). Perhaps the very fact that they are ageing hints that they are of a generation now passing.

In intimate culture, something alien is felt where borders of geography and time and culture might instead have held. In that sense, the intimacy feels out of place, both disregarding and disrespectful of established bounds. Del Campo has 'profaned ... the sanctuary of the sublime poem', Guido y Spano says, just as 'the impious hand of the composer', Gounod, has turned Goethe's masterpiece into an opera (profanado ... el santuario del sublime poema; la mano impía del compositor) (del Campo 1870: 221–2). To *profane a sanctuary* is not simply desecration, even as the vulgar language of the *gauchos* or Gounod's stripping away of Goethe's gnomic complexities has something of that. It is above all to gain entry to a holy place where access has been forbidden. The problem with the pseudo-religious status of Goethe's *Faust* in Germany is that it keeps everyone else away, prevents the poem from speaking to anyone but Germans. The irruption into the sanctuary of an Argentine from the future enables intimacy with the alien: both insofar as a *gaucho* might enter the sacred domain of the Germans, and insofar as German mysteries are opened to the Pampa and its language. We are where we might otherwise feel uncomfortable or unwelcome, like El Pollo in the Colón Theatre.

Meeting: coming together and taking shape

The classical is not, of course, always the same as what is alien, but there is an association, because of a shared reaching out from the past so as to breach the bounds of place and time. 'The category "classics" names the idea that literature once communicated with the gods', Christopher Wood has said (2012: 169). The 'communication with the gods' – I take it – both underlines the alien nature of the most ancient European literature (dealing with matters not even recognisably human), and its lack of a notion of confinement to human, historical time and its bounds. On both counts, on its own terms, it exceeds a mentality that seeks to explain and interpret by situating and historicising. This, putatively, is what renders it compelling beyond the limits of contexts. So far as *Fausto* is concerned, we have seen already the notion that it opens up something sacred, a sanctuary. This alludes in turn to the non-secular character of the Faust tale itself: 'the other night, I saw the Devil'. For the early commentator, Juan Carlos Gómez, the *gauchos* of the poem are themselves 'a race of disappearing centaurs', mythological creatures of ancient Greece (una raza de centauros que desaparece) (del Campo 1870: 212), recalling the poem's image of a man seamlessly connected to a horse.

As Gómez's comment suggests, this is not just a matter of the supernatural *per se*, but more broadly of things that are both atavistic and of a scale that, exceeding usual human affairs, is compelling beyond their originating context. In his introduction to the 1870 edition of del Campo's complete poetry, the author José Mármol remarked that it is easier for writers to attain immortality (inmortalidad), to have survived after their own era (sobrevivido a su tiempo) (1870: iii–iv) if their own period was one of grand events or of great mythologies. He gives as examples classical legends, the medieval crusades, the glories of India, the Trojan War, and, in Argentina, the wars of independence and the battles for freedom in its aftermath. While Mármol dwells on the difficulty with which this presents writers such as del Campo who live in less epic times, other commentators evoke a resonant archaism and atavism in *Fausto*. Ricardo Gutiérrez says that del Campo has gone to the 'most grandiose terrain' (al terreno … más grandioso), that of the souls of Argentina's primitive Americans, the *gauchos* (1870: 217–18). Juan Carlos Gómez remarks that in giving us an Argentine version of *Faust*, del Campo has, for the first time, enabled the 'muse of epic' (la musa de la epopeya) to tread the Pampa. Gómez signals here the folkloric sources of the Faust story itself, their depths in the European middle ages, calling *Fausto*, among other things, the 'importation of [the] medieval legend' (importación de la leyenda de la edad media) (1870: 209–10).

The *gauchesque* and the medieval and all that is grandiose across place and time thus dovetail. It is less important for our immediate purposes whether this is an accurate account of the *gauchos*. What matters is the notion that some such compelling emotive force could exist, and the effort to conjure it up. Put another way, what renders all this epic is a breach in the time frame for a distinct modern era, even as it is established. 'Les rois s'en vont', the kings are departing, del Campo says of the *gauchos* in his own reply to Gómez's comments, melancholically citing a famous French revolutionary song, and wondering if we really need to let go of their remnants (1870: 215). The *gauchos* are being sentenced to belong in an historical context alien to the present, and are classified as creatures of another age, as if in a museum's exhibits. But, precisely because this is happening, first, they evoke an antique majesty ('the kings') and, second, they are still present, even if departing, clearly not gone, certainly not from the poem.

Intimate companionship runs through such an experience of the classic. The latter takes shape in the echoes across time and place that constitute poetry itself. As something classic, the *gauchesque* resonates with medieval Germanic myth, with the fallen French monarchy, with the ancient centaurs. It is a coming together, a meeting. Surveying the hodgepodge of a movie that is *Casablanca*, the Italian novelist and theorist Umberto Eco remarks: 'When all the archetypes burst in shamelessly, we reach Homeric depths …. It is a phenomenon worthy of awe.' A 'telluric force' arises from the component elements, the aspects of the blend, 'talking *among themselves*, celebrating a reunion' (1985: 38; original emphasis). It is a disposition and character that unleashes their combined resonance, not a causal connection, nor an explanation, nor a systematic structuring uniting them, nor a detailed discourse on what they have in common. It is not even an attempt at a full account of any of them. Eco points out that it is the sketchy, mix-and-match, unelaborated composition of *Casablanca* that enables its component allusions to 'burst in shamelessly' and encounter each other with 'telluric force'.

In *Fausto*, likewise, the *gauchesque* style of telling strips back the component parts of its own blend, leaving them in resonant outline. In turn, this sketchy simplification echoes with an atavistic grandeur. There is a taciturn forcefulness in the eight-syllable lines, what Mármol called 'a tendency, innate in their [the *gauchos*'] spirit, to reveal their thought with the fewest number of words possible' (una tendencia, innata en su espíritu, a revelar su pensamiento con el menor número de voces posible) (1870: vi). The entirety of the Walpurgis Night scene – a lengthy ballet in Gounod – is swept away, a distraction from the main action. El Pollo habitually hurtles through events in a whirl of verbs: there are twenty-five alone in the first five stanzas after the Devil appears to Margarita's brother (2000: 70–1). A series of images and comments, evocative of aspects of the *Faust* myth, are scattered through the poem's seemingly simple telling, its apparent primitive austerity, set in each other's company. The tall story about Laguna's horse involves death and a waiting until the Day of Judgement, themes that echo with the mortality, salvation or damnation of Margarita and Faust. Elsewhere, in describing the staging of changes between night and day, El Pollo observes that 'the stars were heading onwards / to die, without anything remaining of them, / not even a sad, smudged-out trace' (caminaban las estrellas / a morir, sin quedar de ellas / ni un triste rastro borrao) (2000: 100). When he looks out onto the sea, El Pollo compares the waves to humanity crashing against its own destiny, the fierce ocean to God's anger at sin, and the calm waters to divine mercy (2000: 65–6). Aside such intimations, one finds the presence of beauty: 'es linda la mar', the sea is pretty (2000: 63), we are told laconically.

Beauty, death, desire, judgement, trust, sentiment, harmony, the ancient, the passage of time, the male and the female, the philosophical and the worldly: such large concerns are cast up in *Fausto* in many passing references and varying scenes, their full sense habitually undeveloped, the relationship of each mention to another often left unspoken, each instance stated with simplicity. Here is 'the fog of our *pampa*' that enables us to traverse 'the nebulous metaphysics of the *highest poet*'. Such Homeric depth is what *Fausto* shares with Goethe and Gounod, and with ancient legend, Argentina with medieval and modern Europe. It is a telluric force resistant to the passage of time even as its antique majesty is of the past. *Fausto* offers us a celebration of reunion, a keeping company, where places and times, authors and myths, travel and blend together, skilled horse riders traversing the mist of life in friendship.

Meeting: coming together and taking shape

Interlude

It is a day between 20 June 1866 and 25 July of that same year in Madrid. A group of friends have gathered in the studio of the painter Francisco Sans Cabot to hear one of their number, the composer and musician Juan Bautista Pujol, play a fantasia based on Gounod's *Faust*. Present are three other artists: Agapito Francés, Lorenzo Casanova and Mariano Fortuny, the latter the most internationally successful Spanish painter of his time. The scene appears in a painting by Fortuny of that year, *Fantasia on Faust* (Barón 2017: 142; Plate 1). The painter does not himself feature directly in the painting, but his presence seems implied by the unnervingly intense gaze of one of the company, straight out of the image towards an otherwise identified person: the viewer and painter. In the painting, a scene from *Faust* – a floating Mephistopheles and Marta, and in the distance Margarita with Faust – coexists in the room with the group of artistic friends. Through friendship, we once more experience a series of companionships across place and time: Gounod and Pujol's music, Fortuny's art with that of Sans Cabot hanging on the wall, the latter two with the first two, the visual and musical arts, and – through *Faust* – literature and Goethe. The composition of the painting reflects Goya's etching, *The Dream* [or, *Sleep*] *of Reason Produces Monsters* (Barón 2017: 143): across a diagonal from an artist by a piece of furniture, his head down, a fantastical scene rises with no clear distinction between the everyday and the supernatural, between the (imaginary) representation and external reality. So, in turn, through this meeting, *The Dream of Reason* encounters *Faust*, Spanish culture that of the German lands and France, and (in the form of the Fortuny) Catalonia, the end of the eighteenth century with the middle of the nineteenth, the time of Fortuny's painting with that of the performance.

If friendship is found through music here, it is in fantasia: improvisation upon something pre-existing, that does not, even so, entirely depend upon a template of pre-existing rules and principles. Such is Pujol's response to Gounod's score at the apparent heart of the image, and of Fortuny's echo of Pujol: after all, the paint must riff off the sound rather than in the most literal sense recording it. In each case, that echoing must entail a kind of listening or heeding: Fortuny of Pujol, Pujol of Gounod, and so forth. There is something here of the notion that – as the philosopher Richard Sennett puts it in his *Together* – being 'a very good listener' involves 'restating "in other words" … but the re-statement is not exactly what they have actually said …. The echo is actually a displacement.' It 'does not resemble an argument, a verbal duel' (2013: 361). Taking up a musical reference, Sennett remarks that 'the players are sparking off one another – as true in classic chamber music as in jazz' (2013: 378). But, if we what we have here is a 'displacement', it is so in the sense of a continual elision of one thing into another, rather than of a subtle shifting of one thing out of the way to make room for another that is similar but distinct. Fortuny's paint guides us here. The gentle transitions of sober colours in the wash of loose brushwork create a misty haze, only by degrees more or less fantastical, enveloping the whole in a single modulation of paint from the bright white near Margarita, running seamlessly through greyish blues, to the dark suits and brown furnishings of the nineteenth century and back again. Despite the apparent allusion to distinctions in the form of lines – like the diagonal of light across the piano – these are in fact effects of that gentle, overall, porous modulation. The experience offered us here is fluid. In that sense, the distinction drawn by Sennett between 'the converging agreement in dialectic' and its 'opposite' does not really hold (2013: 377). Sennett (like so many others) invokes the dialogic approach of the Soviet literary theorist, Michail Bakhtin, so as to evoke 'a discussion which does not resolve itself by finding common ground' (2013: 367). In the wash of Fortuny's paint, there is no question of locating or not locating 'common ground', for commonality is found in the continual elision among things: neither that solidifying, bounded imagery of ground, nor its implied opposite can hold. Pointedly, the three friends' dark garments seamlessly connect, like El Pollo with Laguna.

Friendship as *fantasia* here is a version of blending, *mixtura*, a seamless coming together of mists. Its improvisation upon the work of others flows out of these, does not set them aside or supplant them. Key to it is an experience of reasoning and of beholding or observing – and, more broadly, attending. Reasoning is implied both by the echo of Goya's *Capricho 43* with its title's reference to reason, and in *Faust* itself, where the eponymous character seeks unbounded knowledge; in turn, these two resemble one another. We are drawn to beholding and observing by the friend staring right at us as we look back, just as Fortuny putatively returned the gaze as he painted. In his account of the Panopticon, Foucault (1991) famously connects looking in the nineteenth century to a controlling knowledge secured from a position of total surveillance of the world. Correspondingly, in many studies of the nineteenth century and its legacy, the logocentric and the scopic are twinned: controlling through looking is paired with securely founded reasoning based on epistemological guarantees. In turn, in *Techniques of the Observer*, Jonathan Crary links mid-century notions of observation both to the separation of beholder and world – the growing autonomy of the individual gaze – and to efforts to discipline how we see so as to serve socioeconomic structures and their regime of knowledge in a technological economy. Specifically, Crary refers to efforts by scientists to show and dispel how optical illusions and errors arise, because we do not see the image on our retinas, but rather what is processed from them autonomously in the brain (1990: 126–32, 150). Phantasmagorias are an example. In the projection of the scene from *Faust*, with the cone of light from the piano resembling that of, say, a magic lantern, Fortuny's painting pointedly recalls such optical displays, but does so in order to blend them into the rest of reality. There is no distinction here between an inner and an outer world: the images from Faust that might come to mind or be recalled mentally at the sound of music are now physically present in it. The staring friend may be taken as both looking outwards at us and as so absorbed in the music as to be oblivious. His way of gazing lies beyond theatricality and absorption, subsuming both, and suggests that subjecthood here is not bounded in such a way for us to be able to define what is inner or outer to a self. Any such distinction runs against the flow of Fortuny's paint.

Insofar as we are supposed to engage with the friend's staring gaze, our knowledge – and Fortuny's knowledge – of what is happening does not arise from a position of autonomous, controlling looking from the outside onto the world. Rather, it is found intersubjectively between gazes which themselves are neither inner nor outer realities. To recall Shane Butler's words, this is not Narcissus's knowledge, in which a beholder looks upon the image of their own gaze, as in a sense Crary's observer will if they behold what their autonomous brain processes. As befits the musical setting, Echo once more prevails, as we experience 'players … sparking off one another': Pujol, Gounod, Goethe, Fortuny, Goya, and so forth. Nor then can this friendship offer us knowledge as control through surveillance: it requires a relinquishing of such mastery. That is all the more so because the gaze in which we might seem to be locked – between the individual who stares out and ourselves – is off-centre, and our eyes are drawn, not just to its apparent lode-line of viewing, but elsewhere, to the more nearly centred piano or to the flight of Satan. If we were to look in that direction, we would follow the gaze of the other seated friend, looking out of the side of his eyes like Goya at the start of *Los Caprichos*. If this effect guides us in seeing the image, it leads us to look in both ways at the same time, which would entail our slipping out of a way of seeing in which we discipline our gaze so that it heads in solely one direction. Equally, to see all that, our looking would need at the same time to settle in all the directions needed: we would not, for example, break the exchange of stares with the other friend. Such a feat would involve a reconfiguration of looking consonant with the flowing, dispersing paint: a way of seeing that seamlessly gazed in multiple directions at once, and that was constituted among self and others in a meeting. In the place of the harsh light of the surveillance gaze, we find here a pervasive, softening modulation.

If reasoning is to help us in encountering others, it will be through a version of reason: its eclipse or subsumption in sleep, but also its dreaming state, *El sueño de la razón*. Friendship as fantasia offers us an hallucinatory thinking: a finding of patterns of similarity across place and time that are not reducible to logical rules or causal connections. We find this in the patterns of analogy drawn in the multiply focused gaze. The various figures take shape in locations across the canvas that echo one another in rhythmic movements of resonance across place, time, and the various arts. The two friends facing us are back to back, their bodies all but merged, resembling the red and blue harmonic conglomeration of the Devil and Marta in the air. The single figure of the pianist gazing towards our left is mirrored by the lone Margarita turned towards our right. In looking both ways the Devil and Marta echo this pattern, the canvas divided either (and both) between the musician and the aerial scene, or in two sections between Marta and Margarita, on the one hand, and the Devil and the pianist, on the other, each facing the other. Equally, Faust's and Margarita's bodies can be rotated visually into those of the Devil and Marta. The outstretched leg and inclination of Satan suggests in turn the shape of the seated musician and then his two companions – and, vice versa. These similarities take shape across the intervals in the metamorphosing line of bodies. Through sensual elisions, erotic sensations slip free of conventional moral divisions of the time, and pervade and flow across the vision. On either side of the Devil and Faust, the different-biological-sex desire of Faust and Margarita echoes the two seated men, one of whom stares intensely at Fortuny to form a further pairing. Along his legs, crossing his groin level and pointing up is a phallic stick, whose symbolic arousal could be as easily from his male company as from thinking about the Faustian legend.

Ultimately, the arts and the rest of reality (which is no longer either 'external' or 'internal'), and the various media of the arts (music, visual art, literature), meet each other in this way. Sans Cabot wondered at the 'marvellous exactitude' (maravillosa exactitud) with which Fortuny's image evoked his studio (cited in Barón 2017: 142). In turn, the scene from *Fausto* resonates with and cannot be disentangled from the event of the performance. Fortuny's painting itself echoes Pujol's music: it is a fantasia on *Faust*. Like a musical *fantasia* of that kind, it riffs on pre-existing things (say, the Pujol score in the foreground, or the story of Margarita). It works through rhythmic patterns and echoes that evoke but exceed conventional schema of composition: we cannot settle on a main line of sight. The entire painting, then, is a visual analogy to, an echo of Pujol's sound. Better put, it is a pouring of the one through the other, evoked in the wash of the paint. Its passage continues in spite of apparent boundaries and distinctions. Friendship's fantasia enables the different media of art to come together as they would in opera – the visual and non-visual, the Apollo and

Dionysus of the opening of Nietzsche's *Birth of Tragedy* – not merely in parallel, but by flowing rhythmically in and out of each. The same occurs with the arts and the rest of reality.

In the final words of her final book, Susan Manning evokes 'the particular poetic sense in which analogy may be argument' (2013: 269). But 'is analogy argument?' ask the sceptics, as her opening words recall (2013: xi). In this dream of reason, we experience a Faustian bursting of the bounds of knowing, and with it a sensuality, an erotics that the ageing, scholarly Faust had been denied. Here arises the prospect of intimacy through fantasia. With it, there is a letting go of distinctions, and there is no safety net of epistemology to catch us. To the side of the piano, a Goyesque owl begins to soar, a creature alternately of wisdom and of threat. In this 'unlimited intimacy', there is and must be risk.

Part 2

At the end of 1871, in Basle, Switzerland, the philosopher Friedrich Nietzsche envisages his friend Richard Wagner at home in Lucerne, 'perhaps after an evening stroll in the winter snow'. This would be 'the moment when you, my honoured friend, would receive this essay', Nietzsche says in the preface to that very same prose work, *The Birth of Tragedy* (2003: loc.602). Already at the point of transmission from one location and time, the reception at another is included. Moreover, the composer, Wagner, would be 'immediately convinced that ... he [Nietzsche] was communicating with you [Wagner] as the ideas came to him, as if you were a real presence, and was only able to write what was appropriate to your presence' (2003: loc.607). Even though the two men are physically apart, even though – unlike in *Fausto* – *The Birth of Tragedy* might appear to be a monologue, even though the work is not the upshot of a specific dialogue and was written alone, it is offered as the outcome of a real coming together. It is, as it were, a conversation piece that takes place without the exchange of words through the air or in writing, but rather through the 'real presence' of one man to another across place and time. In such circumstances, the distinction of what is spoken spontaneously and what is written is set aside. The book is conceived 'as the ideas came to him [Nietzsche]': orality and text, like here and there or then and now, are not relevant distinctions in this realm of meeting.

Within the exchange itself, Nietzsche is a submissive to Wagner's dominant, uttering only what is 'appropriate' in his master's view. The latter becomes a 'privileged reader', in the words of the American philosopher John Sallis (1991: 11). But it does not follow from such a submissive-dominant relationship that there is not what Sallis describes as 'equivalence' between the two sides (1991: 12). Nietzsche immediately afterwards mentions the publication of Wagner's study of Beethoven at the time he 'was assembling [his] thoughts', as if the two things were of the same order (2003: loc.607): *The Birth of Tragedy* is thus asserted in its own right as Wagner's equal, his likeness even. Similarly, we are told of the essay's compelling effect on the composer, such that he 'will ... read my [Nietzsche's] name, and be immediately convinced that ... the author has something serious and urgent to say' (2003: loc.602–7). 'Equivalence' runs through the interplay of dominance and submission in this meeting. While, on the one hand, the emphasis may seem at one point to be on how the text is in its reception – from the standpoint of the 'privileged reader' – conversely one cannot simply distinguish between the receiving and the creation and transmission, for these are the outcome of the two presences together, Nietzsche and Wagner. A sameness, a likeness, has thus been brought about. That sameness arises at a moment both of the reconfiguration of Europe's power balance – north and south of the Rhine – out of division and conflict, and of dramatic unification. As Nietzsche recalls, Wagner published his work on Beethoven 'amid the terrors and glories' of the opening of the Franco-Prussian War (2003: loc.606). This was to bring the second Napoleonic Empire to an end, with the fall of France and the rise of a newly unified German Empire out of many of the German states. It would reconfigure the perceived power relationship between the Germanic and 'Latin' peoples, the north and south. Nietzsche alludes to the latter development in urging that his study aims 'to discover the seriously German problem that we are dealing with, a vortex and a turning point at the very centre of German hopes' (2003: loc.610).

In one of the most influential works of late twentieth-century cultural study, *Allegories of Reading*, Paul de Man observes how 'the prologue, an invocation to Richard Wagner, names the epiphany and vouchsafes the truth of the narrative' through this notion of 'presence'. Likewise, at the ending of Nietzsche's essay, we encounter 'the same incarnate spirit' (de Man 1979: 95–6). However, through a characteristic reading, de Man argues that the text 'compels the reader ... into an apparently endless process of *deconstruction*', the term with which he, like the French philosopher Jacques Derrida, became closely associated (1979: 101; my emphasis). Through *deconstruction*, a text that appears to assure us of 'presence' comes undone, leading us to the awareness that no such 'presence' is ever fully possible, that signs always involve absences, and 'presence' is an effect of signs. For de Man, a key factor in *The Birth of Tragedy* is the treatment of 'representation' and 'subjectivity' in the main body of the text. As Nietzsche explores tendencies that he sees in ancient Greek culture, associated variously with the gods Apollo and Dionysus, the narrative voice 'argues against the subjectivity of the lyric and against representational realism' (1979: 98). This gives us 'a statement about the limitations of textual authority' (1979: 99), which runs contrary to other tendencies in the text where 'presence' is affirmed. There is, therefore, a to-and-fro as presence is undone in its very affirmation through 'representation'.

To read *The Birth of Tragedy* this way is to suppose that discussion of 'representation' in the main body maps back onto Nietzsche's act of writing in the Preface. Put another way, it is to envisage that Nietzsche's 'absence' from Wagner corresponds to the kind of 'absence' that de Man supposes is characteristic of signs. It is easy to see how that would be a tempting thought within the intellectual circles in which de Man moved. The circulation of autonomous signs could be invoked as a continual exchange of letters and exemplified in epistolary correspondence, just as Nietzsche sends his text. A piece of such writing is physically separate from its originator and receiver, and each of these are 'absent' from one another. Famously, Edgar Allan Poe's 'Purloined Letter' became the subject, in those terms, of a debate between Derrida and the psychoanalyst Jacques Lacan (Woodward 1989). Both were responding to an interpretation of the thinking of the linguistician Saussure, in which no word has anything but an arbitrary relationship to the external world ('table' just happens to be the sound and inscription for a *table*) and as such words can only be distinguished from each other by their differences from one another (*table* is not identical to the sound and inscription *chair*). There is thus a continual play of deferral, as no word can actually be pinned down either to the external world or to a fixed meaning of its own. There can, in turn, be no subjecthood for human beings, linguistic creatures, free of that play of deferral.

Even so, the Preface does not, of itself, invite us to make such an equation between one kind of 'absence' and another, or even between the writing that Nietzsche sends to Wagner, and 'representation' as set out above and (putatively) described in the course of the main body of the essay. The Preface might invite us instead to suppose that the exchange of writing between philosopher and composer – their conversation piece – is simply of a different order to the notion of 'representation' as considered in the Apollonian world of appearances. It might invite us to envisage that its vision of the 'presence' of each to the other, despite apparent 'absence', has nothing to do with the notion that the sign is autonomous of a sender and transmitter. That is to say, it invites us to step beyond one picture of the world, and its categorisations, into another. After all, this is a very different kind of conversation, in apparent defiance of what might habitually be thought impossible: to have a dialogue without speaking, to have a monologue that is a dialogue (and vice versa), to be together in two different places and times. There is an invitation here to let go of distinctions that we might take for granted outside the new experience. The suggestion is that such a vision pervades, more still actually *is* the essay *The Birth of Tragedy*, not that it relates to any part of subsection of its contents. In short, what is front and centre here is not a tension of 'presence' and 'absence' as de Man might imagine them, but sameness and likeness felt in an encounter.

The Preface offers us an experience of how a meeting might be, and as such maps most obviously, connects most evidently, to a whole series of meetings that figure in the text: the 'mysterious marriage' of the gods Apollo and Dionysus (2003: loc.845) which gives us the titular birth of tragedy; the way in which, in the German-speaking world of late 1871, 'we seem to be experiencing the great epochs of Hellenism in *reverse* order', so that then as now we have 'the birth of a tragic age' (2003: loc.1994–9); an effort – in George S. Williamson's words – to 'overcome the divide between antiquity and the present, a venture with uncertain consequences for both' (2004: 239). Where *Fausto* projected cultural intimacy over time and across the Atlantic in the face of Argentine internal divisions and of the war with Paraguay, *The Birth of Tragedy* seeks it over the depths of history and across northern and southern Europe, as Germany arises from the Franco-Prussian conflict of 1870. If we read the Preface in this fashion, the entire experience of the 'mysterious marriage', of the traversing of time toward the birth of tragedy, of the likeness of the contemporary German and the ancient Greek, is inherent in the way that Nietzsche and Wagner encounter one another. For, all of these things are of the essay, *The Birth of Tragedy*, and the essay *is* that meeting of the two men. Nietzsche and Wagner's category-defying encounter offers us a pervasive experience of equivalences, and, more still, *is* that sort of 'equivalence'. It is worth dwelling on such phrasing as this to describe late 1871: from an 'abyss the Dionysiac song rises up to us, telling us that this German knight is still dreaming his ancient Dionysiac myth in blissfully serious images' (2003: loc.2327). Put at its boldest, Nietzsche in Basle and Wagner in Lucerne, returning home from his stroll in the winter snow, would together experience the marriage of two ancient gods, through the connection between themselves.

In the opening sentence of the main essay, we read: 'We shall have gained much for the science of aesthetics when we have succeeded in *perceiving directly*, and not only through logical reasoning, that art derives its continuous development from the duality of the *Apolline* and the *Dionysiac*' (2003: loc.617; my emphasis). Nietzsche goes on to tell us that: 'These terms are borrowed from the Greeks, who revealed the profound mysteries of their artistic doctrines to the discerning mind, not in concepts but in the vividly clear form of their deities' (2003: loc.617–22). It matters, then, that the gods were gods. Within a few sentences of the opening, Nietzsche has juxtaposed, on the one hand, an opposition of 'perceiving directly' to 'logical reasoning' with, on the other hand, an opposition of 'the vividly clear form of their deities' to 'concepts'. At a minimum, the perception rendered possible by the meeting between Wagner and the philosopher follows the same pattern as the distinction between conceptual thought and the role of deities. In turn, the 'discerning mind' will have revealed to it 'profound mysteries', thus discarding any distinction between intellectual discernment and the experience of mystery.

If El Pollo saw the Devil, have Nietzsche and Wagner, then, seen Apollo and Dionysus getting conjoined, married? Does their category-defying dialogue offer something like communication with the gods, the 'classic', in Christopher Wood's terms? There is plenty in *The Birth of Tragedy* to make us doubt anything so literal, at least at first blush. In what is a notoriously uneven piece of writing, other sentences find Apollo and Dionysus described in terms more palatable to the secular mind: for example, as 'different tendencies' (2003: loc.622), or 'the vivid and concrete representations of *two* worlds of arts' (2003: loc.1660). Nietzsche also offers us non-supernatural explanations of the genesis of divinities. Of the Olympians, he tells us, 'The Greeks knew and felt the fears and horrors of existence: in order to be able to live at all they had to interpose the radiant dream-birth of the Olympians between themselves and those horrors' (2003: loc.761). The apparent interest in the gods as gods seems to sit uneasily with such aspects of the text. The tension perhaps echoes what Matthew Rampley describes as Nietzsche's wider 'problem of reconciling both belief in meaning and also a radical scepticism' (2007: 103). And, yet, there the gods are at the very start of *The Birth of Tragedy* in 'vividly clear form'. Put more boldly, if the point is that there are two drives, or tendencies in aesthetic life, which happened once to be associated with two gods, there would be little point in being interested in this 'vividly clear form' at all, for it is entirely reducible to those drives and tendencies. The divine manifestation would, then, be something very much like a 'concept', which Nietzsche says it was not. The continual referencing of Apollo and Dionysus would be some rather crude sort of extended metaphor, entirely unnecessary to the point of the essay, and done for erudite show. The same could be said of the interest in the ancient world of the Greeks, which would be little more than a cipher for what would actually be a general treatise on aesthetics. Or, at best, historical interest in the Hellenic would be reduced to an exercise in abstract theorising.

Conversely, if the gods matter as such – if it is really important to speak of Apollo and Dionysus and their mysterious marriage – that would be so in two ways. First, the gods would be something genuinely atavistic, of the depths of time, seemingly far from the German-speaking peoples of late 1871, and intensely foreign. In *The Smile of Tragedy*, Dominic R. Ahern starkly sets out, 'from Nietzsche's point of view, ... how strange and alien the Greeks of the tragic age are to us' (2012: 17). They 'embraced and honoured virtually everything that his own Europe, at least in principle, considered immoral' (2012: 16). Second, the experience of the gods could not be wholly explained through the 'priority' of something else, to borrow Manning and Taylor's term. If there are naturalistic understandings of them, if they can serve as ciphers for something else, the gods must even so be experienced as something irreducible to all that. Put another way, for something truly to be a god is for it not to be explicable or accountable in terms of something beyond or behind it, prior to it. In this vein, from the vantage point of the Indian subcontinent, Dipesh Chakrabarty has noted 'the assumption in modern European political thought and social science that the social fact is prior to the gods and that they are "social facts"' (2001: 16). The two points dovetail: it matters to experience the Hellenic gods as atavistic and alien because they are not then reduced to the terms of a bounded present-day context or epistemology or science, which would be 'prior' to them. Writing in the essay collection *Nietzsche and the*

Gods, Lawrence J. Hatab remarks that 'the sacred element of a myth – usually embodied in a deity – exceeds both the ordinary, profane world and the human sphere in such a way that a mysterious "other" is indigenous to a mythical mode of disclosure' (2001: 47).

To experience these Hellenic gods is to experience an alien culture without priority: it is to experience alien experience itself. And conversely, perhaps, to experience alien culture without priority is to experience the gods. Intimately to encounter the gods is to experience an 'intimate culture'. Through the meeting experienced by Nietzsche and Wagner, not only are we enabled to have such an encounter with the gods, but we are given the pattern of such a meeting. Conversely, the marriage of the gods maps back onto, gives us the pattern of the meeting of Nietzsche and Wagner as it does that of ancient Greece and the Germany of late 1871, and, again, vice versa. History and geography map back and forth across each other through the birth of tragedy and the category-defying conversation of the composer and the philosopher in Lucerne and Basle at the end of 1871. 'Equivalence' runs through all of these things: these are meetings in sameness through apartness. For the encounter is not simply with one god, any more than *The Birth of Tragedy* is presented as the outpouring of a simple monologue. It is a meeting with, and of, two gods who are fundamental rivals for the prize of ancient Greek culture, 'in violent opposition to one another … perpetuating the struggle'. And what we ultimately meet, at the birth of tragedy, and in its return, in Lucerne, in Basle, is their 'coupling' (2003: loc.622).

My interest here lies more in the manner of these meetings and that marriage, the qualities of the experience of equivalence that they offer, than in the specific implications for aesthetics or philosophy that arise from the combination of the Apollonian and the Dionysiac, and that have much preoccupied academics. My approach comes in somewhat at left field from such concerns. I am interested in the sensibility, the disposition towards the world that we would find in the meeting of Nietzsche and Wagner that would enable us to experience the marriage of two ancient rival male deities which 'was finally blessed with a child' (2003: loc.845). We read that a person 'need only ask himself [*sic*] honestly about the feeling with which he responds to *miracles* portrayed on the stage: whether his historical sense, aimed at strict psychological causality, is insulted; whether he accepts miracles, with a benevolent concession, as a phenomenon intelligible to children but remote from himself; or whether he responds in some other way. He will thus be able to tell whether he is at all capable of understanding *myth*' (2003: loc.2214). That is to say, if we are to have an intimate encounter with the gods, and to experience their intimate meeting, we need to set aside a series of terms of reference, just as we did in not associating absence with the autonomous sign and deferral. The question is not whether Nietzsche and Wagner directly perceived the divine wedding as an historical event, because that issue could only arise were we to test our experience of the world against 'historical sense', or 'psychological causality' or its intelligibility to a supposedly mature understanding. To be clear, it is not asserted either that the gods exist in the sense that, say, a rabbit exists, for the question simply lies outside the realm of this kind of meeting. It is a matter of not looking behind or beyond, of not trying to explain the gods in terms of something else. That would be no way to enter into intimacy with them, or to experience how they could be intimate with one another.

At stake here is the definition of *rigour* in the practice of understanding others, in our experience of meeting something. The warning against the desire to explain away is just one instance of this larger question. *The Birth of Tragedy* alerts us to how we might assume we have found a way to comprehend something because we seem to have sets of guidelines or technical procedures for doing so. *Rigour* is conflated with an apparent intellectual safety net that might speak more to the emotional aversions of those who believe in it than to a genuine guarantee of certainty. Famously, Nietzsche rejects the German philological tradition in which he was trained: the painstaking study of linguistic usage and texts as evidence through which to understand and piece together the ancient past, 'the reliable corrector of old texts, or ... microscopic examiner of language' (2003: loc.2014). The same applies to sequences of logical thought. It is not obvious that working through a line of formal reasoning is a more reliable route to understanding than other ways of apprehending things. Pondering the legacy of the Greek philosopher Socrates, whom he blames for this outlook and for killing the marriage of Dionysus and Apollo, Nietzsche refers to 'the limitations of logic' (2003: loc.1578). Certain claims of 'rigour' involve a given single way of envisaging the world that is projected as the only true and secure foundation of knowledge, excluding such other ways of apprehending it as perceptive intuition. The latter is impeded by what Rampley memorably paraphrases as 'the mummifying practices of academic historical discourse' (2007: 152). On this account, that is an insidious phenomenon, reappearing even in scholarly practices that appear, at first blush, transgressive of those very standards.

A case in point is the notion that our encounter with a culture must be constituted by constructs if it is not underpinned by logical foundations or psychological systems or the rigorous explanatory framework of historical philology or historical contextualisation. De Man's *deconstruction* is, as the word suggests, ultimately dependent on that view. The constructionist outlook simply replicates the notion that unless there is a guarantee of truth in the form of epistemological (or similar technical) rules, there is only unreliable artifice. From this vantage point, Foucault's anonymous discourse that, in *The Order of Things*, wipes away the face of Man is as much the twin as the opponent of the historical philology it seeks to erase. In *Nietzsche, Truth and Redemption*, Ted Sadler aptly notes that: 'according to the epistemological assumption that truth is knowledge, dogmatism and relativism are the basic alternatives in philosophy' (1995: 17). Conversely, James I. Porter neatly observes of *The Birth of Tragedy* that 'Nietzsche has no philosophy in the proper sense of "having" or "philosophy"' (2000: 4). Even so, it is noteworthy how many academics seek to reconstruct the text as in the terms of a philosophical treatise, or to have recourse to a notion of 'primordiality' of one or other kind (Sadler 1995: 35–6, 44), or to dwell on the problematising of metaphysics within *The Birth of Tragedy*, or simply to talk in terms that have reassuring echoes of constructionism or deconstruction.

We are invited instead to attend to the intimate meetings in an experience of 'myth'. Such a meeting needs no justification other than itself. Dwelling on the marriage of Apollo and Dionysus, and the birth of their offspring Attic Tragedy, Nietzsche famously asserts: 'existence and the world seem justified only as an aesthetic phenomenon' (2003: loc.2311). While this is, no doubt, a specific claim about tragedy and its potential rebirth now, it is also resonant with Nietzsche's whole way of proceeding through *The Birth of Tragedy*. He attends to the aesthetic insofar as this may be conceived as 'experience in its integrity', as Dewey puts it, or, phrased another way, the experience of experience as such, its sensual qualities (1934: 274). These things are justified in the way that Wittgenstein's forms of life are, for as the latter says, 'explanation comes to an end' (*PI* §1).

Tyler T. Roberts has compared Nietzsche's overall approach to Stanley Cavell's notion of *acknowledgement* (which we have seen echoed by Fried and Foster Wallace).

Instead of modernity

It is, Roberts says, not an epistemological system, but 'a practical, artistic engagement' (2013: 146), 'a practice of placing oneself in the life of the world by encountering it in the reality of its otherness, which is a precondition for acknowledging it in its relation to us' (2013: 120–1). There is a sense even in which the exemplary meeting of Wagner and Nietzsche might appear to evoke a virtue-based ethics found in friendship. That is, it might seem to draw on a notion of virtue based not on principles, nor 'reduced to rules', but rather on 'character', 'dispositions', as Jennifer Welchman puts it in *The Practice of Virtue* (2006: xi, xiii). Epistemology and metaphysics themselves would give way to 'character' and 'disposition'. Welchman finds *The Birth of Tragedy* to be consistent with this in its rejection of 'theories of values' (2006: 110). But if this is so, we have here a notion of *virtue* and of friendship far removed from any notion of the latter as 'an instantiation of a general good', for there is no 'general good' to instantiate beyond the meeting itself. We cannot be caught in what the philosopher Alexander Nehamas (2016) sees as Aristotle's legacy in the understanding of proper friendship. That would suppose a kind of *philia* (love) that involves *arete* (excellence in realising the goals of morality, at least in Nehamas's rendering). After all, Aristotle belongs to the post-Socratic world, back beyond through which Nietzsche seeks to return onwards to the marriage of Apollo and Dionysus. *The Birth of Tragedy* recalls instead a broader, older sense of *virtue*, a kind of potency or prowess. The power, though, would come from our renunciation of mastery, of letting go of efforts to subject experience to frameworks of understanding and to supposed standards of rigour. Nietzsche baulks at 'the superior demeanour of our cultured historiography' (2003: loc.2020). In this vein, Roberts once more echoes Cavell, saying that 'Our words continually lead us to desire a grasping relationship with the world, so we must just as continually unsay them' (2013: 124–5).

It is in this way that we meet the encounter that is 'the birth of tragedy', which is 'out of the spirit of music', as the subtitle tell us. Such an experience of music thus lies at the heart of meeting, of the coming together of Nietzsche and Wagner in their apartness in 1871, 'the mystery of the union of German music and German philosophy … of which we can only gain an inkling through Greek analogies' (2003: loc.1994). It is here that 'existence and the world' are 'justified … as an aesthetic phenomenon'. Once more we may think of Shane Butler's and Carolyn Abbate's thoughts on sound and opera, urging resistance to transforming music into narrative. Once more, though, the meeting must be something other than the incommensurable alone. It is a transfiguration. For the incommensurable sound cannot be at the expense of all else that is present in the meeting: the 'non-visual Dionysiac art of music' will be married to the 'Apolline art of the sculptor' (2003: loc.622). If Wagner and Nietzsche's meeting is musical, and, by extension, so is the entire essay – surely, it must be – that will not be to the exclusion, but rather the transformation of Nietzsche's academic erudition. After all, at the age of 24, he had become the Chair of Classical Philology at the University of Basle. His lecturing on classics there preceded the publication of *The Birth of Tragedy*.

Nietzsche's essay offers us a sort of scholarly hallucination, born of meeting: knowledge of the ancients is set loose from historicism and psychology and philology into a transfigured realm of music and tragedy. 'More focus should be given to his cherishing of the poetic genesis of the sacred theme', Scott Freer (following Karl Jaspers) has said of Nietzsche in *The Birth of Tragedy*, for 'mythos is opposed to discursive or naming language and allows for an understanding that cannot be completely unfolded' (2015: 19, 9). If this is the case of the essay itself as well as the myth it tells, the former cannot be cast in conventional academic prose. There can be no careful progression through sequences of developing argument and assembled evidence. At times, the essay sounds like the kind of theoretical treatise it elsewhere denounces, while at others 'slipping toward the very discourse of Wagnerian music drama' (Sallis 1991: 144). When it evokes 'figures' of gods, it is not to produce a logical or conceptual argument but 'to transcribe … a certain movement between them and through them, an enactment of a certain figural discourse' (Sallis 1991: 17). Sallis aptly remarks that 'Since it [the book] is directed toward a theoretical presentation *of art*, it must arrive, not merely at logical insight, but at immediate certainty of intuition' (1991: 15). Structurally and in its myth, the essay evokes but departs from a 'genetic pattern', Paul de Man notes (1979: 101). At a minimum, the story appears to travel in one direction explicitly as a way of making that same journey in reverse. In Frances Nesbitt Oppel's words, 'it moves in a double orbit, from ancient times to the present and back again, and then back to the present once more. The narrative effect is not only that of a double orbit, but also of a double exposure, with ancient and modern superimposed on each other' (2005: 67). Modern German and ancient Greek music come together in this 'double exposure', such that the antique exists as what Zielinski calls a 'dynamic moment'. The question (on this account) is not whether *The Birth of Tragedy* describes what ancient music amounted to within its own bounded context, or whether it presents instead a projection back from the modern day (Porter 2000: 149–52). What we experience is its potentiality, what it might become when released into an encounter across time and place.

As befits its intimate encounters, the characters – divine and human – of the essay's myth lack secure boundaries that keep them distinct. After all, they are, not logical categories nor are they carefully delineated concepts. Sallis traces the blurring between the pair of Apollo and Dionysus: for example, since both arise in flight from 'the terror of existence' of the time of the Titans, Apollo derives from something Dionysiac (1991: 37). At the very core of Nietzsche's myth, the delineations of gender (at least as generally understood in Basle in 1871) give way: two males marry, and are 'blessed with a child', who in turn, in this realm of meetings, is two girls, 'Antigone and Cassandra' (loc.845–50). From the very outset, the masculine gods are overlain with the pairing of man of woman, but with no indication of which is which or if both are both: their duality echoes 'the duality of the sexes'. Nietzsche suggests even that when they are 'in violent opposition' they are 'inciting one of another to ever more powerful births' (loc.617–22). In *Nietzsche Beyond Gender*, Oppel shows how – in an essay from which woman is largely absent and in which two males dominate – female sexual and maternal imagery is scattered across the entire text, and particularly accumulates around references to Wagner (2005: 73, 75).

As with the encounter between our two *gauchos*, we lose something of the strangeness of this to ourselves now if we describe it solely as a queering of the myth; in that sense, we ourselves would not meet it intimately. *The Birth of Tragedy* cannot be mapped or transposed onto a generalised denial of sexual categories, any more than it can be translated into an abstract treatise (and I doubt, alas, any image of Nietzsche and Wagner as joint advocates of the LGBT+ agenda). The essay is rather an intimate working through a series of meetings in myth, in transfigured music. Boundaries give way, not on principle so much (there is no ethical principle), as in the enactment of given encounters. In each of these, a bounded self gives way – in the ecstasy of Dionysus, 'a being outside oneself' (Sallis 1991: 53), or in the intoxication of Apollo, or in the Nietzsche-Wagner that writes the book. On each occasion, we would have the pleasures of self-shattering, as Romana Byrne (following Bersani) puts it in her *Aesthetic Sexuality* (2015: 77–9, 80–1, 85). At least, that is so insofar as we would lose the bounds of our selfhood, rather than, perhaps, any sense of self at all: Wagner and Nietzsche like Apollo and Dionysus, Greece and Germany are present to each other precisely through such intimacy.

The ultimate challenge would be to meet intimately with, to find a way through what most refuses the very notion of doing such things. That would be the person of Socrates whose legacy pervades all that impedes Nietzsche's course, from philology to logical sequencing. It is here that we again encounter the figure of Faust. For Faust at once experiences the 'urge for knowledge', while – precisely because of his unbounded, Satanic pursuit of such things – he feels 'the limitations of the Socratic delight in knowledge' and 'yearns for a shore from the wide and barren sea of knowledge' (2003: loc.1840). If Faust points us to how, by embracing the Socratic, we might open its bounds, and, conversely, how the anti-Socratic might fuse with its opposite, such a possibility is implicit in the person of Socrates himself. For, as Oppel observes, 'Socrates' tendency to logic is Dionysian, creating "the myth of scientific rationalism"' (2005: 83). That is to say, if Socrates's rationalisation of the world is no more than an assumption, it has the same character of ungrounded wilfulness as does the behaviour of the god Dionysus. But conversely, as we meet Socrates within the myth (in both directions through time), he retains his role as destroyer of the central meeting, the marriage of Apollo and Dionysus, for that is key to his selfhood and person. So, the myth narrative enables us to have Socrates with us 'as if he were a real presence', even as his very presence would refuse that, and even as we acknowledge his wish for its rejection. If the essay is truly to be one of likeness and sameness, this challenge too must be navigated: the essay must seek commonality with its apparent opposite.

In returning to *The Birth of Tragedy*, James I. Porter had among his aims 'to unravel some of the ways in which Nietzsche's strands of narrative and logic were never intended to "work" or cohere, and in this way to determine some of the "impossibility" of what remains Nietzsche's most underread and underinterpreted text' (2000: 88). In *The Birth of Tragedy*, there is no real test of what 'works' or 'coheres' and what does not, made against criteria that lie beyond the realm of an intimate meeting, of encounters with gods. I am suggesting, rather, that Nietzsche and Wagner's encounter takes us on a journey, finding ways to make connections back and forth across time and place, even where these seem to defy other standards of what counts as a legitimate, rigorous link between them. It is an exploration of textures of likeness, to borrow Manning's phrase, a feeling a way through as experiences arise and may clash, eliding their boundaries without erasing their existence. Language twists and moulds as each challenge arises, seeking a path. 'He was communicating to you as the ideas came to him', Nietzsche says of the conversation piece that is the Preface (2003: loc.607). Such a thing, of its very nature, cannot be reduced to or predicted by or tested against some map of a narrative other than its own travelling. It is a passage through equivalence in the realm of the gods.

Taking shape

Un cuadrado, una esfera, un triángulo ideal
Geometría polisentimental entre nosotros
Alaska/Fangoria

Meeting: coming together and taking shape

The form of the performer

In 1853, the Spanish performer Matilde Díez (1818–83) left for the Americas, arriving first in Cuba. Two years later, she headed on to Mexico City. A short, anonymous biography was issued in May of that year in anticipation of her arrival, ending with the excited words: 'Welcome to the land of Montezuma and Cortés, leading dramatic [female] artist of the century, PEARL OF THE SPANISH THEATRE' (¡Sea bien venida a la tierra de Montezuma y de Cortés la primera artista dramática de nuestro siglo, PERLA DEL TEATRO ESPAÑOL!) (1855: 20). The author describes Díez's journey as that of an unlimited force finding freedom from bounds of place and time: 'For many years now the agitated theatre of Europe has seemed too narrow for great artistic geniuses .... The Old World is not sufficient to contain creatures in whom God has placed a spark of the infinite' (Hace muchos años que el revuelto teatro de la Europa parece estrecho para los grandes genios artísticos .... Criaturas en quienes ha colocado Dios una chispa de lo infinito, el mundo antiguo no basta para contenerlas) (1855: 3). 'There is', a Spanish witness assures us, 'no resistance against her power' (No hay resistencia contra su poder) (1855: 19). Díez, we are told, exercises absolute dominion on an enraptured public, over whose bodies and minds she takes control. Within the auditorium, she is the dominant partner, the audience the enraptured passive. This is what Mexicans may expect, and what makes her so seductive a figure: 'she always attracts to the theatre hall a numerous gathering, and that gathering finds itself continually dominated by the inflections of her voice, by her energetic action or by the delightful mobility of her countenance' (ella atrae siempre a la sala de teatro un concurso numeroso, y este concurso se ve dominado continuamente por las inflexiones de su voz, por su acción enérgica o por la graciosa movilidad de su semblante) (1855: 19). Her total control extends over all genres of drama: 'everything is subject to her eminent faculties, and, the absolute queen of the stage, she dominates everything' (todo se somete a sus facultades eminentes, y todo lo domina, como reina absoluta de la escena) (1855: 20).

At first blush, this vision of a controlling Spanish doyenne might seem to run counter to assertive strains of Spanish-American ideology of the mid-century, and to recall instead old imperial relations. Culminating in the 1860s, James E. Sanders has explained, 'a broad consensus ... emerged in many parts of Spanish America that the future of the world lay in their societies'. The continent, on such accounts, would give rise to a new universalism – reversing that of the old imperialism – so as 'to challenge old hierarchies ... between the imperial power of the Old World and the weak and struggling young nations of the New World' (2014: 6). Conversely, the pamphlet suggests that Díez is utterly dependent on the expansiveness of the New World fully to realise her own expression: her need to be dominant is constrained within Europe, which is 'too narrow for artistic geniuses'. This is a matter not simply of physical expanse but of a willingness to release constraints, such as might be echoed precisely in the kinds of thinking that Sanders describes as the *Vanguard of the Atlantic World*. The sentiment echoes with the focus on Spanish America as a place of futurity, such as Carlos J. Alonso finds widespread in post-independence Creole culture (1998: 11). If the Spanish-American audience plays the role of the 'submissive' here, it does so neither in the sense of an inferior, nor in a negative sense a 'passive'. Nor is the point that it will be dominated when European audiences have not been. Rather, Mexicans may look forward to being an enabling partner more gifted than the European submissives for whom presumably Díez has performed in the past. This is as crucial to Díez as her own exalted dominance is to the audience. Transatlantic cultural expression comes about not through conquest or its reversal, from which notions of dominance are here uncoupled. Rather it arises in togetherness, through the boundlessness of the dominant and submissive: unconstraining America with indomitable actress. At all events, it is not just a case of Díez controlling theatrical experience and her audience. Her supreme gift, the pamphlet says, is that she performs and transmits 'the intention of the author' and 'the soul of the drama' (la intención del autor, el alma del drama) (1855: 19). Her power, then, lies in rendering herself submissive, pervaded by another's mind, by a spirit. Put another way, her own dominance depends in turn upon her submission. Three years earlier in 1852, the highly successful comic dramatist, Manuel Bretón de los Herreros, published one of the few original Spanish treatises on performance of that time. Bretón states bluntly that actors do not create characters; authors do, and there is 'great merit in the faithful and genuine interpretation of the thoughts written by them' (harto mérito en la fiel y genuina interpretación de los pensamientos escritos por aquél) (1852: 7).

In a knee-jerk, twenty-first-century reaction, we might rapidly dismiss these views with well-rehearsed objections. An oppressive, authoritarian subject is endowed here with mastery over all around them: the writer dictates the meaning of the text, and others – audience and actor – bow down to it. It has become common practice to contrast with this the view that a performer is a creator and interpreter in their own right, and so is the audience; performance itself is a reality above and beyond authorial intention or imitation. We can, of course, note such commonplace observations and their relevance here. We can also pause over the implications of the supposedly antique viewpoint. Bretón explicitly denies that performance is in any way of lesser value than writing (1852: 8). He envisages, rather, an equal, non-hierarchical sharing-out of activity. This is consistent with the interest of the wider public in acquiring and keeping images of celebrity performers such as those of Matilde Díez and many others produced by photographic companies such as Laurent & Co., as much or more than of the authors of plays. The merit of the actor, according to Bretón, lies in their specific way of being a human subject, subjectivity in that sense. The performer is a creature of constant and almost infinite transformation. It is only because of this extraordinary degree of mutability that they can take on so many varied roles and scripts. Their subjection to continually changing dictates requires a chameleon-like existence, physical and mental. For Bretón, this means that star performers are very special creatures, born with a capacity for metamorphosis that goes beyond that of other people. The actor is physically, biologically constituted and organised in a way that enables continual mutability, having 'a privileged organisation that gives them the aptitude to imitate every variety of affects and passions' (una privilegiada organización que le dé aptitud para imitar todo género de afectos y pasiones) (1852: 57). In the words of the scholar Nina Auerbach, theatricality could connote 'a fluidity of character that decomposes the uniform integrity of the self' (1990: 4).

Precisely because the performer takes on the shape of others' dictates, they are released from any fixed subjectivity in their own sense of self. The subjecthood of the performer thus consists in a continual ability to become someone and something else. The actor's self is always other. If this were not so, Díez could not take on 'the soul of the drama'. For Bretón, the actor is able to 'comprehend and express others' thoughts as if they were their own; ... to mould their face to every variety of sensation and the inflections of their voice to every family of tones' (comprender y expresar los pensamientos ajenos como si fuesen propios ...; amoldar su rostro a todo género de sensaciones y las inflexiones de su voz a todo linaje de acentos) (1853: 9). In such a vision of performance, there are echoes of what the American philosopher John Sallis terms 'a Dionysian mimesis': 'Nietzsche calls it the primal dramatic phenomenon ...: to see oneself transformed before one's own eyes and then to act as if one had actually entered into another body, another character.' This is ecstasy, that stepping beyond our own subjecthood, and beyond all the collective identities to which we might otherwise belong (1991: 91–2). An openness to being dominated – but also, necessarily, the corresponding act of domination – may thus offer what Leo Bersani calls 'self-abolition' (1987: 218): an end to the submissive's being limited by supposed boundaries effected by their own sense of identity. From a less obviously sexological perspective, Michaud has likewise spoken of the way the art historian Aby Warburg deliberately exposed himself to 'the risk of a complete loss of self' in pursuit of cultural encounters (2007: 13–14). From the perspective of the audience rather than the performer, Laura Marks has observed that in 'spectatorship', 'the pleasure of yielding may be that the self is broken down only to be rebuilt again, larger and even more porous' (2002: loc.182).

Through the force of the dominant, our bodies and persons are broken out of categories of gender and age, into a form of life that is both inherently androgynous and free of chronological time, like the coupling of Apollo and Dionysus and the birth of tragedy. Bretón tells us of great performers that they are able 'today to be old and tomorrow young ... and, what is more, a woman in Madrid and a man in Barcelona' (hoy ser viejo y mañana joven ... y lo que es más, mujer en Madrid y hombre en Barcelona) (1852: 9). His remark echoes the obsession with cross-dressing on the mid-nineteenth-century Spanish stage (as elsewhere), captured among others by the international photographic company, Laurent & Co. The mutability that arises from such subjection to the dominant may undo the secure adscription of a gender to a body just as it involves the abandonment of a securely bounded self. '*In imitating gender,*' Judith Butler famously wrote, '*drag implicitly reveals the imitative structure of gender itself – as well as its contingency*' (2007: 187; original emphasis).

In a Laurent photograph of the soprano Dolores Custodio (1863; Figure 1), we find the performer staring at us impertinently, seated at a desk in a vast Victorian dress, a top hat on her head; her clothing from the waist up could as easily be that of a man or a woman. One hand rests between her legs, while the other, its arm forming an upward V shape, holds a horizontal cigar: in associating one hand with another, we would connect her groin both with the phallus-like cigar and with her genital area. In nineteenth-century illustrations, such insinuations, effected by the posture of women in impressive dresses, are far from uncommon. Sharon Marcus has shown how the 'erotic atmosphere' of fashion images (for example) exceeded any narrow categorisation of appropriate sexual preference. We might see, for example, 'a seated woman, one hand buried deep in a small bag that rests on her thigh just below and alongside her crotch, the other hand resting on a table but also tangled in the fur trim of the woman standing' nearby (2007: 131).

Such mutability in gender and in sexuality parallels the role of penetration in the Mexican pamphlet about Matilde Díez. We learn that 'When with a heart-rending ah!, she expresses a deep sentiment, she *penetrates* even into the most hidden fibres of the heart of all those who are listening', presumably both men and women (cuando con un ¡ay! desgarrador espresa un profundo sentimiento, penetra hasta en las fibras más recónditas del corazón de cuantos la escuchan) (1852: 19; my emphasis). The act of being penetrated may (I stress *may*), thus in a positive sense, enable a person '*to abdicate power*' (Bersani 1987: 212; original emphasis), that is, to relinquish all efforts to know the other based on

1 Juan Laurent, *Dolores Custodio in Entre mi mujer y el negro*

subjection to our own frameworks. Comparing the unprotected penetration of barebacking with some notions of religious love, Bersani toys with the possibility that 'the subject allows himself [*sic*] to be penetrated, even replaced, by an unknowable otherness' (Bersani & Phillips 2010: 53; Bersani himself has reservations). It is, not, however, simply a matter of being penetrated, for the latter experience then enables its own reversal: our penetration by the other becomes equivalent to penetrating them. Precisely because the actress is now within the most hidden parts of the audience's own self, the latter is able to effect, with her, entry into the author and the drama. Such is the key to accessing esoteric knowledge, the sense of the 'other': 'she makes the public *penetrate* into the hidden [or, occult] thoughts that are the soul of the drama' (hace al público penetrar en los ocultos pensamientos que son el alma del drama) (1855: 19; my emphasis). By implication, all parties here are within each other's most intimate selves, their hidden thoughts and the most hidden fibres of their hearts. The author and drama are in Díez who is in the audience who are, with Díez, in the author and drama, and around in a circle. In this scene of deep mutual penetration, everyone becomes the same. It is as if in a fantasy scene of bareback fisting described by Dean in which 'one partner dominates the other by sliding his arm ever deeper into the narrator's bowels, until, 'for an instant, we shared the feeling of occupying the same place at the same time' (2009: 46).

If I invoke so graphic a similarity, it is to shock us out of assumptions about the naïveté of mainstream nineteenth-century performance practice. By dominating the audience, just as they themselves submit in 'ecstasy', the actress transmits the experience of liberating subjection. All those involved physically and emotionally in the performance enter into a transfiguration, in which any authoritative self they have vanishes. In the auditorium, the actress thus engenders intense togetherness, physical and mental, conjoining the local audience, the visiting performer, and the play and author from whichever place or time these came. European notions of 'sympathy', of shared feeling, were, after all, often conceived in terms of a play of dominance and submission, Laura Hinton has shown. In visions of the Paris of the mid-century, Hinton finds, for example, a fantasy of submission in the openness to 'global cosmopolitanism' (1999: 2, 118).

This new state, free of prior, entrenched subjectivity, is described as having near-occult properties, like Nietzsche's mysteries or del Campo's blending of souls or Fortuny's evocation of a dream of reason. It is an hypnotic, living-dream experience. The pamphlet on Díez describes the audience as dominated 'in the same way as the freedom of a somnambulist is by the caprice of a magnetiser' (del mismo modo que lo está la libertad de un sonámbulo por el capricho de un magnetizador) (1855: 19). We are possessed. The Spanish hypnotist Modesto Costa y Turell observes that by impregnating a hypnotised person with their magnetic fluid, the practitioner's will 'annihilates, absorbing them, all the other faculties of our being' (aniquila, absorviéndolas, todas las demás fuerzas de nuestro ser) (1857: 12). Through this transfiguration and emptying out of our selves, we become party to hieratic knowledge of the play, what the pamphleteer calls the 'ocultos pensamientos' – concealed/occult thoughts – of its soul (1855: 19). This is perhaps the sense of the pamphleteer's remark that Díez 'surprises' (*sorprende*) the intention of play, that she takes us into its occluded thought (1855: 19), just as the *gauchos* violated Goethe's Germanic sanctuary so as to set its resonances free.

'Spirit theories fundamentally challenged the idea of the bounded person', Marina Warner remarks in her *Phantasmagoria* (2006: 247). Likewise, the boundaries of dominance and submission in mesmerism were far from unyielding. This is apparent in Robert Browning's poem 'Mesmerism' (from *Men and Women* (1855)). The practitioner's dominance involves a submission, a yielding to the forms of the woman he summons. His own being must spread beyond its prior bounds to take on her contours. His active concentration entails passivity: 'While I – to *the shape*, I too / Feel my soul dilate / Nor a whit abate, / And relax not a gesture due, / As I see my belief come true' (2004: loc.1470; my emphasis). On some nineteenth-century accounts, 'mesmerism becomes not the imposition of an active will upon a passive patient', Alison Chapman has commented, 'but a more open and fluid circulation of influences as the stability of the psyche falters' (1998: 309). If Díez is a magnetiser, she is, after all, dependent both upon the responses that her audience gives, and upon the 'soul' of the author that she is able to conjure and transmit. Her very status as the hypnotist is, at the very least, unusual in the gendered terms of the time, for the mesmerist (unlike the medium) was habitually male, and the image of a woman under the masculine hyponotist's power was commonplace, then as now. Costa y Turell warns that, while, women could magnetise people, they did so weakly and with some risk to themselves, because they were the delicate sex; conversely, they were well suited to being hypnotised (1857: 17–18). That said, even conventional mesmerism resonates with the fluidity of gender in such practices, for – Chapman notes – 'the masculine dominance is coterminous with a heightened emotive power, a sensibility usually associated with feminine cultural norms' (1998: 305). We might think of Díez's 'heart-rending ah!'

The taking on of forms, the making of shapes, seems to have been crucial in effecting Díez's dominant force, as if these made a kind of imprint upon the audience: 'to the shape, I ... feel my soul dilate', as Browning put it. In collectable photographs (*cartes de visite*) issued after her return to Spain, the actress strikes domineering poses. In one portrait (Figure 2), regally dressed, and resting an arm on an ornate pedestal, she looks out haughtily, her chin very slightly raised, her head utterly upright and unyielding, her free hand directing us down to her feet. The gesture is familiar from aristocratic portraits such as Goya's paintings of the Duchess of Alba. In her dress, Díez has the robust, bold outlines of a decorated human pyramid, shimmering white, occupying a disproportionate part of the card. The actress is serenely certain in the forcefulness of her presence. Close to the foreground, her body presses out onto the viewer from a near-blank backdrop; were anything to approach her, it would break and disperse as if upon the column glimpsed at her side. She fixes us with her gaze.

The photographs are the work of the French-born Jean – or Juan – Laurent's firm, running an international operation out of Spain, and ultimately circulating thousands of images of the country: its monuments, infrastructure, art, celebrities, cities and peoples. This was a vast enterprise of cultural translation. Established and run by a French-born artist, the company used the new technology to transform Spanish culture and society into piles of two-dimensional, reproducible objects – photographs – for onward transmission beyond and across Iberia. Laurent is particularly renowned for doing so by presenting his subjects to audiences as geometrical shapes, seen here in the near-straight lines of Díez's form. Her formidable triangle is thus projected out from its point of origin onto the world, just as her irresistible power had burst forth from Europe to dominate Mexican theatregoers. Taking all the thoughts above together, Walter Benjamin's 'work of art in the age of mechanical reproduction' becomes a vehicle for channelling quasi-occult powers, a means to burst subjectivity's limits across place and time. The association between mesmeric experience and photography was, after all, not uncommon. In her vast study, *Victorian Glassworlds*, Isobel Armstrong notes the powerful voicing of the parallel in Browning's verses: 'I imprint her fast / On the void at last / As the sun does whom he will / By the calotypist's skill' (Armstrong 2008: 352; Browning 2004: loc.1438). It was said that primitive peoples believed the camera stole the soul, but Warner suggests that this oft-repeated tale

2 Juan Laurent, *Matilde Díez*

arises largely amid Western preoccupations about photography and the spirit. The medium could be envisaged, for example, 'as a kind of camera, receiving and transmitting light's action upon matter' (2006: 230).

Yet 'the shape' of an actress such as Díez – the bold, geometrical patterns formed by a performer's body on a nineteenth-century photograph – tends now to make us laugh. Our amusement is consistent with the view of humour set out by the French philosopher Henri Bergson in his volume on *Laughter* (*Le Rire*) of 1900: that it is a reaction to humans behaving as if they were objects or automata, exhibiting fixity rather than the flow of life (Bergson 1962). In many photographs of nineteenth-century performers, the poses struck may seem stiff, the movements of limbs lacking in fluidity, the gestures exaggerated and crudely simplified, bodily and emotional nuance lost. This is all the more so with such geometrically fixated photographers as Laurent & Co. In one melodramatic image of an angry sheikh, the actor Ludovico Mancini raises a fist to our right so that it stands parallel and at a distance to his scowling face and its false beard. His left arm runs out to the clenched hand through black cloth, counterbalanced by his other arm in a white sleeve which bends down in awkward symmetry at the opposite point to where the fist was formed. Bergsonian laughter at such effects is an extension of a wider suspicion of fixity, and potentially of all photography. Kaja Silverman notes Bergson's belief that the photographic image was the antithesis of all change in time (2015: loc.1210). The French thinker was thereby moved to an abjure even 'the cinema as an adequate representation of time', Mary Ann Doane observes (2002: 175).

Against such a dichotomy between bold geometrical form and the life of the body may be set a notion of immanent transfiguration. In an experience of that kind, human figures would have a quality of being 'both flesh and not'. The phrase was coined by David Foster Wallace, especially with regard to the tennis player Roger Federer (2012: 5). It is worth dwelling here on the parallel between still shots of sports stars in a dramatic moment and the photographic depiction of an actress such as Díez. In both cases, we find the human body stretched out of its usual appearance into shapes of exaggerated, geometrical boldness (Foster Wallace insists on 'kinetic beauty', but for reasons set out below, any distinction between still and mobile becomes somewhat moot here). Presumably for reasons of present-day cultural preferences, this kind of posture proves admissible in sports photography, perhaps because it is taken that, in the normal course of things, sports people adopt such forms, as nineteenth-century performers in their own way once did. Dwelling on Federer's body movements, Foster Wallace invokes 'mystery and metaphysics'. He evokes 'preternatural athletes who appear to be exempt, at least in part, from certain physical laws' (2012: 18).

Put another way, this kind of 'human beauty' involves the reconfiguration of corporeal form into something that defies habitual human movement and its limitations. For Foster Wallace, an aesthetic experience of this kind enables 'human beings' reconciliation with the fact of having a body' (2012: 8). Running through the footnotes of Foster Wallace's essay is an account of a dying child, interlaced with that of Federer, such that the fragility of the human form, and its ultimate mortal limitations, are interwoven with the capacity to take that body beyond the confines of its usual shapes. In this way, the transfiguration is immanent, for it is realised in and through the mortal body, and gestures back to the habitual limitations that it momentarily exceeds. It 'reconciles' us by showing us of what the body is capable, for and within all its frailty. By extension, on this account, what would be at stake

Meeting: coming together and taking shape

for the nineteenth-century performer would not be whether bold geometrical forms were at odds with living experience. It would be whether the actress transfigured lived experience from within, so as to realise radical metamorphoses and effect a mesmeric force. In the terms of Michael Fried, 'theatricality' would here be pushed to an extreme, such that the experience of 'absorption' is to arise, not by tempering or modifying the form, but out of its very boldness, in its assertive geometrical shapes, tipping us over into an experience of possession.

To do so would be to court the limits of embodied existence in the interplay of dominance and submission. Only that way could a performer attain 'the shape' that is crucial to intimate communication. Transfiguration through performance is not, then, some simple state of ludic freedom. Not only must actors come to believe things 'even when these are repugnant to their own convictions', but they end up, Bretón tells us, 'doing daily violence to their nature, their character, their personal habits' (aunque repugnen a su coviccíon; haciendo cuotidiana violencia a su índole, a su carácter, a sus hábitos particulares) (1852: 9). They become other than themselves through a self-inflected and willingly accepted assault on their very being, mental and physical. As they do so, they set aside their own standards of judgement, the whole frame of reference within which they live ('their own convictions'). 'Through an ordeal of self-chosen 'torture', a human being might get beyond conventional ways of thinking', James Miller remarks in *The Passion of Michel Foucault* (1994: 277). Through dominance and submission, 'a game played with the body itself', the influential theorist of sexuality 'sought out potentially transformative "limit-experience" … deliberately pushing his mind and body to the breaking point' (1994: 269, 30). In this fashion, he looked death in the face (1994: 88). What Bretón sees in a performer is not entirely unlike that: forever taking their own self to the point of its extinction through the adoption of another 'shape'. This must entail risk: 'in this shadowy ordeal, putting body and soul to the test … the outcome was always in doubt', Miller remarks (1994: 279). Likewise, mesmerism – Chapman comments – risked 'moments of psychic crises' (1998: 307). Among the dangers is that the self would be utterly subjugated to its dominant: killed off, in that sense. If we return only to the opening remarks of this section, the willingness of the Mexican audience to yield before Díez risks a neo-colonial oppression. For all the allure of submissive erotics – Amber Jamilla Musser has noted in *Sensational Flesh* – we cannot assume it is always subversive (2014: 3).

In the geometrical image of a nineteenth-century performer, to be thus transfigured would involve the body adopting such forms that, on the one hand, it continued to evoke the physical nuances of our lived existence ('flesh') while, on the other, articulating the bold geometrical shape through them ('not'). Were this state attainable, the Bergsonian distinction between fixity and life would fall away, for both would be subsumed within 'the shape'. A Laurent photograph of Díez with the actor Antonio Pizarroso (Figure 3) evokes that quality of the actress in comparison with other performers of her time. The two are in a scene of tense confrontation, adopting near-identical, but mirror-image poses: in profile, their feet apart, one arm at their side, the other at a diagonal heading towards the other actor, their heads turned with still precision to one another. Yet, there is something more remarkable about Díez's appearance, compared to her fellow thespian, something other even than the shimmering white triangle of her dress and head. Her arms are both tensed and, at the same time, slightly flexed, the hands extended and suspended almost exactly above her midriff, their slight diagonals forming transformations of each other and

3 Juan Laurent, *Actors in Venganza Catalana*

expansions and mirror outlines of her skirts below. Her torso and legs are turned more pointedly at the viewer, the chest pushed forward, and her head is taken further round over the shoulder as a result. Her shape manages to embody within itself the tense equilibrium to which the scene aspires. Her presence presses itself more forcefully towards us. Her pose, with its near-invisible straining – out of which it might spring – is on the brink of violent movement while attaining near-perfect geometries.

Shape and geometry

Such geometrical 'shapes' could be understood as a universal language, capable of transmitting and communicating beyond the boundaries of places and times. This involved descriptive geometry: the practice of undertaking geometrical tasks by tracing lines and shapes. In the following discussion, I will draw upon ideas and evidence that I first set out in a discussion of universal language and photography (Ginger 2012b), recasting these and setting them in relation to the wider discussion of 'shape' in this present chapter. Photographs, mechanically reproduced, had vast potential to distribute these forms widely across geography, while preserving them over the decades, just as they broadcast Matilde Díez's 'shape'. As is implicit in the notion of a transfiguration, such communication would need to overcome a series of oppositions: abstract and particular, fixed and moving, inanimate and animate. By extension, this includes the distinction between the living and the dead, not just in relation to an individual existence, but as regards historical periodisation: it is, in the end, mortality that renders something definitively of the past. In the discussion that follows, the tension of abstraction and particularity, of fixity and movement leads us to a further opposition between taking and receiving a photograph, between the organisation of the image by its maker and the disclosure of the world's shapes in photographic vision. Through such issues run the erotics of geometrical shapes and of photography, taking us back once more to penetration, to dominance and submission, and to the sensual effect of analogous shapes. The continuous projection from one such form to another evokes once more a sensation of 'drag', of freedom from gender boundaries. A notion of the vagueness of shapes is crucial to all these matters, to whether the various oppositions hold, or to whether a transfiguration might be possible. Through all these issues, we are led once more to the mesmeric resonances of the 'shape'.

In the words of an artillery captain, Luis Felipe Alix, in 1866, descriptive geometry constitutes 'a true language, its alphabet is made of the representative signs of the elements that are to be combined; reading and translation of it, the interpretation of these combinations and composition in it, the means to effect them' (Verdadero idioma, su alfabeto son los signos representativos de los elementos que se van a combinar; su lectura y su traducción, la interpretación de estas combinaciones, y su composición el modo de realizarlas) (1865 I: 5) The words *traducción* (translation) and *trasladar* (to transfer, to translate) were used to describe how geometrical drawings transformed an object into two-dimensional form (Lozano y Ascarza 1866: 9; Cardona y Escarrabill 1865 II: xii). In general, such descriptive geometry involved projections: the metamorphosis of the lines of one shape into another. This language was, in principle, something anyone anywhere could pick up and learn. Applied to scenes from a particular city, region, country or culture, it could transform what was shown into something universally comprehensible by drawing out its patterns. The subject matter would, thereby, be released from limiting boundaries of place and time into a realm of shared experience. These geometrical arts were fundamental and widespread in

European and Europeanised societies of the mid-century. They were exercised by anyone from artisans through schoolchildren to soldiers. In a country such as Spain, undertaking efforts at reform and redevelopment, the practical nature of descriptive geometry made it a crucial tool from the cutting of stones, through urban reconstruction, to military planning, as well as the encouragement of the fine arts.

The similarity of descriptive geometry to photography did not escape contemporary observers such as the military topographer Pedro Borja y Alarcón, among others. Photography – literally drawing with light – likewise projects lines from three-dimensions onto two. Borja went so far as to recommend cameras as a time- and labour-saving mechanical device for projecting an image onto a plane, and for magnifying or reducing it through projections (1876: 1–2, 18–21, 39–40, 64). The highly geometrical nature of widely distributed images of Spain – notably by Laurent and the Valencian José Martínez Sánchez – uses these shapes for cultural translation, communicating a vision of the country to their audiences. Such photographs range from regional and national types, through historic buildings, objects and landscapes to new infrastructure, and encompassing famous performers such as Matilde Díez. In their national and international circulation, they appealed to distinct perspectives on Spain's integration into and place in the wider world. Broadly speaking, on the one hand, they could serve the growing interest abroad – in Britain, the United States, France and elsewhere – with Spain's historic legacy as a world-shaping empire, and – through the culture of its Golden Age – as an untapped source for inspiration in the arts, now eclipsed by its supposed decline. On the other hand, the images could project Spanish preoccupations, not just with historic glories, but with the affirmation of contemporary renewal, both to its own people and others: an assertion that it was a dynamic and important part of the Europeanised world. Such aspirations are exemplified in the photographic collection *Public Works of Spain* (*Obras públicas de España*), and – pointedly – in the display of images of infrastructure by Martínez Sánchez at the 1867 Universal Exhibition in Paris. Recent writers – María José Rodríguez Molina and José Ramón Sanchis Alfonso – note how these included such masterpieces as *Sariñena Bridge (Alcanadre Bridge)* (1867) (2014: 91).

The notion of such a universal visual language cast from geometry has fallen far from fashion during recent decades in cultural studies, with very occasional exceptions such as Martin Kemp's *Structural Intuitions* (2016: 23). This is, in part, because of a generalised suspicion of universalism. But it is also because of a specific hostility to images – not least photographic images – that are structured around the lines of two-dimensional geometries like those of Díez's shimmering pyramid. (The latter are often referred to casually as *Euclidean geometry*, though, in fact, not all nineteenth-century versions took Euclid as the authoritative theory (Richards 1988: 143, 164 170).) To the extent that geometry is more positively evoked – for example, in contemporary European philosophy deriving from Deleuze and others – it has tended to be by analogy specifically with non-'Euclidean' space (Plonitsky 2003). It is widely held that the rendering of the world into abstract shapes in the nineteenth century served a bourgeois, capitalist order, that sought to organise the world for purposes of consumption and exploitation. Geometry is a means to exercise disciplinary control and surveillance. In the process, the specificity and particularity of cultures and of life is emptied out into homogeneous forms.

For example, Suren Lalvani in *Photography, Vision, and the Production of Modern Bodies* remarks that 'the railroad, by assimilating previously accessible places into the coordinate geometry of a systematised grid, had transformed landscape into disciplined and disciplinary geographical space. What is manifest in this systematisation of geography is the disciplinary architecture of the panopticon' (1996: 177). Such an outlook characterises the thinking about urban life that derives from Michel de Certeau (2000) and Louis Marin (1984). In *Utopics*, Louis Marin affirms that '*Geometry* inserting itself into the city's map has profound political and social implications: it signals the presence of bourgeois rationality' (1984: 219; original emphasis). Derek Gregory likewise refers in *Geographical Imaginations* to 'the cartography of objectivism, which claimed to disclose a fundamental and enduring geometry underlying the apparent diversity and heterogeneity of the world .... Ostensibly "scientific", "objective" maps cannot escape their (sometimes unwitting) complicity in ideology', he avers (1994: 70, 74). For the influential theorist, Henri Lefèbvre likewise, 'Capitalism and neocapitalism have produced abstract space' (1991: 39). In *The Victorians and the Visual Imagination*, Kate Flint segues smoothly into a consideration of perspectival optics from an echo of John Tagg's emphasis on 'practices of surveillance' (Flint 2000: 30). For Tagg, photography was, at the very least, part of the 'unremitting surveillance of ... new, disciplinary institutions' (1988: 63). Writing subsequently, Allan Sekula notes with a critical eye 'the homology between the function of the photograph as a universally exchangeable "abstract equivalent" of its world referent and the circulatory function of paper currency' (2002: 22). Underlying many of these observations is an outlook such as that expressed by the philosopher Martin Heidegger in his essay 'Building, Dwelling, Thinking': 'the fact that they are *universally* applicable to everything that has extension can in no case make numerical magnitudes the *ground* of the nature of space and location that are measurable with the aid of mathematics' (1971: 156). So, geometry could not translate these realities, and neither could geometrical photographs. Even as we seemed to connect outwards across place and time, we would be alienated from, not at home in the world.

It is easy to see how geometric photographs could serve socio-economic purposes of this kind. Laurent's photographic enterprise effectively put the image of Spain on sale – from its landscapes, through its local customs, to its performers like Matilde Díez. In John Urry's famous words, 'places themselves are in a sense consumed, particularly visually' (Urry 1995: 2). Geometrical communication could be seen to render an individual such as Díez transmissible through international markets, turning her into a commodity. The connection between geometrical images and large movements of capital is manifest in the many images of railways and other infrastructure made by photographers such as Laurent and Martínez Sánchez. As Elizabeth Anne McCauley notes in her *Industrial Madness*, similar French photographers like Collard produced images that closely resembled 'the technical drawings' of the engineers, as if the photographs were part of the same endeavour (1994: 212). Such is one possible outcome from the affordances of this universal visual language.

Conversely, many nineteenth-century treatises and manuals of descriptive geometry envisage it as a practice through which to work with things, their textures and properties, making shapes, as we do (for example) in carving a stone (Cardona y Escarrabill 1865 II: 165). Many people valued geometrical illustrations because of the very limits to their abstraction: as physical drawings and lines, they are attuned to embodied existence. Unlike theoretical statements and mathematical formulae, graphic images 'enter through the senses', Borja remarks (entra por los sentidos) (1876: 52–3). Such an outlook echoes with that of the twenty-first-century philosopher Peg Rawes in her *Space, Geometry and Aesthetics*: a 'geometric encounter ... is embodied in the act of drawing geometric figures'

(2008: 2). Looking in her *Atlas of Emotion* to a more antique allegory of Geometria holding measuring instruments, Giuliana Bruno observes, in a not dissimilar way, that 'the nature of her mapping is tactile' (2002: 254). By extension, the geometrical forms in a Laurent photograph are not in any simple sense abstractions: they are brought about in the photographer's craftwork and the light of the world through chemical reaction on a material surface. Like the artisan exerting their craft with a rock, the geometrically minded photographer works through and with all this specificity to draw out and trace lines and shapes, hands-on as it were. In the same way, when a performer like Matilde Díez (or a tennis player like Federer) transfigures their body through geometry, they do not abandon their own corporeal existence but project it into new, communicable form ('both flesh and not'). Far from abstracting us from life and the world, the adoption of such shapes involves intense engagement with our physical and psychological realities. That is how Díez's shimmering pyramid materialises and is transmitted through its reflected and projected light in the *carte de visite*.

Crucially, the lines that are traced and seen are characterised by what philosophers call 'vagueness', of which geometrical treatises and manuals often took a positive view. It is this lack of interest in a putatively perfect, abstract precision that opens a route beyond the dichotomy of controlling, fixed form and rich, lived experience. In valuing vagueness, we suppose that the ways in which we understand the world to be organised often do not have specifiable exact boundaries, and are at the same time perfectly serviceable. Often as not, when we see something as a geometrical shape, its lines are actually quite rough. Borja puts it bluntly: in drawings, 'all the exaggerated demands of exactitude will be little short of ludicrous' (todas las exigencias exageradas de la exactitud serán poco menos que ridículas) (1876: 52–3). Another geometer, Antonio Lozano y Ascarza, writing in 1866, closely associates vagueness with our practical ability to engage with and act in the material world. The 'exact results' of 'algebraic calculation', he observes, 'lose much of their advantage due to the imperfection of the instruments or means that we have to employ' (del cálculo algebraico; la exactitud de sus resultados; pierdan mucha de su ventaja a causa de la imperfección de los instrumentos o medios de que tendremos que servirnos) (1866: 50). The transfiguration of Díez into geometry involves such vagueness. In the *carte de visite*, the bottom of the pyramid shape is formed by the hem of Díez's dress, but this hangs unevenly to the ground, curving in and out, sometimes touching, sometimes rising above the floor. Overall, the actress and outfit look cone-shaped, but the line upward to our left has to take into account the performer's prominent right breast.

Lozano and Borja are highlighting a much more fundamental reality even than that much of our day-to-day use of geometry is rough-edged. They are pointing out that the moment a line is actually drawn in the physical world, the moment that any physical measurement of any kind is applied to a line, there can be no ultimate precision. In his book, *Not Exactly*, the computer scientist Kees van Deemter makes the point bluntly: 'even the most sophisticated definitions [of measurement] have some residual imprecision, and it is unclear how this imprecision can ever be got rid of completely. … This observation casts doubt on the standard division between vague and crisp concepts' (2010: 35, 52). Taken, as it were, positively and expansively, vagueness implies that it would not be possible to distinguish absolutely the geometrical lines of the object from the latter's peculiarities and particularities. Wherever we sought to make the distinction, however apparently finely, there would not be an absolute, discernible gap between where the latter ended and the former began. For this reason, the specific character of, say, an individual piece and kind of stone would not be removed by geometrical patterning. Rather the one would be present in the other. Likewise, there could be no line that we could project, with however fine a set of instruments, from the hem of Matilde Díez's dress that would complete a perfect cone.

The question is not – as philosophers have often debated – whether such vague shapes are a fundamental element of reality. The question is what the vagueness might enable us to do or not do, what its 'affordances' are. As Wittgenstein remarks in *Philosophical Investigations*, to dismiss something as 'not an area at all' because it has 'vague boundaries' 'presumably means that we cannot do anything with it'. Conversely, he affirms an 'indistinct picture' might be 'often exactly what we need' (*PI* §71). In a similar vein, in *The Pragmatics of Mathematical Education*, Tim Rowland observes that 'vagueness is not a limitation but a means to do things which are inhibited by precise communication' (2000: 64). What would be 'inhibited by precise communication' here is our capacity to experience and articulate geometrical shapes vaguely in the world, such that they are neither disembodied abstractions, nor simply exceeded by particularity. 'Why cannot the line be just as real as whatever passes along it, if indeed the two can be distinguished at all?' asks Tim Ingold in *Lines* (2016: xv). At least insofar as we might attend to the vague shapes themselves, we would let go of Roland Barthes's classic distinction in photography between 'punctum' and 'studium', between 'that accident which pricks me', and the general scheme that it escapes (2000: 26–7). We would be able to comprehend the detail of Díez's dress and the curve of her breast as part of the cone area that is projected on and from the photograph. We would be able to experience, and she would be able to project, her 'shape'.

The question is whether, in seeing such patterns, our disposition is to experience possible structures of power and control as hierarchically prior to the vague geometrical forms, or whether, the former might be taken simply as possible outcomes of the latter. Considering Frith's photography in her *Scenes in a Library*, Carol Armstrong has suggested that we might take as a 'superstructure' the ideologies that nineteenth-century photographs express or with which they might be complicit. These, she says, rest on 'the base', including 'the logic of its illustrational foundation', which she describes as its 'subideological workings' (1998: 280). In the images we are considering here, the 'subideological workings', 'the logic of its illustrational foundation' would lie at the level of the means of communication and transmission itself: the vague geometries of the image, how they are drawn, and how they are perceived, in embodied existence. If one is disposed towards the photograph in this way, whatever is specifically articulated in the universal visual language will always be exceeded by the potential of the forms of the language themselves, its capacity to connect. The contemporary art and design movement Patternity has observed in a similar vein that 'pattern' is 'an antidote to humankind's mounting sense of disconnection and sense of isolation'. 'Patterns speak a powerful universal language', they remark, enabling us 'to better understand life' (Murray & Winteringham 2015: 18).

Martínez Sánchez's *Guadalfeo Bridge* (Figure 5) – from the *Public Works of Spain* – evokes an overcoming of any opposition between the organising, controlling gaze of a dominant subject and the fluid disclosure of the world's mobile forms out of itself. Kaja Silverman associates the former with the 'taking' of likenesses and the latter with the 'receiving' of shapes generated out of the world. Silverman has sought to reclaim the notion of receiving, which – she notes – was widespread in the early years of photographic endeavours (2015:

353, 466, 482, 560, 572). Martínez Sánchez's image suggests that the 'taking' and 'receiving' might be continuously interchangeable: that they might conjoin, as they would in Díez's enraptured auditorium. It is in this way that they would communicate Spain to the wider world. On the one hand, the forms of the natural world, and with it of the depths of time, take up most of the image, giving it key shapes. The sky down to the river banks and land forms a near-blank six-sided polyhedron. The banks and the bulk of the river and its shimmering shale provide a glistening parallel form. The sensation that the world is disclosing the geometrical patterns through the photograph – as Silverman might have it – is evoked by the vantage point of the camera, mid-river, through which the expanse of water flows. At the same time, the near-regularity of the image clearly depends upon the photographer's positioning of the camera in precisely that spot, so as to frame the natural scene. The beginning and end point of the horizontal, within which the image is framed, are defined pointedly by the start and finish of the human-built bridge meeting the landscape. If the river evokes an outpouring of disclosure, the bold horizontal of the bridge and arches suggests the forceful drawing of a technical diagram in the natural scene.

An ability to switch between both disclosure and framing, to experience both at once, as if to subsume both, is key to the sense of intimate connection between subject and other that the photograph offers. It gives us all the image's geometrical shapes, and their capacity to communicate in the putative universal language. In accordance with the practice of descriptive geometry, this suggests that, if there is no ultimate choice to be made between the specificities of the world and the shapes we draw in it, we may 'take' and 'receive' at once. The relationship of sky to water in the photograph evokes such a thought. The blankness of the first suggests a vision of geometry as absolute abstraction, while the textures of the shale, the reflected light on the river offer a rich, sensual texture. It is as if the photograph were a demonstration of the relationship between abstraction and real-world geometries. Perhaps better put, it is a testing of a limit-case: using the sky to explore how close physical reality can come to pure geometrical abstraction, and then how, amid the waters, such a shape can take on more fleshed-out forms. Where we both 'take' and 'receive' the world, we encounter something that is both material and not, to paraphrase David Foster Wallace.

Like Díez's performance and reception, such photographic imprinting and transmission of a 'shape' may evoke both penetration and being penetrated. Across a series of contested theories, the camera and the viewing of photographic images have been associated with both experiences. Whether through the assumptions of particular varieties of psychoanalysis, or mere stereotyping, the two stances have at times been linked to dominance and submission, masculinity and femininity. This is so from Laura Mulvey's essay of 1975, 'Visual Pleasure and Narrative Cinema', with its sadistic, scopic, masculine lens (Mulvey 1985), through the violent phallic camera of Michael Powell's movie *Peeping Tom* (1960), to the vagina-as-camera in Luis Buñuel's Last Supper scene from *Viridiana* or the masochistic, pre-Oedipal identification with the mother in Gaylyn Studlar's 'Masochism and the Perverse Pleasures of the Cinema' (1985). In some images of Spanish practitioners associated with bold, geometrical photography, we find intimated something beyond narrow ascriptions of the sexual resonances of photographic vision. To that extent, these images have an affinity with efforts – like those of Rhona Berenstein – to uncouple the gaze from 'familiar binaries' and 'bifurcated concepts' such as she finds even in 'most feminist models' (Berenstein 1996: 44).

In his own self-portrait and *carte de visite* (?1867; Figure 4), Martínez Sánchez sits absorbed in thought at a curtain-covered table. The image recalls the geometrical patterning

4 José Martínez Sánchez, *Self-Portrait*

of his wider work, from the near-mirrored triangles formed by his arms to the neatly perpendicular legs, and the regular shapes on clothes and floor. The photographer's right hand is shoved deep into a trouser pocket to form a bulbous triangular shape coming out between his legs from the genital area. It is this phallic protrusion that most directly faces the viewer, not Martínez Sánchez's eyes that look to the distance. The effect at once links Martínez Sánchez's enterprise to his penis while impeding a simple association of the latter with his gaze. Our attention is drawn in turn to the curtain, its potential larger significance underscored by its dreamlike peculiarity, seeming to merge or fuse with the table cover. If we are to follow the sexual resonances of the image, the curtains' almost fleshy, thick textures and folds might be taken as vaginal. In turn, the emphasis on the fabric's material substance obviates any simple distinction between the camera actively seeing the world by penetrating it, and passively receiving it through an open orifice. As Maggie Nelson has observed, if we are to describe aesthetic experiences in vaginal terms (and we might add, those of any orifice), we should recall that is not an empty channel but rather a textured place of flesh (2011: 197).

Martínez Sánchez's gaze itself projects a diagonal line between the two sexual insinuations, as if his undertaking drew on and channelled both in order to go beyond the distinction. More unsettlingly, his nephew and successor Eduardo Blasco Martínez thought to emblazon a promotional *carte de visite* (*c.*1869–76) with two *putto*-like males, one completely naked, the other nude but for a top hat and boots. The seated and hatted *putto* firmly grips a long stick terminating at groin level between his legs. Of the other, we can see only the naked buttocks and lower legs towards us. The rest of him is bent over and covered by the camera's hooding, such that the apparatus's protrusion appears to arise from his lower body. The photographer takes his near-naked sitter by pointing the camera at him, but also displays his anus as the posing individual raises up their phallic stick. At the same time, one 'phallus' (the camera) meets another (the stick) in the making of the image. By implication, photography would effect connections between self and other through continual switching, working its way through the possibilities. It is in such ways that the artisanal craft of making lines might be imbued with the continual switching, so as to effect mesmerically forceful 'shapes'.

In the projections from one shape to another, this switching may become generalised, disclosing a sensation of similarity in the world. Silverman has sought to draw attention away from a vision of still photography concerned with stasis and fixity, towards one based around 'development'. This is what she calls *The Miracle of Analogy*, in the title of her book of 2015. Photographic images – especially earlier images in the nineteenth century – emerge from the world as an analogy of it, and the images themselves 'develop' as a series of analogies. The dynamic of photography's form lies in its ability to articulate relationships through comparisons, ultimately leading us to the 'vast similitude' evoked by the mid-nineteenth-century American poet Walt Whitman (Silverman 2015: loc.250, 1008), to whom we will return in Chapter 2. The approach to geometry in Martínez Sánchez or Laurent's photographs suggests that such dynamic analogy is not limited to the 'liquid intelligence' that Silverman champions – and that we see vividly evoked in the river of *Guadalfeo Bridge* – resisting mastery by the optical subject and evading fixity in the final image (2015: loc.1245, 2145). Bold, vague geometrical photographs offer instead a pulsation in which the geometries of 'the shape' may be projected into other similar shapes, both in and beyond the image, just as the three-dimensional forms of the world have been projected into the two-dimensional forms of the image. The very notion of projection here – the main technique of mid-nineteenth-century descriptive geometry – conveys an implicit motion.

We may explore internal transpositions as easily in the image of Matilde Díez in action with Antonio Pizarroso (Figure 3) as in Martínez Sánchez's photograph of the Guadalfeo Bridge (Figure 5). Most obviously, Díez's stance closely matches that of her fellow thespian, but in mirror image, such that if the photograph were folded along an equidistant line between them, their shapes would press together neatly. In the context of the drama being performed, the symmetry here suggests conflict and tension: two apparently equal but opposed forces. Yet, the patterning has effects that are not so easily constrained to interpretation in context. For instance, the projection between the two similar shapes suggests a woman turning into a man, and vice versa. It can be experienced at the level of formal play: a flipping back and forth of two roughly triangular entities. This is true of other patterns: Pizarroso's spaced-out legs may be projected into those of the table and back again, the decorative horizontal of the table might be transposed with the embroidered strips on Díez's dress. Here, as in Fortuny's *Fantasia on Faust*, we have a visual equivalent to Shane Butler's Echo in poetry: sequences of repetition and resemblance transfiguring the scene into a rhythmic chorus that resists interpretation. Pondering Walter Benjamin and Proust's exploration of similarity, Silverman speaks likewise of 'correspondences' that 'are dynamic and unmasterable' (2015: 2496). Such an experience may suggest a disposition towards connections made by analogy: a giving of ourselves to these without seeking to justify them primarily through causal connection or chains of influence, without what Manning and Taylor call 'priority'. The universal visual language presents the world's transfiguration into a pattern of similarities which we appreciate in an aesthetics-led comparison.

Such images, preserved from a moment in the past, pulsate: their forms forever projecting and transposing into others. We are disposed to experience relationships in place and time, somewhat like Aby Warburg's collage – the *Mnemosyne* – a continual, shifting pattern of analogies (Michaud 2007: 244). The continual implicit pulsar motion gives shapes the quality of Zielinski's 'dynamic moments', never exhausted in the potential that they disclose through time. In turn, as the projections suggest pulsations into other forms, they realise connections across apparently separate categories. Where one biological gender forms a shape that could be another, the implied transposition suggests a moving into and out of gender distinctions. In the photograph of Dolores Custodio (Figure 1) seated with her (phallic) cigar and top hat, wearing a dress, the outline of her clothing from the waist up would not be entirely out of place on a male character – something that is accentuated by her sitting position, which obscures, by folding it, the longer cloth of the upper body of a dress. Her curved right arm, finding its way down her torso and to her midriff, helps create a near-rectangular oval, dominantly coloured with a darker grey, and topped with the two parallel forms of the hat and head. It is possible to imagine this shape detaching from the skirts to make the upper part of a man. The forms traced by the performer in the photograph could correspond as easily to a male wearing a skirt, a woman adopting masculine headgear, or an androgyne. The pulsating shapes are what constitute this effect of drag, 'the moment' – in Judith Butler's words – 'when one is no longer sure whether the body encountered is that of a man or a woman' (2007: loc.318). In the pulsation, the simple division of humanity into separated genders is supplanted by their contingent emergence and mutation

5 José Martínez Sánchez, *Guadalfeo Bridge*

through the effects of shared geometrical projections. A person could indeed be a woman in Madrid, and a man in Barcelona, as Bretón had it.

It is this effect of similitude that renders possible a more generalised eroticisation of sensual experience, in the 'vacillation' between animate and inanimate things – but one which, because of the pulsation, takes the form of a flirtation, a continual offering and denying, there and not. 'Denial and accommodation, retreat and advance, absence and presence – just like the teasing interplay of the flirt's alternating tactics – mark the *capriccio* dynamics of analogy's jumps', comments Barbara Maria Stafford in her *Visual Analogy* (1999: 2). A case in point is Martínez Sánchez's *Pamplona – Six Byzantine Capitals, Remains of the Cathedral Destroyed in the 15th Century* (*Pamplona – Seis Capiteles Bizantinos, restos de la Catedral destruida en el siglo XV*) (1867). Here we behold three sets of two column tops; in each pair, one sits upon the other. All are lined up in parallel along a thick piece of wood or table. The structure is at once neat and detached from any original context, lending it an air at once forceful and mysterious. The capitals each take the same shape and are roughly the same size: two stumps with a gap between, widening until they merge into a single piece that arches over the hole, with a further, broader piece of stone atop. Their intricate decorations delineate each from the other even as the resemblances between every piece are clear. The wood on which they ultimately rest has a thick, fleshy texture, rugged, curving, and wrinkled like skin. The capitals look like nothing so much as severed midriffs of human beings, the thighs emerging from the groin area, the body widening up into the hips. These could as easily be the buttocks of any sex as the genital area of a woman. In their possible human universality, they offer us the utopian potential that Jonathan Allan finds in *Reading from Behind* (2016). The eroticised analogical thinking that such shapes facilitate has the quality that the Surrealist artist Salvador Dalí calls 'paranoid critical' vision: a taking seriously of contingent comparisons that we might draw from an image, such that these become meaningful (Dalí 2013). We can see this, for instance, in Dalí's testicular musings on cherries. But necessarily, the eroticisation that finds experiences of animated flesh in the inanimate is just one mutable outcome of the affordances of geometrical projection: in the end, the photograph is a mechanical copy of a collection of capitals from ruined pillars. The sexual implication is only one possible insinuation of the flirtation – as, arguably, are all erotic theorisations of photography. The effect is subsumed within the chorus of echoing resemblances in the immanent transfiguration as the world becomes both material and not, both flesh and not.

Martínez Sánchez's photography is pervaded by such flirtations with eroticisation, where the shapes of the animate and inanimate, of the human and non-human potentially project into one another. This effects a dynamic, sensual experience of connection between the human and wider physical world: it implies its own variety of 'natural contract' (to borrow Michel Serres' phrase), beyond the social contract that binds people together (Serres 1990). In a photograph from the 1867 Universal Exhibition – the *Tómalos Bridge* (literally 'Take Them Bridge'; Figure 6), the symmetries and shapes of the infrastructure and landscape might evoke a vast female figure, without ceasing to be literally themselves. The vision might resemble Mother Earth herself, an ancient goddess alive, not just in the natural but the industrial landscape, persistent through changing time, her presence revealed in the photographic image. The two sheer cliffs at diagonals heading inwards to the white bridge resemble two thighs ending at the midriff. Between them at their closest point is the narrow vertical opening, replete with lush vegetation, out of which liquid

6 José Martínez Sánchez, *Tómalos Bridge*

pours. Beyond, a huge belly-like mass of earth rises up as if in pregnancy, flanked at its apex on either side by two pyramidal lumps suggestive of breasts. The vision is evocative variously of a scene pregnant with the camera's penetration, of a mirroring of the instrument's fecund aperture, and of an outpouring gushing into the camera, photographer and viewer, disclosing the world in Silverman-esque fashion. The possible convergence of photographic vision and the maternal might find an echo in Studlar's masochistic, pre-Oedipal understanding of the medium.

In turn, by evoking life in the inanimate, geometrical pulsation may conjoin the living and the dead: as Robert Pogue Harrison has observed, because the deceased are part of the inanimate, our living relationship to them, and culture's perpetuation through them, is connected to our wider contract with the natural world (2003: 16). By extension, the transfigured realities offer us a point of connection between the present and the past. The photographic medium has long been associated with such effects, because of its indexical character: its preserving the light that materially reflected from living beings. The quality has a double edge, the French theorist Roland Barthes famously explains. On the one hand, 'by shifting ... reality to the past ... the photograph suggests that it is already dead' (Barthes 2000: 79). On the other hand, 'photography has something to do with resurrection' (Barthes 2000: 82). 'At once dead and alive, it [photography] opens the possibility of our being in time', Eduardo Cadava avers (1997: 128). But what I want to emphasise here is how it is specifically the resemblance between shapes, drawn by the light, that make this so. The effect is an 'affordance' of the 'logic of its illustrational foundation'. This would be true even in the most basic recognition of a human being preserved in the two-dimensional, small-scale imprint such as Matilde Díez or Martínez Sánchez in their *cartes de visite*. We experience here projections into a smaller scale of something that, by implication, might then be projected back into three dimensions and life.

The Welsh-born photographer Charles Clifford, with offices in Madrid, had as his business to transmit and translate culture, like Laurent and others such as Napper who visited Spain. Clifford served both the British and Spanish markets, as well as the monarchs of both countries. In his book, *Photographic Scramble through Spain* (London, 1863), he was concerned with remnants of the receding Spanish past, a time of Catholic majesty and empire ('Les rois s'en vont'). Clifford saw in the camera a means for conservation, Rachel Bullough Ainscough remarks (2012: 178). His *Statue of St Bruno in the Monastery of Miraflores* (1853) shows the monument placed at a doorway facing outwards, mitre at its feet, having been temporarily relocated there during refurbishment. A diagonal angle upwards brings out the relief of the figure in light, the black and white of the print. The effect renders the outlines of the statue indistinguishable from St Bruno himself, had he ever been photographed in person. We are given the experience of meeting with the saint: he is coming out of the doorway, perhaps he will descend the steps, we are approaching him, as he extends his arm towards us as if in blessing. Perhaps – quite likely – we are about to feel his hand upon our head. We have the sensation of being with a person who wanders the centuries, freed from mortal confines, even as the past about them slips away in passing time. This is, Lee Fontanella remarks, photography as discovery and surprise (1999: 54), not least in the double sense – the unexpected but also the revelatory – in which Matilde Díez was said to 'surprise' the intention of the author. The camera discloses an experience unsuspected but immanent in historical realities.

Instead of modernity

In evoking such things, Clifford's photographs – and those of his partner Jane, who succeeded him in the business – explore how visual 'analogy provides opportunities to travel back into history ... to leap across continents', as Stafford puts it (1999: 11). Here, the photographer as historian is less a dominant subject mastering the past, than – as Philippe-Alain Michaud suggests – a photosensitive plate responding to it (2004: 260). The images suggest intimate contact, however slight, with world historical forces: that is, powers which effect major, decisive transformations of life of relevance across the globe, their repercussions resonating down through time and countries, even as they may originate in a specific context. Clifford affirms that his photographs of Spain 'may serve as mementos of an epoch when this naturally favoured kingdom swayed the destinies of nearly all the then discovered world' (cited in Bullough Ainscough 2012: 178). The significance of Spain's Golden Age had been set out for the British not least in twin volumes by the eighteenth-century Scottish historian William Robertson: the one recounted Carlos V's life as Holy Roman Emperor, the other the history of Spanish exploits in the Americas. Together they show in action the reshaping of the world from the Atlantic through to the Pacific, interlocking through Carlos V with the early modern European system of the Holy Roman Empire. They articulate an historical aspiration, for better and for worse, to appeal enduringly to all peoples: to be a universal monarchy, 'that elusive dream of ... ultimately global, unity' (Pagden 1995: 43).

Jane Clifford explores a connection to such realities in her photograph of the armour of Christopher Columbus (c.1865; Figure 7), the leader of Spain's first expedition across the Atlantic, an image made for the Kensington Museum (now the Victoria and Albert). Placed against an utterly black backdrop and fully illuminated, the metal suit and closed helmet appear as if suspended, hovering in the night or a dark room, emitting their own light. The evenly cast, powerful lighting gives us all the detailed textures and relief of the object, and with it 'the shape' of musculature and bulk, as well as of ornate splendour. The suit tips slightly to one side, as if moving with Columbus's gait; the arm to our left, lifted a little, seems to rise. The helmet's curved, narrow eye slits stare. Columbus may have died centuries before, but his embodied, energised 'shape' – which encountered a New World and transformed the destinies of the globe – appears to be encountered here freed from mortality, or rather, pulsating back and forth between life and death, a relic-like suit of armour and the action of the living dead. Through Jane Clifford's image we reach out to Columbus's power like Nietzsche to the Apollonian and Dionysiac or Estanislao del Campo to the Faustian.

Numerous theorists of photographic media have associated such effects with the *unheimlich* as envisaged by Sigmund Freud, among others. Laura Mulvey affirms that 'the invention of photography and its diffusion in the mid-nineteenth century introduced an element of the uncanny that was part of its material process' (2006: 45). In 'the convergence between the arts of reality and the arts of deception', 'the threshold between life and death becomes a space of uncertainty in which the boundaries blur between the rational and supernatural, the animate and the inanimate' (Mulvey 2006: 34, 37). Here the modern world and a modern medium become haunted by archaic beliefs (Mulvey 2006: 52–3). Valid as such reflections may be in their own terms, they entail mapping the phenomenon onto a rigorous explanatory framework – with roots in psychoanalysis – and thereby determining its interpretation. They tend to assume that the presence of atavistic sensations, or simply of the dead, is inherently untoward in the supposedly distinct modern era, and that this apparent

7 Jane Clifford, *Armour of Christopher Columbus*

error may, through rigorous study, be elucidated. In so doing, they may conflate 'vacillation' with 'uncertainty', rather than any number of other kinds of affect. They risk establishing 'priority' over the expansive effects of the experience, which – it is well known – was far from always deemed 'uncanny', historically anyway. This is the case – Andrew Smith has shown – even in Gothic literature, among whose concerns through the century was the relationship between aesthetic form and the reanimation of the dead (2016: 2–5, 75). Warner notes how many people linked the camera's ability to communicate with transmissions from the spirit world, and vice versa (Warner 2006: 229–30). In that light, we may attend instead to how lines and shapes are being drawn and projected here, such as to effect through their pulsation a continual journeying back and forth across the grave, between distant historical ages and places, without foreclosing on their possible resonances.

The lines and shapes to which we attend act as force lines or force fields. After all, it is they that articulate recognisable, transmissible form through and in specificity and particularity, they that transfigure the world into 'both flesh and not', into both matter and not, they that take the place of any notion of a sovereign subject. In a photograph, the active chemicals are mobilised in shapes and lines, so as to give us a vision, such as that of the animated armour in Jane Clifford's image. We might aptly say that the lines and shapes galvanise our experience of the other. At the outset of this part of the chapter, we saw how Matilde Díez was said to act upon her audience like a magnetiser. We saw too, through Browning, how 'the shape' that appears on a photograph might be resonant with mesmerism. We observed how the compelling forms adopted by the hypnotic Matilde Díez and transmitted onwards might constitute such a 'shape', 'both flesh and not'. As is well known, magnetism – like other putatively occult forces – was supposed to be latent in the organisation of the universe and could both direct and animate all things, living and dead, lending them both structure and dynamism. The hypnotist Costa y Turell, writing in 1857, remarks that 'it was not just men who were subjected to magnetic power, for trees also were magnetised, it enchained them so to speak; and even the most inanimate bodies, such as a cup, a glass, a bottle, etc., were thought capable of contracting magnetic virtue' (No eran solo los hombres los sometidos al poder magnético, porque se magnetizaban también los árboles, los encadenaban por decirlo así; y hasta los cuerpos más inanimados, tales como una taza, un vaso, una botella etc. se creyeron capaces de contraer la virtud magnética) (1857: 23).

This meant that the power of magnetism could be transmitted across boundaries that might otherwise seem categorically firm, such as that between the dead and the living. The condition for belief in such occult practices – written into them – is the notion that the physical world as we actually experience it can be immanently transfigured, however momentarily. In a not dissimilar vein, one R. Molina, writing about another occult belief system – Spiritism – observes that it 'puts, then, into communication, the beings it evokes with those who inhabit our planet by means of materials perceptible to our senses, and, not content even with that, places immaterial beings within a material envelope' (pone, pues, en comunicación, a los seres que evoca con los que habitan nuestro planeta por medios materiales perceptibles a nuestros sentidos, y aún no contento con esto, coloca a los seres inmateriales dentro de una envoltura material) (1869: xviii). Molina (a sceptic about these things himself) underlines how this implies that the animated spirits are like living human beings and all matter: they follow basic geometry and physics, having extension and limits (length, breadth and depth) (1869: 25).

Meeting: coming together and taking shape

'Communication' relies upon the configuration and reconfiguration of shapes as they are articulated in the world: this is what enables it to discard apparently rigid boundaries in our experience. Some mid-century photographs resemble occult practice precisely because both rely on the similarity in shapes of light and shadow between inanimate and animate entities, and on the potential to project the forms of the one as the other. 'The camera's early shadow play appeared to communicate … ghostly semblances', Warner comments (2006: 16). Where the occult practitioner might conjure up ectoplasm or a phantom, the photographer, mediating light onto the plate, may give us visions in material form, offering – Isobel Armstrong notes – something at once ghostly and made of matter (2008: 352).

Charles Clifford's photograph *San Miguel de Lillo* (1854; Figure 8) shows us a medieval chapel as patches of shadow and shimmering, intense light against a dark landscape akin to that shadow. The building comes to resemble some transparent entity, or cloth. Even as we observe its existence, it is as if we see through to the earth behind and beneath it. The blur where the chapel meets the ground, and the sharp contrast there of whiteness and dark suggest a less than solid connection to the land. The appearance of a phantom is perhaps reinforced by the two joists and windows at its front: we might see two eyes poking out, a long nose, and a downward curving, distressed mouth. We may compare these light effects to how a woman sees the form of her dead sister articulated in a shadow in Costa y Turell's account of a session conducted by the American hypnotist Dr Phillips:

> The biologised person was asked whom she wished to *see* among the dead persons she had most loved.
> 'My sister', she replied after a few moments reflection.
> 'Very well, you are going to *see* her right now.'
> The person was led with *a hand over their eyes* to some distance from the door beside the screen. Placed facing this door, she was told:
> '*Look* at your sister, over there, against the door of the screen … *look* at her closely.'
> The person's *gaze stared* with visible emotion at the location indicated; in the shadow formed by the screen, she *saw* her sister, standing dressed in white (my emphasis).[2]

The speculative notion of hypnotism *in articulo mortis* powerfully evokes the analogy between mesmerism and the articulation of such forceful, animated shapes. In 1857, Costa y Turell rendered into Spanish, from a French translation that had appeared in *L'Illustration*, Edgar Allan Poe's story, 'The Facts in the Case of M. Valdemar'. (For reasons that will become apparent, Costa y Turell's framing of the work is important here.) In the tale, Valdemar is on his deathbed in Harlem, New York. The narrator comes to his side,

---

[2] Se preguntó a la persona biologizada a quién quería ver entre las personas muertas que más había amado.

– A mi hermana, respondió después de algunos instantes de reflexión.
– Bien está, vais a verla ahora mismo.

La persona fue conducida con una mano encima de los ojos a alguna distancia de la puerta que estaba al lado de la mampara. Colocada enfrente de esta puerta se le dijo:

– Mirad a vuesta hermana, allá, contra la puerta de la mampara … miradla bien.

La mirada de la persona se fijó con visible emoción en el sitio indicado; en la sombra formada por la mampara vio a su hermana, de pie vestida de blanco (1857: 55–6).

8 Charles Clifford, *San Miguel de Lillo*

and mesmerises him just as he is about to depart this world. So long as the mesmeric force holds, Valdemar's body remains intact but rigid, his tongue alone able to vibrate, and his person capable of verbal utterances, all this despite the lack of respiration and Valdemar's own admission that he is not, in fact, alive. Here, then, is an entity that resembles both a living being and a dead one, something animate and something inanimate. What interests me most is that the alternative to this state will be the instant and complete loss, not just of what passes for his existence, but with it, Valdemar's shape. By extension, therefore, the force holding him together, maintaining him – like a photograph (Riordan 2018) – in a state that is neither quite death nor life, is the same as Valdemar's recognisable form. While in this shape, he exists as the near-still projection of a particular place and time outwards from its confines, traversing the future: the moment he was about to die. But this can only happen so long as the electricity – the *luz* in Spanish, the light – enables the particularities of his body to maintain their rough lines. Without it, he will literally, instantly dissolve into a liquidy mass, just like chemicals not fixed in a photograph, and with them the conserved light from the moment gone:

> Señor Valdemar was obviously answering the question I had addressed to him some minutes before. The reader will not have forgotten that I said, was he still sleeping? To this he answered:
> 'Yes, – no, – before I was sleeping, and now, and *now* – dead.'
> None of those present sought to contain or deny the inexplicable horror that those few words were able to induce. …
> From that time to the week just gone by, – *an interval of some seven months* – we continued visiting Señor Valdemar on a daily basis.
> [Finally, the narrator decides to awaken Valdemar] But what truly happened exceeded all expectation; for it is impossible for a human being to conceive what took place.
> When I was most occupied with making magnetic movements, amidst the exclamations of 'dead!' emitted no doubt by the tongue and not the lips of the somnambulist, his whole body suddenly – and this in the interval of hardly a minute – shrank, crumbled, positively decomposed beneath my hand. The bed offered to the eyes of those present no more than an almost liquid mass of repellent, horrible putrefaction.[3]

---

[3] El señor de Valdemar contestaba evidentemente a la pregunta que le había dirigido unos minutos antes. No se habrá olvidado que le dije si seguía durmiendo. A esto respondió:

Sí, – no, – antes dormía, y ahora, y *ahora*, – muerto.
Ninguno de los concurrentes procuró contener ni siquiera negar el horror inesplicable que aquellas pocas palabras eran capaces de infundir.

…

Desde aquella época hasta la semana próxima pasada, – *intérvalo de unos siete meses* – seguimos en visitar diariamente al señor de Valdemar.

…

… me esforcé en dispertarlo …

Pero lo que verdaderamente aconteció sobrepujó a toda esperanza; pues es imposible que ser humano alguno concibiese lo que tuvo lugar.

Cuanto más ocupado me hallaba con los movimientos magnéticos, en medio de las esclamaciones de 'muerto!' lanzadas indudablemente por la lengua y no por los labios del somnámbulo, de repente su cuerpo entero – y esto en el intérvalo de un minuto escaso – se encogió, se desmenuzó, se descompuso positivamente bajo mi mano. El lecho no presentaba a los ojos de los circunstantes más que una masa casi líquida de repugnante, de espantosa putrefacción. (Costa y Turell 1857: 63–70)

Costa y Turell frames the story – which had at times been taken for fact – with an apparent denunciation. He has copied it, he says, 'so that our readers may form an approximate idea of how much the results obtained by means of magnetism and somnambulism are exaggerated and distorted' (para que nuestros lectores puedan formarse una idea aproximada de lo mucho que se exageran y se desfiguran los resultados obtenidos por medio del magnetismo y somnambulismo). He introduces the tale as a 'farsa magnética': a magnetic farce (1857: 61–2). This might seem to encourage the reader to approach the vision of M. Valdemar ironically and from a distance. However, Costa y Turell follows his brief opening remarks by simply providing the translation of the tale in full, for several pages of his book, with no further comment during or after. It takes up the entire remainder of that particular chapter of the volume. This means that, once they have got past Costa y Turell's few introductory words, his public has the same experience as they would were they simply to read a Spanish translation of Poe's story anyway (unless they sustain a huff against its nonsense for the full duration). This suggests that the effect of Costa y Turell's framing (intentional or otherwise) is to separate that experience, not just from a claim of literal truth, but from any attempt to reduce it to a credible explanatory system. It sits – as it were – as a protrusion from his putatively didactic treatise, there to be appreciated of itself.

I mention this, by way of concluding, because, like Poe's tale itself, it seems suggestive of how we might experience the visions of connecting forces that I have traced in the present section of this book. The fate of Valdemar's body is resonant with intimations of union and division through aesthetic experience: for Manning, it speaks to Poe's sensibility in the Ante-Bellum southern United States, weighing up unity and separation; for Andrew Smith, it evokes the pattern of the universe's plot line, posited on an ending (Manning 2002: 237; Smith 2016: 75–80). The question, once more, is not how we might judge the connecting forces, not how we might assess them against a framework, not how we might account for them by some ultimate cause or explanation, or recommend them that way. (I would baulk even at reducing matters to descriptive geometry as 'explanation' or 'cause', as such: its projections are simply a way in which we might see things.) We have no need to indulge ourselves in what David Foster Wallace scathingly terms 'impressions of epistemological privilege' (1997: loc.3379). It is here that this chapter takes leave even of a stance such as that taken by Silverman in *The Miracle of Analogy*, as much as anything out of abstention. The analogies of which Silverman speaks amount to the disclosure of the world out of itself. She is making a strong philosophical commitment to them as the basis of a large theory.

I have been interested rather in what it would be to give oneself over to such experiences, to explore them, to seek an intimacy with them and with the intimacies that they promise, without commitment. This book, after all, is pedagogical, not didactic. Poe's tale of Valdemar is once more suggestive here. The somnambulist's repeated statement that he is dead has made it an occasional reference point for perplexity and debate around phenomenology, at least since it was referenced in Derrida's *Voice and Phenomenon* (Ffrench 2007). The statement 'I am dead' seems impossible, since anyone who is dead should not be able to make it. For Barthes and Derrida, each in their own way, Valdemar's use of language, his 'tongue', is critical in understanding the significance of his fate: signs, *écriture*, do not depend upon the presence of a living subject, they claim (Derrida 1967: 108; Barthes 1988: 194). For Jari Kauppinen, this suggests that the sentence 'I am dead' depends upon and invokes the imagination, a place where one's own death might be conceived within life, and thus a 'chiasmatic transcendental subjectless place, like writing' (Kauppinen 2000: 342).

I would reframe this. The story of Valdemar invites us to explore what an experience would be like in which, through the way that a 'shape' was articulated, we were able to discard apparently secure distinctions, such as that between life and death, past and present. 'Look at your sister', the hypnotist assured us, 'You are going to see her right now.'

Coda: Laurent's *Las Meninas*

Laurent's 1875 image of Velázquez's great work of the Spanish Golden Age, *Las Meninas* (Figure 9), is a machine-made reproduction of a two-dimensional use of oil paints on canvas to show a scene at the seventeenth-century royal court, the very heart of the old empire. In the medium it employs, in its authorship, and in its point of completion, it stands at two removes from the vision it evokes out of the 1650s. The camera has drained the colour from that moment, leaving only greys, whites and blacks, a shadowy after-image of what once was there. Much that made Velázquez's painting so lively slips from view: the energy of his loose brushwork, his translucent palette. It is as if *Las Meninas* were dying or had died. The seventeenth century acquires the parchment skin of a dessicated corpse, as Columbus's armour hovers empty in Jane Clifford's image, and Martínez Sánchez's Byzantine capitals are remains of a shattered temple, lost to time.

Yet that same shedding of colour and of brushwork is what brings Laurent's *Meninas* so close to the anecdotal scene of the 1650s. The dying is a resurrection, as when Columbus's outfit is conjured into movement, or when Byzantine fragments mutate into erotic beings. When we look upon this image – 'you are going to see', said the hypnotist, 'look' – we may behold what appears to be a photograph taken in the 1650s at the court of Philip IV of Spain. We see human bodies and their surroundings transfigured into patterns of grey-scale forms; we see the outlines of their shapes carefully delineated, as was Laurent's wont. This is just what we would view, had Laurent turned up with his camera, in the company of the King and Queen, to visit the Spanish princesses, their servants, a pet dog, and their painter Diego Velázquez. It is what we would see had the light reflected off them through a lens onto the chemicals of the negative, there to linger on. The present and the past fold seamlessly together, as, in *The Birth of Tragedy*, modern Germany did with ancient Greece. When he opened his aperture, Laurent let himself be taken by Velázquez's composition, his image utterly occupied by that of the Old Master, as Matilde Díez was possessed and transformed and penetrated by an author and a character and entered her own audience likewise in turn. Velázquez's work has long been understood to assert the high status of the painter and of painting (Brown 1986; Knox 2009). Now a co-author of the vision of *Las Meninas* with the seventeenth-century artist, Laurent becomes a dominant artist through submission: like Díez, he takes his public to a state like hypnotic somnambulism, where they feel and think what he projects upon them, a contemporary's record of his visit to the past, a seeing of what was seen through Velázquez's eyes.

For many in the nineteenth century, what stood out in the painting *Las Meninas* was its evocation of reality. The official catalogue of the Prado (1872) pronounced it to be 'without a doubt, so far as a facsimile of nature goes, the premier painting in the world' (sin duda alguna el primero [cuadro] del mundo como facsímile de la naturaleza) (Madrazo 1872: 604). It captured brilliantly the life of an anecdotal moment: a painting session, a young princess coaxed to pose, the canine lazing, the boy provoking it, the chamberlain appearing through a back door, the monarchs glimpsed in a mirror, the painter and others spotting them, the

9 Juan Laurent, *Las Meninas*

ephemeral light and shadow of the room. Later commentators have drawn attention to an apparent paradox in the image: for Velázquez to paint himself painting the scene, he would need to have looked into a mirror that is not there. The scene is depicted from an impossible point of view. In the first chapter of his *Order of Things*, Foucault sets out a line of thought about the painting's paradoxes that has continued to resonate. *Las Meninas* – he argues – draws attention to pure representation, both exposing and signalling a break from discourse in which art was thought to offer a mirror of the world (1970: 1–16). We might conclude that Velázquez's *Las Meninas* points to an irresolvable tension: apparently real, yet self-evidently a painting (Robbins 1998: 61–2, 74). Such sentiments would be of a piece with the endless ping-pong (*vaivén*) Ludmer and others found in Del Campo's *Fausto*: an ever-balanced play between fiction and reality.

We cannot simply assume that nineteenth-century spectators did not notice this rather obvious feature of the image, and it is not inconsistent with their conclusions that they should do so. We could as well conclude that the painting offers not an impossibility but a transfiguration, like that which we saw in *Fausto*. To the remark that Velázquez could not have observed this scene, we might respond that nothing stopped the artist painting it. His artistry, his genius, was to give us the sensation of being with him within his painted room, as he paused from his work, as the royal couple arrived, as the princess was coaxed, and the dog was provoked, and the chamberlain looked around the door. Velázquez, with his broad brushstrokes, and oils, and translucent colours, rendered possible that experience, that sense of being there, in the studio, in the court, in the 1650s. The French social scientist Daniel Dayan took *Las Meninas* to be exemplary of a situation in which 'the receptive freedom of the spectator is reduced to a minimum – he [*sic*] has to accept or reject the painting as a whole' (1974: 27). Put another way, the viewer may notice that they have the option of accepting Velázquez's dominance over place and time, and willingly, lovingly submit.

As Velázquez possesses Laurent, so the photographer takes on the painter's power of transfiguration. The partitions of place and time melt before his force, as Velázquez was master over the laws of what he could or could not see. Laurent takes on Velázquez's energy. Redoubling it, he does what the painter could not do. There is now no canvas, there are no daubs of oil. There is only now the sensation of light from the mid-seventeenth century, given to us by a photographer who appears to stand there, a companion to genius, court and royalty. We are transported there. We are possessed by an hallucination. And we too are intimates.

2

Departure: to leap beyond yet nearer bring

Plus ça change, plus c'est la même chose
Popular

Let us imagine things separating, departing from one another, so that their likeness is intensified. Let us imagine their moving apart as a form of attraction that brings about their commonality. The notion is present in the most clichéd versions of psychoanalysis: as we repress something, so it returns, as we seek to avoid a situation, so we fall into it. More subtly, the very fact of leaving behind a signal memory, such as a trauma, points to the latter's persistent importance in the present moment (Caruth 1996: 17). The phenomenon does not have to be cast in negative tones: it may be a route back, a way to effect a connection that might otherwise have been lost. In the words of the US poet Walt Whitman, we may 'leap beyond yet nearer bring' (1995: 74). At stake here is something fundamental to similitude. For us to suppose that two different things are, in some way, the same, that they have something in common, we must also suppose their difference, that is their departure or separation from one another. It is taken to be significant that X is the same as Y, precisely because X is or appears to be unlike Y. Put at its strongest, it might be thought essential that something departs from another if those things are ever to be experienced as the same. In some cases, this may be supposed even of the way that something or someone is the same as themselves. The ancient philosopher Heraclitus famously asked whether the river that flows is ever the same river, whether anything that changes is ever the same thing (2001: loc.318). By extension, it might be ventured that, for the question to be explored – whether something is the same as itself – that something must differ from, depart from itself. Put at its strongest, we might ask a question like that posed by Heraclitus, not for its own philosophical sake, but because it is our only hope of experiencing the sameness of a thing or a person to themselves.

Departure may take many forms. In its guise as the question of 'representation', it is the apparent lack of connection of a sign (a word, say) to the world it evokes, and its seemingly endless difference from all other such signs, the 'dissemination' of which Derrida speaks. We saw in the introduction, how such a vision may draw on an understanding of mid-century *modernité* in France. In its shape as the broader question of 'modernity', it is the supposed 'step change' that, perhaps anywhere at any point in history is experienced as splitting one historic form of life from another (Stanford Friedman 2015: 33). In the matter of 'temporality', it might emerge – as Doane suggests – in the guise of Zeno's ancient paradox, how time, split into separate moments that differ from another, could flow. The issue could be felt all the more pressing, where rapid change in life, a 'modernity', was felt to be occurring: Walter Benjamin perceived this in the poet Baudelaire's vision of mid-century Paris (2002: 204–5). We find it likewise in ethical dilemmas or simply between a supposed 'self' and an 'other', – or relatedly – in the traditions of 'analogy' (Stafford 1999: 2) where a bridge might be sought between those who differ.

It is possible to draw a – by now familiar – distinction between two 'pictures' of such departures, to use the later Wittgenstein's word. On the one hand, we might experience them as 'deferrals': the necessary and continual difference between the one and the other, which forever postpones their full coincidence. Conversely, in the picture drawn by Cavell's vision of 'intimacy', our picture of such things would be such that experiences of deferral, even if it takes place, might be overcome through some form of 'return', a guiding back: as each departure occurs, we might be able to find our way back 'home', as Cavell puts it. In such circumstances, deferral here would ultimately be something like 'being lost'. In Wittgenstein's vision – Cavell suggests –, this appears as the danger of insanity in the modern world, the darkness of the mid-twentieth-century of totalitarianism, war, and global tension, in which clarity of thought might be lost (2013: 33–7).

The experiences set out in this chapter form a somewhat different 'picture' from the two set out above. Here, we explore how various ways are sought for 'departure' itself to bring about sameness, and for it to do so ultimately without any of the effects of ultimate 'deferral'. In these experiences, 'departure' actually gives us 'intimacy' as Cavell might understand the latter notion. Such a phenomenon is all but unthinkable, and it would certainly appear as a paradox, in many pictures of the world. So far as I can discern, it goes far beyond what Cavell himself contemplates in his patterns of departure and return, because of its insistence on the act of departing as the very path to similitude without deferral. As Toril Moi notes in her *Revolution of the Ordinary*, any fundamental change of 'picture' is hard to communicate, and, for many, hard to accept, leaving its proponents at times in a state of melancholy (2017: 9). In evoking (rather than advocating) such transformations of the 'picture' – that is, in exploring their possibilities – I set to one side claims made by various forms of 'deferral' to primacy in the discussion of the mid-nineteenth century, or in the theorisation of culture more broadly. I have in mind, for example, the very notion of *modernity*, or the 'question of representation'. On the one hand, this is because these things fit into the alternative picture precisely as varieties of 'departure' that effect intimate sameness: we will encounter them, therefore, in that guise, in the poet Baudelaire and the painter Édouard Manet. On the other hand, their being set to one side is crucial to a picture of mid-nineteenth-century culture at odds with the oft-dominant vision of a new Post-Romantic era, with its combination of a putatively radical split from the past, and an embrace of the medium itself, the sign, awakening us to deferral. Instead, the picture of 'departure' evoked in this chapter entails at least the possibility of intimate sameness across place and time, sign and world, self and other, the same and the different. In their assertion of the modern, Manet, Baudelaire, Marx, and others, will be seen conjuring up the very depths of time.

We will set out with Karl Marx, as Spanish and European empires, and the rise of Capital, shove the past away, only for ancient powers to be fully manifest. This spectacle takes us to the experience of time in Manet's art, echoing with the centuries, in a world of reproductions and equivalences across place and time. Through the challenge of seeing such distinct places and times as the same, our passage leads us to optical toys and devices of the mid-century. In these technologies, in a flickering effect, separate locations struggle to combine as if in a single image that might permit us to travel across geography and history. From a collection of such items found in Madrid, we head on to the journeying of the US poet Walt Whitman's 'Me myself' in the tense circumstances of the United States of the build-up and aftermath of the Civil War, racially and politically divided. In this centrifugal and centripetal force we find sensually, promiscuously ventriloquised the living and the dead, the diversity of the world. From nineteenth-century practices of voice throwing, we move to another intensely material means of passing from one entity to another: free copying with paint. In the Spanish artist Eugenio Lucas, this practice crafts passageways across disturbed relationships in history: the fallen glory of Imperial Spain, the search for national renewal in the post-revolutionary world, the border relationship with France. Through all these experiences, we are returned to the reality of a gap that opens up between places and times and people as departures occur. This takes us once more to Manet's art, and to universalist aspirations and violent realities in France's interconnections with global events. The latter include the US Civil War, the historic relationship with Spain, and the end of Maximilian Habsburg's brief empire in Mexico, as well as the effects of French colonialism and class divides. We encounter an effort to transfigure into affection the violence of dominance and submission, turning the gap of separation into love. We set out from here into experiences of contrasting harmony, an aesthetic quality that may supersede more apparent similarities of form or content. We move between Baudelaire's 'double vision' (Meltzer 2011: 6) of a changing Paris and the depths of time, and the promiscuous oval gallery of the Prado Museum. There, images from Spain's old 'universal monarchy' are gathered, evoking across their differences an erotic cosmopolitanism that transfigures the imperial legacy. In exploring such sensations of continual departure, we venture to Baudelaire's vision of *modernité* as a recurrence across history. Time appears as an ever-fleeing exile, that, conversely, finds harmony in its attraction to the classic. Just as Chapter 1 took seriously the invocation of Lucifer and of Greek gods, here the Romantic vision of Satan suggests that departures in time are a continually dilating atavism. We find too that insistence on promiscuous harmony is not a simple opposite of groupings based on more apparent similarity, but rather draws upon them. Its cosmopolitanism is in interplay with the family resemblances of and between nations, and with the effects of historical context. Drawn back to the Prado Museum of the mid-century, we experience the promiscuous oval room as a bubble in time and place, an opening beyond chronology and location that remains within a single place, flowing into and out of national galleries.

Finally, we step back and consider the disposition to experience departure as sameness through three degrees or modalities of separation. In so doing, we ponder a dilemma. If these visions – not least their erotics – are shaped by historic prejudices that we find parochial and alien, can we really take them seriously as invitations to commonality? I will argue that the debate is irresolvable, even at the level of historical evidence, and that it comes down precisely to a disposition that inclines us either way. We explore three sets of images of departure that express, in turn: the likeness of a being to itself, a vision that brings sameness to the very fore; the close similarity between two distinct beings, to the point of fusion as they depart from one another; and a clearer emphasis on departure itself, where sameness is found in the movement that opens up between beings. We set out from an image of female masturbation in post-independence Buenos Aires, moving to paintings of erotically entwined male and female pairings by Courbet, before ending with Rosa Bonheur's charged visions of men and animals at the Franco-Spanish frontier, and of the horse market in Paris.

Paths to sameness are traced through the troubled ground of class, race, nationality, sexual practices and gender.

As we depart, across the chapter, from one subject to another, so each of these comes nearer to another, as if bringing back its memory through recurrent motifs such as Marx's push and shove away, Whitman's 'Me myself', or the opening gap. Rather than forcing or forging the diverse historical situations into a single system, the chapter by turns departs from and returns to mention of each of them, respecting the irreducible complexity of history's structures, its divergences and convergences. Rather than reducing all patterns to such contexts, or eliminating reference to them, the chapter departs from one location to another so as to bring to the fore resemblances across them. But, in this meandering, it finds its way, once and again, back to connections with previously mentioned contexts – like mention after mention of the legacy of Imperial Spain – in a delicate intertwining, leaping beyond to nearer bring.

Bringing the depths of history out of itself

In Karl Marx's *Capital I* (1867) we encounter one of the starkest examples of such a 'departure'. A revolutionary exile from Prussia and then (twice) from Paris, Marx laboured in London, and in near-poverty, on his analysis of the economic and social changes wrought about him in industrialising Britain and beyond. By 1865, he was effectively leading the General Council of the International Working Men's Association. Gestation of his account was slow and patchy, and he would publish only volume 1 in his own lifetime (Wheen 2006: 7–36). In Marx's narrative, to be brought together in the age of financial capital, the world must be severed from its past. In chapter 31, the new era appears as '"the strange God" who perched himself on the altar cheek by jowl with the old Gods of Europe, and one fine day with a shove and a kick chucked them all of a heap' (2013: loc.11622). Marx dates this transformation to the establishment of the large Spanish and other kingdoms in the Americas, effecting an interlinking across the seas between the world's continents, through which commodities and currency would circulate: 'The modern history of capital dates from the creation in the 16th century of a world-embracing commerce and a world-embracing market', he declares in Part II, Chapter IV (2013: loc.2609; see also loc.11574). In his book *Local Histories/Global Designs* (2000), the Argentine theoretician Walter Mignolo underlines this dark side of 'modernity', often hidden away in later accounts – as if Spanish imperialism had not been integral to it – but providing 'the economical foundation of the world system' (Mignolo 2000, 131). This was but the first of a wave of global colonialism by European peoples, which would brutally integrate ever more of humanity into the ways of Capital. In David Harvey's words, 'The tendency of capitalism … is to establish a universal set of values, … on a global scale', even as these 'equalisations' leave the planet a far from an equal place (2012: 256). This is a 'new epoch', Marx declares in chapter 6 (2013: loc.2966).

The bonding of human beings together requires, then, that they be split violently ('with a shove and a kick') from their ancestors and ancient rites and ways. If necessary, the departure from earlier forms of life must be accelerated in a 'hothouse' (2013: loc.9755). Older modes of being must go the way of defunct species, for this moment depends on 'the extinction of a whole series of older forms of social production' (2013: loc.2953). Reading Marx, the French thinker Louis Althusser goes so far as to evoke 'a history punctuated by radical discontinuities ..., profound re-organisations which ... inaugurate with their rupture the reign of a new logic' (1970: 44). All that might remain is the illusion that the present way of life was always so, natural even: 'neither is its social basis one that is common to all historical periods', Marx warns in chapter 6, appearing to dispel that mirage (2013: loc.2948). It is as if a section of time has been broken off, or at least sped away from all the rest, but shaped in so doing so as to seem to include all places, and perhaps even all times, within its new and artificially aged enclosures, so that everything is alike. Frederic Jameson has remarked how, at the very core of Marx's vision of *capital* and its transactions is 'the riddle ...: how can one object be the equivalent of another[?]' (2014: loc.364). The new age is built around equations in which two utterly disparate things are treated as worth the same amount. Marx's prose style, with its use of chiasmus and bold juxtapositions, resonates with this pursuit of similitude through departures so as to conjure up 'objects of equivalence' (Jameson 2014: loc.369, 385).

At the same time, and in apparent paradox, Marx's dawning era is fundamentally archaic. Put another way, it offers another kind of likeness: with the centuries past. To comprehend Capital, 'we must have recourse to the mist-enveloped regions of the religious world', Marx tells us in the opening chapter (2013: loc.1556). Only by acknowledging its 'religious, if pre-theological and animist character' (Jameson 2014: loc.638–43) could we hope to experience any of the sameness Capital now realises around the globe. In the words of Stavros Tombazos's *Time in Marx*, the whole of the new era is become 'a living organism, ... a living notion ... that escapes conscious human control ..., animated from within by a "soul" ... with its own will' (2014: 4–5, 309). Colonialism, after all, is manifest as a 'strange God'. The new age is populated with divinities, supernatural forces and magic, along with ancient and antique forms of worship and dominion. 'Modern society,' Marx declares, '... soon after its birth, pulled Plutus [the Greek god of wealth] by the hair of his head from the bowels of the earth', and 'greets gold as its Holy Grail' (2013: loc.2451). Marx's vision echoes with later sci-fi films where technology is wielded by long-bearded magicians (Méliès's *Journey to the Moon*), old-style monarchs (*Flash Gordon*), or religious orders with occult powers (*Star Wars*). There is 'magic and necromancy that surrounds the products of labour' (2013: loc.1624) and phenomena 'far more wonderful than "table-turning" ever was' (2013: loc.1535). 'Fetishism' – the worship of objects – is the order of the day. Machines are repeatedly described as 'cyclopean', that is, of the lineage of a one-eyed Greek demi-god (for example, 2013: loc.5997). Industrial capitalists reign as 'new potentates' and '*chevaliers*' (2013: loc.11114), with the powers of 'Asiatic and Egyptian kings, Etruscan theocrats' (2013: loc.5432). Chronology is irrelevant here, not just because of the contact with the very depths of time, but because of the multitude of timescales and places that coexist together, from mythological creatures of the ancient Mediterranean through to the Middle Ages, and including an array of world religions. The full range of archaisms invoked scatters far across the reaches of time, even if the fetish cults themselves arose – as some claim – in the collision of capitalist and non-capitalist worlds during early European expansion across the globe (Pietz 1985: 7).

Capital I evokes a world in direct communication with the gods, not as something lost and gone or even departing, but rather as the very nature of the here and now: this is, by Christopher S. Wood's definition, a 'classic' world (2012: 171; see introduction to this present book). Wherever even Marx himself aims to go after establishing this vision (to dispel it or not, and if so, in what sense), it is clear that, for him, first we need to be able to experience the world this way. The French philosopher Étienne Balibar has remarked that in *Capital*, 'fetishism is not a subjective phenomenon or a false perception of reality, as … a superstitious belief would be. It constitutes, rather, the way in which reality (a certain form or social structure) cannot but appear' (1995: 60). It is, in Geoffrey Pilling's words, 'an objective phenomenon' (2009). I am interested less (at least *per se*) in Marx's technical explanations for the phenomenon or even what he ultimately concludes about it, than by the very fact that *Capital* enables us to perceive time and place this way, in how it does so, and in the affordances that such a form of experience offers. Magic and the supernatural are now entirely and immediately real. In a sense, the modern is more purely atavistic than any previous time. The very force – Capital, the god of colonialism – that bonds humanity horizontally around the globe emanates, as it were vertically, from the very depths of time.

What we experience, then, is a violent movement forwards in time, a rupture, that brings about the intense presence of ancient things. It is as if humanity's acceleration through history had finally collapsed distinctions of time and place so that the gods may roam once more among us. To put it another way, departures across time and place in human history are such that they may bring their own furthest depths out of themselves. The forms evoked in *Capital I* are – the Marxist literary theorist Frederic Jameson notes – neither the work of philosophical nor of economic theory (2014: loc.66). What Wai Chee Dimock (2006) calls an experience of 'deep time' – a sense of intimate connectedness between remote points – is generated by and out of the leaps and bounds of history itself, out of the very material realities that constitute historical time. The forms of the modern world have it in themselves to metamorphose into – more still, actually to be – the shapes of older times, and vice versa, as (for example) industrial machinery and the Cyclops mutate into and out of one another, becoming one another. A similar phenomenon is vividly apparent in the mid-century paintings of the French artist Édouard Manet, which scholars so often associate with 'modernity': T.J. Clark (1984) shows the many references in Manet's 'painting of modern life' to the consumer culture of a transformed Paris. The appearance and life of the city were utterly transformed and dislocated by Haussmann's reforms as Prefect under the Second Empire, the intense mobilisation of state resources providing new opportunities for commodities and commodification. The working-class, but wealthy prostitute *Olympia* (1865), for example, lies on sale in the same posture, and on the same layout of pillows and sheets as the Italian Titian's *Venus d'Urbino* (1538), which, in turn, conjures up the ancient goddess.

It is as if Manet's paintings of the mid-century had been traced over lines and shapes drawn elsewhere in place and time, as if the works were conceived in some impossible collaboration with dead artists who guide his hand, such that beings in diverse timescales act as one. In his famous article, 'Ointments, Makeup, Pollen', Jean Clay goes so far as to describe Manet's identity as continually fused identity, there being a 'Manet-Velazquez', for example, or a 'Manet-Hals' (1983: 6). So perceptible is the presence of such outlines that many contemporaneous critics dubbed the paintings pastiches, exercises in skilled emulation. Michael Fried remarks on 'the literalness and obviousness with which he [Manet] often quoted earlier paintings' (1996: 24). Titian (among others) runs through the veins of a Manet, as Gounod and Goethe shape del Campo's *Fausto*. As the elements of *Fausto* follow one another's rhythms, so here the artists are like voices in a choral work, the one (Manet) coming in a little later than the other, blending with from one another even in their distinctiveness, their patterns overlaying each other. In her essay, 'Manet and the Multiple', Anne Higonnet underlines how such phenomena evoke what she calls a 'culture of visual reproduction': Manet is preoccupied not solely with the original works of other artists, but with the proliferation of copies of them in 'mass-reproduced images of past art', the history of painting ever more a commodity. This is apparent on the walls depicted in his portrait of the novelist Émile Zola, displaying not originals but reproductions, even of Manet's own *Olympia*. 'Perhaps what allowed Manet to slam together so many kinds of image', Higonnet muses, '… was the equivalence among them made newly possible by the reproduction techniques of the 1860s.' In the 'aesthetic potential of exchangeability' (2016: 199, 200, 210), we find something akin to the world of similitude conjured up by Marx's God of Capital and its equations.

It is easy to overlook – perhaps because it is so very obvious – how all this happens on the canvas. One experience of the contemporary world can emerge in the material forms of older times – and mutate back into them – because our ordinary experience of physical and social realities – of being in time – allows for this. As in Marx, there is only what can be generated in and out of the materials of history themselves, the bodies, the objects, the physical images, and no system is looked to beyond these. Moments flow into and take shape as one another, back and forth. Ordinary human movements imply potential shifts: instead of lingering suggestively between the legs, the fingers of Titian's nude now clasp the right thigh firmly, blocking any view to the vagina. The basic forms of biology have the potential to be shaped into distinct outcomes. In Titian's Venus there are fleshy curves, and a gently prominent belly, in Manet's Olympia there is taut, hard musculature; in Titian the servant is white, and in Manet she is black. Accoutrements and objects can be likewise be moved or swapped: the flowers move from Venus's hand to her maid's. The categories through which we navigate the world admit of variants: where 'pet' in Titian is a dog, in Manet it becomes a cat. And Manet and the world of mid-nineteenth-century France can thus extend into and emerge out of Titian and early sixteenth-century Italy, and both of these from Greco-Roman divinity.

Flickering and resolution

If our very existence in history, in time and place, enables us to find the modern to be atavistic, to experience a sharp departure as intensified resemblance, this is nonetheless no easy thing to perceive. It has this at least in common with Capital's conjuring of sameness around the globe. The latter, Jameson remarks, involves 'the sudden grasping and holding together, in one decisive central paradox, of the impossible riddle of the equation (how one thing can be 'the same' as an other) and its resolution' (2014: loc.577). Likewise, even as the world of machines and that of supernatural beings appear to be the same, their difference is manifest. We must be able to hold as one and perceive without contradiction – as if in some strange stereoscope – a vision of the world as riven from the past and utterly modern, and a panorama of an atavistic earth peopled by gods and demi-gods, visited by magic. Or, for that matter, nineteenth-century Paris and sixteenth-century Italy. There is a risk that we will not be able to keep that likeness in view, and that the vision will begin to flicker between diverse images. All of place and time would then be experienced like a hand-cranked early cinema projection or a 1960s avant-garde 'flicker film': the 'flicker phenomenon', as Mary Ann Doane describes it, exposes the blank gap between juxtaposed but separate images (2002: 199). In that case, we may reach for modes of interpreting the world that insist upon the impossibility of such sameness. Such (Marx supposes) is the debility of liberal political economists who – in denial of how things are, of what equivalent form is – seek 'to explain away the mystical character of gold and silver' (2013: loc.1294). They are engaged in what some psychologists call *deflection*: they develop a whole complex of reasoning, plausible to itself, whose sleight of hand is to dismiss what most evidently troubles us, what escapes that very same complex of reasoning. 'They cannot bear to look into the moral, social and psychic abyss that their creativity opens up', Marshall Berman observes, for there they would find a world of demons and magic, as if from a medieval past they thought buried (1983: 100–1). Whereas, the force bringing about commonality truly does have an 'enigmatical character': truly it is a 'riddle' and a 'mystery' (2013: loc.1290, 1297, 1124). So it is too with a mid-century Manet: how absurd, and yet how true (*Olympia* suggests), that, in some sense, nineteenth-century Paris is seamlessly an extension, an equivalent of sixteenth-century Italy, Manet of Titian, Olympia of Venus, and vice versa.

To be able to see that sameness – *Capital I* supposes – is truly to perceive what is actually before us without distraction or deflection, steadily, as it were ('you are going to see', said the hypnotist, 'look'). This entails the acceptance that we really are seeing what we are seeing (the 'objective phenomenon'), and a willingness to allow it to shape our appreciation of the world. I use the words *to appreciate* and *appreciation* here in their aesthetic sense: that we experience sensually the forms that the world may take for us. This is akin to the 'power of passiveness' and 'passive practice' that Cavell describes (2013: 114, 116). It involves a renunciation of our ways of mastering things ('thinking as clutching' in order to understand (Cavell 2013: 108)) that opens us up to experience so that we are transfigured. In Marx's *Capital I*, it is not just that nineteenth-century political economists must give up on their way of seeing the world and their projection of that through history. It is that the age of Capital itself, when beholden without such a veil, is a renunciation of all the ways that human societies have taken form historically, precisely such that it provides an intimate experience both of what peoples now have in common and what resonates from the very depths of time. Likewise, in renouncing the actual forms taken by Goya or Titian's art, Manet channels the history of culture powerfully, just as del Campo enters Goethe's sanctuary by giving up on a Germanic *Faust*.

On the account I give here, to experience this folding together of time – the echo, resemblance and overlap of what is most ancient to what is most far flung in its future – entails 'perceiving directly', as Nietzsche was soon to put it, when he himself conjured Greek gods as if into Richard Wagner's home in the wake of the Franco-Prussian War (2003: loc.617). Such an experience makes sense in the fashion of Velázquez's great painting *Las Meninas* and Laurent's photograph thereof: what we perceive as an impossible paradox is, in fact, quite possible, for we do see it and it was drawn in paint and in light, just as here the 'mystery' is sketched in Marx's writing and by Manet's brush and (putatively) by history itself. This is something other than what Derrida famously described as an *hauntology* (*hantologie*) in the *Spectres of Marx* (*Les Spectres de Marx*) (1993: 255): a continual and characteristic moving back and forth (a *vaivén*, as Ludmer put it of *Fausto*) – a deferral – between the persistent haunting of a past and a modern desire to exorcise it. It is not a wish to be done with this 'very queer thing, abounding in metaphysical subtleties and theological niceties', as Marx famously describes it in his opening chapter (2013: loc.1529). Rather, we must accept that time and place can indeed be transfigured from within in defiance of the rules we think we know. When, in chapter 5, Marx claims to be able to 'at last force the secret of profit making' (2013: loc.3047), it is not simply that he exposes capitalism's mechanisms, but that he enters into it and shares in its sacred knowledge, just as Estanislao del Campo would be said to violate Goethe's sanctuary, not because he destroyed *Faust* but because he opened it up to the Argentine. To paraphrase Jean-Luc Nancy, it is not so much that the secret of history is dispelled, as that we must come face to face with that very secret (2004: 144).

The challenge involved in attaining such a state is apparent in many nineteenth-century optical devices and toys. In these new technologies of vision, the very status of human agents in the world could be at stake and shaped, through what Jonathan Crary (1990) calls the 'techniques of the observer'. In such devices, images from distinct locations are habitually superimposed upon one another. The spinning thaumatrope – with which this book began – is a case in point. The front and reverse of the card are in different physical positions. They cannot be to the fore of the rotating object at the same chronological instant. Yet, we often experience them as seamlessly together: the visual studies theorist, Tom Gunning, has remarked on how two supposedly static images are thus transformed into something else that fuses them (2011: 31–3). The optical phenomenon exemplifies what Doane describes as 'the incessant invasion of the present moment by the past' (2002: 76), for something that has happened earlier is seen simultaneously with something seen now.

In the 1990s, the American researcher Lee Fontanella rediscovered and reconstructed in Madrid a collection of photographic images for a megalethoscope from the mid-century. The device itself had been designed by Carlo Ponti in Venice, some time prior to 1862. In the Madrid version, a photograph would be slightly curved in a mount, so as to create a panoramic effect through graduated depth. A painted sheet was fastened to the reverse of the photograph, and (sometimes) holes were pierced in the latter to let through light. Finally, within the box, behind all this, would be a source of illumination, such as a candle. The effect of overlaying the two images and the light was to bring the scene further to life, whether through colouring, intensified and complex illumination, or the addition of elements such as passersby or lamps. Through such megalethoscopic images, we visit locations far away, and other people (as if by proxy) are seen doing so (Fontanella 1995: 14). It is no coincidence that the Grand Tour – that source of European knowledge through travel for the elites of the time – became such a fashionable source of such entertainments (Fontanella 1995: 12). We encounter, coming together in multiple layers of time, the legacy of lengthy histories.

Unlike painted diaphanoramas, the photograph offered a literal, physical trace of the scene it showed, preserving the light that had fallen upon its chemical surface from the monuments and surroundings. In the words of Laura Burd Schiavo, describing another machine – the stereoscope – the photographic image presents 'the actual visual equivalent of the object or objects', thus 'reconstituting the very visual circumstances that would have presented themselves to the eyes had the viewer witnessed the scene herself' (2003: 128). In many of the images recovered by Fontanella, views of historic monuments, redolent with the passage of centuries, appear in identifiably contemporary scenes. In the Madrid collection we find, for instance, a meticulous photograph of Pompeii's Street of the Tombs (Plate 2) acquiring a sullen, dusty-coloured sky through which the sun barely breaks, casting its jaundiced light onto tiny nineteenth-century figures in the road. With this physical presence comes the material reality of centuries past, the Roman-built street in Pompeii, its burial, rediscovery, and traversing of time. In turn, in the present moment of viewing, in an intense living instant, the candlelight and painted sheet revitalise what had been – in André Bazin's word – 'embalmed' in the grey photographs. The contrast would be all the more poignant in this image. Tourists entering the ruined city down this street habitually associated the present-day place with death and the transience of all things, even as they viewed it 'bifocally', imagining at the same time its ancient life (Beard 2008: 309–10; Nichols 2015: 117).

As this occurs, the spectator might step out of the confines of their own world into that of the image, and the image seep out of the past into the present. Speaking again of the stereoscope, but it could as easily be of the megalethoscope, Pauline Stakelton remarks: 'These simulations aspired not simply to present a copy of a physical site but to reproduce the experience of travel' (2010: 408). The journeying would not be simply across place, but through time. Through the photographic megalethoscope, we experience threefold the 'presence' evoked by many currents of media archaeology. In the words of media theorist Vivian Sobchack, '*Presence* is defined as the *literal* transhistorical (not yet ahistorical) transference or relay of metonymic and material fragments or traces of the past through time to the "here and now" – where and when these can be activated and thus realised' (2011: 324; original emphasis). First, the device reanimates its fragment of the Street of Tombs, and together with it, all the other layers of time found in the combined image it displays. Second, its so doing transfers to whosoever uses it the possibility of experiencing such 'presence', the coming together of layers of time. Third, when this occurs, the potential of the image is 'activated and thus realised', as happened when Fontanella rebuilt the Madrid collection. There is something magical about an experience of this kind: 'we must have recourse to the mist-enveloped regions of the religious world'. In his essay on 'Animated Pictures', Gunning observes how the genesis of the latter 'derives from an intersection between a Renaissance preoccupation with the magical power of images … and a secular discovery of the processes of light and vision' (2004: 102). In the Street of the Tombs at Pompeii, human figures appear as translucent silhouette shapes, through which the ground and surroundings can be seen. It is as if the power of the archaic were so overwhelming that it left the later moment as only a spectral trace upon it, or as if there were some reverse haunting afoot, in which visitors from the modern age and other places extended a tenuous presence into distant history, taking shadowy, insubstantial form.

The viewer might easily slip here into an awareness of something untoward, and with it a heightened consciousness of things overlain upon one another, of detached elements: the light source, the painted sheet, the photograph. Speaking of the much larger painted dioramas, with light effects behind them, Sophie Thomas (2005) has spied the uncanny in their doubled images, at once static and animated: disconcertingly these evoke a combination of life and death. Such hallucinogenic qualities might point likewise to the distance between modern technologies and the intimacy across history and geography that they profess to offer. As time and place are converted by Marx's new god into commodities for consumption in real, but now also virtual tourism through visual technologies (Urry 1995: 2), so we are left, unsettled, alienated even, only with the machine components of a simulacrum. Jonathan Crary's celebrated remarks on the stereoscope in his *Techniques of the Observer* (1990) may more broadly be applied to fusions of two images, whether that is in Marx, or Manet, or an optical toy. 'The "reality effect" of the stereoscope was highly variable', Crary notes, 'The stereoscope discloses a fundamentally disunified and aggregate field of disjunct elements' (1990: 40). More fundamentally still, he argues, rather than giving us a sense of a world 'out there', the optical device underlines how the image is the product of an unstable interaction between and within an individual observer and a machine. This leaves us with a de-centred observer and with a 'dispersed and multiplied sign severed from a point of external reference' (1990: 128). Not dissimilarly, in her *Victorian Glassworlds*, Isobel Armstrong avers both that 'motion toys' – such as the thaumatrope – 'make visible the traces of the past' and that, from the observer's point of view, 'the comparative inefficiency of the incitement to involuntary receptiveness and the effort required to achieve it reminds us that effort can never be quite edited out of the scopic experience' (2008: 348, 350).

A person may acknowledge all this, and still avoid the deflections against which Marx warns, or the *vaivén* with which we might be lured. We must not lose sight of the obvious ('you are going to see', said the hypnotist, 'look'). Many viewers, gazing through their optical devices, seeing their megalethoscopic visions, did and do strive to experience a coming together. Moments of wonder may arise when they attain this, or something like it: when they see depth traced through a single image in a stereoscope, or perceive the light falling upon modern visitors amid old Pompeii. Some will insist that this is just an optical illusion, and draw our attention back to the component parts, the distinct images. For a number of nineteenth-century inventors of optical toys – notably John Ayrton Paris back in the 1820s – the whole point of these devices was to show the true workings of human vision, by the standards of the latest scientific knowledge, disaggregating its elements. It was to expel error and illusion in human perception in the name of science (Gunning 2011: 31–2). Considering such perspectives, Gunning notes that they risk 'driving a wedge between what we know and what we see – and decidedly valuing what we *know* over what we *see*' (2011: 33; original emphasis). For Gunning, what is at stake in nineteenth-century special effects – then and now – is whether there should really be 'a prejudice towards perception as a static process' (2011: 34): that is, towards supposing that movement is an error or invention, and that static component images are real. The issue may be stated much more broadly. The question is whether we experience the world as a series of separated parts, or otherwise. It might be said that periodisation of history favours the former, and 'deep time' the latter. Considering the effects of his rebuilt apparatus, Fontanella remarks that, for all the devices' limitations, what was on offer was 'the illusion of being present at something real into which a person could enter/penetrate to the point of giving themselves over to it. We've seen that, in the case of some diaphanoramas, this is not entirely beyond what is possible' (la ilusión de presenciar algo real y en el que uno penetrara hasta entregarse. Hemos visto ya que en los casos de algunos diaphanoramas, esto no se sale del todo de lo posible) (1995: 15–16).

We could say that many viewers' very use of the equipment, or an observer's encounter with a Manet, may suppose a firm commitment: that they will indeed be able to see in this way, that they will seek to attain that state and so will others. Gunning's willful phrasing is indicative when he speaks of the cycling motions of the phenakistocope, a spinning disc covered with successive images: '*I do not want to say* that when the wheel is spun and I look through the aperture I do not see the figure of a dancer moving' (2011: 39; emphasis added). Schiavo has underlined how far such a commitment could – and can – go in the nineteenth century, to a '*confidence* in vision and in the transparency between object and representation' (2003: 113; emphasis added). Strictly speaking there is no 'representation' here, only a desire for intimacy – and not just with the expanses of place and time but with the optical device itself. Together, the human and apparatus open up an extension of experience: 'Why', asks Gunning, 'shouldn't the ability to see the superimposed image be viewed as a faculty, an ability, rather than a defect?' (2011: 34). For a media archaeologist such as Jussi Parikka, there is here no longer any sharp distinction between physiology and machine.

That is true well beyond the sense of sight (2012: 31). The viewer's posture, position and way of sensing the world are transfigured in company with the machine.

This does not obviate the flickering, the dissipation and separation, but rather subsumes them into the overall experience, just as the irony in del Campo's *Fausto* is integral to overarching companionship. Forms emerge out of and vanish into the pulsations and mutations of the image's parts, just as the geometrical shapes of nineteenth-century photographs translate dynamically, continuously into one another in recurring patterns. If there is a craft to perceiving the superposition – a striving and working with our bodies and the device to attain it – then, as Richard Sennett says of artisans, there is no elimination in the final outcome of the traces of the effort; the latter's sensations, rather, are integrated into the outcome (2008: 268, 262). We might think of this experience in the way a person might approach meditation on a single thing: the dispersal that we at times experience is integral to what we are experiencing. It is no obstacle, in itself, to valuing those moments when everything comes together, however rare they may be. This is what it is to seek and attain intimacy between overlaid images of place and time. There is something of a 'learnt naïveté' about such an experience, to borrow a phrase revived by the Spanish philosopher Javier Gomá (2011). In our pursuit of cleverness, we may seek and emphasise the many qualifications and problems, the many departures from a coming together. Instead, we might learn to take these as a way through which we can attain the vision of togetherness.

This involves an acceptance of one kind of limitation: that we hope to see what others have offered us – the maker of the device, say – what (in a sense) is expected of us. Here 'to limit oneself is to extend oneself', in the words that Gomá fondly quotes from Goethe, he of Faust, the tester of the boundaries of mortal being (2011: 12). In *Techniques of the Observer*, Crary shows how optical technologies could subject their users to discipline, training them in obedience to the needs of a mechanising world, of a new socioeconomic order. While that may in some respects be so, the claim risks reducing everything to social discipline, Gunning notes (2011: 42). More still, it risks the assumption that all forms of discipline are negative, undesirable and undesired, rather than potential sources of pleasure and of liberation. An alternative perspective on optical devices may be found in Luis Buñuel's film *Belle de Jour*. Here, Séverine adjusts her posture to peer through a peephole and observe a masochistic gynaecologist. 'How can one fall so low?', she asks, less as a rhetorical outburst than as a request for instructions. By adjusting her body to the needs of the viewing system, she has already begun her descent. The viewer learns to 'give themselves over' (*entregarse*) as Fontanella puts it, just as an actress like Matilde Díez might give up their self to others in pursuit of freedom.

The fact that we might not see the coming together of two locations perfectly, absolutely stably is somewhat beside the point. To return to the words of the military engineer, Borja, whom we met in Chapter 1, in practical matters, 'all the exaggerated demands of exactitude will be little short of ludicrous'. To commit to experiencing the coming together is specifically to accept that we do so vaguely. This is not a concession, an admission that something cannot be attained. Rather, it is an affirmation that, by accepting vagueness as inherent to our experience, we become open to rich possibility. The viewer of a megalethoscope, wondering at modern visitors in the Street of Tombs, the reader of *Capital I* perceiving atavism in modern universals, does not fixate on what might hold them back, but gives themselves over to what has been conjured in its full, hallucinogenic qualities. In that great novel of a mutating world, *Alice through the Looking Glass* (1871), the protagonist protests that one simply cannot believe impossible things. In reply, Lewis Carroll has the White Queen aptly retort: 'I daresay you haven't had much practice' (1965: 251).

Lavishness, ventriloquism, slippage

When Cavell speaks of the 'power of passiveness' and 'passive practice', he asserts that these will – and should – bring us 'home' from 'exile' as we cease to clutch at the world (2013: 33–7). On this account, human beings and their language are constantly and in multifarious ways drawn away from a sense of being at 'home' in the world, and must counter that by seeking to return. In a suggestive passage of *This New Yet Unapproachable America*, Cavell asks us to consider the multitude of voices and speakers that populate Wittgenstein's *Philosophical Investigations*. These putatively lure us with a corresponding multitude of confusions in the use of language, entangling and bewitching us. The voices together supposedly evoke human culture and history become sick. Cavell asks us how it would be were there no countervailing voice in the text, and conjures up a vision of accelerating danger in human society (2013: 75). He is not inviting us to take refuge in some fundamental rules of epistemology, nor by following a single, given path through our lives and through time. Much less does he suppose that our forms of life should have defined, fixed boundaries that guard against error. His point, rather, is that if we do not have those things, then some voice, some call, must – and must be able to – steer us from danger, to keep us to some kind of path. For, the alternative – a kind of 'lavishness' that lacks any 'the path of philosophy' (2013: 72) – cannot guard us against anything that we may do to ourselves and others in our confusion: we are utterly exposed to all the voices of our cultures. The possibility of 'poverty' – of shedding all that departs into confusion, all that takes leave of our form of life, all that pathless 'lavishness' – becomes a necessary supposition, where the alternative is a helpless scepticism. There must be a way back 'home', even if (specifically if), 'home' does not look like a set of foundational rules and fixed boundaries. Humanity's continual, erratic motion would then consist of 'many journeys, many middles, of repeated losses and recoveries of oneself' (2013: 37).

In addressing these questions, Cavell is frequently concerned with mid-nineteenth-century thought of the United States, not least Ralph Waldo Emerson and Henry David Thoreau, in whom he finds notions of poverty and home. He is preoccupied here with nineteenth-century notions of 'America', a place supposedly discovered by Columbus (dispatched, as we know, by the Spanish monarchy), and, post-independence, potentially free of prior, unquestioned authority. If 'America' is 'new yet unapproachable', he muses, that is in part because it evokes the unfulfilled promise of discovery: as if (I take it) we were not truly to realise we were already in the supposedly New World, and by extension, as if there were some unbreachable distance that prevented us from being at home there, just as scepticism keeps us from believing we can be at home in our forms of life, from discovering that we truly can inhabit them anew, and that we need no mandate from any founder figure, no obedience to foundational rules so to do (2013: 91–3, 116–17).

The intricacies of Cavell's own philosophy and ethics aside, the distinction between unconstrained 'lavishness' and 'poverty' matters to this chapter because it throws a dilemma into stark relief. Without a notion of 'poverty', can we experience the continual departures from one culture and time, from one voice or person to the next, as anything but a constant 'exile', a constant separation, in which nothing is ever settled and everything is always deferred, in which, in growing confusion amid the cacophony, we can never feel 'at home'? If our 'power of passiveness' solely opens us up to this, does it not simply fail, turned to corrupted ends of lavishness? Do our perceptions of overlaid voices and images and entities from across place and time – in megalethoscopes or in Capital or in Manet – lack any real integrity and lead us only astray? Yet, if we do not let go of 'poverty', can we truly be open to all departures across place and time, across language? If we cannot be at home in all these departures precisely as they continually differ, how can they really constitute a shared experience, a commonality? It might become impossible to envisage an authentic way of existing simultaneously through a multitude of ways of talking and envisaging things from across place and time.

Whitman's self-titled 'Walt Whitman' – now generally known as 'Song of Myself' – suggests a way through such dilemmas. In an independent United States whose very constitution was at stake in the mid-century – the years of Civil War, before and after – the poet does so in a vision of how to inhabit 'America', and of how to be at home in a diverse world. 'Not words of routine this song of mine / But abruptly to question, to leap beyond yet nearer bring', Whitman exclaims in the 1867 version (1995: 74). The poet's bounding may be taken as an injunction to step beyond the printed book (Perrin Warren 2009: 384), but it is more still than this. His words bring explicitly and directly into focus the dual movement traced in this chapter: he is, as he puts it, 'one of that centripetal and centrifugal gang' (1995: 75). If his thoughts 'are not just as close as they are distant they are nothing' (1995: 43). Ivy G. Wilson has remarked on how the very patterns of Whitman's language offer a 'sonic oscillation between the here and there. The repetition of words ... creates a sense of reverberation, an echo that anchors the speaker in his present locality at the same time as he is gravitating elsewhere' (2011: 93). Like the beating hooves of the *gauchos'* horses and the fantasia on *Faust* in Chapter 1, this is suggestive of the role of Echo, rather than Narcissus, in the mythic origins of poetry: a vision based not on a narrowly delimited identity (the mirrored face of Narcissus) but rather on a transfigured sharing in which the bounds of self and other fade.

The key to how we could at once be at 'home' and be 'lavish', 'centripetal and centrifugal', here and elsewhere, 'as close as ... distant' is to be found in Whitman's evocation of being 'Me myself'. At first blush, to be 'Me myself' is to reject attempts to understand who we are by contextualising ourselves and others within our place and time and history, by historicising ourselves and others in that sense, or by seeking other things that provide the evidence for who we and they are. That would always be a regressive movement: looking to other things by way of explanation, as if constantly seeking behind or away from something, as if using those things to 'clutch' at experience and master it, and thereby not apprehending what we have before us (including ourselves). The 'people I meet, the effect upon me of my early life or the ward and city I live in, or the nation', are 'not the Me myself' (1995: 29). Likewise, we alienate 'Me myself' by apprehending experience in the terms of other voices and frameworks: 'You shall no longer take things at second or third hand, nor look through the eyes of the dead, nor feed on the spectres in books' (1995: 28).

We encounter here a distinction between, on the one hand, taking 'things at second or third hand', and, on the other, apprehending 'Me myself' as something unconfined in place and time. Yet, the latter must, by definition, be found precisely through a multitude of voices and subjects across geography and history. The song offers 'a series of impersonations', as Kerry Larson puts it (2009: 478). Peter Bellis observes that 'the "I", no longer privileged, becomes the site of a circulation of different roles and identities' (2003: 81). The question, therefore, is not so much whether we should experience the world through other people and things (dead or alive, or not yet born, or in books), but how we might do so. If our disposition is to define ourself in terms of what we read in books, treating these as a self-contained world, we will reinforce the divide from 'Me myself'. Conversely, if we experience the things we read in books and find among the dead (for example) as 'Me myself' and vice-versa, the divide would vanish. Whitman is even moved to declare, 'I beat and pound for the dead, / I blow through my embouchures the loudest and gayest for them' (1995: 43). 'These are really the original thoughts of all men in all ages and lands', he affirms, 'they are not original with me. / If they are not yours as much as mine they are nothing or next to nothing' (1995: 42). In this respect, a true rupture of the locations of the past and of geography would entail their more authentic reiteration, because stripped of confines, any place and time may extend into any other, and be universally shared. 'Walt Whitman' would be 'a kosmos, of Manhattan son' (1995: 48). In this light – as if instances of 'Me myself' – Marx's Capital, shattering the context of the old ways, unleashes the latters' atavistic energy, becoming them as they become it. Manet, busting the lines drawn by Titian around his Venus, allows the Italian to flow in and out of his own art. The very phenomenon of leaping beyond to nearer bring, of being 'Me myself' is itself reiterated from and through the depths and breadths of time and place.

If 'Me myself' offers sameness through continual departures, and does so without deferral, it invites us to set aside a series of 'pictures' of the world within which such an experience would be ultimately unthinkable. To do so is to speak with the world – 'To Foreign Lands', as Whitman puts it in the title of a short poem of 1860 – so as 'to prove this puzzle the New World, / And to define America, her athletic Democracy' (1995: 5). The teasing through discarded pictures is at once offered as a way through the challenges of that mid-century United States, and (putatively) as such, a passage to being 'at home' in diversity, without some prior authority or rule. In his essay on Whitman, 'Promiscuous Citizenship', Jason Frank has eloquently set out the challenge as Whitman saw it, from the growing tensions of the 1850s onwards into the Civil War years and beyond. 'In the United States democratic attachment could not be achieved by Romantic appeal to a common tradition, language, ethnicity, or race, but reasoned allegiance to common principle was also too thinly cognitive, and obligation based in economic interest too narrowly calculating, to achieve the binding precondition of democratic self-creation. For Whitman, the conditions of democracy, America, and the modern required … a radical re-visioning of inherited images of political belonging' (2011: 156).

A series of distinctions in other 'pictures' of the world – however nuanced – may easily obviate an appreciation of 'Me myself', and yet appear tantalisingly close, in their own terms, to describing it. 'Me myself's' claim to constitute a 'language of justice', and its version of universality, do not suppose a breach between a proper embrace of contingency and something 'purified, abstracted, turned into a categoric idea, so that it can remain structurally inviolate … even as it entertains an infinite number of contingent terms' (Dimock 1996: 70). Rather, 'Me myself' must be forever the same precisely in and as a result of continual departure into the varying contingencies of diverse places and times and people and cultures and language. There is nothing 'structurally inviolate' about it, because it is not an abstract principle: it lingers in openness to the very details of life that surge up from moment to moment, perspective to perspective, of the poem, from 'the moth and fish-eggs' to a 28-year-old woman admiring 28 male bodies bathing to a 'leaf of grass' (1995: 42, 35, 55) 'To be in any form, what is that?' Whitman appeals (1995: 53). By the same token, what is at stake in 'Me myself' is not quite whether some unmediated form of experience would 'annihilate differences' between representation and the world, 'the imaginary and the actual'. It does not quite involve the question of whether the poem exists 'in and for itself, prior to any system of exchange or representation' (Bellis 2003: 71, 91). Rather, each departure through the forms of language or media or society articulates 'Me myself's' sameness, and does so without these things ceasing to be departures from something else – from other words, other media, other things. It is 'the connoisseur who peers along the exhibition-gallery' as much as it is 'the President holding a cabinet', or Deacons taking orders, or a 'pike-fisher' (1995: 39–41). Put another way, in the experience of 'Me myself', the foundational distinction between the unmediated and the mediated would not exist, and neither would the debates that stem from that 'picture' of the world.

 Readers of the poem – and of *Leaves of Grass* in its entirety – have drawn attention to the complexities that develop with the volume's evolution: these echo with the tensions about Whitman, that turned to violence, and then to the aftermath of war. They involve, in uneven ways, a growing assertion of the realities of self and other, and of the loss and mutilation of bodies in the war – especially by the time of the inclusion of 'Drum Taps' in *Leaves of Grass*. Peter Bellis traces the process of change as early back as 1855–56, with the conflicts of the mayoral elections in New York and then fighting on the city streets (2003: 111). For Susan Manning, the fragility of Whitman's constant juxtapositions – his parataxis – is apparent in the very tensions these reveal (2002: 14). Increasingly, there is what Michael Moon calls a 'dynamic relationship between powerful tendencies toward both disintegration and recursivity', not least in 'Drum Taps' and its disconcerting array of dead and living bodies (1991: 181, viii). But, the increased nuancing of 'The Song of Myself' after its original 1855–56 version could not amount as such to a growing scepticism about the potential to be free of distance or mediation or loss. After all, such a distinction did not exist in its fundamental 'picture' of the world, even in the first version: it is foundational to 'Me myself' that it does not exist. Rather – and whatever one makes of its implications – the increased complexity constitutes a texturing, a bringing out of 'Me myself', of its continual leaping departures. By extension, in the experience of 'Me myself', it is no longer important to fixate on the question of whether or not a given mediating sign can be attached to a supposedly separate referent – determinate or otherwise – of whether or not the sense of the sign is deferred. While 'Me myself' may be a step away from what Kerry Larson calls 'the tyranny of meaning' (2008: 104), this is not *per se* because its words offer indetermination and opacity as opposed to clarity of intent. That is to say, 'Me myself' is not a 'picture' of the world in which the supposed problem of 'interpretation' arose in the first place, in which the challenge was to seek to relate a sign to something signified. If we are invited to 'enjoy the charms of interactivity itself, the radical equality of speaker and listener', this cannot strictly be – as Larson puts it – 'anterior to the establishment of sense and the assignment of fixed roles' (2008: 99). In short, ultimately at stake here is not a question of mediation or non-mediation, of representation or referent, of contingency or necessity. At stake is how to realise, in all its complex textures, a disposition towards the world in which we are 'at home' in 'lavishness', authentic through our very appreciation of the outpouring of differences across place and time.

'Philosophy,' Wittgenstein famously said, 'leaves everything as it is' (*PI* §124). History, here, is likewise left as it is. It is not that nothing changes, less still that we will not act differently. It is rather that our disposition towards what is (and what has been, and will be) has been refreshed, so that we are 'at home' with these things, and have a new starting point. We become ventriloquists. We speak now in the manner of others, and others find a voice through us (we are 'in the game', in Whitman's words), without making of that manner the defining characteristic of who we – or even ultimately they – are (we are 'out of the game', Whitman says) (1995: 30). We could say, for example, that Marx seeks to become the ventriloquist of the age of Capital, or Capital of the ages of humanity, or Manet of Titian (and Titian of Manet), or a megalethoscope the ventriloquist of old Pompeii. 'Whitman's aesthetic practices' offer us 'a form of choral ventriloquism', Ivy G. Wilson has observed (2011: 83). In *Dumbstruck* (2000) – reflections on ventriloquism and its history – Stephen Connor remarks how, for much of the nineteenth century, practitioners did not just throw their voice into a single dummy, but rather across a multitude of locations, sounds and identities (2011: 253–4). Instead of invoking a 'disabling "splitting" of the self', such as intrigues Derrida (2011: 6), Connor dwells here on 'the power to speak through others ... the experience of being spoken through by others ... the power of unlocated or mobile voices' (2011: 14). Able both 'to remain itself over distances' and 'to multiply itself into different forms', he observes, 'the ventriloquial voice is powerful both because it is able to retain its individuality and because it is able to lose it' (2011: 327).

Connor finds this capacity in the potential of 'voice' itself: it emanates from my (or any) person and travels beyond me, 'at once cleaving to and taking leave from myself' (2011: 7). It is, in Whitman's terms, 'centrifugal and centripetal', forever departing, and in its very departures finding its sameness (it is always the 'ventriloquial voice'), like the singing and the 'Song' of 'Me myself'. It is of a 'me' without being limited by the latter's context. 'Voice goes out, and returns to me,' Connor writes, 'changed and yet the same. It allows me to connect here and there, and then, now and then' (2011: 34). The experience of being in and out of a *game* – as Whitman puts it – is thereby transfigured. The *game* is neither something artificial, misleading nor distracting, a construct from which we must distance ourselves, nor is it something that we engage in at any one time as if it were the only possible way of experiencing things (in the way we might imagine someone lost in the playing of a game). It is akin rather to El Pollo's assertion that, the other night, he saw the Devil – and, conversely, for El Pollo to say this in the sense in which it is true – is for him to be 'Me myself'.

It is inherently difficult, in the everyday phrase, to 'get' all this. I use that colloquial expression here precisely because it does not suppose anything so specific or restrictive or even obviously active as *to grasp* or *to understand*. This is a way of being in the world, not a reasoned explanation or analytical account of things, nor a specific identity or definition nor an ontology nor an interpretation. It can be justified and defended in none of those terms. 'You will hardly know who I am or what I mean', we are told in *Song of Myself* (1995: 85). The same may be said of beholding the supernatural qualities of Marx's god of Capital, or of managing to see a three-dimensional image in an optical device like a stereoscope, or a living scene in a megalethoscope. There can be no theory of this, because there can be nothing that we might habitually think of as a substantial philosophy: no epistemology, no ontology, no metaphysics. Were we to commit to any of these things, we would be inhibited in our experience of 'Me myself': we could not be both in and out of the game of that particular system. We could not be ever open to potentiality. If anything at all is substantial, it is the renunciation of those very things, the 'power of passiveness', our opening up, like the lens of Martínez Sánchez's camera to the world. To the extent that philosophical theories (for example) may assist us at all in getting 'Me myself', that is because they are apprehended as 'Me myself', not the other way around (shortly, we will encounter Aristotle and Lucretius in this guise). In this way at least, 'Me myself' is very like Hegel's Spirit as described by the philosopher Michael Rosen: we may accept or reject its claim to truth, but no case for or against can be demonstrated in interpretation of it (1984: 179).

Were we to get all this (what this 'power of passiveness' is, what it is to be We ourselves), then we could ourselves 'go on' with it, in Wittgenstein's phrase. That is, it evokes how, in our forms of life and of language, we can continue to use this form of life in a whole variety of circumstances, without watertight definitions, without ultimate justifications whose reasoning overcomes all scepticism, and without knowledge of all the situations and ways in which the form of life may be used. From this perspective – Cavell shows – not to say all that could be said in this form of life does not demonstrate that anything is being deferred or withheld (Cavell 2013: 23). To continue the dialogue with Wittgenstein, the point of going on, of embracing such 'lavishness', of being a ventriloquist, would not really be 'to show the fly the way out of the fly bottle' (*PI* §309). That is, the objective is not (just) to release human beings from how they entangle themselves in ways of talking and being that strive to make sense of the world. Rather, the point of 'Me myself' would be to arrive at an appreciation of what it is, how it is, to talk and be in those multifarious ways, those 'forms of life' of diverse places and times, to be able to 'go on' with them. The question is what each of these brings and offers, to explore what every one may give us. To have an open disposition towards history, then, is to allow these many ways to take shape. Such is the 'power of passiveness', to borrow Cavell's phrase once more. 'I resist any thing better than my diversity', says Whitman (1995: 42).

Such ventriloquism involves something other even than fellow feeling or empathy or even affective juxtaposition, touching and caressing, important as those things are to Whitman. He puts it graphically in those years of tension with the South: 'I am the hounded slave, I wince at the bite of the dogs' (1995: 63). This is an intense, physical, often eroticised intimacy, not just with but in others: 'my voice is the wife's voice', 'I turn the bridegroom out of the bed and stay with the bride myself. / I tighten her all night to my thighs and lips' (1995: 62). In *Upheavals of Thought*, the philosopher Martha Nussbaum finds such an outlook to echo with 'the Aristotelian view that the body is the soul, coupling it with the view that the body is itself a poem' (2001: 660; she has particularly in mind *I Sing the Body Electric*). It follows that 'all our acts are bodily acts, and all our art is naked meat, and all our sympathy is blood' (2001: 661). Our body, our voice, our breath, our writing or painting or sculpting arm, our photographing eyes and fingers, take on the forms of others, and can transform into yet others still. In this we are like the mutating actors and actresses of Bretón that we met in Chapter 1. Put at its strongest, our soul physically becomes the soul of others, without our being confined to them or them to us. The physical act of voicing is crucial to the poetics of 'Me myself', E. Fred Carlisle and others have emphasised: it is there that the 'meeting' beyond self and other occurs (1973: 8, 23–7). Reflecting on the legacy of Aristotle's notion of *Logos*, the classicist Shane Butler remarks that 'any conviction that what is in our soul … and what is in our voice are the same thing' need not amount to the 'metaphysics of presence' that Derrida denounces. Rather, one may look to a 'simpler belief': 'we really do feel some very important emotions in our (racing) hearts and (quickening) breath and (tightening) throats, and we really do hear their effects not only in our own voices but also in those of others' (2015: 50). Connor finds voice and voicing to be key to this Aristotelian view of the soul (2011: 24–5), while observing that (as ventriloquism underlines) 'voices are produced by bodies: but can also themselves produce bodies' (2011: 35). What Butler and Connor say of voice and the soul might be extended to all varieties of expression and their physicality. Associating Whitman rather with Lucretius, Max Noble invokes 'the materiality of experience as the means for knowing what one is and who else is out there' (2015: 61): such is the source of our experience of similitude, in potential at least. (This book that I am writing is an act of ventriloquism.)

The artistic practice known as 'free copying' is indicative of the intensely physical sense in which 'Me myself' flows in and out of others across place and time, in which 'I am large', as Whitman famously says, 'I contain multitudes' (1995: 84). 'Free copying' was a common aspect of artists' training in which they would produce variants on a work that they otherwise imitated (Boime 1971: 123, 129). No painter in the mid-nineteenth century so obsessively explored this practice as did the Spaniard Eugenio Lucas Velázquez (1817–70). A leftist sympathiser, Lucas had risen to become a court painter by 1851, and in 1853 was awarded the title of Knight of the Order of Carlos III (Arnáiz 1981: 10–20). He became an 'artist who was not', as I have put it elsewhere. His continual concern with reworking and reimagining the works of artists was at odds with the widespread belief – from the academy to the vanguard – that an artist should grow into a fuller, authentic, original being through independence from the antecedents from which they learnt. Mainly focused on a multitude of lucrative private commissions and sales, largely in this vein, Lucas attracted little commentary, as if he were not, in the full sense of the word, an *artist*, as if had defied the very category of *art*. Conversely, his works appealed to wealthy buyers preoccupied with their own place – and that of their time – within national and European traditions (Ginger 2007a: 45–56, 49–50, 56–62, 73–4). At times, his paintings so closely resembled Goya's as to be bought and sold as such, posing problems for generations of curators and experts (largely now unpicked by the valiant efforts of José Manuel Arnáiz (1981)). At other times, he paints in the manner of Andalusian commercial painters of customs, or of a landscape artist from the seventeenth-century Low Countries. No other painter so gave their self over to others, and to history, as did Lucas. In his most Goya-like paintings, notably some of his bullfighting scenes, he closely follows Goya's composition and drawing, but, in so doing, increases the thickness of paint (the impasto), blurs the image further, and often breaks it into near-discontinuous lumps (Arnáiz 1981: 102, 106; Ginger 2007a: 150–2). We might call this a *slippage*, that is, a movement in particular directions which then departs from the earlier motion of brushwork (in this case, Goya's). This is a way of intimately inhabiting the potential exhibited by a chronologically prior work of art or artist. It physically explores and shows where the dynamic of the paint and of the painter's bodily movements might have taken them. To do this, Lucas must himself take on Goya's motions, while slipping through them away from the limitations of what Goya actually produced. The artist finds their own way of painting through what another artist might have become but did not. Insofar as Goya was the possible futures of his own paintings, Lucas's art resurrects the Aragonese artist. In turn, the resuscitated technique of Goya guides Lucas's arm so that, through him, Lucas may be a painter in his own right. He penetrates Goya's physical manner of painting, and Goya penetrates his. Through the material of the paint, both find a way 'to go on'. Lucas brings Goya nearer by leaping beyond him, and leaping beyond himself to become

Departure: to leap beyond yet nearer bring

Goya, Lucas himself is brought nearer. Both are in and out of each other's game, both are 'Me, myself'. Like Laurent's photographic version of *Las Meninas*, this is active, explicit artistic collaboration across the centuries.

Here we find radicalised – stripped of any framework outside itself, of any foundation – the notion that subjecthood is conceived through and out of the materials of history, in their endless reconstruction. There is no Being beyond this. After the Napoleonic invasion and the counter-uprisings of 1808, with the disruption of the transoceanic monarchy and the domestic order, successive intellectuals and politicians pondered how to reconstitute a Spanish culture, society and state. They sought to do so out of what remained, out of its inheritance, out of its tense relations, present and historic, with other cultures too, not least a powerful, influential France to its north. The 'nation' proclaimed in the first constitution (1812) is, in this sense, an act of creative pastiche, made out of remnants of ancient laws and legal notions imported or home-grown. If the notion of a Spanish 'nation' was always an inherently conflicted, contested proposition, laced with heterogeneity, it was all the more so at the mid-century. By then, the Progressive Liberals had split after a failed 1848 rising, a new Democratic Party had arisen; the 1854 revolt against harder-line conservative liberals (*moderados*) had been rolled back in 1856 only for the two old liberal parties to split and a new Liberal Union to form and, for a time, govern. Intractable challenges of political and economic policy, of how to balance and reach out to powerful groups, including the wider population, shattered such little consensus there had been around 'oligarchic liberalism': the rule of an elite, governing the state, in combination with large-scale capital, so as to redevelop the 'nation'. If this was unsettling, in some observer's eyes the pace of change was an indeterminate blur as social mores altered and cities redeveloped (Ginger 2007a: 181–206, 114–17). The 'surprise' of the presence of the past in the Cliffords' photographs was a way, both to acknowledge this unsettling of foundations, and to find a way once more to communicate with and through history in ghostly meeting (see Chapter 1). In setting aside the question of clarity of meaning, of interpreting or grounding history beyond the experience of its materials, Lucas's continual impersonations – his enigmatic, painterly ventriloquism – embrace endless departures from what we were, while remaining the same. His repeated ventures into Velázquez and Goya interlace him with the splendours and vicissitudes of Spain – from imperial splendour on the cusp of decline, to troubled rebirth as the Ancien Régime reached its collapse (Ginger 2007a: 120–9). As he does this, his frequent dwelling on French colourism, references and styles takes him to the borderland where two cultures, and two histories, overlap in tension and in mutual fascination (Ginger 2007a: 94–107, 120–9).

Vividly, in *Felipe IV, His Court, and Las Meninas* (Plate 3), the physical paint of the latter Velázquez image at the very back seeps and leaks through a wash into the wider Lucas composition – and vice versa, the latter flows into it through the perspectival depths of the image. In continual slippage, the image pulsates back and forth through transformations and transpositions, forming a Lucas–Velázquez or Velázquez–Lucas. Its dynamic of visual projections echoes that of the universal visual language found in Martínez Sánchez and Laurent's photography. The multi-directional flow involves being able 'to go on' all at once through a corresponding multitude of pathways. The Velázquez painting diminishes in size as if it had travelled back through the line of perspective, distancing itself from the viewer; in the foreground Velázquez's dog too shrinks. But the royal couple, seen in miniature on a mirror in *Las Meninas*, now emerge out of the seeping paint of Velázquez's masterpiece to loom large in the foreground, the whole cast making way for them, as the number of characters seen multiplies into a vast crowd about them. In the foreground, figures from *Las Meninas* reappear in full size. *Las Meninas* thus shrinks and expands alternately like something from *Alice in Wonderland*. Meanwhile, the sober palette of Velázquez's colourism flows in and out of the more garish colourism of a French Romantic through the shared loose brushwork.

It is through such slippage and ventriloquism, in a lavish 'Me myself', that history brings its own depths out of itself, each arrangement of place and of time exhibiting its capacity to morph into another, just as *Venus d'Urbino* may become *Olympia*, just as Nietzsche's post-war conversation with Wagner becomes the rebirth of pre-Socratic Greece. By visibly repeating again and again the tasks involved in his artistic training, Lucas shows how, like the White Queen, he has had 'much practice' in effecting things otherwise deemed 'impossible': making the seventeenth century part of the nineteenth century and the latter a home for the former, finding Delacroix through the Golden-Age Spanish court, and enabling *Las Meninas* to leak out of its frame to form another reality. The result has the internal harmony and cogency of an hallucination, just as the art of *Las Meninas* itself, or of Laurent's photographic version of it, was to give us a supposedly impossible point of view. To 'get' Lucas as 'Me myself' is to give ourselves over to that daydreaming experience, to accept the fact of our beholding the multitudes as a single reality. ('The other night I saw the Devil.') The painting shows us less a defined image of the seventeenth-century court than the continual releasing of energy that is pulsation, back and forth across place and time. Ultimately, all of history and geography might be in companionship with one another.

The gap as violent love

Yet – and for all of this – rarely can we escape the sensation of the gap opening up in the flickering, between places and times, wilfully created 'with a shove and a kick', as Marx put it. To dwell upon this 'flicker effect' would indeed be to perceive history as a passage from one distinct vision, one distinct take, one present moment, to the next. 'A gap or interval is required and is found', Doane remarks of cinema, as she might of earlier optical devices, but this 'generates its own anxieties about discontinuity and absence' (2002: 105, 185). Even in Lucas, the 'French' colours seem almost nauseatingly at odds with the Spanish source in *Las Meninas*, insinuating discontinuity amid the 'slippage'. Many contemporary Spaniards would have found the effect repellent, alien to Velázquez's legacy (Ginger 2007a: 95). While Manet's *Olympia* may be a kind of mutation of Titian's *Venus d'Urbino* or his *Execution of Maximilian* a version of Goya's *Third of May*, there is a leap from the one to the next, an abyss within which the mutation itself is quite invisible, a jump that leaves no evident trace on the Manet itself, now far from its origins. Carol Armstrong is perhaps the scholar who most proclaims Manet's indifference to the supposed 'unity of the mature artist's style' (2002: 27). But even she says of his 1867 retrospective that 'picture by picture, it declared its "handwriting" openly and for all to see, as the work of a markedly individual hand' (2002: 27). More bluntly, but no less aptly, James Rubin observes: 'there was never confusion about … authorship; no one mistook him for a Spanish or a Dutch painter' (2010: 112). (The same could clearly not be said of Lucas.) The creation of such a gap in place and time opens the space into which the new image can be formed, and within which resemblance can find expression.

Departure: to leap beyond yet nearer bring

We must attend to that gap itself, to the feelings evoked in the dramatic 'leaping beyond', in the aggressive opening of an abyss, in the shove and the kick. In Lucas's Frenchification of Velázquez, we are hurled back and forth across disparate centuries, and between violently opposing if related ways of making art, cultures even. Through this, we encounter their capacity to work together, for Velázquez's images of the court may indeed be traced in the colours of Delacroix, as they have been in Lucas's painting. The tension is constituent of, does not violate, the intimacy presented to us, like a bickering but enamoured couple, like the wedding of Dionysus and Apollo. The potentially aggressive presence of Delacroix – and of all that is French – surges into the heart of historic Spanish art, and is pushed back insofar as his role seems out of place in Spain. This swaying between dominance and submission expresses allure and desire. In turn, there is only the slightest allusion to Lucas's admired Goya. The Queen's hand points downwards to the ground, its shape tracing the unseen forms of Goya's *Duchess of Alba*, presenting us with a flickering between the two. The kicking away of Goya in favour of Velázquez in this painting, the former's utter submission, reduced to such a detail, is consistent with, draws on the affection in which Goya is held, the desire for him, right at the centre of Lucas's work.

In Manet, likewise, places, populations and times interconnect back and forth through webs of violence as much as of attraction, stretching out from and into France across the globe and through time, from the US Civil War as witnessed off the French Atlantic coast (*The Battle of the Kearsage and the Alabama* (1864)), to the (related) legacy of Atlantic slavery in the West-Indian maid of *Olympia*, to the aftermath of Japan's forced entry into global markets by US warships (the Japanese print on the wall of Zola's portrait in 1868) (Boime 2007: 705–12, 696–8), back to the death of Jesus of Nazareth (*Christ with the Angels* (1864)). By resonating with Goya's *Third of May*, the 1869 version of Manet's *Execution of Maximilian* (Plate 4) evokes violent transformations on a vast global scale. Emperor Maximilian of Mexico's Habsburg ancestors had been the rulers of Spain in its imperial Golden Age which reshaped the globe. With his death we behold a restored link to the old Hispanic order just as it is once more severed. The allusion to *The Third of May* recalls the previous shattering of imperial Spain with the French invasion of 1808. By the same token, it echoes with French imperial violence and defeat: Maximilian had been backed and then abandoned by Napoleon III as a supposed solution to the problem of how to constitute a post-independence Mexican state, reigning only from 1864 to 1867. If the world had been transformed by the Spanish Empire and its fall, the execution of the French-backed Mexican Emperor was often seen in Spanish America as 'a world-historical event', James Sanders has observed, 'the triumph of a vision of modernity that celebrated republicanism, rights, and even democracy – all achieved in the Americas – as defining modern civilisation' (2014: 3–4).

Manet offers an 'inclusive and global aesthetic', Higonnet observes (2016: 198). His paintings are too enigmatic to extract from them some social or political treatise, however many references they may accumulate and we may observe, resonating richly with the textures of their context. In his art, we experience the interconnections over place and time, not through an act of interpretation of the dense allusions, but through a quality of experience. *Olympia* is suggestive of the sensation that Manet seeks. Where Titian's painting seems to give way, to invite the viewer in, Manet pushes us back. The soft flesh of Venus – Goddess of Love, the very embodiment of affection and attraction – hardens; the arm closes off access to her genitals; the dangled flowers are thrust towards us; the maid looms up rather than visiting the receding distance; the pet looks ready to pounce. T.J. Clark notes how many contemporaneous viewers found it all 'too much the opposite of Titian', 'a kind of travesty of the old language of the nude' (1984: 96, 131). Likewise, in the 1869 version of *Execution of Maximilian*, Goya's crowd moving forwards is cut off by a high wall over which it must now peer. The hill behind now towers up so vertically as to be about to tip over into the viewer's space. There is an emotional severing that accompanies these changes. Where Goya conjures atmospheric, melodramatic shadow and illumination, Maximilian's execution takes place in even unremitting sunlight that falls upon prisoners and executioners alike. Where Goya's figures are bent with emotion and grotesquery, Manet's are stiff, almost cut-outs. In the flickering of Manet's *Olympia*, it is as if Titian were being thrust away; in his *Execution of Maximilian*, it is as if Goya were being frozen out with heat and light, and a brick wall.

We encounter here a resolution into provocative dominance, akin to the shove and kick delivered by the God of Capital. Manet's art – says Rubin – 'was viewed nearly always as a confrontation and sometimes as an insult' (2010: 9). Fried speaks of 'an assaultive force' (1996: 329). There is a specific sensual, even erotic charge to that experience. This is most straightforwardly apparent in *Olympia*: the viewer is set upon by their subordinates in a place ostensibly of pleasure. (In the penultimate section of this chapter, we will turn to the vexed question of the gendered and sexualised gaze upon the woman here, its apparent assumption of the perspective of a wealthy male on a naked female, its turning this into the essence of modern art (Pollock 2018).) Olympia's attractions are those of disdain, quiet contempt, even. The West-Indian maid presses herself up against us, looking out at us, ignoring any racial taboos, to the disgust of several critics of the time (Boime 2007: 696). It is as if the painting's allure, its provocation, lies in its apparent indifference. The sensation is likewise manifest in *The Execution*: the painting does not care to give us the kind of emotional prompts offered by Goya, to let us visit depths literal or metaphorical that the Spaniard gave us: the space seems closed where in Goya it opens out. For the poet and thinker Georges Bataille, Manet exhibits here 'an almost callous indifference': 'he deliberately rendered the condemned man's death with the same indifference as if he had chosen a fish or a flower for his subject' (1983: 46). The issue, though, is not the intractable question whether Manet's paintings express emotion, whether *The Execution of Maximilian* carries an emotional charge. At stake, rather, is what Manet has done relative to Goya, how he has pushed away Goya's passions of *The Third of May*. Precisely the point of the pushing away, the apparent indifference to the feelings in the earlier painting, is the generation and expression of attraction, like the tension between Nietzsche's Apollo and Dionysus. Goya is, after all, manifestly of critical importance to Manet in this image. Titian and Goya are so clearly present in outline precisely in order to be shoved and kicked away, and the shoving and kicking away is what draws them close, reels them in, perhaps we might even say, desires them. If we can feel this to be so, we could experience how the absence, the distance, the gap *is* the intimate connection. In the moments when we have that sensation, the flickering ceases or, perhaps better put, resolves. One place or time does not overcome another. It is this that, amid French obsessions with things Hispanic, gives us a 'complex dialectical movement' between the two (Armstrong 2002: 98). It is this that offers us the dream of French thinkers like Michelet and Thoré: a universality born of the specifics of things French, and its affinities with others, a legacy not least of its revolutionary claims to renew the world after 1789 (Fried 1996: 123–9).

'The mighty dead return,' says the literary theorist Harold Bloom, 'but they return in our colors, and speaking in our voices, at least in part, at least in moments, moments that testify to our persistence, and not to their own. If they return wholly in their own strength, then the triumph is theirs' (1973: 141). Such, for Bloom, is the violent struggle of present and past, between the later and the earlier creative artist: one or other must live or die. With this comes what he calls *The Anxiety of Influence*, for he holds that 'a poet's … whole being' – but it could as well be a painter's – '*must* be unique to him [*sic*], and remain unique, or he will perish' (1973: 71). In Manet, as in Marx, as in Lucas – I am suggesting – it is otherwise. In appearing to prevail over earlier paintings, Manet's works effect intense bonds with them, expressed in content as much as form: by turns, love, desire, vengeance and violence, heroism and blood sacrifice. In his lengthy meditation on the *Execution* in all its variants, John Elderfield notes that 'subjects of violence had to have a special place in an art that both sought to destroy and itself tempted destruction' (2006: 47). When undertaken in such a spirit, our departures from things place them at our very heart, just as the outline of Titian and Goya is seen in a Manet. Anything else would be at odds with the Frenchman's adoration of Goya, or, for that matter of Velázquez – 'the painter Manet admired above all others', Rubin comments, and whose *Venus* is one of the sources of *Olympia* (Rubin 2010: 97).

The actress Matilde Díez intimated a liberation of subjectivity through voluntary domination by other people, places and times (see Chapter 1). Manet here offers us specific ways that out of experiences of domination among people, places and times, a vital, liberating energy might emerge. This is absolutely not to be confused with any celebration of violent oppression. I mean rather that, acknowledging force in its many directions around the globe, Manet's art of the mid-century offers an intimation: that the violence and cruelty might be transfigured utterly if love were retrieved amid dominance and submission and its attachments. If, as Fried argues, Manet splits art from the person beholding it, offering 'theatricality' in the face of 'absorption' (1996: 262–5), if – as Clay supposes – his works are possessed by a 'differentiating drive' (une impulsion différentielle) (1983: 9), such separations are not the end of the story. Rather, the gap is opened so that love may emerge.

Promiscuity and family resemblance

The experiences inherent in the gap may thus be opened wide across all history. The very term *modernité* evokes a fundamental and vast breach in our conceptions of time: that is what Baudelaire had in mind when he first used it in his celebrated essay 'The Painter of Modern Life' (Le peintre de la vie moderne) (1863). At one extreme, there exists a notion of the eternal: effectively akin to an atavistic communication with something divine, insofar as it is something beyond history, like Wood's account of the classic (Wood 2012). Baudelaire speaks of the eternal part of humanity. At the other extreme, there are the most ephemerally fascinating of things, the fashions of a moment, evoked with the speed of sketching. This is *modernité* itself (1965: II, 442, 452, 485). In the passage of history, Baudelaire suggests, the latter continually pulls far from the notion of the former, forever opening a divide. His art consists of experiencing such radical apartness, in and of itself, as a form of togetherness. It would be as if we attended to a spinning thaumatrope, and rather than seeing the bird in the cage, we saw the bird and cage as distinct, in their different place and time, and yet, even so, for that very reason, took them to be together. To borrow the evocative words of

Françoise Meltzer, the poet sees through 'double vision: one of the world as it was, and one as it is' (2011: 6). Rather than a fusion of the images as such, the perspective is 'rigorously dual' (2011: 239). In 'The Painter of Modern Life', Baudelaire explicitly rejects a notion of the absolute unity of beauty: rather, it is always a double composition – he says – but such that it creates one impression (1965: II, 441). Like others going back to Walter Benjamin, Meltzer writes evocatively of the changing France and Paris that appears in many parts of Baudelaire's writing. Faced with an accumulation of transformations, Baudelaire – she says – struggles, flailing to piece together the successive parts of time, faced as he was with 'the modern industrial city, the changing face of Paris, the upheaval in social classes, the aftershocks of the revolution, the rise of a bourgeoisie grounded in murder and committed to bienséance (as if decorum could disguise the bourgeoisie's guilt with respect to the urban working class), the still fresh memory of the guillotining of the king and his aristocratic retinue, the rise of poverty in the city' (2011: 239–40). Meltzer's phrasing may be applied, not only (as she often has it) to the passage of time in a changing world, but to the 'double vision' of things supremely atavistic – even before history – and of the fleetingly present. If later nations have beauties unknown to the ancients – he muses in the poem, 'J'aime le souvenir' (I love the recollection) – they still pay homage to the nude purity of an Edenic humanity (1972: 17–18).

A marked shift thereby occurs in the nature of connections that we perceive across time and place. For things to link intimately in this *modernité*, they would need to do so, not through direct relations of cause and effect, nor even through surface similarity, but through the aesthetic and sensual qualities of a given juxtaposition. It is this that Baudelaire calls 'harmony', 'the simultaneous sounding of several notes ... the sounding of two visions' (Meltzer 2011: 239). A person must possess aesthetic refinement to find a harmony in such contrasting extremes, a lingering on 'Correspondances': 'like long echoes that blend from far away', as Baudelaire describes them in the poem of that name (comme de longs échos qui de loin se confondent) (1972: 16). The Echo that takes the place of Narcissus as the source of poetry, the rhythm so important in blending humanity from del Campo to Whitman, accentuates the texture of its differences. It is in this way that we appreciate intimate interconnections – as perhaps Marx does with the 'double vision' of machine and Cyclops in *Capital I*. A wondrous straining across divergence is apparent: 'Franciscae Meae Laudes', present from the first edition in *Fleurs du mal* (1857), presents a woman dedicated to making fashionable dresses, a mid-century *modiste*, in a poem in a classical language, ancient Latin. Delighting in combining extremes, this sensibility involves a kind of 'débauche' as Baudelaire sometimes puts it (1972: 130–1): a 'kink' we might now say. Responding in insinuating terms to Manet's painting of the Spanish dancer, *Lola de Valence* (1862) – an encounter between the Hispanic and the French, an echo of Goya's *Duchess of Alba* – Baudelaire enjoys 'the unexpected charm of a pink and black gem' (le charme inattendu d'un bijou rose et noir) (1972: 247). In turn, the question of how to juxtapose such distinct colours is 'subsumed in the idea of comparison', Bernard Howells notes (2017: 191). It goes to the heart of how we might bring together very different things. The very clash of opposing forces across history, over the expanses of place and time, presents us with 'antagonism', which is 'a form of symmetry, therefore of harmony'. In Baudelaire's continually double vision, Howells notes, 'the only solution to the antinomies is aesthetic' (2017: 161, 159).

The upshot of this alternate historiography is aptly expressed in the distinction between 'family resemblance' and 'promiscuity' (aire de familia, promiscuidad), drawn by the Madrazo brothers – Pedro and Federico – scions of Spain's most powerful artistic dynasty with good connections in France. Their father, José de Madrazo, had recommended Lucas for his role at Court, and family members provided expert evidence in a case concerning the authenticity of some Goyas, now thought to be by the later artist (Ginger 2007a: 44, 55); Fortuny, whom we met in Chapter 1, married Cecilia de Madrazo, the daughter of Federico. In the 1872 catalogue of the Museum, we see the difference between 'promiscuity' and 'family resemblance' explained in relation to two areas of the Prado Museum at that time: those galleries dedicated to eight supposed major national schools (Madrazo 1872: xxii), and an oval room (the Room of Isabel II) where, in better lighting, those works considered the greatest masterpieces were hung irrespective of date or place of origin (1872: xix). The oval room had been so arranged since the Museum reopened in 1853 after reforms (Géal 2001: 143). In her history of the Prado, Eugenia Afinoguénova relates how the door to this 'sacrosanct' space, half-way through a walk along the galleries, was covered in curtains. It occupied a central position, connecting two floor levels, like an altar space, Afinoguénova remarks (2018: loc.3151, 3222). Together, the two approaches exhibit contrasting ways of organising place and time in the history of art, and by extension the histories of culture.

Without functioning in an identical fashion, family resemblance is akin to a logical set. To appreciate a grouping of images in such a way as to experience that 'similarity' (semejanza) entails a practice: that 'one disregards the secondary dissimilarities of the various families, so to speak … compared with one another, just as the classification by families omits the dissimilarities of individuals from one another' (se desentiende de las desemejanzas secundarias de las varias familias, por decirlo así, de cada nación, comparadas las unas con otras, como la clasificación de familias omite las desemejanzas de los individuos entre sí). That does not make these groupings any less there: it is, Federico de Madrazo says, just like when 'we say "John must be the son or brother of Peter, because they have a family resemblance"' (decimos: «Juan debe ser hijo o hermano de Pedro, porque tiene aire de familia con éste») (1872: xxv–xxvi). When Wittgenstein takes up the idea of *family resemblance* many decades later, he famously speaks of 'a complicated network of similarities overlapping and criss-crossing' (*PI* §66). We might find, say, four characteristics recurring, but not all members of the group would have all of them, and some might not share any of these features in common with one another. Wittgenstein seeks thereby to show how we see commonality across groups even where we cannot pin down a single characteristic shared by them all: he is giving us an account of one important kind of vagueness. We must turn away from continual subdivisions and analytical contrasts – 'this endless, motiveless dividing and subdividing' (este dividir y subdividir sin término ni motivo), as Federico de Madrazo put it (1872: xxv) – to behold the broad-brush picture. We must recognise that trying to find an example of things that form a family group without any differences and individualities would be 'endless'. So would any effort to justify why we have identified a group based on such an analysis. 'Explanation comes to an end somewhere', as Wittgenstein observes (*PI* §1). Like Nietzsche, Madrazo suggests it would be factitious to suppose that continual dissection through analysis will offer more of a guarantee of reaching a truth than would apprehending a reality in other ways.

There is at the same time a specific kind of erotics to histories drawn through family resemblances: Pedro de Madrazo assures us that the eight sections are set up with 'no mixing or promiscuity between one another' (sin mezcla o promiscuidad de unas con otras) (1872: xxii). Intercourse is only to take place here within the domestic sanctity sanctioned by the family unit: so far as practical, only there can our eyes linger upon the shifting of one painting into the next. Alongside this invocation of respectable domestic life, we find an evocation of a racist taboo on miscegenation (*mezcla*): (reproductive) sex between those of supposedly distinct 'races and descent' (razas y procedencias) (1872: xx–xxi). Yet out of the Prado protrudes the large '*oval room*, known before the Revolution [of 1868, which overthrew Isabel II] as the *room of Queen Isabel*' (*sala ovalada*, llamada antes de la Revolución *sala de la Reina Isabel*) (1872: xix; original emphasis). Here a very different sexual experience is on offer:

> That the *Oval Room* offers promiscuity itself must never occasion censure, not even were it possible to avoid this amalgam would it be right to destroy it, for it is expressly set out such that, as with a bouquet of select flowers, or in a treasure of unusual jewels, it delights the sight and aesthetic sense of the intelligent and studious individuals who come to contemplate and learn from the marvels of colour and light created by the palette of great painters.[1]

While the term *promiscuity*, in Spanish as in English, could simply mean a mixing together of disparate things, the insistent use of what Afinoguénova calls 'naturalising metaphor' in the Madrazo texts makes its sexual resonances fully apparent (2009: 328): this is a world of families, genealogies and races, out of which promiscuity erupts. The contrast made with the moralising term *censure* similarly reinforces the emphasis. (The phrasing is, perhaps unintentionally, even more suggestive in the light of the earlier name of the room, given that Isabel II was famous, and at times pilloried, for her own adventurous sexuality.) *Promiscuity*, Mosche Barasch notes, likewise appears in the French Goncourt brothers' description of the studio of the artist Coriolis in *Manette Salomon* (1867), in apparent celebration of the detachment of aesthetic vision from originating contexts (Barasch 1998: 22; Goncourt n.d.: loc.1890). In turn, it was in *Manette Salomon* that art historian Carol Armstrong found inspiration for her own book *Manet Manette*, with its 'wandering vision and multiple viewpoints', 'internal alterity: disrupting the boundaries between the native and the alien' and 'radically decentered image' of gender, race, time and nation (Armstrong 2002: 51, 58, 63).

The joy of this libertine sensuality is found not just in any individual work or artist or place or time – the 'flowers' or 'jewels' – but in our viewing them together: the 'bouquet' or 'treasure'. The delight is in the movements across the gaps between them, in our viewing the diverging patterns of the room, as if in some great abstraction through and from the images proffered to us, and, by extension, of art history. The viewer finds pleasure both in heterogeneous company, and in the way others – of 'diverse races and descent' – engage in intercourse with disparate others. In the flickering between highly diverse paintings, in the projections through and across them, we behold 'the marvels of colour and light'. In this way, we find in the whole what was found locally in a painting or part thereof: the harmony that arises through contrast and transition, 'considering colours, not now in isolation, but

---

[1] 'Que el *Salón ovalado* presente la misma promiscuidad, no deberá nunca censurarse, ni aunque pudiera evitarse esta amalgama, convendría destruirla, porque está expresamente dispuesta para que, como ramillete de selectas flores, o en tesoro de joyas peregrinas, recreen la vista y el sentido estético los inteligentes y los estudiosos que acuden a contemplar y a aprender en las maravillas de color y luz creadas por la paleta de los grandes pintores' (1872: xvi).

placed in relation with one another', as one Spanish treatise put it (considerados los colores, no ya aisladamente, sino puestos en relación unos con otros) (Milá y Fontanals 1857: 12–13). In the ovaloid's orgies, we might well encounter the 'unexpected charm of a pink and black jewel'.

The objectives of 'promiscuity' are overwhelmingly aesthetic: its outcomes can be assessed only in terms of the quality of the experience furnished, not primarily in terms of pseudological groupings. The question is what of value may be brought about through the interaction of those who have, on the face of it, little in common. This necessarily entails a commitment to and faith in qualitative judgements, centred on interplay and dialogue, as a fundamental part of our existence. To that extent, the Oval Room finds an echo in the late writings of Susan Sontag, and her assertion that another art form, literature – taken not as an individual work but as 'an accumulation' of such works 'that *matter*[*s*]' – exhibits 'promiscuity' (Sontag 2008: 149; emphasis added). Barbara Ching and Jennifer A. Wagner-Lawlor underline how such an 'erotics of art', involving 'motion and emotion', is shot through with a rejection of 'laziness' and an assertion of 'commitment' and 'seriousness' (Ching & Wagner-Lawlor 2009: 2–3). The room's libertinage is refined. Its promiscuity is enjoyed by being 'intelligent' and 'studious': that is disposed and alive to exploring carefully the patterns we might encounter and discover there. Irrespective of whether the judgements reached in setting up this particular room were actually correct, the disposition informing it is this: that the joy of such a place would depend upon a discriminating sense of value. Only certain works and particular arrangements of them can provide such a pleasurable orgy of colour and light: a load of flowers stuffed together does not a delightful bouquet make.

The vision – put at its most general – is of a panorama of cultural history in which divergences play off one another, not in just any way, but specifically so as to have a valuable, common creative force, a multitudinous 'harmony' that forms out of them. If the Madrazos' 'promiscuity' – their erotics of art and history – is an example of what Ken Plummer (2015) calls 'cosmopolitan sexualities', it ultimately points beyond either the shared institutional structures or common discourse of ethical principles to which cosmopolitans might habitually turn. Likewise, in Whitman – Jason Frank avers – the response to a critical moment in the United States is to look beyond institutions and laws and towards the potential inherent in a broader lived experience. In the 'promiscuous citizenship' and 'aesthetic democracy' of Whitman's 'Me myself', 'the fact that we remain strangers is not something to be overcome, but rather the very condition of our affective bond … the basis of erotic attachment' (2011: 155–6, 171). In poetry's casual cruising from one affection to another, fluidly from encounters between men to those with women, many find evoked the street life of a burgeoning mid-century metropolis, New York City: Manhattan's 'city of orgies', in Whitman's words from 'Calamus' (Whitman 1995: 117; Bellis 2003: 90; Frank 2011: 165). Such opportunities proliferate far beyond across the many states, in the vast open ground as much as in the urban conurbations, inland on the plains of California or by a tree in Louisiana, reaching out through this, further than this, into the promise held by other peoples in other lands, and to future times (1995: 114, 118–19, 121). The promiscuity is 'intelligent', 'studious', 'serious', discerning, precisely in the textures, the complexities and nuances of the erotic experience. It offers no simple utopia, homoerotic or otherwise, any more than the 'blend' (mixture) of *Fausto* eliminates all irony in its encounter between men, across cultures. Vivian R. Pollak cautions against conflating erotic visions with real experiences on the streets or elsewhere (2000: xxii). After all, were we now 'Me myself', we would not need to 'get' it, to learn to 'go on'. Readers in the wake of Michael Moon (1991) have worked through the psychosexual uncertainty, fear and loss in Whitman's work. Even in such successful encounters as we find in 'Calamus', there may be isolation from the collective, a need in practice for privacy, secrecy even (Bellis 2003: 115). In opening up to a stranger, Whitman intends 'to begin with a warning, I am surely different from what you suppose' (1995: 115).

Likewise the Madrazos do not invoke what Paul Gilroy aptly derides as 'banal invocations of hybridity in which everything becomes equally and continuously intermixed, blended into an impossibly even consistency' (Gilroy 2000: 275). Rather, attention turns to discerning appreciation itself, a discriminating capacity to enjoy the flickerings of history's patterns through divergences. The term *promiscuity* has a very specific resonance in the Madrazos' writing, loosely evoked in the catalogue of the Prado. It arises from the Spanish Monarchy's openness to 'all nations' (todas naciones), as Pedro de Madrazo puts it in an earlier catalogue (1854: v). Quite unlike in the English-speaking empires, the Spanish monarchy in Europe as in the Americas was notable for the degree of sexual mixing among people of 'races' and ethnicities, for *mestizaje*. While the circumstances of this were far from always savoury, the creative potential latent in its sexualised legacy has been a contested source of aspirations subsequently. We find these sentiments continuing through the Mexican thinker José Vasconcelos and his prophecy of a Cosmic Race in 1925 (Vasconcelos 1967), to the latter part of the twentieth century in the queer writings of Chicana Gloria E. Anzaldúa (2012) and her invocation of *Borderlands/La Frontera*.

Exile and dilation

As such qualitative factors come to the fore, the distinction between Cavell's 'exile' and 'being at home' collapses; or, at least, it putatively vanishes if and when good taste and refinement are displayed in the harmonies that we identify. Time is a constantly fleeing exile – in the etymological sense of *ex-ire*, to go away or forth – dashing from fashion to fashion, from masterpiece to masterpiece, from sensation to sensation, from affection to affection. That moving away – leaping beyond – is what we bring ourselves nearer to when we attend to harmonious disparity. It is where we find a way to accept our being in time, in history's lavish multitude of voices and images, of forms of experience. Our capacity to experience departure and nearness, exile and home aesthetically is vividly seen in the British artist Ford Madox Brown's famous painting *Last of England* (1864–66). In a circular image, as if through a telescope, we perceive a couple, economic migrants, set on their boat for Australia: 'Thrust away!' as the accompanying poem had it. European colonisation, expanding to the further reaches of the world, reverberates with the precarious realities of society back home, with which it is intertwined, and with all that is left behind, As the couple move far from the putative viewer, back in England, they loom into close-up, visages pressed towards us in the cramped image, as if approaching.

The very sensation of constant exile, of never-ending departure, crystallised in Baudelaire's *modernité*, may itself be experienced as ancient and atavistic, as well as perpetual and recurrent. 'There has been a modernity for every ancient/earlier painter', Baudelaire tells us in *The Painter of Modern Life* (Il y a eu une modernité pour chaque peintre ancien) (1965: II, 452). Writing over a century and a half later, in her *Planetary Modernisms*, Susan Stanford Friedman speaks likewise of *modernity*, not as a specific historical period in the 'West', but as 'the condition or sensibility of radical disruption and accelerating change wherever and whenever such a phenomenon appears' (2015: 33). Seen this way, every leap from the old to the new becomes, in and of itself, an expression of the former: it is antique. Atavism thus pervades all time and place. It is manifest even in any departure from itself. In *Les Fleurs du mal*, Baudelaire's exploration of *mal* – his bouquet made of the 'flowers of ill/evil' – is an expression of all this. It is inherent in his evocation of an ancient, biblical Fall. Elissa Marder puts it well: 'this "Fall" – although irrevocable – is not something that happened "once" and "only once," but something that keeps happening in every lived moment. Thus, one meaning of the "Fall" in Baudelaire is the fall into the present moment' (2001: 22). By that very token, every present moment is the ancient Fall.

In an article published in 1998 – 'Baudelaire's Satanic Verses' – Jonathan Culler made an incisive, and too rarely answered, observation. 'There are many competing accounts of what is most particularly modern and important about Baudelaire,' Culler notes, 'but the one thing on which contentious critics seem to agree is that there is a side of Baudelaire that is of no interest today … and is the very antithesis of Baudelaire's modernity, of Baudelaire the founder of modern poetry: this is the Baudelaire who invokes demons and the Devil. Most critics today pass over this in silence, but even those who explicitly address this Baudelaire seem to find him an embarrassment' (1998: 86). To take this matter seriously is more than to treat such things as mere 'personification', Culler observes (1998: 99). It is more than to subsume them within prevailing theories of the 'modern'. It is to note their apparent literalness ('we must have recourse to the mist-enveloped regions of the religious world', 'the other night, I saw the Devil.'). Exile – *ex-ire*, the going out, the departing, the leaping beyond – is Satan's business, and each iteration of it brings Him back, brings this Ancient 'home'. Banished from Heaven, he is the very 'Prince of exile' (Prince de l'exil), as Baudelaire declares in 'Litanies of Satan' (1972: 148). Atavistic *mal* and its exile drives us, surging out of the depths of time: 'it is the Devil who holds the strings that move us' (C'est le Diable que tient les fils qui nous remuent), we are told at the outset of *Les Fleurs* (1972: 6). Baudelaire's verse collection correspondingly pullulates with antique, often supernatural forces. Our brains are peopled with daemons (1972: 12). Satan, God, Heaven and Hell recurrently appear. There are classical gods and demigods, and Muses, angels and vampires. Beasts resonant with ancient lore, folkloric power, watch or prowl: sphinxes, cats, owls, serpents. The poet brings forth legendary figures and artists of other ages: sorcerers, Leonardo de Vinci, Don Juan.

History thus becomes a continual dilation of *mal* and its atavism. As is true too of 'Me myself', we cannot really speak here of a reception or reinterpretation of the term, for it is already there to be found in every movement from every place to every time. It is not as if it were thought of in one location and reworked in another, or that we could speak of its belonging to one context, for it is itself the endless crossing through time and place. That is what exile is. We behold the term's inherent, expansive accretion of possibilities. The very elasticity of a word like *mal* is inherent to its use, to our capacity to 'go on' with it. *Mal* can evoke anything from murder (1972: 157) to looking at a cat and being reminded of the beloved (1972: 51), from engaging in Satanic rites (1972: 148), to drinking alcohol on one's own (1972: 160). To 'get' this we must experience a recognition (*anagnorisis*): a taking stock of the sensations we may have through the passage of history, through the juxtaposition of departures, harmonic contrasts. We either think it is that way, or we do not, but there is no rational or empirical kernel here on the basis of which such things may be determined. We would need to assume as our realities Satan, the sorcerers, the Muses, the cats, even as

Nietzsche must apprehend Apollo and Dionysus, and the political economists must look away from their intricate arguments to behold the living gods of *Capital*. ('Look', said the hypnotist, 'you will see.')

There is a temptation to conflate such an experience of 'harmony' with notions of unity belonging to quite a different 'picture' of the world. It precisely does not involve imagining *unity* – in opposition to *irony* or *crisis* – as some cognitive resolution, intellectual reconciliation, identity of meaning, or – in any of those senses – transcendence. It is not – as we have seen – even a question of similarity and thence analogy as such, at least not as is habitually understood. If we try to conceive of 'harmony' through those pictures, we will rapidly find ourselves confronting dilemmas that its own picture (right or wrong) does not suppose. If our very consciousness of each present moment causes us to depart from that very presentness (Marder 2001: 21), if, as Paul de Man (1979) famously supposes, each representation of an instance defers us from its presence, if Baudelaire were indeed to cultivate 'the self-reflexivity of irony', as Sanyal concludes (2006: 36), none of that resolves whether or not we are at 'home' in 'exile'. It is only by supposing that the question should be set in such terms that we could end up in the kinds of debate that we find, for example, between Meltzer and Poulet, or Hiddleston and Hannoosh – whether the 'eternal situation' of the Fall means we live in a 'huge space of undifferentiated time' or rather in 'temporal parataxis' (Poulet 1980: 9; Meltzer 2011: 234), whether one must choose between the disruptive force of endless ironies or accepting these and 'having one's cake and eating it' (Hiddleston 2011: 133). It is likewise only in such terms that we might worry – as Walter Benjamin did – whether Baudelaire's notion of *correspondances* was 'crisis proof', that is, resistant to any real rupture in time (1997: 140). Instead, the question, within the 'picture' of 'mal', is whether departures can be experienced and appreciated, in the debauchery and extremity of their contrasts even, as harmonic, and thus each departure taken as a coming home, as 'long echoes that blend from far away'.

In his essay, 'Rewriting Modernity', the French philosopher Jean-François Lyotard remarks that 'the aesthetic grasp of forms is only possible if one gives up all pretension to master time through a conceptual synthesis' (1991: 32). Our experience of history here is 'beyond interpretation', in Sontag's notorious words, because the question of clear meaning as such (for or against) has been parked. As with 'Me myself', so with *mal*, there can be no theory of such a thing, no guiding framework, no 'grasping' or 'clutching' at the world in reducing it to anything of that sort, but rather the 'power of passiveness' that enables appreciation. Jonathan Culler dwells on words from Baudelaire's diary: 'To give oneself to the Devil, what is that?' 'It seems likely that Baudelaire himself did not have an answer', Culler muses (1998: 89). I would add that to answer the question would be to miss the point, because it would confine what *mal* is, and prevent us 'going on'. 'A system', Baudelaire remarks in his review of the 1855 Universal Exhibition, 'is a kind of damnation that drives us into perpetual abjuration' (un système est une espèce de damnation qui nos pousse à une abjuration perpétuelle) (1965: I, 188). We would need rather to attend to *mal*, to perennial *modernité* and its antiquity, the 'shadowy, deep unity' (ténébreuse et profonde unité) (1972: 16), and not turn from it to deflections. In eroticised acknowledgement of our ephemeral, mortal being, our endless exile – Lisa Downing avers – Baudelaire evokes an 'equivalence' of our 'life and death'. The upshot is a necrophiliac longing, all-pervasive, breaching limits of any bounded mortal life, overcoming otherness (2003: 73, 77, 88–9). In the final poem of the first edition, 'The Death of the Artists' (La mort des artistes), the poet aptly warns us:

Departure: to leap beyond yet nearer bring

'We will wear out our soul in subtle plots / … Before we contemplate the great Creature / Whose infernal desire fills us with sobs!' (Nous userons notre âme en subtils complots / … Avant de contempler la grande Créature / Dont l'infernal désir nous remplit de sanglots!) (1972: 165). Such is mortality, the persistent guarantor of impermanence, endless antique voyager through history and geography.

Bubbles

Promiscuity is not, even so, the simple opposite of family resemblance – or, at least, it need not be. On a simple level, wherever we perceive *mal*, for example, we must see similarity: the poet of *Les fleurs* calls out in the prelude to 'my likeness' (mon semblable) (1972: 7). More subtly, promiscuity may depend upon or extend from family resemblance. This is apparent in the Madrazos' account of the Prado Museum. Commonalities are exhibited in the arrangement of the paintings and the building: 'there are in the Prado Museum, eight separate localities for the different cardinal or fundamental schools', we are told (hay en el Museo del Prado ocho localidades separadas para las diferentes escuelas cardinales o fundamentales) (1872: xxii). To view the collection this way is to experience every painting in any 'family' section as a kind of free copy of every other image exhibited there, as a flicker involving every other, as having the potential to be carried on into the other. Out of each 'complicated network of similarities overlapping and criss-crossing' comes the further *semejanza* of their all being *schools*: a commonality exhibited in the pattern of eight like spaces. Finally, travelling through the creative interplay of the schools' divergences, we come in the Oval Room to *promiscuity* as an alternative cosmopolitanism.

These various levels do not exclude one another, but rather lead back and forth through each other: the Prado is 'of the centripetal and centrifugal gang', as Whitman put it. The path of 'family resemblance' is that of 'poverty', to borrow once more Cavell's words. We purge ourselves of entangling thoughts about what groups might look like: that they either have a single element in common, or that they absolutely do not derive from others. In this way, we are able to come back 'home' to experience clearly the shape of 'schools'. The path of 'promiscuity' is that of 'lavishness', in which we find ourselves at 'home' through an experience of harmony thrown up by creative divergences, through a breaking out of family groupings. Yet, 'poverty' provides the grounds for 'lavishness', for it gives us the elements that we juxtapose, like the black and pink of Lola de Valence's gem. Together 'poverty' (seen in membership of a school) and 'lavishness' (the rampant cutting across such membership) give us the effect apparent in the promiscuous room: lavishness is a flickering across and out of poverties. There is a pulsation in the Prado, evoking a twin sexual opening and restraint – promiscuity, family – in both of which we may find good companions of differing kinds.

The extending structure of the building, and its internal design, give us a shape wrought out of a history – the mid-nineteenth century, on the Paseo del Prado – that even so contains a vision opening beyond chronology and location. The structure has something of the heterotopia, as envisaged by Foucault (1986): it is at once a real place, and yet beyond the bounds of location, overcoming such limits. In the oval, it is as if place and time themselves form a bubble emerging from the building within which they themselves are transcended without closing off the exits back into their own confines. In his *Salut au monde!* (1856), Whitman likewise exclaims: 'Within me latitude widens, longitude lengthens' (1995: 126).

In such a bubble, our local home has a passage out into cosmopolitan desire and back again, whether that be in the Prado or in Whitman's dream of America's potentiality, his vision of what emerges from its streets, its expanses, its multiple States, its alternate 'manifest destiny' (Manning 2002: 229), 'embracing carrying welcoming all', as he affirms in his later 'Song of the Universal' (1874/1881) (1995: 210). A bubble forever leaps beyond and nearer brings. Just as we head out, so we return. To walk around the Oval Room is always to end up back in the corridors of the Prado; and the latter may always lead us to the Oval Room. Our 'going on' through passages beyond particular places and times, whether through slippage or family resemblance, whether through gaps or promiscuity, does not obviate the specificities of time and place, but rather works through them. This is the only way that such a bubble – or any like formation – could be formed, or that history could bring its own depths out of itself. Such effects depend on what the ethnologist Anna Tsing calls *friction*. There are phenomena, Tsing remarks, each of which 'spreads through aspirations to fulfil universal dreams and schemes', with 'a particular kind of universality: It can only be charged and enacted in the sticky materiality of practical encounters'. 'This practical, engaged universality', Tsing remarks, acts 'as guide to the yearnings and nightmares' of history (2005: 1). 'Not a claim to explain everything in the world at once' (2005: ix), it is fundamentally a way of continuing, of opening out to other times and places, like Whitman's piles of metonyms, or Baudelaire's flashes of anecdote, or the multiplying images of Lucas's paintings. The accreting layers of history themselves may be thought of this way: in Jules Verne's *Journey to the Centre of the Earth* (1864) (*Voyage au centre de la Terre*), the globe itself contains its own galleries of prehistoric pasts, all coexisting, the legacy of centuries with their wonders and hazards, which the modern-day travellers traverse, only to pop out once more into present-day Europe.

The Prado – shaped out of historical accidents and legacies – is a case in point. The promiscuous gallery came into being not least because the curators had inherited a building they found inadequate. The edifice, first designed by the celebrated architect Juan de Villanueva in the late eighteenth century, was originally intended to host the Cabinet of Natural History, but was then deployed to house the royal art collection. Among the challenges was that 'unfortunately the grandiose building of the Prado Museum, despite the nobility of its external lines and the capacity and majestic proportions of its inside sections ... in most of its rooms lacks the direct light from above that so suits works of painting' (desgraciadamente el grandioso edificio del Museo del Prado, a pesar de la nobleza de sus líneas exteriores y de la capacidad y majestuosas proporciones de sus partes internas ... carece en la mayor parte de sus salones, de la luz cenital, tan conveniente a las obras de pintura) (1872: xv). It was on those grounds – the 1872 catalogue claims – that the curators compromised, putting what they saw as masterpieces in the Oval Room with its overhead lighting, and then distributing the rest in surrounding schools, giving us that flowing in and out of 'families'.

The inherited collection likewise presented obstacles and opportunities in tracing the commonalities and promiscuities of cultural history. On the one hand, Pedro de Madrazo lamented that 'the nature of this Museum ... is not the most favourable for putting together the living history of the art of painting, for there is nothing in it, good or bad, before the fifteenth century' (la índole de este Museo, por otra parte, no es la más favorable para formar la historia viva del arte de la pintura, porque nada hay en él, bueno ni malo, anterior al siglo XV) (1872: xiii). Pierre Géal has shown how visitors not infrequently went further in criticising the lack of breadth of the collections, compared to the Louvre or London's National Gallery (2001: 145–6). On the other hand, as noted in the earlier 1854 catalogue, the country's rulers were 'guided by the generous idea that the cult of the beautiful is not subject to the mean limitation of soils and climates, nor to an exclusive nationalism at odds with the propagation of enlightenment' (guiados por la generosa idea de que el culto de lo bello no está sujeto a la mezquina limitación de suelos y climas, ni a un nacionalismo esclusivo y contrario a la propagación de las luces) (1854: v). On this account, what is most distinctively, historically 'Spanish' is the rejection of confined understandings of context, and, conversely, what enables 'Spanish' culture to come into being is a transmutation of this art beyond frontiers, what Federico de Madrazo later called a transfiguration of other legacies (1872: xxxv).

We find in the Prado, then, those key characteristics of Tsing's 'friction': something partial, something made out of concrete conditions, but something also, and if only in principle, opening out from the local into the universal. There is a reminiscence in the Madrazos' words of the old, contested aspiration that the Spanish domains might have formed the basis of a Universal Monarchy, a global moral and cultural order, putatively open to 'all nations' (see Pagden 1995: 31–112). With much of this territory, and more still that tarnished dream now lost, Madrazo extracts from it the 'generous idea' that finds its shape in the Prado's buildings and displays, made from the material relic that is the royal collection. Likewise, Lucas's artworks trace their slippage through the art of Spain into that of the Low Countries, which had rebelled against the old Monarchy, or that of France, the long-term European and Atlantic rival and occasional ally, and back through these into Spain. His images, after all, trace routes back and forth through the centuries of Spain's changing achievements and aspirations, through its artists but also its landmark events. The 'sticky materiality' of such connections is made vividly apparent in the thick oils of many of his works, such as his extrapolations from Goya, as he teases through the friction of his paint and canvas between what a Goya was and what it might be, working pathways through the impasto. The paintings run from the spectacle of the aspiring and failing 'Lords of All the World' in *The Court of Felipe IV* through to the bloodied, atrocity-filled efforts to rescue the grand Monarchy from French invasion in 1808 in the garish near-grotesque impasto of his scenes from the War of Independence (1808–14).

The structure of the Prado itself, with its eight core sections for its 'families', moves back and forth, pulsates in two historical directions, each passing through the other: the overarching 'generous idea' and the 'nations'. Graphically experienced in this pulsation are (in broad-brush terms) the tension and aspiration apparent from the outset of the unified Spanish monarchy in the fifteenth century. We find both the awareness, in Pagden's words, that 'the 'world' was now composed of a multiplicity of cultures and of independent states' (1995: 38), and the belief of Golden Age philosophers such as Francisco Suárez (1548–1617) in 'humanity ... as a political and moral community', as Headley summarises it (2008: 107).

Beholding sameness, beholding the gap: degrees of a disposition

To experience how divergence may entail an intimate connection, we have attended to the gap that opens up when one thing leaps beyond another. Both 'family resemblance' and 'promiscuity' foreground a relationship of separation from and convergence with others. In the final section of this chapter, I step back to consider three degrees of separation in which a disposition to find commonality might arise. In the first – the most apparent degree of sameness – something departs from itself so as once more to be itself. In the second – in a greater departure – two entities that appear very similar, but are distinct, are juxtaposed closely, to the point of blending, of *mixtura*, as del Campo might have it. In the third, the departure from one thing to another is very clear, but they echo and resemble one another. Each of these degrees permits of its own erotics, from self-stimulation, to desire for sameness with another, to longing laced with division. We will explore, in turn, the possibilities afforded by a series of visual images: Prilidiano Pueyrredón's *Siesta* (1865; Plate 5) from Buenos Aires in which we see a doubled, eroticised image of a single woman, then from France, Gustave Courbet's *The Wrestlers* (1852–53; Plate 6) and *Sleep* (1866), and finally Rosa Bonheur's *Spanish Muleteers Crossing the Pyrenees* (1857; Plate 7) and *The Horse Fair* (1852–55).

To dwell so directly on the very disposition towards 'departure' is to bring into view a dilemma implicit in much of this chapter so far, and with it, fundamental criticisms of mid-century 'Western' culture. On the one hand, sameness through departure, like 'Me myself', offers a way beyond a constraining contextualisation that carves up place and time into locations or outlooks. In Pueyrredón's *Siesta*, one nude image of his housekeeper (known as 'La Mulata' (Hanway 2003: 21)) is not an utterly, unbreachably distinct entity from her double in a different position, and this suggests that sameness through departure is possible. We have seen this claim made through variants across this present chapter. On the other hand, the imagery we see – for example in *Siesta* – may seem, of itself, clearly constrained to a specific worldview and its limiting assumptions. The painting was almost certainly destined for titillating private viewing by male members of the social elite who were sexually attracted to women, Hanway has noted. Pueyrredón was a scion of one of the most powerful families in the founding of independent states on the River Plate. Such a painting effected 'homosocial bonds ... around and against the eroticised bodies of women', and 'a private space of erotic knowledge about the female body, which is possessed by public men' (2003: 21, 23, 43). Furthermore, Pueyrredón appears to exercise race- and class-based power, using his *mestiza* servant as a model to purvey sexual pleasure. The work may reasonably be said to imply both what Griselda Pollock (2018) calls 'a masculine viewer/consumer' and 'the normalcy of that position'.

It has this in common with other sexualised depictions of nineteenth-century females, and with the contested claims made on the behalf of such works to a revolutionary departure in the arts, a 'modernity'. Writing of Courbet's *Sleep* – to which we will turn shortly – Linda Nochlin doubts there is any so fundamental difference between supposedly conventional and non-conventional art, when both perpetuate the assumption that the female body is 'opened to and designed for the pleasure of the desiring male gaze' (1988: 34). Olympia's very assertiveness and her muscular, presumably low-class body are hardly inconsistent with such constraints, her dominating stance conceived primarily to please a male with such tastes. Nochlin has suggested something similar of Courbet's images of working women (1988: 33). Throughout *Les Fleurs du mal*, we encounter examples of Baudelaire's misogyny: starkly, in 'Sonnet d'Automne', he tells the woman to be charming and shut up (1972: 200). In Elissa Marder's words, the poet fears 'the painful knowledge that is communicated through ... feminine apertures' (2001: 19). For all the celebrations of Whitman's sexual and democratic fluidity, his 'understanding of the emotional, educational, political, and legal needs of nineteenth-century American women was self-interested and incomplete', Vivian R. Pollak notes (2000: xix). Like many 'white' people of his time, he was quite capable of infusing his writing with discriminatory sentiments towards other 'races' (2000: 177). His open-armed greetings to the world may be juxtaposed with his one-time support for the invasion of Mexico, and – in *Song of Myself* – the stark portrayal of Mexicans as brutal oppressors and murderers of rebel Texans, as if underlining the exclusion the Hispanic from the creation of a free modern world (1995: 64–5). Following the earlier independence of Texas (1836), in events of 1845–48, the United States took possession of the state and other lands north of the Río Grande. In his poems, Baudelaire's women of African descent, from territories once or still in the French empire – like the one-time object of his affection, the Haitian Jeanne Duval – are obsessively exoticised as an appropriately perilous attraction for decadent, refined male pleasures: bizarre, demonic, prone to witchery, a drug more alluring than opium in 'Sed Non Satiata', for example (1972: 39–40). In a study of the notion of a 'Black Venus', T. Denean Sharpley-Whiting explores how Baudelaire treats it is an equal and fair transaction if a Caucasian European male can get pleasure in this way, because the women concerned are thus privileged to obtain the honour of some fraction of their whiteness (1999: 70). In turn, Afinoguénova (2018) observes, the Madrazos' vision of the normality of 'family resemblance' serves a conservative ideology of Spanish national unity and a rejection of decentralisation. In celebrating the Prado's rejection of exclusive nationalism, Pedro Madrazo was seeking to exalt the traditions of the Spanish monarchy (2018: loc.3169). The insistence on aesthetic discernment may well resonate with the often elitist attitudes that the family adopted towards the museum's function and its visitors (2018: loc.3419). In its implicit erotics, the catalogue of the Prado suggests too an exclusionary vision of what a proper family is, notably with its overt rejection of so-called miscegenation.

The question posed by 'departure' is not as such whether such constraints exist, as they all too evidently and deplorably do. The issue often at stake in critical debate is whether the latter are such that nothing of note reaches from texts and images out of such limitations, whether those texts and images can, as result, effect no intimate connection with other places or time, with us here and now. If we appreciate their appeal to sameness in the terms set out here, we might experience their confines undoing themselves, as it were. That is to say, whatever the relationship between their vision of similitude and any given ideological constraint, whatever the political and gendered origins of their evocations of likeness, their invocation of sameness through departure must imply a potential movement out of such confines. This is so even as the latter are acknowledged, even as they constitute one of the multitude of ventriloquial voices. Put another way, in noting their ideological specificities, we may appreciate these works both in and out of the game. Otherwise – on this account at least, – they – and everything else – must only be what they are (or are said to be) in their originary place and time. These texts' and images' offerings of experiences of sameness are both, and at once, a general denial of narrow contextualisation, and a specific route out of their own constraints. It is in this way that they might – perhaps in spite of themselves – become 'dynamic moments', to borrow once more the words of the media theorist Siegfried Zielinski: they open up possibilities to other places and times. To be able to live their form of sameness is to be able to 'go on' with it, in Wittgenstein's phrase, employing it out of their own specific utterances and images even. I have said *out of* rather than *beyond* their specifics, because this would not simply involve discarding, as if it were a husk, the historical particularity of their vision, so as to keep only a remaining nugget of goodness. We would still be recognising the oppressions wrought within them, and, much more broadly, the reality that these are voices and images that are truly other than our own. The past would not be subject solely to our own terms. In this uncomfortable, uneasy perspective, we depart from these past voices as we are ventriloquising them.

Within debates that take this form, above and beyond any divergences in empirical evidence and its analysis, it is a disposition that separates those who, on the one hand, emphasise an ideological constraint in the mid-century as an ultimate limitation, and, on the other, those who have highlighted complexities and ambiguities that might in some way exceed such confines. The latter vision has been apparent in some innovative studies on this period during the past two decades. In her *Victorian Babylon*, for example, Lynda Nead baulks at the stark judgements of feminist historians of a different ilk. She denies that 'women were necessarily passive victims of a voracious male gaze', pointing instead to 'women who looked at and returned the gazes of passers-by' (2000: 71). In *Between Women*, Sharon Marcus considers fashion illustrations of the time, claiming that 'these disprove the still influential claims that men look and women are looked at', and that 'they activate a female pleasure in looking at women' (2007: 135). Two decades earlier than Marcus, in response to Nochlin, Fried argued that 'Courbet's paintings of the nude can fully be understood only in relation to a larger project in which beholding as such is repeatedly and ambitiously called into question' (1988: 51). In a subtle essay, Cliff Hudder (2012) has suggested how the splattering of blood on the Mexicans in Whitman's depiction, in *Song of Myself*, of the Goliad Massacre in Texas (1836) might imply a potential for blurrings of the divides, and a growing intimation of the complexities of the wars with Mexico – and, by extension, a respect towards the Hispanic Americas.

All this is very well. Yet I am not persuaded that there is anything in all this that could actually convince someone who says: 'In the end, in the final analysis, the imperial, white, male, elite gaze and its interests were overwhelmingly powerful. Whatever happened, happened within the framework of this dominance.' On the one hand, there are those who are disposed to look to the existence of such frameworks, to see the past as suffering all too apparently from their confines, on the other, are those like Marcus who seek, delicately and with care, a contact with the nuances of history. It is in such a spirit that Marcus trawls through a wide body of Victorian evidence to find 'the most surprising commonality … between Victorian society and our own: in the past, as in the present, marriage and family, gender and sexuality, are far more intricate, mobile, and malleable than we imagine them to be' (2007: 262). My approach in this book is pedagogical not didactic, and I am considering the disposition towards departure as sameness in that spirit, rather than in an effort to resolve the matter definitively. As I step back here to consider three degrees of separation, I am interested in the dilemma over historical constraints because it illuminates what is involved in following dispositions of that kind, in seeking to 'go on' with them. By the same token, I am interested in acknowledging, before setting out, what is set aside, rightly or wrongly, in such an endeavour.

Taken as a departure into sameness, Pueyrredón's *Siesta* addresses the challenge of how to depict the commonality of something with itself. If difference is too marked, the immediate impression of identity would be under threat. Yet without a departure from one thing to another, we cannot dwell on how they are alike. By showing one person twice, this artistic and perceptual tightrope may be walked: it could not be addressed so directly even by offering us a doppelgänger or copy, for, however alike these are, they are not actually the same body. In the image, there is one woman upon a bed, to the viewer's left on her back masturbating, to the viewer's right, rolled over and sleeping. In her luxuriation, the person, having moved from one position to another, most visibly resembles herself. As we saw in the introduction to this chapter, in testing our notions of self-likeness, the ancient philosopher Heraclitus famously wondered if a flowing river – or, by extension, any changing thing or person – is ever the same as itself. The question may be related in turn to Zeno's paradoxes: if the movement of the water is split into atomised moments, how can the single moving entity be there? Conversely, if we were to take the gambit and perspective offered by this chapter, we might assert that only where there is departure is sameness experienced. Only by moving into (at least) two differing positions, could La Mulata be herself. This is not what Connor calls 'disabling self-splitting', nor is it an affirmation of continual deferral of identity, the impossible presence of a person to themselves. Rather, in this 'picture' of the world, the very departure of a self from itself is where we encounter and bring into view intimate self-sameness in its own right.

Pueyrredón's skill involves keeping the doubled figure within one location: the scene depicted in the painting. Even portraying the body in two different places would attenuate the intensity of the sameness. The art consists in keeping the images of La Mulata apart, while maintaining an unchanged backdrop, and not to merge them in our vision as the mechanical stereotype does. Only certain circumstances could permit such a vision, like an afternoon's rest, when a body rolls over: not so much time elapses that the location changes, and the movement of the human body ensures that neither one of La Mulata occupies the space of the other. It is as if Pueyrredón has found in our normal sight of the world, and in the habitual depiction of a two-dimensional scene in oils, a way to see time on a single plane, such that before and after rest together, are no longer before and after, just aspects of time, without disturbing the physical order of the scene. Through such artistry, a 'bubble' can be formed with its own heterotopia: a specific location (a room in mid-century Buenos Aires) extends out beyond chronology, enabling us to see La Mulata's sameness to herself, without ceasing to be that unchanging location. The very properties of ordinary space and time provide the means on which the artist may draw to trace this form, just as (we have seen) history may bring its own depths out of itself.

By evoking female masturbation as the very image of self-sameness, Pueyrredón draws on some historic assumptions and prejudices about women and their solitary pleasures. In an essay entitled, 'Playing with Herself', Kelly Dennis recalls how artistic images of self-pleasuring, self-absorbed women often assumed that 'lacking masculine self-difference woman ... cannot pose her own ontological question'. Unlike the penis, female genitals touched themselves, it was supposed (1995: 66). Out of this questionable notion, and its historical 'friction', *La Siesta* invokes the fundamental possibility of sameness in a larger sense, implying that any moment in time and place may not be confined to itself – and, by extension, that the image of La Mulata is not constrained to the terms of its origins. That image of sameness itself becomes the way to channel a whole range of connections across place and time: free copies, flickers, allusions. It affirms not merely their similitude, but the experience of sameness found as they come to accompany one another. In the *Siesta*, the masturbatory woman and red drapes echo with Titian's *Venus d'Urbino* once more; the nude from behind and the blue sheets with Velázquez's own Venus and Ingres's *Grand Odalisque* (1814); and all of these with each other. The single finger pointing down slyly recalls (again) Goya's portrait of the Duchess of Alba. Through the doubled woman, the Spanish School, the culture of Buenos Aires's founder imperial power, has a pathway back and forth to the Italian Renaissance which it had 'transfigured' (as Madrazo was to put it) over time from its own high point of global glory (Titian and Velázquez) to the moment of its impending decline (Goya). It reaches out to the rival empire (Napoleonic France and Ingres) that would seal the Spanish Monarchy's fate, indirectly freeing Buenos Aires. The evocation of Venus takes us to ancient Rome, of Odalisques to its Islamic successor in the east, the Ottoman Empire. The *Siesta* thus shares a longing to revisit global interconnections through, across and beyond the Americas, their origins and aftermath, with Manet, Marx, Whitman. It parallels Lucas and Pedro Madrazo's gazing through the remnants of the Universal Monarchy. And all these possibilities echo with the battle over Argentina's likeness to and departure from 'civilised' Europe. The very image of the woman presents us with the lower-class offspring of American 'miscegenation', and ultimately of the Atlantic slave trade, luxuriating in the apartments of an established creole family, descendants of one of the founding patriarchs of Latin American independence: Juan Martín de Pueyrredón, Supreme Director of the United Provinces of the River Plate (Hanway 2003: 47, 49). The act of masturbation itself might imply a stark contrast with a Europeanised nation on the model of France: Vernon A. Rosario II has observed how, in that latter country, self-pleasuring was considered a threat to 'the health of the state' (1995: 121). In his monumental history of solitary sex, Thomas Laqueur underlines how its self-obsession could be understood in nineteenth-century Europe as a menace to social order, such that 'the onanist thus becomes the alter ego, the nasty bad brother or sister, of the modern self' (2003: 357). But here sameness is suggested even in the apparent threat to collectivity, as if the image sought to move beyond a dualism. Hanway notes that, by association with European traditions of erotic nudes which in Argentine were still widely considered beyond the pale of the civilised elite, Pueyrredón confounded (European) civilisation and supposedly threatening barbarism within the relatively new American state (2003: 45).

The painting intimates that all these many likenesses may be subsumed into the experience of intense sameness: in La Mulata's doubled body itself. In the 'lavishness' of all these possible ways of being, there is something not far removed from 'poverty', for we centre in on sameness in and of itself as a 'form of life', not allowing ourselves to be distracted from what it involves. We experience a multitude of similarities only insofar as they are integral to what 'resemblance', as a form of life, involves. The interest lies not primarily in what it means for one thing to be the same as another: that is, the intellectual content of the notion or what the term might signify. Rather, as with *promiscuity* as with *mal*, what comes to the fore is a quality of experience, the sensual appreciation of likeness. In the vision of self-pleasuring and luxuriating repose, the image evokes a dwelling on and enjoyment of such self-sameness in its own right – its erotics and aesthetics – as a way of apprehending geography and history. In so doing, the image resonates once more out of nineteenth-century understandings of masturbation, so as to bring to the fore the joy of creativity in the pursuit of likeness, 'a poetics-led comparison', to borrow Susan Manning's words. Paula Bennett and Vernon A. Rosario II have observed how 'women in particular ... found in autoerotic fantasy a means to sexual and authorial autonomy ... energising psychological forces, enabling their art' (1995: 10–11). For Laqueur, masturbation – the 'crack cocaine of sexuality' – was closely associated with the imagination, and female self-pleasuring specifically with 'pure libidinous pleasure' (2003: 21, 340). In the *Siesta*'s bubble, pleasure itself revolves through likeness, through waking and sleeping, consciousness and unconsciousness, before and after, circling endlessly, back and forth, flickering and pulsating with one another.

If, instead, a similarly slight departure is presented from one individual to another (or more), we are able to behold, as if stripped back to its own core, the sensation of pairing distinct things in companionship. We neither leap far into heterogeneity nor hold so tightly to sameness itself. A vivid example is to be found a year after *The Siesta*, in the French painter Courbet's *Sleep* (1866), and earlier in his *The Wrestlers* (1853), both of which bring two diverging individuals into intimate proximity within a single location. In *The Wrestlers*, we encounter a pair of near-naked men pushing and pulling at one another. Within the scene of conflict, 'the two antagonists have been fused together in a single compound entity,' Michael Fried remarks, 'the four legs seeming to compose a single system of support and the two upper bodies all but merging in a darkish expanse of striving limbs and sculpted flesh' (1990: 228). *Sleep* offers us two undressed women so entangled that no gap is visible between their heads and their middle sections, as if blended like El Pollo and Laguna in *Fausto*. Only one arm of each is visible, making them seem all the more a single doubled creature, their position and even the pose of the hand paralleling each other, one on a leg, the other on the gaping, pink, vagina-like opening in the bedding. Their bent-back legs are likewise projections of one another, to the extent that the angle of the lower limb of the woman to our left follows that of the other's thigh. Yet, they are clearly different – in hair colour, in skin tone, and in physical position – and their bodies extend away from one another. From one body to the other, we move very slightly away in order to return to sameness, return in order slightly to move away, subsuming that same pattern across great swathes of history and geography as we do so. Flickering again with the traces of earlier artists – Titian and Velázquez and their successors – the two women are stretched out nude upon a luxurious nineteenth-century bed at a diagonal, with a curtain over an opening to the back. Now the drape takes up the use of blue – seen in Ingres's *Grand Odalisque* and in Velázquez's *Venus* – while some red – seen in fabrics in both Titian and Velázquez and emphasised too by Pueyrredón in his curtains – is echoed instead where Velázquez employed blue, in the bedding. In turn, the locked bodies of Courbet's men flicker across the depths of time with tautly balanced sculptures of fighting nudes, tightly embraced in sexually suggestive postures, from the Uffizi *Wrestlers* to Vincenzo de' Rossi's penis-grabbing *Hercules and Diomedes*.

'How does a man's love of *other* men become a love of the *same?*', Eve Kosofsky Sedgwick asks in her influential book, *The Epistemology of the Closet* (2008: 160). Sedgwick underlines how historically contingent is the assumption that people's sexual desires are defined by the identity or otherwise of their biological gender: homo-sexual (same), hetero-sexual (different). With that notion came 'the aspect of "homosexuality" that now seems in many ways most immutably to fix it – its dependence on a defining *sameness* between partners' (2008: 158). On the one hand, this insistence on 'the love of the *same*' amounts to a limiting account of sexuality born of an historical context. Conversely, and resonating beyond any such narrow confines, the notion provides us with an affordance, an opening of a possibility: an erotics of close resemblance. To rephrase Sedgwick's question, we might ask: how might we find a way to love sameness through a man's love of other men, a woman's love of other women? *Sleep* offers this in its suggestions of earlier same-sex activity between two naked young women, their vaginas now coyly concealed, hinted at by the reddening fold of cloth. Meanwhile, if the muscled men of *The Wrestlers* are not quite nudes, their thongs lend a prominent outline to the all-too-evident genitalia. In this 'single compound entity', a penis rubs against legs and buttocks, limbs stretch past genitals as if to extend the phallus into rippling muscle, a head is pushed down in suggestion of fellatio, and the approach of a dark-trunked groin to buttocks intimates the possibility of anal intercourse. Sedgwick speaks of 'the foundational impossibilities of modern homo/heterosexual definition' (2008: 213): that is to say (among other things), that it makes no cogent sense to suppose one kind of similarity (biological gender) is more relevant than another in a sexual pairing, or to imagine that this kind of resemblance any more eliminates the differences between individuals than would any other. Conversely, in the erotics of close resemblance, it is precisely because there is difference, because the two men are separate persons, because the two women are separate persons, that their sensual coupling in sameness is possible at all.

The possibility opened up in such images is that their difference is not deferral, but rather an opening into their intimate blending, the 'mixtura' we encountered between El Pollo and Laguna. In Courbet's paintings, this notion finds expression across the entire composition, just as in Whitman, the leaping away and returning echoes through the poem's formal features and its sound. Michael Fried finds in *Sleep* patterns of similarity scattered across the whole canvas. For the viewer who, like some of Courbet's adversaries, assumes dispersal to be the opposite of unity, this suggests a fracturing, or, at best, a structure brought together additively, that is, by juxtaposing associated things. Fried notes a consequent 'universal impression of lack of *unity*'. If that supposition is set to one side, however, we may experience a 'mode of *unification* through rhythmic repetitions, thematic continuities, and metaphorical equivalences across the pictorial field' (1990: 234). Like El Pollo and Laguna too, taking respite in good companionship, the blending of the women in *Sleep* incorporates their distinctiveness, combining their differences in the rhythmic movement that would project the shapes of one into the other. There is an implicit movement back and forth in the image like that of the twofold La Mulata. The tumbling blonde hair could transform into the dark locks, the more tanned body into the paler. The affordance here, in lazy, post-coital sensuality, is the pleasure of being blended, of experiencing the rhythm of such a circle. We might linger and dwell, as these two women linger, on sameness lived. Not unlike in Pueyrredón's *Siesta*, similitude is found in what Klaus Herding calls Courbet's 'somnambulist sensuality and timelessness' (2010: 10), almost as if entering an hallucinatory state. We might enjoy what a 'blend' (mixtura) is, and feel settled, satiated in its 'telluric power'.

Pre-echoing Manet, *The Wrestlers* intimates, as an affordance of the 'love of the *same*', the sensation of pushing away and desire to dominate that would differentiate the two bodies. Fried aptly notes that for all the violence, outright conflict is not seen in the painting (1990: 228). The bodies are locked as if in taught equilibrium, each shoving at the other's head, with no victor so obvious as there had been in the Uffizi *Wrestlers* or in *Hercules and Diomedes*, and neither showing signs of uncoupling from the other. What comes into view is the fusing force of their struggle. In sculpted muscle, the four-legged creature draws from imagery of ancient times; in compelling spectacle, it pulsates out of and into the Champs-Elysées of the 1850s, projected forth from them, departing from the context in which, even so, it is clearly set. If the bodies of the wrestlers emanate from the canvas into the world and time of the viewer, these paintings are also testament to what Fried calls 'Courbet's repeated, obsessive attempts to transport himself as if corporeally into the canvas before him' (1990: 286). The 'absorbed' posture of the human figures – the faces of the men occluded, the women at rest – both invites commanding voyeurism, and yet intimates that the viewer might themselves be absorbed into the image, ceasing then, in any usual sense, to be its beholder (1990: 206–7, 257–8). Such pulsations into and out of the canvas are themselves departures that bring similarity firmly into view, whether as a sensual, lingering, rhythmic movement, or as the loving effect of forceful separation.

In this way, sameness between spectator and spectacle, between the viewer's location and the painting's origin, resonate with the works' evocation of resemblance and its sensations. Just as, in this erotics of sameness, we move between beholder and beheld, so we move between a series of sexual roles, experiencing these primarily in their similarity to one another. In *The Wrestlers*, Fried notes, neither of the two men is obviously the active to the other's passive (1990: 228), or, perhaps better said, they are both both. In *Sleep*, the painter – and viewer – are invited to become absorbed in the female body, rendering them, if male, 'bi-gendered' (1990: 206), as is true also of any female spectator of *The Wrestlers*. Same-sex and different-sex desire must, by the same token, also now appear similar: a man who desires women might look at *The Wrestlers* as if a man desiring men, a woman who desires women might look at *The Wrestlers* as if a man desiring a man, and so forth, and in all the possible variants. Among the images with which *Sleep* flickers, in turn, is James Northcop's print of the two princes asleep and embraced in the tower, but also Achille Devera's two women, *Minne et Brenda*, dormant together in a novel by Walter Scott (Faunce & Nochlin 1988: 176). It would be less true to say that these comings together erase a series of oppositions in gender, than that we might experience them as departures from each other that leap beyond, only to nearer bring.

If there is more clearly a step from one similar thing close to another, we may bring departure itself more explicitly into view, while retaining a focus on sameness. The intimacy of the two is thus suggested: sameness within an image of departure, departure within an image of sameness. Two paintings by Rosa Bonheur – *Spanish Mule Drivers Crossing the Pyrenees* (1857) and her most famous work, *The Horse Fair* (1852–55) – intimate as much. The two men to the fore of the former painting adopt quite different stances – one standing, one astride a mule – while, at the same time, closely resembling one another in looks and dress. They could be, but are not quite, transpositions of each other; they could, but do not quite look set to move to occupy each other's position. Their bodies do not quite touch, but the outstretched arm of the one behind the other suggests that they might. On the one hand, the men might seem to confront their putative French art viewer, standing right in front of the painting, with difference, barbarism even. Exotic-looking, rough-edged, working-class foreigners with an air of defiance, deploy an antique mode of transport, bearing the dominant red and more limited yellow of the Spanish flag. That we are at a line of separation – the Pyrenean border splitting two nations – is underlined by the parallel presence of the colours of the French tricolour, picked out across the heart of the painting: white, blue, and red. Yet, the colours of the two banners are not set clearly apart from one another: the Spaniards on view are wearing the white and blue of France, while the red required to make up the tricolour is found only aside the yellow of the Spanish flag where it also belongs. The Pyrenees here evoke an opening, shared expanse, beyond such distinctions and differences.

With so close an association between the muleteers and France, it as if, were the muledrivers other to the French – exotic, of another class, not a part of elite French civilisation – then, through the intimation of equivalence, so might the putative French viewers be other to themselves, as if this difference were constitutive of them. This pattern of difference and similarity resonates over centuries through to the mid-nineteenth century: the rivalry, mutual influence, and encounters between France and Spain across the ages, the repeated claim that 'Africa starts at the Pyrenees' (no-one seems quite to know who is responsible for the phrase). The rough and ready realism of Bonheur's image itself parallels the qualities sought by French painters like Manet among historic Spanish artists, even as such a quest underlines supposed differences between two national schools. Sensations of tension pervade so close a juxtaposition of sameness and departure. Difference gets only so far before it is held back, but, even as it is constrained, it pulls away, as if champing at the bit, and vice-versa. In this erotics of resemblance, fluidity and accessibility are in tension with resistance, while resistance, in turn, becomes the allure that draws us across frontiers. Open-shirted, with their toned, hair-strewn chests exposed, one of them leaning somewhat back, the two men might be taken as available, on offer for erotic pleasure to a viewer of any gender. One of them inclines from groin height, as if in a rising erection, a hard implement, a spade. The other places one hand between his legs, while gesturing with the other towards his genitalia. The one already has his hand on the buttocks of the other's mule, just behind his seated companion's rear. The rising or falling spade is sexually allusive certainly, but ambiguously so: its phallic hardness is combined with the space for entry offered by the trowel itself. Even its direction of movement is uncertain or doubled. The mules themselves – neither horse nor donkey – embody defiance of boundaries. In a celebrated essay on Bonheur – '"Disagreeably Hidden"', originally published in 1992 – James Saslow remarks that 'for her, as for many of her contemporaries, animals figured simultaneously as symbols of freedom in their own right … and as surrogate for a parallel desire on the part of gender-deviant women (and men) in particular for release from constricting norms' (2018: 196). At the same time, though, the muleteers resist and set themselves apart: their seated and standing positions seem at odds with the relentless march of their mules out of the painting and into the place we occupy. They look away from one another, as if to evoke the notion of separation. As they stare at us, their expressions are surly, aggressive even. This is likewise their attraction.

This pattern of resistance and multiple intimacy, of pulling away while affirming sameness, has intense force where there is tautness between stasis and departure, the changing and unchanged. The ancient fresco form, adopted in Bonheur's *The Horse Fair* (her 'Parthenon Frieze'), offers just such a possibility, with its apparent posed stillness and yet depiction of movement. Following the early twentieth-century thinker Aby Warburg, Philippe-Alain Michaud observes how classical shapes may be characterised not simply as sculptural stasis but as tending towards dance, as pulling in contrary directions between the 'contemplative' and the 'ecstatic', that is being beyond one's own self. This thought explicitly echoes Nietzsche's experience of the Dionysian amid the Apollonian – that meeting of those two gods in marriage (2003: 28–33). The reverse is also the case: the dance depicted tends to unchanging sameness, the Apollonian is found amid the Dionysian. The circular shape of Bonheur's image is formed by a forceful thrusting away and a continual pulling back. Horses rush or lurch forward wilfully as working-class men seek to tug them into order. Violent struggle alternates with instances of calm. The movement overall is circular, taking the horses and riders back to where they began, and, contrariwise, the circle impels them forever forwards. Even as they vary and differ, men look like transpositions of other men, horses projections of other horses. This twin movement gives shape to the sexual offering which diversifies while forming a single pattern. Two of the males nearest the foreground have their white shirts wide open, offering their chests to the viewer. Each holds a whip whose handle protrudes, penis-like, from his groin and through his grasping hand. Another's blue jacket rises up, fluttering, allowing us to contemplate his rear. Nearer the centre of the picture, another man in blue battles with a vast dark horse that looms up from between his legs like some giant animal erection. Some individuals are aggressive to the point of violence, others, the calm reverse. And at the heart of it, Saslow shows, is Rosa Bonheur herself, a cross-dressed, tranquil woman, aligned with the bridling head of a lusty white horse (2018: 200).

This is not simply a matter of a *vaivén*, a coming and going, between opposing emotional possibilities. The contrasting aspects of these paintings – resistance and intimacy, separation and similarity – are not in contradiction. Rather, the kicking out – the pushing away that allures and draws nearer, so central to Manet, Marx and Baudelaire, to the wedding of Dionysus and Apollo – is presented here as the beating heart of resemblance and its possibilities. It is offered in *Spanish Mule Drivers* once more as a telluric force, not just in the ancient, atavistic practice of mule-driving, but in the transition of colours and rough but sensual brushwork out of the very rocks and vegetation of the mountainscape, the ancient earth, into the animals and the foreground figures, in the parallel between the staring, advancing mules themselves and the humans (and vice versa). It appears in the taking shape of Athenian art in the forms of mid-nineteenth-century Paris, amid the working-class men of a fair. Like 'Me myself' and *mal*, it is experienced as of the very depths of time.

3

Sacrifice: everyone must die

*They were trying to cut through the membrane between them,
and bleed one into the other. ... Bellis was left aghast by it.*
China Miéville, *The Scar*

Let us imagine the destruction of a being, literal or figurative. Let us imagine that, as it is destroyed, its mortal bounds, like the contours of a body, are torn away, and it finds itself in intimacy with what lies beyond it over place and time, as if in an outpouring. Or, let us imagine that this ultimate pain is so intense that, like an endless scream, it persists and is prolonged, compelling other beings across geography and history. Or, let us imagine that, as something dies – literally or figuratively – it is preserved and continues, as if transfigured, travelling across time and place. In such sacrifice, the very marking of a mortal limit – the end point of a being in history and geography – becomes, in apparent paradox, the means by which to escape the bounds of context, to join with what lies beyond it. In such experiences, there lies the temptation of a 'negative utopia', to borrow a phrase from Michael Roth (2012: 87). Griselda Pollock speaks of a 'collective wounding' that might offer us 'a social but also human bonding with, and responsibility for, others' (2013: 8–9). This would occur through 'psychic trauma', whose 'characteristics are timeless presentness, semantic absence, belatedness and transmissibility' (2013: 162). Any effort to leap violently beyond may solely nearer bring. Frank Ankersmit describes how attempts to break with the past and establish a new era in history may be cut across by the destruction of the old that they inflict, breaching the periodisation it seems to establish (2005: 324–5). On some accounts, we might experience what Julia Kristeva calls a 'jouissance of destruction': the constraints through which linguistic systems contain and crush free being are themselves shattered, in a mirror-image murdering (2002: 76, 58). The chronological order of supposed civilisation's development is thus undone, its origins are broken open, and its entry into the systems of signs that constituted it is lost. Our habitual temporality disappears and atavisms return (2002: 429).

We may find combined here the notions of an ethical intimacy, of a resistance to confines of representation and clear interpretation, and of an escape from chronological time. Cathy Caruth speaks of 'the story of a wound that cries out, that addresses us in the attempt to tell us of a reality or truth that is not otherwise available' (1996: 4). The language of this cry resists comprehension; time becomes characterised by repetitions; and, as past and present are interconnected, so are cultures across which the cry reaches (1996: 5, 11, 56). It points to and beyond the painfully mortal limits of representation and interpretation (Saltzman & Rosenberg 2006: xii–xiii; Wallace 2006: 8–9, 14, 20). With release from systems of interpretation or representation we may even be promised intimate contact with and the return of an elusive Real in the arts, Hal Foster (1996) has supposed. Media that, like photography, preserve some physical trace of a being may be experienced as containing and exposed to some pained reality unassimilated into structures of signs and significance. In Margaret Iverson's words, 'exposure, itself a photographic term, is tied up with the indexicality of the medium and links photography with the vulnerability of the subject of trauma' (2017: 9).

Among the temptations of communion in sacrifice are a tendency to sacralise, drawing variously on Christian and on non-Christian legacies. With some scepticism on their own part, Bersani and Phillips have reflected upon the death-courting sexual practice of barebacking, where a person may give up their own being and secure the transmission of a virus. This they link to the Catholic mystical heresy of Pure Love with its utter abandonment of self to Christ's sacrifice (2010: 50–1). In his famous essay, 'Is the Rectum a Grave?' (1987), Bersani himself evokes a willing self-sacrifice in the penetrated homosexual male, putatively opening himself through a symbolic dying to intimacy with others, the bounds of his own subjecthood renounced. In a Pagan vein, writing of *The Birth of Tragedy*, the American philosopher Sallis recalls the dismemberment of the god Dionysus, in a vision of the Death of the Author as ecstasy, breaching the limits of subjecthood (1991: 53, 51). Looming over many of these discussions is the shadow of the twentieth-century French writer, Georges Bataille, and his dwelling on a kind of sacrifice that would rend all bounds of selfhood, of language, of structure, with no prescribed purpose: to have some defined finality would restore those bounds. 'Sacrifice', he declares, 'has the power to contest everything in the instant that it takes place, to summon everything, to render everything present' (2014: 137).

The prospect of sacrifice may lead to a converse desire for safety, even if only relative safety. That is implicit even in many of the utopian longings described above, which seek an ethical communion born out of destruction. Prominent among anxieties that sacrifice may provoke is the obliteration of particularity, annihilation in the cause of transcendence. Citing Jan Patochka towards the start of his *Gift of Death*, Derrida warns of a sacralising passion that eradicates all individual responsibility (2008: 3). Such thoughts echo the broader fear of universalisms often found in cultural studies: that these entail the destruction of all specificity and difference. To render sacrifice safe would be to reject all that while retaining the allure of the death of the bounded subject and of an ethics of shared mortality and suffering. For Derrida, truly to take responsibility in the face of death is to eschew generalisable laws: the only valid universal would be that same responsibility. In some quarters, there is the hope even of undoing sacrifice from within. If the latter does indeed evince a violent longing for what is generalised and self-same, its universality would be exclusionary of difference and uniqueness. Its sacrificial victim would be a scapegoat killed to justify a putative generalised system, and to exclude all that does not fit. The French philosopher René Girard's *The Scapegoat* details such a sacrificial culture and its supposed undoing in Christ's own sacrifice, which is a call to abandon all scapegoating, to be truly inclusive and loving of each unique other (1986: 212). Prophecies such as this amount to the command 'sacrifice sacrifice', in Robert Keenan's words (2005: 1). Like the Italian philosopher Giorgio Agamben, we might then come to accept that our entire collective world is our own social praxis, that beyond us there is no foundation (1991: 106).

Ultimately, all flirtations with sacrifice risk an unending, undying pain in the name of the 'negative utopia', a ceaseless, unyielding attachment to suffering and to death, literal or figurative. We may become entangled in what Maggie Nelson calls *The Art of Cruelty*: 'the conviction that violence is the privileged means by which we come into ourselves *or* lose ourselves as human subjects' (2011: 142). Memorably, Dominick LaCapra has warned against *acting out* in response to mortal suffering: 'a fidelity to trauma, a feeling that one must somehow keep faith with it' (2001: 22), an obsession with and repetition of past suffering, beyond chronological time, beyond clear comprehension (2001: 21). For LaCapra, the alternative is a *working through* towards lucidity and understanding that might release us from the trauma.

To reverse that logic is to set safety aside. The reality is that mid-nineteenth-century 'Western' cultures often took that very path: they were not infrequently sacrificial cultures, we might say. We may dismiss or downplay this as an historical embarrassment, or we may explore its implications. If a person wished to confuse self and other, to collapse distinctions, to conflate past and present, to escape the bounds of the unique mortal self, to embrace forever what has died, that person could indeed hold tight to the destruction of being, could subject even their own being to a kind of obliteration, keeping the wound open. 'Images of death and dying were closely linked to models of creativity', Andrew Smith observes in his *Gothic Death* (2016: 2). To acknowledge such a possibility and its history is absolutely not to endorse the 'negative utopia' and its doubtful ethical promise. On the contrary, it is, as it were. to look the danger in the face, to explore where such perilous paths might lead. Nor is it to deny the all-too-reasonable anxiety that LaCapra and others express, nor even the aspirations of 'negative utopia' itself. Rather these too must be be acknowledged as constitutive of such psychological journeying. My interest here is in the affordances of such perilous experiences, as efforts to release things from whence they came, so that something might extend over time and place or facilitate linkages over geography and history. In this spirit, I offer no theory, and no tight definition of sacrifice. Rather, I explore the possibilities afforded by experiences that share family resemblances with one another in associating destruction with commonality and persistence. I contemplate seriously the violence inherent in such possibilities. I take them rather as a kind of dreamwork through which to travel, using the works of the mid-century as if they were guides.

The Scapegoat (1854–55; Plate 8) – a painting by the British Pre-Raphaelite artist William Holman Hunt – is one such guide, resonating with many of the preoccupations that we will find in this chapter. It portrays a salty Middle-Eastern wilderness containing a goat, left there to die alone. Inspired by Leviticus 16 – where a scapegoat is sent away to atone for the sins of Israel – the vision is a fusion of loss and of unification, of destruction in one location and of persistence beyond it, set at the borderline of life and death. The image is redolent of the scapegoating that Girard describes: one being is not merely sent to die in utter exclusion for the sake of the collective's unity, but its dying takes place beyond the very bounds and limits of habitation of any society, as if to make us see the existence of that deathly, cruel dimension on which – at once and as if in paradox – the continuing order of life depends and that must rest outside it. The goat is envisioned as dying there and then, but its dying projects it beyond the very context that is killing it and defining its fate. The animal is to be seen in mid-century Britain turning its head somewhat towards us, perhaps eyeing us with one eye, looming in suffering, urging its connection to viewers there, and beyond to all who look at it subsequently, persistent and enduring. The force of its pained demeanour engages gazes across place and time in communion.

As it does so, it resists any mastering interpretation arising from its context, whether at its place of demise, or in English Christianity. On one level, certainly, the image suggests suffering for atonement: heretically or otherwise, the goat from Leviticus and from annual Jewish ritual is treated as a pre-echo of Christ (Giebelhausen 2006: 161–2). At the same time, we are confronted with an animal that cannot understand and does not exist within the world of human ideas that have determined its fate, whose death is incomprehensible to it in those terms. We experience the sensation of looking across that divide and of being compelled by the gaze of the beast beyond us, beyond the scheme of interpretation that seeks to incorporate it. Reviewers at the time remarked on the difficulty of seeing so naturalistic a creature as anything but an animal; the art historian Albert Boime has remarked that it would not look out of place in a nineteenth-century manual of natural history (Boime 2007: 325, 327). *The Scapegoat* is an image likewise of wider tensions that frustrate a single viewpoint, between belief and materiality, between heroic redemption and fleeting realities, Carol Jacobi has eloquently shown (2006: 4–8, 75–6, 265–8). Visually, the image is violently disruptive of efforts to master or situate its sense. The landscape that Hunt set out so meticulously to record appears, in its garish colours, like a 'drug-induced hallucination', Boime aptly observes (2007: 324), the transfiguration of the real jarringly apparent. The image defies existing schema in its fusion of 'religious, landscape, and animal painting' (Boime 2007: 324). It evinces characteristics Prettejohn finds in other Pre-Raphaelite work of this time, and that she describes as potentially 'disconcerting … stressful … frightening'. Its multitude of finely painted detail, unmixed colours and hard, even light prevents visual mastery of the whole, impedes the imposition of hierarchies on what appears before us. There is an abrupt transition from foreground to depth, creating an awkwardness of angle (2000: 136, 140 145, 150–1, 163).

It is as if the whole painting were a wounding, a tearing apart, brought about in the violent awkwardness of rendering something in its context persistent and compelling beyond its place and time – as if the painting itself were sacrificial, as if it were itself a scapegoat. In all of this it evinces and is an accomplice of dangerous impulses. The projection of the scene, in transfiguration, out of its context towards Britain implies that the true sense of Judaism's place in history and of the 'oriental' scene was there for those like the British to understand, not its peoples. Scholars have remarked both on this aspect of the work, and on its correspondence with Hunt's aggressive attitudes while abroad: his demeaning view of the Jewish and Arab populations, his identification with the violent force of British men, as the Crimean War raged not so far away, the suggestion even that the truly sacrificial victim was Britain in the cause of good (Prettejohn 2000: 112–13; Boime 2007: 319–23). The very grandiosity of Hunt's artistic vision, his effort to find Christlike transcendence in the contemporary world, his sense of his own redemptive suffering amid corruption, as if to colonise and purify also his own homeland, are suggestive of insanity, as Jacobi has shown. Friends even knew him as 'the Mad' (Jacobi 2006: 5–6, 11, 63–6).

This chapter journeys through the deaths and the dying of the dead and the dying, which are like pathways to others akin to them. It opens a wending path formed of stuffed animals, novels of death, pieces of glass, photographed brains, corpses, nebulous paintings, and accounts of slaughter, among other portals through destruction. Each catastrophe opens a way to the next across place and time, as if in a roll-call or lament. The circumstances of mortal suffering interconnect, not in a simple reductive pattern, but as if through labyrinthine pathways of an underworld, threading back and forth through one another: British imperialism, US expansionism, revolutionary aftermaths and violence, French universalism, the treatment of women and children, the encirclements of capital, commerce and infrastructure, the displacement of the peasantry and the suffering of workers, scientific analysis of humans, and once more the legacy and renewal of imperial endeavour in Spain and its transoceanic monarchy. We pass through the passionate renewal of Christian exaltations of sacrifice in Britain, France and Spain, with the revitalisation of religion in the century – its 'triumphal reemergence', in Bayly's words, anything but a time of simple secularisation (2004: 325). We traverse the slaughter of animals, and the violent confrontations of humans and the wider natural world – aspects of colonialism, of global traffic, but, with these, of long-term global realities, the encounter of the human and non-human that may characterise the poetics of an Anthropocene era (Clark 2019: 39–69).

From the outset of the chapter – in the photography of Julia Margaret Cameron and the prose of Antonio Ros de Olano – life and death telescope into one another, the arc of life narrative stripped out, forming a point in limbo that is projected out across time and place. The sacrificial imagery associated with Ros de Olano's novel leads us to the tearing away of the bounds of the body, and – in Millet's painting, as in Cameron's photographs – the social and economic forces that bring about such destruction. We linger here upon the obsession with holding to pain and to trauma, rendering it persistent, enduring, eternal, an unending sacrifice. A statue of Andromache in Madrid embodies the pain of the vanquished. Nineteenth-century historicism and history painting offer us a heterotopia of demise, resisting all chronology. In Spanish concerns with reconstructing the nation, victims of the new imperial order from sixteenth-century Spain project into our future. The lure of enduring significance – of being classic – takes us to photographic depictions of the actress Sarah Bernhardt and the painter Mariano Fortuny as dead, their immortality dependent on their demise. In offering persistence, death appears as the bringer of copies; we observe its work in Ros de Olano's search for the authentic copy of a human, in a revised Death of the Author, in taxidermy and in human mummification, in the reproducibility of a painting (Millet's *Angelus*), and in a gender-fluid statue entitled *Nineteenth Century*. Through the nineteenth-century obsession with preserving the dead we experience a shift from interpretation to an appreciation of enigmatic textures born of an endless dying, resistant to context, in the sensuality of *Moby-Dick*, taxidermied animals, and the removal and restoration of Goya's Black Paintings. Post-Structuralist theories – the dissemination of signs – are recast in this light; pastiche emerges as a deathly ventriloquism, like a breath through a dying world.

We ponder the qualities of character necessary to experience such things, and dwell upon the 'simple heart' of Flaubert's Félicité – with her stuffed taxidermied parrot – and of Alice in her Wonderland. The conditions for such experiences point to an unsettling conclusion: that the greater the danger to life, the more resistant is the aesthetic effect to context. We turn to visions of desolation in which everyone must die: the singing of the Argentine *gaucho* in *Martín Fierro*, the poetics of destruction in *Moby-Dick*, the epic poem that is Marx's *Capital I*. We consider a dying humanity turning to abstraction, an everything that is a nothing, in the pained longing of the Puerto Rican character Bayoán to redeem the world from imperial violence, and in Whistler's visual response to the Spanish mid-century assault on Chile. We find humanity and the animal world turning to a promiscuously aesthetic abstraction as the French scientist Luys takes to photographing corpses' brains, in the conditions of Madrid's Cabinet of Natural History, and in the still life of the Mexican

Hermenegildo Bustos. Visions scatter in analogies, in abstract sameness, through Isobel Armstrong's 'glassworlds', spectral and redolent with death, in the vitrines of exhibits, in the Crystal Palace, and in the glass paintings of the Mexican Agustín Arrieta. In our quest for commonality, we come to the point of insanity.

Limbo and compression

In 1867 the Anglo-Indian artist, Julia Margaret Cameron – gifted since the age of 48 with a camera – made a photograph entitled *'Call, I follow, I follow, let me die!'* (Figure 10). The quotation is taken from the Alfred Lord Tennyson's *Idylls of the King* (1859–85), a cycle of poems about Arthur and his knights that the image was to illustrate. The title words are from 'The Song of Love and Death', which is invented and performed in the poem cycle by Elaine, a martyr to her love of Lancelot. Elaine is seen in profile, turned almost flat to the viewer's right, the image cropped so as to show only the head and upper torso, against a black backdrop that near merges with the featureless shawl wrapped around her and the tumble of dark hair that falls upon it. The image of her illuminated head might plunge into the beckoning darkness, there to be extinguished in the softening focus, as easily as the obscurity might highlight, in chiaroscuro, the sensuous forms of her well but softly lit face and neck, the textures traced in light and shadow. The photograph, like many others by Cameron, evokes how the persistence of an image, its vitality across place and time beyond the point of its conception, may prove utterly dependent on the imminent threat of physical death or of the destruction of a person's sane mind – even their personhood – or both. While the delineation of a context in time requires an ending, resistance to confinement in it arises precisely from the ultimate tightening of that constraint. Aesthetically, the emergence of the sensual forms of an enduring image may entail the imminence of total loss.

On the one hand, Cameron's practice and her writing about it pushes against the association between the photographic medium and mortality. In famous remarks to the polymath John Herschel, Cameron said of her portraits that 'they are not only *from* the Life but *to* the Life and startle the eye with wonder & delight' (cited in Olsen 2003: 184–5). Cameron's techniques resist any link that might be made between the fixing of a photographic image in clear, defined forms, and the removal of living dynamism. Blurring of the former suggests movement (Olsen 2003: 155). Victoria Olsen comments that 'her work defied what she considered the "skeletal" outlines of sharp-focus photographs in favor of the round modelling of flesh out of light, shadowing, and soft-focus' (Olsen 2003: 185). This is an effect in part of extremely long exposure times, Robin Kelsey notes. Memorably, Herschel observed of an allegorical image by Cameron that it is 'really a most astonishing piece of high relief – She is absolutely alive and thrusting out her head from the paper into the air. This is your own special style' (cited in Kelsey 2015: 87).

'Thrusting' itself 'from the paper into the air', the vision may be experienced as continually, forcefully emerging through and out of the photograph into other places and times where it is viewed. For Marina Warner in her *Phantasmagoria*, the images seem to 'preserve the vital energy of its long-vanished subject' (2006: 202). However, the very same effects are resonant with mortality, such that they emerge in a 'picture' of the world where an opposition of deathliness and vitality – however nuanced – does not hold. Speaking of Cameron and Tennyson's collaboration on another collection – *Enoch Arnold* – Alison Chapman aptly evokes 'a space of loss that, perversely, defies death' (Chapman 2003: 48). In the very

Instead of modernity

10 Julia Margaret Cameron, *'Call, I follow, I follow, let me die!'*

blurring of fixity – Kirsten Hoving observes – there are intimations of self-dissolution, not least in the blankness that we find in *Call, I Follow* … (Hoving 2003: 55). Likewise, the very play of shadow that offers 'thrusting' relief is what suggests its disintegration, its falling away into nothingness.

Sacrifice: everyone must die

The apparent identifiability of a personality – 'Elaine' – combines with the latters's utter undoing. Olsen has written eloquently of Cameron's 'fluid, mobile, ever-dying selves' (2003: 86). Where the grounds of an opposition between death and life are thus discarded, the erotic experience of the flesh becomes inherently deathly. Hoving remarks of *Call I Follow...*, that 'in this remarkably sensual photograph, the exposed throat and lifted chin play off against the dark clefts of folded drapery that obliterate the body, converging *eros* and *thanatos*' (Hoving 2003: 55). In Tennyson's poem, Elaine herself treats the two as equivalents: 'Sweet is true love, though given in vain, in vain,' she sings, 'And sweet is death who puts an end to pain; / I know not which is sweeter, no, not I' (2012: 211). It is not necessary to frame such an experience in psychoanalytical terms to find in it 'the obscure collusion of life and death' that Lisa Downing observes in nineteenth-century necrophilia (2003: 1). This is a convergence, without distinction, both of what fundamentally limits existence and what ultimately impels it to endure. Downing comments that 'to ignore, to sanitise or to dismiss the very real fascination offered by erotic material pertaining to death is ... to cut us off even further from an approach to that end that we, as beings in time and space, are compelled to make' (2003: 131).

Looked at aesthetically, it is the photographic image itself that we see, seeking to emerge and endure and, at once and without contradiction, vanishing into nothingness, the print of Elaine's head and shoulders that is desired in this state of necrophilia. We encounter here 'the pulsing of presence and absence' that conditions an image, to borrow words from Michaud. Inspired by Warburg, Michaud notes how the subject matter ('Elaine', or simply the model), by becoming an image that persists, may find enduring life ('presence') at the moment of its apparent loss ('absence'), for it is replaced by its own image (Michaud 2007: 72). In that sense, the dying away of the moment in time implies the life of the image – and vice versa – just as Cameron's photograph brings to the fore both the thrusting flesh of 'Elaine' and its dissolution. As in the photographs we encountered in Chapter 1, the image is not simply static, but is forever traversing the boundary of life and death, just as it at once evokes its origins in a localised context: it forms a 'dynamic moment', in Zielinski's phrase. Such visual mobility arises from the photographic 'shape' that the image gives us, for the pulsating is an effect of the form, realised on the plate, which can at once be construed in multiple ways.

The gaze of many of Cameron's subjects is crucial to how their image may be experienced as 'thrusting out ... from the paper' into other places and time. In Carol Hanbery MacKay's words, the 'dampening forces around the face act as a visual magnet, and we as viewers are almost forced to zoom in to the eyes' (MacKay 2001: 21). Drawing on Walter Benjamin's thinking, Kaja Silverman has spoken of the 'transhistorical chiasmus' realised as a later viewer is drawn to the eyes of subjects vividly imaged on early photographs through 'long exposures' (2015: loc.2746, 2605). This brings about what she describes as a '*reversibility* of the visual relationship between sitter and viewer: the sitter looks back at the viewer and invites him [*sic*] to reciprocate'; in Benjamin's words, there is here 'something that cannot be silenced' (2015: loc.2617). What 'cannot be silenced', what gives force to the gaze of many Cameron images is closer to a thousand-yard stare, or to a look of a self on the verge of its destruction. MacKay describes the gaze of several of Cameron's sitters evocatively: 'The figures she depicts stare out at us intensely yet blankly, their visages suggesting a trancelike or meditative state' (2001: 21). Often, Hoving notes, 'their eyes are out of focus, downcast or closed' (2003: 52). In Cameron's famous image, *My Niece, Julia Jackson* (also 1867), the eyes are so illuminated as to be drained transparent, as if turned to glass, or as if reanimated just as they were sucked of life. If this is indeed some kind of 'waking trance', in Chapman's words, it is (to repeat that phrase) 'a space of loss that, perversely, defies death' (2003: 48). The perturbing emotional effect resonates with what we learn from some of Cameron's young female models. Her great- niece Laura Gurney observed: 'No wonder those old photographs of us ... look anxious and wistful. This was how we felt' (cited in Ford 2003a: 65).

The force that effects the 'transhistorical chiasmus' is not unlike the *Limbo* evoked by the much-admired Spanish novelist and thinker, Agustín Fernández Mallo, in his 2014 novel of that title (2014a: loc.37, 132, 136, 378, 513). 'Neither a beginning nor and end', Fernández Mallo has commented, it is a frontier 'where the poetic fact itself materialises', giving us 'a slightly out-of-focus reality' (Ni un principio ni un final; donde se materializa el propio hecho poético; una realidad ligeramente desenfocada). The beginning and end – he has remarked – are not birth and death as such, but rather 'the instants just before death' (los instantes justo antes de la muerte): this is a dying, where perhaps a 'Sound of the End' (Sonido del Fin) will be heard (2014b). Hoving has pointed to the number of Cameron's protagonists whose lives are in a 'state of disintegration', inviting us to dwell on how Coleridge's Christabel felt upon turning into a snake, or Beatrice beholding her own demise, or Ophelia her own insanity (Hoving 2003: 52). Pointedly, in Cameron's vision of Madonnas, sacred life-giving is combined with its own dying, maternity with the very real threat of loss: 'These photographs imply an umbilical cord stretched to snapping point, as mothers gaze on children they know will eventually leave them', Olsen remarks, 'Every Madonna and child implies a pietà, especially for Victorians who faced high infant mortalities' (Olsen 2003: 171). Even beyond such direct allusions, Cameron associates the powerful, loss-filled gaze with fertility, whether in the sombre stare of Alice Liddell as Pomona, or that of the young females of *May Day*.

Within this 'limbo', we find a further intimation. Not only may continual dying – the very bounds of any mortal context – 'thrust' images out across place and time. Not only may the deathly gaze of 'limbo' bind humanity forcefully in a 'transhistorical chiasmus'. But – put at an extreme – precisely through all this, the narrative arc of humanity would be stripped out; for, with life and death in such convergence, there is no story as such to tell of anyone's journey from birth to their mortal end. As each individual narrative arc is foreshortened, so all the narratives of every individual life together must be so, such that all human existence is crushed together. So it is that we would be conjoined. The result is aptly expressed in the Spanish writer, Antonio Ros de Olano's use of the adjective *compressed*, with which he describes his hauntingly schematic prose work *Doctor Lañuela* (1863) (un libro comprimido) (1863: 118). Pondering the scant, diffuse outline of an epic plot, concentrated into so little place and time, the volume's prologuist, Manuel Ascensión Berzosa, speaks of 'the perilous novelty of making literature travel at full blast, devouring kilometres of life, on the train of death' (la peligrosa novedad de hacer viajar la literatura a toda máquina, devorando kilómetros de vida, en el tren de la muerte) (1863: 19). The work's narrator evokes a a telescoping of divides between birth, life and death: 'baptism and epitaph have been brought together' (el bautismo y el epitafio se han acercado) (1863: 25–6). We might say, by extension, that many of Cameron images are compressed photographs, perilously traversing human existence at 'full blast': each life already dead, each death already fertile, each epitaph a baptism, and each new birth an epitaph. Every narrative longs for its own ending, its own death, Peter Brooks has famously suggested, but plots work by deviating from the inevitable, so as to postpone it, and avoid 'the collapse of one into the other, of life into immediate death' (1984: 93, 102–4). Here narrative itself is dissipating, and we are left only with the longed-for dying across all place and time.

'Instants group together; spaces disappear,' Berzosa observes, 'and all life gathers itself and piles up in an imperceptible point' (los instantes se agrupan; los espacios desaparecen; y la vida entera se recoge y apiña en un punto imperceptible) (1863: 19). The 'compressed' work of art in its 'limbo' resonates with every life and death everywhere, now concentrated and expressed in just one singular, necrophiliac 'pulsing'.

Violent transfiguration and the opening of space

Berzosa is a vivid guide to the violence inherent in these sensations, describing *Doctor Lañuela* as 'a book opened with chisel blows to the palpitating entrails of the victim' (un libro abierto a golpe de cincel sobre las entrañas palpitantes de la víctima) (1863: 12). If only metaphorically, limbo is brought about by blood sacrifice. Berzosa's choice of language is resonant here in speaking of a book that has been 'opened' (abierto) through such slaughter. This is much more than the physical brushing of the surface, the touching in pursuit of mimesis, that is prominent in the more tempered, influential writings of Laura Marks (2002: loc.37–9, 76–9, 98–9) To reach the entrails with a chisel, the graphic image reminds us, we must breach the surrounding skin. The assault is on the notion that a self has a spatial limit, the tendency to imagine it as 'a kind of glassy blob that exceeds so far and no further', in the philosopher Simon Blackburn's words – and, by extension, the notion that we can only conceive of things in terms of our own confined 'context'. The chiselling forcefully relieves us of that conceptual fallacy, 'the comic question', as Blackburn puts it, 'of whether an American mind can stretch as far as Europe, or a twenty-first-century mind can embrace the Renaissance' (2006: 169). Conversely – and as others would have it – giving up on that notion may be experienced as a violation, a stripping away of our particularity and even of our agency as specific beings. 'Unison collapses life into death', in Marks's resonant words (2002: loc.44–7). The two sensations – of danger, and of liberation, universal love even – are here compounded, as they are in the Prado's long shadow of Spain's Universal Monarchy or in Manet's turning of border-crossing violence to affection.

The energy of limbo may emanate from social, historical and global phenomena experienced as so wounding that they either literally kill or engender a living death. This, in turn, conjoins them with historical developments that stretch far beyond their local context, just as occurs in Marx's Age of Capital. Overwhelming forces break open limits within which people might otherwise be confined to their own place and time, or, indeed, to their own body. We find the effect amid the transformations of infrastructure, in economic reorganisation and the fate of the poor, through gender roles and in imperialism. In *Doctor Lañuela* itself, the accelerating and intensifying communication structure, entwining the nineteenth-century world, is redolent with a crushing of life's duration and extent, an impending merger of living and death: 'We live less;' we read in *Doctor Lañuela*, 'we feel and think more in less space ... There I go at great speed down the fatal line which has but two stations: the cradle and the grave' (Vivimos menos; sentimos y pensamos más en menos tiempo. ... Allá voy yo a grande velocidad por la vía fatal que solo tiene dos estaciones: la cuna y el sepulcro) (1863: 25–6). Transport brings us paradoxically together at the single, 'imperceptible point' as regions and countries are ever more deeply connected together.

The changing patterns of economic life could have a similar effect upon the working class, fuelling 'limbo' with their living deaths. The French painter Jean-François Millet obsessively revisited scenes from central France, evoking the dislocation that peasants experienced as large-scale farming moved in to their local region, pushing many to the edge of survival, even as it enhanced links from the local land to the wider economy (Murphy 1999: 12). In his most famous painting of the countryfolk – *The Angelus* (1859; Plate 9) – death and life merge in a single stark image with powerfully contained and sober energy, forming its own 'imperceptible point'. The prayer itself is a 'compressed' narrative of Christ's sacrificial life from conception to death to resurrection, of His mother's fertility and His demise. The intimation of life in the peasant woman's curved fertile belly (Pollock 1977: 18) rests within a scene of nearly lifeless stillness, its lack of contact or interaction between the proximate man and woman unsettling, the Spanish Surrealist Salvador Dalí remarks (2013: 56). For his part, Dalí believed the two figures to be praying over a concealed corpse, their buried baby (Dalí 2013: 15–20).

In turn, the deadening patterns of nineteenth-century European gender roles are manifest in the 'transhistorical chiasmus', of Cameron's gazing women, in their being thrust forth 'to the life'. Again and again it is woman that is sacrificed before us, or an allegorical figure gendered as female. Notoriously, abnegation was expected of many women. Where she is fertility (*Pomona* (1872), *May Day* (1866)), woman appears to be suffering some overwhelming loss and pain. Where she is mother (*Madonna Adolorata* (1864)), she looks out with a saddened stare. Where she is trained to be an Angel of the House, as with the winged girls of *The Turtle Doves* (1864), she is dulled, bereft, ultimately lost in an endless deferral of living. In her own poem 'The Portrait' – about the beautiful image of a woman – Cameron writes of 'a mouth where silence seems to gather strength / From lips so gently closed, that almost say / Ask not my story, lest you hear at length / Of sorrows where sweet hope has lost its way' (cited in Weaver 1984: 158).

The fate wrought in European policy around the globe parallels and exceeds that of many Europeans, as it did in Marx's *Capital*. In Cameron's image of *Prince Alámayou* on the Isle of Wight (1868), the pose and the gaze into the distance have the same compelling effect, the same compression of life and death into limbo, as with Cameron's bereft female sitters. Aláymayou's father had sought to unite Abyssinia as an African Christian polity and to link it to the European Christian powers. British colonial forces, with their own imperial view of Europe–Africa connections, assaulted his power base, leading to his suicide, leaving Aláymou orphaned and captive. *Spear or Spare* (1868) – a more direct image of a Briton assaulting an Abyssinian – leaves the latter in 'limbo' between life or death. In turn, Jeff Rosen has shown how the *Idylls of King Arthur* – where we find *'Call, I Follow...'* – echoes with preoccupations about Britain's 'imperial course and in particular, its effect on modern women' (Rosen 2015: 232–62). In Nina Auerbach's words, 'receding from the land he could not rule, King Arthur becomes, like Dracula, an undead creature, the vitality of whose protracted dying sucks life from the ordinary world. Death, not the king, is Tennyson's hero' (1990: 97).

Photographic practice brings home the physical nature of such sacrifice. Cameron's sitters – like all sitters – literally give over some of their mortal life for the sake of the image. The camera collects the residue of light that bounces off them, the outline of their bodies in physical nature, preserving it chemically, as André Bazin (1960) notes in 'The Ontology of the Photographic Image'. Cameron went further: remnants of the human body can be found in her images: 'hair, oils, dirt, and fingertip smudges were eternally suspended in the plates' cutaneous layers', Julian Cox observes (2003: 53). Kelsey has underlined how she thus associates 'the intimate materiality of her process and the living presence of her subjects' (2015: 82). The very fact of photographic 'exposure' may resonate with 'trauma' – Margaret Iverson, like others, has explained – preserving at least some unfiltered trace of an originary event from the past, automatically recorded and transmitted (2017: 1–15). Just as pertinently, Cameron held sitters through extremely long exposures, and without physical supports. The residue that is thus collected is often that of real pain and subjection to a kind of tyranny. 'I felt as if I must scream', one sitter said (cited in Ford 2003b: 63). In a resonant choice of words, others referred to the 'chosen victim' and to how parents were unable 'to rescue their infant' (cited in Ford 2003a: 62, 65). With a not dissimilar turn of phrase, Tennyson said to Longfellow, 'You will have to do what she tells you. I'll come back and see what is left of you' (cited in Chapman 2003: 53).

It is this residue that Cameron and her camera transfigure into images of deathly life, through the softening of the focus and the evocations of allegorical, historical and mythical figures on the edge of dissolution. Ksenya A. Gurshtein (2007) observes that many nineteenth-century viewers, like their later counterparts, were unsettled or even upset by such artistic effects occurring in a medium so literally connected to the physical world as was photography. Likewise, Gurshtein notes, spectators were often attentive to the way photographic detail reminds us of the all too physically real nature of the sitters and of the staged scenes. In *Beatrice*, Gurshtein says, 'the drapery threatens to reveal itself as a piled-up rag'. Such untidy physical realities are inherent to what transfiguration is. To omit them, in the conjuring up of limbo and compression, would undo the physicality of the violence done. To borrow Kelsey's words, the many 'glitches' in Cameron's images 'operate as sacred wounds': they are 'the signs of the material limits that nail all transcendental efforts to the world' (Kelsey 2015: 95–6). But also vice versa, they are signs of the transcendental effort involved in nailing the material limit of the world, binding it to the generalised, unending dying.

Immortal looping: pain freely accepted

There is something like a deliberate embrace of trauma here, the 'acting out' of which, LaCapra warns, the unceasing repetition of disturbing past moments and emotions in which the integrity of a person is fundamentally threatened. Through such looping, things are both forever of their time and never-ending, turning in an endless bubble. They are thus simultaneously highly contextualised and resistant to contextualisation. This is visible in the deathly eyes of Cameron's subjects, in the perpetuated intimations of violence and of demise. So long as this experience is not let go, 'limbo' and compression persist. Looping makes the past immortal, extending it beyond its place and time. The cost exacted is high: the pain and loss are ever present, even as transfiguration occurs.

What we behold in images of 'limbo' is not some attempt to attain release from suffering by rehearsing it, working through it – or at least, it is not just that. The last thing that tortured immortality seeks is to be cured, for this would end its eternal repetition. 'Only pain freely accepted purifies us and makes us grow in stature, for it bears hope in its breast', Berzosa tell us (Sólo el dolor libremente aceptado purifica y engrandece; porque lleva en su seno la esperanza) (Ros de Olano 1863: 7). This is literally an unhealthy thought. We are invited voluntarily to become unwell, to refuse to let go of our sickness, physically and mentally, in order to reach beyond our place and time: 'The philosophy of pain is

1 Mariano Fortuny, *Fantasia on Faust*

2 *Pompeii: Street of Tombs* (image for megalethoscope)

3 Édouard Manet, *The Execution of Maximilian*

4 Eugenio Lucas Velázquez, *Felipe IV, His Court, and the Meninas*

5　Prilidiano Pueyrredón, *Siesta*

6　Gustave Courbet, *The Wrestlers*

7 Rosa Bonheur, *Spanish Muleteers Crossing the Pyrenees*

8 William Holman Hunt, *The Scapegoat*

9 Jean-François Millet, *The Angelus*

10 Antonio Gisbert, *The Comuneros Padilla, Bravo and Maldonado on the Scaffold*

11 James McNeill Whistler, *Nocturne in Blue and Gold: Valparaíso Bay*

12 Insects from the Pacific Expedition

13 José Agustín Arrieta, *Disorderly Table – Green Glass Decanter, Bell-Glass Vase and Candelabra*

14 Hermenegildo Bustos, *Still Life with Frog, Watermelon, and Scorpion*

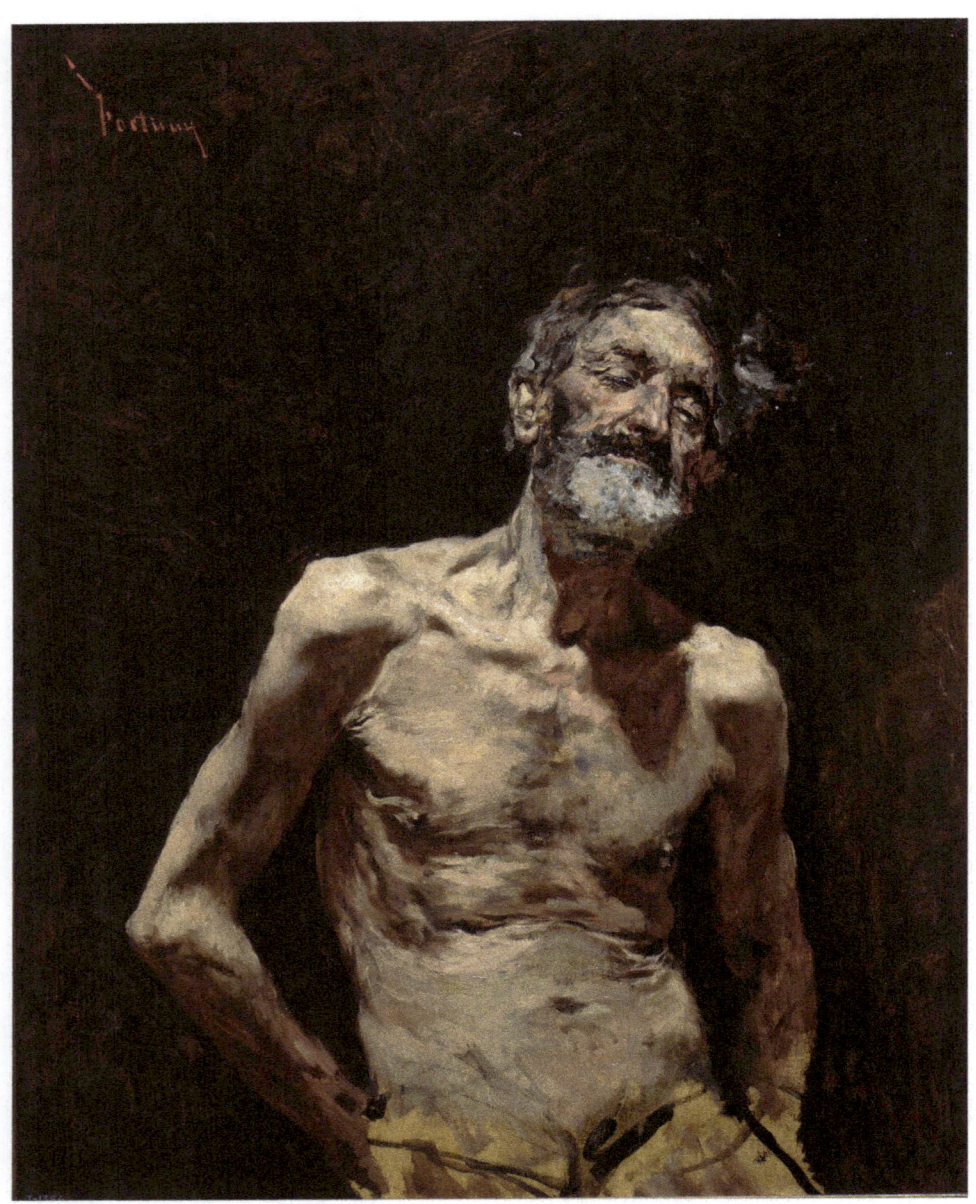

15 Mariano Fortuny, *Old Man Naked in the Sun*

16 Mariano Fortuny, *Choosing the Model*

17 Gustave Courbet, *The Painter's Studio: Real Allegory*

18 Eduardo Rosales, *Presentation of Don Juan de Austria to the Emperor Carlos V in Yuste*

19 Francisco Laso, *The Three Races (Equality before the Law)*

20 Eduardo Rosales, *Isabel the Catholic Dictating Her Will*

the universal philosophy', Berzosa's prologue begins (La filosofía del dolor, es la filosofía universal) (1863: 5). This involves much more than a call to empathy or sympathy brought about by shared suffering. It has an appalling, sacrificial intimacy. Berzosa tells us that the 'photograph of sentiment' involves 'writing with blood from the wounds of the lacerated heart' (fotografía del sentimiento … Escribir con sangre de las heridas del corazón lacerado) (1863: 8). Such words find an echo in Cameron's images and their vivid collection of the residue of human bodies.

Just as Berzosa's 'photograph of sentiment' forms a singular 'imperceptible point', so Walter Benjamin's Angel of History sees only 'one single catastrophe which unceasingly piles rubble on top of rubble and piles it at his feet'. There is a 'storm' that blows towards the Angel through all history from the past. Silverman underlines the parallel of this vision to Benjamin's account of the photographic, 'propelled … towards a particular look …. It travels through time and space to reach this look' (2015: loc.168–78). The agonies of history, the episodes of suffering, then, enable all humanity across the centuries to engage in a 'reciprocity' of gazes, seeing the 'single catastrophe' as if through the eyes of the Angel. But whereas – on Silverman's account – the Benjaminian photographic vision promises potential, messianic release (2015: loc.178), the 'photograph of sentiment' becomes universal precisely by keeping the wounds forever open: that is its hope.

This is not an invitation to reverse the direction of travel, to pass back through the experience of 'catastrophe', the hurling rubble of time, to some point that preceded them, perhaps to some imagined early childhood state of humanity. It is not untempting – for example – to seek a parallel in Cameron's photographs to something like Julia Kristeva's vision of creativity. Carol Mavor traces such a comparison between the photographer and the latter's *Stabat Mater* (Mavor 1995: 60–4). For Kristeva, the artist is inherently involved in 'murder', but is distinguished 'from all other sacrificial murderers and victims' by 'returning, through the event of death' such that the artist 'sketches out a kind of second birth' (Kristeva 2002: 56). In so doing, they undo disciplined structures of sign-making that form in the supposed Oedipal phase. In many of Cameron's images, such as her Madonnas, 'the generative link between mother and child is tied, erotically, to the process of photographic generation'; soft-focus resists patriarchal mastery, Carol Armstrong suggests (1996: 136, 126). Kelsey observes likewise how 'the sticky wetness of the collodion process eroticises and maternalises her photography' (2015: 78). But this no more takes us out the other side of the enduring sacrifice than Cameron sought to overthrow the imperial system or the domestic order, neither of which she wished more than to nuance (Rosen 2015; Armstrong 1996). Rather the maternal bond, like all else, persists in the moment of its sacrifice: 'the womb is never far from the tomb', Mavor laconically observes (Mavor 1995: 54). In *Doctor Lañuela*, the desolate ending likewise offers allusions to the love of originary bonds solely in their very destruction: the male protagonist loves only the parents he has lost and the children he does not have; his female counterpart (Camila) embraces him like a mother, but has no offspring (Ros de Olano 1863: 174, 277).

The experience of violence that unites place and time is not safe and does not, in itself, lead to any place of safety. Sensuously held forever at the moment of mortal pain, we would be engaged in history's 'edge play'. Writing of the practice of erotic asphyxiation, Downing evokes 'the dissolution of the self in SM scenes … extreme experiences that push us to the limits of consciousness and shatter rationality, … to the literal level of potential bodily death' (2007: 123, 128–9). Not dissimilarly, 'Elaine' – singing '*Call, I follow, I follow, let me die!'* – cannot determine which is 'sweeter', which she would enjoy more: to lose her sanity in self-destructive desire, 'shattering rationality', or a 'bodily death'. Pondering 'the lifelessness of many of Cameron's sitters' and 'their lush tresses', Kelsey finds himself moved to comparison with Browning's poem 'Porphyria's Lover' (Porphyria, the woman's name, also denotes a disease that leads to insanity). Here, the poet throttles his female lover with her own hair, supposedly to the satisfaction of both (2015: 91). Aesthetically – the ending of *Doctor Lañuela* suggests – such courting of destruction gives birth to an erotic poetics: a dance and sung poem of courtship, a *seguidilla*, in which we are invited to join. In this song, 'our existence' – its bounds breached by Berzosa's chisel, its guiding structures gone – forms 'pathless wastelands' where we walk by 'rivers of lamentation and blood' (nuestra existencia; páramo sin sendero; de llanto y sangre ... ríos) (Ros de Olano 1863: 282). Such, in its full sensual allure, might be the landscape of all place and time at the 'imperceptible point'.

A graphic image of endless trauma is to be found in the statue of *Andromache* (1853) by José Vilches, which has ultimately found its way onto Madrid's Paseo de Recoletos. There it stands forever silently wailing its tragic fate, as people walk by, trees grow, and the urban scene changes about it. It grasps at its head, staring to one side with a look of pained incomprehension, as if unable to process the enormity of its suffering, bent over in agony, desperately and irrationally gripping for safety at the cloths that drape it. In 'The Swan' (Le Cygne), Andromache surges to Baudelaire's mind too, recalling all those whose melancholy does not change with changing time: the captives, the vanquished, the Africans torn from their homeland. The suffering Homeric widow appears in 'ecstasy' (en extase) – beyond the limits of her own self – by a tomb amid the transforming city of Paris that Baudelaire sees through 'double vision' (1972: 211–13; Meltzer 2011). The unintended setting of Vilches's work underlines how, like all such statues, it is extracted from the original conditions of life of its subject matter, and, in that way, persistent through time. In a treatise of 1865, Vilches describes great sculptures as composites of spirit and matter, into which the artist has infused 'the breath of life' (el soplo de la vida) (Vilches 1865: 13). It is easy to look past such phrasing, perhaps because it is so unsettling, with its suggestions of ancient magic, its evocations of antique myth from Egyptian Ka statues to Pygmalion. For Vilches, the very act of transforming the given (matter such as stone) through what is not given ('el convencional', feeling and thought) resonates with what it means to be a human person (1865: 13–16). By the same token, such a fusion is never more resonant than in depicting 'the figure of the thinking being' (la figura del ser que piensa) (1865: 16). This very notion suggests we encounter in the statue an experience of a person that is not reducible to something for which it stands, in crude allegory. Representation is not understood here in opposition to the natural, as a conventional construct might be to a given nature (1865: 16), but rather as matter, feelings and thoughts are fused in a person. In the presence of a statue, we are in company with personhood itself, with the 'breath of life'. Alongside *Andromache*, we keep company with a humanity forever suffering, always distraught, endlessly repeating trauma.

Such encounters were fundamental to much of what we now call *historicism*. For at least two decades, they had been commemorated on a massive scale in history paintings, like the influential French artist Paul Delaroche's quietly terrified *Princes in the Tower* (1831), awaiting coming murder, or his sober and sobering *Lady Jane Grey* (1833) bowed for her beheading. Images of this kind draw out from the past fragmentary moments of mortal intensity. The very efforts of painters such as Delaroche at authentic historical detail, and reconstruction from past documents, give us scenes that are detached from their before and after, while still projecting out of the context of their place and time. In them, similar moments of 'limbo' are repeated again and again in diverse events over the centuries, and now held before our eyes. Scenes of this kind – all these individuals at the moment of their demise – are collected together for us in our present, irrespective of their time of origin, becoming each others' alike contemporaries. While in France, this kind of historical representation was in crisis by the time of the 1855 Salon (Çakmak 2017: 1), efforts in Spain redoubled with the support of the state (Vázquez 2001: 115–20). National Exhibitions with prizes were instituted as of 1856 and works collected for a new national museum (Díez 1992: 81). The images were part of a widespread, post-revolutionary obsession with reassembling the country by reconstructing the remnants of its histories, such as we saw in Eugenio Lucas Velázquez (see Chapter 2).

The point at issue was not, as such, whether such pasts were accessible in representation, as a signified might be in a sign. Rather, the assumption was that, in and through the present, the legacies of many timescales – including signs and cultural forms – exhibit multiple and complex relationships and tensions. The intricate challenge was how these interconnections might be reconfigured now, effecting a subtle, contested experience of time (Ginger 2012a). The nineteenth-century present was, then, inherently 'anachronic', to borrow Alexander Nagel and Christopher Wood's term (Nagel & Wood 2010). The 'present' moment consisted of compounded layers of time, rather than being bounded off from other pasts of which it would provide autonomous representations. In assembling collections and in mounting exhibitions of history paintings, largely (though not exclusively) populated by the dying, the dead and the slaughtered, the state organised a kind of 'heterotopia' of demise.

This ultimate disregard for chronological divides is powerfully evident in the prizewinning painting *The Comuneros Padilla, Bravo and Maldonado on the Scaffold* (1860; Plate 10) by Antonio Gisbert. In this image, we see the execution of major figures from a sixteenth-century rebellion against Carlos V of Habsburg that was a continual reference point for Spanish Progressive Liberals. Juan de Padilla, their leader, appears before us centre-stage as the principal protagonist, awaiting decapitation. Already his eyes are closed like those of photographed corpses. This pose not only presents him as a vision of the living dead, but it separates him from the scenes unfurling about him through chronological time, as if he were immune to it, and it finally irrelevant to him. Two monks look upon him, imprecating him from each side. All the characters about him are, in Fried's terms, absorbed, avoiding the gaze of the beholder, wrapped up in the action. The historic narrative unfolds to its conclusion, as if in a diagonal from the viewer's lower left to upper right before him, from a companion being prepared for the block to the head of another held high. While Padilla is framed within this past moment, yet he stands wilfully impassive, upright, arms crossed, at once at the centre of the historical action and now detached from it. His closed eyes echo Delaroche's blindfolded Lady Jane Grey. The aversion of gazes – Stephen Bann has observed – prevents any closure of the past narrative, because there is no pattern of exchanged looks that could provide the requisite combination of oppositions and resolutions (Bann 1997: 29, 117, 126). Outside the interchanged gazes that make up the story around him, Padilla appears to escape finality. It would not be hard to imagine him floating out of the painting directly into our contemporary space, emerging across the dais which tips almost out of the image.

The very deathliness of Padilla thus evokes pastness, not as gone, but as continuing potentiality, a 'dynamic moment': his corpselike demeanour, the closed eyes, suggest that the mortal loss of passing time may be identical to its persistence, as if presenting us with a supposition informing an anachronic historicism. The effect obviates the very conditions of a broader dilemma that Bann has described: that of 'having a "desire for history" while being forever barred from consummating it' (Bann 1995: 53). In so doing, it throws into relief a dependence of anachronic vision upon slaughter, like the galleries of simultaneous death and murder to which it belongs. In an influential ode to Padilla (1797), the Spanish revolutionary poet Manuel José Quintana depicts the fall of the hero as the dawning of imperial violence, the moment of Hispanic and Habsburg *monarchia* in Europe and beyond: the assault on the indigenous peoples of the Americas, the (connected) enslavement of Africans, the violence against France, Italy and the Netherlands. In turn, Padilla's demise obviates any freedom won from the imperialism of Islamic powers in the Middle Ages. Quintana writes that, faced with the degradation of Spain, his own 'desire courses … through the continual revolving of times' (discurre mi deseo por … el continuo / revolver de los tiempos). The result is that he is able to attain – and offer us – a new kind of perception in which Padilla is not simply dead: 'vedle', see him, Quintana says, 'how full of generous ire he swirls crying out about us' (cuán lleno / de generosa ira / clamando en torno de nosotros gira) (Quintana 1978: 119, 122). ('Look at your sister', the hypnotist said.) In ensuring that we behold the deadness of Padilla, even as he is among us, in meeting our gaze with closed eyes, Gisbert emphasises the vicarious relationship of that *see him* to the violent death that Padilla met.

It is as if to recognise that Benjamin's Angel of History needs the past to be filled with cataclysms, so that it can watch history's rubble being hurled continuously towards it. At once theatrically beheld upon the stagelike dais, and absorbed – in Fried's terms – Padilla evokes, not just an alternate kind of vision that escapes both of these, but an insistence on not deflecting from a murder that enables us to behold the past as present. In the clinging to the living dead, in the intimacy with those passed or passing away, with death itself, there is an urge once more to bring out of the world what is 'classic' in it, those 'powerful pulsations … that are transmitted … across place and time', as Wood has it. *Victorian Afterlives* amounted to a preoccupation with 'how voices might linger beyond the grave', Robert Douglas-Fairhurst remarks (2002: 1). We might reverse this observation: only by dying could a person truly affirm their immortality, for only then would their voice 'linger beyond the grave', only then would their work be felt fully 'classic'. In *Secure the Shadow*, a study of mortuary photography, Jay Ruby recalls how, by the early 1870s, the famous French actress Sarah Bernhardt evoked the genre when still alive by repeatedly posing in a coffin (1995: 34). If this is – as Ruby supposes – a parody, it is so in the sense of a homage, an amused but brazen assertion of her status as a classic. The shape of a corpse pulsating with the forms of life, as if asleep, is a live person pulsating with the forms of a corpse that pulsates with the forms of life – and so on, ad infinitum. It is by embracing the 'catastrophe' found by Roland Barthes in 'every photograph' (2000: 96) – the person's death now or yet to come – that the actress traces her future passage back and forth across the grave, and, at the same time, shows us what it is to undertake such a passage through a mortuary photograph, even the necrophiliac desire that informs the wish for immortality, a longing to be dead and to be desired as a corpse. The ironies of Bernhardt's mortuary performance suggest the textures of relationships among timescales, the intricacies of the notion of 'influence' that Douglas-Fairhurst (2002) delicately explores. But, as with the jokes of *Fausto*, these are inflections of an affirmation – that something is experienced as shared across history – not a placing of it forever in doubt in a *vaivén*, a ping-pong between assertion and denial.

Through the forms of a corpse, an artist's vital power may thus be experienced as projected out across place and time, as resonant with the very depths of time, like some fallen and ever-resurrected god. This is especially apparent in efforts to bind the newest of media with antique images and visual techniques, as we find in Cameron's images of the impending death of her performers, like *'Call, I follow, I follow, let me die!'* A case in point is the photographic record of Mariano Fortuny – the painter of *Fantasia on Faust*, which we saw in Chapter 1 – lying dead. Fortuny had been the most internationally successful of Spanish artists, his works sought out by purchasers across Europe and the Americas. His brief life had, for a time, fulfilled the dream of reconnecting the arts of Spain with a culture that reached out across the globe, an echo of the fantasy of universal monarchy, as entertained by his in-laws, the Madrazos (see Chapter 2). Likewise, his passing through history was perceived both as of lasting significance and as placing him anachronically among other layers of time. He was the very image of renewed commonality across place and time.

In an obituary in the newspaper *La Época* on 4 December 1874, Eusebio Blasco remarks that Fortuny was one of a very few artists who truly revolutionised painting. It is precisely this departure that makes him a good companion of the classics that he now joins. Blasco expresses terror at the 'empty place' (sitio vacío) where Fortuny was, while affirming, 'he cannot die, his death is yet another dream/sleep' (no puede morir, su muerte es otro sueño). Likewise, Blasco declares: 'I have felt the breath of Raphael or Michaelangelo in the *loggias* of the Vatican' (he sentido el hálito de Rafael o Miguel Ángel en las logias del Vaticano). These words echo with the title of Spain's most famous play, *Life is a Dream* (*La vida es sueño*) (1635) by Pedro Calderón de la Barca. It insinuates not merely the identity of such a life and death, but, like Bernhardt's performance, the disposition that informs such an experience. It is only by denying that life is truly, substantively life, and death truly, substantively death, only by treating both as a 'dream', that one can have an intimate experience of their commonality, of an empty space filled even so with a corpse's breath. It is through this dreaming that Fortuny is in the living company of dead artists.

In his mortuary photograph, Fortuny lies, his eyes shut, with mouth pursed as if breathing gently like Blasco's departed Raphael or Michaelangelo. He exhibits what Caruth describes as 'the uncanny similarity … between the unconsciousness of sleeping and the unconsciousness of dying... *not knowing* the difference between life and death' (1996: 36–7). Beyond his individual persistence, the image, with its white cloths and laurel crown, overlays shapes from across the centuries: medieval tomb sculpture with reclining bodies of the great; public statuary of laureates, such as the monument to Dante erected in Florence in the mid-1860s, draped in the classicising sheet of a toga; and the domestic nineteenth-century memento scene of the freshly departed. The particularities of nineteenth-century Spanish existence are not lost, but rather merge into something both antique and enduring (and vice versa), something both of the past and the future, as the body flickers between life and death. The moment is anachronic: the revolutionary departure is layered with, takes shape in, centuries of history. All these lines and forms are drawn using light that is literally, physically extracted from the corpse and its surroundings. The dead body, duly arranged, provides the material for its own escape from mortal limits, feeding its own copy.

Death: bringer of copies

Often what is encountered in the channels opened across the worlds of life and death, in what Quintana called the 'revolving of times', are resemblances and echoes, manifest at the critical moment of mortality and fundamental loss. Copies formed out of the literal or figurative death of the 'original' may ensure the latter's persistence beyond its apparent end point in time, like Michaud's 'presence' of the image that is an 'absence'. Gisbert's image of Padilla extending out into our era suggests not only the similarity of the two moments, but that Padilla's likeness – as conjured up in the artist's paint – manifests itself in the nineteenth century. 'I thought of copies' – one of Fernández Mallo's characters says resonantly in *Limbo* – 'because copies are everything' (pensé en copias porque las copias lo son todo) (2014a: loc.1892). This is less a phenomenon that can be reduced to a single, causal explanation (such as the indexical properties of photography, or the rules of physics) than it is a way of exploring and making connections, a practice that offers affordances. The shared effects of copying may be traced 'more often by similitude' between different kinds of copy, Hillel Schwartz suggests in his layered and textured volume *The Culture of the Copy* (2014: 17). Death appears again and again as the bringer of copies, less in one single guise, in expression of a single theory, than through 'family resemblances' that enable us to 'go on'.

Doctor Lañuela evokes the quest for true resemblance – the authentic copy – beyond chronology and place, echoing its folding of time, of birth, life and death together into a single point. The problem facing humanity – the first-person narrator tells us – is that after it emerged from a single mother and dispersed into diverse peoples, 'the ties of fraternity lay broken by dissimilarity' (el lazo de la fraternidad estuvo roto por la desemejanza) (1863: 57). Remedying this involves a destructive encounter with candidates for universality, envisaged either as an emptying out – a deterritorialising – or as an allegory of shared loss brought about in the violent interaction both of located European cultures and of that very force of deterritorialisation. While each of these passes through a living death, each evoking its own destructions, neither proves adequate to the task of restoring true similarity. This is at once a teasing through of how true copying may arise and of the latters' genesis from violence, literal and metaphorical. In that, at least, *Doctor Lañuela* resembles more recent reflections on sacrifice that seek to discern between varieties of such slaughter, and – in a sacrificial act – to overcome the versions that oppress us. In that sense, at least, it offers what Dennis Keenan calls 'a sacrifice of sacrifice' (2005: 8).

The Doctor of the title is repeatedly referred to as 'the world' (el mundo), meaning both *worldliness* and the entirety of the globe and the totality of people and things. Lañuela exists in one version of 'limbo' as a 'symbolic statue raised as a boundary line between the region of the living and the mansion of the dead' (estatua simbólica levantada como término entre la región de los vivos y la mansión de los muertos) (1863: 221). At this point of passage between life and death, we find all specificity, all content emptied out of the world, to form a universality that is applicable indiscriminately, indifferently to any situation, rather than by transfiguring particularities. This truly is Laclau's '*empty place*' of '*empty signifiers*' (Laclau 2000: 57). 'I am just as French as I am Moorish;' Lañuela tells us, 'and I can pass as easily from Moorish to Spanish and Greek; and I come and go through languages as I pass the frontiers of all nations' (lo mismo soy yo francés que moro; y tan me paso al moro como al español y al griego; y entro y salgo por los idiomas como paso las fronteras de todas las naciones). He does so because he has freed himself from any need to know what the specific signs might amount to: 'To be from everywhere (he added), two things are needed: to walk straight ahead, and not to speak any language well' (Para ser de todas partes (añadió), se necesitan dos cosas: marchar de frente y no hablar bien ningún idioma) (1863: 231).

An alternative sacrifice is offered by the magnetised woman whom he controls. Luz (light, or electricity), is the 'woman of all nations' (mujer de todas las naciones) (1863: 57), associated with nineteenth-century sacrificial images of femininity, such as we have seen in Cameron's photography. She has attained this state through the excruciating pain of her existence, formed in a story that interconnects civilisations of Europe and the Mediterranean through the destruction of those very bonds. The broad pattern of these preoccupations echoes with Ros de Olano's concerns in his *Legends of Africa* (*Leyendas de África*) published three years previously, just after he helped lead Spanish troops into Tetouan, Morocco in 1860. There he dwells on the relative merits of seeking foundations in 'European' and Christian as opposed to Islamic cultures, on the historic relationship of Spain with the Muslim world given the long history and legacy of Islamic Iberia, and on the merits and perils of reviving Spain's imperial past (Ginger 2000: 194–200). Luz's life, in turn, evokes the legacies and afterlife of such foundational cultures of the region: the classical, the Islamic, the relationship of north and south in Europe (which Nietzsche was soon to ponder) and the sometime great rivals for Oceanic and American empire: the Spanish and the English. Her relationship with Lañuela is resonant with visions of deterritorialising cosmopolitanism mixed in with these. She exists like a fault line along the connection between all these, an experience of loss emanating from the contact between them. Now taken to the capital of Spain, she is the illicit orphaned child of a Hellenic mother married to a North European, English father living in the land of the Moors. The mother passed away in sorrow after conceiving Luz with the exiled, deterritorialised Lañuela, who, stealing his child back, revealed the truth to the father who likewise died of a broken heart (1863: 192–3).

Perpetually hypnotised, a glowing presence, Luz exists in her own limbo: her hands are rigid like those of a corpse, cold as marble; her touch invades Josef with deathliness (1863: 178). Magnetisation befits her being a transmission point between life and death, as it does the destruction of 'the idea of a bounded person' (Warner 2006: 247), the demise of her personal integrity, even as it gives her the universalising, electrical force that we met in Chapter 1. She is now less a person than a universalising force and 'shape', a *Luz*. Turned through mortal pain into an abstraction, she has become an allegory. Reflecting in his account of *Moby Dick* on Benjamin's vision of allegories, Bainard Cowan observes how dying – literal and figurative – may be experienced as an emptying out of specific and particular sense, such that what remains may become a focal point for all 'the community of the bereft' (1982: 178). 'Allegory dries out … the living things of this world in order to turn them into emblems. If it empties them of all life, it fills them with significance' (1982: 161). But if this realises a kind of alternate commonality, it leaves Luz now at a remove from her own existence, as it does from the lived experience of the suffering that traced its connections across Europe. The fusion of the particular with the universal is only apparent. When her personal existence truly intrudes, as she falls in love with Josef, she definitively dies, and Allegory falls.

Lying beyond such generalising visions of universality is an experience of being wounded by them and coming face to face with a person's own mortality. This is evoked in the protagonist Josef, who declares that 'sometimes, I think it may be that it all must amount to my being the last link in the magnetico-living chain and I resign myself to this; because it is certainly true that after me come only Nothing and Nobody' (A veces, creo si todo consisitirá en que yo sea el último eslabón de la cadena magnético-viviente y me conformo; porque lo cierto es que tras mí sólo vienen la nada y el nadie) (1863: 60). In *The Gift of Death*, Derrida reflects that for each being, there can be only one death that is truly a death, its own. After each of us comes only Nothing and Nobody, as Ros de Olano would have it: 'My irreplaceability is therefore conferred, delivered, "given", one can say, by death.' 'To have the experience of one's absolute singularity and apprehend one's own death' (2008: 42) is to realise a new universal law, that replaces the universalised rules of systems of ethics (2008: 67). In *Language and Death*, the Italian philosopher Giorgio Agamben suggests that with such a realisation comes an awareness of two things that together both fundamentally inform our experience of being, and are impossible to experience and articulate within it. On the one hand, there is the very ground of being, of which nothing can be said: there can be no being beyond being, no terms outside being in which to explain it (1991: xiii, 18). On the other hand, there is our own death, which – Heidegger observed – is both essential to and beyond our experience of being, marking its limits (Agamben 1991: 1–2). Accepting that, after us, beyond each of us, is only Nothing and Nobody, we find what Agamben calls the '*completed foundation of humanity*' (1991: 106; original emphasis). In *Doctor Lañuela*, to 'apprehend one's own death' is to renounce even the notion of an extensive, unfurling being. The 'compressed' structure of *Doctor Lañuela*, tracing Josef's life, is pointedly at odds with philosophies, whether in Hegel or in Heidegger, that set out 'an expansive and extensive giving of form to being (even where that paradoxically meant incorporating chaos)' (Ginger 2000: 202).

Here we encounter an alternate universalism and, in the very singularity itself, the authentic copy. 'We all bear within ourselves an authorised copy of our sentence rendered into pieces', Berzosa says. 'The rare privilege of the true poet consists in making us read it through the ordered bringing together of its agglomerated fragments' (Todos llevamos dentro de nosotros mismos copia autorizada de nuestra sentencia hecha pedazos: el raro privilegio del verdadero poeta consiste en hacérnosla leer por la ordenada juntura de sus fragmentos aglomerados). In isolation, each individual is a 'dead letter' (letra muerta). That is to say, they would simply mirror their apparent opposites, empty universals and allegories, that evacuate, kill off the experience of our living death: they could not articulate the 'authorised copy of our sentence' in the way that Josef or the book do. Humanity is constituted rather of a 'multitude of trivialities grouped together in the shape of a cone' (multitud de pequeñeces agrupadas en forma de cono), Berzosa affirms. That is, it is the combination (combinación) of all individual lives: the 'grouping together' implies the singularity of each being (1863: 12). But this is not a matter of contiguity alone, of juxtaposition of separate things, for the 'grouping together' entails the articulation of each as an 'authorised copy of our sentence', each being followed by Nothing and Nobody. It is in the imminent death of each recognisably singular life – Ros de Olano suggests – that we encounter the 'universal philosophy' of mortal pain, as we do through Cameron's portraits. The blood sacrifice of *Doctor Lañuela* enables us to see through and in each individual how they echo with all humanity, how they are copies.

At times, the thing that appears as if alive through the moment of death is a copy of itself, its own similitude: that is, it is its own self repeated. Photography is perhaps the most famous case in point, 'embalming' the transient moment as it dies away, giving us an hallucination that is an ordinary reality, Bazin observes (1960: 4–9). Taxidermy – a parallel and much more ancient art, more dependent still upon the singular being – underwent a new flourishing in the nineteenth century, becoming an obsession for amateurs as much as professionals (Poliquin 2012: 10, 68–71). It was very often made possible by human violence against other species, the killing of animals. Historically, the practice in Europe had taken wing on a fascination with non-European worlds, and was energised by European colonisation in the Americas, following Columbus's voyage from Spain (Poliquin 2012: 14–16). In her book, *The Breathless Zoo*, Rachel Poliquin speculates on the fascination, from pleasure to repulsion, produced by taxidermied animals, and what motivates human beings to create them. She notes how such objects have an irreducible quality that shapes the observer's experience: 'Viewers can never escape the startling realisation that this static thing in a very real sense is an animal still' (2012: 50). Taxidermied animals possess what Poliquin (perhaps echoing Heidegger) calls *thingness* and *thereness*: the quality of truly being other entities before us in the world (2012: 13, 39). This is – we might say – an encounter with the degree zero of mimesis: the animal itself, not even the light reflected from it and received in photographic reproduction. When assembled in museum collections of the nineteenth century, in the quest for the scientific order of the world, these individuals become specimens (Poliquin 2012: 111–15). Each taxidermied animal, like every part of Berzosa's cone of human life, thus exemplifies and embodies the whole species: in seeing a rat in 'limbo' as an example of *Rat* we see how it is 'an authorised copy' of a general case, of a commonality, of all rats that will individually live and die and that have done so. By the same token, like the parts of Berzosa's cone, like Josef, what we have before us is not a generic type or concept of an animal: it is a particular, specific creature that lived in this world, as Poliquin urges (2012: 168, 223). Only in the singularity of its dying can we encounter the 'authorised copy'.

On the one hand, the particular becomes general and vice versa, extending a commonality out of the individual animal through a species across place and time. On the other hand, it is through the very literal persistence of those qualities that the beast is projected outwards beyond its originating context, journeying across time, its life now connecting moments across generations (at least, if the taxidermy has been done well). As with a photograph, the degree zero of mimesis of each individual remains whatever adjustments are made to the animals, and even in our awareness of such modifications. The raw material is very evident and present, Poliquin notes (2012: 50). Conversely, in its most fundamental form – the removal of entrails, the use of preservative chemicals, for example – the act of artistically altering the beast is inherent to its persistence beyond the limits of its originary time and place, and its own mortal span. Such are 'the techniques that aid the passage into an afterlife', as Samuel Alberti puts it (2011: 6) The Spanish taxidermist Juan Grau Bassas observes in 1849 that the 'infinite duration' (duración infinita) of the object depends on whether it is 'kept away from light, dust, and humidity' (resguardado de la luz, del polvo y de la humedad) (1849: 35). Its eternal life depends on its separation from the conditions of biological existence. Samuel Swinney has gone so far as to say that 'reconstruction[s] ... absolves the animal of the necessity for ... base functions'. It is thus purified (2011: 221). Put at its most brutal, the vast majority of taxidermied creatures were slaughtered and their flesh and innards pulled out precisely so as to render them persistent. Looking at them is akin to viewing the aftermath of some animal sacrifice in the pursuit of magical ends. We may observe the now putatively redeemed creature, but cannot be unaware of the violence that took it to where it is, a mixture – as Poliquin suggests (2012: 10) – of immortality and death. The stuffed beast lives off its own slaughter.

Preserved human remains may create a like effect of immortal limbo, exercising a similar fascination and persistence in their 'thingness' and 'thereness', finding persistence and commonality though singular deaths, specific bodies. In this way, the physical victims of history's catastrophes might travel towards Benjamin's Angel. Amid liberal Spain's obsession with the material reconstruction of history, the supposed mummies of the medieval Lovers of Teruel were put on view, twice embalmed: in the flesh, as it were, and in the mid-century photographic record by Jose Martínez Sánchez, whom we met in Chapter 1 (1867) (Figure 11). Here, risen from their grave, are two figures portrayed as martyrs in the most celebrated version of their tale: the Progressive Liberal, Eugenio Hartzenbusch's Romantic drama, *The Lovers of Teruel* (Los amantes de Teruel) (1837). The doomed pair were associated with the projection into the future of a loving liberty – truly inclusive of women – precisely through its own destruction under the pressures of a medieval past, such that a later time could reconnect to it. Their erotic love takes them each to suicide, one upon the other's body, in the face of the pressures of Christian–Islamic conflict, prejudices masked as historic religion, and the conflicts of the states that later become a united Spanish kingdom (Ginger 2012a: 169–83). The force of the three-dimensional object, as of the photograph, evokes the looping refusal to let go, to allow the bodies to disperse and the lifelike 'shape' to be gone. It has something of what LaCapra describes as a 'bond with the dead, especially with dead intimates', which 'may invest trauma with value and make its reliving a painful and necessary commemoration or memorial to which one remains dedicated or at least bound' (2001: 22).

The mummies' catastrophe and limbo become those of all human history. The resultant dark, nondescript bodies could as easily be the larval form from which all living humans might emerge, as the dessicated death into which we all fall (Ginger 2015). The dead may be experienced as undifferentiated copies – Marcus Boon has suggested – and, conversely, a newborn is not yet a differentiated being (2013: loc.923, 1074). The couple are both specifically themselves and, in the generic outline of their corpses, lovers in general, the one tipping a head to heed the other. Skirted, their genitals concealed, their biological sex shrivelled, they at once recall the man and woman they were, while forming an androgynous pair, their image pulsating too across gendered divides, like the photographic 'shapes' we met in Chapter 1.

In such obsessive attachments to the departed, the singular mummified body might fuse private life with the public understanding of the human species, as scientific displays burgeoned. Doctor Velasco, renowned physician, co-founder of Spain's Economic Society of Embalming (Sociedad Económica de Embalsamiento) and director of the country's anatomical museums from 1857 to 1864, vividly created such an effect in his mourning for his daughter. By 1875, Velasco had established Spain's Anthropological Museum in Madrid, which was the same building as his private residence, such that he lived his own life amid preserved remnants of the dead, specimens of the species that were copies of themselves. Once the institution was inaugurated, in a conflation of public vocation and private grief, he had his embalmed offspring dug up, and was delighted to find how successful his efforts had been. Her body was not just preserved, but flexible. After allowing the mummified corpse to dry out, he installed her in the Museum chapel, initially personalizing her disfigured features once more with make-up and a wig (Dorado Fernández et al. 2010: 18–20). It was as if she

11 José Martínez Sánchez, *Mummies of the Lovers of Teruel*

were one more exhibit, another piece of the cone, as it were, and uniquely, belovedly singular in her dying.

Amid Downing's 'obscure collusion of life and death', amid passionate attachments, we may find an erotics in the deathly bringing of copies. In *The Nineteenth Century* (aka *The Wounded Bullfighter*) (1871; Figure 12) by the Spanish and Catalan sculptor Rossend Nobas, the fallen individual clasps their lower stomach, their back arching in pain, their head pushed back, mouth open, eyes gazing at the heavens. Death throes enliven the statue, lending it dynamic curves, its knee pushed out beyond its constraining pedestal. Forever in 'limbo', the vision's unending mortal suffering is also its undying pleasure. Penetrated by a bull, it alluringly thrusts out its buttocks, its hand slides down towards its groin. Its arched back and open mouth evoke writhing delight, orgasm even. The bullfighter offers something akin to what Bersani once described as 'the *jouissance* of exploded limits ... the ecstatic suffering into which the human organism momentarily plunges when it is "pressed" beyond a certain threshold of endurance'. In his celebrated essay on anal sex, 'Is the Rectum a Grave?', Bersani relates such experiences to 'self-abolition' and 'an infinitely loved object of sacrifice' (1987: 217, 218, 222).

As the figure dissolves limits in its implicit animation, its gender and identity, like those of Bonheur's muleteers, shifts through resemblances beyond any single fixed vision. It is thus freed to be mimetic of and available to multiple human forms of intense intimacy, pulsating across them, as if forming a fluid, but generalised copy of the species, an authorised copy of our collective erotic sentence. It could as easily be a person poised to thrust forward with its genitals, as to receive, or both. More still, its genital region is remarkably flat, even though a bullfighter would, at the time, be male. A slight vertical fold of clothing appears between its legs, lending the figure an androgynous appearance with its reminiscence of a vagina. The effect is reinforced by the gentle relief of the shirt and jacket, which might suggest the outline of small breasts. As the apparition's suffering flows across life and death, and through genders and sexualities, it moves through specificity and universality, past and present, layering time anachronically with the force of something 'classic' like the dead Fortuny. The generalising label 'SIGLO XIX' emerges from and merges into the extraordinarily elaborate particularity of the detail: the intricate delicate patterning of the trousers, the little dangling baubles, the fine creases of the shirt. The statue claims to be mimetic at once of something closely associated with Spain (bullfighting) and something general to humanity (the century). In turn, the thrown-back head, the open-mouthed face, and upper body closely match the outlines of a sculpted woman: Gian Lorenzo Bernini's mystically orgasmic *Ecstasy of St Teresa* (1647–52), penetrated by an arrow in a religious wounding. The statue is in the altarpiece of Santa Maria della Vittoria in Rome. The face thus flickers with the image of a sixteenth-century Spanish patron saint, at the heart of the Universal Church.

In such a vision, the erotic dissolution of limits is brought about by the instances of historic and particular violence that the dissolution enables the image to copy; and, conversely, the things copied offer us the instances of historic and particular violence that bring about the dissolution of limits. It was not uncommon to believe that the hope, violence and suffering of the revolutionary and post-revolutionary age – the 'siglo' – echoed the 'saeculum' (siglo) of the Christian era. The crucifixion bound together hope and pain, dying and the future (*porvenir* in Spanish means both the afterlife and the time to come). Understood through an emotive recognition – an anagnorisis – such an apprehension of history might

12 Early photograph of Rossend Nobas, *The Nineteenth Century* (a.k.a. *The Wounded Bullfighter*)

unite all humanity through shared feeling (Ginger 2012a: 114–16). The struggles occurring in 1871 offered an opportunity to explore such sentiments once more. The latest uprising of the unstable era since 1808 unseated the Bourbon monarchy in 1868, and turbulence was growing, while in neighbouring France, the Prussian victory (on which Nietzsche reflected) saw the Third Empire fall. In turn, for social elites, the practice of bullfighting was resonant with the hopes and anxieties associated by a taste and capacity for violence among the Spanish populace, both in the controversial sport itself and its association with the 'nation', and in broader terms, including political uprisings (Ginger 2007a: 276–95). Strikingly, a poem published alongside a photograph of Nobas's statue in 1886 associates the vision of the 'siglo' with recurrent violence, from the 'gallant Hispanic' (gallardo hispano) who enters the present-day bullring to the larger, historic struggles with the rival English, Islamic Ottoman and Spanish empires – evoked likewise in *Doctor Lañuela*. The poem proves ambivalent, speaking of glory based on the barbaric pursuit of honour wherever it may be found, and the pathos of glory secured by killing a bull (1886: 3).

The very quality of being copiable may be evoked amid history's deathly, erotic dissolution, its erasure of clear limits. The Spanish Surrealist Salvador Dalí found this in Millet's *Angelus* – a painting redolent with the fate of France's peasantry, as we have seen. The pause for the prayer, the intimations of death, are overlain with symbolism of sex and fertility: the man's hat covering his genitals, as if his penis were erect (Dalí 2013: 134); the phallic fork rising beside him; the slightly bulging belly of the woman (Pollock 1977: 18). *The Angelus* is an obsessively, repeatedly reproduced image, the Surrealist observed (2013: 47). What makes the central figures so copiable, so easy to imitate (and parody), is their tendency to indifferentiation, as if emerging out of and into more nondescript shapes (Dalí 2013: 80–1), just as the Lovers of Teruel suggest the undifferentiated dead. The blurred sketchiness of the faces in shadowy half-light renders their features vague and all but interchangeable. What Murphy has said of Millet's *The Sower* may be said of *The Angelus*: we have individuals becoming the 'unindividuated peasant as an extended emblem', depicted in what many saw as Millet's 'crude, ugly' style (1999: 14, 2). The latter rough-edged realism of this Catholic-inspired image might in turn evoke the recurrent relationship of mid-nineteenth-century French to Spanish Golden-Age art: Millet had been a frequent visitor to the *Galérie espagnole* in Paris (Tinterow et al. 2003: 513–14) Not only could the 'shape' of each of the two figures be projected so as to form the other, but so vague are their features that it is easy to imagine them transposed into any number of different people – the paintings' viewers included – and vice versa. The composition of the work, with its doublings and parallels, is suggestive of repetitions and superpositions, an invitation to copy: the man and woman, both praying; the upright fork analogous to the male, the curve of the barrel and its contents shaped like the bent female. Dalí was moved to describe it as a kind of 'stereotype', a double vision, such as we found in Chapter 2 in Marx and Baudelaire, and in optical toys. In this reproducibility, the image exhibits what Marnin Young finds to be a double temporality at the heart of the painting's fascination. There is – Young argues – an excessive absorption of the two figures in the instant of time – their contemporary moment of agricultural change – which is at the same time an excessive absorption in the sempiternal customs of the tolling of the bells, its ancient duration (Young 2015: 8, 37–40). Likewise, the symmetrical composition echoes with the Great Tradition with the effect of 'recording a dissolving present and attempting to express a concept of the timeless', in Murphy's words (1999: 2, 17). In transfiguring into copies at this 'compressed' instant of living death, the man and woman are both of their context and projected out and beyond from the depths of time.

The claim of 'sincerity' in literature – later so often scorned or ironised by scholars – could itself be a form of self-slaughter and mummification so as to create something copiable. The creator plunges themselves into and gives themselves over to loss and death, so as to be preserved and perpetuated in their own likeness, in the ever-reproducible letters of their text. This is the sense of the first-person voice's words in *Doctor Lañuela*: 'Do not seek me in any personification in the tale, for I am not there; judge me through sensation in the entire book' (No me busques en ninguna personificación de la fábula, porque no estoy; júzgame por sensación en todo el libro) (1863: 27). The author *is* the overall enactment of death and mortal suffering throughout the work, its folding together of baptism and epitaph into an 'imperceptible point'. For Roland Barthes (1988), the death of the author would be the birth of the reader: the former must be killed off to allow texts to be autonomous of their presence. Here, in ritual self-sacrifice – chiselled entrails – the text is made autonomous of the author and given over to the reader, precisely through its creator's willing experience of loss, which characterises the text itself: it is a 'gift of death', to reuse Derrida's phrase. 'May my book go out into the world and myself remain alone with myself', the first-person voice declares: his whole life is now a memorial in the form of a tear, and his Luz of light (or Light of Light) is snuffed out (vaya mi libro al mundo y quede yo a solas conmigo) (1863: 281). Each reader will need to incubate its egg of sense (1863: 32); each reader, Berzosa tells us, will now find in it 'the moral construction of our own figure' (la construcción moral de su propia figura) (1863: 12). The death of the author and the latter's sincerity, the autonomy of the text and the intimacy between writer and reader, become identical, for the book is born of the dying that constitutes it.

Deathly attachments: beyond interpretation

The effect of such moments of slaughter, mortality and fundamental loss – resisting confinement to the time and place of demise – may be such that it eludes any single, contextualised interpretation within an originary location. It is not that we could not apprehend it. Rather, doing so involves shifting our disposition towards one of sensual appreciation, a lingering on its deathliness as it is felt beyond the limits of a given place and time. In Chapter 70 of *Moby-Dick* (1851), by the US writer Herman Melville, the ship's master, Ahab, considers the head of a massive decapitated whale. 'It was a black and hooded head,' we read, 'hanging there in the midst of so intense a calm, it seemed the Sphinx's in the desert. "Speak, thou vast and venerable head," muttered Ahab.' The captain claims that the head must contain many truths from the whole 'world's foundations' unknown to humanity. He suspects it of holding some universal, atavistic knowledge occluded from us. Yet, Ahab is left to exclaim, 'not one syllable is thine!' (2002: 259). Poliquin remarks likewise that when faced with the preserved corpse of an animal, we may become aware of something that escapes interpretative schema and cultural contextualisation. Like Ahab, we may have the sensation that there is some long history of the animal's experience here forever untold, but suggested in the muteness of the surviving remains: 'taxidermy always holds a secret back' (Poliquin 2012: 168). In broader terms, Bill Brown remarks in *A Sense of Things* that 'Melville's novel produces a world replete with things, but with things that refuse to disclose their meaning' (Brown 2010: 126).

We have here an experience of meeting an entity in the world – perhaps even the world itself – something that, from its own perspective, does not exist in terms through which any of us might understand things, but with which we nonetheless have vivid encounters. Poliquin observes that 'things are material entities. And because they are material, they generate encounters … intimacies between you and an animal-thing that is no longer quite an animal but could not be mistaken for anything other than an animal.' This, she suggests, is a 'visceral knowledge: a bodily knowing that … may even defy reason, logic, and explanatory language' (2012: 38). 'Animal-things', in their degree-zero mimesis, specifically present a kind of living death, the sensation of meeting something that not only had but continues to have a life that goes on beyond the encounter. 'Dead yet still animate,' Poliquin says, 'these animal-things offer something more than words alone can describe' (Poliquin 2012: 198). In their embalmed remains, too, the staring figures of Cameron's images, with pained detachment from any simple message, offer feelings that are expansive in their very muteness: no syllable is theirs either. *Doctor Lañuela*'s 'photograph of sentiment' can no longer speak with its author's voice so as to give us its definite meaning. The author is alone and ultimately silenced, but we encounter him as a preserved thing – his book – as we read 'thinking that he wrote as he felt'. In a bold reflection upon the medium of photography, James Elkins goes further still than such associations of the camera's images with death: in its machine thingness, he finds rather an experience of solitude before all this inarticulate matter, confronting us with something other than ourselves (2011: vii, xii, 166).

All this may be taken as something other than an invitation to endless interpretation, to the unending and never complete assigning of ever more and never enough meaning. The classicist Shane Butler has remarked on the obsessive belief that signs must yield up sense, from psychoanalysis through to hermeneutics. The difficulty with endless efforts at analysis, he comments, 'is not that it tells us too much but, rather, that what it does tell us crowds out all perceptions of what it cannot' (2015: 83). If there is a 'visceral knowledge' here, it is not something to be had by 'grasping' at it, to use that verb from Cavell, that is, by seeking to subject it to a system of understanding or interpretation, however open-ended. Rather we would need to be open to the less cognitive experiences that the encounter might offer us. Melville's sailor Queequeg – a global traveller from beyond Europe and the Americas and their knowledge systems – embodies just such an experience. From the outset, Queequeg is intimately associated with dying: his is a kind of living deathliness. He carries about with him his own coffin, and the narrator Ishmael takes him at first to be a cannibal, one who both kills and lives off other human bodies. Late on in the book, in chapter 111 ('Queequeg in his Coffin'), we find him carving upon the wooden casket the shapes of his own tattoos, which themselves were carved upon his own material being, and will 'moulder away' once Queequeg's own corpse decomposes. They are 'hieroglyphic marks' made by 'a departed prophet and seer of his island', supposedly amounting to 'a complete theory of the heaven and the earth'. In parallel with the Sphinxlike head of the whale, his body intimates a universalist foundation. 'Queequeg in his own proper person was a riddle to unfold, a wondrous work in one volume', we are told, one that no interpretation will ever decipher, not even a little. These 'mysteries not even himself could read, though his own live heart beat against them' (2002: 396). In his recent book *Whipscars and Tattoos*, Geoffrey Sanborn looks to Pacific-island traditions of such tattooing, evoking an embodied sign of selfhood, resistant both to interpretation and to pain unto death, indexical of something in the world (2011: 119–23).

If these 'mysteries', like the whale's head, are to be 'unsolved to the last' – we read – 'this thought it must have been which suggested to Ahab that wild exclamation of his, when one morning he turned away from surveying the poor Queequeg – "'Oh, *devilish tantalisation of the gods!*"' (2002: 396; emphasis added). We are invited to linger here on the 'devilish tantalisation' of the sign's continual resistance to our interpretations. In that way, the hieroglyphic living dying that is Queequeg engages in a never-ending flirtation with its viewers, who linger on their pleasurable despair, despairing pleasure when they seek to understand. The emphasis shifts from the interpretation itself to the sensation of interpreting, and its erotics. The ironic phrasing evokes the 'devilish tantalisation' of the textures of Queequeg's body, carved with those tattoos. Delight in his tempting body would subsume the sensation of ever-failing interpretation, which is now simply one aspect of such appreciation. By implication, a sensual, even sexual experience of textures might become a way to experience an animate deathliness that extends beyond the confines of a given context, 'a complete theory of the heaven and the earth'.

This would become the manner and quality of our attachment to such a thing, its quality of intimacy. There is something here of what Foucault – after Bataille – sought through transgression: 'permitting a person (in Bataille's words) "to look death in the face and to perceive in death the pathway into unknowable and incomprehensible continuity"' (Miller 1994: 88). Such an experience would, Miller notes, 'get beyond conventional ways of thinking, and also beyond a "valorisation" of genitalia, into a wider dispersal of pleasure' (1994: 277), such as might be found by following the lines and shapes of Queequeg's tattoos. Intimate friendship with Queequeg dilates, in turn, beyond limiting gender roles or even biological difference. After a night sharing a bed, the narrator Ishmael famously tells us that, 'upon waking next morning, I found Queequeg's arm thrown over me in the most loving and affectionate manner. You had almost thought I had been his wife.' 'I ... never slept better in my life', our narrator pronounces (2002: 22).

The apparent queerness of such an episode, like the embrace of El Pollo and Laguna, is not something that can simply be assimilated into twenty-first-century notions of gayness, especially given Melville's own prejudices about such matters (Snediker 2013; Martin 2006). Rather, such incidents as the night-time embrace are offered as ways beyond 'conventional ways of thinking', and are imbued with a sense of their own supposed strangeness. Thus, Snediker notes the phantasmal quality of Queequeg's arm as described by Ishmael (2013: 166). As in Nietzsche's *Birth of Tragedy* nearly two decades later, the boundaries do not so much give way on general principles of ethics, of gender inclusivity, say. Rather they do so in the enactment of a vital deathliness extending out across place and time. Such an experience has its own variety of necrophilia, of convergence in desire of life and death. In chapter 94, 'A Squeeze of the Hand', we find the narrator compressing the whale's 'sperm' in his hands alongside other companions, and, in the sensual textures, finding himself drawn to all others in a sexualised vision of harmonic universalism: 'let us all squeeze ourselves into each other; let us squeeze ourselves universally into the very milk and sperm of kindness' (2002: 345). Like Dean's unlimited intimacy of barebacking, the enjoyment of the flesh is shot through here with a dealing in death (Dean 2009: 5, 22, 45, 177). What is being squeezed and fondled, that 'milk and sperm of kindness', with its sensual textures, its 'soft, gentle globules of infiltrated tissues' with 'the smell of spring violets', is a slaughtered animal (2002: 344).

Among the 'devilish tantalisations' is a wish not so much to interpret as fully to explain how the tantalisations themselves arise, to situate them within their proper theoretical frame, in some fundamental explanation for their resistance to interpretation. The many allusions to signs and words and interpretation may lure us in this direction. For example, for John T. Irwin in *American Hieroglyphs*, the core is said to lie in the foundational relationship between human consciousness and an external world that, by definition, must always lie beyond it, but which it seeks to understand. This is what is afoot in the suicidal pursuit of the whale (1980: 287). It is tempting, likewise, to think here in terms of Jacques Derrida's *Voice and Phenomenon*: that every sign that we inscribe – like every mark on Queequeg's body – has the capacity to survive the death or disappearance of whoever assigned a meaning to it. On this account, the very use of any sign involves representation, which is something other than the present subject of the utterer, and by extension implies their absence and, ultimately, their death. As a result, any such marking – any word, any picture – ultimately floats free of any given sense, its significance forever deferred, released from its originary context (1967: 60, 98, 104–8). Seen this way, the physical sign – the written word, the drawing, say – is itself akin to other material remains of the dead: their decapitated heads, or taxidermied bodies. Or, if we are to leave interpretation behind, we might be drawn once again – as Shane Butler is – to Julia Kristeva's *Revolution in Poetic Language*, where art is envisaged, psychoanalytically, as a sacrifice that undoes symbolic sense.

In fully adopting any of these viewpoints, we would need to embrace some generalised explanation of signs and of human understanding, something that underpins all instances across place and time, what Toril Moi has called an 'Arche-Writing' (2017: 68–9). There is, though, no call nor any unavoidable need here for explanations of this sort. They would take us once more to what Susan Manning calls 'priority', a systematic cause to which connections across place and time are subject. 'Our usual interpretative strategies, the task of assessing meaning by fixing cause, may not be well suited to the epistemological structure of Melville's ambiguous fears', Paul Hurh has aptly said (2015: 162). After all, if there once were a general theory in Queequeg's tattoos, there is not now. Rather, what we might take from Irwin or Derrida or Kristeva or Hurh, are the very resonances that they find among signs: suicide, sacrifice and ultimate loss, the persistence of mortal remains, 'the unknown that is death' (Hurh 2015: 189). Derrida's 'difference' is, in that sense, an evocation of literal or metaphorical death's compelling force beyond a literal or metaphorical grave, and thus beyond a confining location. In turn, Kristeva's 'sacrifice' evokes a violent release through a kind of dying. In the opening 'Etymology' of *Moby Dick*, we are told of the 'late consumptive usher', a dying man who supplied words and reflections upon them. He is 'ever dusting his old lexicons and grammars, with a queer handkerchief, mockingly embellished by all the flags of the world'. He 'loved' to do so, for it 'somehow reminded him of his mortality' (2002: xli). We find here evoked intimations of impending death, of love, of cruel comedy, and with them an air of universalism ('all the flags of the world'), all clustering around signs and structures of language ('old lexicons and grammars'). But there is specifically no suggestion that we should explain this conjunction through a fundamental theory of language or cognition. On the contrary, we are told that such an experience may arise 'somehow'.

Seen in this light, pastiche – like the usher's collection of etymological entries – evinces an obsessive attachment to mortality, to limbo, and to a living death as aesthetic experiences, irreducible to narrow context or to interpretation or to fundamental underlying conditions. By pastiche, I mean both the direct copying of other signs, and the copying out of references, allusions, chunks of information collected as if from the flotsam and jetsam of cultural history, irrespective of their origin, from across the extent of place and through the depths of time. Such a sensibility is powerfully evoked in *Moby-Dick*. The book is piled high with such items, from talk of phrenology and physiognomy (2002: 289), to scientific authorities like Olassen and Cuvier (2002: 150), to the Indian god Vishnu and the Vedas, the Bible and the ancient Greeks and Romans (2002: 302), and to Byron's Childe Harold (2002: 131), to mention but a handful. The novel mimics now one, now another literary manner or style from theatrical dialogue (2002: 142–8) to informative treatises on pictures of whales and whaling (2002: 223–5).

In *Chasing the White Whale*, David Dowling remarks on Melville's 'literary ventriloquism, the capacity to assume a stunning array of voices, tones, and attitudes'. Through his 'love of mixed sound, or polyphony ... language came to mean more than message', Dowling says (2010: 197). As with the beating of *Fausto*'s hooves, we have once more a transfiguration of the history of culture into echoes of sound. As with Whitman's 'Me myself' and its ventriloquism, we again experience what Connor called 'the power to speak through others ... the experience of being spoken through by others ... the power of unlocated or mobile voices' (2011: 14). But now this would be a song of continual demise, something akin to Fernández Mallo's 'Sound of the End', as if all those 'unlocated or mobile' voices were dying breaths, that persist across place and time. In a not dissimilar vein, Robert Pogue Harrison remarks in *The Dominion of the Dead* that 'while it is true that we speak with the words of the dead, it is equally true that the dead speak in and through the voices of the living' (2003: 151). As in *Fausto*, this would not suppose our attending to the signs as opposed to their referents, nor to human conscious meaning as against the external universe, for we have left aside such 'pictures' of the world. Rather, the vast transfiguration is that of all the shapes and patterns of matter, from the hieroglyphs carved in the whale's flesh through the textures of those of Queequeg's body to the printed marks of Ishmael's narrative. Human culture is but one aspect of all this: it is one 'form of life', in Wittgenstein's phrase. We would attend, then, to the sound patterns of the whole world forever dying, and humanity with it, the silences included: even as the *Pequod* finally goes down, 'the great shroud of the sea rolled on as it rolled five thousand years ago' (2002: 469).

The commonplace and antique notion – lurking in Melville's novel and its pastiche – that artists and authors should imitate past masters as models (*imitatio* and *aemulatio*) is redolent with that refusal to let go, that clinging to a living death which renders something classic. Such classical *topoi* were not so much abandoned as reinvigorated in the eighteenth and nineteenth centuries (Siegel 2000). Drawing on the eighteenth-century Italian philosopher Giambattista Vico, Pogue Harrison comments that to speak 'of the poetic wisdom of the ancients' is to invoke 'the tropes of reanimation and personification by which the voices ... of the dead are carried beyond the boundary that separates them from the living' (2003: 150). Taking as his example Baudelaire's evocation of Poe, Pogue Harrison remarks that 'to gain an affiliation of this sort, it does not suffice to imitate or translate or admire Poe; one must meet him, retrieve him, and inherit him in that place where the fate of the past has yet to be decided by the descendants' (2003: 103).

The Spanish writer Peregrín García Cadena puts it very directly in 1875, remarking that 'Goya had died a little under half a century earlier; but his restless spirit still fluttered about' (Goya había muerto hacía poco menos de medio siglo; pero su espíritu inquieto aleteaba todavía). The words appear at the start of a short story, 'The Disenchanted House' (La casa desencantada) – which appeared in *Los Lunes del Imparcial* on 13 September 1875 – in which García Cadena describes what we now call the *Black Paintings*. These images carried resonances of an intimate connection to the dead artist, because they were integral to a personal and private place: Goya's home, the Quinta del Sordo. They were literally part of his walls on which they were directly painted. Their own mortality had been all too evident in the walls' dampness and decay: the images threatened to go the way of Queequeg's tattoos. In 1874, the new owner of the building, the Franco-German financier Baron d'Erlanger, had paid for the transfer of the frescoes from the walls, engaging to that end the Prado's Chief Restorer, Salvador Martínez Cubells. Initially, they were taken to be displayed at the 1878 Great Exhibition in Paris, before being donated to the Prado (Glendinning 1975: 466). Cubells's restored paintings, made between 1874 and 1878, are what we see today in the Prado under Goya's name, set adrift from their original conditions, in wooden frames and on a mount against blank walls, carrying with them component shapes and colours from Goya's private domain, saved from time's ravages. They are, as it were, a degree-zero imitation, a taxidermied version of bits of wall. Cubells's was not the sole attempt to secure a copy of Goya's Black Paintings. The photographer Laurent took pictures of them between 1863 and 1866, directly from the walls (Torrecillas Fernández 1992), collecting the residue of their shadowy light. Both Cubells and Laurent sought to constitute and reconstitute the cultural history of Spain. We have in both Cubells and Laurent a form of pastiche, and with it of co-authorship, taken to an extreme. The boundaries between the nineteenth-century individuals and the work of Goya dilate, just as Eugenio Lucas sought ways to 'go on' through Goya's paintings (Chapter 2). Laurent's images reveal co-authorship too with the physical, mortal, decaying world, with death itself, in the contingencies of how the photographs turned out: the technical limitations of lighting, the distortions of colour in photographic reproduction, the level of humidity and deterioration of the walls.

Laurent's version of *Saturn Devouring His Son* (*c*.1863–66) (Figure 13) offers us the god's powerful body rendered out of cloudy patches of light and dark that almost merge with the backdrop, resolving and dissolving before us, emerging from and disappearing into a wash of shadow and light, but surging violently out into blazing eyes, fierce mouth and decapitated victim, like a phantom, semi-substantial, terrifying form, a nightmare appearing and vanishing. In 'The Disenchanted House', García Cadena speaks eloquently of how, while the frescoes were on the walls, Goya's spirit lived on 'with a life of undefined/indefinite actualisation in those energetic and horrifying ghosts' (con vida de indefinida actualidad en aquellos enérgicos y horribles fantasmas). Evocatively, García Cadena recounts how the monsters 'were ever dragging themselves painfully towards life in an incomplete genesis, which seemed still to be being enacted by the creator's breath' (se arrastraban penosamente hacia la vida en medio de un génesis incompleto que parecía hallarse todavía bajo la acción del soplo creador). We may see in Laurent's *Saturn* a similar after-image of Goya's creativity, a forever mutating and ill-formed, but dynamic presence, preserved in negative and print. The energy exceeds death without resolving definitively in a life-form. Its failure is its very force: it is forever in 'limbo'. If the image shares nothing else with Laurent's geometrical concoctions, it partakes of their powerful, endless pulsation. That potential for pastiche to evoke what is in 'incomplete genesis' and 'still being enacted' is apparent in Lucas's Goyesque paintings. It was part of Lucas's contribution to the reconstruction of historic Spanish culture that he had been engaged to evaluate the Black Paintings in 1855 (Ginger 2007a: 52). Unrooted and mutating beyond his mortal span, Goya's images take on perplexing and unsettling new resonances in his wider work. In Lucas's take on

13 Juan Laurent, *Saturn Devouring His Son*

the *Capricho* 'Sleep overcomes them', the female prisoners are, bizarrely, now not only awake, but apparently cheerful, flirtatious even, and sexualised, for reasons unknown. The viewer's response is very visibly put into question, because, echoing many *Caprichos*, two of the women at the back stare at us and confer, as if discussing our reaction. In other instances, fragments of Goya's oeuvre conjoin in enigmatic new combinations, scattered and reconnected across time. In *The Knowledge of Good and Evil*, the Enlightenment-era minister of Justice Jovellanos – portrayed by Goya in association with Minerva, the goddess of wisdom – holds up the allegory of Truth from the engraving 'Truth died'. Yet the allegorical woman is now unable to emit her own light, and requires a nearby lantern, and as Jovellanos supports her body, he takes the shape of Goya's *capricho* of sexual temptation and despair, *Tantalus*.

If we are not able to explain what the piles of pastiche mean as their 'voices ... are carried beyond the boundary that separates them from the living', we may instead give ourselves over to their 'still being unenacted', the unexplained force of their ever 'incomplete genesis'. In *Moby-Dick*, the narrator Ishmael's always-informed manner sits aside his frank acknowledgement that he does not understand the central drive of the story itself, the self-destructive pursuit of the murderous Moby-Dick. 'How it was that they [the crew] so aboundingly responded to the old man's ire ... what the white whale was to them, or how to their unconscious understandings, also, in some dim, unsuspected way, he might have seemed the gliding great demon of the seas of life, all this to explain would be to dive deeper than Ishmael can go. The subterranean miner that works in us all, how can one tell whither leads his shaft by the ever shifting, muffled sound of his pick?' 'Who does not feel the irresistible arm drag?', he asks of the tale's central drive. 'What skiff in tow of a seventy-four can stand still? For one, I gave myself up to the abandonment of the time and the place' (2002: 155). The piled-up allusions and pastiches might, in this light, be experienced as integral to that force, as elements of the irresistible drag, of what carries the skiff along: we abandon ourselves to them and are taken beyond cognitive understanding, beyond all that can be contextualised, beyond the time and place of their being uttered. Lawrence Buell aptly remarks that 'the *Pequod*'s encounter with the monster of the deep is a mysterious, deeply inexplicable, and magic-suggesting event that ... supersedes the telling in the sense that reflective commentary becomes largely displaced by the force of the narrative relation' (1986: 65).

The whole text of *Moby-Dick* spirals back and forth through its own 'limbo', in the wake of the slaughter of sea beasts and the death of all the *Pequod*'s crew in Moby-Dick's attack, but for the narrator, Ishmael. The latter emerges to tell the tale. He is *'another orphan'*, clinging to Queequeg's coffin and its hieroglyphs, drawn in a whirlpool towards a *'button-like black bubble'* and then spun out again by its own *'cunning spin'* (2002: 469). Having undertaken this final journey that flowed seamlessly through life and death, Ishmael recounts the narrative – the novel *Moby-Dick* – that leads us back again to that spot and again to his own telling of the tale, ad infinitum. The loop is not, however, a simple or perfect spiralling through the point of death, the ending of the tale. The final short chapter 'EPILOGUE' seems pointedly set beyond the rest of the text, Bainard Cowan has observed (1982: 176). It alone is set completely in italics, and begins with the words: *'The drama's done. Why then does any one step forth?'* (2002: 469), as if it lay beyond the curtain call. The 'irresistible arm' of the narrative seems at once to drag us to the end point of its death drive. But – as William V. Spanos puts it – 'at the moment when the temporal circle is expected to close on itself, it dis-integrates' (Spanos 1995: 144).

A number of scholars from Cowan and Spanos to Edgar A. Dryden (1968) or Christopher Sten have consequently sought a kind of anagnorisis in the ending, a recognition of what the patterns of the tale have meant and how to step out beyond them. Accounts range widely. Ishmael fulfils the perennial sacred role of epic hero, confronting death (Sten 1996: 200). He is resurrected so as properly to inhabit the textual world of words (Dryden 1968: 109). In his 'stepping forth – his "ek-sisting", in Heideggerian terms – he becomes "the author as mortal being-in-the-world"' (Spanos 1995: 151, 179). He has joined 'the community of the bereft ... at the feet of the Angel of History' (Cowan 1982: 178). For all their resonance, such accounts seem to map once more back onto a single, recommended generalisable theory, to something with 'priority', whether the core elements of human sacred epic or Heideggerian or Benjaminian philosophy or the fundamental nature of literary texts. And 'all this to explain would be to dive deeper than Ishmael can go'. There is no indication of any such exhaustive lesson learnt.

'I cannot tell why it was exactly that those stage managers, the Fates, put me down for this shabby part', Ishmael notes early on (2002: 7). The one clear reason we are given for Ishmael's stepping forth is this: '*Because one did survive the wreck*' (2002: 469). To borrow terms once more from Michael Fried, as a character on stage, Ishmael is not completely absorbed in the narrative's death drive, but nor is he simply theatrically distanced from it, because he is of it. 'Call me Ishmael', the main story famously begins (2002: 3). Like 'Me myself', like a ventriloquist, he is in and out of the game. Having survived, Ishmael can tell the story and keep it looping, but he is not freed from its continual dying in so doing. He offers intimate companionship with all those who die about him, even with death itself. When he is shot out of the whirlpool, he is still clinging to deathliness and to its hieroglyphic signs that so tantalise erotically, in the form of Queequeg's coffin, which he holds tight just as Queequeg once held him. Out of the cataclysm, there is neither complete closure in death nor – any more than in *Doctor Lañuela* – is there any return back through sacrifice to some earlier origin in a safeguarded family. The final words tell us that another ship, the *Rachel*, 'in her retracing search after her missing children, only found another orphan' (2002: 469). Held in this loop, in 'limbo' and 'incomplete genesis', Ishmael's prose continually passes through violent death without ever finishing its living-dying, its endless transfiguration of the world into something like the 'Sound of the End'. Such is its own immortality, its own persistence.

The character of a simple heart: conflation, deathliness, sickness

The formation of deathly attachments involves an aptitude to experience these as taking shape in patterns of analogy: the dying bullfighter as St Teresa, a living body as a dead one, the disparate allusions of *Moby-Dick* welding with one another and with the story of the whale. This is a matter of character, just as in Chapter 1 we saw cultural encounters dependent on the friendship of the *gauchos* and of Nietzsche and Wagner. The 'poetics of character' involve 'the expression of taste and sentiment', of 'judgment', Susan Manning suggests (2013: 13). The writings of Gustave Flaubert in France and of Lewis Carroll in Britain intimate that it is a simplicity of heart that will give us deathly experiences of similitude: such is its taste, sentiment and judgement. We might come to say that it is with a simplicity of spirit that we have been reading Melville or pondering taxidermy or viewing the fate of Goya's Black Paintings.

Sacrifice: everyone must die

At the very point of death, in the culminating image of Flaubert's *A Simple Heart (Un coeur simple)*, the protagonist Félicité has a vision that, through analogy, conflates the biblical Holy Spirit with her taxidermied pet parrot: 'and when she exhaled her last breath, she believed she saw, in the opening heavens, a gigantic parrot, floating above her head' (quand elle exhala son dernier souffle, elle crut voit, dans les cieux entr'ouverts, un perroquet gigantesque, planant au-dessus de sa tête) (2019b: 39). The tale – published in 1877, but written and rewritten through the mid-century – shows its readers what it might be to get to such a point, to have the qualities of personality necessary to perceive such a vision. In the words of Lewis J. Overaker, '*Un Coeur simple* is written to make vital to the reader what can actually happen within the believing heart of a very simple woman. … We are invited to experience Félicité's spiritual elevation through her own feelings and capacity for faith' (Overaker 2001: 130, 142). In turn, to teach oneself to read the story that way entails a kind of 'learnt naïveté' (to borrow those words again from Gomá and Goethe), just as we may practise any number of apparently impossible things. Diane Knight concludes that it invites, 'with bare effrontery, a literal reading of the illusion of reality …, a stance of ingenuous affirmation … "*Lisez-moi littéralement*" (Read me literally) (Knight 1985: 101–2; original emphasis). Suspending our judgement in this way, we once more encounter culture intimately, like Nietzsche's gods, as a thing akin to divine creation, just as Flaubert wished (Jenson 2001: 25); that is, requiring no justification and subject to no 'priority'. The invitation to experience likeness is not an offer of ultimate explanation or cause.

The key to having a 'simple heart' – Flaubert's story suggests – is not to be as alive as other people. Like the 'irresistible arm' of Ishmael's narration, like our dwelling on deathly enigmas, this character – this attitude of deathliness – is not convertible into a single treatise-like theory about literature, whether in relation to mimesis (Prendergast 1986: 181), or the arbitrariness of signs (Culler 1974: 209), or a post-secular modernity rooted in Catholicism (Vinken 2015: 17), or (once again) a Kristevan experience of the maternal (Israel-Pelletier 1991: 42–3), to suggest but a few possibilities. It takes shape as a series of family resemblances, as does death's bringing of copies. It is a way of being, a bundle of qualities and tendencies, not a systematic philosophy. If, for Foucault and Barthes – among others – Flaubert's prose became emblematic of the Death of the Author and the erasure of the face of Man, that was through the assimilation of wide-ranging characteristics into a notion of denial – a death, an erasure – of 'presence'. Such notions of 'absence' and 'presence' are less like philosophical categories and more like a personality or a dream.

In Barbara Vinken's words, Félicité is 'transformed into a mechanical and soulless thing' (2015: 292). We read that Félicité 'seemed a woman made of wood, functioning automatically' (semblait une femme en bois, fonctionnant d'une manière automatique) (Flaubert 2019b: 13). She ceases to undergo physical change over time: from her mid-twenties, she appears statically to be in her forties, and from her fifties she stops showing any identifiable age at all (2019b: 13). Her whole life becomes a fatal repetition of bereavement: if not quite lacking development, it accumulates in a looping and pile-up of fundamental losses. It is all a kind of dying, literal and metaphorical. After the demise of the parrot, 'a weakness stopped her in her tracks; and the wretchedness of her infancy, the disappointment of her first love, the departure of her nephew, the death of Virginie, like the waves of a tide, came back at once, and going up to her throat, suffocated her' (Alors une faiblesse l'arrêta; et la misère de son enfance, la déception du premier amour, le départ de son neveu, la mort de Virginie, comme les flots d'une marée, revinrent à la fois, et, lui montant à la gorge, l'étouffaient) (2019a: 33–4). Félicité thus shows us a way of living at the very limit of life, held in agonised 'limbo', at the point of asphxiation. Hers too is a kind of edge play.

The simple heart's lack of human life enables an experience of things beyond interpretation, for it 'somehow' involves an incapacity to interpret – to echo Melville's 'somehow'. Not without apparent reason, Félicité's mistress declares her to be stupid, and Félicité agrees (2019b: 29). In a spirit of deathly stupidity – it might be said – we have been tantalised by Queequeg's tattoos, we have found echoes across shapes, we have lingered on silent stuffed animals, we have felt mortality to bring forth copies. Félicité's connections to the New World, putatively discovered by Columbus, as seen in the emblematic parrot itself, and her links to the continuing Hispanic empire, are evoked in this way. Confronted with a map that should show her the location of her nephew in Cuba, 'that network of coloured lines tired her sight, without her learning anything from it' (ce réseau de lignes coloriées fatiguait sa vue, sans lui rien apprendre) (2019b: 19). The abstracted vision of the map is pointedly set next to news of the nephew's demise, Arden Reed observes (Reed 2003: 223). Barely capable of attributing anything but the simplest meaning, Félicité tends to mimic the things around her, and to be literal when faced with imagery and metaphors. She talks like her parrot, an animal of mimicry that historically might be thought at the limits of personal existence, lacking a human soul (Schwartz 2014: 139–43). Her religious devotion begins with her simply copying the practices undertaken by Virginie. 'The Copy is the emblem of artistic and spiritual death', Christopher Prendergast observes (1986: 182). Félicité becomes devout, but 'as for dogmas, she understood nothing of them, did not even try to understand' (quant aux dogmes, elle n'y comprenait rien, ne tâcha même de comprendre) (2019b: 21).

The adoption of others' words becomes a continual self-sacrifice – that sometime feminine ideal – a self-obliteration akin to dying. Félicité's life exemplifies a 'living exclusively for others', in Overaker's words (2001: 134). Barbara Vinken has shown the parallels between such an outlook and the heretical doctrine of Pure Love, with its long history in Catholic France; spiritual dying and living here become one. Vinken recalls Charles de Condren's doctrines of the Mass, where 'we must annihilate ourselves and become nothing but Christ's limbs, offering and doing what he offers and does, as if we were not ourselves' (2015: 261). There is – Vinken suggests – a parallel 'surrender of the text to otherness, where the self can only be traced through the other' (2015:11). As with Berzosa's freely accepted suffering, this involves giving oneself over to 'the flowing of the sacrificial blood in us, this everlasting pain' (2015: 261). The narrative's effect is redolent with the renewal of nineteenth-century Catholicism in continental Europe: by the 1870s in France – Deborah Jenson has shown – the extending celebrations of the Sacred Heart brought 'devotion to the *wound*' (2001: 216).

With this death-infused pastiche and attention to surface shapes, the simple heart elides distinctions and connects things through formal likeness, its sacrificial mood causing 'the world to come into view in a certain way', to borrow Rita Felski's words (2015: 20). There is a surface similarity between the taxidermied Loulou, and God imagined as a dove: with this resemblance (ressemblance), 'they were associated in her thought, the parrot becoming sanctified by its relationship with the Holy Spirit' (Ils s'associèrent dans sa pensée, le perroquet se trouvant sanctifié par ce rapport avec le Saint-Esprit) (2019b: 35). Just as in Manet, Olympia's dog can replace Titian's cat, each flickering into, overlaying the other, because both are pets, so a parrot can be the Holy Spirit, for both are birds that talk. A character with a simple heart, then, is the ideal person to perceive the things we have seen in this chapter: apparently unconnected individuals as the same, words from one book as echoes of another, the shapes of one image as identical to another. Just as we have looked upon the living remnants of Fortuny's corpse, so she kisses the eyes of her mistress's dead daughter, 'and would not have experienced any great surprise if Virginie had opened them again' (et n'eût pas éprouvé un immense étonnement si Virginie les eût rouverts) (2019a: 27).

Even as – precisely as – it is wooden, parrot-like and stupid, the simple heart is an expression of intense intimacy. It is forged through close emotional attachments infused with, perpetuated in death and loss. If Félicité's recitation of dogma reverses St Paul's call for the spirit over the letter (Vinken 2015: 18), it does so such that what might seem heart-less is done with the fullness of the heart, in 'superabundant plenitude', as Ross Chambers puts it (1984: 143). The sacred heart and wound are incarnate; Félicité dies during Corpus Christi. Loulou embodies 'a desire to remember in a physical, tangible way', Poliquin remarks (2012: 203), as do other 'relics' like the decaying hat of Mme Aubin's daughter (Jenson 2001: 230). Rather than suggesting some radical autonomy of language, this sensibility – in Jenson's words – 'defies the abyss between representation and reality' (2001: 211). The cherished, taxidermied parrot, at the degree-zero of mimesis, alike to itself in a supreme conflation, offers a 'visceral' encounter, whose sense resonates beyond constraining contexts and systems of explanation, and across the divide of life and death, like Ahab's decapitated whale, or the indexical signs of Queequeg's body, or the bodily remnants in Cameron's photographs. Affection is expressed in these extreme evocations of mimicry. Félicité is drawn to the parrot in the first place because it is from the Americas, which she associates with her defunct nephew's naval travels. Her concern with religion arises when she responds imitatively to Virginie's preparations for first communion; and she was drawn to Virginie not least because the girl had lost her father. 'With the imagination given to us by true tenderness', we are told, 'it seemed she was herself that child' (avec l'imagination que donnent les vraies tendresses, il sembla qu'elle était elle-même cette enfant) (2019b: 22).

Amid the deathly affection of an exemplary sacrificial character such as Félicité, social, geographical and historical boundaries fall away, for disparate things are conflated. A global aesthetic arises, a world united in death. 'The altar on which the parrot is placed at the time of Félicité's death throes', Vinken observes, 'is heaped with knickknacks of all kinds, bric-à-brac from China to South America, a motley collection from all four corners of the earth' (2015: 310). The parrot that the maid embraces often served as an emblem of the New World (Schwartz 2014: 122), and is originally brought by an official, once a French consul in the Americas, who arrives accompanied by a black servant – a reminder of the legacy of transatlantic slavery (2019b: 25–6). In visceral, wounding experiences of 'social likeness', Jenson shows, parallels are effected between the supposedly 'primitive' thought patterns of the past and non-West with contemporary France, across distinctions of social class (between Félicité and her employers), and between ancient and revived religious belief and revolutionary violence (2001: 211–50).

In its 'Pure Love' or 'unlimited intimacy', the exemplary character ultimately gives us, through all these echoes, something like the aesthetics evoked in *Moby Dick*: the sounding – through resemblance and pastiche – of a dying breath, reflections of impending demise. In its culmination, as Félicité dies, the prose offers a deathly recollection of Narcissus but also of Echo, those myths of creativity and poetry, 'as a fountain runs out, as an echo disappears' (comme une fontaine s'épuise, comme un écho disparaît) (2019b: 39). The sound and rhythms of the prose form a ghostly equivalent to the mesmeric 'meetings' we found in Chapter 1. Knight observes the 'characteristic repetition of certain stylistic effects … seducing the reader into the hypnotic state' (1985: 68). The associative experience is less restrained than the rhetorical device of metonymy that so many critics discern in it, one word standing in for the other. In the life of a 'simple heart', disparate things are assimilated to one another, the Holy Ghost is a parrot. 'The tendency of Félicité's mind is to … eliminate differences', Israel-Pelletier notes (1991: 41).

It was Manning's hope that 'critical literary history' would 'manifest … correspondences without collapsing "likeness" into "identity"' (2013: 233). In its poetic rigour, analogy would avoid conflation. Contiguity would be to the fore. Conversely, in the exemplary 'simple heart', there is an invitation to give up on that notion of what it is to have critical faculties, to be like the loving, ever-dying Félicité, to enter an 'hypnotic state' ('Mon Dieu, comme vous êtes bête!' – My God, you're so stupid (2019b: 32).) The 'simple heart' is not quite unthinking, but its thoughts, its ways of living and perceiving, are astray from their ordinary use: lines of a map are no longer for mapping, equations run rampant; the Holy Spirit is a bird, a parrot is a bird, the Holy Spirit is a parrot. This is unhealthy. '"A Simple Heart" is the story of the evolution of a delirium,' in Shoshana Felman's words, 'it is "simple" to "lose one's head"' (1978: 168). Such is its pain freely embraced. Its world of conflations and hollowed-out equivalences are born of a culture on the verge of sickness and decay: post-revolutionary France, with its webs of global interconnections, where the Sacred Heart looms large. In Vinken's words, Flaubert's France is a 'ruined world … sentenced to death' (2015: 283). Its stupidity is evinced, amid 'signs of the times, traces of ruin and decay' (Vinken 2015: 281), like the passing allusions to the conservative liberal regime of July 1830 or to talk of the revolutionary Terror (Flaubert 2019b: 25).

For Wittgenstein, likewise, over 70 years later, it is not the abandonment, but the misuse of our forms of life, our ways of talking, that have led the world into danger, lines of thought going off the rails, 'on holiday', always resembling their correct usage. (How can the verb *to sleep* be active, wonders a child, when sleeping is passive?) We end up 'tormented by questions', and needing, not even one single form of treatment, but 'different therapies' (*PI* §133). Put at its starkest, our culture, our very way of experiencing the world, has it in us to make us sick. In his preface to the *Philosophical Investigations*, Wittgenstein talks of 'the darkness of its time' to which the work might have some remote chance of bringing light. 'Its declaration of its poverty', says Cavell, 'is not a simple expression of humility but a stern message: the therapy prescribed to bring light into the darkness of the time will present itself as, will in a sense be, starvation; as if our philosophical spirit is indulged, farced to the point of death' (2013: 60–70, at pp. 69–70).

To have 'a simple and loving heart', like Félicité, like Alice in her Wonderland (Carroll 1965: 164), is not to respond to this sickness with therapies that seek to take us back 'home' in 'poverty'. We would fill ourselves with things that make our forms of life mutate, just as Alice drinks and eats and finds her body distorted and changed; we become 'indulged, farced to the point of death'. For Wittgenstein, an admirer of *Alice*, it is in childhood that we may begin to get lost as things go 'on holiday'. Conversely, for Carroll, by holding onto a childish 'going on holiday', up the river on a summer's day in Oxford, we may defy the divisions of chronology by resisting the onset of adulthood, and reach out across the generations. The book is 'circular, ever renovating', U.C. Knoepflmacher has remarked (1998: 180). As Alice ages, she will retain her 'simple and loving heart', and the story of Wonderland will be told and retold, as Carroll has told and retold it for his wider readership (1965: 164). This, though, is a death-infested immortality, where on each retelling of the tale, as if from Ishmael's whirlpool, we come again and again back through the moment where Alice 'gave a little scream, half of fright and half of anger'. Wonderland threatens her with execution and she assaults it in a final never-ended confrontation (1965: 162).

The perpetual childhood is itself forever in the shadow of its own demise (Roth 2009: 26), 'in memory's mystic band / like pilgrim's withered wreath of / flowers / Pluck'd in a far-off land' (Carroll 1965: 23). Wonderland's mutations of forms of life into similar things, its continual conflation of the disparate, offer an unrelenting embrace of mortal threats. 'The integrity of the body is ... constantly threatened', Laurence Talairach-Vielmas observes (2007: 54). When Alice's 'shape' begins to shrink for the first time, she ponders what would happen if this geometrical projection ended with her 'going out altogether, like a candle' (1965: 32). In a mutation of reasoned justice, the final sanction – the power of authorities over a person's life – is repeatedly invoked: '"Off with his head!" or "Off with her head!" about once a minute' (1965: 112). In the continual metamorphoses through resemblances, the integrity of the person is menaced: Alice doubts there are boundaries that separate her identity from that of other people. 'Who in the world am I?', she wonders, 'I must be Mabel after all' (1965: 38). When it is not directly threatening, Wonderland is maddening, driving Alice eventually to fury: its creatures are insane.

All this is an 'affordance' of our very forms of life – biological, linguistic and cultural – and their capacity to generate new equivalences. Natural shapes may be geometrically projected into others, as they were in the photographs we saw in Chapter 1: a flamingo (say) may become a croquet mallet, and vice versa (1965: 111), just as the avian Holy Spirit might be a parrot, or in Manet a dog may become a cat. English, with its rules and specificities, may break into a Nonsense that resembles it, for there is no ultimate metalanguage or set of fixed meanings constraining it. Nonsense – Jacques Lecercle avers – 'tells the reader to abide, and not to abide, by the rules of language' (Lecercle 1994: 25, 35). In the shifting use of one adjective, a new being emerges: the Mock Turtle is an animal that, in its own words, 'once ... was a real turtle' (1965: 126). From it, we are told, 'Mock Turtle Soup is made' (1965: 24). Non-literal uses of language are mapped to their literal equivalents: a Queen of Hearts, a Mad March Hare. Along with the national language, mid-century British culture and imperialism are transformed through and out of themselves. Lecercle finds in Carroll's work a pile-up of Victorian 'clichés, *idées reçues*, preconstructed thoughts' (1994: 195): it offers us 'pastiche – a polyphony' (1994: 176). In patterns of similitude, British institutions are inverted. If fair trials involve a verdict followed by sentence (B follows A), a similar sequence – A follows B – offers us a sentence that precedes a verdict, which the Queen of Hearts prefers (1965: 161).

The world of the home nation and that of overseas colonialism now map back and forth into one another, becoming equivalent. Nancy Armstrong – among others – notes that the 'far-off land' (1965: 23) and its exotic beasts and customs recall writings about colonial adventure and about travels in pursuit of natural history (Armstrong 1999: 201, 206). 'There is nothing in the British household', Armstrong comments, 'that cannot undergo the inverse cultural logic that would relocate that object in an atavistic wonderland' (Armstrong 1999: 233). Wonderland becomes a projection of and resembles English customs (tea parties, cake, croquet). It echoes, not just with the lives of the English elite, but with the children's literature read at home, with its talking animals and songs, Ronald Reichertz

(1997) shows. If such a transformation is redolent with attempted Anglicisation of colonies, the reverse holds true: Britain becomes an 'atavistic wonderland', just as Flaubert's France becomes similar to its overseas territories. In invoking, but transforming boundaries, the simple heart thus pulsates forever beyond the limits of what Gubar calls 'the colonisation paradigm' (2009: 40), even as it also recalls it. As explicated in part by Jacqueline Rose in *The Case of Peter Pan* (1992), children, women and the indigenous inhabitants of the colonies could be treated, in parallel ways. They could be imagined as similar primitives available for the service and amusement of the British male elite (Talairach-Vielmas 2007: 54; Straley 2016: 2–13; Robson 2003: 136). Instead, in Wonderland's mutations and equivalences – Robson notes – 'a little girl is just as likely to devour as to be devoured, while her equally frequent changes in size destroy the conventional arrangement in which an older male can be sure of being bigger than a younger female' (2003: 146). Born of Victorian clichés about women – Auerbach explains – Alice, as the woman who falls and the female child, becomes a person where 'extremes meet, and the demonic energy of the fallen woman shares some of the preternatural purity Carroll located in girls' (1982: 167). Even were such an unstable realm to be supposed typical of women, children, and so-called primitives, it has come now to subsume and be projected out of elite Victorian England and the vicarish don of an Oxford college, Lewis Carroll.

In its continual traversal and transfiguration of distinctions, the 'simple and loving heart' preserves and perpetuates, not some 'pitifully brief era of bliss and innocence', some 'sealed idyll', in a simple sense (Robson 2003: 136–7), but rather everything there is in Wonderland and Alice's adventures underground. The heart must be filled with the 'perversity' and 'comedy and terror' that Nina Auerbach detects (1982: 65, 167), the flipping between 'cat and mouse' that Marah Gubar notes (2009: 96). If we proceed with a simple heart, if we read literally – *lisez-moi littéralement* – we will find no place of safety lying beyond this world of equivalences. There would be no vantage point of irony, no elite adult male position from which to offer a final judgement upon the uninstructed female and other 'primitives'. For better or for worse, to act with a 'simple heart' would impede later readings that criticise the novel ethically. *Alice's* disposition towards imaginative analogy parodies and undoes informative and didactic texts and genres – the very embodiment of the text with a message – with which Victorian children would be familiar. In Straley's words, putatively edifying 'literary forms' are 'simultaneously altered and preserved within the new, mutated forms' (2016: 28–9).

The tale frustrates any moment of anagnorisis, by forever repeating itself, never enabling the death wish of narrative, the desire for an end, to be fulfilled, precisely by continually repeating that necrophiliac wish. Mortality and the many forms of mortal violence, so pervasive in Wonderland, never actually reach their culmination amid the mutations and reversals. 'It's all her fancy,' the Gryphon observes of the decapitation-crazy Queen, 'they never executes nobody, you know' (1965: 125). Death itself has gone 'on holiday': executed or not executed is now very similar. The same is true of all the other threats on all their levels. Wonderland is forever in 'limbo': neither quite fatal nor quite not, as if terminally ill or continuously on Death Row. Our culture, our whole form of life is now perpetually sick: we have the capacity to experience biological shapes stretched out of shape, language and reasoning gone threateningly rampant, a world in which a sentence 'seemed to have no sort of meaning in it … yet it was certainly English' (1965: 97).

Everyone must die

Out of everything we have seen in this chapter, a disturbing prospect comes into view. If the force that drives us beyond our context surges from 'limbo' – from the clash of life and its end – then the more that humanity is in peril, the further the whole world is under sentence of death, and facing imminent slaughter, the greater the aesthetic energy, the more resistant the art to context, the more capable it is of reaching out across place and time. 'Everyone must die' becomes more than a matter of fact. It becomes more than an obligation to accept our shared mortality, as Pogue Harrison suggests (2003: 70–1). Rather – on this unnerving line of thought – it appears as an aesthetic requirement, in which demise must be held in limbo with life energies. The basic, if unsettling thought, has since inspired any number of sci-fi plots, in which drama depends vicariously upon the ultimate stakes in destruction.

The great Argentine epic poem, *The Gaucho Martín Fierro* (*El gaucho Martín Fierro*) (1872) by José Hernández, speaks of an unending, unstoppable song. 'If I start to sing / there is no moment when I must end …/ the couplets go bubbling out of me / like water from a spring' (si me pongo a cantar / no tengo cuándo acabar …/ las coplas me van brotando / como agua de manantial) (2018: loc.684). The key intuition of the poem, John Hughes has remarked, is found in the opening words where being 'is solely voice' (no es más que cantar) (1970: 87): 'Aquí me pongo a cantar', here I start to sing (2018: loc.6530). Singing is said to carry the 'voice', from mortal biological life, through death, and thence beyond the grave, 'at the foot of the Eternal Father' (al pie del Eterno Padre). 'You'll find me singing / even if the earth opens up', the narrator proclaims (cantando me han de encontrar / aunque la tierra se abra) (2018: loc.677). Even the first-person singer himself proves unable to prevent its outpouring: he smashes his guitar (2018: loc.2296), only for Hernández's poem to continue and the narrative to be left open-ended (year later, Hernández sought to address this with a poem on the *gaucho*'s return). 'Voice', once unleashed, pours out beyond bounded subjectivity, and is renewed by its own apparent destruction. The singer tries, and fails, to identify the limits of the poem with the bounds of his self. 'Not no-one is to sing / when this *gaucho* sang' (naides ha de cantar / cuando este gaucho cantó) (2018: loc.2296), he declares, but the continuing of the verses, now as narrative – 'relación' (2018: loc.2304), makes explicit what is apparent at the outset. The words 'I start to sing' seem at once to be uttered through the mouths of Hernández and of Martín Fierro, the limits of their respective identities blurring, slipping away.

The inspiration of this unending verse is the clash of two violent international orders experienced in the life of Martín Fierro, both instances of a 'practical, engaged universality', as Tsing puts it, and thence a 'guide to the yearnings and nightmares' of history (2005: 1). On the one hand, there is an effort to build Argentina on a model akin to nation states run by Europeans and by descendent settler populations elsewhere in the Americas in the nineteenth century, to make it part of the vast expansion of 'Greater Europe' as the historian John Darwin has dubbed it (Darwin 2007: 245). Whether in the thoughts of Sarmiento or his rival Juan Bautista Alberdi, this involves an integration of the population into a 'civilised' Argentine state, with strong links to Europe, capable of military action against other such states and against indigenous peoples. This is what happened both in the extraordinarily brutal war with Paraguay (1864–70) – which just preceded publication of the poem, and which we encountered in *Fausto* (chapter 1) – and in campaigns against the free indigenous tribes to the south. In the former, Paraguay lost over half its population, and the vast majority of its men. Martín Fierro sings of the *gauchos*' integration into this new order as a relentless violence and cruel desolation. 'A persecuted *gaucho*', Tulio Haleperín Donghi observes, is 'sacrificed on the altar of the new state' (un gaucho perseguido … sacrificado en el altar del nuevo estado) (1985: 293). The fate of Fierro thus exposes what Girard sees as fundamental to the notion of the sacrificial scapegoat: a 'concealed relationship between persecution and the culture as a whole.' It is by declaring others who are like us to be unlike that we can bring a culture into being, affirming our own sameness to ourselves but not to them (Girard 1986: 21–2). Notoriously, that most influential of Argentine intellectuals and politicians, Sarmiento, said in 1861 that it was fine to spill *gaucho* blood as it was the only human part of them (cited in Hanway 2003: 152).

Fierro, like many others, is arrested on an offence designed to target and bring *gaucho* customs under state regulation: drunkenness in a *pulpería*, a kind of rural bar. He shares with many others the fate of being forcefully conscripted into frontier armies in the service of the central government (Giménez Vega & González 1975: 57–8, 153–4, 184–5). 'Lo miran al pobre gaucho / como carne de cogote', he says: they look on the poor old gaucho, literally, as the meat on the neck of a cow, a scrap of discarded flesh (2018: loc.2170. The process aims to eliminate the distinctiveness of his origins, which are wiped away in a homogenizing effort to create a modern Argentine nation: 'I found not a trace of the ranch', Fierro says of his attempted return home (No hallé ni rastro del rancho) (2018: loc.1385). Ultimately, this state violence conjures up a vision of a future pervaded by death, an aftermath of mass slaughter: 'if things carry on / as they're going up to the present / mayhap of all a sudden / we'll see the countryside deserted / and the bones of those who've died / jus' whitenin'' (si siguen las cosas / como van hasta el presente / puede ser que redepente / veamos al campo disierto / y blanquiando solamente / los güesos de los que han muerto) (2018: loc.2190).

On the other hand, through the killing fields, in displacement and fundamental loss, we are presented with an alternate globalizing vision in which, as Fierro puts it, 'all lands is good' (todas las tierras son güenas) (2018: loc.2279). In showing the barbarism of putative civilisation, its scapegoating sacrifice, in effecting that reversal – Julio Ortega notes – Fierro ends up in 'nameless space' at the 'margins' (2006: 143). Ultimately fleeing south of Argentina, out of the reach of Greater Europe, Fierro projects beyond the borderline, the context, of one world order, another on the outside of its frontiers. The departure of the sacrificial victim seems to evoke something like what the thinker Alain Badiou calls an Event. This is the point where a system based on its own one-ness enters into contact with a reality: that it is one of multiple possible orders, and that there is (literally) nothing underpinning it (Badiou 2007: 29, 175). Here, Žižek comments, it reaches 'the moment of confrontation with its *immanent* limit …, something that cannot be integrated into the existing ideological frameworks … signs of the New' (2008: 270). The violence of Greater Europe thus brings forth the prospect of its potential collapse, of all that lies beyond itself. Fierro breaks with the international order of nation states even as Greater Europe severs his origin, leaving him without a home, a confining origin to which to return: 'I, driven by my [pains] / wanna get out of this hell' (yo, empujao por las mías / quiero salir de este infierno) (2018: loc.2235). His involuntary rootlessness, his being scapegoated, enables what, at first blush, seems like a refusal of belonging. The scene of his razed home offers a near-sacred conflation of sacrifice and renewal: he is 'sadder than Holy Thursday' (más triste que Jueves Santo) (2018: loc.1392).

Out of this all-consuming clash, an alternate experience of likeness opens up, the affordance of its sameness seeming to break with gender norms, like Melville's sperm-squeezing sailors, like the wedding of Apollo and Dionysus, like the *Wounded Bullfighter*. As in Courbet's *Wrestlers*, the pushing against one another brings about a new blending (mixtura), In a scene of assault by and betrayal of the Argentine state, of violence by and against Greater Europe in its furthest southern frontier lands, another man – Cruz – battling to capture Fierro, changes sides. Cruz – literally the Cross – thereafter becomes Fierro's double: they are 'astilla del mesmo palo', chips off the same block (2018: loc.2206), Holy Thursday and crucifixion. The poem itself switches to Cruz's voice and his parallel *gaucho* tale, the verses advancing through patterns of similitude. Like El Pollo and Laguna, the two characters intimately blend together, here through the workings of the poem, to the point that the patterns of their voices are close to interchangeable. This is, Hanway notes, 'the only domestic love story that occurs in the narrative' (Hanway 2003: 165). Violence – suffered and inflicted – tears Fierro out from his monogamous heterosexual home: when he returns his wife has gone. Instead we have the pairing of two men riding at the same trot, the delight of aggressive males on horseback with one another, as they tussle with other men. The supposed 'sameness' of same-sex affection offers an affordance of wider similitude.

Here, though, this transfer from one international order (that of nation states), and one version of resemblance to another, is experienced as the transfer of one form of slaughter to another, the repetition of mortal menace. In the worst possible sense, we leap beyond yet nearer bring. Far from recognizing the fallacy of Oneness – the danger of scapegoating – Fierro's alternative affirms, in reaction, its own version of self-sameness. In the poem, the 'reason' of 'non-citizens'– that is, the fundamental justification for a social and cultural system– is itself what Ludmer calls 'the one-culture', from which there can be no remainder (la cultura toda-una del canto es la razón de los no-ciudadanos; no parece dejar restos (1988: 158–8). A destructive outcome is suggested in Fierro's denial of his own anxiety when he seeks to cross the border out of Greater Europe: 'why go getting alarmed?' (¿A qué andar pasando sustos?), he wonders (2018: loc.2241). We might well ask the same question as we contemplate the murderous Fierro himself, self-appointed emissary of freedom beyond confines, born of the *gauchada* and its resistance to the state: 'I am a *gaucho* … the earth is too small for me … I make no nest on this ground' (Soy gaucho … para mí la tierra es chica … no hago nido en este suelo) (2018: loc 712). The passage out of the nation state is literally carved with the violence of a petty criminal, as Fierro cuts down his fellow humans: 'I will open with the knife / the path t' follow' (yo abriré con el cuchillo / el camino pa seguir) (2018: loc.1666).

The energizing source of deterritorialised universality is a projection of insularity, now putatively transfigured into a variant of internationalism, as Fierro passes from his early hatred of the indigenous to his desperate quest for their embrace. Ultimately, Fierro embodies the threat that – as many cultural theorists see it – any universal notion involving anything specific and substantive must, by definition, serves specific, particular interests to the violent exclusion of others. His homoerotic attachment to Cruz, far from an inclusive queering, is a projection of his own self and an aggressive, macho rejection of difference, Gustavo Geirola observes (1996: 322). His attack on the Atlantic system of Greater Europe – from the legacy of slavery from West Africa (Sluyter 2012: 144–52) to recent encouragement of European migration – takes shape in vicious xenophobia. He brutally kills a man of African descent in a fight, after hurling racist insults (2018: loc.1500–57). He denigrates immigrants from Naples, uttering sexual abuse against them (2018: loc.1269–321). For the educated elite,

Ludmer explains, to hear such sentiments in a gauchesque poem was pointedly to hear a repudiation of egalitarian universalism. The latter outlook had been at the very origins of the genre in the poems of Bartolomé Hidalgo (1788–1822) (1988: 159).

Both versions of universalizing 'friction' – the Greater European order and resistance to it – drawing humanity ever closer, uniting the globe, are riddled with abuse and violence, strewn with corpses. Yet, taken together, they provide a vision of potentially all-encompassing slaughter from which the boundless singing – the poem of *The Gaucho Martín Fierro* itself – arises. It is not in any sense the case here that art condones, less still applauds, the violent forging together of the globe. The poem, the final verses affirm, tells us of 'ILLS KNOWN TO ALL / BUT THAT NOT NO-ONE SANG' (MALES QUE CONOCEN TODOS / PERO QUE NAIDES CANTÓ) (2018: loc.2323). The 'voice' sings out from what is silenced by the sacrifices: it is literally telling what 'no-one' tells, as if it came from the void obscured by but informing every vision of collective oneness. Yet, it is not truly akin to Agamben's 'Voice' which brings, in its recognition of the void beyond our being, *'the definitive elimination of the sacrificial mythogeme'* (1991: 106). Nor – at least in the 1872 poem – is the sacrificed Fierro sacralised as the mythical origin of an Argentine Greater Europe, a paradoxical 'pillar of society', in Girard's words (1986: 42). Instead, the poem's very aesthetic power, its reaching out beyond bounded contexts, depends insidiously upon all the kinds of slaughter and violence of which it sings. And singing is its *raison d'être*. 'Aquí me pongo a cantar', here I begin to sing, as if only out of all this, as if through this juncture in place and time ('aquí', here), the boundless Voice may come. We find before us the spectre of a general sacrifice, in which 'we'll see the field deserted / and the bones of those who've died / jus' whitening'.

That origin-story of poetics, the legend of Narcissus, combines obliteration with sameness. In *Moby-Dick*, the narrator recalls the tale of Narcissus, gazing upon his own reflection in the water, and drowning as he seeks to grasp it. The story, from Ovid's *Metamorphoses*, had long been a trope of *mimesis*, sameness, reflections in that sense (Butler 2015: 87). Melville finds in it 'the image of the ungraspable phantom of life; and this is the key to it all' (2002: 4–5). The death of Narcissus as he snatches at an image, the life of art – 'here is an artist' (2002: 4) – the uninterpretable prose and a murderous force that dominates and joins the globe, are as one. Reflecting on this passage, Bainard Cowan remarks that the 'sublime absolute always bears the hidden face of the Gorgon' (1982: 111). The Ocean's inscrutable waters into which this Narcissus looks are a menace to all life. 'We know the sea to be an everlasting terra incognita ... however much, in a flattering future, that science and skill may augment; yet for ever and for ever, to the crack of doom, the sea will insult and murder. ... The first boat we read of, floated on an ocean, that with Portuguese vengeance had whelmed a whole world without leaving so much as a widow. ... The sea ... is also a fiend to its own offspring' (2002: 229). Whaling – the work's key pursuit – is said to join the world across the seas through mortal peril and in violent killing, the brutal exploitation of resources on which the global economy and societies depend. 'I freely assert, that the cosmopolite philosopher cannot, for his life, point out one single influence, which within the last sixty years has operated more potently upon the whole world, taken in one aggregate, than the high and mighty business of whaling', Ishmael declares (2002: 91).

Scholars have found here swathes of allusion to Ante-Bellum America and its connections to and place within the wider world. Spanos finds in all this both the resonances and the undoing of a 'totalizing' American 'imperial' vision (Spanos 1995: 46, 77). Imagining an advertisement for his own story of whaling, Ishmael foresees it sandwiched between '*Grand Contested Elections for the Presidency of the United States*' and the Great Game between imperial Britain and Russia, 'BLOODY BATTLE IN AFGHANISTAN', on the other side of the globe (2002: 6). He himself speaks of how the commerce of whalers opened up the Spanish imperial system, ultimately leading to independence in Peru, Chile and Bolivia (2002: 92). 'Melville's language of freedom resonated with Jefferson's; it resonated, just as surely, with the language of freedom in antebellum expansionist discourse', Dimock comments. 'Such an empire was to be one of both "space and time"' (Dimock 1989: 9, 14). In *Melville's Major Fiction*, James Duban traces a series of close parallels in wording and imagery, from interest in the acquisition of whaling ports in California, to Prentiss's designs on Mexico and Cuba, to millennialist abolitionism and its notion of a chosen people, to Jackson and Polk's expansionism or Calhoun's efforts to extend slavery southwards. The name of the ship – the *Pequod* – recalls the assault on the indigenous Pequot people of America (Duban 1983: 83–7, 135).

All these clashes in recent and contemporary history provide 'friction' – to borrow Tsing's word – for the literary ventriloquism of *Moby-Dick*, the creative act that unfurls through the 'insult and murder' of the seas. Faced with the waters and the whale, those very humans who violently exploit the globe experience their hunt as nothing less than the battle of all their kind against all that imperils it. Their assault channels even the abuses that global humanity inflects upon itself. The crew famously appear as an inclusive 'deputation from all the isles of the sea, and all the ends of the earth, accompanying Old Ahab in the *Pequod* to lay the world's grievances before the bar from which not very many of them ever come back' (2002: 100–1). Against them is ranged the whale Moby-Dick itself, in some quarters reputed ubiquitous, if not indeed immortal, an animal of all place and time (2002: 151). The creature – rebelling against all human exploitation, across history and geography – is a bringer of death to any human indiscriminately, in defiance of any human moral order, a sempiternal enemy of all humanity. 'Retribution, swift vengeance, eternal malice were in his whole aspect, and spite of all that mortal man could do' (2002: 467). In the enormity of a clash in which everything is at stake, the crew dies, as if the deputation from all humanity had in that moment fallen, and Ishmael can write the tale – or, as it were, sing the epic song, 'here I start to sing' – evoking a bringing of all the world and all of history together beyond even humanity.

'It is a very cheap sort of sentimentality', Marx pronounces, 'which declares … a method prescribed by the very nature of the case, to be a brutal method' (2013: loc.3016). His *Capital I* can be read as a transformation of the whole world into an all-encompassing literary vision. This entails the brutal, life-threatening physical modification of all humanity, the making of the 'sacred wounds' we saw in Cameron's photographs, necessary for organic beings to be transfigured. 'In modern history,' – Michael Taussig writes of Marx – 'the fetishism of commodities rejuvenates the mythic density of the space of death' (1987: 5). *Capital I* explores how a universal abstraction stretching across place could be rendered real in the present-day world (see Chapter 2): the living allegory that is the god Capital, myths emanating from the depths of time (vampires, fetishes, cyclopean creatures), in short what Marx calls 'metaphysical subtleties and theological niceties'.

Seen in this light, Marx's vision of 'capitalism' concerns the creation of a vast, global, *sui generis* poetic epic, evincing a violent poetics. 'It is surprising', Francis Wheen observes, 'that so few people have even considered the book as literature.' Wheen calls attention to 'Marx's own declared ambition – in several letters to Engels – to produce a work of art' (2006: 74). For Stanley Edgar Hyman in *The Tangled Bank*, what truly made Marx's masterpiece compelling was less his economic theory, than 'the imaginative construct' (1974: 149). The god of Capital, and the atavistic forces let loose with it, draw their life from the constant dying, the continual slaughter, of all workers. 'Capital is dead labour,' Marx famously claims, 'that, vampire-like, only lives by sucking living labour, and lives the more, the more labour it sucks' (2013: loc.3968). We might say the same of *Capital I*. It is the poem of a culture and society, existing in defiance of human mortal limits, that, unchecked, will leave the planet devoid of life, like Martín Fierro's fields of blanched bones. 'In its blind unrestrainable passion, its were-wolf hunger for surplus-labour,' Marx tells us, 'capital oversteps not only the moral, but even the merely physical maximum bounds of the working-day. It usurps the time for growth, development, and healthy maintenance of the body. ... Capital ... is in practice moved as much and as little by the sight of the coming degradation and final depopulation of the human race, as by the probable fall of the earth into the sun' (2013: loc.4432, 4489–93). Dying humanity now becomes 'both flesh and not', to return to David Foster Wallace's phrase (see Chapter 1). Marx's voice gives us that transfiguration, and is itself transformed. It too is 'both flesh and not', the writer's hand, arm, larynx even, shaped in their movements into evocation of the tortured, now abstracted world.

Like *Moby-Dick* or Manet's world-embracing violence, *Capital I* is a hodgepodge of voices conjured up in a chorus of deathly pastiche. There is – in Hyman's words – 'a whole menagerie of supernatural horrors' (1974: 134). Wheen finds in the book sections from 'the Gothic novel ... Victorian melodrama ... black farce ... Greek tragedy ... satirical utopia'. There are vast numbers of quotations from a mass of literary sources across many languages (2006: 74–5). The text flows in and out of the words of others, themselves in turn assimilated to literary tradition, especially that of the heroic ode. We hear, for example, from 'Dr Ure, the Pindar of the automatic factory' (Marx, 2013: loc.6643). The British liberal politician William Ewart Gladstone offers us a 'Pindaric dithyrambus on the advance of surplus-value-making' (2013: loc.10163–7). For all the irony, we are not to dismiss the force of the literary allusions. Rather, as with 'the irresistible arm drag' of *Moby-Dick*, we experience how they carry us away from one vision of the world – that of the liberal political economists, say, and their supposed delusions – and into Capital and its world-shaping, world-sacrificing majesty, the reality of its horror. Hyman finds in it 'four acts of a drama', each a descent into hellishness, at times comparable to Dante or Hieronymus Bosch (1974: 143). The allusions and styles, like the gods and mythical creatures, are, as it were, reincorporated into the epic of Capital, put in their true place, where they exercise their real roles. We may then apprehend their reality. If the world's sacrifice is the song, Marx is its singer.

Abstraction (I): nothing and everything

Obliteration, totality and the historical reality of human life may, then, converge in efforts to realise universality in the world. In *The Pilgrimage of Bayoán* (1863) (*La peregrinación de Bayoán*), by the Puerto Rican writer Eugenio María de Hostos, the notion is eloquently summarised in the description of the protagonist, offered by a friend: 'Nothing: that was Bayoán; the nothing of an everything' (Nada: eso era Bayoán; la nada de un todo) (2015: loc.3488). Discussing Hegel, Slavoj Žižek likewise remarks that the One (everything) is 'void' (nothing): it cannot, without becoming particular, have any specific traits

(2008: 52–3). Through Bayoán's life, we encounter a continual effort to turn a human being into such a universal abstraction: not entirely to remove them from this existence to some higher plane, but to draw out of them (*abs-trahere* in Latin) the universal. The aspiration is that this transfiguration will be that of all humanity. The description that we are offered of the story calls to mind the vast philosophical histories conceived in the nineteenth century, from Hegel's *Phenomenology of the Spirit* onwards, unfurling *Geist*, Spirit through history. It does so through ambiguity in the Castilian language, where history and story may be the same word, and the tale *of man* (all men) is written the same as the tale *of the* (specific) *man*. 'When Bayoán said to me, "Take this manuscript; keep it and remember me", I did not see in the manuscript the history / story of a man, the memoir of a love affair; I saw the history / story of the spirit of man / the man' (Cuando Bayoán me dijo: 'Toma ese manuscrito; consérvalo y acuérdate de mí', yo no vi en el manuscrito la historia de un hombre, la memoria de unos amores; vi la historia del espíritu del hombre) (2015: loc.3499). With alarming literalness, *The Pilgrimage* parallels the vision of mid-century Democrats like the Spanish and Catalan leftist post-Hegelian, Francisco Pi i Margall. For Pi i Margall, in his response to the 1854 Revolution, the latest turbulence in the wake of 1808, Spirit can only be that of an individual being, and, therefore, the universal absolute can only be realised in the singular Spirit. Individuals – he claims in *Reaction and Revolution* (*La reacción y la revolución*) – are entirely sovereign (Pi i Margall 1982). The bold gambit of *The Pilgrimage* is that if the universal is to occur in history, that must occur from, through and out of a body, a person's feelings, and their thoughts, the accidents of their life. Somehow, then, the singular individual, while still so remaining, has to become a void, the nothing of an everything. 'Impossible and necessary', is how Žižek has described the universal and its realisation in history (cited in Butler, Laclau & Žižek 2000: 10). 'Universality', he says, '*appears* as the distortion of the particular' (2008: 294).

Bayoán evokes something like the agony of that distortion of the particular, that putatively necessary impossibility. 'I want to possess that supreme reason', he declares, 'that leads to derision, to sacrifice' (quiero poseer esa razón suprema que conduce al escarnio, al sacrificio) (2015: loc.1174). This involves a continual courting of annihilation, of nothingness, of a ceasing to be a human person. Murderous pain pervades the attempt: 'Can I commit suicide?' (¿Puedo suicidarme?), Bayoán asks, assessing what his journey across the Atlantic must amount to (2015: loc.1313). There is continual violence: the torturing of the individual body and mind into something it is by definition not, holding it continuously at a point of self-destruction: 'my reason is so cruel', Bayoán exclaims, '… my soul is so cruel' (es tan cruel mi razón … es tan cruel mi alma) (2015: loc.1507). In his 'self-tortures', he is, as Ramón Sotos-Crespo says of Hostos, both 'the Law and the Scapegoat'; 'he erases the constraints … between the punished and the punisher' (1998: 226). The whole work is akin to a sequence of moments, each of reasoning hallucination or hallucinatory reasoning, a blend of reflection and sensation, generated by a person assaulting themselves to the limit of their own integrity. It is as if immediate reality were becoming ever less substantial, turning into something dematerialised: 'Bayoán was no longer a man:' we read, 'he was a conscience / consciousness' (Bayoán no era ya un hombre: era una conciencia) (2015: loc.3475). Yet Bayoán is still, always a man, and the narrative form expresses the intense discomfort of attempting to achieve the transfiguration, like the clumsiness of Cameron's photographs and their 'sacred wounds'. The physical world and human beings, the specifics of events and places, are perceived only through Bayoán's words of aspiration to universal justice.

Conversely, the latter arise only through and out of concrete incidents and events. The journey of spirit takes as its most immediate form the contingent shapes of an individual's life – but also vice versa – responding now to the weather, now to personal encounters, or accidents of travel. The genres of philosophical history, autobiography and romance uncomfortably fuse before us. The effect is to place chaos at the heart of the novel's efforts at order, Ángel A. Rivera observes: the narrative and Bayoán both fragment (1993: 529).

These discomforts of the journey of Spirit become those of world history. Bayoán sets out from one of Spain's continuing overseas territories in the Caribbean: Puerto Rico. Alongside Cuba and the Philippines, this territory was critical to the imperial status that remained so vital to nineteenth-century Spain, as Christopher Schmidt-Nowara has shown (2006: 9). 'The everything of a nothing' would ultimately reverse the violence that has played so great a role in bringing together the globe, dematerialising the world. 'Universal justice' (justicia universal) (2015: loc.538), realised through Bayoán's individual person, would invert the oppressive universalisms that have so often forged humanity together. The protagonist mocks as an 'imposture of history' those like the English, Spanish and Romans, who claim to perfect and civilise humanity through imperialism (2015: loc.87). But just as a person can only be abstracted into 'conciencia' if this is drawn out of their mortal being, so history can only be transfigured from the basis of its own realities. It is a 'verdad aterrradora', a terrifying truth (2015: loc.879), we read, that without Columbus's arrival in the Americas, and the subsequent abuses, human fraternity across the Atlantic would never have been feasible. In vivid recognition of this, Bayoán seeks to overturn imperialist violence, not simply by rejecting it, but by literally reversing Columbus's journey, and travelling inversely down its paths of history. In this 'viaje a la inversa', this reverse journey (Rodríguez de Laguna 2015: 747), he voyages through the desolation of the Antilles and out across to Spain. His voice comes 'as it were from beyond the grave' of a now silenced indigenous history, Sotos-Crespo observes (1998: 229). In this way, the present day seeks to double the past moment, the present individual aims to double the historic personage who joined the Atlantic together. Perceiving Guanahaní in the distance, Bayoán exclaims: 'With the same anxious desire that Columbus awaited it, I await it' (Con la misma ansiedad con que Colón la esperaba, yo la espero) (2015: loc.1729). In this way, the *Pilgrimage* seeks to configure its vision out of the tense debates in Spain, in Puerto Rico and in other territories about the legacy of Columbus. In their self-understanding, many creole patriots delicately balanced the influence of Spain, resistance to it, and distinctive colonial and pre-colonial realities, Schmidt-Nowara shows, such that emblematic figures of conquest became contested icons (2006: 4–5, 14, 54–5). Bayoán's aim ultimately is to transfigure from within the legacy of the putative universal monarchy, persuading Spain instead to seek forgiveness of the Americas while its former children (the American states) become its siblings in a new family resemblance (2015: loc.557).

The point is not that we ever see anything of the sort, but that we experience the effect of attempting it: the cruel suicidal torment, a person's deliberate self-exposure to abuse, the agony of their efforts at global transfiguration through an individual life. The reverse Columbine journey reiterates, in Bayoán's humiliation, the punishment of Columbus as he (supposedly) tried to redeem the effects of Spain upon the Americas (2015: loc.538). Like the endless singing of Martín Fierro, like Melville's Narcissus contemplating the waters in which he will drown, this is pain freely accepted. It is not just that the words of *The Pilgrimage* represent the suffering of Bayoán, but that they present it to us: we encounter a voice, 'the spirit that moans in these leaves of paper' (el espíritu que gime en estas hojas de papel) (2015: loc.3493). The medium of the book, like the voice in Butler's understanding of the *Logos*, is emotion that exists as a material. Speaking of ancient literature, but it as well might be of *The Pilgrimage*, Butler remarks that the voice and any record of it relate to one another, not as 'original and copy' but in a 'more basic resemblance', the fact that both are formed in matter (Butler 2015: 29). *The Pilgrimage* offers a vision of what the medium of literature might become, all those signs and marks and blanks. We have physically before us, in the pages, matter that is trying to be 'conciencia' while still remaining in the world, matter that is lovingly tortured in its desire for self-destruction, matter that 'moans', the agonised dematerialisation of the world, the Sound of the End.

The longing for nullification finds expression in a searingly tense and destructive experience of sexuality and love, the 'historia de unos amores', the story of a love affair. Such might be the aesthetics of an everything that is nothing, nothing that is everything, its mode of sensual appreciation, its erotics. It is in the actual physical desire for another human being in the world that we confront the concrete effects of realising 'the voice of universal love' (la voz del amor universal) (2015: loc.1590). 'Your love is cruel', Bayoán's fiancée Marién exclaims all-too accurately, in a moment of desperation (tu amor es cruel) (2015: loc.1495). *The Pilgrimage of Bayoán* gives us sexuality lived as pain, fusing the intensity of physical lust with utter terror at it, transfiguring worldly existence into sexualised dreaming turned nightmare. In the most physically intimate moment of the volume, Bayoán contemplates Marién asleep. He is tempted by her even as he protests he can resist, devouring her charms with his gaze (2015: loc.3998). Marién, talking in her sleep, has a lust-filled dream about Bayoán: 'Every time he looks at me ... I shiver, and the fire in his eyes stirs me, sets my blood aflame' (Cada vez que me mira ... me estremezco, y el fuego que en sus ojos me turba, enciende mi sangre) (2015: loc.4004). Bayoán can resist no more: 'I gave it to her; a kiss of fire, from hell' (se lo di; beso de fuego, de infierno) (2015: loc.4017). At this,

> The memory of the dream still alive, she thought a dream what was reality, and ran her hand over her eyes: meanwhile mine, leaping from their sockets, sought out delight in her uncovered breasts; she spotted that gaze, covered her breasts, huddled up her body, looked at me and terrified by the disorder found in me, gave out a pitiful cry, a terrifying scream.[1]

To all effects, the consummation of human love has turned, in Bayoán's distorted vision, into sexual assault.

Shortly afterwards, the ailing Marién expires, her body unable to sustain being nothing that is everything that is a person, both flesh and not. 'She will die,' her mother had prophesied to Bayoán, 'and you will live to suffer' (morirá, y Vd. vivirá para sufrir) (2015: loc.1387). So he does, setting out once more on his quest to realise universality, perhaps an unending pilgrimage (2015: loc.4233). We know already that Bayoán's cherished vision is a panorama of recurrent sacrifice, a history become ever-looping misery. '¡Otra vez, otra

---

[1] Vivo aún el recuerdo de su sueño, creía sueño lo que era realidad, y se pasaba las manos por los ojos: mientras tanto, los míos saltando de sus órbitas, buscaban el deleite en su seno descubierto; ella sorprendió aquella mirada, se cubrió el seno, recogió el cuerpo, me miró y espantada del desorden que había en mí, dio un grito lastimero, un alarido aterrador (2015: loc.4017).

Instead of modernity

vez!' – again, again! – are the novel's opening words (2015: loc.485). As Bayoán departs, so the second narrator, left behind in Spain, is unable to keep his own company and 'flees from himself', as if unable too to maintain the integrity of his subjecthood (huye de sí mismo). The latter's suggestive final words evoke an endless journeying into loss in a transfigured vision of the Atlantic seascape: 'I walked over to the beach, and when the boat blurred into the horizon, I lowered my head in sadness, and I reflected that the horizon of life is much more obscure than that of the sea' (Me dirigí a la playa, y cuando el buque se confundió con el horizonte, bajé entristecido la cabeza y pensé que el horizonte de la vida es mucho más oscuro que el mar) (2015: loc.4233).

The horizon is obscured. Nothing is everything. The darkening world of James McNeill Whistler's *Nocturne in Blue and Gold: Valparaíso Bay* (?1874; Plate 11) vividly evokes abstraction through transoceanic violence and the legacies of imperial connections. The American artist arrived in the Chilean port city of Valparaíso on 12 March 1866 from Britain, on a shady – and ultimately failed – mission to supply torpedoes to the government. Floating in the bay was a Spanish fleet under the command of Casto Méndez Núñez, at war with Chile and an alliance of Spanish American states. Alongside were neutral naval forces – including British, French and US war vessels – seeking a ceasefire. The day before Easter, as a deadline expired, the Spanish opened fire on the defenceless city, targeting government buildings in a three-hour bombardment. The neutral fleets, forewarned, had abandoned the scene, returning only at a signal from the Spanish, as issue 13 of the military journal *Assembly of the Army and Navy* reported (*Asamblea del Ejército y de la Armada*) (Sutherland 2014: 95–6; *Asamblea* 1866: 468–73). Though later Whistler made rather light of the episode, at the time he fled the city for his life (Sutherland 2014: 96). In these events, there is something of the recurring pain that *The Pilgrimage of Bayoán* discerns in the long history of encounters between Europe and the Americas, the legacy of Columbus. Whistler witnessed a confrontation between a renascent Spain, reasserting its authority in the hemisphere, a South-American state, and a coalition determined to preserve the reconfigured order of the post-independence world. In a series of endeavours undertaken from the late 1850s – an attack on Morocco, actions in Cochinchina, the temporary recovery of Santo Domingo and abortive support for French intervention in Mexico – Spain had sought once more to project itself as a global power (Martínez Gallego 2001: 117–61). Against it were ranged what its own officials in the *Assembly of the Army and Navy* called an 'Americanised' alliance of independent states. Trying to dissuade it from interrupting global trade via Valparaíso and from operating so far from home base were its historic rivals for dominion in the hemisphere, the English-speaking peoples and the French, alongside the Russians, one-time rivals for the North-East Pacific.

The stay in Valparaíso, during which Whistler was to begin a series of paintings of the bay, came at what was to prove a crucial moment in his development as an artist. This would culminate in an assertion of 'the materiality of paint' (Peters Corbett: 2004: 119) in its own right, emptying out what Elizabeth Prettejohn calls 'verbalisable content' (2000: 190). The trip itself 'may have been partly an attempt to force a complete break with his past', Prettejohn comments. By 1867, on his return to Britain, Whistler had already repudiated the French Realist Courbet with whom he had worked as recently as 1865 (2000: 168). The importance of the 1866 episode is further suggested by Whistler's exhibiting just one painting during a period of transition through to 1870: the *Crepuscule in Flesh Colour and Green: Valparaíso* (Staley 2011: 180). Of the paintings of Valparaíso, two directly reference the events of March 1866 by depicting the neutral fleets. In *Crepuscule*, a French military vessel is identified by its tiny flag, perhaps as the combined force leaves the bay. In the painting oddly known as *Morning after the Revolution* – presumably showing the aftermath of the assault – we see the standards of the various neutral nations on a selection of boats (Dorment & MacDonald 1995: 117–19). In turn, the latter painting's striking compositional structure and view of the bay, pier and ships are directly paralleled in *Nocturne in Blue and Gold*, as they are in the painting generally known as the sketch for the *Nocturne* (in fact, it portrays broad daylight). The *Nocturne* thus emerges from a vision conceived in the wake of the bombardment, and to which it owes its bold formal structure. Katherine Emma Manthorne observes how dramatically Whistler alters his previous structuring of space, as he draws here on Japanese art: 'so near vertical is the plunge ... that the piers and harbor architecture seem to protrude out of nowhere' (1989: 172). That availability of Japanese compositions in turn draws on US intervention on the other side of the Pacific Ocean which had opened up Japan to commerce. The *Nocturne* proper seems to have been completed later: the Freer collection assigns it to 1874, noting that it was owned by Captain Henry Hill who died in 1882; a letter of 1874 refers to Whistler's efforts to complete a Valparaíso nocturne (McLaren Young et al. 1980: 45). The emanation of the *Nocturne* from the war images is thus suggestive of the long transformation of his art towards an abstraction from the world, triggered from that key moment in 1866 to the early 1870s. Prettejohn notes that in the latter half of the 1860s, Whistler's work 'remained tentative', breaking with Courbet but without 'a cogent alternative' (Prettejohn 2000: 168).

The Easter intimations of demise at the meeting point of hemispheric powers – the assault on a defenceless city – ultimately allow us to experience the world dying away, and to dwell upon it. Already in the hazy *Crepuscule in Flesh Colour and Green* (1866) everything is awash with delicate, sweeping shades of cloudy blue, as if the whole scene were liquefying, and the ships hardly in existence. There is a 'fluid tonality', Sutherland comments, 'Whistler enveloped ships, sea, and sky in mist, fog, and twilight' (2008: 68). In its near-dissolution, the *Crepuscule* seems to intimate what was to come in the 1870s: a use of paint that was so liquid, David Peters Corbett notes, that it ran from the canvases (2004: 118). In the *Nocturne* itself – a painting aspiring to the abstract form of music – the whole scene is dissolving softly, or whispily appearing out of very visible but lightly executed strokes of paint. The seascape before us has become a dark, all-enveloping, delicate, complex harmony: the scant light of the sky, the touches of illumination of the lamps, the reflections on the water, merge with what might otherwise be more substantial, the landscape and the ships, and these with those. The effect is 'to weave the same basic hues throughout the canvas' (Prettejohn 2000: 176). Forever held in limbo, the world is dissipating and hardly materialising before our eyes. Everything is on the verge of nothing, and very nearly nothing gives us everything. In Prettejohn's words, 'Whistler is the finest painter of nothingness – of the night, of ghosts, of the air' (2000: 199).

There is a suggestion here of something like Foucault's erasure of the face of 'Man': a 'thoroughgoing rejection of humanism', as Prettejohn puts it (2000: 189). The material medium of paint is taking the place of human presence, or for that matter the presence of the world as we know it. But, it *is taking the place*: it has not done so and does not do so. Recognisable shapes, after all, give us the compositional structure of the image: the boats, the pier, the people on the pier, the shape of the bay, the sea, the sky. Reflecting on this dual aspect of Whistler's art, Peter Dayan dwells on an apparent tension between 'the principle that art is harmony and is independent of subject-matter', and, on the other hand, that principle's 'untenability' (Dayan 2011: 12). The point is rather that, by dying, dissolving, dissipating, the world flows in and out of specificity and abstraction, taking on what García Cadena was to call a ghostly 'life of indefinite actualisation', 'an incomplete genesis', which is also a haunting, an incomplete death, 'limbo'. The association of a mortal ending and a conjunction of the figurative and the abstract recurs in Whistler. The image of his ageing mother, the *Arrangement in Grey and Black* (1871), was key to his 'breakthrough' at the end of the 1866–70 transition (Prettejohn 2000: 169). Back in 1864–65, just before the excursus to Valparaíso, the *Little White Girl* – later to be called *Symphony in White No. 1* – was accompanied by a poem by Algernon Swinburne, 'Before the Mirror'. In the final verses, the young woman looking in the mirror perceives 'all sweet life that was to lie down and lie', 'dead mouths of many dreams that / sing and sigh', and 'the flowing of all men's tears / beneath the sky' (2014: loc.28824–52). Dayan observes that, while Whistler increasingly invoked music in his titles, his own images of musicians evince a disconnection from actual performance on their instruments (2011: 22–3). The music of painting is – as it were – a falling silent, in which we encounter Whistler's own Sound of the End.

The universal emerges here not so much as Ernesto Laclau's '*empty place*' of '*empty signifiers*' (Laclau 2000: 57; original emphasis), but as a continual emptying out, an unending demise, which is also a continual coming into being, as if it occurred at Berzosa's 'imperceptible point'. Anna Greutzner Robins has remarked on Whistler's pursuit of 'universality' in the deployment of form, through his use of the term *axiom*, perhaps with its geometrical resonances (2007: 17). 'The Nocturnes endlessly repeat the same simple patterns', Prettejohn observes, so much so that one location could easily be mistaken for another (2000: 180–1). Each of the images relates to the others now as 'ever-changing spatial configurations' (2000: 177), a sameness that comes about through their varying specificity, and could be continued across place and time, that could 'go on'. So it is that in *Nocturne in Blue and Gold*, traces of Whistler's vision of the port after its bombardment in March 1866 fuse with configurations that could be found in other Nocturnes, like the familiar splash of light that might be a rocket. The port of Valparaíso in 1866, through its destruction, is now ceasing to be its own bounded self, so as to enter into 'simple patterns' of similitude. It has – as it were – met its demise twice, once at the hands of the Spanish, and now of Whistler. As this happens, the medium of paint seeks to 'enact the sensuous character of experience, claim to *be* it with an unmediated directness', in Peters Corbett's words (2004: 122). If this attention to the artistic medium resists the modern world – Peters Corbett suggests – it does so in complicity with it, as its transformation (2004: 123). Sign and referent become the same thing in the transfiguration: the *Nocturne is* the experience of Valparaíso bay dissolving in paint, the location abstracting into universalising patterns out of destruction.

In the 'sensuous character of experience', Whistler brings forth, not the dynamic drama, all that is 'energetic and horrifying', as García Cadena put it, not the tormented wrestling of Bayoán nor the epic mythos of Marx, but a melancholic meditation. The emphasis falls on the moments before and after the abuse and loss, not its occurrence: the scene is almost still. We experience a fading out and in, not Berzosa's chiselling away at entrails. The energetic pulsation of forms has given way to a gentle pulsing. The soft-edged, blurry, irregular shapes do not lead us through a single or interlocking dynamics of violent movement, but rather allow our eyes to amble here and there in diverse directions, with no purposeful destination.

The very imminence of demise allows us to experience the whole world dying away, and to dwell upon it, not without awareness or rejection of abuses, but now without turbulence. To philosophise – said Montaigne, after Cicero – is to learn to die. To experience the world being abstracted is to do the same. Through the threat and fact of violence emerges a sensation beyond violence, not divorced from the world as we know it, but drawn out from it, offering us a refreshed disposition before what we behold. We care for the matter of paint, as we care for Bayoán's printed words and their voicing. The sensual forms of our experience of the world do not vanish, but rather re-emerge through the flow of paint. Through our lingering, dallying in the wash of shapes before us, we experience a becalmed love of them. If we have not leapt, we have stepped beyond to nearer bring: we have passed through the dying of the scene so as to return to it. For, in *Nocturne in Blue and Gold*, Whistler emphasises for us the experience of the potential forms of experience in their own right – 'Blue and Gold' – above and beyond their specific sources, and, yet, without letting go of how they are found through such sources. So far does this go, that at the very centre of the painting there is a virtual blank space of colour. This aesthetic exploration of the world in its nullification is our loving born of its dying.

Abstraction (II): the dreamworld of the dead

Once dead, the preserved remains of biological creatures may become their own kind of nocturne dreamworld, not just persisting through history past death, but enabling connections through new aesthetic patterns. They may become doubly abstracted, drawn away (*abs-trahere*) from their original place and time, and into configurations of shapes beyond their original form of life, or at least our immediate experience of it. In 1873, the French scientist Jules Luys offered to the public his *Photographic Iconography of the Nervous Centres* (*Iconographie photographique des centres nerveux*). The book contained the first such images of human brain slices, 'substituting' – as he put it in the prologue – 'the action of light for my own personality' (substituant l'action de la lumière à ma propre personnalité) (Luys 2016a). Such visions of 'aperspectival objectivity', Lorraine Daston suggests, came to inform a notion of 'coherent scientific community … stretching over time and space' (1999: 116). Luys's *Atlas* emerges with universalist aspirations of this sort, and, with them, a notion of 'mechanical objectivity', that was – Jennifer Tucker shows – a troubled and contested aspect of nineteenth-century thought (2005: 2–23).

Embalmed here on the plates – to borrow Bazin's description of a photograph – are magnified forms reflected, not just from the generic human brain, but from a singular individual whose death facilitated the image-making. The visions before us have the thingness and thereness that Poliquin found in taxidermied beasts, but what we behold here are cross-sections of the very seat of thought and feeling, the nearest we have to the core of the physical person. As the techniques of taxidermy provide us with a copy of something that is itself abstracted into a new life, so Luys's staining and photographing of the brain structures present the shapes of a map which is, nonetheless, the original, individual terrain itself, giving 'topographic knowledge of those very regions which until now had been hardly explored and were imperfectly known' (la connaissance topographique de ces mêmes régions jusqu'ici à peine explorées et imparfaitement connues) (Luys 2016a). Just as taxidermied animals may evidence imperial conquest, so here the reach of French colonial exploration extends through the inner world of all humanity, even as it was probing the external globe and even as the home nation had been defeated by Prussia. The dream of a universalism born of France is thus renewed.

What we see is hardly recognisable, not only as a human being, but even as a biological organ, even though we know it is literally the preserved light of these, even as that light could scarcely have emanated from anywhere more intimate. In an essay on Luys, Sarah de Rijcke shows how his efforts at objectivity left visions of little use to medical mapping. In their very literalness, their lack of interpretation, they fail 'to emphasise the basic characteristics of the brain's gross anatomy' (de Rijcke 2008: 358). Characteristically, in Plate XVIII (Figure 14) we see something that forms a contained place, or series of confined locations, with a firm boundary and boldly contrasting, demarcated areas of light and dark within. In Plate XVIII these shapes are suggestive of some simpler life form, like a vegetable: the top two pieces have something about them of a split cauliflower, the bottom two a root formation or pair of cabbage leaves. On the whole, like the large inkblots of a Rorschach test, the photographs invite such psychological associations, with recognisable shapes of our world appearing and disappearing before the viewer. At the same time, in their deathly abstraction, they take us to a limit point of humanity, where interpretation falters. James Elkins has written eloquently of how the mechanical vision of the camera is, of itself, unlike the human way of looking: it has no inherent affect, it is 'not made to human measure', but exhibits instead a 'creeping cessation of meaning' in the 'dead and deadening stuff of the world' (Elkins 2011: 173, 91, xii). As we are faced with this, 'the metaphors flood in, and again they fail, and then they flood back' (2011: 173). What is so unnervingly inhuman in its shapes, so resistant to us and yet rich with possible association and texture, is a mechanical record of the inner core of a human.

'We all bear within ourselves an authorised copy of our sentence rendered into pieces', Berzosa said. As we look upon these remnants of another human person, which are maps to unknown regions of humanity, we apprehend that we are abstracted beings. In the intimate, physical seat of myself, I am something like an inkblot – we might reflect – and so was this individual. Every person pulsates and projects into similar bold, abstracted, unfamiliar forms, each individual flickering into every other. This is what that person's dying gives us, what their opened-up brain reveals, preserved now in light and chemicals and reproduced. Luys, after all, envisaged metonymically that 'each particular slice … stood for numerous alternatives of that slice in nature' (de Rijcke 2008: 357). As we appreciate the forms aesthetically, exploring their sensual shapes, we enter a dream-world conjured by our fleshy biological realities even in their demise. By photographing slices of the human brain, Luys preserves their light, gifting it survival beyond death, and in so doing, abstracts the seat of our very humanity into something that is both fact and hallucination. In *Victorian Glassworlds*, Armstrong evokes the effects of precision optical instruments as visions like hallucinatory dreams even in their exactness (2008: 319). This is a reality in which we look like cabbage leaves, certainly, but one in which we are, above all, suggestive patterns 'of indefinite actualisation … in incomplete genesis'.

The corpses of taxidermied animals are likewise abstracted aesthetically into dreamscapes, while retaining forms that we more immediately recognise: the body, skin, fur, scales of the now atemporal beast. This combination was peculiarly apparent in the Cabinet of Natural History in Madrid. Since the late eighteenth century, the Cabinet had been installed in the very same building as the Real Academia de San Fernando, the official training academy

Sacrifice: everyone must die

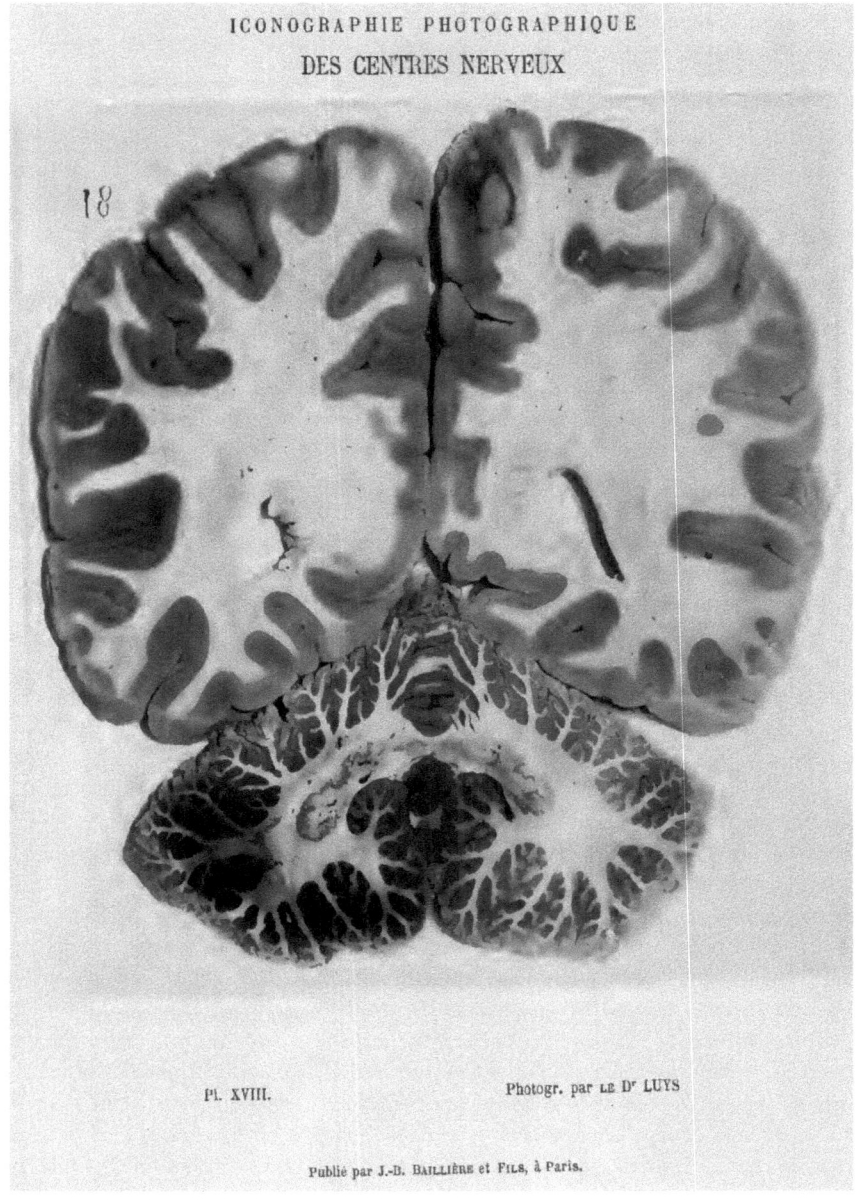

14 Jules Luys, *Photographic Iconography of the Nervous Centres*, Plate XVIII

for artists. In his guide to the Cabinet of 1871, José María Solano y Eulate reminds us that this had not been the intention during the first part of the nineteenth century. The Prado building was originally constructed as a museum of natural history, but was given to painting and sculpture at the urging of Fernando VII's wife. The Cabinet was left in its dark and limited accommodation, and starved of funds (1871: 5–7, 17, 21). As we saw in Chapter

2, this decision was also to have consequences for the patterning of images in the Prado Museum, not entirely suited to being a gallery of that kind. Conversely, the outcome meant that – as Solano y Eulate acknowledges *malgré lui* – visitors found 'lodged under the same roof nature and art' (albergadas bajo el mismo techo la naturaleza y el arte) (1871: 8). Back in the eighteenth century, a plaque had been installed above the entrance, celebrating that combination as a glorious achievement of the monarch, Carlos III, with a Latin motto to that effect by Juan de Iriarte. It is still there.

The effect was an invitation to explore back and forth the flow between dead animals and aesthetic experience. Far from rigorously organised around scientific classifications and schemata, even by 1871, the Cabinet's rooms offered a visual experience of miscellaneous multitudes, as if in a sprawling cabinet of curiosities. For example, Room V was putatively given to the reptile family, but on the central dais stood a number of female ostriches from Africa, a pair of the same species from the Americas, and some birds from the Indian Ocean islands described as having stubby wings and a body like a sow. For good measure, alongside dangling crocodiles, enormous snakes and great tortoises, the walls of Room V were hung with boards of insects, many in a state of decay, including a beautiful assemblage of butterflies donated by María Isabel de Braganza, Fernando VII's spouse. Meanwhile, on the floor, a visitor could observe the cultivation of silkworms in an urn (1871: 73–4). The visual patterns offered by the contents of Room V would suggest associations, similarities, connections and disconnections that escape the realms of science, or for that matter biological normality, but that were made up by real animals and insects. The 1871 catalogue itself, with its long metonymic list of items and their position, leaps from one anecdotal aspect to another, from the position of eyes on one fish, to how tasty another has proved to be (1871: 74).

Into the Cabinet, items had poured initially from the territories of Spain's global monarchy, supplemented by connections to museums and collectors active across the world, and various confiscations (Cabello Carro 2011: 218, 224–32). In the second half of the eighteenth century, 'a flurry of scientific expeditions crisscrossed the empire' in a 'project to make the empire visible', Daniela Bleichmar observes (2015: 249). All the collected objects, with their diverse provenances, were configured into aesthetic patterns that, as in the Prado, spilled out from family resemblances (say, 'reptile'), and from imperial networks and exchange, into visual 'promiscuity', to borrow Madrazo's word. In the mid-nineteenth century, the renewal of Spanish interest in the wider natural world was to be seen in the mid-century scientific expeditions to the Pacific. These became entangled in the naval assertiveness, dreams of renewed Pan-Hispanic leadership, and ultimately the conflict that Whistler witnessed in the 1860s (Puig-Samper 2013: 30, 243–56; López Ocón Cabrera 2003: 13). Among other things, this latter venture brought back boxes of insects from Latin America (Plate 12) in which our eyes may leap from the emerald colour of tiny insects to the similar hues of the left-hand side of a large bug found in Rio de Janeiro, or flit between the browns and whites of two big butterflies, one from Buenos Aires, the other from Rio, which are almost inverse images of one another, and so forth in multiple combinations. Likewise in a nineteenth-century fantasia of American birds, we see a range of avians improbably perched on a minuscule, fragile tree. We may trace visual similarities and differences back and forth across them in multiple directions, with no real central focus or correct pathway to follow. The birds are at once irreducibly themselves, while creating a complex visual dance far removed from the natural environment to which they belong.

Sacrifice: everyone must die

The *Still Life with Frog, Watermelon, and Scorpion* (1874; Plate 13) by the indigenous Mexican painter Hermenegildo Bustos brings to the fore a similar potential for multiple patterns of interconnection in the assemblage of objects of natural history. In what is called in Spanish a 'dead nature' (naturaleza muerta), a variety of plucked fruits, one insect and one reptile are set out as if in a series of horizontal lines on a blank backdrop. There are intimations of fertility – the prodigious produce, some of which is split as if cut for eating – and of threatening mortality, such as the scorpion, or the very fact that the fruit has been sliced into. The insect and reptile exist in a limbo: they might be taken to be alive or dead or both. The objects are of ostentatiously diverse origin: some are indigenous to the Americas, but the prominent watermelon has a long history of transmission from Africa through Iberia to that continent. We see an affordance of Mexico's global position in the wake of its conquest by the Spanish, as if it were a gathering from the criss-crossing of the Americas and the wider world. But like the most isolated of taxidermied animals, or Madrid's collection of American insects, each item has now been stripped from its originary environment, and lives in a blank place. There are considerable gaps between the items displayed and no obvious taxonomic link between many of them: the scorpion lies between the top two sections, as if connecting two sets of fruit, and the frog sits to our top left as though it began a sequence mainly involving the produce of plants. The stark simplicity of the patterning means we cannot default to more everyday explanations of their proximity, such that they just happened to be together on someone's table. We are left to ponder any number of visual suggestions: the elongated item to the bottom right might hint at penetration of the bottom-like peach beside it; the watermelon may form a bright smile, to another split fruit's crooked, sinister grin. Deprived not only of their originary life, but of their ordinary place in human affairs, and yet conserving their biological form, each item undergoes a lonely transfiguration into a world of resemblances, most tragicomically in the frog's mysterious solitude.

In collections of taxidermy, the abstract effects are made possible and compounded by the fact that dead creatures are so starkly extracted from their originary conditions before being put together in a museum space. On the one hand, a preserved, puffed-up fish might exemplify the degree-zero mimetic realism of such conservation practice. Yet, it is literally a fish out of water, abstracted from the seas, and surrounded by non-figurative planes, some, like shelves, opaque, and others, like the glass, transparent. Glass is a key part of this abstraction because it was frequently a fundamental component of taxidermic and embalmed objects, whether because it protected the animal from the air or because it contained preserving fluids. The very guarantee of the beast's newly eternal life exhibits a series of optical effects that are autonomous of the animals themselves. In jars of bright birds, for example, we see aleatory reflections of light and colour, of objects and people around them, which are superimposed on the animals and mix phantasmagorically with them. We see through the glass into other planes of reality to which the animals did not originally belong, whether the room and its furnishings, or other abstracted creatures. The curvature of some glass containers and the liquids they contain necessarily inflect the course of light, magnifying or reducing different parts of the animal in a new metamorphosis, as often happens with preserved snakes. Our very perspective on these creatures is mobile: we can stand at different angles, or move around them, provoking more variants of light, colour and vision.

In Madrid's Cabinet of Natural History, the way creatures are laid out would cause such effects to combine with one another across the miscellanies in the rooms, augmenting still further the visual promiscuity amid the shadowy setting. This was scarcely just an accident, whatever the contingent factors also involved. It was thought well in Room V to hang the longer creatures by one another whether or not they were closely related, evoking resemblances in scale and form. Someone considered it looked good to put some ostriches in the middle. The most absolute form of realism converges here with the most absolute optical abstraction, each flowing out of the other: 'nature and art' are 'lodged under the same roof'. Such is the endpoint of the mass sacrifice of creatures, the death and the slaughter, of which we are so fully aware as we behold the taxidermied victims. Our habitual ways of perceiving the world – we see 'a bird' – transfigure into a capacity to value connections beyond territories or times, or even the categories of science.

The world turned to glass: we're all mad here

The glass inhabited by so many of these creatures was itself redolent with death and transfiguration out of which its transparency emerges, as if, like Bayoán or the scene in Valparaíso Bay, struggling to dematerialise. In London's Crystal Palace (1851), the material was central to offering a vision of an interconnected world of trade and peoples forged amid British Imperial dominance (Hoffenberg 2001: 20; Young 2008: 5–6). In her extraordinary book *Victorian Glassworlds* (2008), Isobel Armstrong evokes the burgeoning 'glass consciousness' and 'glass culture' in the nineteenth century, due to improvements in manufacture and extended use of the material. This was spectacularly displayed in the Palace. The glass literally contained traces of workers' breath within it, and was born of the residue of their lives, often shortened by the task. For Marx and others, it was a supreme example of 'crystallised' and 'congealed' labour, the latter made ghostlike and abstracted in manufacture. More still, the material itself was resonant with dead, residual matter – the sand from which it came – turned into a form of life, 'a form of resurrection seizing the imagination with aesthetic wonder', in Armstrong's words. Ostler's great glass fountain at the heart of the Crystal Palace, Armstrong observes, is like an inversion of the Great Exhibition's many chandeliers and their resemblance to water, conjuring 'the magical transformation of sand into the very element that brought about its being by erosion and dissolution, gave them a mythical reference, an association with birth and with death' (Armstrong 2008: 1, 4–6, 92, 212).

Amid the multitude of shifting reflections and refractions, across the viewing angles of this living-dead medium, visitors to the Palace experienced a vast array of objects of diverse origin around the globe, a mixture of colonialism and of networks of exchange. The effect was reinforced by the geometrically patterned interior design work, based around primary colours, and undertaken by Owen Jones, in the spirit (as he saw it) of the Islamic cultures of Spain as exemplified in the Alhambra (Thomas 2011: 148). Armstrong aptly describes how the overall effect 'flattens out the diachronic and assimilates it into the synchronic. But space and time were not neutralised. The enfolding of multiple times and histories within one another meant that heterogeneous objects with different histories occupied the same gigantic space.' Visitors were faced with strange re-creations of the earth's geography: to get to China you had to go up stairway 5. The catalogue itself was a work of unprecedented multiple authorship, with some fifteen thousand writers. In Armstrong's eyes, the effect was one of sublimity born of difference, not homogeneity (Armstrong 2008: 148, 150, 193). If anything, the phenomenon intensified once the edifice was reconstructed in Sydenham from 1854, with displays and reimaginings of civilisations over the centuries. In a kind of reflection from within the building on historic lessons for design, Owen included here the once-famous Alhambra Court and its polychrome geometrical shapes (Thomas 2011: 150–1). The overall layout at Sydenham created what Kate Nichols describes as 'evident engagement with, but refusal to play by, chronological time' (2015: 4). In 1851, there was 'tension between the Exhibition's elaborate "philosophical" classification system and its material floor plan' (Buzard, Childers & Gillooly 2007: 9). The same occurs – Andrea Hibberd remarks – between efforts to direct how the public viewed things and the temptations of a 'promiscuous, roving eye' (Hibberd 2007: 162). For Eileen Gillooly, 'faced with ... an overabundance of objects', even 'the catalogue writer (and the viewer before him, and the reader after him) makes sense of the experience, not by comprehensive calculation, but by apprehensive analogy' (Gillooly: 2007: 25). On a grand scale, family resemblance now spills in and out of promiscuity, as it did in the Prado Museum.

As with other optical media and devices – the stereoscope, the thaumatrope, the diaphanorama – it is possible to be deflected here, through complexities and qualifications, from more obvious, but expansively dilating experiences. Fundamentally, glass can and could evoke sameness itself, both insofar as it gives us reflections, and insofar as its transparency enables us to see things together. From this perspective, it is not so much that sameness is contradicted or in tension with heterogeneity or mobility, but that the latter comes to be experienced through similitude, as constitutive in attaining it. The issue, from that perspective, might not so much be whether any display in glass could be a 'totalisation' – that is, an exhaustive and systematic summary of everything – but how its promiscuous resemblances can enable us to 'go on', to 'leap beyond yet nearer bring' through the flickering of resemblances across the panes, within the bubbles the glass building formed beyond chronology and geography. Such an experience may be taken as a call – implicit and otherwise – to social commonality, on an overlapping spectrum from the putatively cosmopolitan (Nichols 2015: 229–30) through the complex internal relations of the Empire (Hoffenberg 2001: 14, 17, 205–8), to the imperial violence, racism and discrimination that was implicated in securing the global trade network (Young 2008: 5–6). Through Jones's involvement, all these patterns are interrelated and channelled through efforts – summarised in *The Grammar of Ornament* (1856) – to recentre global architectural and design on a culminating moment in southern Spain in the Islamic middle ages, tipping the balance away even from the ancient Greeks or the Renaissance (Spanish Christian contributions are notable for their absence) (Jones 2016: 185, 187). This is as one with Jones's provocative enthusiasm for wider non-European – especially Indian – design in the offerings of the Great Exhibition as much as in earlier ages, at a point when British imperialism extended ever more over the economy of the subcontinent (2016: 239; Heide 2009: 69). But just as the displays as whole mingle cosmopolitanism with colonialism, such an endeavour – Claudia Heide notes – cannot be taken as an unalloyed immersion in the Islamic world. Against the manifest evidence of an inscription in the building, Jones assimilates the styles of the Alhambra to his own beliefs about the importance of polychromy (Heide 2010: 211–12). *The Grammar of Ornament* itself patriotically asserts the exceptionalism of the British Isles through all known history (Jones 2016: 239, 287).

At the same time, we may attend to what Carol Armstrong calls 'the base ... the logic of its illustrational foundation', the 'subideological workings' of the visual object (1998: 280), like the geometrical patterns we met in Chapter 1, and which Jones saw as the universal basis of art, of its music-like patterning (2016: 24, 193, 204–5). From the latter viewpoint, a glasswork like the Crystal Palace, with all its inherent associations with death, goes beyond an interpretation of the world or a conduct manual or treatise on life amid globalisation. Like Manet, like Whistler, like Cameron, it can give us a disposition towards sameness, one that is shot through with awareness of death and dying as forces that unite the world, often in cruelty and dispossession.

'We're all mad here', the Cheshire Cat tells Alice (1965: 89). There is a thread of insanity, and more broadly of illness, running through this chapter. This is what advocates of careful distinction, of difference, of particularity and location, those wary of analogy or conflation, rightly seek to hold at bay. We are never so far from people believing they have seen the Devil in an opera house, or Greek gods on the Rhine, or their dead sister around and about. We are a little too close to people adoring flowers of evil, or thinking nineteenth-century Paris is really Renaissance Italy, or that they alone are 'Me myself'. In this present chapter, the menace looms to the fore in the explicit violence, the abuse, the willing embrace of sickness, the overriding urge for all-too-literal sacrifice. 'I want to be mad', declares Bayoán ('Quiero ser loco') (Hostos 2015: loc.1174); 'I am undoubtedly ill', admits Josef (Ros de Olano 1863: 146). We might do well to take their words fully and painfully at face value, not as literary affectation. Telling too is the maddened force of conviction held by so many of those we have beheld here: 'As the unsetting polar star, which through the livelong, arctic, six months' night sustains its piercing, steady, central gaze; so Ahab's purpose now fixedly gleamed down upon the constant midnight of the gloomy crew' (Melville 2002: 437). Two threats of insanity criss-cross and often converge. The first is an ancient belief that through death, sacrifice or violent affliction, humanity will be redeemed. The atavistic nature of that conviction is presented, often as not, directly. It is part of the claim that things may resonate across great swathes of time and place. The second is an obsessive pursuit of patterns and their possibilities, in which our forms of life may easily – as Wittgenstein puts it – 'go on holiday', and through which the world is perceived to find its commonalities.

The two are brought powerfully together in the treatment of glass by the Mexican painter, José Agustín Arrieta, culminating in his mirror painting of the late 1850s. Already in earlier still-lives, known as *Disorderly Tables* (*Meses revueltas*), Arrieta had explored visual patterns of resemblance across objects from Mexico and abroad, perceived at the time – Erica Segre notes – as 'an eloquent allegory of the confusion of ideas, values and classes that characterised Mexican society' (2007: 49). Like Bustos, Arrieta is responding to the confluence of global and local factors in his country's culture, with its ocean-born trading links to the Atlantic and Pacific, the Anglophone dominance to its north, the long presence of Spanish descendants, and longer still of indigenous peoples in the Americas, alongside mixed ethnicities, its blending of new techniques and ancient traditions. Segre places Arrieta's efforts within a broader concern with 'a kind of "discordia concors" which yokes together the apparently unlike in order to convert heterogeneity into an enabling, shifting ground … a practice rather than a place or destiny' (2007: 1).

In one example of a *Dining Room Painting* (*Cuadro de comedor*), we even find an apparently live, if unmoving, cat and bird perched alongside ceramics, some intricate glassware including a vase and full decanter, several pieces of commonplace fruit and the carefully arranged spectacle of bright flowers. The sharpness of the depiction and delineation of these multitudinous objects, combined with the marked gaps between them, gives us something like a seventeenth-century Spanish still life – a Zurbarán, say – but with far less restraint in the multitude of combinations. The fairly even light and Arrieta's tendency to tip the shelf or table towards us, defying perspectival realism, invites us into a game of finding what the objects might have in common, even as we pointedly perceive their tendency to separate into disorder. Our eyes move back and forth across the image and the many possible similarities among its forms: the head of the cat is like an apple or an orange or the small ceramic jug, the opacity of one receptacle placed within the glass recalls both the other ceramic pots, and, in its combination of two objects, parallels a white cup precariously placed upon a jug. The very ordering of experience becomes here its own kind of disorder, a sort of delirium. Its pitfalls are underlined by the reality of the gaps. The latter point to the importance of making sharp distinctions, but, even so, lure us into seeking commonalities. In Arrieta's work we find starkly presented the pulsation and flickering that are key to so much sameness, the opportunity and the risk of similarity.

In his later mirror painting – *Disorderly Table – Green Glass Decanter, Bell-Glass Vase and Candelabra* (Plate 14) – Arrieta intensifies the presence of decorative glass objects, and places them on shiny reflective shelves, right in the foreground, but with a vast reflective surface behind them. The nineteenth-century social elite acquired ever more ornamental glass, and social customs involved its use, Armstrong notes (2008: 221). The centrepiece is a tall intricate glass vase, topped with a nearly equally tall bouquet of flowers, and standing on a small stand within a huge, bulbous glass cover. By it there are half a dozen pieces of glassware. Each of these, because so close to the mirror, has a reflection at a very tight angle to and just behind itself, so that in some cases, like the bulbous cover, the glass object appears to have a double outline just offset against it, as if it were singular and plural at the same time. The only large area of opaque matter depicted is formed by the wooden panels of the room, but these are seen only in the mirror, meaning that even they are experienced primarily as a play of reflection and light. The same happens to the perspectival depth that might appear as a sign of real physical space. It too is only markedly present in its reflection, which we know to be two-dimensional.

The effect is to render the whole scene somewhat spectral – 'quasi-phantasmagorical', Segre says. These later 'dead natures', still lifes, are evocative of the resonances of mortality, the residues of dying human life, of death and resurrection, that Armstrong finds in the 'glass culture'. That is all the more so because the very genre of Spanish still life had long associations with *desengaño* (disillusionment): the attempt to see mortal experience as filled with illusions, made so and rendered apparent by the face of death. Segre links such allusions to the '*vanitas*' of 'promiscuous disorder' criss-crossing Mexico, with which Arrieta's work as a whole is redolent. For Foucault (1986), a mirror is a heterotopia, where, in reflections, things were at once real and unreal. The quest for similarity across the shapes and objects itself now has this ghostly, deathly quality, as our eyes dart around 'optical distortions …, multiplying reflections and complicated perspectives' (Segre 2007: 50). For Armstrong, as surfaces are enlivened with reflected imagery so they appear ever less solid and substantial. When we see things through and on glass and in mirrors, our sense of their identity and of ours may easily become fractured, and fragmented (2008: 9, 105–9, 111). This is apparent in the slippage between the boundaries of the duplicate objects in Arrieta's work, in the lack of any clear distinction between what is substantial and what a reflection – the room in which a viewer putatively looks and its reflection – in the diverse, discontinuous angles from which we see disparate visions of supposedly the same thing.

Instead of modernity

In its visual sharpness and clarity, Arrieta's work evokes what it might be to experience commonality: to turn the world to ghosts, to dissolve our selves and it, to dally with delusion and illusion and confusion, to court sickness, to lose sharp distinctions and welcome death, to experience the world as a single plane through which we may go on, to find patterns through the disparate, even to find no difference between an image and the thing itself. To borrow words from R.D. Laing, 'psychiatrically, this would appear as … helping future patients to go mad' (1990: 106). Possessed by such perilous hallucinations, we become intimates.

4

Repose: forms of shared distraction

Let us imagine a letting go, as if not to clutch at, or hold to, or dominate the heart of the action in the world, the dynamic force that controls it. Let us imagine that all existence is released from even having such a core or soul. Let us imagine that, free of the force of any dominance in ourselves or in the world, we find our way gently, delicately, without strong emotion, through multitudes dispersing in all directions, without centre, exploring freely their connections. Or let us imagine that we step aside to a tangent from the heart of things, so as calmly to contemplate and apprehend the patterns of history, people, the world. Or let us imagine that where there might have been forceful, violent domination, we find a distinct, serene core to which to hold and through which we apprehend anew the linkages across people, between things.

Some such sentiments are familiar from, but not reducible to, aspects of late twentieth- and early twenty-first-century thought. This is particularly so where such musings pair an affect of gentleness or weakness with a notion of de-centring or of offsetting any Being or *Logos* that might inform or direct life or the world. Variants of such a notion have become widespread, from Derrida's 'dissemination' to Deleuze's and Guattari's 'rhizome', 'an acentred, non-hierarchical, non-signifying system without a General and without an organising memory, or central automaton, defined solely by circulation of states' (1987: 23). As the description of a 'non-signifying system' suggests, the 'acentred' is often associated with the autonomy of signs from signified meaning or *logos*, from any sense that is present to consciousness, and by extension with the Death of Man. That outlook evokes the supposed Post-Romantic turn – that classical account of cultural modernity, or of its undoing from within – which was echoed through so much of High Theory, as we saw in the introduction to this present book. The broader suggestion of continual distraction – a constant moving away from any centre or focus or anchored meaning, escaping synthesis – is likewise resonant with many established theories of modernism (Crary 2000: 48).

The insinuated release from controlling power may easily be conflated with a weakness that is positively embraced, and with gentleness in place of violence and cruelty. In the *pensiero debole* – 'weak thought' – of Gianni Vattimo and others, 'the enfeeblement of (the notion of) Being' leads us to *pietas* for our mortal, ephemeral state, 'compassion for these ruins' (2012: 45, 47, 51). As cruelty is repudiated so we may reject not just sacrifice's bursting of the bounds of being, but the rigorous, forceful assertion of our core identity. As we saw in Chapter 3, Maggie Nelson affirms that cruelty arises from the belief that violence may authentically realise, as much as it may dissolve, human subjecthood. In the place of this notion, she evokes a nuanced, mediated set of relations through which we may come together (2011: loc.610). The emotional and ethical allure of weakness is apparent in the conjuring of patterns in cultural connections beyond any sovereign authority and its supposed rigour. This is the case with the weak networks that Wai Chee Dimock (2013) pursues across place and time. Out of all this may emerge a compassionate experience of 'sameness', without violence, aggression or mastery. Drawing on some Buddhist thought, Marcus Boon speaks of a vision of endless similarity free of efforts to 'fix impermanent flux' (2013: loc.337–9, 1146, 1039).

It is tempting to privilege similitude and commonality in this vein over all others, precisely because the turn of thought feels so familiar, reassuring even in many quarters. It is not my intention here to do so, any more than to relegate its claims below other moods. This present book is a work of pedagogy, not didacticism, after all. I am engaged in the craft of tracing 'affordances' through and out of the materials of history. No less than any other mood, repose may take shape in things we might find alien, prejudiced, constricting, unappealing, even in its apparent queerness. Its affordances may likewise prove dogmatic and controlling, even in spite of itself. Flaubert's prose, so significant in the genesis of Theory, is a case in point, and we return to it in this chapter. With Jonathan Culler (1974), we may find in it a cool turning from controlling *Logos*, being, or *Telos*, a floating world of autonomous signs. But, with Mary Orr (2000), we may find that its exaltation of the surface signifier may reinstate, as if in reverse, the dominant, controlling effects of the *Logos* that it seems to deny. In this chapter, I have accentuated reference to historical specifics so, as it were, to roughen the texture of the experience of repose, to give it an air as unfamiliar as familiar, so it is not too lightly assimilated. Where – in Fortuny's art – we might find object networks, queerness, and a release from being, we encounter, in the same breath, imperial aspiration and sexual prejudice. If in Juana Manuela Gorriti we find skilled evasion of the 'art of cruelty', it takes shape in constraints upon elite women and advantages of elite men, and in the global circumstances of mid-century Spanish America. Often as not, repose appears like a shadow of other moods, pervaded with departure, sacrifice and meetings. In its Coda, this chapter ends with the coming together of all these moods in a vision of Faust, through Juan Valera's novel *The Illusions of Dr Faustino* (*Las ilusiones del doctor Faustino*, 1874–5).

If, at times, repose offers release from a notion of Being or centre or soul, the latter concepts are both historically specific and variegated, rather than constant, essential features of a putative 'Western' metaphysics. A number of authors have explored the specific circumstances of the emergence of such an outlook. In *Suspensions of Perception*, Jonathan Crary explores how visions of distraction in the latter part of the nineteenth century were co-implicated with a notion that attention was not underpinned by present consciousness, *a priori* categories, or a necessary relationship to the external world (2000: 48–77). Jan Goldstein's *The Post-Revolutionary Self* (2005) shows how nineteenth-century French ideas of a transcendental subject emerged in rejection of looser, associationist visions of the self from the eighteenth century. Goldstein is thinking especially of the philosopher Victor Cousin, then widely influential well beyond France. In turn, Cousin's account was challenged by rival, contemporary ideas, such as those of some phrenologists, for whom the self was constituted by plural components in the brain. Goldstein's observation is particularly pertinent, given how much of High Theory emanates from individuals educated in French or French-influenced education systems, on which Cousin had a considerable impact. The very title of Foucault's *Surveiller et punir* is taken from Cousin's definition of the state, for example. It is Cousin's philosophy of history that gives us the intellectual pattern of thesis, antithesis, synthesis – often wrongly seen as Hegelian – and pervasive in French school-level essay-writing of a certain vintage.

In this chapter, the tension between centres of Being and distraction is evoked solely as a family resemblance across multiple outlooks, not as a cogent philosophical proposition nor as an essential transhistorical reality. What is called repose is likewise no more, and no less, than a family resemblance, traced across and through diverse texts and images. By extension, in exploring the apprehension of commonalities through serenity, I have avoided privileging those versions that depend upon an opposition between distraction and centred Being. Such a preference seems determined by a particular theoretical stance, with its own history, and is wed in no small measure to a specific understanding of modernity. It assumes that the family resemblance that truly matters is the one that most closely matches its own preoccupations. Instead, in the patterns traced here, I find connections between distinct ways of apprehending similitude through repose.

Distraction from a centre wends its way into a quest for an alternate origin or origins in quietude, such as we might see displacing the violence of empire in the Peruvian painter Francisco Laso or the Spaniard Eduardo Rosales. The search for repose takes us out to tangential positions from where Charles Darwin ponders the origins of species, or Henry Thoreau looks upon the depths of time, or writers of the Spanish First Republic dwelt on donkeys. In our awareness that knowledge of the whole is limited, we might apprehend or intuit its interconnections. In this chapter, we will pass through a myriad of historical circumstances, interlacing and interweaving factors, coming and going, echoing other parts of this present book, without a dominant single narrative. Among these, we will encounter, once more, resurgent French and Spanish imperialisms; the legacy of violence from European and Hispanic empire; the struggle to rebuild Argentina and Peru after the first turbulent decades of nation building; the destiny of independence in the United States; the intertwining of the Americas with the wider world; the frontier of Greater Europe and the treatment of indigenous peoples of the Americas; the direction of Second-Empire France, and, as Napoleon III falls in war with Prussia, the fate of First-Republic Spain; the international book trade; the experience of change in European streets and cities at mid-century; the rise of evolutionary science after British journeys to Latin America, and the condition of the Victorian gentleman scientist; and debates on the mapping of the brain and of the universe.

Intimacy with such expressions of repose need not limit us to their historical specifics, even as these shape their character. In coming to rest with them, in sharing their serenity, we find in them a letting go, a 'living laxly to the front', as Thoreau puts it, an apprehension of what is not yet perceived, that may take us through and beyond them, to what they had not been and have not yet been. This not an easy, comfortable experience. Like the intimate culture and intimate meeting of Chapter 1, it takes us into things that are alien, unappealing, at times repellent even. It is possible to hold that anything objectionable, in the final analysis, is so through and through. Conversely, one can maintain that what is tainted can be shed, so that a thought or sentiment becomes purified, as an essence is stripped of what is accidental to it. The choice, alas, is not always quite so simple, as I suggested in Chapter 2. In Charles Darwin, we will see a limit case, where our trust in a person, who may be in so many ways so alien to our principles, seems crucial to a judgement that proves true. To trust here is to have faith that, precisely in their qualities of character, in their sense of repose, in their pursuit of tangents or distractions, there is the potential to let go of their own self.

Instead of modernity

Contemplation and dispersal

The paintings of Mariano Fortuny offer us a contemplative experience. In his visual world, we are led delicately away from any forceful emotional and dramatic dynamic that might dominate the image, and overwhelm us with sentiment. His visions are filled with distractions from anything of the sort, continually drawing us away from any central action and feeling (etymologically: *dis-trahere*, in Latin). Nineteenth-century observers aptly observed the results. 'The soul and passion side of things seemed to escape him,' averred the French critic Charles Yriarte, 'he astonishes more than he moves us.' Fortuny neglected the 'soul of the subject' (le côté âme et passion semblait l'échapper … il étonne plus qu'il n'émeut; l'âme du sujet) (1889: 8–9, 29). 'The bewitchings of form and external spectacle preoccupied him more than the interesting and moving episodes that compel the soul', said his most astute Iberian commentator, Josep Yxart (los hechizos de la forma y el espectáculo exterior le preocupaban más que los episodios interesantes y conmovedores que se imponen al alma) (Yxart 1881: 53). In its release from forceful emotion ('passion', what 'moves us'), Fortuny's work turns away from any commitment to a notion of Being ('soul'), whether expressed through a person or history. It releases itself from any fascination with a supposed depth of Being through its concern with 'external spectacle'.

Compositionally, the heart of his paintings is at times blank or nondescript, as if there were no dominating centre of experience: shades of grey wall in *The Painter's Children in the Japanese Room* (1874), a section of a decorative gate in *La Vicaría* (1870) (the small painting that made his international name and sold for an extraordinary 70,000 francs). The same occurs in the sandy, dusty middle of that most obviously dramatic episode of recent history, the *Battle of Tetouan*, commissioned to celebrate Catalan military prowess in the defeat of Morocco (1860), and pointedly a work that Fortuny was ultimately disinclined to complete. Even where a central image may seem to dominate compositionally, the subtle variations of often similar colours across the rest of the painting, the evenness of the light, and the mass of delicate, irregular little curves of brushwork across the whole work invite our gaze to wander. At times, the image thus dissipates into near-blank surroundings that dominate the picture. In one viewing of the *Old Man Naked in the Sun* (*c.*1871; Plate 15), for instance, the protagonist seems lit up as he lies back on the darker ground. On another glance, across the whole painting there is an irregular, ever-varying play of flesh-coloured, dark, and occasionally white brushstrokes; the edges of parts of the body (the head, for example, or the lower arms) are dissipating into the wider, darker expanse out of which the figure also emerges. The diminutive wedding party of *La Vicaría*, visually alluring and just off-centre, is overwhelmed by the enormous expanse of blank floor and the modulations of dark background colours. In such attenuated remembrances of a 'soul' and its 'passion', we have 'access to Being not through presence but only through recollection' in its 'enfeeblement', to borrow words from Vattimo (2012: 45, 47).

As a dominant centre and imposing emotion weaken, the paintings become invitations to experience the subtleties of similitude themselves across the image as a whole. Before us are an array of interconnections, often evenly lit, everything a modulation of everything else. We enter a world of echoes and repetitions that can be traced indifferently in a multitude of directions. Describing *Choosing the Model* (1874; Plate 16), Yxart comments that 'such multifarious variety diffuses and decomposes to the infinite, leaving the diverse parts of the image iridescently shimmering with mutual and repeated reflections' (tan múltiple variedad se difunde y se descompone hasta lo infinito, irisa y tornasola las diversas partes del cuadro con mutuos y repetidos reflejos) (1881: 127). The mirroring that occurs through this continual distraction once more evokes mimesis as continual transfiguration into Echo's repetitions, rather than as Narcissus's copying of the world, in Shane Butler's terms. Its 'spectacle' offers us an 'erotics' of art's textures (2015: 81–2, 84, 86–7). In its lack of 'soul' – of overt meaning and legible emotional significance – the series of ever-varied resemblances suggest a 'similarity beyond concepts' such as Marcus Boon seeks *In Praise of Copying* (2013: loc.975). But in its extreme 'enfeeblement', this vision has no metaphysical or ontological substance to it: it is indeed a glittering of surfaces. We have here the very image of 'weak networks', 'the off-center and off-focus energy of meandering threads' that Dimock describes (2013: 59).

No 'priority' is given to one thing over another, object, place or person, in all the senses in which Manning uses the term *priority*: the lack of indication of where we should start in any sequence of echoes, of what comes before or after, or the primary cause or the intellectual hierarchy. The dwelling on what would otherwise be 'background' as much as 'foreground', Fortuny's lingering on architectural detail and setting, underlines the point (Yriarte 1889: 29): nothing has a claim to determining significance over all the rest. Vision becomes characterised by gentle, lingering, multi-directional movements that follow patterns of similarity. In his *The Painter's Children in the Japanese Room*, for instance, we find ourselves spending time discerning and dwelling on diverse patterns in a kind of meditation: we might perceive the shapes of the large leaves taken up in the smaller lighter forms of butterflies depicted on the walls, or spy the blue of the sheet in the colours of the wall. Fortuny's evocations of resemblance offer the very sensation of weakness as a way of being in the world: a releasing that is not an absolute letting go, a 'power of passiveness'. A mood of contemplation and a highly nuanced experience of resemblances come together, each providing a disposition for the other.

The paintings underscore the subtle difficulty of attaining such a disposition, the apparent paradox of finding power in passiveness, the capacity to perceive neither in nor out of focus but specifically 'off-focus', so as to find similitude. *Choosing the Model* exemplifies the difficulty. The painting itself depicts a simple, determined form of looking: a group of male experts eye a nude female model who poses for them. The work equates the most attentive and directed gaze with a woman appearing voyeuristically for the inspection of males. But the bulk of the picture is a pink to silver-grey glow of light enhanced by the vast marble surface of the floor. The latter not only reflects but disperses the illumination. To this effect is added a large irregular mirror to our right and, in the distance, a huge entrance. Conventional artistic practice required balance of light and shadow that would bring out the central subject. The levelling out of vision here recalls instead the imagery of philosophical knowledge. Writing in 1849, the thinker José María Rey y Heredia remarks that 'synthetic interlinking requires *equal lighting* in every point of the path it runs' (el encadenamiento sintético exige *igualdad de luz* en todos los puntos del camino que se recorre) (1849: 130–1, my emphasis). But, we saw in the *Fantasia on Faust* (Chapter 1), Fortuny's 'synthetic interlinking' does not offer us an all-illuminating, sharp clarity, a scopic totalisation of the kind diagnosed by Foucault (1991) in nineteenth-century thought. Rather, it is as if we were invited to relax somewhat the focus of our perception without in so doing altogether letting ourselves go. The characteristic brushstrokes neither quite form into precise details nor are quite free of evoking them: the images are neither forcefully crisp in their visual detail, nor freely energetic in their brushwork. The French writer and critic Théophile Gautier famously found in Fortuny a fusion of Goya's sketchiness and fantastical freedom with the detail and accuracy associated with the then-successful French painter Ernest Meissonier (une ébauche de Goya reprise et retouchée par Meissonier; la liberté fantastique; la scrupuleuse vérité) (cited in Davillier 1875: 61).

At first glance easy on the eye, the vision is simply hard to view. Within the near-all-absorbing sheen of light, we find scattered – and only just distinct – an abundance of uneven, decorative shapes running and merging into one another, echoing each other in a myriad of patterns. The similar artistic treatment given to each of the human figures and their relatively small size means they themselves begin to fuse with the scene around them. Fortuny ends up 'placing equal values on each other, illuminating the shadows', Folch i Torres observes (posant valors damont valors iguals, illuminants les ombres) (Folch i Torres 1962: 170). At the time of painting this image, the artist proclaimed his desire to put flesh colour on flesh colour, making the background as alike it could be to the female figure (Yriarte 1889: 38). The glowing pink of the model's body hardly stands out from the wall behind her, and she is positioned so far towards it that she could be taken for a statue or a mural. If we were ever able to look at *Choosing the Model* in such a way as to take all this into account, we would be viewing things synthetically, evenly, through their ever-varying similarities, nothing more central than anything else, but without controlling them with a dominant gaze.

Likewise, the presentation but undoing of a dominant subject and presence; a serene, even dreamy mood; and an aesthetic appreciation of similitude together characterise Courbet's *The Painter's Studio: Real Allegory* (1855; Plate 17). Through its vision of Courbet at work, the painting offers a meditation on art in itself: in Michael Fried's words, it is one of the 'supreme representations of representation', recalling not least Velázquez's *La Meninas* and Vermeer's *Artist in His Studio* (1990: 155). At the very heart of the famous image is the artist himself, resplendent with a vast patriarchal beard, in the act of painting. On the one hand, the male painter, and the centre of the scene, might seem to dominate. Courbet had a notorious reputation as the proudest man in France – Petra Chu observes – going so far as to erect his own pavilion in Paris to house this work, as a rival to the Universal Exhibition itself, as if to challenge the newly installed Emperor Napoleon III (2007: 106). In turn, the French philosopher Jean-Luc Marion has gone so far as to see the landscape painting before the artist – appearing like a slice of sky and nature in the studio – as revealing a true sight, as a 'Eucharistic trace of *real* presence' (une trace eucharistique de présence *réelle*) (2014: loc.1598). Yet, it is not easy for the viewer to keep their focus on the Courbet depicted here, or on the landscape, or for that matter on any part of the painting. The nuanced, subdued palette – echoing the serene image of the artist – characteristically 'no longer depicts a particular object but extends beyond it or even "infiltrates" it, spreading over the whole picture and leaving room for chance effects'. In so doing – Klaus Herding notes – it 'challenged nineteenth-century ways of viewing' (2010: 10). The rather muddy colours spread into a near-blank, ever more vague and sketchy expanse of the room, that occupies over half of the painting, dwarfing the many figures and landscape on which scholars have lavished so much attention, as if these emerged through or dissipated into an attenuated experience of being.

The stance of the many other characters underlines the challenge. Almost none of them pay Courbet any mind, any more than he looks to them. In turn, 'there is no meaningful interaction between the figures', Linda Nochlin notes: they have a 'frozen quality' (2007: 155).

There is no 'soul' to such an image. The overall effect, Nochlin finds, is 'the melancholy of lost presence' (2007: 154; Nochlin herself seems to imply this is unintentional). The full title tells us that the image depicts 'the interior of my studio determining a phase of seven years in my artistic and moral life'. 'My artistic and moral life' – that is, Courbet's subjectivity – is not limited by the outline of the body of the painter at the centre of the image, or even to what that 'Courbet' directly perceives and views. Forever distracted from its own limiting centrality, the very power of dominant artistic subjecthood and assertion of presence becomes here its giving up on its own boundedness. Instead, the painting evokes a form of subjectivity constituted through distraction into multiple criss-crossing resemblances and patterns among objects, animals and people, just as the apparent centre of a Fortuny image echoes and is an echo of a multitude of objects, people and physical brushstrokes about it. Michael Fried observes how interchangeable the elements of the painting are, undoing through patterns of similarity any supposed division between a rejected group of figures on the left (including Napoleon III) contrasting with those to the right (including the critic Champfleury) (1990: 163). To follow but one of the many sequences, Courbet's bearded head – that of an Assyrian, some contemporaries opined – echoes the rabbi to the viewer's far left. He in turn resembles the bearded man at the distant back right in a very similar posture. The tilted heads of both of these take us to the shawl-wearing woman looming to the right front – her garment recalling Spain – who leans back to spy us as viewers. The shape of her figure flipped around gives us that of a blonde lady in white, sharing something with a companion.

It would be easy to go on, continually leaping beyond to nearer bring. The painting is an invitation to go on rather than the image of a closed single system, and to do so not simply across place but time also: these are seven years displayed simultaneously. There is no telling which of the visions occurred when (or if), nor their full story, nor which have a direct causal link to one another. There is no hierarchy either in physical scale or in the potential interest aroused by anything here. James D. Herbert has underlined how there is no attempt 'to order and prioritise actors in a manner reminiscent of academic history painting'. Despite efforts of Marion, Fried and others to privilege the central group around the depicted Courbet, there is little real effort to highlight them and separate them from the rest, in the way one would expect in a more conventional composition of the time (2014: 376). The point is precisely not that Courbet constitutes 'the sole coherent guardian of any (such) concealed meaning' (2014: 370).

The notion of an autonomous observer of the world – whether the viewer, or 'Courbet' or any of the lookers in the painting – who is able to process perceived diverse data into an homogeneous vision, is becoming undone. In *Techniques of the Observer*, Crary points out the parallels between Courbet's compositions and what happens when a stereoscopic view does not resolve in the viewer's perception, when the data from each eye does not come together with a 'unifying logic or order', and instead gives us disparate planes (Crary 1990: 125). Likewise, in Fortuny's *Choosing the Model*, precisely as there is an invitation for a viewer to stare attentively at something, constituting themselves as a well-trained observer – like the art experts-cum-voyeurs – that attentiveness leads into distraction across the image. Crary argues that attending to things could be imagined as a contingent set of techniques, rather than something guaranteed and secured by a subject being present to itself, or the world being immediately present to it. In consequence, 'attention was shown to constitute within itself the conditions of its own undoing', he remarks in *Suspensions of Perception* (2000: 45).

Above all, the suggestion is that, to apprehend such an experience, we enter into the gentle, complex, almost hallucinogenic movement through which its aesthetic vision arises, the sensation of merger, fusion and emergence within the work's limited chromatic range. Decades ago, Kenneth Clark observed how the *Real Allegory*, by seeming both so unfantastical and yet redolent with possible resonances, is intensely dreamlike in its realism (1960: 167). The experience, like that of seeing a Fortuny, takes the form of a subtle delusion, akin to Arrieta or Bustos's still lifes, in which connection and disconnection become interchangeable. Logic is no longer the master in the tracing of 'synthetic interlinking'. 'It is fairly mysterious', Courbet famously remarked of the painting (C'est passablement mystérieux) (cited in Hoffmann 2010: 21). Such is the mood of repose that Courbet, like Fortuny, evokes. 'Inactivity, sleep, introversion and being lost in contemplation' recur across Courbet's images – Herding observes – and action is most usually noticeable for its absence (2010: 10–11). Far from the torments of a violent insanity, a calmer dreaminess might be found at the heart of being in the world in this way, in working one's way again and again through patterns and similitudes.

In this vein, for us to seek sanity, or – better said – any real perceptiveness, would entail, in the first instance, acceptance of a vision of un-centered subjecthood in the world. This suggestion is at the heart of the speculative neuroscience promoted by Spain's leading medical researcher of the time, Pedro Mata, the Chair of Legal Medicine in Madrid from 1843 to 1874. Mata was particularly concerned with understanding how to distinguish dangerous forms of insanity from other conditions. In a series of lectures at the Ateneo during 1856–57, subsequently published as treatises, he argues that our biological form as humans has no executive governing centre. Any notion of a 'self' or 'consciousness' is, he supposes, a 'chimerical abstraction and chimerical ontological creation' dreamt up by philosophers as a basis of their edifices (han hecho una entidad, el Yo, la conciencia, y sobre esta abstracción, sobre esta creación ontológica, quiméricas, han fundado un edificio) (1858: 48). Mata goes further even than the earlier French phrenologists, who – Goldstein notes – assert the plurality of the physical brain (2005: 305–15). Even such phrenologists assumed both that there was a truly executive set of higher functions, and that the brain, in turn, acted as a presiding controller of the body. In Mata's world, there is no room even for an executive faculty of reasoning in the brain. The latter organ is only a centre insofar as it is the place where the impulses of the body's multiple organs converge, and the place of interaction of a series of functions of its own (Ginger 2018). Humanity is thus presented as a 'complex unity' (unidad complexa) (Mata 1858: xviii), both in each individual body, and through the near-infinite configurations that this same pattern can produce across all the individuals of the species (1858: 239).

The implication is that sanity cannot be attained by subjecting every aspect of every body to a sole controlling centre, nor by settling the parts of every brain into a single, defined configuration. The 'state of reason' (estado de la razón), as Mata puts it, requires continual mobility, the shifting of forces and emphases, across a dispersed and complex pattern. Human thought and emotion has something about it of the form of a Fortuny painting or of Courbet's *Real Allegory*. It shares with such art works both a subtlety and a fragility in its unsettled structure. It has the potential for collapse, for a slide away into insanity, like so many varieties of similitude. Like the hallucinogenic aspect of a Fortuny or Courbet, the brain's ever-shifting configurations are often neither quite sane nor insane: Mata describes them as most commonly 'intermediate' (1864: 27–8). Frequently that condition is the source of our deepest insights, in contrast with the kind of tranquillity that comes with a putative clear-mindedness. 'Our wakefulness is more asleep than dreams,' the good doctor says, invoking Montaigne, 'our wisdom is less knowing than madness; our daydreams are worth more than our discourse' (nuestra vigilia está más dormida que el sueño, nuestra sabiduría es menos cuerda que la locura; nuestros ensueños valen más que nuestros discursos) (1864: 263). Our capacity for insight depends on our ability to navigate the centreless structures that all humanity shares, without slipping utterly into violent insanity, without subjecting ourselves to an oppressive chimera of conscious, executive reason, and without expecting a dominant uniformity when what we have is a subtler sameness.

A weak subject of this kind, built up from atoms through the interplay of matter, and developing through interaction with its environment (Mata 1852: 75, 92–3; 1858: 170), may be envisaged as part of a composition more radical in its endless, distractions and similitudes even than that of a Fortuny or Courbet painting. In their speculative work of science, *Total Organisation of Matter* (*Total organización de la materia*) (1870), the Spanish physicists Enrique Serrano y Fatigati and Salvador Calderón y Arana evoke the universe as an image without a frame, a 'picture' involving 'limitless worlds' (cuadro, mundos sin límite) (1870: 8–9). They advocate the 'intuition of unknown laws that present all beings to us as relatively similar links in the great picture in which everything is a centre with respect to what is most incidental and accidental with regard to what is most elevated' (la intuición de ignoradas leyes que nos presentan a todos los seres como eslabones relativamente semejantes del gran cuadro en que todo es centro respecto de lo más accesorio y accidental con relación a lo más elevado) (1870: 54). The shared patterns of structures, and our capacity to perceive them, depend on the lack of a single, central organising point and on the continual mutation of viewpoints.

Such an 'intuition' is an aesthetic appreciation of ever-varying resemblances without discordant feeling: the two scientists express 'a sentiment of admirable harmony that the universe imposes on our intelligence' (un sentimiento de admirable armonía que el universo impone a nuestra inteligencia) (1870: 7). Put another way, the being of the material universe shows us – better still, discloses through us, for we are part of it – how *harmony* now arises through the abandonment of a structure organised around a privileged, dominant centre, reversing the assumptions of conventional visual composition. We come to appreciate organic and inorganic matter within such an harmonic continuum, just as in Fortuny objects, environments and people are primarily parts of patterns. It is specifically the consequent flattening out of any radical distinction between human subjectivity and agency and that of material objects that so offended Charles Yriarte (and other critics) in Fortuny's paintings. Of *Choosing the Model*, Yriarte declares that 'the obvious vice of this curious canvas … is that man does not play a more superior role than that played in it by things and still natures' (le vice évident de cette toile curieuse … c'est que l'homme n'y joue pas un rôle supérieur à celui qui y jouent les choses et les natures mortes) (1889: 27–8). (The language is revealing: it was *obvious*, it was a *vice* as if morally as well as aesthetically objectionable, and the problem was the neglected role of *man* in an image with a naked woman in it.) The same occurs in the patterns of Courbet's *Real Allegory*. Insofar as everything we see is presented as constitutive of the painter's subjectivity, its similitudes offer an experience of what some philosophers call an 'extended mind', where thinking and feeling are realised through anything that may be involved in so doing. In Andy Clark's words, 'bodily parts (e.g. hands) and biological cognitive elements (e.g. biological memory) end up on a par with external items such as rakes and shopping lists' (2002: 77). If in Fortuny, the panoply of detailed objects become effective as 'actors' in the place of 'soul', Courbet famously draws attention to the material of paint itself, as part of the physicality of the world as a whole through which he exists and sees, often applied 'like mortar, like a common material', as Rosen and Zerner put it (1984: 222). The very body of the painter himself, at the centre of the studio, was by then associated with 'materialism', F. Desbuissons has argued, given 'his rustic manner with earthy materials', 'his way of eating, laughing, and singing' (2008: 255, 257). The rather muddy tones of *The Studio* are testament to this, as is the way that the painter's body appears to be absorbed – in Fried's terms – into the Franche-Comté landscape before him (Fried 1990: 163–4).

The 'harmony' that we experience here has something of the 'symmetry' of the Actor-Network-Theory advanced by Bruno Latour and others as an approach to social existence (2005: 109). There is a 'flattening' (2005: 219) that, by including all manner of entities, 'gives non-humans a type of agency' (2005: 10). In turn, we become able 'to trace connections' through 'a trail of associations between heterogeneous elements' (2005: 1, 5), rather than to engage in 'dispersion, destruction, and deconstruction' (2005: 11). In turn, like the myriad shifts of viewpoint and perspective in Fortuny and Courbet's harmonies, this kind of symmetry is not a flattening out, but an opportunity for continual shifts of scale and emphasis (2005: 219–20). There is no depth of Being (no 'soul') to be plunged here, no behind, above or before that would offer some underlying but hidden forces of truth and meaning (2005: 245–6). In making his case, Latour draws on strands of nineteenth-century sociology that were at odds with Durkheim's later supremacy. While he specifically invokes the French thinker Gabriel Tarde from later decades (2005: 13), there was widespread interest in mid-century in visions of society and wider physical reality as patterns of association. Mata's vision of the brain as a democratic chamber, where the body's plural impulses vote, is a case in point (1858: 340). Herbert likewise sees parallels between Courbet's *Real Allegory* and the Socialist Pierre-Joseph Proudhon's belief in self-organising structures throughout reality and society, a revolutionary alternative to the reigning order. This is not necessarily a matter of reducing the painter to explanation in terms of the thinker, but of an affinity (2014: 378–80; more literal parallels seem to be sought in Rubin 1980: 63, for example).

In her call for an art of compassion and nuance, Maggie Nelson has described how 'by definition there is no master sketch for what such a thing might look like. It can only be an experiment' (2011: loc.182). The experience of nuance obviates a 'picture' of the world where what matters is whether there are or are not self-evidently distinct selves and others, foreground and background, subject and context. Rather this is more a 'worknet' than a 'network' (to borrow Latour's words): it is a continual working through connections out of which such distinctions may contingently, temporarily be made, without these being basic realities (2005: 142). In such a vision, the artist cannot situate themselves on the margins of society, as Bourdieu imagined mid-century modernists to dwell, asserting their autonomous subjecthood. Rather the artist seeks to be manifest through and in the shifting interrelated patterns of the wider world.

The very stylistic features of Fortuny's work that evoke such a disposition to nuanced similarity are themselves expressions of linkage across frontiers, which merge and fuse among themselves across his oeuvre. In turn, just as the conjoining patterns of his compositions distract us from any central, emotive 'soul', so he sought to dissociate art from residence in an 'artistic centre', as he informed the Baron Davillier (un centro artístico)

Repose: forms of shared distraction

(González López & Martí Ayxelà 1989: 111). While Paris and Rome figure in his career, they do not predominate. Rather, Fortuny's work reasserts 'periphery' to 'periphery' relations of a kind that Henriette Partzsch (2014) has traced through lesser-known patterns in the geography of nineteenth-century European culture. The characteristic even brightness of Fortuny's painting, which obviates a single focal point, has its origins in his encounter with Morocco during the Spanish invasions (1859–60) and subsequently (Carbonell 1999: 146), to the extent that Yxart described Africa as 'his true muse' (su verdadera musa) (1881: 49). Arguably too, the concern with endless, multi-directional patterns of similarity echoes Islamic design: by way of comparison, Owen Jones asserts that their continual, gentle modulation of shapes brings about 'repose' (2016: 188). In turn, this vision connected with the southern atmospherics of formerly Islamic Andalusia, and with those of Portici in Naples (González López & Martí Ayxela 1989: 107), formerly part of the Spanish crown, likewise at the border of Christendom and Islam, and associated with the light effects of the Golden-Age Spanish-Italian artist José de Ribera. All three locations are widely portrayed across Fortuny's oeuvre – both directly and in echoes of Ribera's depictions of undressed older males such as *Old Man in the Sun*. In turn, Fortuny looked beyond this peripheral triad to other linkages. If a concern with sketchy patches of paint echoed his association with Domenico Morelli and the contemporary Italian *machiaiolli*, the love of complex ornamentation spoke to his admiration and awareness of British Pre-Raphaelites (Millais – whom he met, – Alma-Tadema and Leighton) (Davillier 1875: 118, 126). To give but one more instance, with the forced opening of the Japanese ports by the United States, Fortuny sought to merge European line and modelling of form with composition studied from artists from Japan (Vives 1993: 24–5). The latter effort gives us the structure of *The Painter's Children in the Japanese Room*, starkly and statically counterposing the domains of the two resting infants, with no centre point or action in the composition binding them.

If Fortuny displaces the Paris in which he sold so many works, Courbet seeks as if to undo the 'artistic centre' from within, by binding specific references to his own compositional structures and innovations. In placing his *Real Allegory* in a pavilion in Paris – in thus challenging Imperial French authority and the institutional universalism of the *Exposition Universelle* – the painter raised a monument instead to the provincial Franche-Comté, so vividly depicted in the landscape (Rubin 1980: 9). The echoes of the awkward sequences of poses in the Le Nain brothers, championed by Champfleury, suggest just such a reorienting at the heart of French universalism towards something with a rustic flavour. Through the depths of remote time as much as of marginalised place, the painter's vaunted 'Assyrian profile' connects this transformation to an ancient culture. Assyrian aesthetic achievements, uncovered in recent archaeology, were proving hard to assimilate to French assumptions about the hierarchies of antique civilisation and the role of the Middle East (Bohrer 1998). In the disparate patterning of the *Real Allegory*, these dimensions sit between and interlink with more established notions of French civilisation and its visual culture: a classical nude and the Christian crucifixion. At the same time, in the structure of substitutions, Courbet's form may be projected back and forth, equally, to a Jewish man, or to a woman whose shawl might make us think of Spain. Amid the miscellany, there is an Irish woman. Seventeenth-century Spain looms large: 'the huge room is full of echoes of Velasquez [*sic*]', Kenneth Clark observes (1960: 175).

Often, at the dispersing heart of many Fortuny images, we find a parallel unravelling of conventional gender and ethnic boundaries. The *Nude Boy Seen from the Back on Portici*

Beach (1874) is an ambiguous creature with hermaphroditic buttocks (Barón 2018: 334). There are numerous glistening naked and half-naked adult male bodies, many but not all of them older men, in which the painter seems to delight. Some, like the *Opium Smoker* (1869) or the *Arab Chief* (1874), have massive phallic objects emerging from their laps, whether a giant pipe or an 'impressive arsenal' (Martin-Márquez 2008: 180). Others seem to signal their availability, like the figure in *The Rest of the Enchained Man* (1870–72), tied up, naked but for a cloth draped so as to frame his protruding anus. In an early watercolour, the fully dressed *Il contino* (1861) pulls apart the lower reaches of his coat, thrusting his groin forwards, as he averts his gaze, at once beautifully aloof and submitting. Carlos Reyero notes the campness detected both by early viewers of the image, and for which the model Filippo Cugini had a reputation (2017: 229–30). If many of the available males depicted are Moroccans, it is a gypsy, rather than a 'white' woman who appears at the heart of a rare depiction of female undress: the painting of his maid Carmen Bastián (*c.*1871–72) reclining on the furniture and pulling up her skirt. Once again – Susan Martín-Márquez argues – disruption of established composition accompanies a manifestation of intimacy across boundaries of class and 'race'. The abundant pubic hair, framed like a picture in a picture by the woman's clothing, undoes the airbrushed norms of European painting, and thus 'moves to expose ... the laws governing the representation of the nude' (2008: 152–5). In the end – Carlos Reyero shows – Fortuny's most fundamental techniques – the distracting, shimmering brushwork, the details and objects, the luxurious surface effect that draw us away from the 'soul' – became associated with femininity in some influential critics' eyes. This transgression of gender roles was the death knell of his serious artistic reputation, from which one of Europe's leading painters has never truly recovered (2017: 214–24). Fortuny became a kind of hermaphroditic artist.

Equally, just as the same-sex affection of del Campo's *gauchos* (Chapter 1) or the sperm-squeezing sailors of *Moby-Dick* (Chapter 3) cannot be assimilated to our notions of a liberal attitude, so Fortuny's weakening of Being and a mastering gaze cannot simply be identified with opposition to European imperial phallogocentrism. Like other Spaniards, he might nuance the division between Iberians and North Africans because of a shared historic heritage in previously Islamic Andalusia. He might be seeking to re-encounter an 'estranged self' among them, rather than simply othering them as Orientals. He might – like many moderate and conservative Spaniards – also reject outright colonisation of Morocco. But such attitudes were entirely compatible with delight in Spanish victory in 1860 as a kind of surgical strike: it served geopolitical aims in protecting Spain's global position and projection, while avoiding entanglement. It resisted encirclement by France in Algeria and Britain in Gibraltar, while consolidating a global pattern of trade and power that crossed to Cuba and Puerto Rico. It began the process of reassertion of Spain as a world power which led to the Pacific war, as well as intervention in Mexico and Cochinchina (see Chapter 3). The depiction of Muslims as not mastered or assimilated, in turn, could underline their supposed difference as mysterious, even mute Orientals, held in interplay with Spanish Christendom (Ginger 2006, 2007a). Likewise the association of a gypsy female with sexual laxness and availability, and the centuries-old evocation of North Africa as a place of male same-sex activity, drew on stereotypes common in Spain, even as they seemed to undermine other norms (Martin-Márquez 2008: 156, 181).

Similar observations may be made of Courbet's innovations and their connotations. Michael Fried has explored how, in absorption, Courbet might be taken to project the viewing experience into and through the female body and nature, exemplified by the nude of *Real Allegory*. Yet, as Linda Nochlin eloquently shows, the gesture may be taken, like the vast beard and the hand penetrating into nature, 'as fully and unequivocally phallic', born of conventional gender roles (2007: 71). The triad of an admiring child, a naked woman looking on, and an active patriarch rather reinforces this impression, as if merging artistic practice with conventional views of domesticity. Meanwhile, the superficiality of Courbet's gesture towards Assyria – Frederick Bohrer argues – seems rather to echo with French refusals to engage more seriously with the challenge of that ancient culture. The tendency was rather to reduce Assyria to 'a hybrid second-order visual creation' of their own, using their archaeological finds to celebrate the importance of France and its projection of its power in the middle east in imperial rivalry with Britain (1998: 342, 347). Prejudice may be found likewise in the relegation of the Rabbi to the far left, not far from the putative figure of Napoleon III: the positioning may be redolent even with Socialist varieties of anti-Semitism, Rubin suggests (1980: 41).

Rather than an abstract openness to all cultures, Fortuny's sexual and artistic cosmopolitanism is 'rooted' (to borrow Appiah's phrase), as was his in-laws' – the Madrazos' – vision of promiscuous universality in the Prado that we met in Chapter 2. But it is – we might say – weakly rooted. The peripheral axis of Andalusia–North Africa–Portici comes to be predominant in his oeuvre: it forms an image of renewed rebirth of medieval and early modern cultures with which Spain is associated, and in which a Spaniard – and a Catalan – prevails. It suggests renewed glory in a Western Mediterranean civilisation. The painting that made his name – *La Vicaría*, pointedly rendered in Paris as *Le mariage espagnol* – evinces Fortuny's reaching out specifically from Iberia to beyond (here into France): Goya and Meissonier are married the Spanish way, we might say. This alternate, 'peripheral' core – which takes the place of an 'artistic centre', acts in just the same way as the heart of many of his compositions, which take the place of 'soul'. It is forever weakening, becoming distracted into networks of interconnections. The exceeding of gender and sexual boundaries is likewise weakly rooted in and flows from the tripartite peripheral axis and its archetypes and histories.

To rest with Fortuny, letting go of passion and imposing emotion is to begin to let go of 'soul', to weaken Being, from and through that very specific set of positions, becoming distracted through them so as to perceive similitude beyond boundaries, and so to 'go on' (in Wittgenstein's phrase). Likewise, it is through Courbet's self-assertion of a weak centre – as the Franche-Comté patriarch, the alternate Emperor, and 'proudest man in France', with all his prejudices and assumptions – that another letting go begins.

Quietude and the gap

In her story 'The Well of Yucci' (El pozo de Yucci), Juana Manuela Gorriti – a writer born in Salta Province, Argentina – presents us with an indigenous shaman in possession of the knowledge of what was, is, and will be. When consulted, he avers that 'a lake of blood' separates the past and present, as if forming a hidden in-between, joining the two time periods (un lago de sangre) (1876 I: 195, 200). Likewise, in Gorriti's 'Camila O'Gorman', as the female narrator hears the titular character's name, she perceives the present landscape metamorphosing into the past, 'the red anemones of the countryside' into 'drops of blood': a lost link has been restored through violence across the apparent divisions of history (las rojas anémonas de la campiña; gotas de sangre) (1876 II: 371). The words are suggestive of a kind of recognition – anagnorisis – through which the truth about our subjecthood (collective, national, global, and individual) in history is ultimately disclosed in the very violence that has brought it about, connecting timescales. This suggestion goes to the heart of many nineteenth-century views of historical time: to comprehend and be ourselves, we must take cognisance of the historical forces that have made us and will continue to do so. In independent Spanish America – Doris Sommer (1991) has famously shown –, there emerged an obsession with 'foundational fictions', narratives that might give such grounding to states that had just been formed. The violent imagery of that recognition and re-telling – all that conjoining blood – is resonant with the sacrificial visions that we saw in chapter 3, opening up the bounds between time periods and locations.

Faced with enquiries, however, Gorriti's sage is adamant: 'the shadow you wish to illuminate, conceals abysses that will make you vertiginous with terror' (la sombra que quieres illuminar, oculta abismos que te darán el vértigo del espanto). He warns that 'knowledge and pain are synonyms in the book of life.' 'Probing! Inquiring! Knowing!' he declares to be 'that fateful desire which was your race's perdition' (ciencia y dolor son sinónimos en el libro de la vida; ¡Sondar! ¡Inquirir! ¡Saber! … ese anhelo fatal que perdió a tu raza) (1876(I): 388, 391). Or, as the title of another, celebrated Gorriti story more succinctly puts it: 'Whoever listens to this hears their own affliction' (Quien escucha su mal oye). After the shaman's advice is ignored, and just as he predicts, convoluted strands of interlinked narrative across place and time unfurl, soaked with bloody violence and massacres, from the fleeing Spanish loyalists of the transatlantic independence wars, to the continental conflict between the independent Argentina Confederation and the Peruvian-Bolivian state.

The alternative is a form of life that turns away, deflects from the dynamic of violence that joins people across time and geography. We need not assume that a recognition of history's patterns, less still its cruelties and suffering, will reveal who we really are, our true subjecthood. We may suppose instead that such an outlook becomes a self-fulfilling prophecy. It risks determining who we are and what we become as persons: suffering, obsessed with violence and pain. We may affirm, in turn, that to be at home in the world – to have wisdom, even – is utterly distinct from knowing the world, from epistemology. The shaman says that the desire to know is the perdition of Europeans and their descendants. He thus evokes a putative historic error over centuries of culture, from the Garden of Eden through to powerful traditions of philosophy that privileged epistemological foundations: we might think of Descartes, Locke, Kant, among others. On the shaman's account, the key issue is not whether something truly happened, or even whether a particular outcome might or might not be avoided, or even whether we work a trauma through. Rather, to be at home in the world is a matter of letting go of violence and of attending to other things, of opening up other ways of being. In her *Art of Cruelty*, Nelson recalls the following anecdote, recounted by Sharon Salzberg, a Buddhist teacher. Salzberg had been dwelling upon upsetting recollections of her own misdeeds. Her own teacher asked her if this meant that she now saw the truth about herself. Salzberg came to the conclusion that she was not in fact seeing the truth about herself (Nelson 2012: loc.2285–90). She is suggesting – I take it – that no such historical data, no such knowledge constitutes an authentic self, a Being, a 'soul'.

So as better to follow the shaman's counsel, so as to deflect, we might remove from our perception, or at least half-hide, the core around which an historical narrative might otherwise be structured. Gorriti's story 'Camila O'Gorman' exemplifies such a vision. It seems at first that we are to read a 'foundational fiction'. The name Camila O'Gorman – a victim of the Federalist dictatorship of Juan Manuel Rosas in Buenos Aires – first appears in the story just after a list of men considered to be founding fathers in the turbulent forging of the Argentine Republic. She is presented as a female equivalent to them. Yet, the core of her story is as if unseen or only glanced at. The supposed eyewitness, Colonel G., initially only glimpses someone he insinuates to have been O'Gorman. He is away in Europe, to cure him of his infatuation, when the (well-known) critical events of O'Gorman's life unfurl: her elopement with the priest Ladislao Gutiérrez, their detention by the Rosas régime, and the sentence of execution, even though she was pregnant. A gap opens in the tale. In its place, we end up, as if through Chinese boxes, with third-hand information, obtained by the returning, young Colonel G. from other people who themselves got it from others, and then recounted from memory at a distance of over thirty years, before being retold by a female first-person narrator (who resembles Gorriti herself returning from exile to Buenos Aires).

By attending to such plural, partial perspectives, we are able to perceive the violence askance, multiply refracted as it were, just as in Fortuny's images our attention slips away from what is forceful or we spy it off-centre, in a weakening. The final scene of 'Camila O'Gorman' is testament to the ephemeral, passing nature even of the O'Gorman story and its bloodshed. An abandonment, a breaking up and falling away of collective recollection is precisely what opens up fissures of other possibilities. The female narrator and her friends gather about the place where O'Gorman was shot, forming a community that contemplates the past with 'pietas' – to borrow Vattimo's word. This is not a dismissal or forgetting of its place in history, but an appreciation that even so compelling an experience, with all its claims to central importance, is subject to mortality (Vattimo 2012: 47). The ruin they behold is evocatively termed 'the execution wall of our memory' (El paredón de nuestra memoria). We read that: 'At its foot a green carpet of vegetation raised, flower-filled, its exuberant offshoots; in its cracks, the turtle doves nested, and on its black summit a lark sent happy songs into the air' (A su pie una verde alfombra de vegetación alzaba floridos sus exuberantes vástagos; en sus grietas anidaban las tórtolas, y en su negra cima una alonda enviaba al aire alegres cantos) (1876(I): 386).

There is an oneiric feel to such combined impressions of something immediately, violently relevant yet distant, of something at the centre of our attention but that slips away, just as there is to Fortuny's blurring of crucial details, his deflections from focal points, or to the flow of Courbet's studio into a vague and uncertain expanse of nuanced colour. Foundational stories become derealised. In Gorriti's stories, there is an ambiguous slippage between fantasy and reality, Escalante observes (2013: 1069). In the course of 'Gubi Amaya', from the collection *Dreams and Realities* (*Sueños y realidades*) (1865), we meet a character from across the Atlantic, an Italian. He tells his tale, taking our attention to Europe and the Austro-Hungarian imperial occupation of Venice, and then vanishes. He has, for a time, occupied the centre of perceptions among a group of listeners, but without their ever knowing anything about him. 'He arrived silently among us,' the story ends, 'and silently too he departed like one of those images that cross the mind preceding a dream' (Silencioso llegó entre nosotros, y se marchó también silencioso como una de esas imágenes que cruzan la mente precediendo el sueñc) (Gorriti 2000: 201).

In the story 'Gubi Amaya' itself, the female narrator repeatedly dissociates from the painful and intimate experiences she confronts, perceiving the same thing from two distinct perspectives, distanced and near, or derealised and immediate simultaneously. She has returned, cross-dressed as a man, from painful, enforced exile to visit the River Plate region, rejoining the facets of her own transnational identity as she does so. 'I walked about, as if there were two different persons in me, one of them, the rugged daughter of those woodlands, the other, a traveller from far-off countries who had come to contemplate them', she remarks early on. Beholding the graves of those she had loved, she tells us, 'I began to doubt whether I was not myself a ghost/shadow' (caminaba, como si hubiera en mí dos personas, la una, hija agresta de aquellas selvas, la otra, viajera que de lejanos países había venido a contemplarlas, me refería a mí misma la historia de todos esos sitios; comencé a dudar si yo misma no era una sombra) (2000: 124, 134). This dissociation may be linked to the effects of trauma, to the avoidance of reference to painful events, Beatriz Urraca notes (1999: 161). But even as it acknowledges the consequences of violence, the feeling of loss and dissociation may, in so doing, offer a calming, where what was lost may return to the fore as a serene force, precisely in its absence or occlusion. The violence that joined places and times is thus transfigured into a powerful tranquillity that follows but transforms the very same patterns of interconnection. The blood of Camila O'Gorman's death may flow from Argentina's past to its present, and from Buenos Aires out to the border-crossing exile Gorriti, but it is experienced as a missing core that joins us.

The multiple viewpoints and mobile perspectives that deflect from a 'core' narrative evoke interconnections across place and time. In a long essay on Gorriti, Francine Masiello speaks of how the writer conjures up 'multiple sites of focus', 'memory' that 'is never pure in lineage', 'multiple chartings ... in response to the mixed realities', 'pure movement', 'a trail of multiple possibilities'. Masiello remarks on how these techniques evoke the complex mesh of relationships in post-independence Latin America, with its shifting boundaries and state formations as the old order fell. Gorriti expresses her own 'transnational linkage' across this fragmenting and reconfiguring world. Her family went into exile from Rosas's regime; she married Manuel Isidoro Belzú, who would become the President of Bolivia, later to be murdered; she took off to the literary scene of Lima, where she became a patriotic nurse in the defence against Spanish attack in 1866, but still published in Argentina; and she spoke two indigenous languages (Quechua and Aymara) (2003: xvii, xx–xxv, xxxiii, xxxv, xxxvii, xlvii, xlix). In 'Camila O'Gorman', as in 'Gubi Amaya', the female narrator is just such an exile visiting Argentina. In turn, the narrative patterns and gaps of Gorriti's tales recall how Spanish-American states were born from and sustained in the interplay of factors across the globe, giving rise to 'fables of globalisation', in Beckman's words (2013). In 'Camila O'Gorman', the Colonel misses the main events because he has been sent away to study in Europe, to which so many Argentine intellectuals looked. On his return, overlaying past and present Atlantic passages, he compares himself to an anxious Columbus, who had fatefully conjoined the two worlds (1876(II): 369–70, 378–9). In 'Whoever listens ...', the female narrator cannot recount the end of the story, because a male revolutionary – from whom she heard it – ran off to catch his train, taking him on a series of American and European adventures. He now wanders the globe.

The partiality, the kinds of mobility, even the fluidity of these perspectives are affordances of prejudice and assumption in Spanish-American societies, as if to trace a possibility that paradoxically arises from these. If – as Pratt suggests – the narratives challenge 'polarities' of elite creole thinking (1992: 194), it is less through the direct overthrow of widespread beliefs, than the latters' capacity to attenuate and be altered from within. Gorriti's exiled 'female wanderers' offer us visions of past and present through eyes denied the privilege of more secure male vantage points, Grzegorcyk (2002) notes. The travellers gather such knowledge as they can, and are faced with 'displacement and loss' (2002: 56). Conversely, in 'Whoever listens …', it is easy male access to travel and action that ensures the woman cannot complete the tale. In turn, the criss-crossing of identities that is 'endemic to foundational romances' (Sommer 1991: 80) becomes an exacerbated gender fluidity in the partial, mobile perspectives of Gorriti's protagonists. The young Colonel, wandering about Buenos Aires, obsessed with the woman who may be O'Gorman, manifests all the hysteria stereotypically associated with women. In 'Whoever heeds …' – Andrea Castro observes – the male protagonist who departs at the end spies into and becomes identified with a woman mesmerist within a secret chamber associated with another timescale. The very fact of a woman playing mesmerist to a male somnambulist reverses the habitual hierarchy (2002: 88, 132, 134).

If, through a gap in history's narrative, Manet's paintings offer a violent pushing away that joins things, Gorriti suggests we attend instead to the experience of lack in such an opening. In his *Presentation of Don Juan de Austria to the Emperor Carlos V in Yuste* (1869; Plate 18), the Spanish painter Eduardo Rosales evokes just such a sensation in the legacy of Hispanic imperialism, in the person of a King of Spain and Holy Roman Emperor. By extension he invokes (here and elsewhere) the enduring legacy of universalisms associated with the idea of a Spanish *monarchia* (overlordship of the world). Rosales alludes likewise to the related European notion of *imperium* as derived from ancient Rome and reinvented in the Holy Roman Empire, and with it, under the Habsburg Carlos V, the apparatus of continental European statehood. Rosales thus revisits the entanglement of Spain in the shaping of the world as we come to know it. It is not, as it is in Gorriti, a question of deflecting the belief that the recognition of our history constitutes authentic subjecthood. The very use of the genre of history painting rather affirms such concerns. Instead, the effect might be envisaged as a reversal: not a stepping aside from or removal of the Empire's impact, but rather a dwelling on a sense of unfulfilment at its heart, on emotions drained away, a looming emptiness. The very acknowledgement of these sensations becomes an alternate source of energy in the wake of *monarchia* and *imperium*, conjoining us, transfiguring the effect of those legacies from within, like Bayoán's inversion of Columbus's journey, but now beyond overt torment.

The combination of the painting's (oft-remarked) unusual use of scale (Díez 1992: 274–6), and the nature of the scene, is suggestive of a shift in perception. The monumentality of history painting is as if re-scaled through an experience of small-scale intimacy, in a format more usually employed for anecdotal and episodic scenes. We behold the revelation of a private secret, as if the reconfiguration disclosed something hidden in the habitual monumentalisations of the past, but that is more truly monumental. To our far left, we find the now ageing and ill Carlos V, after his abdication. Though he did not claim the title, as formal successor to the Roman Empire as well as ruler on a new continent, he inspired the notion of a new universal monarchy (Pagden 1995: 32, 39–45). To our right is Juan de Austria, his illegitimate son who, in turn, was to lead the Catholic Holy-League fleet at the Battle of Lepanto, the decisive naval victory over the Islamic Ottoman Empire, the successor state to Byzantium and the Eastern Roman Empire. In so doing, he would both mark the future of the Catholic monarchy, and significantly determine the boundaries of Islam and Christendom in shaping Europe and the world. The secret of the intimate connection between these two individuals, and their roles in history, is about to be revealed.

In the middle of the image, where we might expect some memorable or decisive action, there is almost nothing at all. There is an extreme stilling of what little activity there is: a bow from the visiting Don Juan, a gesture from his tutor. While the composition owes something to Delaroche's more violent *Death of the Duke of Guise* (1834) (Díez & Barón 2007: 217), Rosales stretches out the near-empty spaces, pushes his characters far apart, drastically limiting the chromatic range of much of the painting to a mixture of brown, brownish-gold and dark reds. At the heart of the ocean-spanning monarchy, past and future, is a lack of contact between father and his unacknowledged son, resonant with vast emotional deprivation and incapacity: they do not even manage to exchange glances. Such is the crucial masculine relationship in the patriarchal order to which we now return in *anagnorisis*. Out of acceptance of this comes an imperturbable force that might substitute their world of emperors and wars. The painting hints at a harmony of opposites that the Romantic painter Delacroix might have found in the stark contrast of the brilliant blue of Don Juan's outfit and the reds of Carlos's blanket and chair. But set so far apart, so diminutive within the larger room and intervening, nondescript colour, such a violent balance is undone from within, leaving only the black-gloved hand of Don Juan's tutor at the point of equilibrium. The lasting resonance of world-shaping energy is contained force, a serenity, a compelling void, its own 'nothing that is everything'.

To look at such a thing acceptingly is to experience and to attain something of 'the power of passiveness'. Rosales's *Prior's Cell in the Monastery of El Escorial* (1864) suggests how – in an experience of forcefulness in lack, an unaggressive, subtle chromatic scheme – our gaze might relax into a vision's indefinition, without losing completely the outlines of reality, just as our eyes adjust to Fortuny's *Choosing the Model*. Unlike Fortuny's mobile multitude of tiny strokes, Rosales's sweeps of colour enable our eyes to settle more easily in stillness upon the painting's broad, vague shapes, resting in meditation, amid a gentle variation over predominant browns and creams, with large blank areas of near-uniform colour. This is what we now find at the former heart of the empire. The combined religious and palatial complex outside Madrid was built by Felipe IV, and from here he ruled the world's first transoceanic monarchy. Here too its rulers would be buried in a pantheon. Evocations of the building were at the heart of many Spanish revolutionary and later liberal attempts to reconfigure their relationship with the legacy of *monarchia* and *imperium*. At the start of the century, in his then-influential poem, 'The Pantheon of the Escorial' (El Panteón del Escorial) (1805), the revolutionary poet Quintana had set out a vision of the building as a place of ever-growing infamy in the Habsburg monarchy, as if a bifurcation in the course of history, in which present-day Spain was horribly haunted by its past rulers, but from which it should depart (1978: 177–86). For the protagonist, Josef, in Ros de Olano's *Dr Lañuela*, the place was above all stultifying of the soul: he perceives in Herrera's architecture simply stone after stone, intended solely to perpetuate the human fame of monarchs, lacking any mystic place for the indeterminacy of the spirit (vaguedad) (1863: 243). In his own response to the palace-monastery, Rosales leads us not into any of the regal rooms, but rather, off-centre, into a senior cleric's austere habitation, as if displacing imperial authority from within, without mirroring it through direct opposition. There is absolutely no one there – the one visible chair is empty – and nothing is happening. The dead centre of the image is a patch of wall between two indistinct paintings. If El Escorial becomes – as in Ros de Olano – a place of absence and lack, it becomes, paradoxically and for that reason, a place where it is possible to let go of controlling violence and imperial splendour. A serene sensibility reconnects places and times in the wake of empire through its old heart. As the legacy of European *monarchia* and *imperium* shifts off-centre, we encounter a quietude that could pervade the history of global cultures in their aftermath.

The Three Races (Equality before the Law) (*c.*1859; Plate 19), painted by the Peruvian Francisco Laso, presents us with the outcome of violent encounters across the Western hemisphere in the multi-racial city of Lima. We have before us an African-Peruvian maid, a descendant of imported slaves, child of what Paul Gilroy (1993) has called 'The Black Atlantic'; an indigenous servant girl, of whom many were still kidnapped for domestic work at this time; and a wealthy creole boy in expensive European clothes. Though they are playing together, they do not look at one another, nor do they directly interact. If these three are together, they are so in their apartness, in mere contiguity. As Natalia Majluf suggests, the separations dividing them following the recent abolition of slavery, the understated awkwardness of the scene are suggestive of a still conflictive and unequal history, the key to what they really share, beyond their formal equality in law (2003: 43–6). In their mixture of togetherness and division, they have settled into the shape of a composition that is at once triangular and disjointed. By turns, each of them could appear to be the most important apex, and none of them, by definition, can quite occupy the centre of the triangle. This is given over to an uncertain future in the form of a game of chance. Yet in their virtual stillness, and in spite of everything, they suggest a geometrical shape in its serenity, like the designs on the wall or the patterns on the floor.

There is a classical purity to the resultant composition. Though Laso may have learnt such techniques in Europe at Gleyre's Parisian studio (Estrabridis Cárdenas 2004: 83–6), the pattern is formed here by all of the three races in equal part, out of large blocks of colour. In his article of 1859, 'The Palette and Its Colours' (La paleta y sus colores), Laso (2003) suggests that harmony could emerge from contrasting colours, comparing such an outcome to the failure of nation building in the divisions of Peru. The aesthetic vision of *The Three Races*, its composition, intimates that *limeño* life might be transfigured, out of and through its own divisions, releasing its potential for commonality. By implication the values of classicism are shown to recur across places and times and peoples, well beyond the ancient classical Mediterranean and its legacy, the source of many European claims to cultural hegemony. The repeated occurrence of such forms across geography and chronology requires and has no centre, and no order of priority. As in the 'universal constructivism' of the Uruguayan Joaquín Torres García nearly a century later, the specific circumstances and art of Latin America are presented as part of a universal, geometrical classicism. That is not because they derive from ancient Greece and Rome, but because across the globe, such aesthetic patterns trace paths through and into universality (1944: 76, 990–7).

The suggestion is drawn out in Laso's painting of an African-Peruvian laundress, *La lavandera* (1859). As she stretches upwards to hang out (perhaps her employer's) laundry, we see the simple, elegant shapes of her powerful body, draped in equally simple clothing in the sunlight. She could be Athena at Herculaneum, raising her arms to launch a spear, or Aphrodite reaching upwards with a garment in her hands. She is neither: she is an African-Peruvian woman doing the laundry. Her life and movement resonate with the same serene dignity that might be attributed to the ancient Greeks, but likewise vice versa, Hellenistic civilisation is resonant with African-Peruvian laundresses. Back and forth across geography and time, and without any necessary direct influence, serene, bold geometries echo with each other. Like the gap in *The Presentation of Don Juan* or *The Three Races*, the calm central figure takes the place of the violent forces that connected imperial history but does so without repeating their malice. The laundress's pose stretches beyond the atrocities that ultimately brought her across the Black Atlantic, even as these place here where she is now. Hers is what Gilroy later called a 'strategic universalism': a staking of a counterclaim against oppressive versions of universality based upon European superiority (2000: 327–56).

In turn, Rosales's most celebrated history paintings – *Isabel the Catholic Dictating Her Will* (1864; Plate 20) and *The Death of Lucretia* (1871) – suggest that, by returning to the very beginnings of European notions of empire, it is possible to bring to the centre a positive quietude that was obscured by violent forms of connectedness. This goes beyond the acknowledgement of loss and lack at the core of universal *monarchia*. It is not even a matter of de-centring, or of weakening a centre within a system, nor quite of something that lies beyond but defines a socio-historical structure. Rather it is a return to the beginning of an origin story, in which European imperial history can be transfigured and undone from within. These two large paintings putatively offer what Zielinski calls 'dynamic moments': they present at their core a potential in the past that was not realised, but with whose enduring force we can reconnect across time. The implication of Rosales's work is that, where connections are not effected by a more obviously active and directing central principle, a compelling dynamic might emerge. The large history paintings are resonant with the suggestion that this positive lack might, in turn, offer its own unifying force to humanity across place and time.

The first of these two paintings was the work that made Rosales's international name, winning him the French Légion d'honneur. *Isabel the Catholic Dictating Her Will* depicts the monarch who had both led the unification of European Spain and overseen the first ventures into the Americas. The Queen was widely invoked in the mid-century, rendered relevant by the parallel and comparison with Spain's second queen since the fifteenth century, Isabel II (Reyero 1992: 50). On her deathbed, Isabel I pronounces the fate of her new Atlantic kingdom, her husband seated on a chair beside her. A small crowd gathers about her, including her daughter Juana, and the political and religious leader Cardinal Cisneros. She is illuminated in white, contrasting with the darker colours of the surrounding images. The core of the scene is near-stillness: Rosales himself wrote in his letters of its 'perfect repose' (perfecto reposo) (2018: 101); Gómez Moreno goes so far as to describe it as static in its calm (1993: 354). The Queen is lying down, her face serene, inclined a little to one side, her arms at rest and a hand and finger gently pointing to a scribe. Nor are there any very dramatic gestures or movements from other people in the room. Even the bright lighting on the monarch is tempered with sobriety: her clothing is pointedly off-white. The brushwork and drawing are broad and rough-edged, in places darkened with touches of black. Both the technique and the image's sobriety place Rosales likewise as a successor to Velázquez, effecting a bond in Spanish art as well as political and royal history across the centuries. Yet there is nothing here of Velázquez's spectacular translucence or sensual plays of light, and the brushstrokes are thick; the work divided contemporary critics as to whether the artist was a worthy heir (Díez 1992: 281–4). Rosales is less copying Velázquez than releasing an untapped potential from the very core of Spaniards' sense of a national art tradition.

The centre of the image does not connect simply to the rest of the painting or to a continuity in history from Isabel to her successors. In his letters, Rosales underlined the disconnection of this moment from later history, through his rejection of other, violent candidates for a great national story: the rebellion of Padilla and the *comuneros* against Carlos V – a habitual liberal reference point, depicted by Gibsert, as we saw in Chapter 3 – or Carlos's imperial European ventures in Italy (2018: 77). The intensity of light upon Isabel sets her utterly apart. Her will ends up in the darker part of the painting, among her companions, presenting a vision (as Rosales explained) of how she saw the future of her country. This alludes to a frequently expressed notion among Spanish liberals that her reign had been the last gasp of an older order of liberties (2018: 77). So far as the Americas are concerned, the Will itself urges her successors to ensure that indigenous peoples meet no harm and are well treated. Instead of looking at the Queen, her consort looks straight ahead at the scribe. Cisneros, the political leader, lurks in the shadows. Princess Juana, later known as the Mad, likewise gazes at the will, not her dying mother; she would be confined to a nunnery by 1506, her father acting in her place as regent.

Revilla Uceda has observed that the theatricality of form – the visual language disclosing the dramatic significance of history – is displayed here so as to be exposed (1982: 36): the box of the bed with its curtains, its spectators themselves located rigidly within the stagelike confines of a rug. In the place of a meaningful drama created through the interplay of gazes, the painting evokes a positive power found in restfulness, emanating from the Queen's 'limbo' – that juncture between life and death, the very moment at which historical time becomes periodised. This 'repose' would be capable of uniting the vast populations and territories, but is never fully incorporated into later history as evoked by the other characters. It is the viewer who now looks headlong upon the face of Isabel the Catholic, and is invited to feel that unrealised potential: she is anachronistically youthful, as if beginning once again, but by deflecting from emotional intensity. The Queen's eyelids are dipped, impeding eye contact.

Rosales's second and last large history painting, *Death of Lucretia* (1871), is a complex echo of his first. Again we behold a woman's demise at one of the great turning points of history (or at least legend). The suicide of Lucretia, to avoid the sexual attentions of Rome's last king, inspired a revolt and the founding of the Roman Republic (Beard 2016: 121–3). The politics born of this story would resonate through European history and beyond, across geography and time. Lucretia's death putatively gave rise to a state, which, sprawling across Europe, Asia and Africa, would be the continual reference point both for European civilisation and, more specifically, for the notion of a universal polity, *imperium*. Yet even as Lucretia's corpse, like Isabel's body, is brightly lit in white, her death is set apart from the future events which it sparks among the surrounding men and darker colours. She is even slightly off-centre amid the unfurling action. As the virtuous woman falls towards our left, Brutus stands aside to our right, looking up at his weapon and vowing the revenge that will bring about the Roman Republic, his face turned from us.

In a famous letter to a friend, Rosales aptly evokes Brutus's pose: 'he does not even fix his gaze upon the victim ... for him it is no more than an opportune moment ... he is a political man and politicians have no heart' (ni siquiera fija su mirada en la víctima ... no es para él más que un momento oportuno ... es un hombre político y los políticos no tienen corazón). Rosales goes on to describe Lucretia's husband Collatinus as 'imbecilic' (imbécil) (cited in Díez & Barón 2007: 224). The latter's face is again turned from us. He leans in with a gesture of his hand to ask questions of what is, after all, a corpse. He and Brutus together were to be Rome's first consuls, the founders of the Roman state as it came to remembered: SPQR, the Senate and People of Rome (Beard 2016: 127). The male gaze dominates in the painting, taking its place as the source of the new state and the long legacy of its civilisation, as a vehicle of enquiry (Collatinus) and of power (Brutus). But its constitutive power is undone; it appears bogus, at worst self-aggrandising, and brings about no significant dynamic within the image: the contemporary art critic Cañete despaired at the image's lack of meaning, as he saw it (Díez 1992: 288). The only thing that truly matters is Lucretia's mute, unseeing corpse.

It is through, rather than against the grain, of historic gender stereotypes, that Rosales comes to this displacement of patriarchal masculinity, and his dwelling upon the feminine as force to resist it. The catalogue entry for *The Death of Lucretia* at the 1871 National Exhibition recalls Titus Livius's celebration of her inner purity, unsullied by the sex act (Díez 1992: 278). In turn, in his letters, Rosales spoke of Isabel as displaying 'a mother's love' (el amor de una madre) in dictating her will (2018: 77). She is, after all, the very image of tenderness and gentility. The painter seems, in part, to echo the call of the prominent writer, Gertrudis Gómez de Avellaneda in her 1860 essay 'Woman' (La mujer): that we should recognise that characteristics supposedly specific to femininity could become sources of universal value, as seen in figures such as Isabel I. In turn, both images – Lucretia and Isabel – if only in outline, recall the longstanding myth – revived by psychoanalysts – of the founding of a civilisation or an era upon the demise of a woman, habitually with intimations of violence (Nelson 2011: loc.2214).

Once again in *Death of Lucretia*, while the illuminated female figure is linked to later events, she is not fully incorporated into them. Again, her dying force exceeds and resists them, an undoing of their foundations of a civilisation. Not truly seen and known by her male companions, Lucretia offers an alternate disposition to the sweep of later European universalism and its gaze, a path not yet taken, but to which we might return, reconnecting with this moment. If *Isabel the Catholic* offers us a non-action, *Death of Lucretia* presents a kind of anti-action at the core of that experience. That is to say, it retains the features of dynamic, violent events while undoing these with their opposite. The brushwork itself, so controversial at the time, contributes to the effect. Here Rosales takes the loose style of *Isabel the Catholic* and renders it far more extreme. The brushstrokes are larger and more uneven, the use of dark lines and patches is intensified, the forms are often not just blurred, but clumsy and blunt-edged, like Collatinus's stunted foot. The rough-edged textures of the paint give it an air of physical force, both as regards the image and its making: 'vehemence', Rosales said. Yet, the result is intensely sober (Díez 1992: 280). Lucretia herself is decidedly off-white, and, despite her mortal wounds, unbloodied. In the anti-drama, in the reversal at the centre of empire's origin, restraint and force go together.

Deflection and infinite jest

In a verse prologue to an early edition of his *Traditions* (*Tradiciones*) (1875) – brief narratives about historical episodes and anecdotes – Ricardo Palma – a Peruvian of partially African descent – describes his own writing as a 'disguise' or 'mask' (antifaz). The effect of the light joke ('merry chitchat') is 'to mask my poor spirit', and 'the most cruel, bitter disappointments' caused by the present era (broma, feliz cháchara, enmascarar mi pobre espíritu, crudelísimas, / amargas decepciones). The point is neither that we should look behind the mask to the pain, forming an emotional connection, nor only that we should simply disguise it. Palma mocks those who insist on sharing their suffering through their writing, but cautions those who take his jesting for happiness. Anyone who does that – he says – cannot see further than the end of their nose (no ve más allá de su nariz) (1875: xii–xiv). We attend here to something like the *Infinite Jest* that lends its title to David Foster Wallace's great novel. Foster Wallace's novel lingers over the ever-present possibility of ironising things, there being nothing to which irony cannot lend a sense of superiority and distance. The risk to be avoided – the seeing only to the end of our nose – is that 'ironic self-consciousness' can easily become 'the one and only universally recognised badge of sophistication', as Foster Wallace remarks in an essay on David Lynch (1997: loc.3254). In considering historical narrative, we are invited, then, to attend to the very fact of deflecting and distracting, rather than as such to the deflection and distraction. Here it is not solely the absence of emotional intensity ('soul') that matters, but rather, in and of itself, the act of releasing oneself from it through a 'jest'. *Cháchara* offers us attention both to that deflecting, and – through its use of anecdote – to individual, peculiar cases rather than a single large narrative. (This whole book that I am writing is a series of cases, of anecdotes.)

As it evades definition, the deflecting becomes redolent with a crossing of gender boundaries, like the delicacy of Fortuny's artwork. Elisa Sampson Vera Tudela emphasises how Palma's writing implies a 'a retreat … from scientific, masculine history', to a stance 'outside the theoretical certainties of his age'. Noting his frequent use of feminine imagery to describe his writing, Sampson Vera Tudela goes so far as to describe his writing as 'in "drag"' (2012: 47, 52, 74–9; at 52, 78–9). Palma attributes many stories to the oral traditions of *viejas* (old women) of Lima; his first tradition appears in an album for Gorriti. Palma associates women, and racial mixing, with Peru and Lima's popular culture, and these in turn with an untrustworthy mixing of truth and fiction in anecdotes, and with putative deviance extracted from the country's archive, 'lurid, ridiculous, and outlandish titbits', in Christopher Conway's words (Sampson Vera Tudela 2012: 31, 55–6, 71–2, 105–7; Conway 2004: xxxi–iii). These remnants of Peruvian attitudes and narratives – often with their own roots in prejudice – are integral to the historical 'case' of the country, and the place of its culture in the world and time. They evoke the urban humour of Lima with which Palma is so directly associated (Conway 2004: xxi), the legacy of Vice-Regal satirists (Sampson Vera Tudela 2012: 21) and the echoes of contemporary European humorists, like the Spanish satirical journalists Martínez Villergas and Modesto Lafuente, whom he admired (Villanes Cairo 1994: 20; Holguín Callo 2001: 46). It is out of this confluence of attitudes and styles that the writing proceeds, that the distraction begins, disclosing its evasion of pain.

The notion of a 'case' – so important to nineteenth-century historical visions – is crucial to the relationship between attending to such 'merry chitchat' and apprehending connections. At its most basic, an individual *case* is at once a specific, particular historical situation – such as one of Palma's little episodes – and a means of drawing out wide-ranging judgements and connections through it. This occurs in two intertwined ways. First, the 'case' implies an explanation of how the situation arose out of and caused effects in wider events. Second, it entails both an evaluation of the ethical significance of the case in terms of larger principles, and an assessment of how and to what extent our understanding of larger principles may be shaped by it. All of these things, in all their complexity, are implied in the notion of a *case study*, in the use of *case law*, and in the ethical practice of *casuistry*. The *case* is, thus, a delicate attempt to consider what is particular to a place and time in terms of general application, without in so doing eliminating its own specificity. It is this that has made the exploration of its nineteenth-century histories simultaneously a subject of study and a mode of historical writing for writers such as Chandler in his *England in 1819* and Dunkerley in his *Americana: The Americas in the World, around 1850*. Chandler surmises that 'the word *case* ... has to do with ... the world of chance and contingency and with the positing of worlds – normative orders – against which chance and contingency might be established as such' (1998: 39–40; original emphasis).

Palma's earliest *Traditions*, written in the mid-century, often directly evoke the notion of a 'case' by explicitly placing judicial and quasi-judicial processes at the core or culminating point of a narrative structure: their joking concerns matters of judgement about cause, effect and ethics, in relating the particular to the general. In 'Don Dimas de Tijereta' (1864), for example, a lawyer who appears to have sold his soul to the Devil challenges Satan in the courts of Hell, and wins. At the end of 'The Dying Christ' (El Cristo de la Agonía) (1867), a tribunal absolves a great painter of murder despite (or because of) his having killed his male model in order more accurately to depict pain. To paraphrase the subtitle of Chandler's monograph, the *cháchara* is thus an exploration of the 'case of historicism': that is, it is not simply the use of a case to explain and evaluate history. Rather, it explores the historicist outlook as something that had prominence as a mode of explanation and that had arisen historically (as a 'case' in its own right). In Julio Ortega's words, the *Traditions* often focus on 'the story about the story, the genre's reflection on itself ... a hermeneutic of the formations and deformations of the national, produced inside a culture that is plural' (2006: 146–7).

Specifically, the episodes we find in the *Traditions* linger over the past of Peru as a viceroyalty of a global empire, the most frequent topic of Palma's writing. By implication, this supposes the relationship of institutional and ethical judgement as conceived within an ocean-spanning empire, in relation to Palma's time with its post-imperial attempt to create a nation state. The significance of such an undertaking is underlined in an essay by the Peruvian historian Natalia Sobrevilla, 'How (Not) to Make a Durable State' (2018). Sobrevilla explores how the continuous constitutional and institutional crises of the nineteenth-century Spanish Americas (and of Spain itself) are at once a consequence of the shattering of the framework of the global monarchy, and a reiteration of institutional and social crisis over the *longue durée*. The latter both fuelled the monarchy's undoing, and remained fundamental to its aftermath. In turn, Elisa Sampson Vera Tudela has shown how, by the mid-century, historical writers in Peru explored the foundations, and foundational fictions, for their country through its Vice-Regal past (2012: 20).

Such efforts echo both the increasingly assertive establishment of a state apparatus for independent Peru – recovering from the collapse of the earlier oceanic system of governance – and the reality that much of the new elite was intertwined with the older aristocracy and with the Old World. As he penned his earliest *Traditions*, Palma found himself wrestling with where legitimacy lay in contemporary Peru, amid a web of connections between past and present, between Peru and Western Europe. Having supported President Ramón Castilla and the latter's renewal of a powerful state (from a national budget to railway infrastructure), he rebelled against the increasingly conservative regime. By this time, with state-backed concessions of guano exploitation to British enterprise providing lavish revenue, Peru's new elite was indulging in European luxuries, intermarrying with the old Vice-Regal elite and European aristocrats and oligarchs; old families took leading roles (Conway 2004: xxi–xxv; Patrón Boylán 2004: 36–50). Travelling to Europe himself, Palma admired contemporary writers in France and Spain, before joining Americanists in overthrowing President Pezet, and entering the war with Spain in 1865–66 that Whistler witnessed from Valparaíso (Chapter 3). In time, Palma came to reject the post-war Civilists, who favoured freeing up (international) finance and scaling back the Peruvian state and military (Conway 2004: xxi–xxvi; Holguín Callo 2001: 29–78).

The early traditions foreground three intertwined aspects of how cases exhibit interconnections: the verdict, 'sympathy', and what Palma calls *presumption* and *plan* (*presunción, plan*). The first might promise some clarity of judgement about the relevance of the case beyond its local circumstances, with whatever nuances and qualifications that might imply. To this, the *cháchara* offers instead the notion that 'every existence is an epigram' (toda existencia es un epigrama) (1875: xii–xiii). The use of the *epigram* suggests the importance of the genre of a case (what Coleridge, in his definition of the epigram, called 'a dwarfish whole'), the role of wit (jesting), and a double-edge, exemplified in Catullus's famous words 'Odi et amo'. Characteristically, in the *Traditions*, even where an institutional verdict is given, it is often presented as only one of at least two possible judgements. In an exceptionally stark example titled 'The Nazarene' (El Nazareno) (1859), the eighteenth-century protagonist has been unsuccessfully pursued in lawsuits and to little effect by the Holy Inquisition, although he has (for example) offered up a woman he seduced to be raped by his friends (horrified, they decline). At his funeral, a legal officer of a high tribunal (an *escribano* of the *Real Audiencia*) pronounces in pseudo-judicial terms: 'I testify and certify that the blessed captain is already scorched in hell' (Doy fe y certifico que el dichoso capitán está ya achicharrado en el infierno). It turns out, though, that he had lived a double life as the near-saintly Nazarene. The assembled crowd fall to their knees in reverence. The suddenness of this switchover and Palma's deadpan tone are suggestive of core judgement flipping back and forth between opposites, with no middle term, as if allowing both to exist, unmediated, at the core of the verdict.

Not only does Palma's technique prevent ethical transcendence of opposites – for which many in the nineteenth century had hoped – but even any notion that the irony itself offers its own alternative. This is what Baudelaire sought through his vision of the Absolute Comic, in 'The Essence of Laughter' (1855) (absolu comique; L'essence du rire). The very words chosen by Baudelaire evoke transhistorical, philosophical foundations of Being. For Baudelaire, the Absolute Comic is rooted in ironic contradiction, certainly, as the basis of humanity, which cannot be resolved in transcendence (Hiddleston 2011). But this contradiction is, even so, an immanent transfiguration of the human, conjoining aspiration for an ideal with utter fallenness from perfection. In its continual departure from Paradise – whether that be a prior Eden, or a dreamt-future utopia – the Absolute Comic returns forever to this eternal, enduring atavism – the Satanic – as did the flowers of evil that we saw in Chapter 2. To dwell on such an immanent transfiguration is to experience superiority within humanity (however delusionally).

In their continually deflecting ironies, Palma's traditions depart from 'sympathy': the then-widespread notion that collectives are formed across time and place through the sharing of sentiments and through our capacity to experience imaginatively the feelings of other people. On that account, and reflecting on the legacy of eighteenth-century Scottish historiography, the philosopher Simon Blackburn remarks that 'imagination and sympathy … together enable us to reconstruct the influence of the circumstances that act on the mind as motives or reasons' (2006: 210). Not only would that allow a verdict (however complex) to be reached, but it would, in so doing, bond us both to the histories we thereby reconstruct, and to the collective – a society – to which we belong. By describing sympathy as a 'fairy tale', as he does in his story 'The Just and Sinners' (Justos y pecadores) (1861), Palma effects a distraction from it, just as he draws us to a mask and thus away from his own intense emotions: the disguise consists precisely of the text of narratives such as 'The Just and Sinners', where the notion of a verdict sits even in the title.

The many diverse cases cannot, then, be pieced together through narratives built on judgements and sympathy. In Elisa Sampson Vera Tudela's words, 'the anecdote has the quality of allowing the historical gaze to focus on the past's heterogeneity rather than on any sense of totality' (2012: 31). The very structure of Palma's collections of 'traditions' is a continual drawing away from any continuous, cogent structure or narrative core of cause and effect, of influence, of priority. Speaking of the third series, as well he might of any other, Palma remarks, 'I place in it neither presumption nor plan' (No finco en ella ni presunción ni plan). As in Nietzsche – Aníbal González notes – there is neither teleology nor geneaology in this history (1993: 81–2). We have, rather, miscellanies of disconnected anecdotes, jumping achronologically from one period to another. Each comes to dominate our perception as we read it, only then to slip away. To paraphrase *The Total Organisation of Matter*, every tradition can be a central reference point with respect to every other, and thus accidental with regard to every other. But – not least for that reason – the evocation of the 'case' matters still: the suggestion is not that a grand narrative is simply shattered into a multitude of micro-narratives. If 'verdict' and 'sympathy' cease to be what weaves the cases together, or what tests contingency against normativity, this does not mean that nothing now interlaces them.

Through the traditions, the historical case is, as it were, reapprehended as our being deflected through ironies, and, as we experience being deflected, so we trace pathways back and forth across instances of time, interlacing the imperial and post-imperial world. In Sampson Vera Tudela's words, Palma offers a 'voice uniting people, constructing communities across time and space' (2012: 38). This 'voice' distracts from 'soul' in an endless masking of our being's authentic emotion; it does not hold Being forever at a point of violent demise that bursts our bounds into sacrificial singing, as it does in Hernández or Marx (see Chapter 3). When we 'get' the *cháchara* – as we might 'get' 'Me myself' – we apprehend the connectedness of place and time, not as absolute irony, but as the very urge to deflect, emerging again and again, through the cases of history, a longing to evade pain, that extends outwards from Peru and its imperial past.

An endless totality of such deflection is evoked in the image of a 'Book of Books' (libro de los libros), at the end of the *Knight in Blue Boots* (*El caballero de las botas azules*) (1867) by the Spanish and Galician novelist, Rosalía de Castro. It is the revelation of this item that brings together all the narrative's protagonists, in an image of convergence and commonality. The apparently sacred and all-encompassing title replaces every other volume on sale in Madrid: these are all now destroyed, whereas it secures 'universal fame', 'bringing joy to the universe' (fama universal, haciendo la felicidad del universo), and becomes the most read book on the planet (Castro 1995: 344). We experience at the centre of things now, in the all-pervading Book of Books, only its decorative and alluring cover, not anything it might contain. The signifier has triumphed over the signified, turning our attention to the medium of signs themselves, as if in the most canonical accounts of modernity and the Death of the Author (Ginger 2005a). Throughout, the Knight, who delivers the blessed volume, has been a fascinating surface, all flashy footwear and pale make-up, recounting to no one who he is.

Like Palma, he has become a disguise. Such is this fellow of infinite jest: 'a strange spirit, not sublime, but new and joking, animates my whole being', he declares at the outset (un extraño espíritu no sublime, pero nuevo y burlón, anima todo mi ser) (1995a: 106). Jesting becomes the direct substitute of sublime Spirit, the presence of consciousness in the individual subject, and – as the Duke leads us to the Book of Books – in the collective destiny of humanity.

This transformation from man into Knight is a constant effort at letting go of suffering, of 'old memories' and 'eternal venom', a desire 'to live without struggling' (antiguos recuerdos, eterna pozoña, vivir sin luchar) (1995a: 229). In one final joke, once installed as the very centre of the novel and society, he simply departs without explanation: 'he uttered the loudest laugh, and … good night!' (lanzó la más sonora carcajada, y … ¡buenas noches!) (1995a: 344). There is only departure and distraction and deflection, where time is experienced as a constantly fleeing forwards, dashing from fashion to fashion, longing for blue boots or shiny book covers, in the constant exile that Baudelaire evokes. Everyone who pursues such modernity joins in a movement that is constant through the depths of time and across the globe. With the Book of Books, Castro offers us as a 'sovereign' governing centre only the Muse of Novelty, who proclaims her own cunning of history:

> Since the race of Cain spread across the earth, I have been travelling the universe showing my disciples the hidden/occult ways …. Until God calls men to judgement, I will live without ever ageing …. But blind humanity will forever follow my footsteps and will offer me worship, declaring me the sovereign of the world.[1]

In doing the bidding of Novelty, and leading the trajectory to the Book of Books, the Duke transfigures connections across place as well as time. He is linked variously to the Caucasus, the banks of the Jordan, Asia, China and Moravia; he speaks of the fate of women around the world, East and West (1995a: 114, 121–2, 133, 315, 333–4). He moves across the social spaces of Madrid, along the streets of the poor, in the salons of aristocrats, and the houses of the middling sort. Through his closer associates, he echoes Spain's connections to North-African Islam, and its imperial ventures. He is accompanied by Zuma, a Moor. He attracts both Europeans and the Marquise of Mari-Mari, proud Cuban and American, child of Spain's continuing, wealthy empire in the Caribbean, offering herself, a descendant of Montezuma, like the 'virgin America' (la virgen América) as if for colonial conquest (1995a: 150, 189, 195). From this nucleus, the Duke's fashions are desired across nations from English to Russian aristocrats (1995a: 315–16). His Book of Books will replace the flood of the local and cross-border trade (1995a: 259): Spanish publishing was now linked with transnational industry, after all (Martí-López 2002). But the whole form of his tale suggests the lack of any robustly articulated structure to such connections, which accumulate loosely, leaping abruptly from one mention or episode to the next. In the words of Wadda Ríos-Font, the novel 'is barely a story at all': the Duke 'officiates neither as an organising consciousness nor as a consciousness to be organised' (1997: 192). The lack of structured interplay suggests rather the Spanish Left's complaints: despite the revolutions, society has not been organised

---

[1] Desde que la raza de Caín se extendió por la tierra, recorro el universo enseñando a mis prosélitos los caminos ocultos …. Hasta que Dios llame a los hombres a juicio, viviré sin envejecer jamás …. Pero la ciega humanidad seguirá siempre mis pasos y me rendirá culto, proclamándome la soberana del mundo (1995a: 104–5).

Instead of modernity

on clear, correct principles of legitimacy articulated through history (Ginger 1999: 47–83; 2007a: 194–5). This is a grotesque parody of a Spirit of the Age.

Amid all this, we find deflection's counterpart to Baudelaire's dilating atavistic *mal*, to Nobas's gender-bending sacrifice of the nineteenth century, to the violation of our body's limits, to the death-pervaded irony of Melville, and to the switches between dominance and submission that we find in Matilde Díez or Manet. Ancient the Novelty may be, but its continual distractions draw us away from our connection to atavistic forces. There is no transcendent nor even a transfiguring eternal found in fashion. 'The devil?' the Muse exclaims – in stark contrast to Baudelaire – '¡What madness! Has the immortal Béranger (a French poet) not sung with great joy: *The devil is dead, dead is the devil?*' (¿El diablo? … ¡Qué locura! ¿Acaso el inmortal Béranger no ha cantado muy alegremente: *Ha muerto el diablo, el diablo ha muerto?*) (1995a: 99; original emphasis). In a determined effort at mutation for its own sake, the Muse breaks free of gendered limits, but does so in specific rejection of any cult of suffering and dying that might shatter the bounds of a body and let Being pour forth. It is precisely from such 'melancholic and terrorific lamentations' and suicidal longings that the Muse seeks to save the soon-to-be Duke, in the very moments before visible manifesting herself as an 'amphibious being', moustachioed, with long hair trailing over alluring half-naked shoulders (las melancólicas y terroríficas lamentaciones, un ser anfibio) (1995a: 102–3). The constant ironising has a deathliness about it, treating all words and signs as things that are beyond any intended meaning, as it does in Derrrida's *Voice and Phenomenon* (see Chapter 3): the Muse's emissary, the Duke, has a face of mortal pallor. Yet, if we attend to every transient moment as a new distraction, we experience, not the survival of texts and images through their deathliness, but rather their being buried.

There is no pastiche of what is classic, but only its being forever forgotten: there are no restless spirits fluttering in this world, no persistent presence of historic forces, no interest in relics of signs left by the dead, not even truly an interplay between the presence of beings and their absence. The latter is clearly the leading partner, continually erasing the former, ushering it away, rendering it unwelcome. The 'noble shadows' of past greats try to flee in shame, as they hear the taunts of the world (el mundo) saying *'You are gone!'* as 'it moves on' (*¡Ya fuisteis!*, y pasa adelante) (1995a: 91; original emphasis). Domination, there certainly is, in this constant pushing away, and opening of gaps in time, as there is in all the deflection, its continual denial of a connection. With that comes an allure, a bringing near as it forever moves away. The Muse appears with a whip and riding boots; the Knight humiliates his followers, and his admirers end up in chains processing behind the ever-elusive Duke. As readers attend to the enigma of the Knight – Lou Charnon-Deutsch has suggested – they expose themselves to possession by desire, just as characters become obsessed with the same insatiable longing (2010: 88). But this does not merge spirits, fuse cultures or cause history to resonate through its own depths. Rather it is what it is: a continual, mocking domination through irony's elusiveness, the constant, universal, superior sophistication of which Foster Wallace speaks, now relished for its own sake. The novel evokes a succession of literary visions, not least of gender, only to undermine each and every prescription, leaving nothing standing, Geraldine Lawless avers (2012). 'Spectators will wrack their brains to understand its plot, and I swear to you that they will not succeed …. *Bon courage* in laughing at yourself and vanquishing my friends and enemies', the Muse declares (Los espectadores se desvanecerán los sesos por comprender su argumento, y te juro que no lo conseguirán …. Valor, pues, para reírte de ti mismo y vencer a mis amigos y enemigos) (Castro 1995: 105–6).

Repose: forms of shared distraction

If, like the Duke, we are to seek to be free of suffering, to be released from sacrifice, to be without the hauntings of the past, this is what we must do. All of history, all of geography must do this: all of time and place would then belong to Novelty's Muse. Disarticulated, lacking the structure of a sublime Spirit of the Age, something of a joke, Spain would be a beacon to the world once more. But that is to see no further than the end of our nose, as Palma had it: we would attend only to the irony. The infinite jest matches what it seeks to replace, one universality much like the other. The transgender Muse sends out a dominant male who ends up, phallic wand in hand, gathering once proud Amazonian women now dressed as slaves to kiss his boots (1995: 333–4). The sign triumphs over the signified, but, like the *Logos*, offers us its own Book of Books. The male messiah – bringer of this insight – has ascended to 'elevated regions', and his statue now presides (elevadas regiones) (1995: 344). Uncontrolled crowds surge forward for the publication, desperate once more in desire, 'like a savage horde' (como una horda salvaje) (1995: 343). As Foucault's 'What Is an Author?' perhaps implies, the order that appears to replace substantive subjecthood and Being, even patriarchy, may be more of an equivalent to these than it appears; and it too will have been constituted in history. If we are to look further, to achieve repose while sensing all the emotional intensity it abandons, we need to attend instead to how all human history, all human geography might be seeking deflection, until the end of days, just as it sought a sublime Spirit to unite it. We journey through distraction, in the company of the Duke and of the Muse, only so that distraction might come undone. If we could do this, we would let go, stop 'clutching' (to use Cavell's verb), and find ourselves, free of such unending longing, but in awareness of how those desires arose.

In the work of the French illustrator Constantin Guys, it is as if the watercolour and ink were setting before us that longing for deflection and distraction, leaving us a world that is forever fading or faded, hardly realised, 'in incomplete genesis'. Guys was Baudelaire's archetypal 'painter of modern life', a flâneur, a stroller, drawing from observation at street (or room) level. Even in something as intense as a *Bazar of Voluptuousness* (*Bazar de volupté*) (1870), people, objects and surroundings together continuously dissipate. At times – as in the *Bazar* – costumes and bodies are all but transparent, and we see through them into the whiteness of the paper. The emotions involved in scenes, the flirting, the rampant sexuality, the treatment of women as sex objects, the male bravado, become in Guys's images ghostly experiences, barely etched into reality. This is to be disposed towards the world as something that desires its own continual dissolution, its letting go of its own realities, a leaping beyond that brings nearer only its own leaping beyond. We experience what it is forever to be losing our intensity of feeling and to wish to do so. Guys's *Woman with a Parasol* (*c.*1860–65, Getty Museum), for instance, is a subtle haze of blues and mauve tinges, with touches of white and a little pink. The observer seems hardly able to connect to this delicate, near-vanishing world, which seems barely palpable. Through the sensation of dissipation and of ever losing contact we experience the expanses of centuries and of geography, just as the Muse of Novelty presides over all time. In 'The Painter of Modern Life' – an essay later so often associated with the city of Paris – Baudelaire says of Guys that he is preoccupied with 'universal life', and that 'he is interested in the whole world; he wants to know, understand, appreciate all that happens on the surface of our spheroid' (la vie universelle; Il s'intéresse au monde entier; il veut savoir, comprendre, apprécier tout ce qui se passe a la surface de notre sphéroïde) (1965: II, 450, 446). Guys treats in the same manner everything from Queen Isabel at the Spanish Court, to soldiers of the Crimean War – that conflict at Europe and Asia's edge, which so appealed to Hunt, the painter of *The Scapegoat* –, to Guys's own French sense of similarity to Spain, an experience he shared with Bonheur or Manet. His *Girls on a Balcony* (1860) takes up a centuries-old Spanish subject of painting, from Murillo in the seventeenth century via Goya and Lucas in the nineteenth. If we are to be joined with everything across place and time, we must learn paradoxically to feel the letting go, the loosening of our clutching at the world.

Namelessness

At the end of his vast seven-volume evocation of social customs, *Yesterday, Today, and Tomorrow* (*Ayer, Hoy y Mañana*) (1863), the Spanish writer Antonio Flores imagines how the people of 1899 might view the passing of the mid-nineteenth century or the coming of their own descendants. He does so by recalling one of the most famous and influential poems in the Spanish language, Jorge Manrique's medieval verses on the death of his father: 'And since we see things *present*, / how in a moment they are gone / and finished, / if we judge wisely, / we will treat *things not yet come* / as if *past*' (Y pues vemos lo *presente* / cuán en punto se es ido, / y acabado, / si juzgamos sábiamente [*sic*] / daremos lo *no venido* / por *pasado*) (1863: VII, 328; original emphasis). The words appear to call for a tempered outlook free of any belief that history manifests substantive Being, but without giving ourselves in turn to distraction. As in Guys or Castro or Palma, this disposition seems to enable us to experience diverse things together over place and time. The words reference the three parts of Flores's work (past, present future), and, in so doing, present us with a view of the whole that is freed from chronology, for what is yet to come and what is present are all past. The words connect us to the depths of time of Hispanic and of Roman imperial culture through their neo-Stoicism. They remind us of the centuries-long fascination with that philosophy in Christian Spain, and, by extension, the assertion through the ages that Spain was the source of Roman Stoicism, by association with Seneca, born in Corduba (now Córdoba), Hispania. In the contained sobriety of Rosales's *Testament of Isabel the Catholic*, there is just such an echo of Spanish *senequismo*; perhaps in disposition, if not in overt philosophy, that links the *Testament* to its sister, classical Roman image, *The Death of Lucretia*.

All this may seem like an invitation to experience the entirety of transient history as sameness, with a steady, antique temper that has endured through time, to observe its shapes form and pass in ultimate similitude, with no direction or period dominating. Yet it is not quite or not just that. The seemingly conclusive quotation implies a warning: that even such an attitude may manifest and serve the interests of given people at a specific place and time, and that, paradoxically, selfishness is an affordance of a dispassionate sense of sameness. Manrique's ancient words are offered to us as the thoughts of the future when it ignores the people of the past and its own future: 'They [the people of tomorrow) say nothing, and if they were to say anything they would rinse their mouth with these verses of Jorge Manrique' (Nada dicen, y si algo dijeran se enjuagarían la boca con estos versos de Jorge Manrique) (1863: VII, 328). The modern world says, 'what was not of its year is no source of tears' (lo que no fue en su año no es en su daño; literally, 'what was not in its year was not to its harm') (1863: VII, 327). Manrique's ancient verses have been appropriated to a particularly callous version of modernity in which one need care neither about the causes nor the consequences of the present day. To attend to distraction as distraction – in the fashion that Palma and Castro would soon encourage, or that is manifest in Guys's images – may unwittingly hand to deflection its ultimate triumph and self-justification. Apparent release becomes a form of entrapment within a seemingly localised historical outlook.

Always seemingly historicising, *Yesterday, Today, and Tomorrow* presents the quest for repose as one of many urges for similitude that have arisen in history. Manrique's words are simply the last vision in the book, and among the earliest chronologically, of a multitude of experiences of sameness that Flores explores as fascinating and threatening possibilities. It is in this specific sense that *Yesterday, Today and Tomorrow* is presented as a series of 'pictures of customs' (cuadros de costumbres), transient forms of life and their affordances. Martina Lauster (2007) has shown how across Europe such essays offered, through their typologies, a way of understanding the shapes and structures that society adopts in time. In Flores, each and the opposite of each is undermined, serving his moderate conservative outlook by blunting every ideological turn, preventing any too-decisive thrust of society in any direction (Ginger 2012a: 275–6). Towering in the Madrid of *Tomorrow*, for example, we find the emblematic Grand Hotel of Transatlantic Unity (Gran Hotel de la Unidad Tras-Atlántica), covering 2,780,480 square feet, and incorporating a bullring and theatre. Built in a spirit of 'international fraternity' (fraternidad internacional) by French financiers, along with other similar edifices across Europe, it has worldwide shareholders. This variety of futuristic oneness involves a combination of capital, accountability and publicity, rendering every person's business utterly transparent. Flores tells us in a sinister twist that not only do the Grand Hotel's walls have ears, but they also speak. For the sake of smoothness of administration, as of accountability and accountancy (contabilidad), human beings staying at the hotel are assigned colours and numbers instead of names (1863: VI, 212–14). Interchangeable symbols and mathematical figures take the place of persons. 'Madrid becomes no longer a city of people,' Rebecca Haidt has remarked, 'but, rather, a city of residual effects of mass production' (2011: 20).

In a preceding bout of similitude, the transition from *Tomorrow* to *Today* offers a way of living in which a place that was putatively different – Spain – sealed off in its own location, seeks, in opening up, to be like its neighbour. As in the sacrifice that we saw in Chapter 3, this urge is characterised by sickness, death and wounding, destroying a prior way of life, seeking to free a collective subject from its bounds. The cause of *Yesterday*'s death, we are told, is 'French pneumonia, complicated with a touch of gastro-encyclopeditis and philosophical rheumatism' (pulmonía francesa, complicada con algo de gastro-enciclopeditis y reumatismo filosófico) (1863: II, 441). This affliction involves an urge to sudden and dramatic transformation: 'we wanted to make ourselves wise and perfectly wise in a single blow' (quisimos hacernos de un golpe sabios y sabios completos) (1863: III, xvi–xvii). Flores's phrasing underlines the violence and the persecutory mentality lurking in that desire: a wish to purge one thing in the name of another, provoking a converse resistance. 'We have lived half of the nineteenth century in a society of persecuted and persecutors' (hemos vivido la mitad del siglo XIX en una sociedad de perseguidos y perseguidores) (1863: III, xvi). The upshot, by mid-century, is a longed-for sameness sustained only by repression of particularity, a world of deception and falsification. In a vivid image, we see Spanish women engaging in whitening: it is not enough to try to look French if one's skin and hair are dark (1863: V, 48–50).

As the concealed hair and skin colour imply, each historic version of similitude risks being undone from within by particularity. Each is exposed, like Manrique's words, as apparently specific to localised outlooks – the rise of capital, the obsession with Frenchness – reversing the flow from similarity back to the particular. The mid-century desire to see everything in identical terms, found in the mania for statistics rather than persons (1863: III, 152), in the universal grammar and encyclopedic knowledge in which all is to be subsumed (1863: V, 107), is presented as a fashion. If such sentiments echo later suspicions that universalism is a mere projection of local preferences, the resistance to the various similitudes fares no better across the seven volumes. Against *Today* and *Tomorrow*'s version of sameness, Flores holds up a notion of the human person and, relatedly, the specific character of local customs (Ginger 2005b). That notion of personality is core to the forms of life that *Today* and *Tomorrow* replace: the world of *Yesterday*. Boundedness to a place and time, a deliberate lack of openness to a wider world, was what protected person and character from a descent into sameness. Precisely for that reason, it is – as Flores starkly puts it – obscurantist: its last will and testament is signed by Mr Candid Backwardness (Cándido Retroceso), son of Silvestre Terror and Barbara Muzzle (Bárbara Mordaza) (1863: I, 419). For the same reason the happy ending of *Tomorrow* is pointedly unconvincing: the independent woman Safo, previously freed from historical gender roles, is guided by a provincial man – Venancio – to understand the errors of the modern world, and ends up married to him. Not only does particularity fail to offer a plausible alternative, but the very attempt to localise outlooks in specific contexts of place and time turns out to fail: Jameson's cry of 'always historicise', the epistemic breaks of Foucault's *Archaeology of Knowledge*, Bhabha's 'location of culture', would not help us here. Geraldine Lawless (2018) has pointed out how – in multiplying ironies and self-contradictions, amid a multitude of unreliable narrators across *Yesterday, Today and Tomorrow* – the very discourse of historisisation flounders, revealing itself as simply one more possible but flawed form of life (2018).

If all sameness turns out to be limitation, and limitation begs for relief through sameness, we seem to be at the kind of impasse whose overcoming this present book evokes. In Lawless's words (2018) – so at odds with any notion of a 'location of culture' – 'it is impossible for the reader to establish a position, in either a literal or figurative sense. He or she ... is left with nowhere to stand'. Manrique-like repose has not freed us from this. The final thing we might articulate – Flores suggests – is that all such talk about similitude and particularity has ended up as so much nonsense: 'Mad was the world / a hundred years back, / mad they bequeathed it to us, / mad we hand it on, / mad it continues to be, / mad it will die' (Loco estaba el mundo / cien años atrás, / loco nos lo dieron, / loco le entregamos, / loco sigue siendo, / loco morirá) (1863: VII, 327). While providing its own vision of sameness across place and time, the thought appears to offer little by way of immediate guidance. It is as if we were to turn for advice to the Cheshire Cat only to be assured once more that 'we're all mad here'. Worse still, there is no cogent notion of madness without a test of sanity, and, in *Yesterday, Today and Tomorrow*, there is no explicit candidate for reasonableness, or of proper human life, not even the authorial voice itself. There is, as it were, an unchecked 'lavishness' of forms of life – to borrow once more Cavell's choice of word – but without even any embracing of 'deferral', that Derrida-like spawning of differences and divergence. Sameness and difference, centring an experience in a place and time, and opening up its bounds, all lead back to something we cannot even call *insanity*, because we have nothing with which to compare it. We are denied the consolation even of sincerely declaring ourselves mad.

If there is to be relief from this joke world, a way out – Flores suggests – it will come from an outlook that cannot be concretised in words or an explicit mode of behaviour. The moment that we do so, we end up in one of the confounding forms of life. We cannot articulate this alternative form of life, we cannot make it a 'picture of customs', without destroying it. Conversely, the attitude that *Yesterday, Today and Tomorrow* engenders does not set us absolutely outside of the many ways of being across place and time. It is less a detachment from them – which Flores undermines – than it is a manner of experiencing them. Paradoxically, in the vast number of words that constitute *Yesterday, Today, and Tomorrow*, we have, as it were, an inversion of Whitman's 'Me myself': we are both 'in and out of the game', but without giving ourselves in enthusiasm to its verbosity, to its embodied ventriloquised voices, in an outpouring across place and time. We are left with a nameless awareness, suffusing all forms of life, and centred on none of them. Of this, we cannot speak, but we may experience it, and a work of art – Flores's museums of images – may stimulate us to do so. Ultimately, there either is such a viable disposition available to us, or there is not. It is not a matter on which we can engage in further argument. If we not to concretise the experience itself, we could be authentically aware of any place and time in all its lavishness. Out of our silence, we could articulate the galleries of history, of possible forms of life.

Like a shadow of 'Me myself', this notion entails no commitments so great as an ontology, or metaphysics, or even epistemology, with which it might easily be mistaken. In the previous paragraph I echoed Wittgenstein's famous words at the end of the *Tractatus*, 'what we cannot speak about we must pass over in silence' (*TLP* §7). But there is no implication here that at the limits of our cogent speech we encounter 'things that cannot be put into words' that 'make themselves manifest' and are thus 'mystical' (*TLP* §6.522), a 'feeling the whole world as a limited whole … sub specie aeternitatis' (*TLP* §6.45). Nor is this one of the many philosophical claims that all phenomenal Being is founded on its own ultimate absence, as in Boon's Buddhist statement about a universe of endless similarity where 'the emptiness of all phenomena … is what makes it possible for anything to appear at all' (2013: loc.311–15). It is not even an attempt to engage in philosophical discourse with such terms of reference, as we might find in Agamben or in Vattimo's 'weak thought'. The emphasis here on something nameless is, rather, with regard to an attitude, a mood or disposition: a willingness not to concretise by naming which, in its very 'passivity' and 'poverty', enables us to experience – in apparent paradox, to articulate – all ways of being across time (past, present and future) without, in the process, being lost.

Between and among the forms of life, then, we may experience this specific kind of muteness. The latter is made manifest in images showing scenes before and after a point in history, such as we find in the lithographic series, *Yesteryear and This Year* (*Antaño y Hogaño*) by Flores's contemporary, the illustrator Francisco Ortego. A space sits between each successive pairing of images, one showing life before 1808, the other scenes from the mid-century. Thus, a gap rests between a depiction of men and women pre-1808 ('Each one with their one each' (Cada cual con su cada cual)) and another for the mid-nineteenth century ('There are no more Pyrenees' (Ya no hay más Pirineos)) (Figure 15). In the first, each biological gender sits rigidly in line, separated by an austere table; in the other, men and women loll across one another in a lavish setting. Despite the chronology, we have no reason to view one image before the other: both are simultaneous on the page. Through the mutating similarity of their pairings, the visions flicker: the separations closing and opening, the lines straightening and curving, the humans tensing and relaxing, and vice versa. There is not, as there is in Manet, an ultimately dominant image, nor, as in Lucas, the offer of painterly routes from one to the other. Rather, the flickering itself comes into view, on

15 Ortego, 'Each one with their one each' / 'There are no more Pyrenees'

its own terms. We saw in Manet how in any such flickering there is an implied gap: the absence of any tracing of the mutating lines, the difference that splits the two images apart. In Ortego, unlike in Manet, that gap is exhibited directly to us. What we actually see if we look at the illustration's centre with the greatest possible care is the medium of empty paper itself, bereft of ink's eloquence and outpouring. The suggestion is that we might attend to the blankness of the page itself in order to be able to attend authentically to all other things. In drawing back into its blanking, our viewing would expand across place and time, and into the lines that are drawn. To reverse the description of Bayoán, this is the everything of a nothing.

Of extremes

Early in his *Excursion to the Ranquel Indians* (*Una excursión a los indios ranqueles*) (1870), the Argentine military officer Lucio V. Mansilla declares: 'Whatever people say, if happiness exists, if we can specify and define it, it lies at the extremes' (Digan lo que quieran, si la felicidad existe, si la podemos concretar y definir, ella está en los extremos) (2018: loc.457). 'Who understands the satisfactions of middle terms?', he asks disdainfully (¿quién comprende las satisfacciones de los términos medios?) (2018: loc.478). Such sentiments might seem at odds with what we have seen of tempered repose throughout this chapter. Equally, the absence or weakening of a controlling centre depends upon and refreshes our disposition to the contrast between opposing worlds, the lurching between forms of life without transition: the sudden death of 'Yesterday' and 'Today' in Flores, the flipping between now and then in Ortego, Rosales's standoff of Carlos and Juan de Austria, the disconnected elements of the *Real Allegory*, the contrasting destiny of Laso's children. The gap that opens up in any flickering leaves us without visible 'middle terms'. At the very end, Mansilla brings to the fore this relationship between the questing for 'extremes' and the destination of tranquillity: 'the day was calm, my soul joyful', he declares (El día estaba en calma, mi alma alegre) (2018: loc.9891). There is no simple opposition between the more agitated or impassioned moods we have found in previous chapters – the continual leaping, the sacrifice and insanity – and the repose sought here. The way to greater serenity in our experience of connections follows the path of all that is troubling about them, like the citizens of Madrid pursuing Castro's Knight. Mansilla's *Excursion* explicitly offers us a travel guide through such sensations.

The key 'extremes' that Mansilla explores in the *Excursion* are those purportedly dividing humanity into two: the civilisation and barbarism that so fascinated Argentine intellectuals since Sarmiento (see Chapters 1 and 3). Mansilla pursues the dichotomy so as to find the sameness of human beings through them. 'Civilisation and barbarism shake hands;' he comments, 'humanity will be saved because the extremes touch one another' (La civilización y la barbarie se dan la mano; la humanidad se salvará porque los extremos se tocan) (2018: loc.3086). 'I believe in the unity of the human species', he affirms (Creo en la unidad de la especie humana) (2018: loc.692). The point is not that we renounce emotional commitment to 'extremes' by showing, through reasoning and social and historical observation, how apparently diverging viewpoints have things fundamentally in common. To do this would be to pursue 'middle terms', by establishing a *Logos*, or a univocal political and national narrative that could mediate. This, Hernán Feldman (2010) observes, Mansilla seems to eschew. The writer's disdain for the 'theory of historical fatality' implies contempt for a core dialectic from which humanity's future might be deduced (teoría de la fatalidad histórica) (2018: loc.9879). Likewise, if the undertaking has something in common with the deconstruction of binary opposites, it is less in the careful intellectual exposure of unsustainable divides – the mirror image of a *Logos* – than it is in the sensation of such an enterprise, the painstaking groping through oppositions until these collapse upon themselves, just as Flores pursues a given form of life until its death. As Mansilla's notion of an 'excursion' – an 'ex-cursus', a going outwards – suggests, what really matters is the lived experience of the divergence itself, the pulling apart across a gap. The prose – first published in instalments – features extensive meanderings off topic and abrupt juxtapositions.

Mansilla physically transports himself as far as he can out of one form of life – that of his native Argentina – and into its supposed 'other': that of the Ranqueles, an indigenous people to the south of what was then the Argentine frontier. The extremity is not a matter of geographical distance: Mansilla reminds us that he is a seasoned traveller, a global Argentine who has journeyed 'through India, through Africa, through Europe, through America' (por la India, por África, por Europa, por América) (2018: loc.1807). Rather, what matters is the supposed stepping out of one world order of constituted states into another ('barbarism'), across something which, for that very reason, Mansilla does not recognise as an 'international frontier' (frontera internacional) (2018: loc.519). The influential Argentine theorist Sylvia Molloy observes that Mansilla's writing style and his topological journeying evoke an abandonment of origins (1991: 169–73). It is this experience of extreme journeying – literal and metaphorical – in itself that brings forth the latent sameness of 'extremes', the supposedly incompatible forms of life. It is precisely when deep inside Ranquel territory, and having stood before their large assembly to explain Argentine constitutional procedures, that Mansilla muses, 'it seemed to me that between the Indian's manner of proceeding and mine, there was a perfect similitude. … Is it not true that the case was identical?' (me parecía que entre la manera de discurrir de los indios y la mía, había una perfecta similitud. … ¿No es verdad que el caso era idéntico?) (2018: loc.7634–5). Far beyond the frontier, we find ourselves in the world of Buenos Aires.

To the fore here is a mode of perceiving things such that by seeing and sensing things one way, we find ourselves with their contrary: far becomes near, relief becomes torment, barbarism civilisation. It is such a conjunction that Mansilla describes in his final words as 'conciousness of myself' (conciencia de mí mismo) (2018: 9894). Such now is subjecthood. In one passage, Mansilla describes how, as he and his men travelled during a cloudy night, the light effects made distance impossible to judge, leading them into constant error. Branches that seemed far off turned out to be close enough to lash them. 'Does the same not happen to us on the path of life?' Mansilla asks, 'We think we are on the edge of the longed-for beach and we are enveloped by the angry whirl' (¿No sucede en el sendero de la vida … lo mismo …? … Nos creemos al borde de la playa apetecida y nos envuelve la vorágine irritada) (2018: loc.2063). The point is not a delirious erasure of all boundaries, a homogenising of all things, but rather a continual, dreamlike flipping of viewpoints, without the loss of any of them – as if, in Ortego, between today and yesteryear – until we experience extremes as jumping back and forth into one another through their own rival claims. In a resonant, shaggy-dog tale, recounted by one of Mansilla's soldiers, we hear of Siamese twins who 'with one mouth drank cow's milk, and the other a goat's; who with one said yes and with the other no; who with one sang and with the other cried, mounting through that dualism infernal disputes and rows' (que con una boca bebía leche de vaca y con la otra de cabra; que con una decía que sí y la otra no; que con una lloraba y con la otra cantaba, armando mediante ese dualismo unas disputas y camorras infernales) (2018: loc.2082). For all Mansilla's professed scepticism about the particular tale, the image resonates with parallel instances across the *Excursion*.

'We live from surprise to surprise, from revelation to revelation, from victory to victory, from defeat to defeat', Mansilla declares, 'We are something more than a dualism; we are something complex, complicated or indecipherable' (Vivimos de sorpresa en sorpresa, de revelación en revelación, de victoria en victoria, de derrota en derrota. Somos algo más que un dualismo; somos algo complejo, complicado o indescifrable) (2018: loc.3790). In our see-sawing perception of rival viewpoints ('dualism', in Mansilla's terms), we experience primarily the enigmatic shifting itself, just as in Ortego and Flores we come to encounter opposing lifeworlds in the nameless, mute quality through which they are articulated. Samuel Monder and Eva-Lynn Alicia Jagoe have underlined the queerness at the heart of this experience, male gender boundaries giving way as self flips into other: the narrative voice merges with other men gathered around campfires telling tales; Mansilla is tender towards a friend – Máximo Alcorta – who loves both sexes; he wears the marriage cape of Mariano Rosas (the indigenous leader), whose name derives from the dictator who persecuted Sarmiento and was Mansilla's uncle; he lingers over virile gaucho bodies (Monder 2008: 68, 72; Jagoe 2008: 76–8). If Sarmiento sunders humanity into extremes – the civilised and the barbaric (Rosas, the *gauchos*, the indigenous) – homoerotic desire surges from the opposition, pushing away to nearer bring, evoking the likeness of humanity through 'same-sex' attraction, as happens with Courbet's *Wrestlers*. If – as Alonso and Molloy suppose – there is a disturbed family drama here, an Oedipal undoing of Sarmiento's text *Facundo* (Molloy 1991: 161–2, 178–80; Alonso 1998: 82–107), it surges from a troubled desire for father figures, born of rather than collapsing the tensions with and between them.

With the sensation that the very core of our subjecthood (individual and collective) is gnomic, comes reserve, a tempering of judgement. Of the alternating, mutating extremes, Mansilla remarks: 'From the heart are born the great attachments and the great hatreds …. By what impulses? What yesterday beautified my life, today I find dreary …. The thing is we do not understand ourselves' (Del corazón nacen los grandes afectos y los grandes odios …. ¿A impulso de qué? …. Lo que ayer embellecía mi vida hoy me hastía …. Es que no nos entendemos) (2018: loc.3811). 'For myself, when it comes to the thoughts of a fellow human,' he tells us, 'I always keep in mind the saying of a moralist of note …: the law of God that prohibits temerary judgements is not only the law of charity, but of justice and sound reasoning' (Yo, cuando se trata de los pensamientos del prójimo, siempre tengo presente el dicho de cierto moralista de nota …: la ley de Dios que prohíbe los juicios temerarios es no solamente ley de caridad, sino de justicia y buena lógica) (2018: loc.4688–94).

We must approach predominant schemes of explanation in a spirit of failure that leads through them to ostensibly less controlling, less oppressive kinds of similitude. We must become disposed to experience them as flailing. This is not a denial of such narratives and their prejudices, as numerous scholars have pointed out. Joy in homosociality excludes women as supposedly inarticulate (Hanway 2003: 127–31; Monder 2008: 73); encounters with enigmas confirm that women are unknowable and that the indigenous keep secrets and are untrustworthy (Monder 2008: 64; Armillas-Tiseyra 2008: 71). Mansilla sees himself as entering *terra nullius* – land that can be appropriated because it 'belongs' to no one: he speaks of a kind of transculturation and contact zone, a mixing of races, only so that the indigenous might be assimilated and whitened, departing from his origin only to join the other to it (Armillas-Tiseyra 2008). The political dispute in which he is involved is not about the rights of conquest, but about whether to exterminate. More mundanely, it expresses a spat with Sarmiento: the President benefited from Mansilla's support only to refuse him government office, while Mansilla faced charges of unlawful execution of a soldier for which Sarmiento would condemn him (Alonso 1998: 90–1, 98–101).

But, if he rides out under such designs, Mansilla's writing opens up an alternate prospect: that we could be baffled by their fundamental terms. For Jagoe, as for Armillas-Tiseyra, the constant contradictions of the *Excursion* point beyond any authoritative narrative – including white supremacy – that seeks to contain them (Jagoe 2008: 87; Armillas-Tiseyra 2008: 76). Acknowledging this, disposed to flip between extremes, in the expectation that they will fail us, we might attain a restful unity in humility.

Failure, care and the nature of connections

In a disposition towards failure, vast visions of interconnectedness are experienced as coming undone and that coming undone discloses their true interconnection, in a nothing that is everything. Here we discern a potentiality – an affordance – within expansive, encompassing accounts of the world, the possibility for connection and disconnection to resemble one another, to become the same. Caroline Levine suggests that the very extensiveness of long nineteenth-century novels, like Dickens's *Bleak House*, means that their form has the inherent potential to be supreme instances of connectedness (2017: 127). The French writer Flaubert's *Sentimental Education* (*Education sentimentale*) (1869) evokes this possibility only to show its potential to unmake itself, as it sets before us the complex interlocking dynamics of individual lives and of political, social, cultural and economic events. The work undoes from within the very practice of making such nodes of connection. It thus goes to the heart of what – according to Levine – the efforts at connectedness hold in common between a notion of culture as a bounded whole – a form of life with a central principle – and a notion of cultural networks as unbounded, endless successions of linkages (2017: 117–22). Influentially, Jonathan Culler asserts that *Sentimental Education* was 'written *against* the novel as institution' (1974: 105); but one might say, rather, that it goes under the bonnet of the 'novel as institution', into its innermost workings, so as to transform these in detail from within, to re-effect their connections paradoxically through the very process of unmaking.

The novel is on a fairly imposing scale, extending over three parts. The lives of many characters are caught up in the 1848 Revolution and the events that would lead to the Second French Empire under Napoleon III. In turn, 1848 in Paris is pointedly hailed as a 'world-historical' event, like the execution of Maximilian in Mexico some years later. That is to say, whether in actuality or potential, it could reshape all human life, bringing together all humanity, enabling one location in place and time – the French capital – to dilate in significance across geography and history beyond its originary bounds. We hear a voice saying: 'Some journalists, chatting right now in front of me, were saying we're going to liberate Poland and Italy! No more kings, you understand? *The whole earth free! The whole earth free!*' (Des journalistes, qui causaient tout à l'heure devant moi, disaient qu'on va affranchir la Pologne et l'Italie! Plus de rois, comprenez-vous? *Toute la terre libre! toute la terre libre!*)

(2019a: 286; my emphasis). By taking up such cries in its monumental, bold literary form, the very writing of the novel parallels the French cultural universalism that we saw echoed in Manet. Such thinking fed in turn on the notion that Paris might be the capital of the nineteenth century, to borrow Benjamin's phrase (2002: 32).

In scenes late on in Part 3, for example, we find suggested how these wider social and realities might be carefully intertwined with the minutiae of personal lives in a sprawling novel. At such points where the text seems most intricately woven together it can, at the same glance, appear like a miscellaneous collage, mere juxtapositions. Structurally in the novel, we experience a lesson in feelings, a *Sentimental Education*: how, at each detailed turn, the coming together of disparate things, there could be a sensation of a lack, an opening 'gap', like that seen more starkly when Juan de Austria encounters the Emperor Carlos, or as the historical periods of *Today, Yesterday, Tomorrow* are stuck together. Characteristically – Larry Schehr observes – 'failure of desire' is equated with 'failure of style' (1997: 210–11). At one point, the character Mme Dambreuse insists on going to the auction of the goods of the Arnoux family who have fled financial disaster. The main protagonist Frédéric Moreau had met her husband, a wealthy businessman, earlier on at the suggestion of a childhood friend, Deslauriers. Mme Arnoux, in turn, is a woman whom Frédéric met casually and with whom he became obsessed at the outset of the novel. Following the auction, Frédéric refuses to join Dambreuse in her carriage, abruptly breaking with her, then feeling cowardly. The next thing we know – the following morning – a state of siege is declared in Paris. The placing of these things together leaves us with no clear sense of how they are actually joined. Rather, we simply find a series of statements beginning: 'The next morning, his servant brought him the news' (Le lendemain matin, son domestique lui apprit les nouvelles) (2019a: 355).

The linkages come together and disperse, like Fortuny's minute brushstrokes and traces of light, without 'soul and passion'. As this happens, intense emotions and fervent beliefs are continuously lost even as they form. *Sentimental Education* frequently emulates the short paragraphs and at times lapidary sentences and clauses fashionable among many mid-century writers from Émile de Girardin and Alphone Karr in France to Pedro de Alarcón and Agustín Bonnat in Spain. Even when humorous, they evoke powerful but transient impressions, such as we saw in Gorriti or Palma's prose. Yet Flaubert's relentless hopping from one phrase to the next may offer, just as easily, a repetitive staccato rhythm which the words serve to beat out, as if any feelings or meanings, comic or otherwise, were secondary, as if in a hollowing out of Echo's poetics. The great debates of the time float somewhat free of any depth or substance beyond the words in which they are cast, even as ideologies are stacked abruptly against each other, like yesteryear and today in Flores or Ortego. 'Sénécal – who had a pointed skull – thought only in terms of systems. Regimbart, on the other hand, saw only facts in the facts', we read (Sénécal – qui avait un crâne en pointe – ne considérait que les systèmes. Regimbart, au contraire, ne voyait dans les faits que les faits) (2019: 61).

The centrepiece of this structure – just as in Hostos's *Pilgrimage* – is a life that is at once individual and a phenomenology of universal relevance. The mirror image of Bayoán, Frédéric is described succinctly at one point as the 'man with every weakness' (homme de toutes les faiblesses) (2019a: 260). He is presented not simply as typical of the failings of his time, but as a man transfigured into failure itself. He is thus incarnate, that continual letting go, not so much an absence as an ever-slipping grasp, unable to dominate and possess. At the outset of this chapter, I suggested that 'weak thought' and 'weak networks' are apt phrases for repose, not just because they express attenuated yet real connectedness, but because of the feeling of weakness itself, the exploration of what it is like to be weak, in body and in mind. Failing, abortive or just unmotivated connections characterise Frédéric's personal relationships, so crucial to the narrative structure. His obsession with Mme Arnoux, whom he pursues on and off with varying amounts of energy, has no obvious explanation. We are simply told in one short paragraph when he first sees her: 'It was like an apparition' (Ce fut comme une apparition) (2019a: 16). When they are to meet for a tryst in Part 2, she does not attend; and in a crucial meeting where they kiss, his lover Rosannette suddenly interrupts, taking him off to inform him she is pregnant (2019a: 309–10). The child dies not long after (2019: 343), just as so little else lasts in Frédéric's flitting love affairs.

A life that is not simply a failure, but failure itself, is unable to act as a 'middle term' amid contrasting lives and ways of life, 'extremes' (such as Sénécal and Regimbart). It cannot effect any kind of mediation between all the things juxtaposed in a given place and time. There can be no dialectical motor of history here, driving us from 'extreme' to 'extreme' onward each time to a further resolution. Rather, what Frédéric's incarnation of failure brings to the fore is its own version of friendship – of meeting – the very making of an intimate connection that we found in Chapter 1 of this present book. The one attachment that recurs right to the end is with his childhood companion Deslauriers, their reconciliation brought about, we are told, 'by the fatal force of their nature' (par la fatalité de leur nature) (2019a: 362). Among the things they share is an abiding lack of success in love. At the end, Deslauriers has been abruptly abandoned by his wife, Frédéric's once-beloved Louise who has run off with a singer; Frédéric has split up with Mme Dambreuse. Suggestively, when they settle on a favoured anecdote of their finest hour, they come up with an incident back in 1837 when Frédéric, faced with available women in a brothel, ran away, Deslauriers following in his wake. It is a notable non-event, which, we are assured, was not forgotten three years after the event, and on which they now dwell at length (2019a: 364). Its fascination as a form of storytelling echoes the approach taken by the novel as a whole, the affordances of its expansive literary form itself. The entire plot flows out from Frédéric's failed affair with Mme Arnoux – initiated at the start – and in its longer back story from Frédéric and Deslaurier's youthful companionship extending into their interlocking groups of friends.

The intimacy of friendship that we saw in Chapter 1 – Laguna and El Pollo, Nietzsche and Wagner – brings about a closeness to far-off things precisely through its distance from them. Its 'blending' (*mixtura*) unites great swathes of time and place. Here, to care for what happens in this novel and for its protagonists is to care for awkward juxtaposition. It is to care for failure as of the very nature of connections. Undeniably, this vision of friendship as connector is exhibited (exposed even) as a mode of homosociality, leaving powerful women to one side (Orr 2005). In a study of *Sentimental Education*, Mary Orr shows how sentiments expressed by male characters, not least the fraternal democracy of 1848, are habitually iterations of patriarchal dominance. These had been embedded in nineteenth-century French law and society since the Code Napoléon. Out of all that emerges the tender, sensual intimations of nascent notions of homosexuality and bisexuality in Frédéric and Deslaurier's relationship, which informs the novel's whole aesthetic, the work's 'bitextuality' (2000: 89–117, 209). It is tempting to spy here simply a mirroring of phallogocentrism, a reiteration of male control, of an authoritative true language owned by men, even as the power of the phallus seems to be denied. Frédéric and Deslauriers flee the penetration of women in a brothel, a place where females are at the paid whim of men; but this reinforces male togetherness and conversation. In parallel – Orr suggests – even as the order of the great novel breaks down, Flaubert reasserts masculine control through his obsessively crafted style (2000: 116–17, 201–10): those exquisitely realised, intricate patterns of disconnection between one piece of language and another, and between any piece of language and a compelling meaning.

Across some of the profoundest disputes about *Sentimental Education* runs a shared assertion that Flaubert's style offers a recognition – an *anagnorisis* – of the true nature of representation through signs, and with it a new plane of discourse. For Culler, Flaubert exposes all representation through signs as arbitrary and without underpinning sense (1974: 95–156). For Knight, Flaubert positively discloses and embraces the very nature of representation and its literary illusions, as if distilling its purified state (1985: 74–102). As we saw in the Introduction to this present book, such claims rehearse assertions in some key Post-Structuralist texts: a distinct era of cultural modernity was inaugurated in mid-century Paris, for better or for worse. But if Flaubert's style transfigures the form of the expansive nineteenth-century novel, that transfiguration is a giving up. It is weakness, it is failure: that is what is recognised in companionship at the end. D.A. Williams has aptly observed that the final encounter of Frédéric and Deslauriers is anything but an 'apotheosis' (1987: 191). As such it cannot offer anything so robust, so definitive, as the disclosure of literariness, or the cult of the arbitrary sign and its 'arche-writing', or even the emergence of presence through absence such as Unwin (2011) discerns. In this transfiguration, every meeting – every intricate node of connection – invites us to care for renunciation, in its own spirit of friendship. And – as we saw in Chapter 1 – friendship (so understood) is not an instantiation of any general ideal at all, but rather an intimacy with the particular, with no ultimate justification. We care as we let go of each specific instance of connection, simply because we care for it in the awkwardness of its juxtapositions.

With this mirror image of 'meeting' comes a corresponding version of sacrifice and of liberation through domination, just as through their own book of disconnected narrative strands, the Knight in Blue Boots wore the face of mortality and his Muse carried a whip. As failure follows failure, and one thing is juxtaposed to yet another, there is a same-y quality to the whole through all its complex, varied convolutions, forcefully exercised on the reader, and devastating expectations of a novel. The American novelist Henry James famously compared reading *The Sentimental Education* to 'masticating ashes and sawdust': 'the book is in a single word a *dead* one', he pronounced (1984: 176). *Sentimental Education* has everything that enlivens many of the great, long novels of the nineteenth century: the intricate intertwining of lives, the interweaving of large-scale events and individual persons. Yet, the incapacity of these effectively to join up is like massive failure across the organs of a complex being, a death of sorts. Or, better put, it is a kind of 'limbo', as connection and disconnection fuse across the whole text, leaving us with something alive and dead at the same time, not unlike the taxidermied parrot of *A Simple Heart*.

Universalisms may be associated with the annihilation of specific ways of being – of difference – and thence with sacrificial violence at its most brutal. In the repose brought by failure, we find an evening out, less through direct violence than through the draining away of life, the senselessness of endless juxtaposition. In its pale reflection of French universalisms, the *Sentimental Education* brings forth from Paris a mastication of sawdust and ashes that could consume the world, chewing it with the monotony of a cow where *Martín Fierro* offers up bloody slaughter. The same-y quality of the whole text places similitude centre-stage: everything resembles everything else, in a spirit of uninterest that provokes and intimates fascination. Culler speaks of 'homogeneity' effected through 'emptiness' (1974: 156); Dorothy Kelly of an endless oscillation of repeated, hollow forms (1989). In one telling phrase, the novel remarks on 'what broad depths of indifference the world/everyone possesses' (quel large fonds d'indifférence le monde possède) (2019a: 210).

Like Manet, Flaubert makes a show of how little obvious affection his characters or subjects inspire. Like Manet too, with his broad areas of juxtaposed colour, Flaubert does this at the level of technique in a given section as much as of the whole. He does so – again like Manet – in such a way as to suggest a web of intricate interconnections. The emotional pulling or pushing away, the distancing thus acts as a form of attraction (and vice versa): people – readers included – are drawn to one another in their very separation. As in Manet's *Olympia*, disdain is allure, allure disdain. Flaubert relentlessly, dominatingly overwhelms the reader with sentence after sentence redolent with indifference over hundreds of pages, written with painstaking care. Likewise, the anecdote of failure and disconnection with which the novel ends really is memorable, effecting an attachment between the readers and two friends, just as it affirms the latters' companionship.

Beyond interpretation: deathly attachments, analogy and sickness

We saw in Chapter 3 how accumulations of signs and of pastiche might evince an obsessive attachment to mortality, to limbo, and to a living death as aesthetic experiences, irreducible to interpretation or to contextualisation. We found such a thing likewise in the unsettling 'pain freely accepted', in its world of analogy and conflation. In the pursuit of repose, we find shadows of such notions, just as we have encountered shades of grand schemas of sameness, of affordances of vast artworks, of dominant disdain, of delirium and of sacrifice. The poetry and the poetics of the Spanish writer Gustavo Adolfo Bécquer set out starkly, as if on double tracks, the aspiration to insight through conflation, and an escape from the sickness caused by such aestheticising. Each of these echoes the other through the experience of failure; each is on the verge of nothingness. His only manuscript volume involving poetry – *The Book of Sparrows* (*Libro de los gorriones*) (?1868) – is presented only as memories of a lost book ('poesías que recuerdo del libro perdido'). In poem 11/I, the poet famously declares his knowledge of 'a gigantic strange hymn / which announces in the night of the soul a dawn' (un himno gigante y extraño / que anuncia en la noche del alma una aurora). To sing it, he would need a language of pure correspondances – like Baudelairean harmonies – finding identity across diverse, even opposite experiences: 'words that would be at once / sighs and laughs, colours and notes' (palabras que fuesen a un tiempo / suspiros y risas, colores y notas). (Bécquer's friends posthumously published the verses under the title *Rhymes* – *Rimas* – in a different sequence, placing this poem at the very opening, as if to set out Bécquer's vision of literature. Their alternative sequence is indicated in Roman numerals.) Here the world becomes oneiric, as the poet Jorge Guillén (1942) observes in a celebrated essay. Matter is turning to something tenuous, abstract and ineffable, like light itself, Edmund King saw (1953: 111, 119). It has the potential to be an 'everything that is a nothing'.

But, failing, the poet can scarcely mumble something of it, the poem concludes. Conversely, at the opening of the *Book of Sparrows*, in the prose 'Symphonic Introduction' (Introducción sinfónica), Bécquer describes the merging of identities and chronologies as a tormenting chaos, a mental illness, a realisation of the impending insanity we encountered in Arrieta or in *Wonderland*, as if in some terrifying filing system: 'My memory classifies, all mixed up, names and dates of women and days that have died, or have gone by, with the days and women that have existed but in my mind' (Mi memoria clasifica revueltos los nombres y fechas de mujeres y días que han muerto, o que han pasado, con los días y mujeres que no han existido sino en mi mente). Here similitude is a sickness from which he must escape. The poet longs not to be troubled in his sleepless nights by the 'extravagant procession' of images that his mind throws up (extravagante procesión) (1998: 12–16). Bécquer desires self-control and cool, the contemporary poet Luis García Montero has written (2001: 33, 44). If the poet is to be freed from his feverish imaginings, he must cast these creations out into the world as best he can, in the form of fragmentary writing: dressed in rags, as he puts it.

This casting out traces a path parallel but inverse to that of the scattering of signs by death beyond the limits of subject that we encountered in Melville and others. The poet wishes to accept his mortality, from which the verses are a distraction, taking him away from his own subjecthood and its limits: he will soon pack his bags for his final journey (1998: 126). Words thus separate from the intention of an originating subject, an author who wishes to die, and are emitted in a ventriloquised multiplicity of voices that detach from the poet. In an imaginary world where different people and times blend together, and where distinct things can be the same, the poet could not have an identifiable voice of their own, but rather would continually release a motley chorus of others, detaching from them, as if in a shadow of 'My myself'. The literary critic Irene Mizrahi (1998) has shown how the verses emulate a multitude of other poets and kinds of poetry. Now Bécquer is a writer of odes with long, rolling, redolent lines of dramatic imagery: 'You gigantic waves that break roaring / On deserted remote beaches' (Olas gigantes que os rompéis bramando / En playas desiertas y remotas) (poem 35/LII; 1998: 64). Now, he is a narrative poet drawing on literary sources: 'sweet Ophelia, her reason lost / Picking flowers and singing goes by' (la dulce Ofelia, la razón perdida / cogiendo flores y cantando pasa) (poem 57/VI; 1998: 76). Now, the voice seems intimately autobiographical or pseudo-autobiographical: 'I put down the light, and on the edge / of the unmade bed sat down') (Dejé la luz, y en el borde / de la revuelta cama me senté) (poem 34/XLIII; 1998: 63).

We are left with voices freed from chronology and context, incidents, episodes and exclamations, surging up only immediately to pass, occurring in no particular order, with no sense of what comes before or after. As we encounter fragment after fragment of amorous and erotic relationships, we have no way of telling how many women are being mentioned, or in which verses the same person recurs. The *Book of Sparrows* is subtitled a 'collection of projects, arguments, ideas and plans for diverse things that will be concluded or not depending on how the wind blows' (Colección de proyectos, argumentos, ideas y planes de cosas diferentes que se concluirán o no según sople el viento). Like Baudelaire's *Little Poems in Prose* (*Petits poèmes en prose*), these works could be read in any sequence. The whole resists cogent interpretation, leading us instead towards appreciation, not now because of a deep attachment to 'pain freely accepted', but rather through an impulse towards letting go even as we make connections. The world dematerialises into haunting, fragmentary voices and images.

Likewise, the continual failure of connections in the structure of *Sentimental Education*, the obsession with awkward juxtaposition that we find in the novel, lends itself to higgledy-piggledy accumulations of allusions to a multitude of sources and discourses. In Flaubert's novel, we find, for example, suggestions of the French obsession with things Hispanic, a source of reinvention through an exoticised other. Frédéric supposes Mme Arnoux an Andalusian woman at first sight or perhaps a creole (he is wrong) (2019a: 17); Spanish revolutionaries speak their own language in the scenes of 1848 ('personne ne comprend' – no one can understand – a voice complains (2019a: 267)); the friends visit a dance hall called l'Alhambra (2019a: loc.1632). There are mentions of imperialism and the legacy of slavery: in his speculations, Frédéric imagines Mme Arnoux's black nursemaid might be accompanying her from the Caribbean islands (2019a: 17); we are told in cursory fashion that Deslauriers's career path includes his being the head of French colonisation in Algeria and secretary to a Pasha (2019a: 352). Objects from M. Arnoux's business evoke a miscellany of cultures across place and time from Etruscan to Chinese, now simply commodities (2019a: 173); the brothel from which Frédéric famously flees is named *Chez la turque* (*The Turkish Woman's Place*) (2019a: 364). None of it adds up to much. If these are expressions of global relations, they evince little genuine interest in others. Colonial and orientalising languages are exposed as inadequate to global realities, relentlessly ironised, Jennifer Yee has observed; the allusions involve both fakes and mistakes (2016: 115–64). In Manet, universal love is found by transfiguring and redeeming the domination and submission of the world. In this *Sentimental Education*, we take as our starting point – our disposition towards the world – a caring for failed, apparently unattractive global relationships. Such are the cultural encounters that extend out from France into the wider world. We experience this, not in a hermeneutic effort to explain the meaning of the allusions and pastiche, but evocatively in their unrealised coming together, the 'incomplete genesis' of their connections, as a way to start again.

The similitude – convergence even – of encompassing connection and disconnection in such a poetics is apparent in Bécquer's statements about extreme fragmentation. In reflections on another poet – Augusto Ferrán – Bécquer speaks of a universal aesthetics, 'the synthesis of poetry' found among the populace, 'the great poet of all ages and of all nations' (la síntesis de la poesía; el gran poeta de todas las edades y de todas las naciones) (1998: 112). The popular song of Bécquer's native Andalusia and Seville, a manifestation of the 'synthesis of poetry', is presented as one with the ancient Greek Homer, the Italian Dante, the German Romantics, Byron, Shakespeare and – in the poet's prose *Legends* (*Leyendas*) – the mythology of India and the myths of a borderland between Islamic and Christian worlds (Regueiro Salgado 2013). Across social classes, the learned poet draws on the culture of the people, just as – we are told – the aristocratic woman does with popular habits – an allusion to the custom that Andalusian noblewomen at times wore folk dress (1998: 114). Just as popular poetry may synthesise the culture of an era (1998: 112), Bécquer's own short poems resonate with fleeting, fragmentary moments taken from modern Madrid street and interior scenes (García Montero 2001: 64; Lewis 1997: 423), as women pass by, as there are encounters in orgies and in bedrooms.

But poetry – as Bécquer describes it – does not follow a pattern of development from beginning to end like a melody, which unfurls, finishes and fades (se desarrolla, se acaba y se desvanece). Rather, all we have is a single chord of a harp, its continuing vibrations, and then silence. It is as if Being or Spirit were stripped back to a single, isolated moment. This is something other than the perpetual becoming, the Universal Progressive Poetry of fragments of which Friedrich Schlegel famously spoke, for while Being here resonates and suggests, giving rise to 'nameless thoughts' (pensamientos sin nombre), it does not develop along a pathway (1998: 112). Its existence is at once impassioned, rich, and on the verge of nothingness. The same is true of Bécquer's unrealised, failed creations in the 'Symphonic Introduction': they are not even a seed that might grow, but 'dispersed atoms of a world in embryo winnowed by death' (átomos dispersos de un mundo en embrión que avienta la muerte) (1998: 125). In the 'Symphonic Introduction', the 'synthesis' of the elite and the poor, of the voices of the contemporary era, is undone in rejection. The poet's fantasies appear as a repellent revolutionary mob spewing into the world as if from the wombs of the supposedly feckless, ever-reproducing poor. The democratic idea of giving them sovereignty fails, for the poet can supply no purple robe of majesty, only rags (1998: 123–4). In Bécquer's verse, poetry finds itself on the back of banknotes, a novelty of speculative finance with no gold standard underpinning it (7/XXVI; 1998: 48–9); ideologies are cast up and discarded, from the modern cult of liberty to antique glory (5/LXII; 1998: 47–8), and from the binaries of spiritual ideality and prosaic materialism (7, 50/XVII; 1998: 47–8, 73) about which contemporary thinkers obsessed (Ginger 1999: 11–88).

The voicing of prejudiced sexual and gender roles in the poems is at the heart of the meeting of connection and continual disconnection. Woman is to offer us the translucent ineffability of poetry itself (González Gerth 1965: 192), dematerialising into metonymic fragments of her own glimpsed body, and confined to beautifying inarticulacy, Lewis (1997) and James Mandrell (1995) have shown. She is poetry, but cannot speak or know it, for its language is for males (21/XXI; 1998: 55). If she is to be the totalising synthesis, and thus defined as something too pure to be human, the correlate is the recoiling at her body that we saw in the birthing of poetic ideas, and that we find in images of blocked-off penetration: she is a watery ocean and the poet a hard rock and neither will cede (26/XLI; 1998: 58). Where real woman turns out not to be what woman should be, love affairs fail once and again, and she is subject to male anger and efforts at control. Tom Lewis has underlined the violent switchings of domination and submission that all this implies, and with it something of the 'bitextuality' that we see in Flaubert. If the male is to have poetry, he must dominate woman, but he must also, in a way, be woman, splitting his subjecthood so as to make himself at once putatively dominant and submissive. This kind of gender fluidity is certainly not a liberation as we might now understand it, but rather a tormented seeking to control and corresponding failure (1997: 428–42). In turn, in the poet's at-times failed penetration of women, his inability to achieve that kind of 'unlimited intimacy' with them, he finds himself before a vision of same-sex eroticism. As an ineffable woman stands out of reach beyond a grill, two angels guard the way, their clothes undone, brandishing their naked swords (24/LXXIV; 1998: 57).

Through all these explorations of notions of fusion and division, poetry traces the high risks involved in seeking lucid insight through conflation and analogy. Such would be the affordances of a putative 'gigantic hymn', whose vastness echoes that of the webs of connectedness traced in Levine's version of the nineteenth-century novel. As we have seen in the delirium of Chapter 3, and as Bécquer comes to tell us in a further poem (42/III; 1998: 67–8), to give oneself to such a thing is to court insanity (locura), by dwelling in a realm of pure possibility, of might-bes: 'memories and desire / of things that don't exist' (memorias y deseo / de cosas que no existen). In such an orderless dimension, it makes perfect sense that a word could be a sigh and a laugh, a colour and a note, or that – in an image from this very poem – a cadence that lacks rhythm or beat (1998: 68). The alternative presented in the *Book of Sparrows* is to approach such a claim in the spirit of failure. There would be, as Bécquer puts it, 'alas, no cypher / able to encapsulate' the gigantic hymn (no hay cifra / capaz de encerrarle) (11/I; 1998: 50): no such affordances would actually be unleashed in some vast artistic form. There would be no successful endpoint for the kinds of journeying through patterns offered by an artist such as Arrieta. There would instead, for sure, be mental disturbance: the delusion and confusion of the Bécquer of the 'Symphonic Introduction'.

In that spirit of failure, we would still pass through all this, as R. D. Laing was later to urge us to journey through the disturbed mind, or Salvador Dalí was to encourage us to follow the reasonings of paranoia's associations. The prose fragment, 'The Stone Woman' (La mujer de piedra), towards the beginning of the *Book of Sparrows*, shows such a travelling: the poet's steps take him again and again inexplicably to a female whom he finds enigmatic. We follow this path, not so as to connect ourselves robustly to the associations that may form along it, but such that they slip away from our grasp, that we continually release them before they can become even fully formed, as if in rags. The affordance of male prejudice is a failed coupling that points beyond itself, even to its own undoing. The uncentred, multi-directional flow of resemblances, the flawed fusions of pastiche and allusions, become a passage to being free of such things altogether, in order to feel once more at home in the world in the face of mortality, accepting the limits of our worldly existence. Like Josef in *Dr Lañuela*, the poet must renounce any notion of unfurling Being, of 'soul' in that sense. 'When' – a voice asks in the opening poem – 'will I be able to sleep with that dream / in which there is an end to dreaming?' (¿cuándo podré dormir con ese sueño / en que acaba el soñar?) (1998: 45).

At a tangent: the character of the observer

In repose, in tempered renunciation, in awareness of our finitude, we may acknowledge how tangential each of us is to the larger realities of history and of the world. Situated in a local context, a person may expressly lack an understanding of all the intervening, immediate connections to such a whole. Yet acceptance of that tangential position, of that lack of full knowledge, may provide a way to apprehend and thus connect to the larger picture in a spirit of serenity and humility. This is not because of any immediate apprehension of the macrocosm in the microcosm, nor any dilation of the individual into the whole. Rather it is because the form of that person's experience, their character as an observer, renders their judgements abou the whole reliable in the very absence of full information. In a way consonant with their practical limitations, such a person has three qualities that we have encountered since Chapter 1: the virtue of character which we found in Nietzsche and Wagner, in Félicité and Alice; the capacity to apprehend through vagueness and correspondingly to 'go on'; and craft.

The approach to exposition taken in Charles Darwin's *Origin of the Species* (1859) is perhaps the most striking instance of this phenomenon in the mid-century. The work is offered as – and I take it to be – an outline but true account of the genesis and development of all life across our planet. Quite explicitly, such a vision supposes that the place of writing – mid-nineteenth-century Europe – is dwarfed in scale by the subject matter: 'We forget how small the area of Europe is compared with the rest of the world', Darwin observes (2009: 261). Though himself never free of prejudice about non-Europeans, Darwin emphasises how relative, to the point of parody, are the achievements of the civilisation to which he belongs. The ingenious work of advanced geometers is matched by bees shaping structures in wax, 'no more knowing that they swept their spheres at one particular distance from each other, than they know what are the several angles of the hexagonal prisms and of the basal rhombic plates' (2009: 212). His depiction of his own self frequently serves to emphasise the rather modest nature of his vantage point: we find him pottering about his garden, marking up seedlings, collecting 'three tablespoonfuls of mud' and putting them in 'a breakfast cup', labelling weeds and counting how 295 of 357 were 'destroyed, chiefly by slugs and insects' (2009: 340, 69).

The extremity of the contrast is apparent when Darwin insists on 'how incomprehensibly vast have been the past periods of time' (2009: 252). The huge scales of temporality that Thrift finds disclosed here (May & Thrift 2001: 12), the sublimity upon which many have remarked (Levine 2006: 41), are rendered possible through the writer's tangential stance; the very experience of dwarfing immensity depends upon it. The starkness of the contrast brings to mind and exacerbates that which we saw between the two *gauchos* on the outskirts of Buenos Aires and the epic, Teutonic world of Faust, or between Wagner and Nietzsche in imagined armchair conversation and the deeds of Greek gods.

In *Origins*, Darwin makes no claim to offer a fully reasoned account of the 'incomprehensibly vast' history of life. In part, this is because *Origins* is a summary, explicitly brought out in haste due to ill health and the risk that others might publish similar views. Yet – many scholars have noted – it goes deeper than that. 'I am well aware', Darwin says at the outset, 'that scarcely a single point is discussed in this volume on which facts cannot be adduced, often apparently leading to conclusions directly opposite to those at which I have arrived' (2009: 12). This very statement points to a challenge which no account, however long, could have overcome: Darwin's vision is underdetermined by data from the natural world, and the evidence available could be construed into very different accounts. There are whole parts of his explanation, and of the workings of natural selection, for which there is little to no available information. 'Much remains obscure, and will long remain obscure', he notes (2009: 15). This is scarcely a theory arrived at by Baconian scientific induction (Beer 1986: 242; Levine 2006: 191; Stovall 2015: 697).

The point is not that Darwin's conclusions are questionable, but rather that – in the absence of the full story, where the core of a tale so inconceivably huge must be grasped by one small actor within it – the case is decided by judgement: 'I can entertain *no doubt*', he tellingly declares early on, 'after the most deliberate and *dispassionate judgment* of which I am capable' (emphasis added). 'I am convinced', Darwin says again and again, 'I am strongly inclined to suspect', 'several reasons make me believe', 'I am strongly inclined to believe' (2009: 15, 93 *inter alia*). It is for that reason that *Origins* is to such an extent a first-person, even autobiographical text, looking to the individual observer, dwarfed by history and geography. It is key then that the narrative voice be established as reliable, in part through his ways of explaining himself, but also as the kind of person who combines writing to Mr Miller of the University of Cambridge with the acquaintance of cattle breeders, who digs up dirt in his own garden and sails far afield on the *Beagle*, who has attentively read Charles Lyell's latest work on geology and who has, 'after deliberation, taken up domestic pigeons' (2009: 28), who is prepared to admit his own surprise – 'I should never have expected' (2009: 50), 'I can never reflect on them without being staggered' (2009: 158).

Scholars – from Stanley Edgar Hyman (1974) and Gillian Beer (1986) through John Angus Campbell (2003), from Avon Crismore and Rodney Farnsworth (1989) to Benjamin Bradley (2011) – have explored how Darwin renders – or seeks to render – his writing trustworthy, in rhetorical devices, linguistic turns, and by recasting established images and terms of reference. But the point is not simply whether or how Darwin is persuasive in his prose.

It is not just whether the reader, compelled by Darwin's voice, comes to trust where there is no certainty and where existing paradigms will not take us. Rather, the judgement is indeed (broadly) true and offered as such. It is the virtue of Darwin's character that enables him to envisage biological time and place in all their vastness, just as, in quite a different spirit, it is the quality of Wagner and Nietzsche's friendship that enables them to apprehend the ancient (or so Nietzsche claimed). Gillian Beer aptly observes how Darwin appears in the guise of a 'companion'. His oft-conversational tone 'implies the presence of both addresser and addressee' (1986: 225–6). But this 'meeting' with Darwin's voice differs from the 'intimate culture' we saw exemplified in the *gauchos* of Chapter 1. In the latter, friendship is not an instantiation of a general good: in entering into intimacy, for better or for worse, we relinquish such a thing. If among the *gauchos*, we encounter a 'a pure embodiment of value' – in Manning's phrase (2013: 266) – Darwin's 'poetics of character' brings us instead intimate attunement with the biological world itself across all place and time.

In emphasising Darwin's character, George Levine urges us to distinguish between recognising that Darwin's insights emerged from his attitudes, and the claim that such insights are limited to their own time and place (2006: 133, 179–84). In saying this, Levine makes two claims about the enduring force of Darwin's words, about what makes them a 'dynamic moment', in Zielinski's phrase. First, following Hilary Putnam (2004) and earlier Pragmatists, Levine denies that objective insight involves 'absolute disinterest' or that truths are value-free, and that, conversely, anything that is not absolutely disinterested and stripped of feeling is unobjective (2006: 29–30, 242). Second, he argues that it is possible for a turn of thought to be conceived in a given set of terms, but ultimately to undermine and outstrip these, whether when applied by its author or subsequently (2006: 173, 200). Certainly, to accept *Origin*'s account of natural selection may – and should – involve rejecting any prejudiced belief to which Darwin appeals.

But only to say that risks sidestepping the issue. To accept the broad account of nature as it is given in *Origin* is fundamentally to trust Darwin's character because we are so reliant upon it. It is to consider that character trustworthy, reliable, in some ways virtuous, even – however alien it is to us. The pottering character projected by Darwin is – as Levine says – depicted 'entirely from the point of view of a Victorian gentleman' (2006: 40), with his 'humility and honesty', 'modest, hardworking, ready to get his hands dirty' (Levine 2011: 21–2). Put more robustly, here is a male, replete with patriarchal beard, acting in circles of English privilege, and evincing the corresponding manners. Here is a man who, journeying on the *Beagle* to Chile and the Galapagos, benefited from the work of Latin American scientists and indigenous insight (Schell 2013), but whose authoritative voice emphasises his authority. Something like the 'bedrock' of trusting someone's judgement when they observe tangentially is truly to be guided by them, however different – even unappealing – they are to us, in the full awareness that their thoughts may have been conceived in attitudes, in a cultural world, at odds with our own. We might call this experience an 'intimate judgement': we find it in the company of someone who truly is a different person. Though this may seem paradoxical in other 'pictures' of the world, it is precisely through our companionship with such an alien that we go beyond their worldview, for through it we may lead ourselves to judge truly, becoming free of their prejudices.

Key to his character and virtue is Darwin's recognition that his own place in biological nature is tangential, that his knowledge is limited, and that he needs to rely on judgement. This is the only possible starting point. He speaks with assurance and balance from and through his limitations as he confronts the 'mystery of mysteries' (2009: 11). This is a tempered outlook, neither overly assertive of the self, nor overwhelmed by what Darwin beholds. He is, in that specific sense, 'dispassionate'. The 'decentering' of the human subject is 'another aspect of his modesty', Levine observes: it is an acceptance that there are experiences beyond his narrow confines (2006: 150–1). It is the very source of his apprehension of a vast similitude: the 'community' of all beings, the 'abstruse lateral range of interconnections' between them, as Beer puts it (1983: 117, 100). His judgement resides in a 'remarkable capacity to recognise similarities across space and time', in Levine's words (2011: 75). Where Kant's third *Critique* projects a purpose onto order that we trace through judgements, Darwin comes to envisage this as possible in nature without a purpose, forming its own endless self-ordering, Preston Stovall argues. His very process of 'non-deductive reasoning' – that judgement without full knowledge – proceeds by inference from analogy (Stovall 2015).

Put another way around, the ability to perceive connecting patterns may be an affordance of off-centre viewpoints. In the early 1870s, the Spanish novelist, Benito Pérez Galdós – soon to become the country's equivalent of a Dickens or Balzac – began his long series of *National Episodes* (*Episodios nacionales*). The *Episodes*, running to several collections of novels through his career, were to trace the fate of Spain from the start of the nineteenth century, when its place in the world and its internal affairs were so fundamentally reconfigured. Galdós started to revisit this historical narrative during Spain's first Republic, the time of writing of all the Spanish texts in the rest of this chapter and of this book. In a further convulsion of the instability stemming from the fracturing global monarchy of 1808, the Glorious Revolution of 1868 had toppled the country's Bourbon monarchs. The subsequent search for a monarch entangled the country in the rivalry of France and Prussia, helping to trigger the war between these two. This in turn brought about a putative struggle of North and South in the aftermath of which Nietzsche conceived his *Birth of Tragedy*, rejoining the two. The hapless Amadeo of Savoy – whom Galdós backed – briefly became monarch, before losing control, and being replaced by a turbulent republic (1873–74), prior to the restoration of the Bourbons. In a way, this was a further incident in a long international war of the succession to the Spanish Empire and its remains: France and northern powers clashed over the ruling dynasty of Spain in the early eighteenth century, in 1808, and now once more. By the early 1870s too, one of the jewels of the remaining overseas empire – Cuba – was experiencing violent unrest, and Spain was resisting the encroachment of the United States on its valuable Caribbean territories (Dendle 1986: 1–16). The remnants of the old monarchy were once more at crisis point.

In the novels published in the early 1870s, our witness to this large history – Gabriel – is someone who arrives in Madrid in 1805 'with no job or benefice, with no relatives or guardians' (Sin oficio ni beneficio, sin parientes ni habientes) (Galdós 2006: 14), shortly before the Napoleonic invasion in 1808 is to overwhelm the old regime, and set in motion both its fall and that of the larger empire. The hope is that, by placing the core of the viewpoint in a single individual at a remove from apparently leading protagonists, the central core of shared history will be more fully experienced and apprehended. In the second volume, *The Court of Carlos IV* (*La Corte de Carlos IV*) (1873), dealing with the run-up to 1808, we find that aspiration strikingly realised, not even in Gabriel himself, but in an individual whom he admires: the illiterate artisan Pacorro Chinitas. As the machinations of the French Emperor Napoleon intermingle with the efforts of the heir Fernando to seize the throne, only Chinitas foresees how things could turn out. 'I am more and more convinced', Gabriel tells us, 'that Pacorro Chinitas was one of the greatest notables of his time' (Cada vez estoy más convencido de que Pacorro Chinitas fue una de las más grandes notablilidades de su tiempo) (2006: 90).

Late in the novel Chinitas's capacity to perceive is contrasted pointedly with that of Napoleon himself: 'He [Chinitas] alone had foreseen events with a sure eye, and conversely the hero of the age/century, who knew Spain through its monarchs, through its ministers and its your-lordships, wanted to know everything and knew nothing.' Napoleon's later failure in Spain is easily explained: 'alas!, he did not hear the blade-sharpener speak' (Él solo había previsto los acontecimientos con ojo seguro, y en cambio el héroe del siglo, que conocía a España por sus reyes, por sus ministros y por sus usías, quería saberlo todo y no sabía nada. … ¡ay!, no oyó hablar al amolador) (2006: 177). The description of Bonaparte evokes the notion that an historic 'age' and its spirit could be incarnate and recognised in a 'hero'. But, if such incarnation is possible, it no longer constitutes knowledge of the totality: efforts at apprehending 'everything' through it amount to 'nothing'. In contrast, what Chinitas perceives is more than the localised fate of Spain: it is how his country's future intertwines and interconnects with the forces reshaping the continent and far beyond.

A positive preference for the rough impression over the analysis of as much information as possible separates the person who is truly connected to the whole from the grandiosity of one who 'wanted to know everything'. Gabriel wonders at 'how much the *good judgement* of the blade-sharpener penetrated with his *rough* mistrust' (lo que penetró con su ruda desconfianza el buen juicio del amolador) (emphasis added) (2006: 90). In such close proximity to the man's humble profession, the word *ruda* suggests that true sharpness comes from having a rough edge, and from doing things roughly. Chinitas relies on 'gramática parda', literally, 'dark grammar', a phrase implying the insight of those who lack formal education. The extent of the artisan's awareness and embrace of such limitations equips him especially well for appreciating the overall course of events, the detailed workings of which are not really available to any observer, not even Napoleon. Chinitas – out there amid the working classes – becomes akin to the practitioners (female and male) that we saw in Chapter 1, offering, through penetration, the vagueness necessary to fuse particularity and generality.

Darwin likewise looks to approximation and imprecision as entirely viable ways of experiencing the world, and as features of the world. After all, *Origin* is a sketch of biology, a vision of life that is vague because lacking detail and evidence. Like the shapes we saw in Chapter 1, such an 'indistinct picture' is – in Wittgenstein's words – 'exactly what we need' (*PI* §71). The *species* whose origins it shows, and which emerge in this vast pattern of similitude, are discerned with the same quality of judgement. They are 'tolerably well defined', but not for that less real (Darwin 2009: 164). In turn – David Stamos argues – they too are apprehended through the relatively constant similarities through their variations, insofar as the former are pertinent in the large scheme of natural selection (1999: 150, 174). Darwin's judgement is true, not in the sense of mapping out precise structure or complete information, but rather, correctly aligned to the ways of the world, like an arrow launched so as to fly true. It is reliable, for it enables us to 'go on', that is, to continue to be used in ways that describe our experience beyond what it describes in 1859, just as Chinitas's rough-edged vision of the early nineteenth century finds amplifying use as events unfurl.

The vague sense of the course of things, the rough calculation, which are ways to trace the shapes of the complex picture, are skills attained through practice, as we saw with the artisans of Chapter 1. That Chinitas exercises a manual technique is suggestive, for this is a craft. It is, as Sennett has put it, an ongoing 'dialogue with materials' (2008: 268) (in this case, the impressions of history itself, as well as the blade and stone), a 'not knowing quite what you are about when you begin' (2008: 262), and 'a realm of skill and knowledge perhaps beyond human verbal capacities to explain' (2008: 95). There are, ultimately, no precise or systemic rules beyond the practices found in working through and with the material of experience itself. As Ribbans says, Galdós lacks a Tolstoy-like interest in the philosophy of history (1993: 72). The craft of having a 'sure eye' consists in this way of being tangential, of working from limitations themselves.

At home in the world, from a tangent

History may thus be re-grounded in an alternate centre in the tangential person. What might seem to have fallen to one side may become the locus, not just of understanding and apprehension, but of being fully at home in the world. Pointedly, in *The Court of Carlos IV*, such a role is assigned not just to the illiterate male artisan, but to a working-class craftswoman, Inés. Inés – with whom Gabriel falls in love – is a dressmaker, who – unlike Gabriel – has no interest in joining the apparent core of events at Court and among notables. It is given to her to bring restful order to thought. Of her spirit, Gabriel remarks: 'hers had a centre and mine did not. Mine wandered about carried back and forth by diverse impressions' (el de ella tenía un centro, y el mío no. El mío divagaba llevado y traído por impresiones diversas) (2006: 28). The narrative traces Gabriel's zigzagged journey to finding this true centre far from the apparent, turbulent core, a centre which was always there, at a tangent to the main narrative, unchanging in its disposition, and from which Inés predicted Gabriel's trajectory, just as Chinitas foresees the path of history. It is Inés who is able to bring rest (descanso), with her 'imperturbable serenity' (imperturbable serenidad) (2006: 27). Here, then, is a history-transforming quietude akin to that offered by Rosales's Isabel or Lucretia, but now far from such elevated figures. At the end of the novel, Gabriel – like Rosales – commits to it most decisively with a woman's demise: now not a queen or person of rank, but Inés's adoptive mother Juana, who seems, not so much dead, as in a state of 'meditative innerness' (recogimiento meditabundo) (2006: 218), in 'limbo'. Perceiving together the tranquillity of the mourning younger woman and that of the dead elder, Gabriel is transformed into new life, able to breathe normally once more, as if in 'an environment, temperate and regenerative, that lends equilibrium to the atmosphere' (un templado y regenerador ambiente que equilibra la atmósfera) (2006: 219).

The balanced narrative voice that emerges offers an aesthetics of being in the world. Like so many of Galdós's narrators, it combines written with oral registers, the ostensibly literary with 'real and palpitating life' (la vida real y palpitante) (2006: 221). Often, in a book peppered with literary allusion, the overall tone is comfortably colloquial: 'Galdós is never happier than when he is using the spoken word', Geoffrey Ribbans aptly remarks (1993: 64). 'Os hablaré', Gabriel says in the second paragraph: I shall speak to you, as if physically present with his audience, in our company (2006: 7). A very short while later he calls us 'lectores', *readers* (2006: 9). In such a 'picture' of being at 'home', there can be no disclosure of some purely literary language such as many scholars find in Flaubert, nor is it predicated that literature – or signs in general – are arbitrary, performative constructs. Perhaps it is the prestige of such visions of modernity that has led critics to seek out the same in Galdós. In discussions of *The Court of Carlos IV*, scholarly attention has lingered on a scene in which a (bad) translation of *Othello* is performed, and literary and wider realities interact. The celebrated (real-life) actor Isidoro Máiquez goes to stab Desdemona, played by his mistress whom he fears is in a love triangle. He does so with a real weapon, not a theatrical prop. Gabriel steps in, altering the literary work and avoiding disaster. Previously, he has observed and learnt the manipulation of language and letters in the service of the female courtier Amaranta – only to turn it against her designs at the end of the story. Tsuchiya thus discerns in the novel a disclosure that 'history is ultimately language' (1988: 109). In an essay on *The Court of Carlos IV* – citing Derrida, Lacan and Kristeva – Diane Urey (1988) similarly finds in Amaranta a maternal guide to Gabriel, showing him the endless deferral and slippage of *écriture*.

The self-reflexivity does not, however, imply an inherent distrust of the narrative word. Rather, to create a literature that is at home in the world and that blends ordinary and literary language is a craft, in which we learn to judge and tease out where and when ostensible or apparent literary form might coincide with that of other realities, just as the written and oral coincide. 'Every man [*sic*] is the author and actor of something that, were it recounted and written, would but seem written and told for entertainment …. There is no existence that does not have much of what we have settled on calling *a novel* (todo hombre es autor y actor de algo que, si se contara y escribiera, habría de parecer escrito y contado para entretenimiento …. No hay existencia que no tenga mucho de lo que hemos convenido en llamar *novela*' (2006: 221; emphasis in the original). It is not simply a matter of identifying all coincidences between other realities and literary form, but rather of reapprehending that conjunction through a tangent. When Máiquez goes to strike his lover, he is utterly identified with Othello, the title role in the play's key scene: literature and life converge. But he is violent, possessed with passion. It takes an untrained actor in a role that no one wants – Gabriel – to step in and stop him, in a rival fusion of literature with 'real and palpitating life'.

This alternative aesthetics involves a kind of unsaying – not a simple negation – a letting go of narratives and narrative stereotypes from across 'the deep time' of culture, just as Gabriel undoes the story of Othello. Chinitas appears as a male who exhibits knowledge through penetrating blades, but, unlike Máiquez's Othello – tempted by violent images of penetration – he is a gentle person, 'manso' (2006: 86). Conversely, while Inés appears as a domestic angel, and bringer of watery, translucent calm (2006: 19), she is to such a degree at odds with beliefs about lower-class women as to seem made-up (2006: 27). In this dressmaker we find recast the wisdom of the doctors of the University of Salamanca (whom she has not read) and Dante's Beatrice, just as the divine Roman patriarch Jupiter is associated with the lowly, mild-mannered knife-sharpener. In having, then rejecting, delusions of grandeur, Gabriel's life is an untelling of *Don Quijote* (2006: 28, 35, 86).

The form of the historical novel is itself unsaid. The interrelation of the core historical narrative and the protagonist's life, of society and the individual, the particular and general, is experienced only in its offsetting, in Gabriel's departure from the world of the Court and from Amaranta who is 'la intriga misma' – that is, in both senses, the *plot* or *plotting* (2006: 140). If Gabriel initially seems an ideal ultra-realist narrator, with his extraordinary ability to observe and recount, it is this that drew Amaranta to him. Now he must flee her (2006: 188). In turn, the very narrative of Spanish nationhood and history is undone. The desire rapidly to become a leading character (un verdadero y genuino personaje) is said to be typical of 'Spanish blood' (sangre española) (2006: 104, 76). This is doubtless an allusion once more to *Don Quijote*, but perhaps also to the weakness of the socio-economic and especially fiscal foundation on which imperial glory had been sought, and to the frequent pursuit of notable public office over wealth generation. Gabriel must learn to unsay this too. He is well placed to do so: in his own uncertain descent as an orphan, he combines a belonging to a defining genealogy (that national blood) and its unsettling. He has no lineage.

All the above implies that there is a way of being at home in the world that is tangential, intimately connected to larger history, adaptably vague, and that provides true insight. Such is the claim made by the American thinker and writer Henry David Thoreau in his *Walden* (1854). On the one hand, he confidently asserts the need to be 'lax': 'In view of the future or possible, we should live quite laxly and undefined in front, our outlines dim and misty on that side; as our shadows reveal an insensible perspiration toward the sun.' 'The words which express our faith and piety are not definite', he avers (2012: 460–1). Like the artisans we met in Chapter 1, and like Chinitas, Thoreau does not think something is false simply because it is not abstractly exact: in his taste for measuring things, there is an 'open-ended roughness', Maurice Lee remarks (2011: 137). Equally, Thoreau affirms that his outlook meets a clear test for truthfulness: that it should be supported by evidence. 'No way of thinking or doing, however ancient', he rails, 'can be trusted without proof. What everybody echoes or silence passes by as true to-day may turn out to be falsehood tomorrow, mere smoke of opinion.' *Walden* echoes with the language of empirical tests and of science. Life is 'an experiment' (2012: 203–4).

Thoreau claims that the standard of truth might be discovered about a mile away from the madding crowd: in his case, in a self-made home in the relative quiet of the New England forests, near Concord and not far from a railway line. Leo Marx notes how, in so doing, he creates a narrative like 'many American fables' with 'the hero's withdrawal from society in the direction of nature' (Marx 2000: 242). The work is conceived in detachment not simply from the society of New England and the United States, but from the infrastructure that increasingly interconnected the world. He 'could easily do without the post-office' and finds no 'memorable news in any newspaper' (2012: 273). He concludes that 'our voyaging is only great-circle sailing .... One hastens to southern Africa to chase the giraffe; but surely that is not the game he would be after' (2012: 457). Like Mansilla or Hernández in Argentina, Thoreau seeks out the edge of Greater Europe, a borderland where a worldview might reach and test what its limits are and what lies beyond: 'It would be some advantage', he muses, 'to live a primitive and frontier life, though in the midst of outward civilisation' (2012: 206).

The rhythms of life and time in Walden sit beyond those expected of mature men in Concord at the mid-century, for Thoreau resides with no wife or children, and pursues no conventional occupation; there is an awkward conversation – Benjamin Reiss observes – when he meets the married Irishman John Field and family, their patterns of life so at odds (2013: 26). Contemporary claims that Thoreau's book and behaviour were 'eccentric' – literally off centre – specifically referenced this facet, Henry Abelove has shown. A favoured visitor is a French-Canadian woodcutter, with whom he reads Homer's tale of Achilles and Patroclus, ancient masculine lovers; Thoreau goes to town only to seek out males (1993: 17–23). The gender norms of Concord are not so much overturned here, as taken to a limit point, to their own tangent of male independence and erotic homosociality, as they are in Mansilla or among Del Campo's *gauchos*.

By heading to our respective Walden Ponds, by placing ourselves at a tangent to the encircling infrastructure of globalisation, we find ourselves to be truly global beings, truly to experience sameness. The whole world and all of time is ours. Homeric 'queerness' speaks less to whether Thoreau was 'really "gay" all along' than to a vexed longing for meeting in intimate friendship, for community, Robert Óscar López notes (2007: 130, 141). It evokes a 'utopian impulse', Michael Warner observes (1991: 158). As with Courbet's *Wrestlers* and *Sleep*, sameness may become an affordance of same-sex relationships. When approached with such a disposition, physical place and chronological time are locations of, at best, secondary significance: 'Any prospect of awakening or coming to life ... makes indifferent all times and places. The place where that may occur is always the same' (2012: 307).

It is the apparent combination of drawing back so as to challenge established culture, of purging, and of a bedrock for all being that attracts Cavell to *Walden* (1981: 11, 63, 92–8, 112; 2013: 36–7, 44, 81). Here Cavell finds a genealogy for language understood other than as autonomous signs. Where thoughts of Post-Romantic modernity led many theorists to the mid-century prose of Flaubert, Thoreau offers Cavell instead 'some intimacy between language and the world', such as Wittgenstein could only evoke (2013: 81). Thoreau begins with a declaration that he has written and that he will account for having done so (2013: 1). For Cavell, writing is here transfigured by its faithfulness to its being, as if disclosing itself in and through the world (1981: 27–33). *Walden* seems to exemplify the value of 'poverty', and the related capacity to 'go on' authentically. 'Let us settle ourselves,' Thoreau urges, 'and work and wedge our feet downward through the mud and slush of opinion, and prejudice, and tradition and delusion, and appearance, that alluvion which covers the globe ... through poetry, philosophy and religion, till we come to a hard bottom and rocks in place, which we can call *reality*, and say, This is, and no mistake' (2012: 276).

Reaching such an ontological ground ('this is') putatively involves stripping back human existence to things that he describes as *'necessary of life'*, that is 'whatever, of all that man obtains by his own exertions, has been from the first, or from long use has become, so important to human life that few, if any, whether from savageness, or poverty, or philosophy ever attempt to do without it'. These are 'Food, Shelter, Clothing, and Fuel' (they may vary somewhat according to climate, but only as variants of the 'grand necessity ... to keep warm') (2012: 206–7; original emphasis). The point is not simply the preference for material poverty over luxury, but rather that the latter embodies the tendency of human culture to distract itself, to become entangled, to 'go on holiday', in Wittgenstein's terms, precisely because we can invent a world free of the bedrock of being: 'Our inventions are wont to be pretty toys,' Thoreau avers, 'which distract our attention from serious things' (2012: 239). From this perspective, a culture of global travel and communication, of far-travelling boats and newspapers, offers the supreme possibility for deflection.

Retreating provides a refreshed disposition towards such things. Thoreau is not, after all, interested in spending his whole life in a cabin by Walden Pond. He is concerned, rather, with cultivating an awareness of 'reality' that can inform his life once he has physically left the place behind. He is always learning to leave Walden, Cavell notes (1985: 45). Even the apparent concerns with specifiable criteria – with the *'necessary of life'* or 'reality' or 'proof' – are not so defined as they may first appear. In advocating 'poverty', Thoreau declares: 'In proportion as he [*sic*] simplifies his life, the laws of the universe will appear less complex, and solitude will not be solitude, nor poverty poverty, nor weakness weakness.' At apparent odds with his denunciation of inventions, he teasingly proceeds: 'If you have built castles in the air, your work need not be lost; that is where they should be. Now put the foundations under them' (2012: 460). Our very notion of *poverty* has now been transfigured to such an extent that it is, as it were, no longer itself. In what Thoreau calls his 'extra-vagant' prose (2012: 460), its wandering outside, he seeks 'to wrench language from its traditional signification', Malini Schueller comments (1986: 40). *Walden* offers one bold statement and then another, its language trenchant but elusive. Its sudden juxtapositions, like those of Mansilla, leave us with habitually uncertain sense: we often wonder what is meant, Robert Milder observes (1995: 67). Thoreau's words 'will not be' are enough to make one question quite what is being affirmed in his affirmations of a bedrock of being, of ontology: 'This is, and no mistake'. 'This is' now 'will not be' what it was. Even deflection and distraction of the most obvious kind – 'castles in the air' – seem to be no obstacle to 'reality' and its 'foundations'.

A tempting conclusion is that Thoreau means something like this: once we attain true poverty, we will realise it is much more enriching than material luxuries or complexities of thought and feeling. So we will no longer really think of it as *poverty*, that is, a state of deprivation. Approaching life 'laxly and undefined in front' would be a realisation that having come to this refreshed disposition, we may 'go on'. Yet, at a minimum, such a gloss begs some qualification. If we live 'laxly and undefined in front', that must also be true of the very criteria of 'poverty', 'reality' and the 'necessary of life'. The very notion of *poverty* must, at its very core, continually dilate, like Baudelaire's *mal*: put at an extreme, it must be lavish through and through. This is a 'picture' of the world in which to purge ourselves with poverty, to return home, to avoid deferral, may be experienced as continual capacity for departure – and vice versa. If Whitman's 'Me myself' is a disposition to the world in which we are 'at home' in lavishness, Thoreau's 'poverty' is such that lavishness is found in a tangential home, in a hut by Walden Pond, and not in some more obviously expansive movement. In an essay on both Thoreau and Cavell, Paul Standish dwells upon this notion of 'departure' in *Walden*, drawing a distinction between Thoreau's insistent emphasis on 'reality', and 'the siren pressures of postmodernity … in which image displaces substance' (2006: 155), that is the endless difference of autonomous signs. In the line of American thought, Standish finds a stark contrast of tone between Thoreau's urgent call to a 'reality' and the '"laid-back"' style of Richard Rorty in his version of Dewey's Pragmatism (2006: 154) with which Cavell, and pragmatists such as Haack, have taken such issue (as we saw in the Introduction to this present book).

There is no way of knowing in advance of any given moment how such 'poverty' will be instantiated in feeling, thought, or deed. There is no pre-given purpose, no *Telos*, Standish notes (2006: 152). In the lack of plot and character development, there is no unfurling of a given path of being (Cavell 1981: 49). Cavell speaks of an openness to contingency, to strangeness, and to change (1981: 49, 55, 119). Of a person truly living in such a state – 'a poet' – Thoreau asks, 'Who can predict his comings and goings?' (2012: 415). There is absolutely not a single way of living in *poverty*. On the contrary, the latter's dilation supposes near-endless variation, differentiation and individuation: 'I desire that there may be as many different persons in the world as possible; but I would have each one be very careful to find out and pursue his *own* way, and not his father's or his mother's' (2012: 254; emphasis in the original). *Poverty* does not consist of a system of rules whose necessary consequences for any situation may be deduced through chains of reasoning or cause and effect. In Thoreau's laxness and indefinition, in what Cafaro calls his 'living ethics', the resistance to distraction cannot amount to strict epistemological guidelines (2004: 222–3). This would be true even of those that avoid the fallacies of foundationalism, such as Haack (1993) sought to construct in her Foundherentism. Likewise – Standish shows – the experience of living at Walden Pond is not akin to the later Heidegger's 'dwelling' with its 'gravitational force', its seeking to root us in a sense of ultimate belonging in a place. Rather, Thoreau speaks of 'sojourning', a capacity to dwell in a willingness to change circumstance and place, 'a combination of attachments ... with a readiness for departure' (Standish 2006: 156). His urge for 'reality' and 'poverty' is a call to a state of awareness, a disposition that (he hopes) will ward off the risks of distraction and deflection even as we 'sojourn'. This involves an extreme capacity to adapt and change, even to the extent of self-mutilation, which Thoreau calls 'elasticity' as opposed to being 'at a dead set': it is like a fox leaving behind its own tail so as to escape (2012: 250).

Like the photography and performances that we encountered in Chapter 1, Thoreau neither simply 'takes' nor 'receives' an image of the world. His language takes shape – Theo Davis has suggested – much as contemporaneous 'fancy crafts' took shape, 'indirectly ... by kinds of pressure' in the world, giving us ornamental forms that we appreciate, not signs representing a meaning to be deciphered (2010: 578–83). For Jane Bennett, it is precisely by renouncing a unified vision of nature that Thoreau attains his oneness with the world: craft and materials, sculptor and sculpture share in this wildness and their boundaries are elided (1994: xxiv, 52–6, 73). In the 'evanescence' of his prose – Deborah Slicer asserts – Thoreau seeks neither simply to colonise nor appropriate the natural world, but to give it continual voice (2013: 180). He tries not to 'clutch', as Cavell would have it. The very content of our philosophy shifts with our mood and with the changing world, 'as every season seems best to us in its turn' (2012: 451). *Walden* is itself structured loosely across the times of the year. (This present book is structured around repose, sacrifice, departure and meeting.) The prose dwells now on more abstract thinking, now on detail like house building or the cost of seeds, now on the vegetation or on animal life. In Lawrence Buell's eyes, the interest of the first-person writing lies less in evoking a 'unifying consciousness' than in 'the succession of exploits of its crusty, resourceful, unpredictable narrator', from 'hoeing beans' to 'nearly devouring a woodchuck' (1973: 309, 298). With his rich textures of specifics, Thoreau is not even – as Russell Goodman puts it – an Aristotle to Emerson's Plato (2015: 200), for this is no general treatise on ontology or epistemology. It is not even a theory.

Poverty is, after all and above all, always an 'experiment'. It is in this lax, undefined trajectory through life that *Walden* 'flows' – in Wai Chee Dimock's words – 'outward, circumnavigating the globe, gliding past Europe and Africa on its way back to India' (2006: 9, 28). The apparent stepping away from past history and the present global order links us to reference points across history and geography. Not least of these is the classical literature and thought of the Indian subcontinent and the *Bhagavad Gita*. 'Be a Columbus to whole new continents and worlds within you', Thoreau urges in his concluding thoughts (2012: 458). Cavell and others point out that this is a rebuke to Ante-Bellum New England and America, to how 'discovery', religious dissidence and the cry for freedom are subsumed historically in oppression and self-repression, from slavery to the everyday working of the economy. In dwelling on two 'accidents' – so-called 'discovery' itself, and Thoreau inhabiting Walden on Independence Day – Cavell shows us the writer's unsaying (not his rejection) of his own American lineage (Cavell 1981: 7–9, 87), his 'foundational fictions', just as Gabriel's orphaned voice does for Spain and Europe.

But this is not a matter solely of the United States. If the expedition sponsored by Spain's monarchs began a prospective universal monarchy, if, as Karl Marx supposed, the venture launched intense Oceanic globalisation (including the traffic in slaves), aside from it, lying at a tangent, as if in some wood cabin by some remote pond, there is a parallel and truer, Ocean-spanning, history-encompassing kingdom, which may take its place, in which Columbus's fateful journey is at last transfigured. In this retreat to a tangent, Bayoán's dreamt-of reversal of Columbus's voyage will now take place, without the literalness of global travelling through which Bayoán failed, without continual sacrifice. It will resonate with the 'expressions, rhythms, and imagery of the Old Testament prophets', Standish says (2006: 148). The house at *Walden* is filled with ancient presences, as if a metropolis were built upon graves, Pogue Harrison remarks. Its freedom is liberty to inherit the depths of time (2003: 42). This is the domain of what is truly classic, a compelling force across place and time, 'for what are classics but the noblest recorded thoughts of man? They are the only oracles which are not decayed, and there are such answers to the most modern inquiry in them as Delphi and Dodona never gave' (2012: 279).

Perception through anecdotal contemplation; or, heeding the donkey

Some attempts at a global approach to culture emphasise, less an encompassing account, than an outlook that evades national and localising interpretations. They look instead to specific encounters. Thomas DaCosta Kaufmann, Catherine Dossin and Béatrice Joyeux-Prunel advocate such an approach in their *Circulations in the Global History of Art*, for example (2015: 18). At times, mid-nineteenth-century art and literature take another tack. Here the very act of attending to and contemplating something apparently anecdotal – a specific encounter – may, of itself, enable us to apprehend large connections across place and time. In the turbulent early 1870s in Spain, the donkey came to the fore in such efforts. The patient, gentle beast of burden, antique mode of transport, associated with Christ's entry into Jerusalem, guides us through its 'power of passiveness'.

In 1872, Rosales painted a small oil, *Donkey* (*Burro*), which vividly offers such an experience. We see the humble beast now only from behind, at an angle, its face hidden from us, as it stands pointing towards something unseen in the distance. Seemingly isolated and unmoving, it wears gear typical of provincial Murcia, far from the madding crowds of Spain, at a remove from the centres of power in Europe and the world. Its large, nondescript back end disproportionately dominates the image. Not only do we contemplate something apparently incidental, peripheral and passive. We do so from what, by many standards, seems the wrong end. It is out of this off-beat angle, and from this tangential position, that we apprehend how to go on. Stripes across the beast's buttocks even form a broken version of the Spanish flag, disappearing into or emerging from the anus beneath its tail, suggesting the national panorama. We look upon the narrative of Spanish collective life as a protrusion from a donkey's backside, and, in turn, upon transcendent universality as emerging from the rear view of a provincial *burro*.

As befits an animal linked to Christ, to divine sacrifice and to redemption, the image has about it the quality of a transcendent vision. The blankness beyond the donkey's head is bright, like an expanding aureole. It is as if the diagonal line of sight, along the animal, into the depths of the image and beyond, were leading us into some new dimension. The local place – somewhere in Murcia – seems to dilate and open onto a transfiguration in our experience of the world. With its lack of figurative detail, the beckoning emptiness could be anywhere and everywhere: it is 'the nothing of an everything', such as we saw in Whistler.

Instead of modernity

We get there in the gentle, meditative contemplation of vagueness, through which we move back and forth between what is localised and what might be universal, the one dilating into the other. To borrow Thoreau's words, the donkey lives quite laxly and undefined in front', its 'outlines dim and misty on that side'. Through Rosales's imprecise irregular broad brushstrokes, his limited, ochre-tinged chromatic range from grey to creamy golden whites taking in some brownish-reds, the donkey almost melts into and out of the surrounding blankness.

What is it to heed the donkey, we might ask? Let us consider what is at once a fleeting moment and a core incident in *The Three-Cornered Hat* (*Sombrero de tres picos*) (1874), a novel by Pedro Antonio de Alarcón, later adapted as a ballet by Pablo Picasso and Manuel de Falla. Set just before 1808, the tale recounts how the Corregidor – an abusive local oligarch in an Andalusian village – unsuccessfully seeks sex with the miller's wife in the former's absence. The miller, suspecting both the official and his spouse, seeks to take revenge. Two passing donkeys – ridden respectively by the miller and his wife – salute one another in the darkness of the night. Had the beasts' riders attended to this call, the entire narrative would have halted there and then, for the miller would have realised his wife was both un-implicated and unharmed, and she would have impeded his onward passage. The story's shifts between dominant and submissive positions in sexuality, social authority and corresponding violence would have aborted. The miller would not have continued his Othello-like – if failed – pursuit of vengeance on the Corregidor for supposed adultery with his wife, and on his wife for the same. The two men's spouses would not in turn have humiliated them for their folly.

Alarcón himself could be said to heed the call of history's donkey, and to show us how. His light, anecdotal tale of pre-revolutionary, rural Spain – drawn from a folk story – is flanked by references to the vast changes soon to be unleashed after 1808 that would entangle Spain, its empire, Europe and even the village we behold in *The Three-Cornered Hat*. The episode dwarfs these references, its miniature world looming over any larger narrative of history (Ginger 2010: 65–6), and the latter's patterns of domination and submission. We are invited here to pull back, to disentangle ourselves from intricate cause and effect, from what most apparently joins the local and the global, and to linger on the resonances of the former, as if enclosed once more within a little village, a bounded context. This is not a question of simply discarding the larger history – which, after all, frames the anecdote – any more than Inés was to attend only to her local crafts or Darwin solely to gaze upon his garden worms. There are allusions to social change scattered throughout the text (Fernández 1994). Rather, we are to reapprehend the larger picture, to refresh our disposition towards it, by venturing, gently, passively through it like a donkey. The very release from direct connections is what enables us to apprehend what it is to be in the larger whole. In Rosales's painting, the area where donkey meets the wider world is, literally, a blur; in Alarcón, the relationship with a larger history is gnomic because barely articulated. In painterly terms, an anecdotal genre piece jarringly has the air of a grand history painting, even more disconcertingly so than in Rosales's vision of Juan of Austria and Carlos V: 'What's with these melodramatic attitudes in a genre picture?' the narrator asks (¿A qué estas actitudes melodramáticas en un cuadro de género?) (Alarcón 1943: 449; Ginger 2010: 62–3). These anecdotal visions do not engage us in how Being will unfurl: like Bécquer's poems, these are not fragments as envisaged by Novalis or in Friedrich Schlegel's Progressive Universal Poetry. They are not the embryonic seed of a larger history, needing only gestation, nor are they dynamic parts of an infinitely progressing dispersal. They are invitations to a disposition, to what Thoreau calls 'a prospect of awakening'.

The effect may be reinforced rather than attenuated by distancing techniques, as if moving to a tangent of a tangent. In Ros de Olano's autobiographical masterpiece, *Return Journeys Written by An Apparition* (*Jornadas de retorno escritas por un aparecido*) (1873), the events of the main anecdote are neither undertaken by nor inflicted on Ros de Olano. Instead this is an episode that he happened to witness in his adolescence. A donkey – Bunik – decapitates a man as the young Ros de Olano looks on at his family home in rural Catalonia. In place of Ros de Olano, the apparition of the title – an apparent mirror image – tells the story, further distancing it from him. Readers are kept pointedly away from whatever full sense the incident may have had in the unfurling of a life (Ginger 2000: 93–9). The apparition has mutilated the original manuscript, leaving only this fragment. In the prologue, a serpent goes so far as to recommend: 'Make your book a confessional closed to the world.' 'Nobody ever regretted keeping quiet', it declares (Haz que tu libro sea confesionario cerrado al mundo; A nadie le pesó de haber callado) (2008: 322–3). The 'world' – including the readership – is thus left dissociated from the intimate emotions of the autobiographical subject, which are, literally, unarticulated, just as the heart of Ros de Olano's Being in the world is evoked only by something he has beheld.

This is all the more striking given the significance of Ros de Olano's life story, from his birth as the son of a Spanish officer in imperial Venezuela, to his leading role in liberal politics and in the military, including the invasion of Morocco, passing through his orphaned childhood in an absolutist family in Catalonia. An autobiography of Ros de Olano had the potential to unfurl a life narrative within the development of larger history. In its digressions and its framing, the story of Bunik the donkey evades even as it evokes such a possibility. Mention of life in imperial America is aborted, for example: it is too wondrous to be believed (2008: 326), as if the narrative could not incorporate what Ortega calls the 'paradigmatic discourse of Abundance in which America is represented' (2006: 20). References to larger events appear and pass, like the family's support for the uprising against liberal rule in the early 1820s, and Ros de Olano's reflections on the lasting consequences for Spain of the actions of all sides in that struggle (2008: 368–9, 371–2). It is pointedly in a digression that we read his discussion of humankind's dilation from confines – like those of the Catalan village – to a world without frontiers, 'the universal aspiration, called *Idea of the Human*', 'the boundless ideal of universal fraternity' (la aspiración universal, llamada *Idea Humana*, la idea sin término de la fraternidad universal) (2008: 358–9). The same occurs with brief recollections of Spain's global past and its decisive role in joining the hemispheres and completing the earth, as Ros de Olano puts it (completó la tierra) (2008: 370). These are followed immediately by the words 'As I was saying, my uncle came out of his room' (Iba diciendo que salió mi tío de su cuarto) (2008: 371). Conversely, the very retreat into the 'confessional closed to the world' becomes the basis of common experience, just as looking at the back end of Rosales's donkey takes us into all immensity: 'I bind humanity together', the reticent serpent says (enlazo la humanidad) (2008: 321). Perhaps correspondingly, the main action involves a donkey, a mode of transport that pre-dates the accelerating encirclement of railways (Lawless 2011). It occurs in Puig Alegre, a village whose leader resists change, and which is so isolated that some of its women thought the world literally ended with its bounds (2008: 356).

What is observed – but only observed – in the closed confessional, and confined location, is a fusion of the supremely peaceful passive with its dominant opposite, each continually taking the place of the other. As the adolescent Ros de Olano looks on, Bunik attacks his tormentor – the local man Saturní – chewing off the peasant's face before decapitating him. The donkey then nods, as if in assent, while it is executed, the beast's blood mingling with that which floods out of the human. The 'power of passiveness', embodied in the donkey, here inverts the order of nature (as Ros de Olano puts it) (2008: 407). The beast becomes sacrificially dominant, splitting open the limits of the human's body and erasing his individual face, before returning to a posture of submission where bullets can split its own skin open, breaking apart its own bounds in death, so that the blood of human and animal merge (2008: 407–9, 412). In that moment, we appreciate the sensation of humans and animals encountering one another at the point of violent death, the reality of their meeting, and the resistance of the beast to any scheme of interpretation that seeks to incorporate it. Like Hunt's *Scapegoat*, Bunik 'met his death in redress of laws he did not know' (recibió la muerte en desagravio de unas leyes que él no conocía) (2008: 328).

In Ros de Olano – as in Alarcón and Galdós's invocations of vengeful Othello – the sacrifice resonates with the dangers of attitudes from the historic depths of European time. Alongside the violence to the rest of the natural world, it is redolent with violent penetration and abuse of women, the knife wielded towards Desdemona. We witness the male partner claiming possession, the powerful using force against lower-class women. Bunik's revenge follows the absolutist Saturní's assault on the young orphan Marieta, driving the spikes of a comb into her head, just as he has previously tortured the animal. In turn, blaming the woman, and having killed the donkey, the head of the household casts Marieta out onto the roads, beyond Puig Alegre, and she vanishes at its boundary, into an unknown fate. Reminiscent now of a Maria Dolorosa, her wandering evokes release from bounded context only through and into sustained pain towards death. A shared fate for all humanity returns in her departure, just as Ros de Olano – long departed from the ancestral home, unable to return – dwells on the story of Bunik: 'The certainty of pain comes between the fortuitous cases of being born and dying' (Entre los casos fortuitos del nacer y el morir media el dolor cierto) (2008: 413).

The heeding of the donkey, the lingering on tangents, are not a simple rejection of 'the world' and its violent swings from domination to submission, its sacrificial frenzies, its violent universalism, its encounters with death, animal and human. Bunik shows us how passiveness, even peacefulness, without ceasing in the end so to be, traverses the realms of violence: that is what is shocking. Alarcón's donkeys, after all, still do ride on, their riders upon them, through the reversals of power, the longing for dominance and revenge, towards the beckoning post-1808 world which offers the same. We pull back from the grand patterns of history, from the entangled connections of place and time, into the minute particularity of context, precisely so as to sense – as if from a distance – 'the world'. Such an anecdote is – the serpent tells us – 'open to each conscience, so that you may be justified in secret by whoever reads' (abierto a cada conciencia, para que tú seas justificado en secreto por quien leyere) (2008: 323). On this account, microhistory – the detailed study of local moments in place and time – is not an alternative to grand narrative, nor even is it quite a microcosm of the latter. Rather, it is a state of observation from a distance, through whose vague resonance we sense sacrifice and anticipate the leaping beyond, the departure from a context, that nearer brings. As this binds humanity together, it becomes a kind of meeting.

Coda: meeting and friendship; or, two Juans and a lesser Faust

We began, in Estanislao del Campo's *Fausto*, with two *gauchos* meeting in the countryside beyond Buenos Aires. At a tangent to the world of the epic tale, they spoke of Faust, blending themselves together as they did so, merging also with the depths of time, the expanse of place. Now, we find ourselves deep in rural southern Spain, far from the capital, in the village of Villabermeja. Here two people – the author, man of letters and diplomat Juan Valera, and his double, the fictional character Juan Fresco (Montesinos 1969: 135) – speak of a modern 'lesser Faust'. The story is recounted in Valera's long novel *The Illusions of Doctor Faustino* (*Las ilusiones del doctor Faustino*) (1874–75; the suffix *-ino* is a diminutive). Across the many pages of the action (400 in one modern edition), Juan Valera plays no part, and Juan Fresco intervenes but a little. They are as apparently tangential to the action as the village is to Spain or to the wider world. The meeting of Juan and Juan is, as it were, a coming together of disparate ways of coming together, a pairing of similitudes. It brings to the fore, not only how other moods of sameness may be brought together in repose, but the nature of their possible connection, of their encounter with one another. It returns us through repose to a meeting, and evokes how a meeting may enable diverse kinds of sameness to embrace, as if they were El Pollo and Laguna.

Juan Fresco is redolent with a restful fusion of 'poverty' and 'lavishness', finding 'the infinite (lo infinito) within the 'unprepossessing horizons' (mezquino horizonte) of Villabermeja (Valera 1970: 50, 66). A truly global Spaniard, who rode the networks of travel and commerce across the world, he has lived in the Americas before and after they separated from Spain, he has ventured across wider Europe, he has been on the Ganges in India (1970: 65), in the Philippines and Oceania and at Calcutta, his journeys rivalling those of Sinbad (1970: 60). Now he turns from this to deliberate self-confinement in his place of origin, ruthlessly contextualising himself, as it were. Such is his apparent detachment sexually and emotionally that he speaks neither of friendship nor of love affairs from his prior existence; late in life, there is no way that he will marry (1970: 61). His nickname *fresco* – literally, *fresh* – means in Spanish that he is both unconcerned and serene.

The lesser Faust, Dr Faustino, evokes – perhaps even is – all that Fresco renounces and calls *ilusión*, illusion, hoped-for dreams, a denial of what he terms *realidad*, reality (1970: 69, 76). It is as if the story of this Faust were some enduring trauma for *freshness*, and as if his railing against *ilusión*, his retreat to unprepossessing horizons, were efforts to ward it off. (Some have gone so far as to suppose that Faustino is a further alter ego of Valera, as if appearing overlaid in triple, distinct aspects (Trimble 1995: 38–9).) At the end of Fresco's long tirade on *ilusiones*, Valera asks his namesake if his feelings might arise from some unpleasant experience with someone who had them. In a striking phrase, Fresco responds, 'It is true: something unpleasant and worse than unpleasant has happened *to me* (Es verdad: algo desagradable y más que desagradable me ha pasado) (emphasis added). It is as if if he, not Faustino, were the true protagonist of the main narrative, despite appearing in it only towards the end. In this moment, Fresco 'seemed to me [to Valera] another person' (me pareció otro) (1970: 76), as if something other than his constitutive freshness had taken over. These words are echoed in the emotional change that comes upon Fresco as he witnesses Faustino's suicide: 'Don Juan Fresco was disturbed, terrifyingly moved, horrified, despite his freshness' (D. Juan Fresco estaba trastornado, conmovido espantosamente, horrorizado, a pesar de su frescura) (1970: 445).

The traumatic *ilusión* appears in the novel as a failed reaching outwards from originary confines, seeking to break the binds of limitation. Faustino spends most of the work's extension wanting to get out of the village and up to Madrid, to link himself out of the provinces and into the 'centre of intellectual movement' (centro del movimiento intelectual). There he might realise his greatness across a wide range of fields from mysticism to politics (1970: 346). At one point, he identifies his individual spirit with that of progress in the spirit of the age, as if he were a beacon of the *Geist* (1970: 279). Once in the capital, he lives in a hostel, achieves little, and is barely known. He himself recognises that his love both of his nation and of humanity is sterile (1970: 228). His is an unrealised attempt to reconnect a provincial life in Spain to the wider world. It comes at the end of an aristocratic lineage which pointedly failed to tend its own patrimony, while expending effort on a global empire that is now gone (1970: 83). Fausto's subsequent suicide is so traumatic for *freshness* because it is illusion's crazed culmination in attempted sacrifice, in the violent bursting of the bounds of the self, in utter self-destruction of the kind we saw in Chapter 3: 'If my individual persists, selfishness will persist, for it is the essence of individuality' (Si persiste mi individuo, persistirá el egoísmo, que es la esencia de la individualidad) (1970: 444). Faustino echoes in his final words the belief system of his beloved, now dead, María, his *Immortal Friend*, whose heart he broke, and who held that they were eternal consorts, with a love free of earthly life, transmigrating across the ages (1970: 371, 444). The supreme moment of self-destruction appears here as the supreme fallacy of belief in persistence across the depths of time and extent of time. Likewise, in his initial affection for María, there is an insane conflation of likeness with identity, of analogy with truth, that blurs the bounds between the places and times of Hispanic history, in the manner of the sickly analogies that we saw in Chapter 3. Faustino associates her with a figure from a family portrait of La Coya, also called María, from sixteenth-century Vice-Regal Peru, whose money was foundational to Faustino's noble lineage (1970: 188–9).

In the place of empire, of global economics, of territory-spanning intellectual networks and of world-historical posturing, all these things in which Thoreau feared distraction, in the place of self-shattering and endless persistence, Juan Fresco appeals to a bedrock, his 'reality' (realidad), which gives rootedness to 'fantasia' (fantasía), the castles in the air of which Thoreau spoke. His imagination, locked in Villabermeja, is an openness to true potential, to what the real might be. From this vantage point, it is not 'lavishness' or 'luxury' as such that brings down Faustino and his lineage: it is denial of a putative ontology, a basis of Being, which rests on self-limitation in order to dilate infinitely, evading the hazards of inauthenticity. Conversely, through the figure of Juan Valera, in and out of the novel, we perceive the allure of the connectedness that Thoreau and Fresco denounce. A literary eminence in 'the centre of intellectual movement', a one-time diplomat with postings from Rio de Janeiro to Russia, he emphasises the allure of the global and metropolitan locations through which commerce and travel took Fresco (1970: 65). His attachments in sexuality and affection likewise seem the inverse of Fresco. He had visited Russian brothels and casually petted the actress Madeleine Brohan. Aspects of his private affairs had become public when his letters were published (Lombardero 2004: 126–7; Azaña 1971: 186–7). Quite unlike Fresco, at the age of 43 he had married the 20-year-old Dolores Delavert in Paris, having first met her in Brazil (Valera 1970: 9, 167; Lombardero 2004: 181–4).

At Fresco's side, Juan Valera evokes, not as such refusal, but a sidestepping of expansive repose. 'I do not claim to demonstrate ... any thesis contrary to illusions', he declares, having quizzically interrogated Fresco (no pretendo probar ninguna tesis contraria a las ilusiones) (1970: 77). He sets out a tranquil coexistence, akin to movement in parallel lines, and avoids any forceful counterposition: 'Don Juan Fresco follows his opinion, and I my own, which is besides the point here' (D. Juan Fresco sigue su opinión y yo la mía, que aquí no es del caso) (1970: 77). Only with a smile and the astute kindness of a friend does he imply that Fresco's stance of repose may be, not a general good, but a particular mood, born of specific circumstances, 'and for that reason he/you (Fresco) declaims so much against having and losing illusions' (y por eso declama tanto contra el tener y perder ilusiones) (1970: 76). Parallel lines these may be, but there is more to the relationship than contiguity. The village of Villabermeja, like Juan Fresco himself, evokes deflection from, but not an absence of the global connections that were its making. It offers 'unprepossessing horizons' only through the eclipsing of its historic resonances: the violent meeting of worlds, not only in imperial ventures of Europeans in the Americas, but as a frontier in the clash of Christianity and Islam in Iberia (1970: 79). Put more strongly, the former traveller Juan Fresco and his tangential context are redolent with a longing for repose in the wake of the meeting of vast global forces. The figure of Juan Valera evokes the same, but in the opposite direction: a tendency towards global networks and 'the centre of intellectual movement' that, even so, longs for repose. Valera's sentimental education has been to learn that those, like himself, who celebrate rural idyll but do not return, are not guilty of contradiction or hypocrisy. Rather, he finds in them what he calls 'entrañable ternura': engaging tenderness (1970: 50). By extension, such a sentiment, in both directions, is what links together Juan Fresco and Juan Valera, Villabermeja with the wider world: a feeling that embraces both departure and repose.

A gentle sentiment ('tenderness') embodies the combined pull, on the one hand, of direct connections to the large affairs of humanity, and, on the other, of the boundless perspectives found in self-limiting viewpoints. This involves a disposition for our feelings to be wholly defined neither by absorption in a fixation with *ilusión* and its rejection, nor by a stepping away from such sentiment and a giving ourselves to direct connectedness with the world, but rather by an outlook that entails the two together. The structure of the novel is an invitation to reconstitute our disposition toward life in a nuanced, textured experience that blends these two perspectives, as if it were their meeting, like the encounter of Juan and Juan. Unfortunately, many critics have taken these aesthetic textures as a failing: Montesinos complains that it is like reading two disconnected novels, for example (1969: 140). Comparing the work to *Sentimental Education*, the influential late-nineteenth-century writer Leopoldo Alas observed that many readers found it similarly unappealing (wrongly he felt) (Valera 1970: 18–19).

The incapacity and capacity to develop a narrative plot, to unfurl the story of Being(s), here evoke how *ilusión* fails and is destructive as a mode of connection. But the writing also encompasses what is unassimilated within that assumption: the possibility that we could or should not so simply withdraw to a tangent and repose, even as we may not give ourselves utterly to the *ilusión*. Its complex, varying rhythms stretch out, interrupt, curtail, delay and accelerate the plot line by turns and under diverse aspects. Insofar as Faustino seeks to reach 'the centre of movement', much of the novel is a long delay, a lengthy non-event. Some 75 per cent of the novel dwells on a handful of months – DeCoster has observed – before a rapid consideration of seventeen years, and then more detail as we head to the end of Faustino's life (1974: 112). The interval of some 270 pages in a modern edition is largely filled by three love stories with three women (Costanza, Rosita, María). Each of these in turn are abortive tales about transcending limitations, each a Faustian in a Faustian tale (Weaver 2006), whether by seeking funds to reach Madrid, or invocations of an ideal of Arcadia (1970: 270), or of Dante's Beatrice (1970: 244). Conversely, the account of Faustino's arrival in Madrid – the 'centre of movement' – is drastically telescoped as unimportant (1970: 356). Then, as if in accelerating and compressed narrative, the three women reappear in the capital and in Faustino's life, and, through 100 pages of a modern edition, we have plots of jealousy and love triangles, culminating destructively first in a duel, and then in María's death and Faustino's suicide. As they return, the women each evoke a form of connectedness to a larger narrative of history or humanity, hinting at stories that stretch out, only glimpsed, from the tale of Faustino: María through her transmigration and her travels with Juan Fresco; Costanza by being adored across the capitals of the continent, shining 'in the great world' (en el gran mundo) (1970: 207); and Rosita, through marriage to a capitalist, and by exercising power over her lover, a general, who in Spain's political circumstances could change the form of the state at will (1970: 363, 439).

Expressed through this narrative structure, the 'tenderness' that Valera advocates involves neither dispassionate distance from *ilusión* and its opposite, nor a playful oscillation between them, a 'vaivén'. Nor is it quite an attempt to overcome their apparent logical contradiction through dialectical interplay, as some have supposed (Montesinos 1969: 135). Rather it is a lived, affective connection. Beyond the perspective of either side – Juan Valera or his namesake Juan Fresco – we may find such a disposition in their friendship itself. Together Valera and Fresco form, in Whitman's words, a centripetal and centrifugal force, here called, not 'Me myself', but simply 'Juan', the name into which they blend. The narrative voice in the main plot seamlessly combines the two, more still than the rhyming pattern of El Pollo and Laguna's words in *Fausto*: we have no way of knowing who contributed what to the tale of Dr Faustino. In the culminating reaction to Faustino's suicide, the narrative voice blends the fixation with *ilusión* – the trauma and desire to be free of it, 'he was disturbed' – with a teasing smile upon that obsession: 'despite his freshness'.

In this friendship, in such a coming together of comings together, in this blending (*mixtura*), there is something irreducible to either Juan, beyond either of their visions, in their telling, or hearing, or retelling of Faustino's story. There is an intimation of, a disposition towards something unassimilated in their twin accounts of connectedness. Pointedly, there are things recounted by the shared voice that neither Juan seems able to have known, as Marta Remedios Sánchez García notes (2009: 94–5, 99). More tellingly still, in the framing narrative of the two Juans, as in the final appearance of Frédéric and Deslauriers in *Sentimental Education*, women – so crucial to the story – are remarkable for their lack of protagonism, as they are in the pairing of Del Campo's *gauchos*, as if only masculine friendship is the lens through which the question of *ilusión* may be mediated. Yet, as Mary Orr has remarked of Flaubert's novel, 'what has in fact fuelled the plot remains largely unvoiced. Throughout and repeatedly, it was the pivotal actions … of these women that instigated and shaped the history to come' (2005: 22). In Valera's unresolved dialogue, 'Harmonic Rationalism' – written in response to a fashion for philosophy in women's salons (Azaña 1971: 238) – it is not least the quizzical voice of a female interlocutor that points beyond the system-building explanations, of which Valera is so sceptical (Ginger 2010: 68). Costanza, Rosita and María are powerful agents, each of them realising their own version of *ilusión* (right or wrong) to more practical effect than Faustino. Their decisions are fundamental to the novel's outcome, Sánchez García and others have observed

(2009: 191). Teresia Langford Taylor goes so far as to see them as triumphant (1997: 8). Their stories reach out beyond the constraints of Faustino's tale as we have it in the novel, stretching, in details untold, into the Americas, across the capitals of Europe, through the corridors of financial, political and military power, even through imaginary history, so as to shape events. Even as it may seek to define women in its terms, perhaps in spite of itself, the narrative voice, like 'Me myself', intimates the potential of its going on through such connections, the return of the female voice, the surpassing of its own exclusions.

The blended voice resonates from the long depths of time. Even as the world of Villabermeja is tangential, even as Faustino's story is historically and locally specific, they are classic. Fresco blames Faustino's fate on recent *mores* – 'these days ... Dr Faustinos abound' – but he completes the sentence with words to the same effect taken from Juvenal, in the original Latin (En el día ... los doctores Faustino abundan) (1970: 446). Valera ponders his longing for Villabermeja likewise through Horace's poem *Beatus Ille*, and its sixteenth-century Spanish imitator Brother Luis de León, in the company of the poetry of Francisco Martínez de la Rosa, a leading nineteenth-century politician and diplomat. Already in Horace, the individual portrayed both wishes to be far from the madding crowd but stays in the city, as is Valera's fate (1970: 49). This is not, reductively, to telescope the mid-nineteenth century back into the terms of ancient Rome, any more than Faustino is simply the medieval or even Goethe's Faust. In recalling the legend, our lesser Faust is all too aware that there is now no magic and no easily tricked Mephistopheles (1970: 106). His fate is linked to a number of historical specificities of nineteenth-century Spain, from his membership of the allegedly riotous National Militia (1970: 448), through the power of the military as exploited by Rosita (2008: 439), to a trend of philosophic doubt and a desire for unearned social superiority (1970: 448). Nor, though, are the Latin words or the Faust legend – or any number of other historical allusions – just received and reinterpreted in this new context. There is too fluid a slippage between timescales and societies in Fresco's verdict upon Faustino, as there is elsewhere, for that to be so. For instance, Costanza remarks that money is what makes for true aristocracy in this age (en esta época), even as she says that 'in all times it has been the same' (en todos los tiempos ha sido lo mismo) (Valera 1970: 204). The central, Faustian notion of *ilusión* – of overweening connectedness – is presented without contradiction as a persistent, enduring human condition, and in its particularity to Faustino and his time and place, as a story of an historic generation, as Montesinos puts it (1969: 133). We feel the antique dilate in textures across the swathes of history, like Baudelaire's 'mal'.

If there is a 'modern world', we would experience it as an emanation of such atavisms. In the culture of the Spanish First Republic, the recurrent visions of donkeys remind us of as much: a mode of transport burdened with connotations so ancient that it was Jesus's vehicle back into Jerusalem. The tangential viewpoints are redolent with centuries of culture: Ros de Olano invoking Calvary in *Return Journeys*, Othello giving shape to plotlines in *The Court of Carlos IV* and *The Three-Cornered Hat*. However bad the Spanish translation and adaptation, Gabriel muses, Shakespeare's play 'always preserved the dramatic elements from its origin, and the impression it exercised upon its audience was astonishing' (conservaba siempre los resortes dramáticos de su origen, y la impresión que ejercía sobre el público era asombrosa) (2006: 181). In Valera's writing of the 1870s – in his shorter novel *Pepita Jiménez* (1874) as in Dr Faustino – we find a littering of references to antique writers of varied vintage from scholastic theologians and Spanish mystics, to Dante and

Instead of modernity

Petrarch. More recent authors find a place among them too. It is partly this jumbling of authorities that gives his work an antique air, something it shares with Marx and Manet, Melville and Lucas, and many more. We find the effect across writers and artists that we have encountered in this chapter: in Rosales, Isabel the Catholic one day, Lucretia another. Stepping back from individual writers and artists of the mid-nineteenth century, we spy the same phenomenon across the span of culture: one writer invoking Shakespeare, another the Bhagavad Gita.

In none of these coming togethers are voices each assigned their respective location systematically and analytically, contextualised in relation to one another, separated in place and time. Rather, they are all tangents, all a centre with respect to each periphery and vice versa. This is not to diminish the affective attachment felt towards any or all of them. We have seen that it is not in the nature of tangential things that there should be any such total loss. Nor is it to say that other voices could not or should not join them. We may always go on. We may always be released from the confines of our present centre, in submissive domination, dominant submission, in our own dying, in our leaping beyond, in companionship. We may encounter voices from across place and time 'talking *among themselves*, celebrating a reunion'. In tempered repose, we may find 'telluric force'.

References

Abelove, Henry (1993), 'From Thoreau to Queer Politics', *Yale Journal of Criticism* 6.2, 17–27.
Afinoguénova, Eugenia (2009), '"Painted in Spanish": The Prado Museum and the Naturalization of the "Spanish School" in the Nineteenth Century', *Journal of Spanish Cultural Studies* 10.3, 319–40.
Afinoguénova, Eugenia (2018), *El Prado: La cultura y el ocio (1819–1939)*, ed. by Javier Portús Pérez, trans. by Pablo Veyrat, Madrid: Cátedra, Kindle edition.
Agamben, Giorgio (1991), *Language and Death: The Place of Negativity*, Minneapolis: University of Minnesota Press.
Ahern, Daniel (2012), *The Smile of Tragedy: Nietzsche and the Art of Virtue*, University Park: Pennsylvania University Press.
Alarcón, Pedro Antonio (1943), *Obras completas*, ed. Luis Martínez Kleiser, Madrid: Ediciones FAX.
Alberti, Samuel J. M. M. (2011), 'Introduction: The Dead Ark', in *The After Lives of Animals: A Museum Menagerie*, ed. by Samuel J.M.M. Alberti, Charlottesville: University of Virginia Press, 1–16.
Alexander, Jeffrey C. (2006), *The Civil Sphere*, Oxford: Oxford University Press.
Alix, Luis Felipe (1866), *Tratado elemental de geometría descriptiva seguido de una ligeras nociones sobre perspectivas y sombras*, Valencia: Imprenta de Ferrer de Orga, 2 vols.
Allan, Jonathan A. (2016), *Reading from Behind: A Cultural History of the Anus*, London: Zed Books.
Alonso, Carlos J. (1998), *The Burden of Modernity: The Rhetoric of Cultural Discourse in Spanish America*, Oxford: Oxford University Press.
Althusser, Louis & Balibar, Étienne (1970), *Reading Capital*, trans. by Ben Brewster, London: NLB.
Amann, Elizabeth (2006), *Importing Madame Bovary: The Politics of Adultery*, Basingstoke: Palgrave Macmillan.
Ankersmit, Frank (2005), *Sublime Historical Experience*, Stanford, CA: Stanford University Press
anonymous (1855), *La perla del teatro español: Biografía de la actriz Doña Matilde Díez*, Mexico City: Imprenta de F. Escalante y Comp.
Anzaldúa, Gloria (2012), *Borderlands/La Frontera: The New Mestiza*, San Francisco: Aunt Lute Books.
Appiah, Anthony (2005), *The Ethics of Identity*, Princeton, NJ: Princeton University Press.
Armillas-Tiseyra, Magalí (2008), 'Un texto (ex)céntrico: Nation, Narrative, and Archive in Lucio V. Mansilla's "Una excursión a los indios ranqueles"', *Latin American Literary Review* 36.72, 52–82.

References

Armstrong, Carol (1996), 'Pencil of Light: Julia Margaret Cameron and the Maternalization of Photography', *October* 76, 114–41.
Armstrong, Carol (1998), *Scenes in a Library: Reading the Photograph in the Book, 1843–1875*, Cambridge, MA: MIT Press.
Armstrong, Carol (2002), *Manet Manette*, New Haven, CT: Yale University Press.
Armstrong, Isobel (2008), *Victorian Glassworlds: Glass Culture and the Imagination 1830–1880*, Oxford: Oxford University Press.
Armstrong, Nancy (1999), *Fiction in the Age of Photography*, Cambridge, MA: Harvard University Press.
Arnáiz, José Manuel (1981), *Eugenio Lucas: Su Vida y su Obra*, Madrid: M. Montal.
Auerbach, Nina (1982), *Women and the Demon: The Life of a Victorian Myth*, Cambridge, MA: Harvard University Press.
Auerbach, Nina (1990), *Private Theatricals: The Lives of the Victorians*, Cambridge, MA: Harvard University Press.
Azaña, Manuel (1971), *Ensayos sobre Valera*, ed. by Juan Marichal, Madrid: Alianza.
Badiou, Alain (2007), *Being and Event*, trans. by Oliver Feltham, London: Continuum.
Bal, Mieke (2002), *Travelling Concepts in the Humanities: A Rough Guide*, Toronto: University of Toronto Press.
Balibar, Etienne (1995), *Marx*, trans. by Chris Turner, London: Verso.
Bann, Stephen (1995), *Romanticism and the Rise of History*, New York: Twayne.
Bann, Stephen (1997), *Paul Delaroche*, London: Reaktion Books.
Barasch, Mosche (1998), *Modern Theories of Art, 2: From Impressionism to Kandinsky*, New York: New York University Press.
Barón, Javier (2017), *Fortuny (1838–1874)*, Madrid: Museo Nacional del Prado.
Barthes, Roland (1988), 'The Death of an Author', in *Modern Criticism and Theory*, ed. by David Lodge, London: Longman, 167–72.
Barthes, Roland (2000), *Camera Lucida: Reflections on Photography*, trans. by Richard Howard, London: Vintage Classics.
Basu, Biman (2012), *The Commerce of Peoples: Sadomasochism and African-American Literature*, Lanham, MD: Lexington Books.
Bataille, Georges (1983), *Manet*, ed. by Françoise Cachin, trans. by Austryn Wainhouse & James Emmons, Geneva: Macmillan.
Bataille, Georges (2014), *Inner Experience: L'Expérience intérieure*, trans. and ed. by Stuart Kendall, New York: SUNY Press.
Baudelaire, Charles (1965), *Critique d'Art*, ed. by Claude Pichois, Paris: Librairie Armand Colin, 2 vols.
Baudelaire, Charles (1972), *Les Fleurs du mal*, ed. by Yves Florenne & Marie-Jeanne Durry, Paris: Livre de Poche.
Baudelaire, Charles (2008), *De l'essence du rire et généralement du comique dans les arts plastiques*, Paris: Éditions Sillage.
Bayly, C. A. (2004), *The Birth of the Modern World 1780–1914: Global Connections and Comparisons*, Oxford: Blackwell.
Bazin, André (1960), 'The Ontology of the Photographic Image (Translated by Hugh Gary)', *Film Quarterly* 13.4, 4–9.
Beard, Mary (2008), *The Fires of Vesuvius: Pompeii Lost and Found*, London: Profile Books.
Beard, Mary (2016), *SPQR: A History of Ancient Rome*, London: Profile Books.

References

Beckman, Ericka (2013), 'Fables of Globalization: Race, Sex and Money in Nineteenth-Century Latin America', *Journal of Iberian and Latin American Studies* 19:2, 99–116.
Bécquer, Gustavo Adolfo (1998), *Rimas y otros poemas*, ed. by Jorge Campos, Madrid: Alianza.
Beer, Gillian (1983), *Darwin's Plots: Evolutionary Narrative in Darwin, George Eliot and Nineteenth-Century Fiction*, London: Routledge.
Beer, Gillian (1986), '"The Face of Nature": Anthropomorphic Elements in the Language of *The Origin of the Species*', in *Languages of Nature: Critical Essays on Science and Literature*, ed. by Ludmilla Jordanova, London: Free Association Books, 207–43.
Bell, Julian (2007), *The Mirror of the Mirror: A New History of Art*, London: Thames & Hudson.
Bellis, Peter J. (2003), *Writing Revolution: Aesthetics and Politics in Hawthorne, Whitman, and Thoreau*, Athens: University of Georgia Press.
Benjamin, Walter (1970), 'The Task of the Translator', in *Illuminations*, trans. by Harry Zohn, London: Cape, 69–82.
Benjamin, Walter (1997), *Charles Baudelaire: A Lyric Poet in the Era of High Capitalism*, trans. by Harry Zohn, London: Verso.
Benjamin, Walter (2002), *Selected Writings, Volume 3: 1935–1938*, ed. by Howard Eiland & Michael W. Jennings, trans. by Edmund Jephcott et al., Cambridge, MA: Belknap Press.
Bennett, Jane (1994), *Thoreau's Nature: Ethics, Politics and the Wild*, London: Sage.
Bennett, Paula & Rosario, Vernon A., II (1995), 'Introduction: The Politics of Solitary Pleasures', in *Solitary Pleasures: The Historical, Literary, and Artistic Discourses of Auto-Eroticism*, ed. by Paula Bennett & Vernon A. Rosario II, London: Routledge, 1–17.
Berenstein, Rhona J. (1996), *Attack of the Leading Ladies: Gender, Sexuality, and Spectatorship in Classic Horror Cinema*, New York: Columbia University Press.
Bergson, Henri (1962), *Le Rire: Essai sur la signification du comique*, Paris: Presses Universitaires de la France.
Berlin, Isaiah (2013), *The Crooked Timber of Humanity*, ed. by Henry Hardy, Princeton, NJ: Princeton University Press.
Berman, Marshall (1983), *All That Is Solid Melts into Air: The Experience of Modernity*, London: Verso.
Bersani, Leo (1987), 'Is the Rectum a Grave?', *October* 43, 197–222.
Bersani, Leo & Phillips, Adam (2010), *Intimacies*, Chicago: University of Chicago Press.
Bhabha, Homi (1994), *The Location of Culture*, London: Routledge.
Blackburn, Simon (2006), *Truth: A Guide for the Perplexed*, Harmondsworth: Penguin.
Blanco, María del Pilar (2012), *Ghost-Watching American Modernity: Haunting, Landscape, and the Hemispheric Imagination*, New York: Fordham University Press.
Bleichmar, Daniela (2015), 'The Imperial Visual Archive: Images, Evidence, and Knowledge in the Early Modern Hispanic World', *Colonial Latin American Review* 24.2, 236–66.
Bloom, Harold (1973), *The Anxiety of Influence: A Theory of Poetry*, Oxford: Oxford University Press.
Bohrer, Frederick N. (1998), 'Inventing Assyria: Exoticism and Reception in Nineteenth-Century England and France', *Art Bulletin* 80.2, 336–56.
Boime, Albert (1971), *The Academy and French Painting in the Nineteenth Century*, New York: Phaidon.
Boime, Albert (1993), *The Art of the Macchia and the Risorgimento: Representing Culture and Nationalism in Nineteenth-Century Italy*, Chicago: University of Chicago Press.
Boime, Albert (2007), *Art in the Age of Civil Struggle 1848–1871*, Chicago: University of Chicago Press.

Bonilla Cerezo, Rafael (2010), *Dos gauchos retrucadores: Nueva lectura del Fausto de Estanislao del Campo*, Alicante: Publicaciones Universidad de Alicante.
Boon, Marcus (2013), *In Praise of Copying*, Cambridge, MA: Harvard University Press, Kindle edition.
Boone, M. Elizabeth (2007), *Vistas de España: American Views of Art and Life in Spain, 1860–1914*, New Haven, CT: Yale University Press.
Borges, Jorge Luis (1985), *Otras inquisiciones*, Madrid: Alianza.
Borja y Alarcón, Pedro (1876), *Estudios hechos sobre la aplicación de la fotografía a la topografía en general, y en particular a la copia y reducción de planos por el oficial 1o del Cuerpo de Topógrafos D. Pedro Borja y Alarcón*, Madrid: n.p.
Bourdieu, Pierre (1992), *Les Règles de l'art: Genèse et structure du champs littéraire*, Paris: Éditions du Seuil.
Bradley, Benjamin Sylvester (2011), 'Darwin's Sublime: The Contest Between Reason and Imagination in *On the Origin of Species*', *Journal of the History of Biology* 44, 205–32.
Bretón de los Herreros, Manuel (1852), *Progresos y estado actual del arte de la declamación en los teatros de España*, Madrid: Establecimiento Tipográfico de Mellado.
Brooks, Peter (1984), *Reading for the Plot: Design and Invention in Narrative*, Oxford: Clarendon Press.
Broude, Norma (1987), *The Macchiaioli: Italian Painters of the Nineteenth Century*, New Haven, CT: Yale University Press.
Brown, Bill (2010), *A Sense of Things*, Chicago: University of Chicago Press.
Brown, Jonathan (1986), *Velázquez: Painter and Courtier*, New Haven, CT: Yale University Press.
Browning, Robert (2004), *Selected Poems*, ed. by Daniel Karlin, London: Penguin, Kindle edition.
Bruno, Giuliana (2002), *Atlas of Emotion: Journeys in Art, Architecture, and Film*, New York: Verso.
Buell, Lawrence (1973), *Literary Transcendentalism: Style and Vision in the American Renaissance*, Ithaca, NY: Cornell University Press.
Buell, Lawrence (1986), 'Moby-Dick as Sacred Text', in *New Essays on Moby-Dick*, ed. Richard H. Brodhead, Cambridge: Cambridge University Press, 53–72.
Bullough Ainscough, Rachel (2012), 'Charles Clifford en la exposición de la Photographic Society de Londres en 1854', *Espacio, Tiempo y Forma* 7, 173–84.
Burbules, Nicholas C. (2017), 'Wittgenstein's Metaphors and His Pedagogical Philosophy', in *A Companion to Wittgenstein on Education: Pedagogical Investigations*, ed. by Michael A. Peters & Jeff Stickney, Singapore: Springer, 23–34.
Burdiel, Isabel (1998), 'Myths of Failure, Myths of Success: New Perspectives on Nineteenth-Century Spanish Liberalism', *Journal of Modern History* 70, 892–912.
Butler, Judith (2007), *Gender Trouble: Feminism and the Subversion of Identity*, Abingdon: Routledge, Kindle edition.
Butler, Judith, Laclau, Ernesto & Žižek, Slavoj, eds (2000), *Contingency, Hegemony, Universality: Contemporary Dialogues on the Left*, London: Verso.
Butler, Shane (2015), *The Ancient Phonograph*, New York: Zone Books.
Buzard, James, Childers, Joseph W. & Gillooly, Eileen (2007), 'Introduction', in *Victorian Prism: Refractions of the Crystal Palace*, ed. by James Buzard, Joseph W. Childers & Eileen Gillooly, Charlottesville: University of Virginia Press, 1–19.
Byrne, Romana (2015), *Aesthetic Sexuality: A Literary History of Sadomasochism*, London: Bloomsbury.
Cabello Carro, Paz (2011), 'Spanish Collections of Americana in the Late Eighteenth Century', in *Collecting Across Cultures: Material Exchanges in the Early Modern Atlantic World*, ed. by

Daniela Bleichmar & Peter C. Mancall, Philadelphia: Pennsylvania University Press, 217–35.

Cadava, Eduardo (1997), *Words of Light: Theses on the Photography of History*, Princeton, NJ: Princeton University Press.

Cafaro, Philip (2004), *Thoreau's Living Ethics: Walden and the Pursuit of Virtue*, Athens: University of Georgia Press.

Çakmak, Gűlru (2017), *Jean-Léon Gérôme and the Crisis of History Painting in the 1850s*, Liverpool: Liverpool University Press.

Campbell, John Angus (2003), 'Why Was Darwin Believed? Darwin's *Origin* and the Problem of Intellectual Revolution', *Configurations* 11.2, 203–37.

Carbonell, Jordi À. (1999), *Marià Fortuny i la descobert d'Àfrica: Els dibuixos de la guerra hispanomarroquina, 1859–1860*, Tarragona: Museu d'Art Modern.

Cardona y Escarrabill, Baltasar (1865), *Tratado de geometría descriptiva y de sus principales aplicaciones*, Barcelona: Establecimiento tipográfico de Jaime Jepús, 2 vols.

Carlisle, E. Fred (1973), *The Uncertain Self: Whitman's Drama of Identity*, East Lansing: Michigan State University Press.

Carreño-Rodríguez, Antonio (2009), 'Modernidad en la literatura gauchesca: Carnavalización y parodia en el Fausto de Estanislao del Campo', *Hispania* 92.1, 12–24.

Carroll, Lewis (1965), *The Annotated Alice: Alice's Adventures in Wonderland & Through the Looking Glass*, ed. by Martin Gardner, Harmondsworth: Penguin.

Caruth, Cathy (1996), *Unclaimed Experience: Trauma, Narrative, and History*, Baltimore, MD: Johns Hopkins University Press.

Casanova, Pascale (2007), *The World Republic of Letters*, Cambridge, MA: Harvard University Press.

Castro, Andrea (2002), *El encuentro imposible: La conformación del fantástico ambiguo en la narrative breve argentina (1862–1910)*, Gothenburg: DocuSys.

Castro, Rosalía de (1995), *El caballero de las botas azules*, ed. by Ana Rodríguez-Fischer, Madrid: Cátedra.

Cave, Terence (1979), *The Cornucopian Text: Problems of Writing in the French Renaissance*, Oxford: Clarendon Press.

Cavell, Stanley (1981), *The Senses of Walden: An Expanded Edition*, San Francisco: North Point Press.

Cavell, Stanley (2012), *Must We Mean What We Say?*, Cambridge: Cambridge University Press.

Cavell, Stanley (2013), *This New Yet Unapproachable America: Lectures after Emerson after Wittgenstein*, Chicago: University of Chicago Press.

Certeau, Michel de (2000), 'Walking in the City', in *The Certeau Reader*, ed. by Graham Ward, Oxford: Blackwell, 101–18.

Chakrabarty, Dipesh (2001), *Provincializing Europe: Postcolonial Thought and Historical Difference*, Princeton, NJ: Princeton University Press.

Chambers, Ross (1984), *Story and Situation: Narrative Seduction and the Power of Fiction*, Minneapolis: University of Minnesota Press.

Chandler, James (1998), *England in 1819: The Politics of Literary Culture and the Case of Historicism*, Chicago: University of Chicago Press.

Chapman, Alison (1998), 'Mesmerism and Agency in the Courtship of Elizabeth Barrett and Robert Browning', *Victorian Literature and Culture* 26.2, 303–19.

Chapman, Alison (2003), '"A Poet Never Sees a Ghost": Photography and Trance in Tennyson's *Enoch Arden* and Julia Margaret Cameron's Photography', *Victorian Poetry* 41.1, 47–71.

References

Charnon Deutsch, Lou (2010), *Narratives of Desire: Nineteenth-Century Spanish Fiction by Women*, Philadelphia: Pennsylvania University Press.

Ching, Barbara & Wagner-Lawlor, Jennifer A. (2009), 'Introduction – Unextinguished: Susan Sontag's Work in Progress', in *The Scandal of Susan Sontag*, ed. by Barbara Ching & Jennifer A. Wagner-Lawlor, New York: Columbia University Press, 1–20.

Chu, Petra ten-Doesschate (2007), *The Most Arrogant Man in France: Courbet and Media Culture*, Princeton, NJ: Princeton University Press.

Clark, Andy (2002), 'Mind, Brains and Tools', in *Philosophy of Mental Representation*, ed. by Hugh Clapin, Oxford: Clarendon Press, 66–90.

Clark, Kenneth (1960), *Looking at Pictures*, London: John Murray.

Clark, T.J. (1984), *The Painting of Modern Life: Paris in the Age of Manet and His Followers*, Princeton, NJ: Princeton University Press.

Clark, Timothy (2019), *The Value of Ecocriticism*, Cambridge: Cambridge University Press.

Clarke, Liam (2004), *The Time of Therapeutic Communities: People, Place and Events*, London: Jessica Kingsley.

Clay, Jean (1983), 'Ointments, Makeup, Pollen', trans. by John Shepley, *October* 27, 3–44.

Código rural de la Provincia de Buenos Aires (1865), Buenos Aires: Imprenta de Buenos Aires.

Connor, Steven (2011), *Dumbstruck: A Cultural History of Ventriloquism*, Oxford: Oxford University Press.

Conway, Christopher (2004), 'Introduction', in Ricardo Palma, *Peruvian Traditions*, ed. by Christopher Conway, trans. by Helen Lane, Oxford: Oxford University Press, xix–xlv.

Conway, Christopher (2015), *Nineteenth-Century Spanish America: A Cultural History*, Nashville, TN: Vanderbilt University Press.

Costa y Turell, Modesto (1857), *Nociones de magnetismo y somnambulismo*, Madrid: Librería Española.

Coster, Cyrus C. (1970), 'Introducción', in *Las ilusiones del doctor Faustino*, ed. by Cyrus C. Coster, Madrid: Castalia, 7–32.

Cowan, Bainard (1982), *Exiled Waters: Moby-Dick and the Crisis of Allegory*, Baton Rouge: Louisiana State University Press.

Cowling, Elizabeth (2002), *Picasso: Style and Meaning*, London: Phaidon.

Cox, Julian (2003), '"To … Startle the Eye with Wonder & Delight": The Photographs of Julia Margaret Cameron', in *Julia Margaret Cameron: The Complete Photographs*, ed. by Julian Cox & Colin Ford, Los Angeles: Getty Publications, 41–80.

Craig, Cairns (2007), *Associationism and the Literary Imagination: From the Phantasmal Chaos*, Edinburgh: Edinburgh University Press.

Crary, Jonathan (1990), *Techniques of the Observer: On Vision and Modernity in the Nineteenth Century*, Cambridge, MA: MIT Press.

Crary, Jonathan (2000), *Suspensions of Perception: Attention, Spectacle and Modern Culture*, Cambridge, MA: MIT Press.

Crismore, Avon & Farnsworth, Rodney (1989), 'Mr Darwin and his Readers: Exploring Interpersonal Metadiscourse as a Dimension of Ethics', *Rhetoric Review* 8.1, 91–112.

Culler, Jonathan (1974), *Flaubert: The Uses of Uncertainty*, London: Paul Elek.

Culler, Jonathan (1998), 'Baudelaire's Satanic Verses', *Diacritics*, 28.3, 86–100.

DaCosta Kaufmann, Thomas, Dossin, Catherine & Joyeux-Prunel, Béatrice (2015), *Circulations in the Global History of Art*, Farnham: Ashgate.

Dalí, Salvador (2013), *El mito trágico de "El Ángelus" de Millet*, ed. by Óscar Tusquets, trans. by Joan Vonyoli, Barcelona: Tusquets.

Damrosch, David (2014), 'World Literature in Theory and Practice', in *World Literature in Theory*, ed. by David Damrosch, Chichester: Wiley, 1–11.
Darwin, Charles (2009), *On the Origin of Species by Means of Natural Selection*, ed. by William Bynum, London: Penguin.
Darwin, John (2007), *After Tamerlane: The Global History of Empire Since 1405*, London: Allen Lane.
Daston, Lorraine (1999), 'Objectivity and the Escape from Perspective', in *The Science Studies Reader*, ed. by Mario Biagioli, New York: Routledge.
Davey, Nicholas (2006), *Unquiet Understanding: Gadamer's Philosophical Hermeneutics*, New York: SUNY Press.
Davillier, Jean-Charles (1875), *Fortuny: Sa vie, son oeuvre, sa correspondance*, Paris: A. Aubry.
Davis, Theo (2010), '"Just Apply a Weight": Thoreau and the Aesthetics of Ornament', *ELH* 77.3, 561–87.
Dayan, Daniel (1974), 'The Tudor Code of Classical Cinema', *Film Quarterly* 28.1, 22–31.
Dayan, Peter (2011), *Art as Music, Music as Poetry: From Whistler to Stravinsky and Beyond*, Farnham: Ashgate.
de Man, Paul (1979), *Allegories of Reading: Figural Language in Rousseau, Nietzsche, Rilke, and Proust*, New Haven, CT: Yale University Press.
de Rijcke, Sarah (2008), 'Light Tries the Expert Eye: The Introduction of Photography in Nineteenth-Century Macroscopic Neuranatomy', *Journal of the History of the Neurosciences* 17.3, 349–66.
Dean, Tim (2009), *Unlimited Intimacy: Reflections on the Subculture of Barebacking*, Chicago: University of Chicago Press.
DeCoster, Cyrus (1974), *Juan Valera*, Boston: Twayne.
del Campo, Estanislao (1870), *Poesías*, ed. by José Mármol, Buenos Aires: Imprenta Buenos Aires.
del Campo, Estanislao (2000), *Fausto: Impresiones del gaucho Anastasio el Pollo en representación de esta ópera*, Buenos Aires: Emecé.
Deleuze, Gilles & Guattari, Félix (1987), *A Thousand Plateaus: Capitalism and Schizophrenia*, trans. by Brian Massumi, London: Continuum.
Dendle, Brian J. (1986), *Galdós: The Early Historical Novels*, Columbia: University of Missouri Press.
Dennis, Kelly (1995), 'Playing with Herself: Feminine Sexuality and Aesthetic Indifference', in *Solitary Pleasures: The Historical, Literary, and Artistic Discourses of Auto-Eroticism*, ed. by Paula Bennett & Vernon A. Rosario II, London: Routledge, 49–72.
Derrida, Jacques (1967), *La Voix et le phénomène: Introduction au problème du signe dans la phénoménologie de Husserl*, Paris: Presses Universitaires de France.
Derrida, Jacques (1981), *Dissemination*, trans. by Barbara Johnson, London: Athlone Press.
Derrida, Jacques (1993), *Spectres de Marx*, Paris: Éditions Galilée.
Derrida, Jacques (2008), *The Gift of Death and Literature in Secret*, ed. and trans. by David Wills, Chicago: University of Chicago Press.
Desbuissons, F. (2008), 'Courbet's Materialism', *Oxford Art Journal* 31.2, 251–60.
Dewey, John (1934), *Art as Experience*, London: G. Allen & Unwin.
Díez, José Luis (1992), *La pintura de historia del siglo XIX en España*, Madrid: Consorcio Madrid '92.
Díez, José Luis & Barón, Javier (2007), *El siglo XIX en el Prado*, Madrid: Museo Nacional del Prado.

References

Dimock, Wai Chee (1989), *Empire for Liberty: Melville and the Poetics of Individualism*, Princeton, NJ: Princeton University Press.

Dimock, Wai Chee (1996), 'Whitman, Syntax, and Political Theory', in *Breaking Bounds: Whitman and American Cultural Studies*, ed. by Betsy Erkkila & Jay Grossman, Oxford: Oxford University Press, 62–79.

Dimock, Wai Chee (2006), *Through Other Continents: American Literature across Deep Time*, Princeton, NJ: Princeton University Press.

Dimock, Wai Chee (2013), 'Weak Theory: Henry James, Colm Tóibín, and W. B. Yeats', *Critical Enquiry* 39.4, 732–53.

Doane, Mary Ann (2002), *The Emergence of Cinematic Time: Modernity, Contingency, The Archive*, Cambridge, MA: Harvard University Press.

Dorado Fernández, Enrique et al. (2010), 'La momia de la hija del doctor Velasco', *Revista de la Escuela de Medicina Legal* 13, 10–30.

Dorment, Richard & Macdonald, Margaret F. (1995), *James McNeill Whistler*, London: Tate.

Douglas-Fairhurst, Robert (2002), *Victorian Afterlives: The Shaping of Influence in Nineteenth-Century Literature*, Oxford: Oxford University Press.

Dowling, David (2010), *Chasing the White Whale*, Iowa City: University of Iowa Press.

Downing, Lisa (2003), *Desiring the Dead: Necrophilia and Nineteenth-Century French Literature*, Oxford: Legenda.

Downing, Lisa (2007), 'Beyond Safety: Erotic Asphyxiation and the Limits of S/M Discourse', in *Safe, Sane and Consensual: Contemporary Perspectives on Sadomasochism*, ed. by Darren Langridge & Meg-John Barker, Basingstoke: Palgrave Macmillan, 119–32.

Dryden, Edgar A. (1968), *Melville's Thematics of Form: The Great Art of Telling the Truth*, Baltimore, MD: Johns Hopkins University Press.

Duban, James (1983), *Melville's Major Fiction: Politics, Theology, and Imagination*, DeKalb: Northern Illinois University Press.

Dunkerley, James (2000), *Americana: The Americas in the World around 1850*, London: Verso.

Eco, Umberto (1985), '*Casablanca*, or The Clichés Are Having A Ball', in *On Signs*, ed. by Marshall Blonsky, Baltimore, MD: Johns Hopkins University Press, 35–8.

Elderfield, John (2006), *Manet and the Execution of Maximilian*, New York: Museum of Modern Art.

Elkins, James (2011), *What Photography Is*, Abingdon: Routledge.

Epps, Bradley S. & Fernández Cifuentes, Luis (2005), *Spain Beyond Spain: Modernity, Literary History and National Identity*, Lewisburg, PA: Buckell University Press.

Estabridis Cárdenas, Ricardo (2004), 'Academia y academicismos en Lima decimonónica', *Tiempos de América* 11, 77–90.

Faunce, Sarah & Nochlin, Linda (1988), *Courbet Reconsidered*, New Haven, CT: Yale University Press.

Feldman, Hernán (2010), 'La digresión en crisis: *Una excursión a los indios ranqueles* de Lucio V. Mansilla', *Hispamérica*, 39, 25–36.

Felman, Shoshana (1978), *La folie et la chose littéraire*, Paris: Éditions du Seuil.

Felski, Rita (2015), *The Limits of Critique*, Chicago: University of Chicago Press.

Fernández, James D. (1994), 'Fashioning the Ancien Régime: Alarcón's *Sombrero de tres picos*', *Hispanic Review* 62.2, 235–47.

Fernández Mallo, Agustín (2014a), *Limbo*, Madrid: Alfaguara, Kindle edition.

Fernández Mallo, Agustín (2014b), 'Agustín Fernández Mallo presenta "Limbo", su último trabajo', www.culturamas.es/blog/2014/01/24/agustin-fernandez-mallo-presenta-limbo-su-ultimo-trabajo/ [accessed 12 August 2019].

Ffrench, Patrick (2007), 'Valdemar's Tongue: Voice, Flesh and Death', in *The Flesh in the Text*, ed. by Thomas Baldwin, James Fowler & Shane Weller, Oxford: Peter Lang, 229–42.

Fischer, Michael (1989), *Stanley Cavell and Literary Skepticism*, Chicago: University of Chicago Press.

Flaubert, Gustave (2019a), *L'Éducation sentimentale*, Paris: Arvensa.

Flaubert, Gustave (2019b), *Trois contes*, Paris: Arvensa.

Flint, Kate (2000), *The Victorians and the Visual Imagination*, Cambridge: Cambridge University Press.

Flores, Antonio (1863), *Ayer, Hoy y Mañana; o, La fe, el vapor y la electricidad: Cuadros sociales de 1800, 1850 y 1899*, Madrid: Mellado, 7 vols.

Folch i Torres, Joaquim (1962), *Fortuny*, Reus: Asociación de Estudios Reusenses.

Fontanella, Lee (1995), *Diaphanoramas en el Museo Romántico*, Madrid: Museo Romántico.

Fontanella, Lee (1999), *Charles Clifford: Un fotógrafo en la corte de Isabel II*, Madrid: El Viso.

Ford, Colin (2003a), *Julia Margaret Cameron: 19th Century Photographer of Genius*, London: National Portrait Gallery.

Ford, Colin (2003b), '"Mountain Nymph" and "Damned Villain": Posing for Julia Margaret Cameron', *History of Photography* 27.1, 60–5.

Foster, Hal (1996), *The Return of the Real: Art and Theory at the End of the Century*, Cambridge, MA: MIT Press.

Foster Wallace, David (1996), *Infinite Jest: A Novel*, New York: Little, Brown & Co.

Foster Wallace, David (1997), *A Supposedly Fun Thing I'll Never Do Again*, London: Hachette Digital, Kindle edition.

Foster Wallace, David (2012), *Both Flesh and Not: Essays*, London: Hamish Hamilton.

Foucault, Michel (1970), *The Order of Things: An Archaeology of the Human Sciences*, London: Tavistock.

Foucault, Michel (1977a), 'Fantasia of the Library', in *Language, Counter-memory, Practice: Selected Essays and Interviews*, ed. by Donald Bouchard, Ithaca, NY: Cornell University Press, 87–109.

Foucault, Michel (1977b), 'What Is an Author?', in *Language, Counter-memory, Practice: Selected Essays and Interviews*, ed. by Donald Bouchard, Ithaca, NY: Cornell University Press, 113–38.

Foucault, Michel (1984), 'What is Enlightenment?', in *The Foucault Reader*, ed. by P. Rabinow, New York: Pantheon, 32–50.

Foucault, Michel (1986), 'Of Other Spaces', trans. by Jay Miskowiec, *Diacritics* 16.1, 22–7.

Foucault, Michel (1991), *Discipline and Punish: The Birth of the Prison*, Harmondsworth: Penguin.

Foucault, Michel (1997), 'Friendship as a Way of Life', in *Ethics: Subjectivity and Truth*, ed. by Paul Rabinow, trans. by Robert Hurley et al., London: Allen Lane, 135–40.

Frank, Jason (2011), 'Promiscuous Citizenship', in *Political Companion to Walt Whitman*, ed. by John E. Seery, Lexington: University Press of Kentucky, 155–84.

Freer, Scott (2015), *Modernist Mythopoeia: The Twilight of the Gods*, Basingstoke: Palgrave Macmillan.

Fried, Michael (1980), *Absorption and Theatricality: Painting and the Beholder in the Age of Diderot*, Berkeley: University of California Press.

Fried, Michael (1988), 'Courbet's "Femininity"', in *Courbet Reconsidered*, ed. by Sarah Faunce & Linda Nochlin, New Haven, CT: Yale University Press, 43–65.

Fried, Michael (1990), *Courbet's Realism*, Chicago: Chicago University Press.

Fried, Michael (1996), *Manet's Modernism; or, The Face of Painting in the 1860s*, Chicago: University of Chicago Press.

References

García Montero, Luis (2001), *Gigante y extraño: Las Rimas de Bécquer*, Barcelona: Tusquets.
Géal, Pierre (2001), 'El Salón de la Reina Isabel en el Museo del Prado (1853–1899)', *Boletín del Museo del Prado* XIX. 37, 144–71.
Geertz, Clifford (1973), *The Interpretation of Culture: Selected Essays*, New York: Basic Books.
Geirola, Gustavo (1996), 'Eroticism and Homoeroticism in *Martín Fierro*', trans. by Melissa A. Lockart, in *Bodies and Biases: Sexualities in Hispanic Cultures and Literatures*, ed. by David William Foster & Roberto Reis, Minneapolis, University of Minnesota Press, 316–32.
Giebelhausen, Michaela (2006), *Painting the Bible: Representation and Belief in Mid-Victorian Britain*, Aldershot: Ashgate.
Gillooly, Eileen (2007), 'Rhetorical Remedies for Taxonomic Troubles: Reading the Great Exhibition', in *Victorian Prism: Refractions of the Crystal Palace*, ed. by James Buzard, Joseph W. Childers & Eileen Gillooly, Charlottesville: University of Virginia Press, 23–39.
Gilroy, Paul (1993), *The Black Atlantic: Modernity and Double Consciousness*, Cambridge, MA: Harvard University Press.
Gilroy, Paul (2000) *Against Race: Imagining Political Culture Beyond the Color Line*, Cambridge, MA: Harvard University Press.
Giménez Vega, Elías & González, Julio (1975), *Hernandismo y Martinfierrismo: Geopolítica del Martín Fierro*, Buenos Aires: Editorial Plus Ultra.
Ginger, Andrew (1999), *Political Revolution and Literary Experiment in the Spanish Romantic Period*, Lewiston, NY: Edwin Mellen Press.
Ginger, Andrew (2000), *Antonio Ros de Olano's Experiments in Post-Romantic Prose (1857–1884): Between Romanticism and Modernism*, Lewiston, NY: Edwin Mellen Press.
Ginger, Andrew (2005a), 'The 1850s and 1860s: Towards a Comparison Between France and Spain', in *Antes y después del 'Quijote': En el cincuentenario aniversario de la Asociación de Hispanistas de Gran Bretaña e Irlanda*, ed. Robert Archer et al., Valencia: Biblioteca Valenciana, 331–9.
Ginger, Andrew (2005b), 'Modernity, Representation, and Personality in Antonio Flores's *Ayer, Hoy y Mañana*', Hispanic Research Journal 6.3, 209–22.
Ginger, Andrew (2006), 'Some Cultural Consequences in Spain of the Spanish Invasion of Morocco', *Journal of Iberian and Latin American Studies* 12.2–3, 147–58.
Ginger, Andrew (2007a), *Painting and the Turn to Cultural Modernity in Spain: The Time of Eugenio Lucas Velázquez (1850–1870)*, Selingsgrove, PA: Associated University Presses.
Ginger, Andrew (2007b), 'Spanish Modernity Revisited: Revisions of the Nineteenth Century', *Journal of Iberian and Latin American Studies* 13.2–3, 121–32.
Ginger, Andrew (2010), '1873–1874, End of a Century?: Time and Space in Valera's *Pepita Jiménez*, Ros de Olano's *Jornadas de retorno* and Alarcón's *Sombrero de tres picos* and *La Alpujarra*', Hispanic Research Journal 11.1, 59–70.
Ginger, Andrew (2012a), *Liberalismo y romanticismo: La reconstrucción del sujeto histórico*, Madrid: Biblioteca Nueva.
Ginger, Andrew (2012b), 'Universal Language and Cultural Translation in Nineteenth-Century Geometry and Photography', *History of Photography* 36, 385–96.
Ginger, Andrew (2013), 'The Origins of Atlantic Modernism and the Spanish-Speaking World', in *Theorising the Ibero-American Atlantic*, ed. by Harald E. Braun & Lisa Vollendorf, Leiden: Brill, 175–98.
Ginger, Andrew (2015), 'From Cultural Translation to Translation inside Photographs (1860–1930)', *Art in Translation* 7.1, 141–64.

Ginger, Andrew (2018), 'Brain States, Sanity, and Wrongdoing', in *Writing Wrongdoing in Spain, 1800–1936: Realities, Representations, Reactions*, ed. Alison Sinclair & Samuel Llano, London: Tamesis, 69–86.

Girard, René (1986), *The Scapegoat*, trans. by Yvonne Freccero, Baltimore, MD: Johns Hopkins University Press.

Glendinning, Nigel (1975), 'The Strange Translation of Goya's "Black Paintings"', *Burlington Magazine* 117, 464–77.

Goldstein, Jan (2005), *The Post-Revolutionary Self: Politics and Psyche in France, 1750–1850*, Cambridge, MA: Harvard University Press.

Gomá, Javier (2011), *La ingenuidad aprendida*, Madrid: Galaxia Gutenberg.

Gómez Moreno, María Elena (1993), *Pintura y escultura españolas del siglo XIX*, Madrid: Espasa-Calpe.

Goncourt, Edmond & Goncourt, Jules (n.d.), *Manette Salomon*, Paris: BnF Collection ebooks, Kindle edition.

González, Aníbal (1993), *Journalism and the Development of Spanish American Narrative*, Cambridge: Cambridge University Press.

González Gerth, Miguel (1965), 'The Poetics of Gustavo Adolfo Bécquer', *Modern Language Notes* 80.2, 185–201.

González López, Carlos & Martí Ayxelà, Montserrat (1989), *Mariano Fortuny y Marsal*, Barcelona: Ediciones Catalanas.

Goodman, Russell B. (2015), *American Philosophy Before Pragmatism*, Oxford: Oxford University Press.

Gorriti, Juana Manuela (1876), *Panoramas de la vida*, Buenos Aires: Imprenta y Librería de Mayo, 2 vols.

Gorriti, Juana Manuela (2000), *Sueños y realidades*, n.p.: Ediciones elaleph.com, ebook.

Grau Bassas, Juan (1849), *Nociones de taxidermia*, Barcelona: Imprenta de R. Frexas.

Greenberg, Clement (1988a), 'Context of Impressionism', in *The Collected Essays and Criticism Volume 1: Perceptions and Judgments, 1939–1944*, ed. by John O'Brian, Chicago: University of Chicago Press, 233–4.

Greenberg, Clement (1988b), 'The Crisis of the Easel Picture', in *The Collected Essays and Criticism Volume 2: The Arrogant Purpose, 1945–1949*, ed. by John O'Brian, Chicago: University of Chicago Press, 221–5.

Greenberg, Clement (1993a), 'Manet in Philadelpha', in *The Collected Essays and Criticism Volume 4: Modernism with a Vengeance, 1957–1969*, ed. by John O'Brian, Chicago: University of Chicago Press, 240–4.

Greenberg, Clement (1993b), 'Modernist Painting', in *The Collected Essays and Criticism Volume 4: Modernism with a Vengeance, 1957–1969*, ed. by John O'Brian, Chicago: University of Chicago Press, 85–93.

Gregory, Derek (1994), *Geographical Imaginations*, Oxford: Blackwell.

Greutzner Robins, Anna (2007), *A Fragile Modernism: Whistler and his Impressionist Followers*, New Haven, CT: Yale University Press.

Grzegorcyk, Marzena (2002), 'Lost Space: Juana Manuela Gorriti's Postcolonial Space', *Journal of Iberian and Latin American Studies* 8.2, 55–69.

Gubar, Marah (2009), *Artful Dodges: Reconceiving the Golden Age of Children's Literature*, Oxford: Oxford University Press.

Guillén, Jorge (1942), 'La poética de Bécquer', *Revista Hispánica Moderna* 8.1–2, 1–42.

Gunning, Tom (2004), '"Animated Pictures": Tales of the Cinema's Forgotten Future, After 100 Years of Film', in *The Nineteenth-Century Visual Culture Reader*, ed. by Vanessa R. Schwartz & Jeannene M. Przyblyski, London: Routledge, 100–13.

Gunning, Tom (2011), 'The Play Between Still and Moving Images: Nineteenth-Century "Philosophical Toys" and Their Discourse', in *Between Stillness and Emotion: Film, Photography, Algorithms*, ed. by Eivind Røssaak, Amsterdam: Amsterdam University Press, 27–44.

Gurshtein, Ksenya A. (2007), 'The Mountain and the Mole-Hill: Julia Margaret Cameron's Allegories', *Bulletin of the University of Michigan Museums of Art and Archaeology* 17, http://hdl.handle.net/2027/spo.0054307.0017.101 [accessed 28 August 2019].

Haack, Susan (1993), *Evidence and Inquiry: Towards Reconstruction in Epistemology*, Oxford: Blackwell.

Haack, Susan (1998), *Manifesto of a Passionate Moderate: Unfashionable Essays*, Chicago: University of Chicago Press.

Haidt, Rebecca (2011), 'Commodifying Place and Time: Photography, Memory, and Media Cultures around 1850', *Hispanic Issue Online: Debates* 3, 10–29.

Haleperín Donghi, Tulio (1985), *José Hernández y sus mundos*, Buenos Aires: Editorial Sudamericana.

Hanway, Nancy (2003), *Embodying Argentina: Body, Space and Nation in 19th Century Narrative*, Jefferson: McFarland & Co.

Harvey, David (2012), *Spaces of Capital: Towards a Critical Geography*, London: Routledge.

Hatab, Lawrence J. (2001), 'Apollo and Dionysus: Nietzschean Expressions of the Sacred', in *Nietzsche and the Gods*, ed. Weaver Santaniello, New York: SUNY Press, 45–56.

Headley, John M. (2008), *The Europeanization of the World: On the Origins of Human Rights and Democracy*, Princeton, NJ: Princeton University Press.

Heide, Claudia (2009), 'A Dream of the South: Islamic Spain', in *The Discovery of Spain*, ed. David Howarth, Paul Stirton & Claudia Heide, Edinburgh: National Galleries of Scotland, 65–80.

Heide, Claudia (2010), 'The Alhambra in Britain. Between Foreignization and Domestication', *Art in Translation* 2.2, 201–21.

Heidegger, Martin (1971), 'Building, Dwelling, Thinking', in *Poetry, Language, Thought*, trans. by Albert Hofstadter, New York: Harper & Row, 145–61.

Heraclitus (2001), *Fragments: The Collected Wisdom of Heraclitus*, trans. by Brooks Haxton, New York: Viking, Kindle edition.

Herbert, James D. (2014), 'Courbet, Incommensurate and Emergent', *Critical Inquiry* 40.2, 339–81.

Herding, Klaus (2010), 'The Other Courbet', in *Courbet: A Dream of Modern Art*, ed. Klaus Herding & Max Hollein, Ostfildern: Hatje Cantz, 10–18.

Hernández, José (2018), *El gaucho Martín Fierro*, ed. by Carlos Gamerro & Alejandra Laera, Mexico City: Penguin Clásicos, Kindle edition.

Hibberd, Andrea (2007), 'Distracting Impressions and Rational Recreation at the Great Exhibition', in *Victorian Prism: Refractions of the Crystal Palace*, ed. by James Buzard, Joseph W. Childers & Eileen Gillooly, Charlottesville: University of Virginia Press, 151–67.

Hiddleston, J. A. (2011), *Baudelaire and the Art of Memory*, Oxford: Oxford University Press.

Higonnet, Anne (2016), 'Manet and the Multiple', in *Is Paris Still the Capital of the Nineteenth Century?: Essays on Art and Modernity, 1850–1900*, ed. by Hollis Clayson & André Dombrowski, London: Routledge, 195–214.

Hinton, Laura (1999), *The Perverse Gaze of Sympathy: Sadomasochistic Sentiments from Clarissa to Rescue 911*, New York: SUNY Press.

Hoffenberg, Peter (2001), *An Empire on Display: English, Indian, and Australian Exhibitions from the Crystal Palace to the Great War*, Oxford: Oxford University Press.

Hoffmann, Werner (2010), 'Courbet – Artist, Dreamer, and Philosopher', in *Courbet: A Dream of Modern Art*, ed. Klaus Herding & Max Hollein, Ostfildern: Hatje Cantz, 19–25.

Holguín Callo, Oswaldo (2001), *Páginas sobre Ricardo Palma (Vida y obra)*, Lima: Universidad Ricardo Palma.

Hostos, Eugenio María de (2015), *La peregrinación de Bayoán*, Puerto Rico: Puerto Rico eBooks, Kindle edition.

Hoving, Kirsten A. (2003), '"Flashing thro' the Gloom": Julia Margaret Cameron's "Eccentricity"', *History of Photography* 27.1, 45–59.

Howarth, David J. (2010), *The Invention of Spain: Cultural Relations between Britain and Spain, 1770–1870*, Manchester: Manchester University Press.

Howarth, David, Stirton, Paul & Heide, Claudia (2009), *The Discovery of Spain*, Edinburgh: National Galleries of Scotland.

Howells, Bernard (2017), *Baudelaire: Individualism, Dandyism, and the Philosophy of History*, Abingdon: Routledge.

Huberman, Ariana (2011), *Gauchos and Foreigners: Glossing Culture and Identity in the Argentine Countryside*, Lanham, MD: Lexington Books.

Hudder, Cliff (2012), '"A Day of Most Heartfelt Sorrow": Death and Texas in Whitman's "Song of Myself"', *Walt Whitman Quarterly Review* 29.3, 66–80.

Hughes, John B. (1970), *Arte y sentido de Martín Fierro*, Madrid: Editorial Castalia.

Hurh, Paul (2015), *American Terror: The Feeling of Thinking in Edwards, Poe, and Melville*, Stanford, CA: Stanford University Press.

Hyman, Stanley Edgar (1974), *The Tangled Bank: Darwin, Marx, Frazer, & Freud as Imaginative Writers*, New York: Atheneum.

Ingold, Tim (2016), *Lines: A Brief History*, London: Routledge.

Iriye, Akira (2013), *Global and Transnational History: The Past, Present, and Future*, Basingstoke: Palgrave Macmillan.

Irwin, John T. (1980), *American Hieroglyphs: The Symbol of the Egyptian Hieroglyphs in the American Renaissance*, New Haven, CT: Yale University Press.

Israel-Pelletier, Aimée (1991), *Flaubert's Straight and Suspect Saints: The Unity of 'Trois Contes'*, Amsterdam, Philadelphia: John Benjamins.

Iverson, Margaret (2017), *Photography, Trace and Trauma*, Chicago: Chicago University Press.

Jacobi, Carol (2006), *William Holman Hunt: Painter, Painting, Paint*, Manchester: Manchester University Press.

Jagoe, Eva Lynn Alicia (2008), *The End of the World as They Knew It*, Lewisburg, PA: Bucknell University Press.

James, Henry (1984), *Literary Criticism: French Writers, Other European Writers, The Prefaces to the New York Edition*, New York: Library of America.

Jameson, Frederic (2014), *Representing Capital: A Commentary on Volume One*, London: Verso, Kindle edition.

Jenson, Deborah (2001), *Trauma and Its Representations: The Social Life of Mimesis in Post-Revolutionary France*, Baltimore, MD: Johns Hopkins University Press.

Jones, Owen (2016), *The Grammar of Ornament: A Visual Reference of Form and Colour in Architecture and the Decorative Arts*, Princeton, NJ: Princeton University Press.

Kauppinen, Jari (2000), 'Death as a Limit of Phenomenology: The Notion of Death from Husserl to Derrida', *Analecta Husserliana* 66, 323–48.

Keach, William (2004), *Arbitrary Power: Romanticism, Language, Politics*, Princeton, NJ: Princeton University Press.

Keenan, Dennis King (2005) *The Question of Sacrifice*, Bloomington: Indiana University Press.

Kelly, Dorothy (1989), 'Oscillation and its Effects: Flaubert's *L'Education sentimentale*', *Romanic Review* 80.2, 207–17.

Kelsey, Robin (2015), *Photography and the Art of Chance*, Cambridge, MA: Belknap Press.

Kemp, Martin (2016), *Structural Intuitions: Seeing Shapes in Art and Science*, Charlottesville: University of Virginia Press.

King, Edmund (1953), *Gustavo Adolfo Bécquer: From Painter to Poet*, Mexico City: Editorial Porrúa.

Knight, Alan (2007), 'When Was Latin America Modern? An Historian's Response', in *When Was Latin America Modern?*, ed. by Nicola Miller & Stephen Hart, Basingstoke: Palgrave Macmillan, 91–117.

Knight, Diane (1985), *Flaubert's Characters: The Language of Illusion*, Cambridge: Cambridge University Press.

Knoepflmacher, U. C. (1998), *Ventures into Childland: Victorians, Fairy Tales, and Femininity*, Chicago: University of Chicago Press.

Knox, Giles (2009), *The Late Paintings of Velázquez: Theorizing Painterly Performance*, London: Routledge.

Kristeva, Julia (2002), *The Portable Kristeva*, ed. by Kelly Oliver, New York: Columbia University Press.

LaCapra, Dominick (2001), *Writing History, Writing Trauma*, Baltimore, MD: Johns Hopkins University Press.

LaCapra, Dominick (2004), *History in Transit: Experience, Identity, Critical Theory*, Ithaca, NY: Cornell University Press.

Laclau, Ernesto (2000), 'Identity and Hegemony: The Role of Universality in the Constitution of Political Logics', in *Contingency, Hegemony, Universality: Contemporary Dialogues on the Left*, ed. by Judith Butler, Ernesto Laclau & Slavoj Žižek, London: Verso, 44–89.

Laqueur, Thomas W. (2003), *Solitary Sex: A Cultural History of Masturbation*, New York: Zone Books.

Laing, R. D. (1990), *The Politics of Experience and The Bird of Paradise*, London: Penguin.

Lalvani, Suren (1996), *Photography, Vision, and the Production of Modern Bodies*, New York: SUNY Press.

Lamborghini, Leónidas C. (2008), *Risa y tragedia en los poetas gauchescos: Hidalgo, Ascasubi, Del Campo, Hernández*, Buenos Aires: Emecé.

Lange, Charlotte (2008), *Modas de parodia: Guillermo Cabrera Infante, Reinaldo Arenas, Jorge Ibargüengoitia y José Agustín*, Oxford: Peter Lang.

Langford Taylor, Teresia (1997), *The Representation of Women in the Novels of Juan Valera: A Feminist Critique*, New York: Peter Lang.

Larson, Kerry (2008), *Imagining Equality in Nineteenth-Century American Literature*, Cambridge: Cambridge University Press.

Larson, Kerry C. (2009), 'Song of Myself', in *A Companion to Walt Whitman*, ed. by Donald D. Kummings, Oxford: Wiley-Blackwell, 471–83.

Laso, Francisco (2003), 'La paleta y sus colores', in *Aguinaldo para señoras del Perú y otros ensayos*, ed. by Natalia Majluf, Lima: Museo de Arte de Lima, 73–8.

Latour, Bruno (1993), *We Have Never Been Modern*, Cambridge, MA: Harvard University Press.
Latour, Bruno (2005), *Reassembling the Social: An Introduction to Actor-Network-Theory*, Oxford: Oxford University Press.
Lauster, Martina (2007), *Sketches of the Nineteenth Century: European Journalism and its Physiologies, 1830–50*, Basingstoke: Palgrave Macmillan.
Lawless, Geraldine (2011), *Modernity's Metonyms: Figuring Time in Nineteenth-Century Spanish Stories*, Lewisburg, PA: Bucknell University Press.
Lawless, Geraldine (2012), '"At Last I Killed Her": Rosalía de Castro's *El caballero de las botas azules*', *Journal of Iberian & Latin American Studies* 18.1, 77–93.
Lawless, Geraldine (2018), '*Avant la lettre*: Contradictory Affinities in Antonio Flores, Juan Bautista Amorós (Silverio Lanza) and Ángel Ganivet', *Modern Languages Open* (1) 13 http://doi.org/10.3828/mlo.v0i0.180.
Lecercle, Jean-Jacques (1994), *Philosophy of Nonsense: The Intuitions of Victorian Nonsense Literature*, London: Routledge.
Lee, Maurice (2011), *Uncertain Chances: Skepticism, and Belief in Nineteenth-Century American Literature*, Oxford: Oxford University Press.
Lefèbvre, Henri (1991), *The Production of Space*, trans. by Donald Nicholson-Smith, Oxford: Blackwell.
Levine, Caroline (2017), *Forms: Whole, Rhythm, Hierarchy, Network*, Princeton, NJ: Princeton University Press.
Levine, George (2006), *Darwin Loves You*, Princeton, NJ: Princeton University Press.
Levine, George (2011), *Darwin the Writer*, Oxford: Oxford University Press.
Lewis, Tom (1997), 'Gender, Discourse, and Modernity in Bécquer's "Rimas"', *Revista de Estudios Hispánicos* 31.3, 419–48.
Lombardero, Miguel (2004), *Otro Don Juan: Vida y pensamiento de Juan Valera*, Barcelona: Planeta.
López Ocón Cabrera, Leoncio (2003), *Breve historia de la ciencia española*, Madrid: Alianza.
Lozano y Ascarza, Antonio (1866), *Lecciones fundamentales de geometría descriptiva como estudio preliminar necesario para el de la topografía y fortificación*, Toledo: Imprenta de D. Ricardo Romero.
Ludmer, Josefina (1988), *El género gauchesco: Un tratado sobre la patria*, Buenos Aires: Editorial Sudamericana.
Luys, Jules (2016a), *Iconographie photographique des centres nerveux*, www.artandmedicine.com/biblio/authors/Luys4.html [accessed 22 June 2016].
Luys, Jules (2016b), Plates from the *Iconographie photographique*, www.photo-arago.fr/C.aspx?VP3=SearchDetail&IID=2C6NU04N1PM0 [accessed 22 June 2016].
Lyotard, Jean-François (1991), 'Rewriting Modernity', in *The Inhuman: Reflections on Time*, trans. by Geoffrey Bennington & Rachel Bowlby, Stanford, CA: Stanford University Press, 24–35.
MacKay, Carol Hanbery (2001), *Creative Negativity: Four Victorian Exemplars of the Female Quest*, Stanford, CA: Stanford University Press.
Madrazo, Pedro de (1854), *Catálogo de los cuadros del Real Museo de Pintura y Escultura*, Madrid: F.M. Alonso.
Madrazo, Pedro de (1872), *Catálogo descriptivo del Museo del Prado de Madrid: Parte primera. Escuelas italianas y españolas*, Madrid: Rivadeneyra.
Majluf, Natalia (2003), 'Estudio introductorio', in Francisco Laso, *Aguinaldo para señoras del Perú y otros ensayos*, ed. by Natalia Majluf, Lima: Museo de Arte de Lima, 5–32.

Mandrell, James (1995), '"Poesía … eres tú", or the Construction of Bécquer and the Sign of Woman', in *Culture and Gender in Nineteenth-Century Spain*, ed. by Lou Charnon Deutsch & Jo Labanyi, Oxford: Oxford University Press, 53–74.

Manjapra, Kris (2010), 'Introduction', in *Cosmopolitan Thought Zones: South Asia and the Global Circulation of Ideas*, ed. by Sugata Bose & Kris Manjapra, Basingstoke: Palgrave Macmillan, 1–19.

Manning, Susan (2002), *Fragments of Union: Making Connections in Scottish and American Writing*, Basingstoke: Palgrave.

Manning, Susan (2013), *Poetics of Character: Transatlantic Encounters, 1700–1900*, Cambridge: Cambridge University Press.

Manning, Susan & Taylor, Andrew, eds. (2007), *Transatlantic Literary Studies: A Reader*.

Mansilla, Lucio V. (2018), *Una excursión a los indios ranqueles*, ed. by Alan Pauls & Alejandra Laera, Mexico City: Penguin Clásicos, Kindle edition.

Manthorne, Katherine Emma (1989), *Tropical Renaissance: North American Artists Exploring Latin America, 1838–1879*, Washington, DC: Smithsonian Institute.

Marcus, Sharon (2007), *Between Women: Friendship, Desire and Marriage in Victorian England*, Princeton, NJ: Princeton University Press.

Marder, Elissa (2001), *Dead Time: Temporal Disorders in the Wake of Modernity*, Stanford, CA: Stanford University Press.

Marin, Louis (1984), *Utopics: Spatial Play*, trans. by Robert A. Vollrath, Atlantic Highlands, NJ: Humanities Press.

Marion, Jean-Luc (2014), *Courbet; ou, La Peinture à l'oeil*, Paris: Flammarion, Kindle edition.

Marks, Laura (2000), *The Skin of the Film: Intercultural Cinema, Embodiment, and the Senses*, Durham, NC: Duke University Press.

Marks, Laura U. (2002), *Touch: Sensuous Theory and Multisensory Media*, Minneapolis: University of Minnesota Press, Kindle edition.

Martí López, Elisa (2002), *Borrowed Words: Translation, Imitation, and the Making of the Nineteenth-Century Novel in Spain*, Lewisburg, PA: Bucknell University Press.

Martin, Robert K. (2006), 'Melville and Sexuality', in *The Cambridge Companion to Herman Melville*, ed. by Robert S. Levine, Cambridge: Cambridge University Press, 186–201.

Martin-Márquez, Susan (2008), *Disorientations: Spanish Colonialism in Africa and Performances of Identity*, New Haven, CT: Yale University Press.

Martínez Gallego, Francesc A. (2001), *Conservar progresando: La Unión Liberal 1856–1858*, Valencia: Centro Francisco Tomás y Valiente.

Marx, Karl (2013), *Capital, Volume 1: A Critical Analysis of Capitalist Production*, ed. by Mark G. Spencer, trans. by Samuel Moore & Edward Aveling, Ware: Wordsworth, Kindle edition.

Marx, Leo (2000), *The Machine in the Garden: Technology and the Pastoral Ideal in America*, Oxford: Oxford University Press.

Masiello, Francine (2003), 'Introduction', in Juana Manuela Gorriti, *Dreams and Realities: Selected Fiction*, ed. by Francine Masiello, trans. by Sergio Weisman, Oxford: Oxford University Press, xv–lx.

Mata, Pedro (1852), *Examen crítico de la homeopatía*, Madrid: Imprenta de Manini Hermanos.

Mata, Pedro (1858), *Tratado de la razón humana*, Madrid: Carlos Baily-Baillière.

Mata, Pedro (1864), *Tratado de la razón humana en sus estados intermedios*, Madrid: Carlos Baily-Baillière.

Mavor, Carol (1995), *Pleasures Taken: Performances of Sexuality and Loss in Victorian Photographs*, Durham, NC: Duke University Press.

May, Jon & Thrift, Nigel, eds (2001), *Timespace: Geographies of Temporality*, London: Routledge.
Mazlish, Bruce (2006), *The New Global History*, New York: Routledge.
McCauley, Elizabeth Anne (1994). *Indusrrial Madness: Commercial Photography in Paris, 1848–1871*, New Haven, CT: Yale University Press.
McLaren Young, Andrew et al. (1980), *The Paintings of James McNeill Whistler*, New Haven, CT: Yale University Press.
Meltzer, Françoise (2011), *Seeing Double: Baudelaire's Modernity*, Oxford: Oxford University Press.
Melville, Herman (2002), *Moby-Dick; or, The Whale*, ed. by David Herd, Ware: Wordsworth.
Michaud, Philippe-Alain (2007), *Aby Warburg and the Image in Motion*, New York: Zone Books.
Mignolo, Walter (2000), *Local Histories/Global Designs: Coloniality, Subaltern Knowledges, and Border Thinking*, Princeton, NJ: Princeton University Press.
Milá y Fontanals, Manuel (1857), *Principios de estética*, Barcelona: Diario de Barcelona.
Milder, Robert (1995), *Reimagining Thoreau*, Cambridge: Cambridge University Press.
Miller, James (1994), *The Passion of Michel Foucault*, London: Flamingo.
Mizrahi, Irene (1998), *La poética dialógica de Bécquer*, Amsterdam: Rodopi.
Moi, Toril (2003), 'Feminist Theory after Theory', in *Life.After.Theory*, ed. by Michael Payne and John Schad, London: Continuum.
Moi, Toril (2017), *Revolution of the Ordinary: Literary Studies after Wittgenstein, Austin, and Cavell*, Chicago: University of Chicago Press.
Molina, R. (1869), *El espiritismo: Fundamentos especiales de esa doctrina y nueva secta. Juicio sobre ella, controversia espiritista y sus resultados prácticos*, Madrid: Félix Perie.
Molloy, Sylvia (1991), *At Face Value: Autobiographical Writing in Spanish America*, Cambridge: Cambridge University Press.
Monder, Samuel (2008), 'La ley del deseo: Acerca de "Una excursión a los indios ranqueles" de Lucio V. Mansilla', *Iberoamericana* 32, 61–74.
Montesinos, José F. (1969), *Valera; o, La ficción libre*, Madrid: Castalia.
Moon, Michael (1991), *Disseminating Whitman: Revision and Corporeality in Leaves of Grass*, Cambridge, MA: Harvard University Press.
Moretti, Franco (2007), *Graphs, Maps, Trees: Abstract Models for Literary History*, London: Verso.
Mulvey, Laura (1985), 'Visual Pleasure and Narrative Cinema', in *Movies and Methods II*, ed. by Bill Nichols, Berkeley: University of California Press, 303–14.
Mulvey, Laura (2006), *Death 24x a Second: Stillness and the Moving Image*, London: Reaktion Books.
Muñoz, José Esteban (2009), *Cruising Utopia: The Then and There of Queer Futurity*, New York: New York University Press.
Murphy, Alexandra R. (1999), *Jean-Francois Millet: Drawn into the Light*, New Haven, CT: Yale University Press.
Murray, Anna & Winteringham, Grace (2015), *Patternity, A New Way of Seeing: The Inspirational Power of Pattern*, London: Conran Octopus.
Musser, Amber Jamilla (2014), *Sensational Flesh: Race, Power, and Masochism*, New York: New York University Press.
Nagel, Alexander (2012), *Medieval Modern: Art out of Time*, London: Thames & Hudson.
Nagel, Alexander & Wood, Christopher (2010), *Anachronic Renaissance*, New York: Zone Books.
Nancy, Jean-Luc (2004), 'The Two Secrets of the Fetish', *Journal of Visual Practice* 3.2, 139–47.
Nead, Lynda (2000), *Victorian Babylon: People, Streets and Images in Victorian London*, New Haven, CT: Yale University Press.

References

Nehamas, Alexander (2016), *On Friendship*, New York: Basic Books.

Nelson, Maggie (2011), *The Art of Cruelty: A Reckoning*, New York: W.W. Norton, Kindle edition.

Nichols, Kate (2015), *Greece and Rome at the Crystal Palace: Classical Sculpture and Modern Britain, 1854–1936*, Oxford: Oxford University Press.

Nietzsche, Friedrich (2003), *The Birth of Tragedy Out of the Spirit of Music*, ed. by Michael Tanner, trans. by Shaun Whiteside, London: Penguin, Kindle edition.

Noble, Max (2015), *American Poetic Materialism from Whitman to Stevens*, Cambridge: Cambridge University Press.

Nochlin, Linda (1988), 'Courbet's Real Allegory: Rereading "The Painter's Studio"', in *Courbet Reconsidered*, ed. by Sarah Faunce & Linda Nochlin, New Haven, CT: Yale University Press, 17–42.

Nochlin, Linda (2007), *Gustave Courbet*, London: Thames & Hudson.

Nussbaum, Martha (1998), *Cultivating Humanity: A Classical Defence of Reform in Liberal Education*, Cambridge, MA: Harvard University Press.

Nussbaum, Martha (2001), *Upheavals of Thought: The Intelligence of Emotions*, Cambridge: Cambridge University Press.

Olsen, Victoria (2003), *From Life: Julia Margaret Cameron and Victorian Photography*, London: Aurum Press.

Oppel, Frances Nesbitt (2005), *Nietzsche on Gender: Beyond Man and Woman*, Charlottesville: University of Virginia Press.

Orr, Mary (2000), *Flaubert: Writing the Masculine*, Oxford: Oxford University Press.

Orr, Mary (2005), 'Still Life and Moving Death in Flaubert's *L'Education sentimentale*', *Dix-Neuf* 5.1, 16–27.

Ortega, Julio (2006), *Transatlantic Translations: Dialogues in Latin American Literature*, trans. by Philip Derbyshire, London: Reaktion Books.

Óscar López, Robert (2007), 'Thoreau, Homer, and Community', in *More Day to Dawn: Thoreau's Walden for the Twenty-First Century*, ed. by Sandra Harbert Petrulionis & Laura Dassow Walls, Amherst and Boston: University of Massachusetts Press, 127–51.

Osterhammel, Jürgen (2014), *The Transformation of the World: A Global History of the Nineteenth Century*, Princeton, NJ: Princeton University Press.

Oswald, Alice (2011), *Memorial*, London: Faber & Faber, Kindle edition.

Overaker, Lewis J. (2001), 'Manifestations of the Holy Ghost in Flaubert's *Un Coeur simple*',Renascence 53.2, 118–48.

Pagden, Anthony (1995), *Lords of all the World: Ideologies of Empire in Spain, Britain and France c.1500–c.1800*, New Haven, CT: Yale University Press.

Palma, Ricardo (1875), *Perú: Tradiciones. Tercera serie*, Lima: Benito Gil.

Palma, Ricardo (2000), *Tradiciones: Primera Serie*, Barcelona: Montaner y Simón, 1893; e-edition, Alicante: Biblioteca Virtual Cervantes.

Parikka, Jussi (2012), *What Is Media Archaeology?*, Cambridge: Polity Press.

Partzsch, Henriette (2014), 'The Complex Routes of Travelling Texts: Frederika Bremer's Reception in Nineteenth-Century Spain and the Transnational Dimension of Literary History', *Comparative Critical Studies* 11.2–3, 281–93.

Patrón Boylan, Paul Rizo (2004), 'Del aguardiente al *champagne*. La aristocratización de la burguesía peruana en el siglo XIX', in *La experiencia burguesa en el Perú (1840–1940)*, ed by Carmen McEvoy, Madrid: Iberoamericana, 27–55.

Pérez Galdós, Benito (2006), *La Corte de Carlos IV*, Madrid: Alianza.

Perrin Warren, James (2009), 'Style', in *A Companion to Walt Whitman*, ed. by Donald D. Kummings, Oxford: Wiley-Blackwell, 377–91.
Peters Corbett, David (2004), *The World in Paint: Modern Art and Visuality in England, 1848–1914*, Manchester: Manchester University Press.
Pi i Margall, Francisco (1982), *La reacción y la revolución*, Barcelona: Anthropos.
Pieters, Jurgen (2001), *Moments of Negotiation: The New Historicism of Stephen Greenblatt*, Amsterdam: Amsterdam University Press.
Pietz, William (1985), 'The Problem of the Fetish, I', *RES: Anthropology and Aesthetics* 9, 5–17.
Piglia, Ricardo (1986), *Crítica y ficción*, Santa Fe, NM: Universidad Nacional del Litoral.
Pilling, Geoffrey (2009), *Marx's 'Capital' (Routledge Revivals): Philosophy and Political Economy*, London: Routledge.
Plonitsky, Arkady (2003) 'Algebras, Geometries and Topologies of the Fold: Deleuze, Derrida and Quasi-Mathematical Thinking (with Leibniz and Mallarmé)', in *Between Deleuze and Derrida*, ed. by Paul Patton & John Protevi, New York: Continuum, 98–119.
Plummer, Ken (2015), *Cosmopolitan Sexualities: Hope and the Humanist Imagination*, Cambridge: Polity Press.
Pogue Harrison, Robert (2003), *The Dominion of the Dead*, Chicago: University of Chicago Press.
Poliquin, Rachel (2012), *The Breathless Zoo: Taxidermy and the Cultures of Longing*, University Park: Pennsylvania State University Press.
Pollak, Vivian R. (2000), *The Erotic Whitman*, Berkeley: University of California Press.
Pollock, Griselda (1977), *Millet*, London: Oresko Books.
Pollock, Griselda (2013), 'Introduction' and 'From Horrorism to Compassion: Re-Facing Medusan Otherness in Dialogue with Adriana Cavarero and Bracha Ettinger', in *Visual Politics of Psychoanalysis: Art and the Image in Post-Traumatic Cultures*, ed. by Griselda Pollock, London: I.B. Tauris, 1–22, 159–89.
Pollock, Griselda (2018), 'Modernity and the Spaces of Femininity', in *The Expanding Discourse: Feminism and Art History*, ed by Norma Broude & Mary D. Garrard, London: Routledge, 245–67.
Pollock, Sheldon (2009), *The Language of the Gods in the World of Men: Sanskrit, Culture, and Power in Pre-Modern India*, Berkeley: University of California Press.
Porter, James I. (2000), *The Invention of Dionysus: An Essay on The Birth of Tragedy*, Stanford, CA: Stanford University Press.
Poulet, Georges (1980), *Exploding Poetry: Baudelaire/Rimbaud*, trans by Françoise Meltzer, Chicago: University of Chicago Press.
Pratt, Mary Louise (1992), *Imperial Eyes: Travel Writing and Transculturation*, London: Routledge.
Prendergast, Christopher (1986), *The Order of Mimesis: Balzac, Stendhal, Nerval, Flaubert*, Cambridge: Cambridge University Press.
Prettejohn, Elizabeth (2000), *The Art of the Pre-Raphaelites*, London: Tate.
Puig Samper, Miguel Ángel (2013), *Crónica de una expedición romántica al Nuevo Mundo: La Comisión Científica del Pacífico (1862–1866)*, Madrid: Polifemo.
Putnam, Hilary (2004), *The Collapse of the Fact/Value Distinction and Other Essays*, Cambridge, MA: Harvard University Press.
Quintana, Manuel J. (1978), *Selección poética*, ed. by R. Reyes Cano, Madrid: Editora Nacional.
Rama, Ángel (2004), *Transculturación narrativa en América Latina*, Buenos Aires: Siglo XXI.
Rampley, Matthew (2007), *Nietzsche, Aesthetics and Modernity*, Cambridge: Cambridge University Press.

Rawes, Peg (2008), *Space, Geometry and Aesthetics: Through Kant and Towards Deleuze*, Basingstoke: Palgrave Macmillan.

Reed, Arden (2003), *Manet, Flaubert, and the Emergence of Modernism: Blurring Genre Boundaries*, Cambridge: Cambridge University Press.

Regueiro Salgado, Begoña (2013), 'Una nueva forma de orientalismo: Presencia y valores de lo oriental en la obra de Gustavo Adolfo Bécquer', *Bulletin of Spanish Studies* 90.2, 177–94.

Reichertz, Ronald (1997), *The Making of the Alice Books: Lewis Carroll's Uses of Earlier Children's Literature*, Montreal: McGill University Press.

Reiss, Benjamin (2013), 'Sleeping at Walden Pond: Thoreau, Temporality, and the Modern Body', *American Literature* 85.1, 5–31.

Revilla Uceda, Mateo (1982), *Eduardo Rosales en la pintura española*, Madrid: Edarcon.

Rey y Heredia, José María (1849), *Lógica*, Madrid: Imprenta de La Publicidad.

Reyero, Carlos (1992), *El arte del siglo XIX*, Madrid: Anaya.

Reyero, Carlos (2017), *Fortuny: o, El arte como distinción de clase*, Madrid: Cátedra.

Ribbans, Geoffrey (1993), *History and Fiction in Galdós's Narratives*, Oxford: Clarendon Press.

Richards, Joan L. (1988), *Mathematical Visions: The Pursuit of Geometry in Victorian England*, Boston, MA: Academic Press.

Ringrose, David (1996), *Espana, 1700–1900: El mito del fracaso*, Madrid: Alianza.

Riordan, Kevin (2018), 'Photography and First-Person Death: Derrida, Barthes, Poe', in *Narrating Death: The Limit of Literature*, ed. by Daniel K. Jernigan, Walter Wadiak & Michelle Wang, London: Routledge, 46–95.

Ríos Font, Wadda (1997), 'From Romantic Irony to Romantic Grotesque: Mariano de Larra's and Rosalía de Castro's Self-Conscious Novels', *Hispanic Review* 65.2, 177–98.

Rivera, Ángel A. (1993), '*La Peregrinación de Bayoán* de Hostos: Viaje de retorno al caos', *Revista canadiense de estudios hispánicos* 17.3, 525–35.

Robbins, Jeremy (1998), *The Challenges of Uncertainty: An Introduction to Seventeenth-Century Spanish Literature*, Lanham, MD: Rowman & Littlefield.

Roberts, Tyler T. (2013), *Contesting Spirit: Nietzsche, Affirmation, Religion*, Princeton, NJ: Princeton University Press.

Robson, Catherine (2003), *Men in Wonderland: The Lost Childhood of the Victorian Gentleman*, Princeton, NJ: Princeton University Press.

Rodríguez de Laguna, Asela (2015), 'Cristóbal Colón como puente transatlántico en el imaginario de Eugenio María de Hostos', *Revista de Indias* 75.265, 743–70.

Rodríguez Molina, María José & Sanchis Alfonso, José Ramón (2014), *Una nueva visión de la fotografía española: La obra de José Martínez Sánchez (1807–1874)*, Valencia: Railowsky.

Rorty, Richard (1979), *Philosophy and the Mirror of Nature*, Princeton, NJ: Princeton University Press.

Ros de Olano, Antonio (1863), *El doctor Lañuela: Episodio sacado de las memorias de un tal Josef*, Madrid: Imprenta de Manuel Galiano.

Ros de Olano, Antonio (2008), *Relatos*, ed. by Jaume Pont, Barcelona: Crítica.

Rosales, Eduardo (2018), *Epistolario*, ed. by Juan Antonio López Delgado, Murcia: Neocromo Producciones Gráficas.

Rosario II, Vernon A. (1995), 'Phantastical Pollutions: The Public Threat of Private Vice in France', in *Solitary Pleasures: The Historical, Literary, and Artistic Discourses of Auto-Eroticism*, ed. by Paula Bennett & Vernon A. Rosario II, London: Routledge, 101–30.

Rose, Jacqueline (1990), *The Case of Peter Pan; or, The Impossibility of Children's Literature*, Philadelphia: University of Pennsylvania Press.

Rosen, Charles & Zerner, Henri (1984), *Romanticism and Realism: The Mythology of Nineteenth-Century Art*, London: Faber & Faber.

Rosen, Jeff (2015), *Julia Margaret Cameron's "Fancy Subjects": Photographic Allegories of Victorian Life and Empire*, Manchester: Manchester University Press.

Rosen, Michael (1984), *Hegel's Dialectic and Its Criticism*, Cambridge: Cambridge University Press.

Roth, Christine (2009), 'Looking through the Spyglass: Lewis Carroll, James Barrie, and the Empire of Childhood', in *Alice Beyond Wonderland: Essays for the Twenty-First Century*, ed. by Cristopher Hollingsworth, Iowa City: University of Iowa Press, 23–35.

Roth, Michael S. (2012), *Memory, Trauma, and History: Essays on Living with the Past*, New York: Columbia University Press.

Rowland, Tim (2000), *The Pragmatics of Mathematical Education: Vagueness in Mathematical Discourse*, London: Falmer Press.

Rubin, James H. (2010), *Manet: Initial M, Hand and Eye*, Paris: Flammarion.

Rubin, James Henry (1980), *Realism and Social Vision in Courbet and Proudhon*, Princeton, NJ: Princeton University Press.

Ruby, Jay (1995), *Secure the Shadow: Death and Photography in America*, Cambridge, MA: MIT Press.

Ryle, Gilbert (1968), 'The Thinking of Thoughts: What is *Le Penseur* Doing?', *University Lectures* 18, University of Saskatchewan, https://web.archive.org/web/20080410232658/http://lucy.ukc.ac.uk/CSACSIA/Vol11/Papers/ryle_1.html [accessed 26 August 2019].

Sadler, Ted (1995), *Nietzsche, Truth and Redemption: Critique of the Postmodernist Nietzsche*, London: Athlone Press.

Sallis, John (1991), *Crossings: Nietzsche and the Space of Tragedy*, Chicago: University of Chicago Press.

Saltzman, Lisa & Rosenberg, Eric (2006), 'Introduction', in *Trauma and Visuality in Modernity*, ed. by Lisa Saltzman & Eric Rosenberg, Lebanon, NH: Dartmouth College Press, ix–xix.

Sampson Vera Tudela, Elisa (2012), *Ricardo Palma's Tradiciones: Illuminating Gender and Nation*, Lewisburg, PA: Bucknell University Press.

Sanborn, Geoffrey (2011), *Whipscars and Tattoos: The Last of the Mohicans, Moby-Dick, and the Maori*, Oxford: Oxford University Press.

Sánchez García, Marta Remedios (2009), *Juan Valera en la encrucijada: Pensamiento, estética e ideología en la literatura del siglo XIX*, Madrid: Síntesis.

Sanders, James E. (2014), *The Vanguard of the Atlantic World: Creating Modernity, Nation, and Democracy in Nineteenth-Century Latin America*, Durham, NC: Duke University Press.

Sanyal, Deborah (2006), *The Violence of Modernity: Baudelaire, Irony, and the Politics of Form*, Baltimore, MD: Johns Hopkins University Press.

Sarlo, Beatriz (1993), *Borges, un escritor en las orillas*, Madrid: Espasa Calpe.

Saslow, James M. (2018), '"Disagreeably Hidden": Construction and Constriction of the Lesbian Body in Rosa Bonheur's *Horse Fair*', in *The Expanding Discourse: Feminism and Art History*, ed. by Norma Broude & Mary D. Garrard, London: Routledge, 187–205.

Schehr, Lawrence R. (1997), *Rendering French Realism*, Stanford, CA: Stanford University Press.

Schell, Patience (2013), *The Sociable Sciences: Darwin and his Contemporaries in Chile*, Basingstoke: Palgrave Macmillan.

Schiavo, Laura Burd (2003), 'From Phantom Image to Perfect Vision: Physiological Optics, Commercial Photography, and the Popularization of the Stereoscope', in *New Media*, ed. by Lisa Gitelman & Geoffrey B. Pingree, Cambridge, MA: MIT Press, 113–38.

Schmidt-Nowara, Christopher (2006), *The Conquest of History: Spanish Colonialism and National Histories in the Nineteenth Century*, Pittsburgh, PA: University of Pittsburgh Press.

Schueller, Malini (1986), 'Carnival Rhetoric and Extra-vagance in Thoreau's *Walden*', *American Literature* 58.1, 33–45.

Schwartz, Hillel (2014), *The Culture of the Copy: Striking Likenesses, Unreasonable Facsimiles*, New York: Zone Books.

Sedgwick, Eve Kosofsky (2008), *Epistemology of the Closet*, Berkeley: University of California Press.

Segre, Erica (2007), *Intersected Identities: Strategies of Visualization in Nineteenth- and Twentieth-Century Mexican Culture*, New York: Berghahn.

Sekula, Allan (2002), 'Between the Net and the Deep Blue Sea (Rethinking the Traffic in Photographs)', *October* 102, 3–34.

Sennett, Richard (2008), *The Craftsman*, London: Penguin.

Sennett, Richard (2013), *Together: The Rituals, Pleasures and Politics of Cooperation*, London: Allen Lane.

Serrano y Fatigati, Enrique & Calderón y Arana, Salvador (1870), *Total organización de la materia*, Madrid: Imprenta de M. Tello.

Serres, Michel (1990), *Le Contrat naturel*, Paris: Flammarion.

Sharman, Adam (2013), *Otherwise Engaged: After Hegel and the Philosophy of History*, Nottingham: Critical, Cultural and Communications Press.

Sharpley-Whiting, T. Denean (1999), *Black Venus: Sexualized Savages, Primal Fears, and Primitive Narratives in French*, Durham, NC: Duke University Press.

Shubert, Adrian (1990), *A Social History of Modern Spain*, London: Unwin Hyman.

Siegel, Jonah (2000), *Desire and Excess: The Nineteenth-Century Culture of Art*, Princeton, NJ: Princeton University Press.

Silverman, Kaja (2015), *The Miracle of Analogy; or, The History of Photography, Part 1*, Stanford, CA: Stanford University Press, Kindle edition.

Siskind, Mariano (2014), *Cosmopolitan Desires: Global Modernity and World Literature in Latin America*, Evanston, IL: Northwestern University Press.

Slicer, Deborah (2013), 'Thoreau's Evanescence', *Philosophy and Literature* 1, 179–98.

Sluyter, Andrew (2012), *Black Ranching Frontiers*, New Haven, CT: Yale University Press.

Smith, Andrew (2016), *Gothic Death*, Manchester: Manchester University Press.

Snediker, Michael D. (2013), 'Melville and Queerness without Character', in *The New Cambridge Companion to Herman Melville*, ed. by Robert Levine, Cambridge: Cambridge University Press, 155–68.

Sobchack, Vivian (2011), 'Afterword: Media Archaeology and the Re-Presencing of the Past', in *Media Archaeology: Approaches, Applications, and Implications*, ed. by Erkki Huhtamo & Jussi Parikka, Berkeley: University of California Press, 323–34.

Sobrevilla, Natalia (2018), 'How (Not) To Make a Durable State', in *Spain in the Nineteenth Century: New Essays on Experiences of Culture and Society*, ed. by Andrew Ginger & Geraldine Lawless, Manchester: Manchester University Press, 13–38.

Solano y Eulate, José María (1871), *Guía del Gabinete de Historia Natural*, Madrid: Imprenta a cargo de Gregorio Justo.

Sommer, Doris (1991), *Foundational Fictions: The National Romances of Latin America*, Berkeley: University of California Press.

Sontag, Susan (2008), *At the Same Time: Essays and Speeches*, ed. by Paolo Dionardo & Anne Jump, London: Penguin.

References

Sotos-Crespo, Ramón E. (1998), 'Puerto Rican Marginality in Abniel Marat's *Dios en el Playgirl de noviembre* and Eugenio María de Hostos's *La Peregrinación de Bayoán*', *Modern Fiction Studies* 44.1, 215–39.

Spanos, William V. (1995), *The Errant Art of Moby-Dick: The Canon, the Cold War, and the Struggle for American Studies*, Durham, NC: Duke University Press.

Stafford, Barbara Maria (1999), *Visual Analogy: Consciousness as the Art of Connecting*, Cambridge, MA: MIT Press.

Stakelton, Pauline (2010), 'Travel through Stereoscope: Movement and Narrative in Topological Stereoview Collections of Europe', *Media History* 16.4, 407–22.

Staley, Allen (2011), *The New Painting of the 1860s: Between the Pre-Raphaelites and the Aesthetic Movement*, New Haven, CT: Yale University Press.

Stamos, David N. (1999), 'Darwin's Species Category Realism', *History and Philosophy of the Life Sciences* 21.2, 137–86.

Standish, Paul (2006), 'Uncommon Schools: Stanley Cavell and the Teaching of *Walden*', *Studies in Philosophy and Education* 25.1, 145–57.

Stanford Friedman, Susan (2015), *Planetary Modernisms: Provocations on Modernity across Time*, New York: Columbia University Press.

Sten, Christopher (1996), *The Weaver-God He Weaves: Melville and the Poetics of the Novel*, Kent, OH: Kent State University Press.

Stovall, Preston (2015), 'Inference by Analogy and the Progress of Knowledge: From Reflection to Determination in Judgements of Natural Purpose', *British Journal for the History of Philosophy* 23.4, 681–709.

Straley, J. (2016), *Evolution and Imagination in Victorian Children's Literature*, Cambridge: Cambridge University Press.

Studlar, Gaylyn (1985), 'Masochism and the Perverse Pleasures of the Cinema', in *Movies and Methods II*, ed. by Bill Nichols, Berkeley: University of California Press, 602–24.

Sutherland, Daniel (2008), 'James McNeill Whistler in Chile: Portrait of the Artist as Arms Dealer', *American Nineteenth Century History* 9.1, 61–73.

Sutherland, Daniel E. (2014), *Whistler: A Life for Art's Sake*, New Haven, CT: Yale University Press.

Swinburne, Algernon Charles (2014), *Complete Works*, ed. by Edmund Gosse & Thomas James Wise, n.p.: n.p.

Swinney, Geoffrey N. (2011), 'An Afterword on Afterlife', in *The After Lives of Animals: A Museum Menagerie*, ed. by Samuel J.M.M. Alberti, Charlottesville: University of Virginia Press, 219–33.

Tagg, John (1988), *The Burden of Representation: Essays on Photographies and Histories*, Basingstoke: Macmillan.

Talairach-Vielmas, Laurence (2007), *Moulding the Female Body in Victorian Fairy Tales and Sensation Novels*, Aldershot: Ashgate.

Taussig, Michael (1987), *Shamanism, Colonialism, and the Wild Man*, Chicago: University of Chicago Press.

Tennyson, Alfred, Lord (2012), *Idylls of the King in Twelve Books*, n.p.: n.p., Kindle edition.

Thomas, Abraham (2011), 'Owen Jones and the Islamic World', in *Britain and the Muslim World: Historical Perspectives*, ed. by Gerald MacLean, Newcastle upon Tyne: Cambridge Scholars Publishing, 143–63.

Thomas, Sophie (2005), 'Making Visible: The Diorama, the Double, and the (Gothic) Subject', *Romantic Circles*, www.rc.umd.edu/praxis/gothic/thomas/thomas [accessed 1 June 2018].

References

Thomson, Guy P. C. (2009), *From Democracy to Anarchism: The Transformation of the Left in Liberal Spain, 1849–75*, Basingstoke: Palgrave Macmillan.
Thoreau, Henry David (2012), *The Portable Thoreau*, ed. by Jeffrey S. Cramer, London: Penguin.
Tinterow, Gary et al. (2003), *Manet/Velázquez: The French Taste for Spanish Painting*, New York: Metropolitan Museum of Art.
Tombazos, Stavros (2014), *Time in Marx: Categories of Time in Marx's Capital*, Leiden: Brill.
Torrecilla, Jesús (1996), *El tiempo y los márgenes: Europa como utopía y como amenaza en la literatura española*, Chapel Hill: University of North Carolina Press.
Torrecillas Fernández, María Carmen (1992), 'Las pinturas de la Quinta del Sordo fotografiadas por J. Laurent', *Boletín del Museo del Prado* 13, 57–6.
Torres García, J. (1944), *Universalismo constructivo: Contribución a la unificación del arte y la cultura de América*, Buenos Aires: Editorial Poseidon.
Trimble, Robert G. (1995), *Chaos Burning on My Brow: Don Juan Valera in His Novels*, San Bernardino, CA: Borgo Press.
Tsing, Anna Lowenhaupt (2005), *Friction: An Ethnography of Global Connection*, Princeton, NJ: Princeton University Press.
Tsuchiya, Akiko (1988), 'History as Language in the First Series of the *Episodios Nacionales*: The Literary Self-Creation of Gabriel de Araceli', *Anales Galdosianos* 23, 11–25.
Tucker, Jennifer (2005), *Nature Exposed: Photography as Eyewitness in Victorian Science*, Baltimore, MD: Johns Hopkins University Press.
Unwin, Timothy (2011), 'Being There with Flaubert', *Dix-Neuf* 15.11, 15–25.
Urey, Diane F. (1988), 'Engendering Style in the First Series of Galdós's *Episodios nacionales*', *Revista de estudios hispánicos* 22.2, 25–43.
Urraca, Beatriz (1999), 'Juana Manuela Gorriti and the Persistence of Memory', *Latin American Research Review* 34.1, 151–73.
Urry, John (1995), *Consuming Places*, London: Routledge.
Valera, Juan (1970), *Las ilusiones del doctor Faustino*, ed. by Cyrus C. Coster, Madrid: Castalia.
van Deemter, Kees (2010), *Not Exactly: In Praise of Vagueness*, Oxford: Oxford University Press.
Vasconcelos, José (1967), *La raza cósmica: Misión de la raza iberoamericana*, Madrid: Aguilar.
Vattimo, Gianni (2012), 'Dialectics, Difference, Weak Thought', in *Weak Thought*, ed. by Gianni Vattimo & Pier Aldo Rovatti, trans. by Peter Caravetta, New York: SUNY Press.
Vázquez, Óscar (2001), *Inventing the Art Collection: Patrons, Markets and the State in Nineteenth-Century Spain*, University Park: Pennsylvania State University Press.
Vilches, D. J. (1865), *Reflexiones artísticas aplicadas al proyectado Monumento de Colón*, Madrid: Imprenta de Julián Peña.
Villanes Cairo, Carlos (1994), 'Introducción', in Ricardo Palma, *Tradiciones peruanas*, ed. by Carlos Villanes Cairo, Madrid: Cátedra, 11–61.
Vinken, Barbara (2015), *Flaubert Postsecular: Modernity Crossed Out*, trans. by Aarnoud Rommens & Susan L. Solomon, Stanford, CA: Stanford University Press.
Vives, Rosa (1993), *Hokusai como modelo: Precisiones sobre dibujo de Fortuny*, Madrid: CSIC.
Von Zinnenburg Carroll, Khadija (2014), *Art in the Time of the Colony*, Farnham: Ashgate.
Wallace, Isabel (2006), 'Trauma as Representation: A Meditation on Manet and Johns', in *Trauma and Visuality in Modernity*, ed. by Lisa Saltzman & Eric Rosenberg, Lebanon, NH: Dartmouth College Press, 3–27.
Warner, Marina (2006), *Phantasmagoria: Spirit Visions, Metaphors and Media into the Twenty-First Century*, Oxford: Oxford University Press.

References

Warner, Michael (1991), '*Walden*'s Erotic Economy', in *Comparative American Identities: Race, Sex, and Nationality in the Modern Text*, ed. by Hortense J. Spillers, New York: Routledge, 157–74.

Weaver, Mike (1984), *Julia Margaret Cameron 1815–1879*, London: Herbert Press.

Welchman, Jennifer (2006), *The Practice of Virtue: Classic and Contemporary Readings in Virtue Ethics*, Indianapolis, IN: Hackett.

Wheen, Francis (2006), *Marx's Das Kapital: A Biography*, London: Atlantic Books.

Whitman, Walt (1995), *The Works of Walt Whitman*, ed. David Rogers, Ware: Wordsworth.

Williams, D. A. (1987), '*The Hidden Life at Its Source*': A Study of Flaubert's '*L'Education Sentimentale*', Hull: Hull University Press.

Williamson, George S. (2004), *The Longing for Myth in Germany: Religion and Aesthetic Culture from Romanticism to Nietzsche*, Chicago: University of Chicago Press.

Wilson, Ivy G. (2011), *Specters of Democracy: Blackness and the Aesthetics of Politics in the Antebellum US*, Oxford: Oxford University Press.

Wittgenstein, Ludwig (2001), *Tractatus Logico-Philosophicus*, London: Routledge.

Wittgenstein, Ludwig (2008), *On Certainty*, Oxford: Blackwell.

Wittgenstein, Ludwig (2010), *Philosophical Investigations*, Oxford: Blackwell.

Wood, Christopher S. (2012), 'Reception and the Classics', in *Reception and the Classics: An Interdisciplinary Approach to a Cultural Tradition*, ed. by William Brockliss et al., Cambridge: Cambridge University Press, 163–73.

Woodward, Servanne (1989), 'Lacan and Derrida on "The Purloined Letter"', *Comparative Literary Studies* 26, 39–49.

Yee, Jennifer (2016), *The Colonial Comedy in the French Realist Novel*, Oxford: Oxford University Press.

Young, Marnin (2015), *Realism in the Age of Impressionism: Painting and the Politics of Time*, New Haven, CT: Yale University Press.

Young, Paul (2008), 'Mission Impossible: Globalization and the Great Exhibition', in *Britain, the Empire, and the World at the Great Exhibition of 1851*, ed. by Jeffrey A. Auerbach & Peter H. Hoffenberg, Aldershot: Ashgate, 3–25.

Yriarte, Charles (1889), *Fortuny*, Paris: J. Rouam.

Yxart, Josep (1881), *Fortuny: Noticia biográfica crítica*, Barcelona: C. Verdaguer.

Zielinski, Siegfried (2006), *Deep Time of the Media: Toward an Archaeology of Seeing and Hearing by Technical Means*, ed. by Thomas Druckrey, trans. by Gloria Custance, Cambridge, MA: MIT Press.

Žižek, Slavoj (2008), *For They Know Not What They Do: Enjoyment as a Political Factor*, London: Verso.

Index

absence 8, 29, 35, 37–8, 45, 60–1, 63, 88, 121, 123, 145, 152, 162, 174, 180, 204, 215, 223, 225, 230, 235, 240, 242, 246, 248, 253–4, 265, 270
absorption 8, 52, 57, 76, 124, 170, 219, 270
acknowledgement 21, 49, 61
aesthetics 1, 3, 5, 7, 9, 11, 13–15, 17–21, 23–5, 27–33, 36, 58–62, 64, 72, 77, 82–3, 90, 94, 100, 104–5, 114, 119, 122, 124–6, 128, 133, 136, 146–7, 149, 155, 171, 179, 183, 186, 191, 195–6, 198, 200, 210, 212–13, 215, 223, 244, 246, 248, 255–6, 267
affect 17, 59, 66, 90, 115, 125, 196, 205, 268, 270
affordance 16–17, 24, 29–31, 36, 42, 77, 79, 85, 87, 103, 137–8, 144, 159, 181, 185, 199, 206, 220, 234–5, 242, 244, 246, 249–50, 253, 258
Africa, African 7, 29, 133, 140, 152, 155, 157, 160, 185, 198–9, 215–17, 223, 225–6, 231, 240, 257, 260
Agamben, Giorgio 14, 143, 161, 186, 237
allegory 13, 57, 78, 147, 152–3, 155, 159–61, 175, 187, 202, 210, 212–15, 217, 239
America, American 2, 6–8, 14–16, 18, 21, 29, 31–2, 38–43, 45, 49, 51, 56, 65, 67, 82, 88, 91, 101, 106, 119, 126, 133–4, 136, 143, 151, 157–8, 160, 162, 169, 171, 179, 183, 186, 190, 192, 198–9, 202, 207, 220, 224–5, 228, 231, 245, 252, 257, 259–60, 265, 267, 269
anachronism 29, 156–8, 165, 225
anagnorisis 3, 10, 127, 165, 176, 182, 218, 222, 245
analogy 16–17, 23, 30–1, 55–6, 62, 75–6, 82–3, 85, 88, 91, 94, 99, 128, 147, 167, 176–7, 180, 182, 201–2, 246, 249, 253, 266
Ante-Bellum period United States 28, 94, 186–7, 260
Apollo 26, 36–7, 55, 57–64, 67, 88, 119–20, 128, 140–1, 185

Appiah, Kwame Anthony 42, 50, 217
appreciation 1, 3, 5, 7, 9, 11, 13, 15, 17–21, 23, 25, 27–31, 33, 42, 44, 105, 112–13, 115, 126, 128, 136, 146, 168, 170, 191, 210, 213, 219, 247
Argentina, Argentine 10, 13, 17, 25, 28, 31, 36–42, 44–7, 50–2, 58, 101, 106, 136, 146, 183–6, 207, 217–20, 239–40, 257
Aristotle 62, 115–16, 260
Arrieta, Agustín 147, 202–4, 212, 246, 250
artifice 61, 102, 114
Asia, Asian 34, 102, 225, 231, 234, 286
atavism 17, 23, 27, 49, 51–2, 59, 88, 100, 103–4, 109, 112, 121–2, 126–7, 141–2, 168, 181–2, 188, 202, 229, 232, 269
authenticity 46, 111–13, 116, 123, 146, 155, 159, 161, 205, 218, 221, 230, 237, 239, 258

barbarism 136, 139, 167, 184, 239–41
Barthes, Roland 3, 79, 87, 94, 157, 168, 177
Baudelaire, Charles, 3–4, 6, 9–10, 13, 22, 27, 99–100, 121–2, 126–8, 130, 132–3, 141, 155, 167, 172, 229, 231–3, 246–7, 259, 269
Bazin, André 106, 152, 162, 195
Bécquer, Gustavo Adolfo 246–250, 262
Being 16, 117, 205–8, 214, 216–18, 229–30, 232, 248, 250, 262
Benjamin, Walter 3–4, 9, 44, 46, 70, 83, 99, 122, 128, 149, 154, 157, 160, 163–4, 176, 243
Berman, Marshall 3–4, 6, 15, 105
Bernhardt, Sarah 27, 146, 157–8
Bersani, Leo 64, 67–8, 143, 165
Berzosa, Manuel Ascensión 150–1, 153–5, 161–2, 168, 178, 194, 196
blend 32, 37–9, 43, 45, 54, 69, 103, 122, 126, 132, 137–8, 185, 202, 244, 256, 265, 267–9
Bonheur, Rosa 6, 13, 100, 132, 139–41, 165, 234

296

Index

Bretón de los Herreros, Manuel 66–7, 73, 85, 115
Britain, British 7, 28, 42, 87–8, 126, 144–5, 152, 181–2, 188, 192, 200–1, 207, 215, 228
Browning, Robert 37, 69–70, 90, 155
bubble 29, 33, 129, 183, 201
Buenos Aires 32, 37–8, 41–2, 46, 100, 132, 135–6, 198, 219–21, 240, 251, 265
Bustos, Hermenegildo 147, 199, 202, 212

Cabinet of Natural History (Madrid) 27, 130, 146, 196–9
camera 70, 72, 76, 80, 82, 87, 90–1, 95, 115, 147, 152–3, 169, 196
Cameron, Julia Margaret 6, 13, 28, 31, 146–50, 152–5, 158, 160–1, 169, 179, 187, 189, 202,
canon 3, 5–6, 9–10, 12–13, 16, 230
capitalism 4, 15, 76–7, 101–2, 105, 187, 268
Carlos V 88, 156, 221, 239, 243, 262
Carroll, Lewis 110, 170–2, 176
Caruth, Cathy 98, 142, 158
Castro, Rosalía 6, 38, 230–2, 234, 239
Cavell, Stanley 18–22, 25–6, 28, 30, 32, 50, 61–2, 99, 105, 110, 115, 126, 129, 169, 180, 233, 236, 258–60
character 13, 22, 42, 46, 62, 66, 73, 79, 146, 176–7, 179, 207, 250, 252
civilisation 34, 39, 119, 136, 142, 160, 184, 190, 201, 215, 217, 223, 225–6, 239–40, 250, 257
classics 4, 14, 20, 24, 27, 31, 35, 37, 44, 51, 53, 59, 62, 79, 100, 102, 115, 121, 127, 140, 146, 157–8, 160, 165, 169, 172, 205, 215, 223, 232, 234, 260–1, 266, 269
Clifford, Charles 87–8, 91, 117
Clifford, Jane 14, 88, 90, 95, 117
clutch 18, 32, 105, 110–11, 128, 233–4, 260
   see also grasp
colonialism 25, 28, 34, 73, 100–3, 126, 145–6, 152, 162, 181–82, 190, 195, 200–1, 216, 231, 248, 260
Columbus, Christopher 2, 14, 88, 95, 102, 110, 162, 178, 190, 220–1, 260–1
commonality 1–3, 7–10, 12–14, 19, 30, 40–1, 43–4, 46, 48, 54, 64, 98, 100, 105, 111, 123, 129–30, 132, 134, 144, 147, 158, 160, 162–3, 201–4, 206–207, 223, 230
companionship 25, 35–6, 39, 41–4, 48–51, 53, 55, 97, 109, 118, 129, 137–8, 140, 156, 158, 170, 176, 211, 225–6, 244–6, 252, 270
   see also friendship

comparison 6, 8–9, 11–15, 17, 45, 82, 108
connection 1–2, 12–15, 22–5, 27–32, 40, 42, 52, 55, 58, 64, 77, 80, 82–3, 85, 87–8, 91, 98, 101, 103, 120, 122–3, 131, 133, 135, 144, 152, 159–60, 171, 173, 178, 186, 192, 195, 198, 200, 205–7, 212, 214, 221, 224, 226–8, 230–2, 239, 242–5, 247–50, 261–2, 264–9
context 5, 16, 26–9, 36, 46–7, 51, 59, 61, 63, 83, 85, 88, 100–1, 111–12, 114, 119, 124, 127, 131–3, 137–8, 142, 144–7, 149–51, 153, 156, 162, 168, 170–1, 175, 179, 183–4, 186, 214, 236, 246–7, 250, 262, 264–5, 267, 269–70
contiguity 161, 180, 223, 267
   see also juxtaposition
copy 44, 46, 85, 107, 129, 134, 146, 161–2, 165, 167–9, 173, 178, 191, 195–6
cosmopolitanism 16, 35, 42, 69, 100, 125, 129–130, 160, 201, 217
Costa y Turell, Modesto 69–70, 90–1, 94
Courbet, Gustave 4, 6, 15, 17–18, 26, 31, 100, 132, 134, 137–8, 185, 192–3, 210–17, 219, 241, 258
craft 3, 18, 23–5, 28, 32, 37, 78, 82, 100, 109, 206, 245, 250, 255–6, 260, 262
Crary, Jonathan 4–6, 14–15, 54, 106–7, 109, 205–6, 211
Crystal Palace 13, 147, 200, 202

Darwin, Charles 4, 6, 14, 20, 27, 207, 250–4, 262
Dean, Tim 14, 25, 35–7, 43, 69, 170
deferral 19–22, 26–7, 34–6, 39, 57, 60, 99, 105, 111–13, 115, 128, 135, 138, 152, 171, 236, 256, 259
del Campo, Estanislao 13, 17, 30–2, 37–9, 41, 43–8, 50–1, 69, 88, 97, 103, 105–6, 109, 122, 132, 216, 257, 265, 268
Deleuze, Gilles 76, 205, 277, 289–90
Derrida, Jacques 3, 14, 34, 57, 94, 98, 105, 114–15, 143, 161, 168, 171, 205, 232, 236, 256
Devil 19, 21, 23, 27, 32, 38–40, 45, 48–52, 55, 59, 114, 118, 127–8, 170, 202, 228, 232
   see also Lucifer; Mephistopheles; Satan
Díez, Matilde 26, 36–7, 65–7, 69–73, 75–80, 83, 87, 90, 95, 109, 121, 232
Dimock, Wai-Chee 12, 14, 18, 28, 32, 103, 112, 187, 206, 209, 260
Dionysus 26, 36–7, 56–64, 67, 88, 119–20, 128, 140–1, 143, 185
disconnection 41, 66, 79–80, 102, 116, 118, 138, 178, 194, 198, 203, 212, 224, 230, 239, 242, 245–6, 248–9, 267

Index

disposition 17, 23, 25, 28, 32, 38, 46–7, 52, 60, 62, 79, 83, 100, 112–15, 125, 131–2, 134, 158, 168, 182, 195, 202, 209, 214, 226, 233–4, 237, 241–2, 248, 255, 258–60, 262–3, 267–8
donkey 14, 140, 207, 261–4, 269

Eco, Umberto 30, 44, 64, 270
Echo 44, 54, 111, 122, 179, 209, 243
ecstasy 63, 67, 69, 140, 143, 155, 165
embalming 106, 161, 163, 169, 195, 199
empire 13, 31, 57, 76, 87–8, 95, 99–100, 103, 119, 126, 133, 136, 160, 167, 178, 187, 198, 201, 207, 221–4, 226, 228, 231, 242, 253, 262, 266
see also imperialism
endlessness 19, 21–3, 25–6, 30, 34, 57, 77, 97–8, 117, 120, 123, 127–9, 137, 142, 144, 146, 152–5, 165, 169, 173, 176, 181, 190–2, 194, 206, 213, 215, 230, 233, 237, 242, 245–6, 253, 256, 259, 266
England, English 126, 182, 228, 257, 260
epistemology 4, 17–18, 21, 50, 54, 56, 59, 61–2, 94, 110, 114, 137, 171, 218, 236–7, 259–60
equivalence 13, 35, 56, 58, 60, 64, 69, 77, 83, 99, 102, 104–6, 128, 138–9, 149, 180–2, 219, 233, 253
erotics 24, 26, 36–7, 43–4, 55–6, 67, 73, 75, 85, 95, 100, 115, 120, 123, 125, 128, 132–3, 136–40, 149, 154–5, 163, 165, 167, 170, 176, 191, 209, 247, 249, 257
Europe, European 2, 5, 7–8, 15–16, 34–5, 38–40, 43, 49, 51, 59, 65, 69, 76, 88, 99, 101–2, 106, 116, 126, 131, 133, 136, 152, 159–60, 162, 183, 185–6, 207, 215–16, 218, 220–1, 223–8, 231, 250, 264, 267

Faust 12, 36–40, 44–8, 50–6, 64, 83, 88, 105–6, 109, 111, 158, 206, 209, 251, 265, 268–9
Felipe IV 117, 131
Felski, Rita 17, 23–4, 178
Fernández Mallo, Agustín 30, 150, 159, 172
Flaubert, Gustave 3–4, 6, 9–10, 20, 31, 146, 176–7, 180, 182, 206, 242–3, 245–7, 249, 255, 258, 268
flicker 29, 33, 99, 104, 109, 118–20, 124, 126, 129, 135, 137, 139, 158, 165, 178, 196, 201, 203, 237, 239
Flores, Antonio 234–7, 239–41, 243, 279–80, 285
Fontanella, Lee 87, 106–9
form 4–5, 19–22, 28, 32, 53, 58–9, 65, 67, 70, 72–3, 75, 78, 80, 82, 90–3, 98, 103, 105, 107, 110, 113, 115, 122, 129, 133, 135–6, 140, 149, 154, 159, 161–3, 167, 172, 176, 178, 180, 182, 189, 193–6, 199–200, 208, 212, 215, 225–34, 236–7, 242–7, 250, 256, 261, 268
Fortuny, Mariano 16, 26–7, 37, 53–5, 69, 83, 123, 146, 158, 165, 179, 206, 208–17, 219, 222, 227, 243
Foster Wallace, David 23, 49–50, 61, 72, 94, 188, 227, 232
Foucault, Michel 3–5, 11, 29, 54, 61, 73, 96, 129, 170, 177, 193, 203, 206, 209, 233, 236
France, French 5, 9–10, 15, 25, 34, 37–8, 45, 51–2, 57, 70, 72, 77, 87, 91, 97, 100–1, 103, 117–22, 124, 128, 131, 133, 137, 139–40, 143, 146, 152, 155, 157, 159, 167, 179, 192–3, 195, 206–8, 210, 212, 214–15, 217, 224, 232–5, 242–5, 247–8, 253, 257
Fried, Michael 4, 6, 14, 49–50, 69, 73, 103, 120–1, 134, 137–9, 156–7, 176, 210–11, 214, 216
friendship 25, 37, 41–4, 48, 50, 52–5, 62, 145, 170, 176, 219, 229, 232, 244–6, 248, 252, 258, 265, 268
see also companionship

Galdós, Benito Pérez 253, 255–6, 264
gap 21, 27, 78, 85, 100–1, 104, 118–21, 124, 130–1, 199, 202–3, 217, 219–21, 223, 232, 237, 239–40, 243
gaucho 37–42, 44–8, 50–2, 63, 69, 111, 146, 176, 183–6, 216, 241, 251–2, 257, 265, 268
gender 29–30, 36, 63, 67, 70, 75, 83, 101, 120, 124, 133–4, 137–40, 146, 151–2, 163, 165, 170, 185, 215–17, 221, 226–7, 232, 236–7, 241, 249, 257
geometry 14, 26, 37, 70, 72–3, 75–80, 82–3, 85, 87, 90, 94, 109, 173, 181, 194, 200–1, 223, 250
Germany, German 1, 5, 12, 25, 37–9, 44–7, 50, 52–3, 57, 59, 61–3, 69, 105, 173, 248
Gisbert, Antonio 156–7, 159
glass 13, 70, 108, 147, 151, 196, 200, 202–3
Gorriti, Juana Manuela 6, 25, 31, 206, 217–21, 227, 243
Gounod, Charles 37–9, 41–2, 44–5, 48–50, 52–4, 103
Goya, Francisco 27, 53–6, 69–70, 105, 116–23, 131, 135–6, 146, 172–3, 175–6, 210, 217, 234
grasp 18, 62, 104, 114, 128, 141, 169, 186, 243, 250–1
see also clutch

Greece, Greek 7, 51, 58–60, 64, 95, 104, 118, 160, 172, 201, 223
Guys, Constantin 233–4

hallucination 27, 55, 62, 97, 107, 109, 118, 138, 145, 162, 189, 196, 212
Hegel, Georg Wilhelm Friedrich 5, 35, 115, 161, 188–9, 207
Heidegger, Martin 16, 77, 161–2, 176, 260
Hispanic world 1–2, 5–8, 12, 16, 31–2, 37, 39, 119–20, 122, 133–4, 157, 167, 178, 193, 207, 221, 234, 247, 266
historicism 28, 62, 146, 155, 157, 228
Hernández, José 183, 230, 257
Hispanic 1–2, 5–8, 12, 16, 31–2, 37, 39
Hostos, Eugenio de 14, 188–9, 202, 243
Hunt, William Holman 144–5, 234, 264
hybridity 126, 217
  see also mestizaje
hypnotism 22, 69–70, 90–1, 95, 105, 108, 128, 157, 160, 180
  see also mesmerism

Iberia, Iberian 28, 70, 160, 199, 208, 216–17, 267
imperialism 15, 17, 28, 43, 65, 101, 146, 151, 157, 181, 190, 201, 207, 221, 248
  see also empire
imperium 221–3, 225
  see also empire; imperialism
Impressionism 9, 272, 281, 295
indigenous peoples 7, 60, 157, 182–3, 185, 187, 190, 199, 202, 207, 217, 220, 223, 225, 240–2, 252
insanity 22–3, 99, 145, 147, 150, 155, 181, 202, 212–13, 236, 239, 246, 249, 266
  see also madness
insect 31, 198–9, 251
internationalism 14, 35, 185
intimacy 1–2, 11, 13–14, 17, 26–8, 30–2, 35–7, 39, 42–4, 48–51, 56, 58, 60–1, 63–4, 69, 73, 88, 94, 97, 99, 103, 105, 107–9, 115–16, 119–22, 131, 133, 135–43, 153–4, 157–8, 163, 165, 168–70, 173, 176–7, 179, 185, 191, 193, 196, 204, 207, 216, 219, 221, 223, 244–7, 249, 252, 257–8, 263, 269
irony 3, 5, 22–3, 25, 35, 38–41, 46, 48, 50, 94, 109, 125, 128, 157, 168, 170, 182, 188, 227, 229–30, 232–3, 236, 248
Isabel I the Catholic 224–6, 234, 255
Isabel II 30, 123–4, 224

juxtaposition 26, 32, 102, 113, 115, 122, 127, 129, 140, 161, 240, 243–5, 247, 259
  see also contiguity

Kristeva, Julia 14, 142, 154, 171, 177, 256

Lacan, Jacques 57, 256
LaCapra, Dominick 14, 28, 144, 153, 163
Laclau, Ernesto 41, 43, 159, 189, 194
Laing, R. D 25, 27, 30, 204, 250
Laso, Francisco 15, 207, 223, 239
Laurent, Juan (a.k.a Jean) 29, 37, 66–8, 70–4, 76–8, 82, 87, 95–7, 105, 117–18, 173–4
lavishness 21–3, 30, 110–11, 113, 115, 129, 136, 236–7, 259, 265–6
Levine, Caroline 16, 242, 249
Levine, George 251–3
likeness 13–15, 29–31, 40, 42, 46, 48–9, 56, 58, 64, 79, 98, 100, 102, 104, 129, 133, 135–6, 159, 168, 177–80, 185, 241, 266
limbo 30, 146–7, 150–3, 156, 159–60, 162–3, 165, 171, 173, 175–6, 178, 182–3, 193–4, 199, 225, 245–6, 255
localisation 36, 111, 124, 129, 149, 235–6, 254, 261–2, 269
Logos 54, 115, 191, 205–6, 233, 239–40
looping 30, 33, 153, 163, 176–7, 191
Lovers of Teruel 163–4, 167
Lucas Velázquez, Eugenio 9–11, 15, 20, 27, 100, 116–19, 121, 130–1, 136, 156, 173, 175, 234, 237, 270
Lucifer 100
  see also Devil; Mephistopheles; Satan

madness 19, 21, 23, 77, 145, 200, 202, 204, 213, 224, 232, 236
  see also insanity
Madrazo family 95, 122–6, 129–31, 133, 136, 158, 198, 217
Manet, Édouard 3–4, 6, 9–11, 13, 15, 23–4, 26–7, 29, 99–100, 103–5, 107–8, 111–12, 114, 118–22, 124, 136, 138, 140–1, 151, 178, 181, 188, 202, 221, 232, 234, 237, 239, 243, 246, 248, 270
Manning, Susan 11, 13–15, 17, 29, 31, 36, 42–4, 48, 50, 56, 59, 64, 83, 94, 113, 130, 136, 171, 176, 180, 209, 252
Mansilla, Lucio V. 28, 239–42, 257, 259
Marx, Karl 3–4, 6, 12–14, 22–3, 27, 29–31, 99, 101–5, 107–8, 112, 114, 118, 121–2, 136, 141, 146, 151–2, 167, 187–8, 194, 200, 230, 257, 260, 270
Mata, Pedro 212–14
Maximilian I 100, 118–120, 242
medieval period 11, 14, 25, 36, 38–9, 42, 45, 47, 51–2, 91, 105, 158, 163, 217, 234, 269

medium 4, 9, 37, 70, 72, 87–8, 95, 99, 143, 147, 153, 169, 191, 193–4, 200, 230, 239
megalethoscope 106–9, 111, 114
Melville, Herman 13, 31, 168–72, 176, 178, 185–7, 190, 202, 232, 247, 270
Mephistopheles 37–8, 48, 53, 269
see also Devil; Lucifer; Satan
mesmerism 37, 69–70, 73, 75, 82, 90–1, 93, 180, 221
see also hypnotism
mestizaje 126, 132, 271
see also hybridity
Mexico, Mexican 8, 13–14, 23, 32, 36–7, 65, 67, 70, 73, 100, 119, 126, 133–4, 146–7, 187, 192, 199, 202–3, 216, 242
Millet, Jean-Francois 146, 152, 167
mimesis 2, 13, 26, 44, 67, 151, 162, 165, 169, 177, 179, 186, 199, 209
modernism 3–4, 11, 31, 34–5, 126, 205, 214,
modulation 53, 55, 208, 215
mood 23–5, 27, 31–2, 178, 206, 209–10, 212, 237, 239, 260, 265, 267
Morocco, Moroccan 160, 192, 208, 215–16, 263

Nagel, Alexander 11, 34–6, 156
Napoleon I 5, 57, 117, 136, 253–4
Napoleon III 119, 207, 210–11, 217, 242
Narcissus 44, 54, 111, 122, 179, 186, 190, 209
nation 5–7, 15–16, 20, 35, 65, 76, 100–1, 116, 122–3, 126, 131, 133, 139–40, 156, 159–60, 181, 193, 218, 224–5, 228, 231, 239, 248, 256–7, 261
nationalism 28, 131, 133
Nelson, Maggie 82, 144, 205, 214, 288
Nietzsche, Friedrich 3–4, 6, 12–13, 17, 26–7, 31, 36–7, 56–64, 67, 69, 88, 105, 118, 120, 123, 128, 140, 160, 167, 170, 176–7, 230, 244, 250–3
Nobas, Rossend 165–7, 232

ontology 4, 114, 135, 152, 209, 212, 237, 258–60, 266
optics 1, 14, 19, 29, 31, 54, 77, 82, 99, 106–9, 114, 118, 167, 196, 199–201, 203
Ortego y Vereda, Francisco 237–40, 243
Ostler 200
Othello 256, 262, 264, 269

Padilla, Juan de 25, 156–7, 159, 225
Palma, Ricardo 226–31, 233–4, 243
Paraguay 37, 39, 47, 58, 183
Paris 3, 5, 9, 39, 69, 76, 99–101, 103–5, 108, 122, 141, 155, 167, 173, 202, 210, 215, 217, 223, 233, 242–3, 245, 266

passivity 25, 30, 65, 69–70, 82, 105, 110–11, 115, 128, 134, 139, 180, 209, 222, 237, 261–4
pastiche 15, 30, 40, 41, 103, 117, 146, 171–3, 175, 178–9, 181, 188, 232, 246, 248, 250
periodisation 3, 11–12, 28, 34–6, 75, 102, 108, 142, 217–18, 225, 243, 251
periphery 31, 39, 215, 270
persistence 8, 13–15, 17–18, 26–31, 121, 144, 146–7, 157–9, 162–3, 171, 176, 195, 266
Peru, Peruvian 15, 187, 207, 218, 223, 226–30, 266
phenomenology 5, 94, 189, 243
photography 13, 20, 26, 28–9, 37, 66–7, 70, 72, 75–80, 82, 85, 87–8, 91, 97, 106–7, 109, 115, 117–18, 143, 145–7, 149–50, 152–4, 156–63, 169, 173, 179, 181, 187, 189, 195–7, 260
Poe, Edgar Allan 37, 57, 91, 94, 172
poetry 24, 27, 31, 37, 44–6, 51, 83, 111, 122, 125, 127, 179, 246–9, 258, 262, 269
Pogue Harrison, Robert 87, 172, 183, 261
Poliquin, Rachel 162–3, 168–9, 179, 195
Pollock, Griselda 14, 16, 120, 132, 142, 152, 167
poverty 20–2, 30, 101, 110–11, 122, 129, 136, 180, 237, 258–60, 265
practice 3, 7–8, 17, 20, 25, 28, 30, 32, 37, 60, 62, 69, 75, 77, 80, 100, 105, 110, 116, 118, 123, 147, 152, 159, 202, 209, 217, 242, 244
Prado Museum 22, 30, 95, 100, 123–4, 126, 129–31, 133, 151, 173, 197–8, 201, 217
Pragmatism 23, 252, 259
Pre-Raphaelitism 144–5, 215, 289, 293
presence 3, 6, 12, 26–7, 34–5, 37, 42, 52–3, 56–8, 64, 70, 75, 77, 85, 88, 94, 103, 106–7, 115, 117, 119, 128, 135, 139, 149, 153, 155, 159–60, 168, 173, 177, 193, 202–3, 208, 210–11, 231–2, 245, 252, 261
preservation 31, 37, 75, 83, 87, 106, 142, 146, 152–3, 162–3, 168–9, 173, 182, 195–6, 199, 269
priority 9, 15, 28, 36, 42–3, 50, 59–60, 83, 90, 171, 176–7, 209, 211, 223, 230
promiscuity 22, 33, 100, 112, 121–6, 129–31, 136, 146, 198, 200–1, 203, 217
Prussia, Prussian 57–8, 101, 105, 167, 196, 207, 253
psychoanalysis 25, 36, 57, 80, 88, 98, 149, 169, 171, 226

Puerto Rico, Puerto Rican 6, 14, 28, 146, 188, 190, 216
Pueyrredón, Prilidiano 10–11, 17, 26, 29, 132, 134–8
pulsation 29, 83, 85, 87–8, 90, 109, 117–18, 129, 131, 137–9, 149, 157, 163, 165, 173, 182, 194, 196, 203

queerness 25, 30, 37, 50, 63, 105, 126, 170–1, 185, 206, 241, 258
Quintana, Manuel José 157, 159, 222

race 100, 120, 223, 227
racism 124, 185, 201
religion 50, 68, 102, 107, 127, 145, 165, 178–9, 222, 224, 260
Renaissance 15, 107, 136, 151, 201–2
representation 1–2, 4, 9–10, 13, 19, 24, 34–6, 38–42, 45, 49–50, 53, 57–9, 72, 96, 98–9, 108, 113, 128, 142–3, 155–6, 171, 179, 210, 216, 245
resemblance 6, 13, 17–18, 26, 30, 42, 46–7, 53–5, 77, 83, 85, 87, 91, 93, 100–1, 104–5, 116, 118, 121–3, 129–33, 135–41, 144, 159, 165, 177–81, 185, 190–1, 198–202, 207, 209, 211, 213, 219, 242, 245, 250
rhythm 14, 44, 55–6, 83, 103, 138–9, 180, 257, 261, 267
rigour 10, 15, 17, 24, 31, 44, 60–2, 64, 88, 90, 122, 180, 198, 205–6
Romanticism 2, 4–6, 8–11, 13, 99–100, 112, 118, 163, 205, 222, 248, 258
Rome, Roman 136, 165, 172, 190, 215, 221, 223, 225, 269
Rorty, Richard 17–18, 22–3, 259
Ros de Olano, Antonio 14, 26, 146, 150, 153–5, 160–1, 202, 222, 263–4, 269
Rosales, Eduardo 20, 207, 221–2, 224–6, 234, 239, 255, 261–3, 270
Russia, Russian 187, 192, 231, 266

sameness 1–2, 6–8, 12–14, 29–31, 48, 56, 58, 60, 64, 98–102, 104–5, 112–14, 131–40, 147, 184–6, 194, 201–3, 206, 213, 234–6, 239–40, 246, 258, 265
Sarmiento, Domingo Faustino 39, 183–4, 239, 241–2
Satan 27, 39, 55, 64, 100, 127, 228–9
see also Devil; Lucifer; Mephistopheles
scapegoat 143–5, 184, 189, 234, 264
Scotland, Scottish 5, 29, 42, 88, 229
sculpture 62, 115, 137, 140, 155, 158, 165, 197, 260

Sennett, Richard 18, 24, 53, 109, 255
Serrano y Fatigati, Enrique 213
sexuality 14, 37, 63–4, 67, 73, 80, 82, 85, 101, 120, 124–6, 129, 132, 134, 136–40, 143, 165, 170, 175, 185, 191, 206, 216–17, 225, 233, 249, 262, 265–6
Shakespeare, William 248, 269–70
sickness 19–20, 23, 153, 176, 180, 202, 204, 235, 246–7, 266
signified 113, 156, 205, 230, 233
signifier 10–11, 13, 41, 159, 194, 206, 230
Silverman, Kaja 16, 72, 79–80, 82–3, 87, 94, 149, 154
similarity 1, 11, 13–17, 26–7, 35, 40–1, 55–6, 69, 76, 82–3, 85, 91, 98–100, 102, 104, 116, 122–4, 128–9, 133, 135–41, 158–9, 161, 176, 181, 185, 194, 198, 201, 203, 206–15, 217, 234–7, 241, 245, 247–8, 253–4, 256, 265, 267
Sontag, Susan 24, 44, 125, 128
Spain, Spanish 1–2, 5–8, 13–17, 20, 25, 30–1, 34, 36–7, 39–41, 43, 53, 65–7, 69–70, 76–7, 79–80, 87–8, 91, 93–5, 99–101, 109–10, 116–20, 122–6, 131–3, 136, 139–41, 146, 150–2, 156–60, 162–3, 165, 167, 172–3, 187, 189–90, 192, 194, 198–203, 206–7, 211–13, 215–18, 220–2, 224–5, 227–31, 233–5, 243, 246, 248, 253–4, 256, 260–3, 265–6, 268–9
species 4, 101, 162–163, 165, 198, 207, 212, 239, 250, 254
specificity 12, 25, 32, 41, 76, 78, 80, 90, 130, 133, 143, 159, 165, 181, 194, 227, 258, 269
stereoscope 104, 106–8, 114, 201, 211
subjecthood 54, 57, 66–7, 94, 117, 143, 192, 205, 211–12, 214, 218, 221, 233, 240–1, 247, 249
subjectivity 25, 49, 57, 66, 69–70, 103, 121, 183, 211, 213
submission 13, 37, 56, 65–7, 69, 73, 75, 80, 95, 100, 119, 121, 232, 248–9, 262, 264, 270

tangent 33, 205, 207, 250–2, 255–7, 259, 261, 263–5, 267, 269–70
taxidermy 14, 30, 146, 162, 168, 171, 173, 176–9, 195–6, 199–200, 245
Tennyson, Alfred 147, 149, 152–3
thaumatrope 1, 33, 106, 108, 121, 201
theatricality 5, 40, 49–50, 54, 66, 73, 121, 157, 172, 176, 225, 256

Index

Theory 2–5, 9–12, 15–19, 21–2, 25–7, 30, 32, 35, 40–1, 44, 49, 52, 54, 59, 62–3, 69, 73, 76–7, 80, 85, 87–8, 94, 99, 101, 103, 106–7, 114–15, 121, 127–8, 133, 144, 146, 159, 169–71, 176–7, 185, 188, 205–7, 214, 227, 239–40, 251, 258, 260
Thoreau, Henry David 17, 28, 110, 207, 257–60, 262–3, 266
Titian 103–5, 112, 114, 118–21, 135–7, 178
transatlanticism 31, 41–2, 66, 179, 218
transculturation 35, 40–1, 43–4, 242
transfiguration 27–8, 37, 45, 47–8, 62–3, 69, 72–3, 75, 78, 83, 85, 87, 90, 95, 97, 100, 105, 109, 111, 114, 121, 131, 136, 142, 145, 151, 153, 159, 167, 172, 176, 182, 185, 187–92, 194, 199–200, 209, 220–1, 223–4, 229, 231–2, 243, 245, 248, 258–9, 261
transhistoricality 27, 30, 107, 149–50, 152, 207, 229
translation 35, 40–1, 43–4, 46, 70, 75–6, 91, 94, 256, 269
transnationalism 23, 27, 37, 220, 231
trauma 14, 19, 30, 98, 142–4, 146, 153, 155, 163, 218, 220, 265–6, 268
Tsing, Anna Lowenhaupt 130–1, 183, 187

universality 3–5, 8, 11, 13–14, 16, 23, 30, 35, 37, 41, 75–7, 79–80, 83, 85, 88, 100–1, 109, 112, 117, 120, 128, 130–1, 136, 138, 143, 146, 151, 154, 158–61, 165, 168–71, 183, 185–91, 194–6, 201, 210, 215, 217, 221, 223–7, 230, 232–3, 236, 243, 245, 248, 260–4

utopia 29, 85, 125, 142–4, 188, 229, 258

vagueness 20, 75, 78–9, 82, 109, 123, 167, 210, 219, 250, 254, 257, 262, 264
Valera, Juan 17, 31, 206, 265–9
Vattimo, Gianni 205, 208, 219, 237
Velázquez, Diego 95–7, 103, 105, 117–19, 121, 135–7, 210, 224
ventriloquism 22–5, 100, 110, 114–18, 133–4, 146, 172, 176, 187, 237, 247
Verne, Jules 130
Vilches, D. J. 30, 155
virtue 18, 62, 90, 225, 250, 25

Wagner, Richard 36, 56–60, 62–4, 105, 118, 125, 176, 244, 250–2
Warburg, Aby 35, 67, 83, 140, 149
Warner, Marina 69–70, 90–1, 147, 160, 258
West, Western 7–8, 14, 35, 41, 72, 132, 144, 206, 217, 223, 228
Whistler, James Abbott McNeill 6, 146, 192–5, 198, 202, 229, 261
Wittgenstein, Ludwig 1, 18–22, 25, 30, 61, 79, 99, 110, 114–15, 123, 133, 172, 180, 202, 217, 237, 254, 258

Yriarte, Charles 208–10, 213
Yxart, Josep 208, 215

Zeno 98, 135
Zielinski, Siegfried 9, 11, 63, 83, 133, 149, 224, 252

EU authorised representative for GPSR:
Easy Access System Europe, Mustamäe tee 50,
10621 Tallinn, Estonia
gpsr.requests@easproject.com